Lecture Notes in Computer Science 4171

Commenced Publication in 1973
Founding and Former Series Editors:
Gerhard Goos, Juris Hartmanis, and Jan van Leeuwen

Bertrand Meyer   Jim Woodcock (Eds.)

Verified Software: Theories, Tools, Experiments

First IFIP TC 2/WG 2.3 Conference, VSTTE 2005
Zurich, Switzerland, October 10-13, 2005
Revised Selected Papers

 Springer

Volume Editors

Bertrand Meyer
ETH Zurich, Department of Computer Science
Clausiusstr. 59, 8092 Zurich, Switzerland
E-mail: bertrand.meyer@inf.ethz.ch

Jim Woodcock
University of York, Department of Computer Science
Heslington, York YO10 5DD, UK
E-mail: jim@cs.york.ac.uk

Library of Congress Control Number: Applied for

CR Subject Classification (1998): D.1.0, D.2, D.2.1, D.2.6, D.2.13, D.3.1, D.4.5, F.3.1, F.4.1, F.4.3

LNCS Sublibrary: SL 2 – Programming and Software Engineering

ISSN   0302-9743
ISBN-10   3-540-69147-2 Springer Berlin Heidelberg New York
ISBN-13   978-3-540-69147-1 Springer Berlin Heidelberg New York

Springer is a part of Springer Science+Business Media

springer.com

© IFIP International Federation for Information Processing 2008
Printed in Germany

Typesetting: Camera-ready by author, data conversion by Scientific Publishing Services, Chennai, India
Printed on acid-free paper   SPIN: 12282821   06/3180   5 4 3 2 1 0

Preface

A Step Towards Verified Software

Worries about the reliability of software are as old as software itself; techniques for allaying these worries predate even James King's 1969 thesis on "A program verifier." What gives the whole topic a new urgency is the conjunction of three phenomena: the blitz-like spread of software-rich systems to control ever more facets of our world and our lives; our growing impatience with deficiencies; and the development—proceeding more slowly, alas, than the other two trends—of techniques to ensure and verify software quality.

In 2002 Tony Hoare, one of the most distinguished contributors to these advances over the past four decades, came to the conclusion that piecemeal efforts are no longer sufficient and proposed a "Grand Challenge" intended to achieve, over 15 years, the production of a *verifying compiler*: a tool that while processing programs would also guarantee their adherence to specified properties of correctness, robustness, safety, security and other desirable properties. As Hoare sees it, this endeavor is not a mere research project, as might normally be carried out by one team or a small consortium of teams, but a momentous endeavor, comparable in its scope to the successful mission to send a man to the moon or to the sequencing of the human genome. It requires a cogent agenda with both scientific and engineering components; support from the scientific community and from governments; and the collaboration of many groups, spread across many countries and including many specialties, for the advancement of a common goal.

VSTTE — the first conference on Verified Software: Theories, Tools, Experiments —(http://vstte.ethz.ch) was the launching event for this undertaking. Held at ETH Zurich in October of 2005, the conference gathered about 100 participants, the elite of software verification from a dozen countries. The conference was by invitation only. Although of course not every top expert could be invited, and not all who were invited could come, the attendee list makes up a sample of the best work currently being pursued in software verification. The present volume is the record of this memorable event.

We have not just gathered the position papers contributed by most of the participants. Attendees of scientific conferences know well that the benefit does not just come from formal paper presentations; question-and-answer sessions after talks are another prime source of insights, especially with participants as distinguished as those of VSTTE. In an effort to increase the attraction of this book for readers who were not in Zurich, we recorded the discussions and include the transcripts here (with the exclusion of some sessions with no associated paper). To preserve the spontaneity of these exchanges, we have kept the editing to a minimum, essentially removing a few superfluous comments. (Because the process took some time, it also serves as our excuse for the delay between the conference and the present publication.) We hope that you will enjoy the added value of this material, and perhaps even that you will at times feel like you are actually attending a live VSTTE session, including the occasional inaudible comment.

From "Exclusive ors" to Conjunction

The field of software verification has long been marked by competition between approaches, often resulting in binary oppositions—view A vs. view B. The oppositions still exist, and help define a rough multi-dimensional classification of the techniques represented at VSTTE and elsewhere; in attempting this classification, however, we should note that the variants along each dimension are increasingly recognized as complementary rather than exclusive. Software verification is sufficiently hard that a Grand Challenge effort must glean help from every good idea.

The first distinction pits *management*-oriented approaches against those based on *technology*. VSTTE was technology-oriented and this volume emphasizes the latter kind, but you will find occasional references to project management, the political context, model-driven development, process models and the like. Bad management can be as effective as bad technology in destroying software quality. In the rest of this discussion we limit ourselves to technical aspects.

A thick line has long divided proponents of *constructive* approaches to software construction from people who understand "verification" in the same way Reagan did in his reaction to Gorbachev's arms-reduction promises: "Trust, but *verify*." This division can also be called "a priori vs. a posteriori": build the software right, in the Dijkstra tradition of *A Discipline of Programming*, continued today by such techniques as proof-supported refinement, well represented in this volume; or scrutinize the result, with the help of powerful tools, for possible quality violations. This is an example of where opposition tends nowadays to yield to convergence: we need the best techniques to produce software that will have no bugs; and the best techniques to find any bugs that, all these efforts notwithstanding, still slip through the cracks.

Also prominent in this volume is the contrast between authors who concern themselves mostly with *specification*, often to the point of dismissing the advances of modern programming languages, and those who work at the implementation level, using these very programming languages as their basic tool. Even that conflict is not as irreducible as it sounds, since effective approaches using specification languages must go all the way to implementation, and advances in programming languages bring them to a level of abstraction not so far removed from the realm of specification.

The next opposition is between *static* approaches, which work on the basis of the software text only, and *dynamic* ones which require its execution. Examples of the first category are static analysis and proofs; the primary example of the second is testing. Although VSTTE did not prominently feature work on testing, this approach has made significant progress in recent years, and researchers are increasingly recognizing what software practitioners have known for years: that testing is today, and will remain for a long time, a key part of almost any effort to produce quality software.

Among static approaches, you will note the contrast between *full proofs* of correctness, which for any significant software system must command the support of powerful computer-based proof systems (the authors of several of the most famous of these tools were present at VSTTE and contributed to this volume), and *static analysis*, a term that generally describes ascertaining more partial properties of the software. Static analysis uses tools too, sometimes even the same theorem provers.

This is one more distinction that tends to get blurred, as the successes of partial static analysis continue to expand the scope and ambition of the properties they assess.

The distinction between static and dynamic approaches might seem to defy such blurring; but that too would be a wrong guess. The testing community's long-time differences with the advocates of proofs are fading out; a successor conference series of VSTTE, Tests And Proofs (TAP, http://tap.ethz.ch), launched at ETH Zurich in 2007, explores this new convergence. Also significant is the growing popularity of *model checking*, a technique that has enjoyed considerable successes in recent years, first with hardware verification and now with software. Model checking is similar to exhaustive testing in that it attempts to explore all execution paths of a program; but it does so on a simplified version of the program (to make the search tractable) and uses advanced proof techniques to limit the search space and make the results significant. One may further contrast model checking with *abstract interpretation*, also used successfully in large industrial projects; here too, some of the key contributors to both approaches were active participants in the conference and this book.

Competition turning into cooperation, "exclusive or" replaced by "and," initial contradictions revealing complementarity the deeper one digs: this could be the theme of the present book. By exploring the authors' often contrasted contributions, you will discover both the multiplicity of viewpoints that exist today in the field of software verification and the numerous common themes and solutions that justify Tony Hoare's injunction: to join forces and all get to work together.

Acknowledgments. Many people made VSTTE and this volume possible. As Program Chair, Natarajan Shankar composed and orchestrated the event. We are of course particularly grateful to the authors, panelists and other participants who contributed their best work.

ETH Zurich (as part of its 150th anniversary celebrations) contributed a generous donation; so did Microsoft Research. We are particularly indebted to Professor Meinrad Eberle, coordinator of the ETH 150th anniversary, and Dr. Andrew Herbert, Managing Director of the Microsoft Research center in Cambridge.

ETH provided superb infrastructure and services, allowing in particular the recording of sessions as reflected in this book. The organizing team from the Chair of Software Engineering—Claudia Günthart, Bernd Schoeller, Ilinca Ciupa, Andreas Leitner, Manuel Oriol, Werner Dietl, Adam Darvas, Farhad Mehta, Luc de Louw and a number of student helpers—was essential to the preparation of the conference and its smooth operation, including the recordings. The grueling task of transcribing these recordings was performed with remarkable efficiency by Patrick Schönbach. Claudia Günthart helped put the book in its final form.

Our primary debt is to the two conference Chairs, Tony Hoare and Jay Misra, for not only conceiving the vision but also relentlessly pursuing its realization down to the most practical details, with an energy that never ceases to amaze us all. We hope that readers of this book will feel some of that energy, and share some of the excitement that pervaded every session of the VSTTE conference.

February 2008

Bertrand Meyer
Jim Woodcock

VSTTE Chairs and Committees

Joint General Chairs

Tony Hoare, Microsoft Research, UK
Jayadev Misra, University of Texas at Austin, USA

Program Chair

Natarajan Shankar, SRI, USA

Steering Committee

Manfred Broy, TU München, Germany

Butler Lampson, Microsoft Research, UK

Mathai Joseph, Tata Research Development and Design Centre, India

Gilles Kahn, INRIA, France

J Moore, University of Texas at Austin, USA

Amir Pnueli, Weizmann Inst. of Science, Israel

Michel Sintzoff, U. Cath. de Louvain, Belgium

Zhou Chao Chen, Chinese Acad. of Sciences

Program Committee

Jean-Raymond Abrial, ETH Zurich, Switzerland

Dines Bjørner, Technical Univ. of Denmark

Patrick Cousot, École Normale Supérieure, France

Michael Ernst, Mass. Inst. of Technology, USA

David Evans, Univ. of Virginia, USA

David Gries, Cornell University, USA

Orna Grumberg, Israel Inst. of Technology

Masami Hagiya, Univ. of Tokyo, Japan

Ian Hayes, Univ. of Queensland, Australia

Gerard Holzmann, Jet Propulsion Laboratory, USA

Cliff Jones, Univ. of Newcastle, UK

Greg Morrisett, Harvard Univ., UK

George Necula, UC Berkeley, USA

Greg Nelson, HP Systems Research Center, USA

Tobias Nipkow, TU München, Germany

Colin O'Halloran, QinetiQ, UK

Ernst-Rüdiger Olderog, Univ. Oldenburg, Germany

Mooly Sagiv, Tel-Aviv University, Israel

He Jifeng, United Nations Univ.,
    Macao
Connie Heitmeyer, Naval Research
    Laboratory, USA

Carolyn Talcott, SRI International, USA

Jian Zhang, Academia Sinica, China

Publication Chair

Jim Woodcock, University of York, UK

Publication Committee

David Gries, Cornell University, USA
Cliff Jones, Newcastle, UK
Bertrand Meyer, ETH Zurich, Switzerland
Ernst-Rüdiger Olderog, Univ. Oldenburg, Germany

Organization Chair

Bertrand Meyer, ETH Zurich, Switzerland

Organization Committee

Bernd Schoeller, ETH Zurich, Switzerland
Claudia Günthart, ETH Zurich, Switzerland

Tony Hoare, opening session

Rajeev Joshi, Joseph Kiniry, Greg Nelson, Natarajan Shankar, Jay Misra, Tony Hoare,
closing panel

Welcome party in the historic Semper-Aula of the ETH

Panagiotis Manolios, Wolfgang Paul, Amir Pnueli

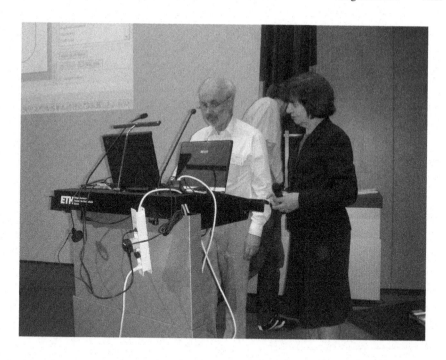

Cliff Jones, Connie Heitmeyer

Anthony Hall, Rod Chapman   Jay Misra, Niklaus Wirth, Tony Hoare
in the "VSTTE Express" (chartered train to Üetliberg for conference dinner)

Photographs by Bertrand Meyer

Participants

Jean-Raymond Abrial, ETH Zurich, Switzerland

Rajeev Alur, University of Pennsylvania, USA

Myla Archer, Naval Research Laboratory, USA

Ralph Back, Abo Akademi University, Finland

Thomas Ball, Microsoft Research, USA

David Basin, ETH Zurich, Switzerland

Yves Bertot, INRIA, France

Ramesh Bharadwaj, Naval Research Laboratory, USA

Egon Börger, University of Pisa, Italy

Manfred Broy, TU Munich, Germany

Tevfik Bultan, University of California, USA

Michael Butler, University of Southampton, UK

Supratik Chakraborty, Indian Institute of Technology, India

Patrice Chalin, Concordia University, Canada

Roderick Chapman, Praxis High Integrity Systems, UK

Marsha Chechik, University of Toronto, Canada

Alessandro Coglio, Kestrel Institute, USA

Patrick Cousot, École Normale Supérieure, France

Michael Ernst, MIT, USA

Kathi Fisler, Worcester Polytechnic Institute, USA

Kokichi Futatsugi, JAIST, Japan

Allen Goldberg, Kestrel Technology
LLC, USA

Cordell Green, Kestrel Institute, USA

Arie Gurfinkel, University of Toronto,
Canada

Masami Hagiya, University of Tokyo,
Japan

Anthony Hall, Oxford, UK

Stefan Hallerstede, ETH Zurich,
Switzerland

Klaus Havelund, Kestrel Technology
LLC, USA

Eric Hehner, University of Toronto,
Canada

Constance Heitmeyer, Naval Research
Laboratory, USA

Michael G. Hinchey, NASA, USA

Thai Son Hoang, ETH Zurich,
Switzerland

Tony Hoare, Microsoft Research, UK

Gerard J. Holzmann, NASA Jet
Propulsion Laboratory, USA

Peter Vincent Homeier, NSA, USA

Andrew Ireland, Heriot-Watt University,
UK

Bart Jacobs, Radboud University
Nijmegen, Netherlands

He Jifeng, UNU-IIST, China

Cliff Jones, Newcastle University, UK

Mathai Joseph, Tata Consultancy
Services, India

Rajeev Joshi, NASA/JPL Laboratory for
Reliable Software, USA

Joseph Kiniry, University College
Dublin, Ireland

Daniel Kröning, ETH Zurich,
Switzerland

Patrick Lam, Massachusetts Institute of
Technology, USA

Gary T. Leavens, Iowa State University,
USA

Rustan Leino, Microsoft Research, USA

Zhiming Liu, UNU-IIST, Macao, China

Panagiotis Manolios, Georgia Tech,
USA

Tiziana Margaria, University of
Göttingen, Germany

Edu Metz, Nokia Research Center, USA

Bertrand Meyer, ETH Zurich, Switzerland

Jayadev Misra, University of Texas at
Austin, USA

J. Strother Moore, University of Texas,
USA

Peter Müller, ETH Zurich, Switzerland

David A. Naumann, Stevens Institute of
Technology, USA

Greg Nelson, USA

Colin O'Halloran, QinetiQ, UK

Peter O'Hearn, Queen Mary, University
of London, UK

Ernst-Rüdiger Olderog, University of
Oldenburg, Germany

Manuel Oriol, ETH Zurich, Switzerland

Wolfgang Paul, University of
Saarbrücken, Germany

Amir Pnueli, Weizmann Institute, Israel,
and New York University, USA

Sanjiva Prasad, Indian Institute of
Technology, India

Ganesan Ramalingam, IBM Research,
India

Thomas Reps, University of Wisconsin-
Madison, USA

Tamara Rezk, INRIA, France

Martin Rinard, Massachusetts Institute of
Technology, USA

Willem Paul de Roever, University of
Kiel, Germany

Grigore Rosu, University of Illinois, USA

Harald Ruess, SRI International, USA

John Rushby, SRI International, USA

Shmuel Sagiv, Tel-Aviv University, Israel

Peter Schmitt, University of Karlsruhe,
Germany

Florian Schneider, ETH Zurich,
Switzerland

Wolfram Schulte, Microsoft Research,
USA

Natarajan Shankar, SRI International,
USA

Natasha Sharygina, Carnegie Mellon
University, USA

Michel Sintzoff, Université Catholique de Louvain, Belgium

Douglas R. Smith, Kestrel Institute, USA

Graham Steel, University of Edinburgh, UK

Bernhard Steffen, University Dortmund, Germany

Ofer Strichman, Technion, Israel

Aaron Stump, Washington University, USA

Carolyn Talcott, SRI International, USA

Cesare Tinelli, University of Iowa, USA

Mark Utting, University of Waikato, New Zealand

Eric Van Wyk, University of Minnesota, USA

Helmut Veith, TU Munich, Germany

Arnaud Venet, Kestrel Technology, USA

Laurent Voisin, ETH Zurich, Switzerland

Georg Weissbacher, ETH Zurich, Switzerland

Niklaus Wirth, ETH Zurich, Switzerland

Jim Woodcock, University of York, UK

Stephan Zdancewic, University of Pennsylvania, USA

Naijun Zhan, Chinese Academy of Sciences

Jian Zhang, Chinese Academy of Sciences

Jianjun Zhao, Fukuoka Institute of Technology, Japan

Table of Contents

Introduction

Verification Tools

Guaranteeing Correctness

Software Engineering Aspects

Verifying Object-Oriented Programming

Programming Language and Methodology Aspects

Components

Static Analysis

Design, Analysis and Tools

Formal Techniques

Position Papers

Verified Software: Theories, Tools, Experiments
Vision of a Grand Challenge Project

Tony Hoare and Jay Misra

Microsoft Research Ltd. and The University of Texas at Austin
thoare@microsoft.com, misra@cs.utexas.edu

Summary. The ideal of correct software has long been the goal of research in Computer Science. We now have a good theoretical understanding of how to describe what programs do, how they do it, and why they work. This understanding has already been applied to the design, development and manual verification of simple programs of moderate size that are used in critical applications. Automatic verification could greatly extend the benefits of this technology.

This paper argues that the time is ripe to embark on an international Grand Challenge project to construct a program verifier that would use logical proof to give an automatic check of the correctness of programs submitted to it. Prototypes for the program verifier will be based on a sound and complete theory of programming; they will be supported by a range of program construction and analysis tools; and the entire toolset will be evaluated and evolve by experimental application to a large and widely representative sample of useful computer programs. The project will provide the scientific basis of a solution for many of the problems of programming error that afflict all builders and users of software today.

This paper starts with an optimistic vision of a possible long-term future of reliable programming. It argues that scientific research will play an essential role in reaching these long-term goals. It suggests that their achievement should be accelerated by a major international research initiative, modelled on a Grand Challenge, with specific measurable goals. The suggested measure is one million lines of verified code. By definition, this consists of executable programs, together with their specifications, designs, assertions, etc., and together with a machine-checked proof that the programs are consistent with this documentation. We anticipate that the project would last more than ten years, consume over one thousand person-years of skilled scientific effort, drawn from all over the world. Each country will contribute only a proportion of the effort, but all the benefits will be shared by all.

The paper concludes with suggestions for exploratory pilot projects to launch the initiative and with a call to volunteers to take the first steps in the project immediately after this conference. A possible first step will be to revise and improve this paper as a generally agreed report of goals and methods of the scientists who wish to engage in the project.

B. Meyer and J. Woodcock (Eds.): Verified Software, LNCS 4171, pp. 1–18, 2008.
© IFIP International Federation for Information Processing 2008

1 The Long-Term Vision (20-50 Years from Now)

Programmers are human and they make mistakes.There are many competent programmers who spend as much as half their time in detecting and correcting the mistakes that they and their colleagues have made in the other half.Commonly used programming tools and languages do little to prevent error. It is not surprising that software products are often delivered late, and with a functionality that requires years of evolution to meet original customer requirements. Inevitable evolution of the requirements, and changes in the environment of software use, are increasingly hard to track by changes made to the program after delivery. The US Department of Commerce in 2002 estimated that the cost to the US economy of avoidable software errors is between 20 and 60 billion dollars every year. Over half the cost is incurred by the users.

In the progress of time, these problems will be largely solved.Programmers of the future will make no more mistakes than professionals in other disciplines. Most of their remaining mistakes will be detected immediately and automatically, just as type violations are detected today, even before the program is tested. An application program will typically be developed from an accurate specification of customer requirement; and the process of rational design and implementation of the code will be assisted by a range of appropriate formally based programming tools, starting with more capable compilers for procedural and functional programming languages. Critical applications will always be specified completely, and their total correctness will be checked by machine. In many specialised applications, large parts of a program will be generated automatically from the specification. Declarative and procedural programming languages will emerge or evolve to assist in reliable program design and verification. Education of software engineers will be based on an appreciation of the underlying science. As a result, inevitable changes in environment and in customer requirements will be more easily and rapidly tracked by changes in the delivered software.

Progress towards these solutions will require many changes in the current prejudices and professional practice of the designers and implementers of software.It will involve a great many interlinked educational, social, commercial, financial and legal issues, which are outside the domain of scientific research.Experience shows that scientific progress is best achieved by postponing discussion of such issues until the underlying scientific issues have been resolved, and the tools are available for its wide-spread application.As scientists, we take the view that the ultimate solution to the problem of programming error must be based on a full and accurate answer to some of the basic questions explored in computing research.They are similar to questions asked about the products of any other branch of pure and applied science, namely: what does a computer program do; how does it work; why does it work; how do we know the answers are correct?Only when these answers are found can we address the issue of how to exploit the answers to make the programs work better.

For many simple but critical applications, we already know the answers to these questions.A formal specification tells us precisely what a program does.Assertions internal to the program define the modules and interfaces, and explain how the program works.The semantics of a programming language explains why programs work.A mathematical proof is what checks that the answers to the above questions are correct.And finally, a theory of programming explains how to exploit the scientific understanding to improve the quality of software products.The continuing challenge is to broaden and deepen our understanding, for application to the full range of computer programs in use, both now and in the future.

Steady progress towards the answers is emerging from the normal scientific processes of competitive research and open publication.Much of this research is already driven by the need to solve immediate industrial and commercial problems.These strands of research must certainly continue.This paper addresses an additional question: whether progress towards the longer term goals could be dramatically accelerated by the concerted effort of an international team of computer scientists.This will be a Grand Challenge project, similar to those that build satellites for astronomers and particle accelerators for physicists.Such a project should not be undertaken lightly, because it will involve commitment of more than a thousand person-years of effort from our most inventive scientists and engineers; their enthusiasm and talent will always be our scarcest scientific resource.The project will involve uncomfortable changes to the current culture and practice of science; perhaps we will have to break down some of the current divisions between our research communities, and abandon some of our favourite controversies between rival schools of thought.Recognition of success will be far in the future, and failure will be an ever-present risk.

But the rewards will be spectacular.The theory of programming will be proved applicable and adequate to explain the workings of most of the kinds of program that people actually want to write and use.Computing will demonstrate its maturity as a respectable branch of engineering science.Its basic scientific discoveries will underpin a comprehensive range of programming tools in widespread professional use.Experiments in the development, application and evolution of prototype tools will give strong scientific evidence of their value and limitations.Evidence of intermediate progress will encourage research in the many other areas of computer science, whose results will make essential contributions to the eventual application of the knowledge and tools developed by the project.Confidence in the availability of tools will also trigger discussion, planning and action on the many issues outside the domain of science that are needed to exploit the results of the research and so to achieve our long-term vision.

As in other branches of science, the achievement of the goals of a Grand Challenge is only a milestone of scientific advance, providing new methods that accelerate research aimed at even broader and more fundamental goals.For example, a program verifier is only a partial contribution to the development of reliable and dependable software: its availability will stimulate intensified research into the reliable capture of requirements and their faithful encoding as specifications.Indeed, the philosophy and technology of formal software verification may be an inspiration and foundation for a new general science of System Certification, covering not only software but also many other aspects of the design and implementation of major technological products that raise critical concerns of safety.

A program verifier, together with its associated toolset of specification aids, code generators, test environments, etc., will eventually be integrated into a single professional support environment, that might play a role as an 'intelligent programmer's assistant'.Its intelligence will be based on the capability of a computer to perform not only numerical calculations but also formal deductions, in a manner fore-shadowed by philosophers in the tradition of Aristotle, Leibnitz and Russell.Such a professional support environment might provide a pattern for similar intelligent assistants in other engineering professions where dependability is a crucial concern, perhaps including even mathematics and medicine.

2 The Contribution of the Grand Challenge Project (20 Years from Now)

We envisage that the Grand Challenge project will deliver its testable and measurable scientific results within twenty years.The results may be classified under three headings: theory, tools and experiments.

2.1 Theory

The project will deliver a comprehensive and unified theory of programming, which covers all the major programming paradigms and design patterns appearing in real computer programs, and nearly all the features of the programming languages of the present and foreseeable future.The theory will include a combination of concurrency, non-determinism, object orientation and inheritance.Many disciplined software design patterns will be proven sound, and analysis algorithms will be developed that check whether a program observes the relevant disciplines.Development of the theory should consume only a small percentage of the total research effort.

2.2 Tools

The project will deliver a prototype for a comprehensive and integrated suite of programming tools for the design, development, analysis, validation, testing and evolution of computer programs that are free of all errors of certain clearly specified kinds.We describe the tools in two classes: programming tools and logical tools.Development of the tools should consume a bit less than half the total effort.

The programming tools will include program development aids such as specification analysers, interrogators, checkers, and animators, as well as a range of application-oriented automatic program generators.They will include type checkers, and program analysers to detect possible violations of theoretically sound design disciplines. They will include test harnesses using assertions as test oracles, and test case generators based on a combined analysis of specifications and program text. They will include aids to evolution and reverse engineering of legacy code, for example, tools that infer assertions from comprehensive regression tests.All the tools of the suite will accept and produce data in compatible formats, and with the same semantics for intermediate specifications and annotated code.

The logical tools will employ a variety of strategies such as proof search, resolution, decision procedures, constraint solving, model checking, abstract interpretation, algebraic reduction, SAT solving, etc.These technologies will work together across broad internal interfaces, and they will share in the solution of each verification problem.They will be supplemented by a comprehensive library of theories which have specifically targeted at concepts of common programming languages, standard libraries, and specific applications.

The pivotal tools in the collection will be the program verifiers. They will exploit the discoveries of research into the theory of programming to transform a program and its specification into verification conditions that can be discharged by the logical tools.

2.3 Experiments

The project will deliver a repository of verified software, containing hundreds of programs and program modules, and amounting to over a million lines of code. The code will be accompanied by full or partial specifications, designs, test cases, assertions, evolution histories and other formal and informal documentation. Each program will have been mechanically checked by one or more of the program verifiers in the toolset. The verification of the code in the repository should consume a bit more than half of the total effort of the project.

The eventual suite of verified programs will be selected by the research community as a realistic representative of the full range of computer application.Realism is assured if the program itself (or perhaps an earlier less fully verified version of it) has actually been used in real life.In size, the individual entries into the repository should range from a thousand to a hundred thousand lines of code. Some of them will be written in declarative languages and some in procedural languages, and some in a combination of both. They will cover a wide range of applications, including smart cards, embedded software, device routines, modules from a standard class library, an embedded operating system, a compiler for a useful language (possibly smartcard Java), parts of the verifier itself, a program generator, a communications protocol (possibly TCP/IP), a desk-top application, parts of a web service (perhaps Apache).The programs will use a variety of design patterns and programming techniques, including object orientation, inheritance, and concurrency.

There will be a hierarchy of recognised levels of verification, ranging from avoidance of specific exceptions like buffer overflow, general structural integrity (or crash-proofing), continuity of service, security against intrusion, safety, partial functional correctness, and (at the highest level) total functional correctness.Each claim for a specific level of correctness will be accompanied by a clear informal statement of the assumptions and limitations of the proof, and the contribution that it makes to system dependability.The progress of the project will be marked by raising the level of verification for each module in the repository.Since the ultimate goal of the project is scientific, the ultimate level achieved will always be higher than what the normal engineer and customer would accept.

In addition to verified programs, the repository will include libraries of bare specifications independent of code.These may include formal definitions of standard intermediate languages and machine architectures, communication and security protocols, interfaces of basic standard libraries, etc. There will also be libraries of application-oriented specifications, which can be re-used by future applications programmers in particular domains (such as railway networks).Some of these will be supported by automatic code generators, perhaps implemented within a generic declarative framework.

The actual contents of the repository will be as chosen by the research community during the course of the project.An overall total of one million lines of mechanically verified code will be a convincing demonstration of the success of the project; it will be sufficient to reveal clearly the capability and limitations of the concept of a program verifier and other associated formal programming tools; and it will give paradigm examples of their effective use.

There will remain the considerable task of transferring the technology developed by the project into professional use by programmers, for the benefit of all users of computers.This is where all the educational, social, commercial, legal and political issues will come to the fore.The scientists will have made their main contribution in demonstrating the possibility of what was previously unthinkable.Scientific research will continue to deliver practical and theoretical improvements at an accelerated rate, because they are based on the achievement of the goals of the Grand Challenge project.

3 The Grand Challenge Project Plans (5-20 Years from Now)

The Grand Challenge project will be planned in outline to take fifteen years, starting perhaps in five years' time, and requiring over a thousand person-years of skilled scientific effort. The project will be driven by the cumulative development of the repository of mechanically verified code.Its progress will be measured by a number of indicators: A count of the total number of executable lines of code that have been verified, the length of the largest verified module, the level of verification achieved, the range of applications that are covered, and the range of programming features that they exploit.According to these criteria, every program and module that is successfully verified will be celebrated as the first of a new kind.That will ensure that the repository eventually covers the necessary wide range of variation.

In order to accumulate a million lines of verified code, it will be essential to exploit all sources of experimental material, and to exploit and develop the capabilities of all available tools.Some of the code and specifications may be collected from critical projects that have already undergone a formal analysis.Some of the code will be developed by rational design methods from specification, using interactive specification checkers and development aids.Other code will be generated automatically, together with its assertions and its proofs, by special-purpose program generators, taking an application-oriented specification as input.Some of the code will be taken from existing class libraries for popular programming languages, and even from well-written open source application codes.In such cases, the specification and other annotations will need to be reverse-engineered from the code, using program analysis, assertion inference, and even empirical testing.In all cases, the resulting code must be checked mechanically against specification by a program verifier.

The experience gained in use of existing tools will be exploited to gradually improve the capability of the tools themselves, including their usability and their performance.For each tool that is mature enough for general use on the project, there will be a research and development group with adequate resources and authority to maintain and develop the tool, to provide support and education, and to control the impact of enhancements to the tool in the interests of existing and new users.On occasion, new tools will be developed, offering a step-change increase in capability and quality, and opening up opportunities for yet further advances.For the purposes of the project, the tools should be as usable by scientists as a routine scientific instrument like an oscilloscope.They can assume a high level of scientific understanding.

An over-riding concern in the development of tools, and in particular of the program verifiers, will be that the algorithms incorporated in the tools must be logically sound and consistent.The second concern is that they should approach more and more closely to completeness.These achievements will require significant contributions from theorists, who undertake to apply their skills in the context of the programs and languages actually included in the repository.For many of these, new concepts in specification, new type systems, and new design disciplines will need to be discovered; and existing knowledge will have to be adapted to the needs of mechanical verification.In some cases, the theorist will be able to test and evaluate new discoveries by making ad hoc changes in existing tools.But the wider testing of the developing theory will depend on the cooperation of tool-builders and tool support groups, who will incorporate new theory into existing and new tools.

Advances in the capability of proof tools will be driven primarily by the needs of their expanding range of users.The first demand of the users will be increased automation and improved performance of analysis and proof.This requirement is readily formalised and promoted by annual competitions, currently conducted by the theorem proving community; they have achieved fantastic improvements in the speed of decision procedures that are needed in the inner loop of all verifiers.In addition to improvements to the capability of individual tools, a strong user requirement will be for the inter-working of all the tools required in a verification experiment, so that each tool accepts the output of the others, and produces its own output in a form acceptable by others.The design of new competitions should be targeted towards this goal; the rules could require broader interfaces than the yes/no of decision procedures; and they could require that counter-examples and proofs be produced and checked by independent tools.In some cases, human inspection of the results may be desirable, to assess comprehensibility.Some competitions could be designed so that they can only be won by combining the merits of the latest versions of different tools. In this way each tool can continue to be developed independently, ensuring that independent improvements can be exploited immediately by other tool-builders and by all users of the tools.Perhaps the most stimulating competitions would be based on the popular programming competitions already set regularly on the web, by simply requiring that the resulting program be verified.A little more time may be needed at first, but the eventual goal would be to develop correct programs just as fast or faster than incorrect ones are today.

It is probable that the practical capability of proof tools will be increased by specialisation towards the needs of particular programming languages.For example, it would pay to incorporate the type system of the programming language directly into the logic of the proof tool.It would also pay to develop libraries of theories to cover specifically the features of the class library of particular languages in widespread use.

At any given time during the course of the project, the repository will contain all the code verified so far, which will be used repeatedly as regression tests for the evolution of the toolset, and as a measure of the progress of the project.In addition, the repository will contain a number of challenge problems, which have been selected by the research community as worthy candidates and ripe for verification.In the early stages, these challenges will include useful programs which already have specifications verified by existing technology, often by hand.For larger and later examples, the challenge may require construction or generation of code from a specification or vice-versa. Some of the problems will be large enough that they have to be solved collaboratively, by an agreed share-out of the work.Smaller problems of a more innovative kind may be set up annually as challenges for scientific competition.

It is the availability of a program verifier that will determine in what languages the initial programs and specifications will be written.A program verifier is a combination of proof tools with the semantics of a particular programming language. Examples of currently mature program verifiers are ESC/Java, Coq, and ACL2; and other proof tools are becoming available for this purpose.In the early stages, the project will be broadly inclusive of all approaches and languages.But the eventual goal will be that nearly all the tools will be readily applicable to nearly all the programs in the repository, and tool providers engaging in the project will collaborate to achieve this goal.Their idealism will be re-enforced by the users of the tools, who will certainly need tools that are highly interoperable; and tool support groups will compete to provide what the users want.Initially, inter-operation could be assisted by mechanical translators, which could be just targeted specifically at the particular challenge material that has been accepted into the repository.The problem of assimilating formats of incompatibly coded data bases is not peculiar to Computer Science – it is also a severe problem in astronomy, physics and biology, and other branches of e-science.The other sciences have exploited the repository concept to tackle this problem, and have allocated the necessary translation and co-ordination effort from their programming support groups.

In the course of time, agreement will be reached between tool support groups for the design and implementation of wider, more efficient, and more convenient interfaces between the tools that they support.In the end, the quality of each tool will determine the numbers of its users.Since users will tend to gravitate towards the most popular tools, it is quite likely that there will be less variety of notation at the end of the project than at the beginning.

We expect that the plans for the project will include a specification phase, an integration phase and an application phase, each lasting around five years.During the specification phase, a network of repositories will be established and populated with challenge specifications and codes.Some of the smaller challenges will be totally verified using existing tools, and some of the larger ones will be verified to a formally specified level of structural soundness and serviceability.A formal tool-bus will establish communication at the file level between the more widely used tools.During the second integration phase, the tools will evolve to exploit even closer inter-working, and performance will be improved by introduction of more inter-active interfaces between them.New tools will emerge as user needs become more apparent.Medium-sized programs will be fully verified and some of the largest programs will be verified to a high level of structural integrity.During the final phase, the pace of progress will accelerate.A comprehensive, integrated tool suite that is convenient to use will permit the collaborative verification of large-scale applications, culminating in achievement of the million-line goal.

4 Pilot Projects (1-5 Years from Now)

The aim of a pilot project for a Grand Challenge is to gather evidence for the viability of the long-term goals, and to gather the experience needed to formulate intermediate goals and more detailed project plans.The pilot projects also lay the foundation for the actual conduct of the project, including recruitment and training of the initial cadres of scientists who will work on it.They do not require the same degree of log-term commitment or global co-ordination as the main project itself.

4.1 The Repository

An early pilot project for this challenge would obviously be the establishment of an initial repository of suggested challenge material for formal verification. It could start by requesting contributions of any available specifications for existing software that can be put into the public domain. In some cases, this could be accompanied by the actual code, and perhaps any existing proofs, constructed earlier by hand.It would remain open to suggestions for further challenge problems, and for accumulating the results of the experimental research.

4.2 Service Centres

A second class of pilot project would be to set up a network of support and service centres for the repository.The centres should have the manpower to curate the submitted material, and to perform any necessary notational conversions to ensure that the announced challenge codes will be amenable to processing by the available programming tools.Such centres could also provide an advisory service to local experimenters and users of the tools. Such a centre could also take responsibility for education; they could organise and deliver summer schools to train scientists in the use of currently available tools, and teach the underlying theories of correctness.

4.4 Tool Inter-Working

The methods and potential benefits and difficulties of tool integration can be explored by a number of ad hoc collaborations between the builders of any pair of tools, whether similar or complementary.There are examples of such collaborations now in progress.

4.5 Tool Repository

For more systematic integration, the concept of a repository could be extended to support the maintenance and integration of suites of existing tools.Such a repository should be responsible for facilitating the combined use of multiple tools from the suite, and ensuring their applicability to the challenge problems.The staff of the tool repository could assist in negotiations of interfaces between tool providers, and they should have the manpower to help implement any standard interfaces that emerge.

4.6 Tool Support Centres

Another important class of pilot project start by the establishment of a recognised support centre for each of the major programming and proof tools that are likely to be used in the initial stages of the project.Such a centre should obtain long-term funding to enable it to discharge responsibilities to a growing community of users.Each centre should have resources to maintain its tool, to improve it in the light of user experience, to integrate it with the latest versions of other tools, to improve its usability, and to incorporate extensions to its functionality that have been suggested by theorists or by users.

5 The First Steps (0-1 Year from Now)

On a long journey, the longest step is the first one.Here are some suggestions on how to take it.Each suggestion is followed by a personal question about your own possible role in getting the project started.I hope that this conference will help you to answer the questions in a positive way.

The first step for every participant is to think deeply whether your personal research goals are aligned to those of a Grand Challenge project; and then to consider what changes to your own research practices and priorities would you be prepared to make to maximise your own contribution to these goals.Then decide whether you are prepared to make these changes? The pilot projects listed above are only rough examples.Can you suggest some more specific ones?Are there any that you would like to make the subject of your next research grant proposal?

These issues should be discussed with other members of each of the research communities whose expertise is necessary to the success of the project.A series of suitable occasions could be at the regular international conferences of your research community.Would you be willing to organise or attend a Workshop at the next conference that you attend; its purpose would be to discuss the general prospect and the detailed progress of this Grand Challenge?Or would you attend such a Workshop organised by someone else?

The most vital contributors to the project will be the experimental scientists, who apply the best available tools to the challenge problems accumulating in the repository, and contribute suggestions for the improvement of the tools.One way to assess and increase the enthusiasm of scientists in your own country or region would be to hold a Working Conference and/or a series of Workshops, to encourage local scientists to contribute their skill and their judgement to the planning of the project.Would you be prepared to sponsor or organise such a Conference?Or serve on the programme Committee?

The teams of experimental scientists will require education in the relevant theories, and training in the use of the best available tools.Would you be prepared to design and deliver Master's courses on program verification?Would it be appropriate to set Master's projects to verify small portions of the challenge material held in the repository?

Education in the technology should begin at the undergraduate level.Would you be prepared to teach the use of specifications and assertions as a routine aid to program testing, as they are currently being used in Industry?Would you use them yourself as an aid to marking the students' practical assignments?

The promises of a Grand Challenge project and the planning of their fulfilment must be based on a deep and wide appreciation of the current state of the art, and the technical and human resources available to advance it.Would you be prepared to draft a survey paper of the current state of the art in your subject, and an evaluation of its potential future contribution to the project as a whole?The paper could serve as an introduction to the relevant parts of the specialist background, for the benefit of those who will participate in the project.

The survey paper might be suitable as the first article in a special issue of an international technical Journal, which could be devoted to technologies relevant for the Grand Challenge Project?Who would you invite as other contributors to the special issue? Would you volunteer to edit such an issue yourself?

For tool-builders, a long-term goal of the project is that all the tools needed for verification of useful software will work conveniently together in an integrated toolset.This process has already been started by pair-wise coupling of proof tools.Can you identify a tool that could usefully be used in combination with yours, across some mutually agreed interface?Who would you approach to start discussion?Is the time ripe for design of interfaces to link larger sets of tools?Would you be prepared to discuss standard interfaces?Or initiate a discussion of them?

For theorists, a long-term goal of the project is that an integration of sound and general theories will be proved adequate for verification of actual programs that people want to write and use.These programs will be written in languages that people want to write their programs in.Elegant and general theories will have to be adapted and specialised to provide an axiomatic (correctness-oriented) semantics for an adequately large subset of existing languages.Further work will be needed to design analysis algorithms that check conformance to the disciplines of the subset.These will then have to be incorporated in tool-sets that are needed for the experimentation; and the results of experiment may require re-evaluation of the theory.Are you prepared to engage in the extra work required to adapt your theories for experimental verification or falsification?

Most of the funds that support research in Computer Science are provided by national funding agencies. In some countries, these agencies have a tradition of favouring shorter-term projects that will give competitive advantage to national industry. For a long-term international project, each agency will have to make a decision on behalf of the country whether and how far to engage in a Grand Challenge project, recognising the advantage of sharing the costs among all nations, in the expectation that the benefits are also shared among all.The modes and procedures for funding the necessary research proposals in some countries may have to be adjusted to accommodate the scale and duration of a Grand Challenge.Would you be able to raise and discuss these issues with your own national funding agency?

The most crucial decisions right from the start of the project will be decisions about the current and final contents of the repository.These decisions could be delegated to an editorial board representing the views and good judgement of the entire research community. The board will lay down criteria for acceptance of new material into the repository, and devise some prestigious mode of publication for the results of each successful verification.In due course, they or their successors would be responsible suggesting priorities, for issuing challenges, and for co-ordinating a reasonable split of the labour of verification among all volunteers.The board might request recognition from IFIP as a new Working Group, as recognition of their international standing and as an aid to obtaining support for regular meetings.Who would you like to see as a member of such a board?Would you be prepared to serve yourself for an initial period?

6 Conclusion

Now is the best time to start this project.Since the idea of a program verifier was first proposed by Jim King in 1969, the state of the art has made spectacular advances.Theories are available for most of the features of modern programming languages. There is already considerable experience of manually proven design of programs currently running in critical applications.Machines are now a thousand times larger and a thousand times faster than they were then, and they are still getting more powerful.The basic technology of automatic proof has also made a thousand-fold advance, and the contributors to the conference show that this advance is also continuing.Finally, the number of computers, the number of computer programmers, and the number of computer users have each increased more than a thousand-fold. As a result, the annual cost of software error is many times greater than the total cost of the proposed scientific project over its entire fifteen-year timescale.The state of the art and the economic imperative convey the same message: the best time to start this project is now.

Acknowledgements. Tony Hoare has presented his original vision to a number of audiences over the last five years. Their comments, questions and criticisms have shaped this document. We are thankful to many individuals who have read and commmented on the preliminary draft of this document. We are thankful in particular to Jim Browne, Fred Chang, Rick Hehner, Jim Horning, Cliff Jones, Mathai Joseph,Bertrand Meyer, J Moore and Natarajan Shankar.

Appendix: Some Frequently Asked Questions

A What Is to be the Ultimate Product of the Grand Challenge?

The ultimate product will be a range of scientifically based programming support tools to assist in the specification, design, development, testing, analysis, evolution of software systems.This will be accompanied by convincing evidence of its successful use in a wide range of computer applications. The essentially new tool, serving as a lynchpin of the entire toolset, will be a program verifier, whose central role will be to certify that software conforms to its stated specification.The wider application of this tool will help to reduce the high costs of programming error, currently estimated at tens of billions of dollars a year.

A.1 Will the Program Verifier Certify all Reasonably-Sized Programs Automatically?

During the course of the project, the program verifier will be applied to a wide range of programs of reasonable size, which the research community has selected as representative of a useful range of computer applications.By the end of the project, this corpus of verified software will amount to more than a million lines of executable code, together with specifications, design history, assertions, test cases and other documentation.The science and technology incorporated in the tools will be generic, so there is good hope that success achieved on the million-line corpus will generalise to previously unseen programs of a similar kind.

The ultimate aim of the project is that the program verifier will certify all programs automatically.In practice, at any given time there will always be a percentage of verification conditions that the verifier cannot prove.For these, the traditional techniques of testing and run-time checking will be employed.The project will measure the percentage of failed conditions, and seek to reduce it, even after the tool is accepted as adequate for practical use.

A.2 If the Verifier Is Not Fully Automatic, How much Human Intervention Will be Needed?

In the initial stages of the project, there will be many verification conditions (perhaps as much as 5% of the total) that cannot be proved automatically.These will be published to serve as a challenge for development of the technology of theorem proving, and the development of specialised libraries of theorems that are targeted at verification of real programs.In the course of the project, the necessary human intervention will be supplied by experimental scientists engaged in the verification of the corpus of challenge codes.When the verifier is more widely used, its more serious failures will still require assistance from a specialist in verification.The tool will not be used in areas where these interventions are found to be too frequent.

A.3 What Kinds of Properties Will it be able to Certify?

The verifier will be capable in principle of certifying any properties that can be formally specified in the relevant subset of mathematical notation.Such properties will include avoidance of software-generated computer crashes, resistance to intrusion from unauthorised sources, observance of privacy constraints, conformity to internal interface conventions.In more critical applications, safety properties will be specified and verified, and in some cases a full behavioural specification will be formalised.

Many important properties are resistant to formal specification, for example 'user-friendliness', early delivery, extensibility.Other properties will be too expensive to formalise; and others will be so complicated that their formalisation is no more obviously correct than the program itself.The decision on how much effort to expend on formalisation of properties will have to be taken by the individual engineer in the light of the circumstances of the individual project.These decisions will limit the applicability of the verifier more substantially than any failure of full automation.

A.4 Will it be Too Onerous for the Average Programmer to Supply the Necessary Assertions and the Lemmas Needed for Their Proof?

Yes indeed.Initially it will be only skilled scientists who can perform this task.As the project proceeds, the verifier will be able to deduce many of the trivial but important assertions from the text of the program itself.Furthermore, the scientists will accumulate libraries of useful theories and theorems, so that that most of the necessary lemmas can be supplied automatically.Finally, the availability of a capable program verifier will motivate the more intellectually lively programmers to use it , and it will support the education of the next generation of programmers.

A.5 Will Programmers Have to Learn a New Language?

No; this is unlikely, and fortunately unnecessary.Certainly, scientists will continue to use and invent new languages to serve as scientific work-benches for exploring the theories under investigation, as it were under laboratory conditions.But the theories will also be extended and adapted to deal with languages in which the corpus of challenge material is expressed.In some cases, only a recognisable subset of the programming language will be verifiable.

Nevertheless, one can foresee ways in which the use of existing languages may gradually change.Programmers will be encouraged to avoid certain combinations of programming language feature which significantly complicate correctness reasoning.They will be encouraged to follow certain well-structured system design patterns, which permit verification by simpler proof patterns.And we may hope to see more program generators, which automatically generate parts of a system from their more abstract specifications.

In this way, it is likely that existing programming languages will evolve further in the direction of support for efficient construction of reliable programs.Such evolution will be based on scientifically supported theories that emerge from this Grand Challenge project.

A.6 Would the Verifier be Partially Available before the 15-Year Time-Line?

Yes; in fact the project will start with verifiers that are already available, but somewhat limited in capability.The main task of the project will be constantly to test and extend their capability.During the course of the project, the primary users of the tools will be the scientists engaged in the project; their task is to test current tools on a corpus of representative software, and determine how they can be improved.The tools will be structured to permit continuous improvement.They will be sufficiently convenient for use by specialised scientist, but probably not for use by the professional programmer.

In the later stages of the project, the emergent scientific understanding will be readily transferable to the developers and suppliers of widely used commercial programming tool-sets.They will be responsible for integrating the technology with current program development environments, for enhancing the convenience of their use, and for marketing and selling the results.That is a reasonable division of labour between the scientific researchers and the commercial exploiters of their discoveries.

B   By What Technical Means Is This Goal to be Achieved?

By collaborative endeavours of scientists from many specialities, who broadly agree on a common outcome, and on the intermediate steps to achieve it in a given timescale.They will work towards agreement on notations for programs and specifications, and on the formalisation of interfaces between tools of various kinds, and on the selection and accumulation of an agreed corpus of representative programs to test the tools.Theorists will work together to ensure that their theories can be applied in combination, and they will adapt their theories for application to the languages in which the programs of the corpus are expressed.Tool-builders will build select theories suggested by others, and build them into their tools; and they will undertake to supply tools of sufficient stability and convenience for use by experimental scientists.And finally, experimentalists will apply the tools to the programs in the agreed corpus.

B.1   Is it Mainly a Question of Improving Current Tools?

Certainly, it is inevitable the initial plans for the project should be based on what already exists.The plans envisage a continuous process of evolution of tools in the light of experimental evidence obtained by their community of users.General experience of software evolution suggests that this is an excellent driver of progress.

During the course of the project, the possibility of emergence of entirely new ideas and tools must be encouraged and welcomed.But by definition it cannot be planned for.

B.2   How Can We Achieve Tool Integration, When They Have Different Interfaces, Internal Data Structures, and Search Methods?

Initially, the goal should be inter-working of tools rather than integration.Inter-working involves translation of formats and data structures whenever information is required to pass between the separate tools.The essential advantage of inter-working is that it permits continued evolution of tools on both sides of the interface.

As understanding of the basic technology matures, and as its implementation stabilises, further efficiency, capability, and convenience of use may be achievable by closer integration of tools.Certainly, closer integration will be a necessary concomitant of actual commercial products.

B.3   Is There any Grounds for Optimism that Combination of Inadequate Tools Will be Found to be Adequate?

The use of tools in combination is essential to the success of the project.Without a full toolset, it will be impossible to reach the goal of a million lines of verified code.Inter-working is required to make combined tool use reasonably convenient.

There are analogies that suggest that inter-working tools can evolve to cover each others' inadequacies.The main ground for optimism is that the individual tools can continue to be improved separately in the light of their substantial use in experiments.

C How Can Different Groups Manage to Co-ordinate Their Activities?

There is plenty of experience of large-scale collaboration among scientists: astronomers build telescopes, physicists build particle accelerators, space scientists build satellites.In all cases, co-ordination is planned by the recognised leaders of the scientific community actually engaged in the project.

C.1 Will There be Top-Down Management Which Will Address Standardisation of Notation, Interfaces for Inter-Operability, and Directions of Research?

In Computer Science, there is less tradition of such a large-scale collaboration as in nuclear physics and astronomy. Consequently, the process of agreement should probably begin with small-scale and relatively short-term agreement among two or three groups engaged in related aspects of the project.When the major contributors to the project have identified themselves, it is likely that wider and more substantive issues will be discussed at regular meetings by the community as a whole.

C.2 Can Individuals and Groups Who do Not Identify Themselves as Participants still Contribute to the Effort?

Yes definitely.New ideas and breakthroughs are more likely to be originated by scientists who (with no need for justification) prefer to work independently of any long-term large-scale project.There will be many who prefer to conduct their research in close collaboration with an on-going engineering or commercial product development.Although the primary responsibility of such scientists is for the timely success of the particular project, the most original and general ideas are often inspired by practical needs.

Those engaged in the project must watch carefully for such advances by non-participating scientists, and be eager to embrace them as quickly as possible.How else can the challenging goals be achieved?

C.3 Who Will Fund This Work?

Funds for an international scientific project are usually contributed by the scientific funding agencies of the nations engaged in the project.The means of obtaining initial funds, and the assurance of reasonable continuity of funding in later years, will have to be planned individually by scientists resident in each country.

In Britain, the Prime Minister has stated that the goals of the national funding of science are:

1. The maintenance of national scientific prestige on the international scene.
2. The promotion of national commercial interest.

Contributions to an internationally recognised Grand Challenge project are a definite source of national prestige.And a scientific project that advances a generally applicable technology is an excellent nursery for technically advanced entrepreneurs, who will adapt and apply the technology in a specific marketplace.Finally, the main benefits of the project will be in the reduction of cost and improvement of the quality of computer software.These benefits will be shared by all nations.

C.4 Will There be an Effort to Get Umbrella Funding?

For international projects in Astronomy and Nuclear Physics, funding agencies in the participating countries undertake to bear some agreed proportion of the costs over an extended timescale, without specifying in advance exactly what the funds will be spent on.The actual spending is decided by the scientists, as the project progresses.This is possible, because the funding agencies have reasonable confidence that the scientists involved can collaborate effectively to produce the results that they promise.

In Computer Science, such collaboration would be unprecedented; but if the early achievements of the project give grounds for the requisite confidence, an effort to get umbrella funding would be entirely appropriate.The important criterion is that the attempt to obtain funding should not dilute or divert the pursuit of the pure scientific goals of the project.

D   Discussion on Tony Hoare's Presentation

Richard Bornat

Tony, I want first of all to waste a little time by congratulating you on a marvelous talk. You will know that I have heard versions of this talk many times, and that I have often disagreed with almost everything you said. Today, I have agreed with almost everything you said, and you made a marvelous clarification of the purpose of this conference. But that is not why I am standing up, because there is only one slide that I think I would like to disagree with. In any case, I think it is only a clarification.

You made a point that the human-genome project did not say that it would generate new drugs and new cures. It said that it would produce a scientific result. And I entirely agree with you. The engineers whom the genome scientists failed to service were the drug companies. For us, the engineers—whether we like it or not—are people like Linus Torvalds, with his attitude to specifications being what it is. (*Editors' note*: this is a reference to a citation by Torvalds shown by Bertrand Meyer during the introductory session: "*a `spec' is close to useless. I have **never** seen a spec that was both big enough to be useful **and** accurate. And I have seen **lots** of total crap work that was based on specs. It's **the** single worst way to write software, because it by definition means that the software was written to match theory, not reality.*") Now, we have delivered many times over the history of computer science—and you have been involved in many of these developments—for the engineers' better computers. We did it with compilers and programming languages first. Well, we did it with computers to begin with, of course, in the 1940s, but after that with compilers and programming languages, later on with types, with structured programming, with assertions. All of these have delivered better computing tools to the engineers. And that seems to me is what we can promise.

Now, if we promise cheaper program development, which is what you have written there, we are unfortunately – as you know as an English person – in competition with a number of charlatans *(Tony Hoare laughs)*, who would claim that by massaging the process of management of the work of a programmer, one can deliver cheaper and more reliable software. And I think, we should distinguish ourselves from those charlatans, and essentially, I am asking you for a mild change of emphasis, that we shall deliver tools, as we have done many times before, that will deliver the kind of advances that we have provided many times before. We shall do it again. And this time – don't you know, because you all use computers – this time, it matters to you! And never in history before did it matter to so many people. When you first did it, there were what? Fifty others? A hundred others? Two hundred others? Now, as you said, there are millions. And this time, it matters to you, and that is what we know we can do, because look, we have done it before, and that is what we will do again. And we will not be able to do what those charlatans—we won't say the word "charlatan"— what those people over there say they can do, but we will do something else. And it seems to me, that is the only point where I hope to see an improvement of what is a truly marvelous description of why I am a scientist and not an engineer. For the first time in my life, Tony, you are the first person who ever explained to me that I am an engineer, and now, you are the first person who ever explained to me that I am a scientist, and I thank you very much.

Tony Hoare

Thank you for your kind remarks. I think the thing that will distinguish us is that when we make those claims that we know that we can do it, those claims will be backed up by scientific evidence, which our competitors generally find difficult. We shouldn't relegate the work of our competitors. For almost every crazy idea for making software better, the alternative is worse. Thank you.

Towards a Worldwide Verification Technology

Wolfgang Paul

Saarland University, Computer Science Dept., 66123 Saarbrücken, Germany
wjp@wjpserver.cs.uni-sb.de

1 Introduction

Verisoft [1] is a large coordinated project funded by the German Federal Government. The mission of the project is i) to develop the technology which permits the
pervasive formal verification of entire computer systems consisting of hardware,
system software, communication systems and applications ii) to demonstrate in
collaboration with industry this technology with several prototypes. During the
fall and winter of 02/03 this project was planned by a task force headed by the
author.

This task force had to face issues very closely related to what we have discussed
in Zurich and we have lived now with the decisions made early in the year 2003
for more than two years. Based on this—mostly positive—experience we make
eight scientific, technological and administrative suggestions for the worldwide
coordination of efforts in software verification.

2 Basic Research Versus Technology

Basic research identifies fundamental effects and laws. It also develops laboratory
prototypes. Laboratory prototypes demonstrate, how newly discovered laws and
effects may be applied: *something like a laboratory prototype is expected to work*
in engineering. Turning this prototype into a component of a technology is left
to the engineers. It requires the elaboration of details which are judged to be
boring from a basic research point of view.

A component of a technology must work as it is. And it does not work in
isolation. All components of a technology must work together as they are. The
world of engineering technology is a binary world; time to work out details is
(or at least should be) over: things work or they do not work. Imagine you are
dying in an airplane crash due to bad software. That fixing a single line of code
would have saved your life is no consolation whatsoever.

In the past, research in the field of verification has stressed the basic research
aspect, very much at the expense of the engineering aspect. As a consequence,
we now have CAV tools which are numerous, ingenious and often even powerful;
because that is appreciated and rewarded in basic research. But i) the landscape of our tools is still very poorly integrated and ii) for many of our tools
it is not clear whether they prove correctness with respect to exactly the right
specifications.

B. Meyer and J. Woodcock (Eds.): Verified Software, LNCS 4171, pp. 19–25, 2008.

Clearly, something like the specifications we are presently using will eventually permit to prove the correctness of big pieces of software. But then, it is also very likely that something like the original software would work in the first place.

3   Right Specifications and Stacks

A specification can be bad for two reasons:

i) It does not capture the user's intention. In general this cannot be discovered by mathematical methods alone. ii) In a computer system with layers, it does not permit to deduce desired properties of the next layer upwards or it cannot be proven using properties from the layer below.

Fortunately there are no principal difficulties to test, whether a specification works together with correctness theorems of other system layers. One simply tries it. That it can be done has been demonstrated as early as 1989 in the famous CLI stack [2]. Experiences since 2003 with far more complex stacks in the Verisoft project are also very encouraging.

We therefore judge it necessary, that the development of a technology for software verification has to be carried out in the context of the verification of entire stacks.

A case study: compilers in stacks. We inspect three well known sources of definitions of programming language semantics: i) the classical Hoare/Wirth paper on Pascal semantics [3] ii) the textbook of Nielson and Nielson [4] iii) the textbook of Winskel [5].

In [4,5] variables can range over the natural numbers. For a program running on a finite processor there is no way to prove this. In contrast, *int* is a finite data type in [3]!

Real programs run under operating systems and they perform I/O. Their computations are *interleaved* with the computations of other programs. Modelling this requires small steps semantics. Thus one cannot rely exclusively on the (big steps) definitions in [3].

Nevertheless the definitions of [3] are a component of engineering technology. Because theorems proven in Hoare logics hold in the corresponding small steps semantics (for the proofs see e.g. [4,5]) they can be used exactly as they are to prove properties of terminating portions of programs. Experience from the Verisoft project suggests that this should by all means be done: productivity with Hoare logics is *much* higher than with small steps semantics alone.

If the verification of an operating system is also part of a project, then conventional small steps semantics alone does not suffice either: one needs to consider in line assembler code for the following reasons: i) arguing in high level language alone is impossible: an operating system written in high level language alone could see in its own variables neither the processor registers nor the user processes. ii) arguing on the assembler language level alone (as was done in [2]) would not be productive enough.

4   Paper and Pencil Theory

Let us assume that we succeed to formally verify a complex stack. Then we can *necessarily* produce a human readable transcript of the formal correctness proof. This proof would be part of a big unified theory of computer science which would i) be (at least!) as stringent as the classical mathematical theories, ii) include in a unified way big parts of what is today called theoretical computer science, and iii) have real systems as examples.

We believe that progress will be faster if this theory is developed first with paper and pencil. In the language of G. Hotz these paper and pencil proofs then can serve as building plans for the formal proofs.

A case study: from gates to user processes i) Hardware is easily specified in the language of switching theory. ii) The random access machines of theoretical computer science are appropriate for specifying instruction sets. iii) Small steps semantics of high level languages is specified by abstract interpreters. iv) various models for distributed computation permit to treat communicating user programs.

Clearly in a verified stack one needs simulation theorems between different layers. Processor correctness is between models i) and ii). Compiler correctness is between models ii) and iii). Operating system correctness—with the scheduler abstracted away—is (because of the in line assembler code) between models ii) and iv). In the Verisoft project the paper and pencil proof for operating system correctness required the introduction of two more parallel models of computation between models ii) and iv): one for operating system kernels and one for operating systems without abstracting away the scheduler.

5   Standardizing Language and Tools

Worldwide cooperative effort is impossible without establishing a common language. In software engineering there is a small number of standard programming languages, among them C and Java. The semantics are admittedly not too well defined, but compilers of a small number of large vendors establish a small number of de facto standards.

For the establishment of a worldwide verification technology we need as a counter part a small number of standard CAV systems. They should be

1. cheap mass products maintained by companies
2. universal: formalization of arbitrary mathematical statements and arguments should be reasonably straight forward. Presently interactive high order logic provers seem the best candidates.
3. easily extendible by automatic tools; interfaces to do this must be open. Without such interfaces we close the door to continuous increase in productivity.

Only with compatible standard tools can different groups of engineers exchange or trade (!) proofs. In the Verisoft project the standard tool is Isabelle/ HOL [6].

6   Standardizing Definitions

Some crucial formal definitions should be standardized and maintained (in standard language) in downloadable form on certain web sites. Examples are i) the semantics of some standard instruction sets (note that this includes the IEEE floating point standard). ii) small steps semantics and Hoare logics for C and Java iii) the semantics of certain standard real time operating systems (such standard systems exist for instance in the automotive industry).

7   Establishing Repositories of Verified Standard Components

For all standard components of computer systems both i) verified constructions and ii) their formal correctness proofs need to be made available in repositories. Clearly, for an *industry* of computer system verification, formally verified components from the following list are indispensable: i) processor with optional memory management units and I/O devices, ii) assembler and linker, iii) optimizing compiler for object oriented languages, iv) operating system kernel, v) operating system, vi) distributed real time operating system, vii) interface compiler supporting port mapper and client-server RPC mechanisms, viii) TCP/IP, ix) mail server, x) electronic signature server, and xi) several cryptographic protocols.

Except for compiler optimization and object orientation all items of the above list are milestones of the current Verisoft project. Whenever possible, constructions and arguments from established textbooks were taken as a starting point for the development of the system components and the correctness proofs.

8   Rewarding Engineering Work

Even the best technical decisions are useless if they are not supported by project members. Students will be reluctant to do work which will not lead to a thesis. Researchers at universities will be reluctant to do work which they cannot publish. We must therefore give proper rewards for the engineering aspect of our work. In particular we have to establish a forum for the following kind of results:

1. The integration of known automatic methods in known interactive provers if that increases the productivity on large realistic benchmarks. This in turn requires the publication of such benchmarks *in a form which is easy enough to read*; putting existing large formal proofs on the web is not enough. In the Verisoft project we are working on such benchmarks together with the Southern Methodist University at Dallas.
2. The 'mechanization' of existing paper and pencil correctness proofs for major system components in a CAV system, if similar proofs were not mechanized before. In an engineering sense one can simply not trust paper and pencil proofs alone; in this respect we agree with [7]. In contrast a mechanized proof establishes not only trust in the verified component. It also shows, that the

line of arguments that is used is complete and hence should work in future similar proofs.

Failing to reward the engineering aspects of our work as highly as the basic research aspects will slow down the development of technology.

9   Summary of Suggestions

In order to help establish a worldwide technology of software verification the author suggests to

1. clearly recognize the difference between basic research and engineering,
2. to study stacks in order to get specifications right,
3. produce paper and pencil proofs first,
4. recognize the need for a grand unified theory of computer science,
5. agree on a small number of standard tools permitting both interactive and automatic work,
6. standardize key definitions,
7. make formally verified standard constructions available in repositories and
8. establish a proper reward structure for results with a strong engineering flavor.

In Verisoft, the standard processor is a DLX machine with memory management units [8]. Formal verification in PVS is complete; proofs are presently being ported to Isabelle/HOL. The standard language is $C0$; in a nutshell this is Pascal with C syntax. $C0_A$ is $C0$ with in line assembler code. We are using small steps semantics for $C0$ and $C0_A$. A Hoare logic for $C0$ is used to increase productivity [9]. Formal verification of a non optimizing $C0_A$-compiler is expected to be completed in early 2006 [10]. Formal verification of an operating system kernel written in $C0_A$ is expected in 2006 [11]. Paper and pencil theory for processors with I/O devices and real time systems can be found in [12] and [13].

References

1. The Verisoft Consortium: The Verisoft Project, http://www.verisoft.de/
2. Bevier, W.R., Hunt Jr., W.A., Moore, J.S., Young, W.D.: An approach to systems verification. J. Autom. Reason. 5(4), 411–428 (1989)
3. Hoare, C.A.R., Wirth, N.: An axiomatic definition of the programming language PASCAL. Acta Inf. 2, 335–355 (1973)
4. Nielson, H.R., Nielson, F.: Semantics with Applications: A Formal Introduction. Wiley, Chichester, 1992, revised online version: 1999
5. Winskel, G.: The formal semantics of programming languages. The MIT Press, Cambridge (1993)
6. Nipkow, T., Paulson, L.C., Wenzel, M.T.: Isabelle/HOL. LNCS, vol. 2283. Springer, Heidelberg (2002)
7. Millo, R.A.D., Lipton, R.J., Perlis, A.J.: Social processes and proofs of theorems and programs. Commun. ACM 22(5), 271–280 (1979)

8. Dalinger, I., Hillebrand, M., Paul, W.: On the verification of memory management mechanisms. In: Borrione, D., Paul, W. (eds.) CHARME 2005. LNCS, vol. 3725, pp. 301–316. Springer, Heidelberg (2005)

9. Schirmer, N.: A verification environment for sequential imperative programs in Isabelle/HOL. In: Baader, F., Voronkov, A. (eds.) LPAR 2004. LNCS (LNAI), vol. 3452, pp. 398–414. Springer, Heidelberg (2005)

10. Leinenbach, D., Paul, W., Petrova, E.: Towards the formal verification of a C0 compiler: Code generation and implementation correctness. In: Aichernig, B., Beckert, B. (eds.) 3rd International Conference on Software Engineering and Formal Methods (SEFM 2005), Koblenz, Germany, pp. 2–11 (September 5-9, 2005)

11. Gargano, M., Hillebrand, M., Leinenbach, D., Paul, W.: On the correctness of operating system kernels. In: Hurd, J., Melham, T. (eds.) TPHOLs 2005. LNCS, vol. 3603, pp. 1–16. Springer, Heidelberg (2005)

12. Hillebrand, M., In der Rieden, T., Paul, W.: Dealing with I/O devices in the context of pervasive system verification. In: ICCD 2005, pp. 309–316. IEEE Computer Society, Los Alamitos (2005)

13. Beyer, S., Böhm, P., Gerke, M., Hillebrand, M., In der Rieden, T., Knapp, S., Leinenbach, D., Paul, W.J.: Towards the formal verification of lower system layers in automotive systems. In: ICCD 2005, pp. 317–324. IEEE Computer Society, Los Alamitos (2005)

A   Discussion on Wolfgang Paul's Presentation

Greg Nelson

Wolfgang, I have one question about the C0 language that you defined. Does it have a storage deallocation function like free()?

Wolfgang Paul

No, it has a new()-operation. And we have a paper-and-pencil proof for a garbage collector. And we are optimistic that it takes about one Russian person-year to verify that thing using the tools we have.

Greg Nelson: Thank you.

Willem-Paul de Roever

A minor question. You did not say in your slides what is the duration of this project. We know that it is three and a half million ECU per year, but is it six or eight years?

Wolfgang Paul

Well, the people who have urged me to run the project are planning for eight years. Now the formula: We are now in the third year. Now, if I get the financing for four-year periods at a row, I lose all power. So, financing is always every two years, okay? Only for two years we do apply for the next money, because other-wise, I cannot convince some of my collaborators to stay within the direction of the entire project.

Willem-Paul de Roever: It's German practice.

Wolfgang Paul

No, I think they would have given me the money in three-year periods. But it is better to reevaluate after two years and say: "You don't agree anymore with this. Do your research elsewhere, and we spend the money in a different way."

Ramesh Bharadwaj

In light of what Amir said, you seem to have missed the word "specification", and you have not explained exactly what is specified and what is not...

Wolfgang Paul (*interrupts*)

It is usually an operational semantics of an operation. So, for instance, [for an] operating system kernel, I am giving you the operational semantics. I am showing you the user-visible data structures of an operating system kernel, I am showing you the operations, and I am defining the effect of the user-visible data structures. So, in these system correctness proofs, most of these proofs are simulation theory, showing that the lower layer of the system simulates the upper layer of the system.

Ramesh Bharadwaj: OK, thanks.

It Is Time to Mechanize
Programming Language Metatheory*

Benjamin C. Pierce[1], Peter Sewell[2], Stephanie Weirich[1], and Steve Zdancewic[1]

[1] Department of Computer and Information Science, University of Pennsylvania
[2] Computer Laboratory, University of Cambridge

Abstract. How close are we to a world in which mechanically verified software is commonplace? A world in which theorem proving technology is used routinely by both software developers and programming language researchers alike? One crucial step towards achieving these goals is mechanized reasoning about language metatheory. The time has come to bring together the theorem proving and programming language communities to address this problem. We have proposed the POPLMARK challenge as a concrete set of benchmarks intended both for measuring progress in this area and for stimulating discussion and collaboration. Our goal is to push the boundaries of existing technology to the point where we can achieve mechanized metatheory for the masses.

1 Mechanized Metatheory for the Masses

One significant obstacle to achieving the goal of verified software is reasoning about the languages in which the software is written. Without formal models of programming languages, it is impossible to even state, let alone prove, meaningful properties of software or tools such as compilers. It is therefore essential that we develop appropriate tools for modeling programming languages and mechanically checking their metatheoretic properties. This infrastructure should provide facilities for proving properties of operational semantics, program analyses (such as type checkers), and program transformations (such as optimization and compilation).

Many proofs about programming languages are straightforward, long, and tedious, with just a few interesting cases. Their complexity arises from the management of many details rather than from deep conceptual difficulties; yet small mistakes or overlooked cases can invalidate large amounts of work. These effects are amplified as languages scale: it becomes very hard to keep definitions and proofs consistent, to reuse work, and to ensure tight relationships between theory and implementations. Automated proof assistants offer the hope of significantly easing these problems. However, despite much encouraging progress in recent years and the availability of several mature tools (ACL2 [15], Coq [2], HOL [10], Isabelle [20], Lego [16], NuPRL [5], PVS [21], Twelf [22], etc.), their use is still not commonplace.

---

* This position paper is adapted from the introduction to the POPLMARK Challenge paper [1].

B. Meyer and J. Woodcock (Eds.): Verified Software, LNCS 4171, pp. 26–30, 2008.
© IFIP International Federation for Information Processing 2008

We believe that the time is right to join the efforts of the two communities, bringing developers of automated proof assistants together with a large pool of eager potential clients—programming language designers and researchers. In particular, we intend to answer two questions:

1. What is the current state of the art in formalizing language metatheory and semantics? What can be recommended as best practices for groups (typically not proof-assistant experts) embarking on formalized language definitions, either small- or large-scale?
2. What improvements are needed to make the use of tool support commonplace? What can each community contribute?

Over the past six months, we have attempted to survey the landscape of proof assistants, language representation strategies, and related tools. Collectively, we have applied automated theorem proving technology to a number of problems, including proving transitivity of the algorithmic subtype relation in Kernel $F_\le$ [4,3, 6], proving type soundness of Featherweight Java [14], proving type soundness of variants of the simply typed λ-calculus and $F_\le$, and a substantial formalization of the behavior of TCP, UDP, and the Sockets API. We have carried out these case studies using a variety of object-language representation strategies, proof techniques, and proving environments. We have also experimented with lightweight tools designed to make it easier to define and typeset both formal and informal mathematics. Although experts in programming language theory, we were (and are) relative novices with respect to computer-aided proof.

Our conclusion from these experiments is that the relevant technology has developed *almost* to the point where it can be widely used by language researchers. We seek to push it over the threshold, making the use of proof tools common practice in programming language research—mechanized metatheory for the masses.

Tool support for formal reasoning about programming languages would be useful at many levels:

1. *Machine-checked metatheory.* These are the classic problems: type preservation and soundness theorems, unique decomposition properties for operational semantics, proofs of equivalence between algorithmic and declarative variants of type systems, etc. At present such results are typically proved by hand for small to medium-size calculi, and are not proved at all for full language definitions. We envision a future in which the papers in conferences such as *Principles of Programming Languages (POPL)* and the *International Conference on Functional Programming (ICFP)* are routinely accompanied by mechanically checkable proofs of the theorems they claim.
2. *Use of definitions as oracles for testing and animation.* When developing a language implementation together with a formal definition one would like to use the definition as an oracle for testing. This requires tools that can decide typing and evaluation relationships, and they might differ from the tools used for (1) or be embedded in the same proof assistant. In some cases one could use a definition directly as a prototype.

3. *Support for engineering large-scale definitions.* As we move to full language definitions—on the scale of Standard ML [17] or larger—pragmatic "software engineering" issues become increasingly important, as do the potential benefits of tool support. For large definitions, the need for elegant and concise notation becomes pressing, as witnessed by the care taken by present-day researchers using informal mathematics. Even lightweight tool support, without full mechanized proof, could be very useful in this domain, e.g. for sort checking and typesetting of definitions and of informal proofs, automatically instantiating definitions, performing substitutions, etc.

Our goal is to stimulate progress in this area by providing a common framework for comparing alternative technologies. Our approach has been to design a set of challenge problems, dubbed the POPLMARK Challenge [1], chosen to exercise many aspects of programming languages that are known to be difficult to formalize: variable binding at both term and type levels, syntactic forms with variable numbers of components (including binders), and proofs demanding complex induction principles. Such challenge problems have been used in the past within the theorem proving community to focus attention on specific areas and to evaluate the relative merits of different tools; these have ranged in scale from benchmark suites and small problems [23, 11, 7, 13, 9, 19] up to the grand challenges of Floyd, Hoare, and Moore [8, 12, 18]. We hope that our challenge will have a similarly stimulating effect.

The POPLMARK problems are drawn from the basic metatheory of a call-by-value variant of System $F_{\le}$ [3, 6], enriched with records, record subtyping, and record patterns. Our challenge provides an informal-mathematics definition of its type system and operational semantics and outline proofs of some of its metatheory. This language is of moderate scale—neither a toy calculus nor a full-blown programming language—to keep the work involved in attempting the challenges manageable.[1] The intent of this challenge is to cover a broad range of issues that arise in the *formalization* of programming languages; of course there are many programming language *features*, such as control-flow operators, state, and concurrency, not covered by our sample problem, but we believe that a system capable of formalizing the POPLMARK problems should be able to formalize those features as well. Nevertheless, we expect this challenge set to grow and evolve as the community addresses some problems and discovers others.

The initial POPLMARK challenge has already been disseminated to a wide audience of theorem prover and programming language researchers. We are in the process of collecting and evaluating solutions. Those results, along with related information about mechanized metatheory, will be available on our web site.[2] In the longer run, we hope that this site, and the corresponding mailing list [3] will serve as a forum for promoting and advancing the current best practices in

---

[1] Our challenges therefore explicitly address only points (1) and (2) above; we regard the pragmatic issues of (3) as equally critical, but it is not yet clear to us how to formulate a useful challenge problem at this larger scale.

[2] http://www.cis.upenn.edu/proj/plclub/mmm/

[3] poplmark@lists.seas.upenn.edu

proof assistant technology and making this technology available to the broader programming languages community and beyond. We encourage researchers to try out the POPLMARK Challenge using their favorite tools and send us their solutions for inclusion in the web site.

References

1. Aydemir, B.E., Bohannon, A., Fairbairn, M., Foster, J.N., Pierce, B.C., Sewell, P., Vytiniotis, D., Washburn, G., Weirich, S., Zdancewic, S.: Mechanized metatheory for the masses: The POPLmark challenge. In: Theorem Proving in Higher Order Logics, 18th International Conference, Oxford, UK (August 2005)
2. Bertot, Y., Castéran, P.: Interactive Theorem Proving and Program Development. In: EATCS Texts in Theoretical Computer Science, vol. XXV, Springer, Heidelberg (2004)
3. Cardelli, L., Martini, S., Mitchell, J.C., Scedrov, A.: An extension of System F with subtyping. In: Ito, T., Meyer, A.R. (eds.) TACS 1991. LNCS, vol. 526, pp. 750–770. Springer, Heidelberg (1991)
4. Cardelli, L., Wegner, P.: On understanding types, data abstraction, and polymorphism. Computing Surveys 17(4), 471–522 (1985)
5. Constable, R.L., Allen, S.F., Bromley, M., Cleaveland, R., Cremer, J.F., Harper, R.W., Howe, D.J., Knoblock, T.B., Mendler, P., Panangaden, P., Sasaki, J.T., Smith, S.F.: Implementing Mathematics with the NuPRL Proof Development System. Prentice-Hall, Englewood Cliffs, NJ (1986)
6. Curien, P.-L., Ghelli, G.: Coherence of subsumption: Minimum typing and type-checking in F. Mathematical Structures in Computer Science. In: Gunter, C.A., Mitchell, J.C. (eds.) Theoretical Aspects of Object-Oriented Programming: Types, Semantics, and Language Design, vol. 2, pp. 55–91. MIT Press, Cambridge (1994)
7. Dennis, L.A.: Inductive challenge problems (2000), http://www.cs.nott.ac.uk/~lad/research/challenges
8. Floyd, R.W.: Assigning meanings to programs. In: Schwartz, J.T. (ed.) Mathematical Aspects of Computer Science. Proceedings of Symposia in Applied Mathematics, vol. 19, pp. 19–32. American Mathematical Society, Providence, Rhode Island (1967)
9. Gent, I.P., Walsh, T.: CSPLib: a benchmark library for constraints. Technical report, Technical report APES-09-, 1999. A shorter version appears in the Proceedings of the 5th International Conference on Principles and Practices of Constraint Programming (CP-99) (1999), http://csplib.cs.strath.ac.uk/
10. Gordon, M.J.C., Melham, T.F. (eds.): Introduction to HOL: a theorem proving environment for higher order logic. Cambridge University Press, Cambridge (1993)
11. Green, I.: The dream corpus of inductive conjectures (1999), http://dream.dai.ed.ac.uk/dc/lib.html
12. Hoare, T.: The verifying compiler: A grand challenge for computing research. J. ACM 50(1), 63–69 (2003)
13. Hoos, H., Stuetzle, T.: Satlib, http://www.intellektik.informatik.tu-darmstadt.de/SATLIB/
14. Igarashi, A., Pierce, B., Wadler, P.: Featherweight Java: A minimal core calculus for Java and GJ. In: ACM SIGPLAN Conference on Object Oriented Programming: Systems, Languages, and Applications (OOPSLA) October 1999. Full version in ACM Transactions on Programming Languages and Systems (TOPLAS), vol. 23(3) (May 2001)

15. Kaufmann, M., Moore, J.S., Manolios, P.: Computer-Aided Reasoning: An Approach. Kluwer Academic Publishers, Dordrecht (2000)
16. Luo, Z., Pollack, R.: The LEGO proof development system: A user's manual. Technical Report ECS-LFCS-92-211, University of Edinburgh (May 1992)
17. Milner, R., Tofte, M., Harper, R., MacQueen, D.: The Definition of Standard ML, Revised edition. MIT Press, Cambridge (1997)
18. Moore, J.S.: A grand challenge proposal for formal methods: A verified stack. In: Aichernig, B.K., Maibaum, T.S.E. (eds.) Formal Methods at the Crossroads. From Panacea to Foundational Support. LNCS, vol. 2757, pp. 161–172. Springer, Heidelberg (2003)
19. Moore, J.S., Porter, G.: The apprentice challenge. ACM Trans. Program. Lang. Syst. 24(3), 193–216 (2002)
20. Nipkow, T., Paulson, L.C., Wenzel, M.T.: Isabelle/HOL. LNCS, vol. 2283. Springer, Heidelberg (2002)
21. Owre, S., Rajan, S., Rushby, J.M., Shankar, N., Srivas, M.K.: PVS: Combining specification, proof checking, and model checking. In: Alur, R., Henzinger, T.A. (eds.) CAV 1996. LNCS, vol. 1102, pp. 411–414. Springer, Heidelberg (1996)
22. Pfenning, F., Schürmann, C.: System description: Twelf — A meta-logical framework for deductive systems. In: Ganzinger, H. (ed.) CADE 1999. LNCS (LNAI), vol. 1632, pp. 202–206. Springer, Heidelberg (1999)
23. Sutcliffe, G., Suttner, C.: The TPTP problem library. Journal of Automated Reasoning 21(2), 177–203 (1998)

Methods and Tools for Formal Software Engineering

Zhiming Liu[1,*] and R. Venkatesh[2]

[1] International Institute for Software Technology
United Nations University, Macao SAR, China
z.liu@iist.unu.edu
[2] Tata Research and Design Development Centre, Pune, India
r.venky@tcs.com

Abstract. We propose a collaboration project to integrate the research effort and results obtained at UNU-IIST on formal techniques in component and object systems with research at TRDDC in modelling and development of tools that support object-oriented and component-based design. The main theme is an integration of verification techniques with engineering methods of modelling and design, and an integration of verification tools and transformation tools. This will result in a method in which a *correct* program can be developed through transformations that are either proven to be correct or by showing that the transformed model can be proven correct by a verification tool.

1 Formal Software Engineering and the Grand Challenge

The goal of the Verifying Compiler Grand Challenge [7,6] is to build a verifying compiler that

> "uses mathematical and logical reasoning to check the programs that it compiles."

This implies that "a program should be allowed to run only if it is both syntactically and semantically correct" [20]. To achieve this goal, the whole computing community have to deal with a wide range of issues, among which are [2]

1. arriving at automated procedures of abstraction that enables a compiler to work in combination with different program verification tools including testing tools,
2. studying what, where, when and how the correctness properties, i.e. assertions and annotations, are identified and specified,
3. identifying properties that can be verified compositionally, and designing specification notations and models to support more compositional specification, analysis and verification.
4. making tools that are scalable even with specified correctness criteria,

In our view, theories and techniques are a long way from being able to solve the first three problems, and solutions to these problems is obviously vital for dealing with the fourth problem.

---

* This work is partially supported by the projects HighQSoftD funded by Macao Science and Technology Fund, NSFC-60573085, NSFC-60673114 and 863 of China 2006AA01Z165.

B. Meyer and J. Woodcock (Eds.): Verified Software, LNCS 4171, pp. 31–41, 2008.

In this position paper, we propose the development *Formal Software Engineering* as a method to develop large software systems using engineering methods and tools that are verifiable. We propose formal modelling of requirements and design, and the automatic generation of code to achieve this. We believe that this effort will contribute towards a solution to the problems stated earlier, in a way that combine techniques and tools of *verification* and those of *correctness by construction* [20].

1.1   The State of the Art in Software Engineering

Software engineering is mainly concerned with the systematic development of large and complex systems. To cope with the required scale traditional software engineers divide the problem along three axes - development phases, aspects and evolutions. The development phases are - Requirements, Design and Implementation. Each development phase is divided into different aspects, such as:

- static data model, control flow and operations in the requirements phase;
- design strategies for concurrency, efficiency and security in the design phase. These strategies are commonly expressed as design patterns [3]; and
- databases, user interface and libraries for security in the implementation phase.

The third axis is that of system evolution and maintenance [9,8] where each evolutionary step enhances the system by iterating through the requirements - implementation cycle. Unfortunately all aspects are specified using informal techniques and therefore this approach does not give the desired assurances and productivity. The main problems are:

- Since the requirements description is informal there is no way to check for its completeness, often resulting in gaps.
- The gaps in requirements are often filled by ad-hoc decisions taken by programmers who are not qualified for the same. This results in rework during testing and commissioning.
- There is no traceability between requirements and the implementation, making it very expensive to accommodate changes and maintain the system.
- Most of the available tools are for project management and system testing. They are not enough to ensure the semantic alignment of the implementation w.r.t a requirements specification and semantic consistency of any changes made in the system.

1.2   The State of the Art of Formal Methods

Formal methods, on the other hand, attempt to complement informal engineering methods by techniques for formal modelling, specification, verification and refinement. They have been extensively researched and studied. A range of semantic theories, specification languages, design techniques, and verification methods and tools have been developed and applied to the construction of programs of moderate size that are used in critical applications. However, it is still a challenge is to scale up formal methods and integrate them into engineering development processes for the correct construction and maintenance of software systems, due to the following problems:

- Each development is usually a new development with very little reuse of past development.
- Because of the theoretical goal of completeness and independence, refinement calculi provide rules only for a small change in each step. Refinement calculi therefore do not scale up in practice. Data refinement requires definition of a semantic relation between the programs (their state space) and is hard to be applied systematically.
- Given low level designs or implementations it is not easy for software engineers to build correct and proper models that can be verified by model checking tools.
- There is no explicit support for productivity enhancing techniques such as component-based development or aspect-oriented development.

We also observe that verification techniques and tools (e.g. model checking, SAT solving, etc.) have only been relatively effective only in the development of hardware systems. An integration of such methods with software development is highly required by the manufacturers of critical and embedded software (avionics, telecom, public transport, etc.). However, the sophisticated nature of software (complex data structures, recursion, multithreading) poses challenging theoretic and practical problems to the developers of automatic analysis and verification methods.

Both formal methods and the methods adopted by software engineers are far from meeting the quality and productivity needs of the industry, which continues to be plagued by high development and maintenance costs. Complete assurance of correctness requires too much to specify and verify and thus a full automation of the verification is infeasible. However, recently there have been encouraging developments in both approaches. The software engineering community has started using precise models for early requirement analysis and design [18]. Theories and methods for object-oriented, component-based and aspect-oriented modelling and development are gaining the attention of the formal methods community. There are attempts to investigate formal aspects of object-oriented refinement, design patterns, refactoring and coordination [12].

1.3 Aims and Objective

The aim of this project is to combine the strengths of software engineering techniques and formal methods thus enabling the development of systems that have the assurances possible due to formal methods and productivity and scale-up achievable by methods adopted by software engineers.

We will focus on the development of a theory of modelling (or specification), analysis and refinement of component and object systems, and a toolset that integrates two kinds of complementary tools: tools for analysis (model checkers and theorem provers) and tools for correctness preserving transformations, including design patterns and domain specific transformations. We will study and verify the correctness of the transformations, aiming at verified designs transformations to scale up formal methods by

- exploiting standard design patterns and strategies existing in large applications, even across applications;
- providing verified design patterns and strategies to reduce the burden on (automated) proofs; and
- proving functionality correctness only at the specification stage.

We can also think this is about the development of a CASE tool that is supported by a formal theory and combines model transformation and model verification.

2   Formal Modelling of Complex Systems

This section gives a brief outline of the technique and solution to be investigated by this project. The techniques are explained using a simple example of a library system, that maintains a collection of books. Members belonging to the library borrow and return books. In order to keep the explanation simple and readable we have not been rigorous in the specification of the library system. For more formality, we refer the reader to the paper [14]. Also in [17], a Point of Sale (POST) system was formally developed, including a C# implementation.

2.1   Requirements Modelling

For an object system or a component, the development process begins with the specification of functional requirements. Functional requirements of a system consists of three aspects: the state, a set of operations through which external agents may interact with the system, and a set of global properties that must be satisfied by the state and operations. This can be represented as a triple $RM = \langle S, O, I \rangle$ where S is a model of the state, O is a set of operations that modify the state and I is a set of global invariants. Each operation in O is expressed as a pre- post-condition pair [12]. A requirements model is consistent if each operation in O is consistent with the state model and preserves the global invariant. The model can be further enhanced by adding descriptions of interaction protocols with the environment [5], timing aspects, features of security, etc. A multi-view and multi-notation modelling language, such as a formalized subset of the Unified Modelling Language(UML) [19], can be used to specify this model and analyzed for inconsistencies using model-checking techniques as demonstrated in [22]. The analysis can be carried out incrementally, a small number of use cases at a time that only involve a small number of domain classes [14]. This is obviously important to development of tool support to the analysis.

Library requirements. The state space of the library system is represented by the tuple $\langle Shelf, Book, Member, Loan : Book \times Member, isIn : Book \times Shelf \rangle$ where, *Book*, *Member* and *Shelf* are set of books, members and shelves in the library. *Loan* is a set of tuples representing the books that have been currently loaned to members. The association *isIn* is a set of tuples representing books that are currently on some shelf. This state space corresponds to a UML diagram and can be formalized as a class declartion section of an OO program [14,13].

The set of operations will be $\{Borrow(Member, Book), Return(Member, Book)\}$. These operations are identified from the use cases [14]. The *Borrow* operation can be described as

$$\textbf{signature}: \qquad Borrow(S, S' : State, b : Book, m : Member)$$
$$\textbf{pre} - \textbf{condition}: \quad \neg\exists m_1 : Member \bullet \langle b, m_1 \rangle \in S.Loan$$
$$\textbf{post} - \textbf{condition}: S'.Loan = S.Loan \cup \langle b, m \rangle \wedge S'.isIn = S.isIn - \langle b, s \rangle$$

Return can be defined similarly.

A sample invariant is *BookInvariant*, which states that every book in the library is either on the shelf or loaned to a member. This can be stated as follows.

$$BookInvariant(S : State) \stackrel{def}{=} \quad \forall b : S.Book \bullet \exists m : Member \bullet \langle b, m \rangle \in S.Loan \wedge$$
$$\neg\exists s : Shelf \bullet \langle b, s \rangle \in S.isIn$$
$$\vee \neg\exists m : Member \bullet \langle b, m \rangle \in S.Loan \wedge$$
$$\exists s : Shelf \bullet \langle b, s \rangle \in S.isIn$$

Details on the formalisation of a use-case model and its consistency relation with a class model (i.e. the state space) can be found in [14].

2.2 Design

Design involves transforming the requirements model of a system to a model with design details, by design strategies or patterns as functional decomposition and object or class decomposition. This model is still platform independent models (PIM) [13].

In a later stage, the PIM is transformed to a model of a platform or a family of platforms (PDM) with desired non-functional properties such as - support for concurrent or parallel execution, performance and usability. The platform may be modelled by a tuple, $\langle S_p, O_p \rangle$ where S_p is a meta-model of the platform state and O_p is a set of platform operations which maybe combined using a set of available operators.

Given a PDM, a system is designed by transforming the PIM state, S to a design state S_d that is an instance of the PDM state S_p and transforming each operation $o \in O$ to an operation o_d, which is expressed as a composition of operations in O_p. The design step also specifies a set of design invariants I_d that the design operations must preserve. Thus the design model is a triple, $\langle S_d, O_d, I_d \rangle$ where O_d is the set of all transformed operations and the design process consists of two transform functions $\langle T_s, T_o \rangle$ where $T_s : S \rightarrow S_d$ is the state transformation function and $T_o : O \rightarrow O_d$ is the operations transformation function. A design is correct if the two transformation functions are consistent that is the diagram in Figure 1 commutes and the design operations preserve the design invariants.

Library design. To simplify the presentation assume the library requirements model to consist of $\langle S_r, O_r \rangle$, where S_r is a set of class and association names and O_r the operations:

$$S_r = \{Shelf, Book, Member, Loan, isIn\}, \ O_r = \{Borrow, Return\}$$

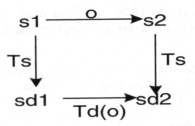

Fig. 1. Design Transformations

Further associate each operation *op* with the set of state objects *obj(op)* it accesses, because for concurrency only the object being accessed is relevant and not the details of the modifications to the object. So

$$obj(Borrow) = obj(Return) = \{Loan, isIn\}$$

Assume the library system is to be implemented on a platform where multiple processes run the library operations and all of these refer to a set of shared objects. The design model will be $\langle S_d, O_d \rangle$, where

$$S_d = S_r \cup \{s_l, s_i\}, \qquad O_d = \{Borrow_d, Return_d, P, V\}$$

where s_l and s_i are semaphores corresponding to Loan and isIn objects, and P and V are the semaphore operations. The operations in the design are defined by a sequence of semaphore operations and objects accessed. Thus,

$$obj_d(Borrow_d) = obj_d(Return_d) = [s_l; s_i; Loan; isIn; s_l; s_i]$$

This design guarantees - correctness, mutual exclusion and deadlock freedom.

Instead of designing each library operation individually we can write two design transformation functions for the library design as follows

$$T_{ls} \stackrel{def}{=} S_r \cup \{S_i \mid S_i \text{ is a semaphore for } s_i \in S_r\}$$
$$T_{lo}(op) \stackrel{def}{=} [P_1; \cdots; P_k; a_1; \cdots; a_k; V_1; \cdots; V_k] \quad \text{if } op \text{ is realized by the sequence} \\ a_1; \ldots; a_k \text{ of accesses to } s_1, \ldots, s_k$$

We can prove the correctness of the transformation as required by figure 1. Also, mutual exclusion and deadlock freedom can be guaranteed. Since the design has been implemented as a transformation we do not have to prove correctness of the design specification for each operation, instead we prove correctness of the transformation.

Design Patterns. Different systems adopt similar design transformation functions. Therefore the process of formal design can be scaled up by abstracting away from individual design transformation functions to a design pattern. A design pattern is a meta-function that maps a requirements model to a design transformation function for that requirements model. A design pattern is correct if the mapped design functions are correct as described above. Design patterns can be proved correct independent of the requirements model making them scalable. In the presence of design pattern a design step will involve selecting and applying the appropriate design patterns.

For the Library example, the design strategy of imposing a total order on the semaphores can be abstracted out into a transformation function. The transformation function takes the total order and a requirements specification as input and transforms the requirements of an arbitrary system into a corresponding design specification. Thus a design pattern for databased applications that supports multiple users and guarantees mutual exclusion and deadlock freedom consists of two transformation functions in the form of T_{ls} and T_{lo} of the library system.

MasterCraft [1] implements a few such design patterns for some select platforms and design strategies. MasterCraft however does not support formal specification and verification of these design patterns. If implemented as a design pattern the atomicity preservation and deadlock freedom will not have to be proved for each application of the transformation. All we need to show is that for a given application there the given total order on objects includes all the objects that are referred to by any of the operations of the system. We believe that is achievable in the framework of rCOS.

rCOS also provide a general refinement calculus for correctness preserving transformation between PIMs. General software design patterns, such General Responsibility Assignment Software Pattern (GRASP) [10], are formalized as refinement rules in rCOS [13]. Here we use UML to represent some of the refinement rules in rCOS:

Functional Decomposition: This is also known as the *expert pattern* which allows us to delegate that part of the functionality of method N in Figure 2, which only refers to attributes x of class M, to the expert M of information x.

Class Decomposition: Figure 3 shows how we can decompose a complex class into a number of related but simpler classes. Figure 4 represents another way of class decomposition. Class decomposition rules are known by OO engineers as High Cohesion Pattern.

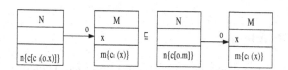

Fig. 2. OO Functional Decomposition

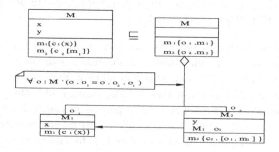

Fig. 3. Class Decomposition 1

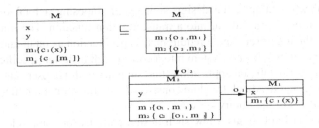

Fig. 4. Class Decomposition 2

Low Coupling: The *Low Coupling Pattern* represented in Figure 5 allows us to obtain the design in Figure 4 from the design in Figure 3.

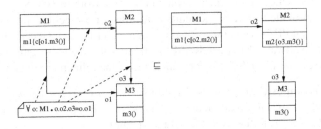

Fig. 5. Low Coupling

More design patterns and pattern-directed refactoring are also studied and applied to the case study POST [17]. We will extend MasterCraft by adding the implementations of these rules.

3   Research Problems

The previous section presented an overview of a proposed method for formal development of large scale systems. To realize this method, we first need to define it more formally. We aim at a logically sound and systematic method (that we are tempted to call a *formal engineering method*) and tools that themselves are provably correct for supporting the method. The method includes:

1. *A language and a logic for specifying and reasoning about a system at different levels of abstractions.* The main task is to develop a notation for describing each aspect of correctness of a model. This will allow a developer to split a model of a system into several aspects making it more manageable. This is important for tool development too. The notation for a particular aspect should be expressive enough for describing all the concerns about that aspect. However, overlapping features among different notations should be kept to a minimum else, problems of inconsistency and integration will become overwhelming[1].

---

[1] This is a serious problem in the application of UML.

The logic should provide a sound link among the different notations to deal with the problems of model consistency and integration. It should support compositional reasoning about the whole model by reasoning about the sub-models of the aspects. Different verification techniques and tools maybe applied to models of different aspects of functionality, interaction and structure of the system.

2. *A Language and logic for specifying the transform functions and reasoning about correctness.* The language should preferably be composable. That is, it should be possible to specify various design transformations independently and compose them to get a design from requirements. The techniques and tools will include formally proved pattern-directed transformations of specifications to scale up the classical calculi of refinement. We will also investigate the use of model checking and static analysis techniques and tools for consistency and analysis of properties of models. For specification and analysis of coordination among components, simulation techniques and tools can be used. Transformation of different sub-models may need different verification techniques and tools. Data refinements will be realized by structural transformations following design patterns that are scaled up from object-oriented design.

3. *Automatic code generators that implement the implementation functions for various platforms.* Refactoring transformation of designs and implementations will be studied and implemented in the tool support.

4. *Techniques and tools for domain-specific languages and their programming* (such as web-based service and transaction system based on internet).

The main theme of the project is to integrate formal verification techniques and tools with design techniques and tools of model (or specification) transformations. Verification and transformation will work complementary to ensure the correctness of the resultant specification. The design techniques and transformation tools are essential in the development to transform the requirements specification to a model that is easy to be handled with the verification techniques and tools. The design and transformation have to be carried interactively between the designer and the tool. Verification tools can be also invoked during a transformation [21].

This project will be conducted in a close collaboration between UNU-IIST and TRDDC. UNU-IIST is particularly strong in theories and techniques for program modelling, design and verification, and TRDDC is the largest industry research development and design centre in India. We will investigate how the research results at UNU-IIST in theories and techniques of program modelling, design and verification can be used in the design of software development tools at TRDDC. A separate position paper by UNU-IIST is also presented at this conference [2].

4 Related Work at UNU-IIST and TRDDC

TRDDC and UNU-IIST have been approaching the above problem from two different ends. TRDDC has expertise in software engineering techniques and has been researching this area for several years now. These efforts have resulted in MasterCraft [1], a tool that generates code for different platforms from design specifications. Current research activities at TRDDC include graph-based languages for specifying requirements [22] and transformations. The requirements group has successfully used model checking to verify correctness of requirements of a few projects. The work on transformation specifications has resulted in a proposal as a standard in response to an OMG request. The proposal is in an advanced stage of acceptance.

UNU-IIST has been working on formalizing object-oriented development. This work has resulted in a relational model for object-oriented design and an associated refinement calculus [13]. The refinement calculus supports incremental and iterative development [14]. The model is current being extended to support component-based development [5]. Initial progress have been made in experimental development of tool support [11,16]. Promising results have been achieved in unifying different verification methods [4,15].

5 Summary

We believe that we need to advance theories, tools and experiments for both verification and design, and to scale them up to meet business and engineering projects need. For this, we propose component-based modelling and design by transformations so that a software designer can

- apply verified model transformations or define a transformation and verify it after applying it,
- model method bodies (hopefully, the methods now are simple)
- generate proof-carrying code from target model

References

1. Mastercraft. Tata Consultancy Services, http://www.tata-mastercraft.com
2. Aichernig, B.K., He, J., Liu, Z., Reed, M.: Theories and techniques of program modelling, design and verification. In: Meyer, B., Woodcock, J. (eds.) Verified Software: Theories, Tools, Experiments (VSTTE 2005). LNCS, vol. 4171, pp. 291–300. Springer, Heidelberg (2008) (this volume)
3. Gamma, E., Helm, R., Johnson, R., Vlissides, J.: Design Patterns, Elements of Reusable Object-Oriented Software. Addlison Wesley, London (1994)
4. He, J.: Link simulation with refinement. In: Proc. of The 25th anniversary of CSP (2004)
5. He, J., Li, X., Liu, Z.: Component-based software engineering – the need to link methods and their theories. In: Van Hung, D., Wirsing, M. (eds.) ICTAC 2005. LNCS, vol. 3722, pp. 72–97. Springer, Heidelberg (2005)
6. Hoare, A.C.R., Misra, J.: Verified software: Theories, tools and experiments. In: Meyer, B., Woodcock, J. (eds.) VSTTE 2005. LNCS, vol. 4171, pp. 1–18. Springer, Heidelberg (2008) (this volume), http://vstte.ethz.ch/
7. Hoare, C.A.R.: The verifying compiler: A grand challenge for computer research. Journal of the ACM 50(1), 63–69 (2003)
8. Joseph, M.: Formal techniques in large scale software engineering. In: Keynote at IFIP Working Conference on Verified Software: Theories, Tools and Experiments (VSTTE), Zurich (October 10-13, 2005), http://vstte.ethz.ch/

9. Kruchten, P.: The Rational Unified Process – An Introduction, 2nd edn. Addison-Wesly, London, UK (2000)
10. Larman, C.: Applying UML and Patterns. Prentice-Hall, Englewood Cliffs (2001)
11. Li, X., Liu, Z., He, J., Long, Q.: Generating prototypes from a UML model of requirements. In: International Conference on Distributed Computing and Internet Technology (ICDIT2004), Bhubaneswar, India. LNCS, Springer, Heidelberg (2004)
12. Liu, Z., He, J., Li, X.: Contract-oriented development of component systems. In: Proceedings of IFIP WCC-TCS2004, Toulouse, France, pp. 349–366. Kluwer Academic Publishers, Boston (2004)
13. Liu, Z., He, J., Li, X.: rCOS: A refinement calculus for object systems. In: de Boer, F.S., Bonsangue, M.M., Graf, S., de Roever, W.-P. (eds.) FMCO 2004. LNCS, vol. 3657, pp. 183–221. Springer, Heidelberg (2005)
14. Liu, Z., He, J., Li, X., Chen, Y.: A relational model for object-oriented requirement analysis in UML. In: Dong, J.S., Woodcock, J. (eds.) ICFEM 2003. LNCS, vol. 2885, pp. 641–664. Springer, Heidelberg (2003)
15. Liu, Z., Ravn, A.P., Li, X.: Unifying proof methodologies of Duration Calculus and Linear Temporal Logic. Formal Aspects of Computing 16(2) (2004)
16. Long, Q., Liu, Z., He, J., Li, X.: Consistent code generation from uml models. In: Australia Conference on Software Engineering (ASWEC), IEEE Computer Scienty Press, Los Alamitos (2005)
17. Long, Q., Qiu, Z., Liu, Z., Shao, L., He, J.: POST: A case study for an incremental development in rCOS. In: Van Hung, D., Wirsing, M. (eds.) ICTAC 2005. LNCS, vol. 3722, pp. 485–500. Springer, Heidelberg (2005)
18. Mellor, S.J., Valcer, M.J.: Executable UML: a foundation for model-driven architecture. Addison-Wesley, Reading (2002)
19. OMG. The Unified Modeling Language (UML) Specification - Version 1.4, Joint submission to the Object Management Group (OMG) (September 2001) http://www.omg.org/technology/uml/index.htm
20. Pnueli, A.: Looking ahead. In: Workshop on The Verification Grand Challenge 2005 SRI International, Menlo Park, CA(February 21–23)
21. Rushby, J.: Integrating verification components. In: Keynote at IFIP Working Conference on Verified Software: Theories, Tools and Experiments (VSTTE), Zurich, (October 10-13, 2005), http://vstte.ethz.ch/
22. Shrotri, U., Bhaduri, P., Venkatesh, R.: Model checking visual specification of requirements. In: International Conference on Software Engineering and Formal Methods (SEFM 2003), Australia, 3003., pp. 202–209. IEEE Computer Society Press, Los Alamitos

The Verified Software Challenge: A Call for a Holistic Approach to Reliability

Thomas Ball

Microsoft Research, Redmond, WA, USA
tball@microsoft.com

1 Introduction

The software analysis community has made a lot of progress in creating software tools for detecting defects and performing proofs of shallow properties of programs. We are witnessing the birth of a virtuous cycle between software tools and their consumers and I, for one, am very excited about this. We understand much better how to engineer program analyses to scale to large code bases and deal with the difficult problem of false errors and reducing their number. We understand better the tradeoffs in sound vs. unsound analyses. The software tools developed and applied over the last eight years have had impact. This list of tools includes Blast [HJMS02], CCured [NMW02], CQual [FTA02], ESC/Java [FLL+02], ESP [DLS02], Feaver [Hol00], MAGIC [CCG+04], MC [HCXE02], MOPS [CDW04], Prefast [LBD+04], Prefix [BPS00], SLAM [BR01], Splint [EL02] and Verisoft [God97], to name a few.

This *bottom-up* approach to improving code quality will continue to be successful because it deals with a concrete artifact (programs) that people produce, has great economic impact and longevity. Furthermore, because many of the tools listed above are specification-based, they are easy to extend to new classes of bugs. Finally, a lot of the science to support the development of these tools has been done; there is now before us a long road of engineering to make these tools truly useful and useable by a wide audience.

To balance these great efforts, we should devote some attention to *top-down* approaches to building reliable software and reconsider how we design software systems so that they are reliable by construction. We want to construct software in such a way that, as a result of its structure, it has certain good behaviors and does not have other bad behaviors. Furthermore, these good behaviors (or the absence of the bad ones) should be preserved as we refine the system to add functionality or improve performance.

I am concerned that Verified Software focuses on the analysis of artifacts (programs) rather than on their design and construction. Instead of just positioning ourselves as software critics ("thumbs-up" or "thumbs-down"), we also must get up on stage and demonstrate methods for designing and building reliable software. A holistic approach to the problem of software reliability that encompasses designing, building and analyzing software systems will offer the greatest challenges and rewards.

B. Meyer and J. Woodcock (Eds.): Verified Software, LNCS 4171, pp. 42–48, 2008.
© IFIP International Federation for Information Processing 2008

2   Perspective: The SLAM and SDV Projects

What is SLAM about? SLAM was motivated by the program of Windows device drivers. What is a device driver? An idealized view of device drivers is that they are programs that interface hardware to the operating system (the reality in Windows is much more complex). The problem with programming device drivers is that the driver API (essentially a subset of the Windows kernel) is very complex and difficult to master and most device drivers are written by third-party device manufacturers, who are not Windows kernel experts. The device driver "monster" is alive and continues to wreak havoc: device driver failures are the source of 85% of Windows XP crashes.

Why is programming a driver so complex? First and foremost, the Windows kernel is a highly concurrent system and this concurrency is exposed to the driver programmer. Asynchronous I/O is a core facet of the Windows kernel underlying the driver API; it allows for high-performance implementations but is hard to program correctly. The API provides many ways to synchronize access to data and resources. Other major features that the driver API supports are Plug-and-Play (the ability to remove devices and OS features while the computer is on and have everything work correctly) and power management (the ability to selectively power-down subsystems, hibernate and restore power as needed). Like many APIs, the driver API evolved in a very demanding and constrained environment where performance and backward compatibility were driving forces. These forces resulted in a complex API. As a result, driver reliability suffered.

The key idea of the SLAM project is that while a device driver contains a huge amount of state, we need only reason about a small amount of this state when checking whether or not a driver properly uses the driver API. The SLAM tool reverse engineers a Boolean program (pushdown automaton) from the C code of a driver that represents how the C code uses the driver API. Bits in the Boolean program represent important observations about the state of the C program (with respect to its usage of the driver API). SLAM then applies symbolic model checking on this Boolean program. The SLAM engine has been packaged up in a tool called Static Driver Verifier (SDV) that has been released in beta form this year to third party driver developers.

The SDV tool is much more than the SLAM engine. The challenge of making an effective "push button" tool was much more than the creation of SLAM's software model checking engine: the real challenge was the creation and refinement of a set of API usage rules that encode the proper usage of the driver API, as well as an environment model to represent the Windows kernel. Because the driver API is so complex, the development of these rules and environment took a very long time. At first, the rules and environment were too simple and resulted in many false errors. Only after much iteration with driver experts, did we end up with a set of rules and an environment that was effective. During this time, the SLAM engine changed very little. Most of the false errors were due to problems with the rules and environment. This effort was deemed to be worthwhile because we have captured a huge amount of domain expertise about device drivers that now can be leveraged in an automated tool that many driver developers will use. In this sense, SDV is a tireless and expert device driver code inspector that will help driver developers to make proper use of the driver API.

3   Will SLAM and SDV Solve the Driver Problem?

The answer is "probably not". Let's try and understand why.

The SLAM project often is held up as a model of success for software analysis. It is nice to receive such kudos but let's not get carried away here! Once, I was invited to give a talk about SLAM at a workshop and saw that in the preliminary publicity materials for the event, the organizer said something to the effect that "SLAM made a significant contribution to improving the reliability of the Windows operating system." I nearly fell out of my chair when I read that, knowing that all the efforts that people in the Windows organization had made over many years to improve Window's reliability and knowing that SLAM's contribution, even if "significant", would pale in comparison to these efforts. (I very quickly got the message removed from the publicity materials, by the way). In reality, it will be years before we can tell what the effect of SLAM on the reliability of Windows will be and it is even questionable, given all the other methods in play for increasing the reliability of Windows, whether we will be able to separate out SLAM's effect.

There are many reasons device drivers fail and SLAM is capable of finding only a certain class of errors. For example, SLAM does not check that a device driver does not write outside the bounds of the data structures it manipulates. A device driver that corrupts the state of the kernel will not be detected by SLAM. SLAM checks the code of a device driver without considering the interleaving of other threads of execution, so it cannot find deep concurrency errors. It does not do performance testing of the driver under heavy volumes or check for reactivity or real-time constraints.

While SLAM is an important tool in the driver reliability toolbox, it is not sufficient to guarantee the reliability of device drivers. There are many other approaches to dealing with misbehaving drivers. For example, some have proposed running the driver in a sandbox where it cannot damage kernel data structures. Now, some may look at this situation and say "so we need more tools". But others may say "we need to design a better APIs for programming drivers". Others may say "we need to redesign the operating system".

My main point is that tools like SLAM and SDV come in very late in the software production process and, as a result, can only have a limited affect on reliability. The tools only are applied after many important decisions have been made (driver API designed, drivers written in C, drivers run in the same address space as the kernel, etc.) that affect driver reliability in ways that are hard for static analysis tools to address.

4   Provocation

A program is a very detailed solution to a much more abstract problem. Leading from a problem to a program is a complex process. By focusing too much attention on the program, we risk ignoring the complicated process that starts with a problem and ends in a program. It is this process that, in the end, is primarily responsible for the quality of the program. The process of design matters greatly, with particular attention to the fact that programs are deeply integrated into our physical world. As is well-known, a critical design mistake made early in this process, once deeply woven into the intricate software tapestry of a program, is not easily corrected.

Viewed from this perspective, program analyzers, model checkers, verifying compilers and tools like SLAM come into play long after a lot of the important work has been done. These tools find errors and suggest minor modifications to the product. Of course, because of the nature of software, these minor modifications can rid the software of crippling behavioral problems. But, in the end, the analysis tools are working at such a low-level of abstraction (the code) that they cannot see the forest for the trees.

An analogy to automatic parallelization was suggested to me by Jim Larus. For twenty years, researchers worked on techniques for automatically parallelizing sequential FORTRAN programs. While this research produced some interesting ideas, it never succeeded in creating efficient parallel programs from sequential ones, mainly because there wasn't a lot of parallelism to be found in these programs in the first place! Today, the parallel program community recognizes that to get efficient parallel programs you need to carefully design parallel algorithms rather than hoping that a tool will be able to extract parallelism from a program that has little of it to offer.

Similarly, we cannot expect verification tools to inject high reliability into a program that was not designed with reliability in mind from the beginning. We must think about reliability at every point in the software production process. If the starting point for verification is that we are given a program and must attempt to verify it, we are in a losing position because we have so little leverage to affect the design of that program. Starting at the "bottom" means our potential energy and potential for success is very low.

5   A Call to Action: Software Design Methodologies

I believe that by designing, building and analyzing software in new ways that substantially increases its reliability, we will face many more challenges and opportunities than if we limit ourselves to analyzing software. This is what I mean by taking a "holistic" approach to issues of software reliability. As an example, at Microsoft Research there is a new operating system research project called Singularity led by Galen Hunt and Jim Larus. Here is part of the "Motivation" section from the Singularity Design Motivation [HL04]:

> Singularity is a cross-discipline research project focused on the construction of dependable systems through innovation in the areas of systems, languages, and tools. We are building a new research operating system, called Singularity, as a laboratory for designing systems, extending programming languages, and developing new techniques and tools for specifying and verifying program behavior.

Singularity is the first OS to enable anticipatory statements about system configuration and behavior. A specific Singularity system is a self-describing artifact, not just a collection of bits accumulated with at best an anecdotal history. Singularity's self description includes specifications of the components of the system, their behavior, and their interactions. One can, for example, examine an offline Singularity system image and make strong statements about its features, components, composition, and compatibility.

The Singularity research team defines operating system research as research into the base abstractions for computing and research into implementations of those abstractions as exposed by the OS. By returning to this basic definition of OS research, Singularity embraces the opportunity to re-think OS abstractions and their implementations.

OS research is ready for a revolution. Modern systems are bound by abstractions largely defined in the early 1970s. OS research has not kept pace with changes in application composition or security needs of everyday usage scenarios.

Now, you can go read the rest of the note to get some more detail about this project. But just reading this motivation gets me excited. This sounds like a challenge problem! Why? This project has several important attributes that catch my attention:

– it focuses on an important domain (operating systems) with high commercial and societal impact;
– it recognizes that reliability depends on many puzzle pieces, such as operating systems design, new languages and software tools (it is cross-disciplinary);
– it recognizes that the search for appropriate abstractions is a key problem in operating systems design.

There is something to learn from Singularity, even if operating systems is not one's cup of tea. First, let's start with a problem domain (or two or three, to keep everyone interested) for which high reliability is a necessity and work our way towards a solution. (To reiterate, software is a solution to a problem. If we start with the solution then we have no control over how the solution came into being.) We may sacrifice claims to generality but we will gain a lot more (especially, credibility). Second, by necessity, we need to form cross-discipline teams. We cannot expect to acquire all the domain knowledge ourselves. By bringing our expertise in what is possible to specify and verify together with the knowledge of domain experts, we can make much more progress than if we work in isolation. Third, let's look into a variety of approaches to ensuring reliability. We have some specification languages and modeling languages, but are they really sufficient for the domains we wish to tackle? We have model checkers, theorem provers and program analysis but are they up to the task? We should let the problem domain guide our search to the abstractions, methods, languages and tools that will be the most appropriate to that domain, rather than letting the technologies we know and love blind us to other possibilities.

6 Conclusion

Based on my experience with the SLAM project, I would like to spend more time thinking about how to design and build reliable software rather than analyzing it after the fact. I don't have a recipe for success or prescriptive advice at this point. However, I am intrigued by the continued success of design patterns and reusable components in helping to construct larger and more complex systems. For example, Microsoft's www.gotdotnet.org site has a community of over 5,000 developers who contribute to the Enterprise Library, "a collection of reusable components that help you quickly build better applications with more features and *higher quality*" (my emphasis). As with the Singularity project, these developers are engaged in the search for better abstractions. We should think about partnering with such people—they are involved in designing and building real applications and have substantial domain expertise. What they are missing is the knowledge we have about verification technology.

References

[BPS00] Bush, W.R., Pincus, J.D., Sielaff, D.J.: A static analyzer for finding dynamic programming errors. Software-Practice and Experience 30(7), 775–802 (2000)

[BR01] Ball, T., Rajamani, S.K.: Automatically validating temporal safety properties of interfaces. In: Dwyer, M.B. (ed.) SPIN 2001. LNCS, vol. 2057, Springer, Heidelberg (2001)

[CCG+04] Chaki, S., Clarke, E., Groce, A., Jha, S., Veith, H.: Modular verification of software components in C. TSE: Transactions on Software Engineering 30(6), 388–402 (2004)

[CDW04] Chen, H., Dean, D., Wagner, D.: Model checking one million lines of C code. In: NDSS: Network and Distributed System Security Symposium, pp. 171–185 (2004)

[DLS02] Das, M., Lerner, S., Seigle, M.: ESP: path-sensitive program verifica-tion in polynomial time. In: PLDI 2002: Programming language design and implementation, pp. 57–68. ACM, New York (2002)

[EL02] Evans, D., Larochelle, D.: Improving security using extensible lightweight static analysis. IEEE Software 19(1), 42–51 (2002)

[FLL+02] Flanagan, C., Leino, K.R.M., Lillibridge, M., Nelson, G., Saxe, J.B., Stata, R.: Extended static checking for java. In: PLDI 2002: Programming Language Design and Implementation, pp. 234–245. ACM, New York (2002)

[FTA02] Foster, J.S., Terauchi, T., Aiken, A.: Flow-sensitive type qualifiers. In: PLDI 2002: Programming language design and implementation, pp. 1–12. ACM, New York (2002)

[God97] Godefroid, P.: Model checking for programming languages using Verisoft. In: POPL 1997: Principles of Programming Languages, pp. 174–186. ACM, New York (1997)

[HCXE02] Hallem, S., Chelf, B., Xie, Y., Engler, D.: Asystem and language for building system-specific, static analyses. In: PLDI 2002: Programming Language Design and Implementation, pp. 69–82. ACM, New York (2002)

[HJMS02] Henzinger, T.A., Jhala, R., Majumdar, R., Sutre, G.: Lazy abstraction. In: POPL 2002, pp. 58–70. ACM Press, New York (2002)

[HL04]   Hunt, G.C., Larus, J.R.: Singularity design motivation. Technical Report MSR-TR-2004-105, Microsoft Research (December 2004)

[Hol00]   Holzmann, G.J.: Logic verification of ANSI-C code with Spin. In: Havelund, K., Penix, J., Visser, W. (eds.) SPIN 2000. LNCS, vol. 1885, pp. 131–147. Springer, Heidelberg (2000)

[LBD+04] Larus, J.R., Ball, T., Das, M., DeLine, R., Fahndrich, M., Pincus, J., Rajamani, S.K., Venkatapathy, R.: Righting software. IEEE Software 21(3), 92–100 (2004)

[NMW02]   Necula, G., McPeak, S., Weimer, W.: CCured: Type-safe retrofitting of legacy code. In: POPL 2002, pp. 128–139. ACM, New York (2002)

A   Discussion on Thomas Ball's Presentation

Kathi Fisler

In this case, are your friends your researchers?

Thomas Ball

Oh, in the case of Singularity?

Kathi Fisler

No, in general, in the project you talk about here.

Thomas Ball

Oh, no, no, no. So, for example, with the Static Driver Verifier, we did a huge amount of work with the driver experts, who did not know what was wrong. We showed up and were like: "Well, we want to find bugs in device drivers, can you tell us something?" So, with SLAM, we started out at zero. With things like PreFast again it took time. Languages like Spec# and Sing# right now have been mainly used by researchers. Again, the adoption of a language is a little bit dicier than the adoption of a tool that is optional or not. But in general, with all the tools we have had to get substantial buy-in from the product groups.

A Mini Challenge:
Build a Verifiable Filesystem

Rajeev Joshi and Gerard J. Holzmann

Laboratory for Reliable Software*,
Jet Propulsion Laboratory,
California Institute of Technology,
Pasadena, CA 91109, USA
{Rajeev.Joshi,Gerard.Holzmann}@jpl.nasa.gov
http://eis.jpl.nasa.gov/lars

Abstract. We propose tackling a "mini challenge" problem: a nontrivial verification effort that can be completed in 2-3 years, and will help establish notational standards, common formats, and libraries of benchmarks that will be essential in order for the verification community to collaborate on meeting Hoare's 15-year verification grand challenge. We believe that a suitable candidate for such a mini challenge is the development of a filesystem that is *verifiably* reliable and secure. The paper argues why we believe a filesystem is the right candidate for a mini challenge and describes a project in which we are building a small embedded filesystem for use with flash memory.

1 A Mini Challenge

The verification grand challenge proposed by Hoare [1] sets the stage for the program verification community to embark upon a collaborative effort to build verifiable programs. At a recent workshop in Menlo Park [2], there seemed to be a consensus that a necessary stepping stone to such an effort would be the development of repositories for sharing specifications, models, implementations, and benchmarks so that different tools could be combined and compared.

We believe that the best way of reaching agreement on common formats and forging the necessary collaborations to build such a repository is to embark upon a shorter-term "mini challenge": a nontrivial verification project that can nonetheless be completed in a short time. An ideal candidate for such a mini challenge would have several characteristics: (a) it would be of sufficient complexity that traditional methods such as testing and code reviews are inadequate to establish its correctness, (b) it would be of sufficient simplicity that specification, design and verification could be completed by a dedicated team in a relatively short time, say 2-3 years, and (c) it would be of sufficient importance

---

* The work described in this paper was carried out at the Jet Propulsion Laboratory, California Institute of Technology, under a contract with the National Aeronautics and Space Administration.

B. Meyer and J. Woodcock (Eds.): Verified Software, LNCS 4171, pp. 49–56, 2008.

that successful completion of the mini challenge would have an impact beyond the verification community.

At the Menlo Park workshop, some participants (notably Amir Pnueli) suggested that a suitable candidate would be the verification of the kernel[1] of the Linux operating system [3]. While the task of verifying the Linux kernel undoubtedly meets conditions (a) and (c) above, it does not meet condition (b). In fact, given that the current Linux kernel is well over 4 million lines of source code, it seems a tall order to write a formal specification for it within 2 years, much less verify the correctness of the implementation. Instead, we propose that a more suitable candidate for such a mini challenge would be the development of a verifiable filesystem. We believe there are several reasons why a filesystem is more attractive as a first target for verification than an operating system kernel.

Firstly, most modern filesystems have a clean, well-defined interface, conforming to the POSIX standard [4], which has been in use for many years. Thus writing a formal specification for a POSIX-compliant filesystem would require far less effort than writing a kernel specification. In fact, one could even write an abstract reference filesystem implementation which could be used as the specification for a verification proof based on refinement.

Secondly, since the underlying data structures and algorithms used in filesystem design are very well understood, a verifiable filesystem implementation could conceivably be written from scratch. Alternatively, researchers could choose any of several existing open-source filesystems and attempt to verify them. This makes filesystem verification attractive, since it allows participation by both those researchers interested in *a posteriori* verification, as well as those interested in "constructing a program and its proof hand-in-hand".

Thirdly, although filesystems comprise only a small portion of an operating system, they are complex enough that ensuring reliability in the presence of concurrent accesses and unexpected power failures is nontrivial. Indeed, recent work by Yang et al shows that many popular filesystems in widespread use have serious bugs that can have devastating consequences, such as deletion of the system root directory [7].

Finally, since almost all data on modern computers is now managed by filesystems, their correctness is of great importance, both from the standpoint of reliability as well as security. Development of a verified filesystem would therefore be of great value even beyond the verification community.

2   Directions and Challenges

The goal of the proposed mini challenge is to build a *verifiable* filesystem. In particular, we are interested in the problem of how to write a filesystem whose correctness can be checked using automated verification tools. After decades of experience with automatic program verification, we know that such an effort inevitably requires that key design knowledge be captured and expressed in machine readable forms that can be used to guide the verification tools. This

---

[1] Actually, Pnueli suggested verifying "Linux"; we assume he meant the Linux kernel.

includes (a) a formal behavioral specification of the functionality provided by the filesystem, (b) a formal elaboration of the assumptions made of the underlying hardware, and (c) a set of invariants, assertions and properties concerning key data structures and algorithms in the implementation. We discuss each of these artifacts below.

Specification. Most modern filesystems are written to comply with the POSIX standard [4] for filesystems. This standard specifies a set of function signatures (such as `creat, open, read, write`), along with a behavioral description of each function. However, these behavioral descriptions are given as informal English prose, and are therefore too ambiguous and incomplete to be useful in a verification effort. The first task therefore is to write a formal specification of the POSIX standard (or at least of a substantial portion of the standard) either as a set of logical properties or as an abstract reference implementation. Such formal specifications have been written in the past: for instance, by Morgan and Sufrin [5], who wrote a specification of the UNIX filesystem in Z, and by Bevier, Cohen and Turner [6], who wrote a specification for the Synergy filesystem in Z (and also partially in ACL2). Although these specifications did not completely model POSIX behavior (for instance, neither completely modeled error codes, nor file permissions), they could serve as starting points for developing a more complete specification.

Assumptions about underlying hardware. In order to provide a rigorous formal statement of the properties of the filesystem (especially its robustness with respect to power failure), it is necessary to rely on certain behavioral assumptions about the underlying hardware. In order to make the filesystem useful, it is necessary to understand what assumptions can reasonably be made about typical hardware such as hard drives or flash memory. These assumptions need to be explicitly identified and clearly stated, as opposed to used implicitly in correctness proofs (as is often the case). In the ideal situation, the filesystem would be usable with different types of hardware, perhaps providing different reliability guarantees.

Properties of data structures and procedures. As noted before, an attractive feature of the proposed mini challenge is that one could either write a verifiable filesystem from scratch, or verify an available filesystem. In either case, however, in order to use automatic checking tools to prove nontrivial correctness properties of the implementation, it will inevitably be necessary to identify and express design properties such as data structure invariants, annotations describing which locks protect which data, and pre- and post-conditions for library functions. Most typical filesystems require use of many common data structures such as hash tables, linked lists and search trees. A proof of filesystem correctness would therefore result in development of libraries of formally stated properties and proofs about these data structures, which would be useful in other verification efforts as well.

3   A Reliable Flash Filesystem for Flight Software

At the NASA/JPL Laboratory for Reliable Software (LaRS), we are interested in the problem of building reliable software that is less reliant on following traditional ad-hoc processes and more reliant on use of automated verification tools. As part of this effort, we are currently engaged in a pilot project to help build a reliable filesystem for flash memory, for use as nonvolatile storage on board future missions.

Flash memory has recently become a popular choice for use on spacecraft as nonvolatile storage for engineering and data products, since it has no moving parts, consumes low power and is easily available. There are two common types of flash memory, NAND flash and NOR flash [8]. While NOR flash is more reliable and easier to program, it has lower density and poor write and erase times, and is therefore less attractive as a data storage device. While it is possible to design flight software to use flash memory directly as a raw device, it is typically much easier to write robust flight software on top of a filesystem layer that provides common file operations for creating, reading and writing files and directories. In fact, the flight software on several recent NASA missions, such as the Mars Exploration Rovers and Deep Impact, uses a filesystem to access flash memory.

Building a robust flash filesystem, however, is a nontrivial task. Performance dictates the use of caches and write buffers, which increase the danger of inconsistencies in the presence of concurrent thread accesses and unexpected power failures. To add to the challenge, flash memory, especially NAND flash memory, requires certain additional issues to be addressed such as arbitrary bit flips, blocks that unexpectedly become "bad" (i.e., permanently unusable), and limited lifetimes (block usually become bad after they have been erased a certain number of times, typically 100,000). In addition, a flash filesystem written for use on a spacecraft must obey additional constraints; for instance, flight software is typically allowed to allocate memory only during initialization.

The goal of our pilot project is to build a robust flash filesystem by following a design methodology that is based on documenting as much as possible in a machine readable form that is amenable to automatic verification. Thus the intent is not only to build a working filesystem, but also to produce key design documents in machine-readable forms that can be used by automated verification tools. Although less ambitious than the mini challenge we have described above (which is aimed at building a general purpose filesystem), our project has similar interests and goals with the mini challenge we have proposed.

4   Summary

An important first step toward the Verification Grand Challenge is the development of a repository containing specifications, models and implementations. We believe the best way to develop this repository is to tackle a "mini challenge" that can be completed in a short period of time, around 2-3 years. An excellent candidate for such a mini challenge seems to be the development of a verifiable filesystem that is both reliable and secure. Since filesystems are well-defined and well-understood, different research teams can take different approaches to building such a verifiable filesystem, from building it from scratch to verifying one of many available filesystems. We believe that the problem is well-suited as a mini challenge for the verification community and will serve as a starting point for the grand verification challenge.

References

1. Hoare, T.: The Verifying Compiler: A Grand Challenge for Computing Research. Journal of the ACM 50(1), 63–69 (2003)
2. Workshop on the Verification Grand Challenge, SRI International, Menlo Park, CA (February 2005), http://www.csl.sri.com/users/shankar/VGC05
3. Pnueli, A.: Looking Ahead, Presentation at the Workshop on The Verification Grand Challenge, SRI International, Menlo Park, CA (February 2005), http://www.csl.sri.com/users/shankar/VGC05/pnueli.pdf
4. The Open Group, The POSIX 1003.1, 2003 Edition Specification, http://www.opengroup.org/certification/idx/posix.html
5. Morgan, C., Sufrin, B.: Specification of the UNIX Filing System. IEEE Transactions on Software Engineering SE-10(2), 128–142 (1984)
6. Bevier, W.R., Cohen, R., Turner, J.: A Specification for the Synergy File System, Technical Report 120, Computational Logic, Inc., (September 1995)
7. Yang, J., Twohey, P., Engler, D., Musuvathi, M.: Using Model Checking to Find Serious File System Errors. In: Proceedings of the Conference on Operating Systems Design and Implementation (OSDI), San Francisco, pp. 273–288 (December 2004)
8. Data I/O, *A Collection of NAND Flash Application Notes, Whitepapers and Articles*, http://www.data-io.com/NAND/NANDApplicationNotes.asp

A   Discussion on Rajeev Joshi's Presentation

Jayadev Misra

[Inaudible question]

Rajeev Joshi

I believe, the specs could be written by a group of five people-any five people in this room-in less than six months. So, how long would it take to write a file system? I think the big problem is getting the machine-verifiability part of it. So, if we go back and think about the level of ambition, I think the first one should be doable by a group of less than ten people in a year. But remember, we are not solving the general problem; we are solving the problem in the context of a filesystem. So, the harder part is as you go down the list. I do not really have an answer. I would be guessing, and I do not know what to guess.

Greg Nelson

Rajeev, when you talked about the options for translating the POSIX English language spec into a formal form, you mentioned two options, neither of which seems to me to be the translation into preconditions and postconditions and modifiers, because this would have been the first thing I would think of. Can you educate me or tell me, how I suffer this disconnect?

Rajeev Joshi

That is because I should have said: "like pre- and postconditions or temporal logical properties or a reference implementation".

Tevfik Bultan

You mentioned, that there was a paper that found errors in the existing filesystems. So, what types of errors, you listed a categorization of types of correctness, could we check? So, did they find null dereferences or...

Rajeev Joshi *(interrupts)*

No, it is more complex. They used a kind of model checking and they found issues where you can have kernel panics, or you could have data corruption, metadata corruption, which should cause losing the system root directory under certain conditions with multiple threads running. So, no, they used software model checking, essentially.

Peter O'Hearn

Isn't this awfully ambitious as a first step? The verification should be automatic, I take it.

Rajeev Joshi

I don't think that in the end we will have a tool that will work on an arbitrary computer program, but we will have something, that will essentially be tailored for this filesystem. I think part of the problem is doing it in a way that all the machine-readable artifacts are published somewhere, which is the issue of setting up a repository. So, somebody who writes the specification has to write it in a format, so that other people know what the format is and have agreed upon it.

Peter O'Hearn

So, you are proposing not to test the proof tools so much as the specifications.

Rajeev Joshi

Well, again it depends on your level of ambition when you say, "proof tools". I don't know how far we can go. If we stop with model checking then, if you write a set of invariants and you say, "well, we model-checked and we guarantee that the model checker has actually covered the entire space", then that is some level of verification I think we could reach. I don't think it is too ambitious from that point of view. I think the harder problem is to make people agree on formats. I mean, that's a fact of life. I have seen this before in other instances that it is not always... *[sentence incomplete]*

Peter O'Hearn *(interrupts)*

Now, if you ask for automatic verification, then the difficulty is very great, but if you would allow manual verification, then I would agree with you. You could do it with some number of man-years. But if the project is to have nearly automatic methods, then your proposal seems like an extremely difficult one as a first step.

Rajeev Joshi

Ok... So, we can check it manually, maybe.

Egon Börger

Since you are speaking about details: I was surprised that you seem to separate the core of specification from what you mention under "design", namely, concurrency, fault tolerance, asynchrony. I think they should be part of the specification, because of the many things you will have to handle at that level. This is something where you have to connect to the operating system somehow, or your scheduling mechanism. And this may break your spec. So, it should be part of the spec, I guess.

Rajeev Joshi

Yes that is of course one of the hard problems in computing science in verification: What assumptions can you make? Under what assumptions is your program going to work? And I think that's hard. Yes, it's true-since the filesystem typically runs as part of the operating system-that how the operating system manages threads, for instance, is an issue. What guarantees the operating system provides against threads writing on each other's data would be an issue. Is that the kind of thing you're asking about?

Egon Börger

Yes, that is exactly the kind of reason why I believe it should be part of your spec. You should analyze this really mathematically, because if you look at what happened to Java, with thread handling in Java, the same you have in C#. When you go to the thread handling mechanism, it is poorly described, and as a programmer, you are left with almost no knowledge of what is going on, except you know all the details of compilers and maybe operating systems. The same thing would happen to your filesystem spec. If you separate specification from what has to do with asynchronous communication or whatever, then you can throw away your spec later on. It does not tell you the real story. It is just a purely functional view under the assumption that all the accesses are safe and secure, or whatever.

Rajeev Joshi

Yes, I think that is an inherent property of specifications. And I think one just writes with a certain model in mind.

Egon Börger

So, you need a communication model and an action model...

Rajeev Joshi

I don't think that is necessary. But for instance, as Greg mentioned, if you write pre- and postconditions, then it's pretty well defined what the *open()*-operation does with the pre- and postconditions. So, you can just check that the code for the *open()* will satisfy the pre- and postconditions. Now, of course, if you are running something concurrently with an *open()*, say if you are running a *create()*, then those guarantees don't hold, but that is a different problem. So, I think it depends on, again, your level of ambition. You can say that we have checked it so that it is correct with respect to pre- and postcondition semantics, but this does not mean, it is correct with respect to everything else.

Egon Börger

The only thing I wanted to point out is that I would not relegate it to just design; I would do this as high up as possible.

A Constructive Approach to Correctness, Exemplified by a Generator for Certified Java Card Applets

Alessandro Coglio and Cordell Green

Kestrel Institute, Palo Alto, California, USA
{coglio,green}@kestrel.edu
www.kestrel.edu

Abstract. We present a constructive approach to correctness and exemplify it by describing a generator for certified Java Card applets that we are building. A proof of full functional correctness is generated, along with the code, from the specification; the proof can be independently checked by a simple proof checker, so that the larger and more complex generator needs not be trusted. We argue that such an approach is a valuable alternative to post-hoc verification, in addressing the Program Verifier Grand Challenge.

1 Position

Our position is that a constructive approach (namely, generating code from specs) can be a valuable alternative to post-hoc code verification. Our goal is to have a proof of full functional correctness of the code with respect to its spec. The automated generation of such a proof, along with the code, is guided by the availability of the code generation/design process. Generated proofs are checkable by a small and simple proof checker. A specification-first approach is made more widely accessible via user-friendly domain-specific notations. Domain-specific restrictions also simplify code and proof generation. Our experience with, and user acceptance of, early versions of the generator described herein, support this position.

2 Summary

Our approach uses automated construction steps (refinements) that are proven to have the desired property, in our case functional correctness. We exemplify this approach with AutoSmart [1], our generator for Java Card applets [4]. AutoSmart converts our domain-specific specification language, SmartSlang, into the Java Card language. This approach does not depend upon verifying the generator – a proof is generated and checked for each applet generated.

AutoSmart first checks consistency properties of the source specification and then applies a series of transformations to the specification. Proofs are generated automatically as the transformations are applied. Each proof can then be

B. Meyer and J. Woodcock (Eds.): Verified Software, LNCS 4171, pp. 57–63, 2008.

checked by a simple proof checker. The correctness of this approach rests upon the correctness of the checker and of the formal specification of the semantics of both source and target language, and of course the logic language used to express the semantics. Only these artifacts need be trusted.

Our Metaslang language [3] is used to express the semantics of both source and target languages and to express the correspondence between the source and target, i.e. "correctness". Metaslang includes an executable subset that was used to implement the generator.

2.1   Progress and Outlook

The system is working and in use. The current release (August 2005) includes the automatic translation from source to target and also includes the semantics of the source and target languages. Consistency properties of about half of the axiomatization of the target language have been automatically checked by a theorem prover, Snark [2]. Autosmart now includes a proof checker.

We believe the full system will be completed early next year. We foresee no scalability problems, having sampled proofs of the various parts. Scalability results from the simplicity and restriction of the domain-specific language, and the inherent simplicity of the applets generated. Since we need not deal with legacy code, we can employ a correct-by-construction approach, which simplifies the complexity of achieving a correctness guarantee. New tasks being undertaken, which also appear to be tractable, include the automated generation of a correct Java Card run-time environment, and the automated generation of the ancillary materials necessary to achieve certification.

Will this system, Autosmart, when completed, satisfy the Grand Challenge? Well, it will indeed provide proofs of both functional correctness and also security properties of software it produces. And the proofs will be tied to the software generated. The generator itself need not be proven. It will scale to reasonable Java Card applets. However, the input specification language is domain-specific and precludes certain features found in general-purpose languages (e.g. no recursion, no concurrency).

3   The Approach

Consider the automatic translation TR of artifacts written in a source language S into corresponding artifacts written in a target language T. "Corresponding" means that a certain relationship must hold between the artifacts. Such a relationship can be formally expressed in a logical language L, including formalizations of the semantics of S and T.

An approach to ensure the correctness of TR is to formalize TR in L, and prove a theorem stating that TR translates S artifacts to T artifacts such that the desired relationship holds. A concern with this approach is the gap between the formalization of TR in L and the actual implementation of TR. If TR is handwritten, then its formalization in L is only a model of the code that implements

TR, and there is the possibility that the code does not behave exactly according to its model in L.

This concern can be overcome by deriving the code of TR via a provably correct refinement process that starts from the formalization of TR in L. However, if TR is sufficiently complex, performing such a derivation can be daunting, despite the relative maturity of current correct-by-construction technology. In addition, to play devil's advocate, the correctness of the TR code would depend on the tools used to derive it from the formalization of TR in L: who ensures the correctness of those tools?

Another approach to ensure the correctness of translations operated by TR is to have TR generate, along with the translation of an S artifact SA into a T artifact TA, also a proof P in L that the desired relationship between SA and TA holds. We also need a proof checker for L and two simple "encoders" that map respectively S and T artifacts to their representations in L. The proof checker is used to verify that P is a valid proof. The encoders are used to construct the formula in L that expresses the desired relationship between SA and TA. Finally, we check that the conclusion of P is the constructed formula. We do not ensure the correctness of TR in general, but just the correctness of particular artifacts produced by TR.

In this approach, we only need to trust the following items:

1. the proof checker for L;
2. the formalizations of S and T in L;
3. the formal expression of the desired relationship between S and T artifacts;
4. the encoders of S and T artifacts into their representations in L.

The size and nature of these items makes them easier to trust than the larger, more complex TR. A proof checker is usually quite small and simple; it can be derived straightforwardly from a mathematical definition of the logic of L. The formalizations of S and T in L may be large (depending on the complexity of S and T), but they can be inspected better than code can; in addition, expected formal properties about them can be proved (this may include testing, especially if the formalizations are executable or can at least be refined to executable versions). Similar remarks apply to the formal expression of the relationship between S and T artifacts. The encoders are also small and simple.

Of course, TR may generate a proof P that fails to pass the proof checker. Such a failure would typically uncover some bug in TR. However, if a proof P is valid and proves the formula derived from the artifacts SA and TA via the encoders, then we know that TA is a correct translation of SA, no matter how many bugs TR may have.

4   The Generator of Certified Java Card Applets

The source language S is SmartSlang (= <u>smart</u> card <u>s</u>pecification <u>lang</u>uage), a domain-specific language tailored to smart card applets. SmartSlang features high-level constructs to express smart card concepts (ranging from communication with card readers to personal identification numbers) in a concise and convenient way. It also features an expressive type system (which includes, for example, integer ranges and enumerations with optional argument), built-in cryptographic operations, global invariants, and Java-like expressions and statements. Users find the domain-specific language simple and easy to use.

The target language T is Java Card, a version of Java tailored to smart cards. Java Card features a subset of the Java language (e.g. floating point numbers and dynamic class loading are left out), a different set of library APIs than standard Java (e.g. to handle communication with the card reader and to perform cryptographic operations), and a specialized runtime environment with its own security model. Even though Java is relatively high-level, developing Java Card applets requires the programmer to deal with fairly low-level details, greatly increasing the potential for bugs.

The translator TR is AutoSmart (= automatic generator of smart Card applets), which consists of two components that operate one after the other. The first component checks various consistency properties of the SmartSlang specification, such as type safety. For instance, expressions assigned to state variables with integer range types are statically checked to always yield results within the ranges. A linear arithmetic decision procedure and a propositional reasoner are used to check type safety. The second component of AutoSmart generates Java Card code from the checked specification. Some of the results of type checking are used by the code generator: for example, the integer range types inferred for intermediate arithmetic results are used to decide which Java Card types to use to represent those values.

Translating SmartSlang into Java Card is not trivial. While some SmartSlang constructs almost directly correspond to Java Card constructs (intentionally), others are realized by multiple constructs spread through the Java Card code. For example, Java Card allocates objects from the heap but does not support garbage collection. Since memory is a very scarce resource in smart cards, Java Card programs must not willy-nilly allocate new objects during normal computation: all objects must be allocated during applet installation, and suitably re-used during normal computation. On the other hand, SmartSlang has no notion of objects and allocation, it just deals with values. Since some of these values are represented as objects in the Java Card code, AutoSmart must figure out, for the generated Java Card code, which objects to allocate and how to re-use them.

In the example applets we have worked on so far, the expansion ratio of SmartSlang into Java Card, measured in lines, is about 3-5; we expect it to rise to about 7 with the introduction into SmartSlang of additional high-level constructs that we have planned. The generated code is quite readable and not artificially verbose, rather close to what a human developer would write. The key to generating good-quality code is domain-specificity: despite the differences between SmartSlang and Java Card (e.g. explicitly allocated objects vs. just values), the two languages are relatively close to each other (after all, that they both describe smart card applets). In addition, smart card applets are relatively small (typically, only a few hundred lines), making their analysis and manipulation tractable.

The logical language L is Metaslang, the specification language of Specware™ [3], a system for the rigorous development of software from formal specifications via provably correct refinement to code. Metaslang is based on higher-order logic; its features include predicate subtypes (as in PVS), first-order polymorphism (as in HOL), pattern matching (as in ML), and quotient types. Like the languages of popular higher-order theorem provers, Metaslang can be conveniently used to formalize the semantics of other languages. The logic of Metaslang has been formally defined and a proof checker for Metaslang exists.

In order to express the desired correspondence between SmartSlang specifications and Java Card programs, we must understand which features of those artifacts are relevant at the top level. The interaction between a smart card and a card reader is a master-slave one, where the reader is the master and the card is the slave. Accordingly, a smart card applet is a passive entity that maintains an internal state. When the applet receives a command (coming from the reader through the runtime environment of the card), it processes the command, possibly updating its internal state, and produces a response (sent to the reader through the runtime environment). Thus, the semantics of a smart card applet can be expressed, in essence, as a function that maps a state and a command to a new state and a response (i.e. a state machine).

A SmartSlang specification precisely describes the state of the applet, the commands it recognizes, and how each command is processed (command processing is expressed partly operationally, partly declaratively). We have developed a formalization of the SmartSlang language in Metaslang. We have formalized the abstract syntax and associated a formal semantics to the syntax. The top-level semantics of a SmartSlang specification is a state machine of the form described above.

A Java Card program consists of a set of classes. Each program must include methods that constitute the interface with the Java Card runtime environment. When the card reader sends a command, the runtime environment invokes a certain method, supplying the content of the command as argument. The method can perform arbitrary processing, including updating the state of the objects in the heap, using the library APIs, and constructing a response. When it terminates, a response is sent to the reader. We have developed a formalization of the Java Card language and APIs in Metaslang. The formalization currently covers the constructs and APIs targeted by the AutoSmart code generator. The top-level semantics of a Java Card program is also a state machine: the objects in the heap constitute the state, and the transition determined by a command is the net effect of the method invocation with that command.

The desired relationship between a SmartSlang specification and the corresponding Java Card program generated by AutoSmart is that they exhibit the same observable behavior. The internal state is not observable; the command-response exchanges are observable. So, in our formalizations of SmartSlang and Java Card, we associate the respective state machines with the set of all their possible command-response exchange traces in time (since we are not interested in real-time properties, traces are simply sequences conveying the relative time ordering of the exchanges). The formula that expresses the correctness of a particular Java Card program with respect to a particular SmartSlang specification says that the two artifacts have the same set of traces.

Note that the equality of the specification's set of traces with the program's set of traces (as opposed to the latter being a subset of the former) guarantees the preservation of certain security properties that are generally not preserved by subset inclusion. For instance, if the specification requires an applet to respond with a random challenge to a command (as part of a challenge-response authentication protocol), the specification has traces with all the possible challenges. If the program systematically generated a constant challenge (which would defeat the protocol, enabling a simple replay attack), the program's set of traces would be a strict subset of the specification's, violating the required equality; in order for the sets of traces to be equal, the program must be able to generate all the possible challenges. Equality of trace sets still allows the program to generate certain challenges more often than others, violating "randomness". We plan to address this issue, in the future, by adding probability information to (our formalization of) certain SmartSlang and Java Card constructs (e.g. a call to the random-number generation Java Card API yields a value with uniform probability distribution in a given range) and hence to traces. So, the program will have to exhibit the same probabilistic behavior as the specification. Another direction for future work is the addition of timing information to SmartSlang, Java Card, and their traces.

As of August 2005, AutoSmart does not yet generate proofs, but we are actively working on that. The code generation component of AutoSmart consists of various sequential phases. To reduce the complexity of proof generation, we are generating a proof from each phase, and obtain the end-to-end proof by composing the sub-proofs.

Once the proof generation capability is completed, we will be in a position to check the correctness of the translations performed by AutoSmart using the proof checker and the encoders. The encoders simply map the SmartSlang spec and the Java Card program to their abstract syntax representations in Metaslang, in order to construct the formula stating correctness (i.e. that the sets of traces associated to the two artifacts are equal). The proof checker is used to check the proof, yielding a formula that is the conclusion of the proof (if successful). A simple syntactic check finally ensures that the conclusion of the proof coincides with the correctness formula.

The capability to establish the correctness of smart card applet implementations with respect to the specifications without having to trust the generator is particularly valuable for achieving third-party certification. Information technology security standards such as the Common Criteria and FIPS 140-2 (for cryptographic modules) require the developer to provide, for the highest levels of certification, proofs of correctness of the code with respect to requirements.

5   Why a Constructive Approach?

In many software situations we must deal with assurance of legacy code, which is verified by a post-hoc method of proving certain properties, or possibly functional correctness. But the combinatorial difficulty of a post-hoc approach has generally prevented the community from being able to prove full functional correctness, i.e. that the program actually does what is intended. For example, we may know with high assurance that some glue code between programs does not overflow a buffer, but not have a proof that it correctly glues components so that the ensemble is correct.

But often we need not be relegated to just analyzing legacy code, and instead are allowed to develop new software. Here the approach of applying constructive design knowledge offers advantages. Most significantly, the intrinsic problem complexity is reduced so that we can prove full functional correctness. This complexity reduction is a consequence of a synthetic versus an analytic approach. That is, the number of ways one functional specification can be implemented is large. On the other hand, while most of these implementations are redundant or differ in unimportant ways, an analytic approach must be able to capture any implementation given. But a generator need only generate a reasonable and smaller number of implementations. Then evolution and maintenance are carried out on the source specification, avoiding the need for target code analysis. Further understanding this question of verification-complexity reduction is a suggested research topic. Empirically, we typically find a factor of about 3-5 increase in complexity or size moving from spec to code.

6   Conclusion

We have described a constructive approach to correctness, in which a generator generates checkable proofs from the transformations that it performs. We have exemplified the approach with the description of a generator of smart card applets. A key feature of the approach is that the generator need not be trusted. We need only trust the proof checker as well as the axiomatization of the semantics of the source and target language and of the correctness relationship between them, which appears to be a "minimal" set of artifacts to be trusted in order to formally establish correctness. We have also discussed potential advantages of a constructive approach over post-hoc verification, for the case where we have the opportunity to develop new code as opposed to using legacy code.

References

1. Kestrel Institute. AutoSmart, www.kestrel.edu/jcapplets
2. SRI International. Snark, www.ai.sri.com/~stickel/snark.html
3. Kestrel Institute and Kestrel Technology LLC. Specware^{TM}, www.specware.org
4. Sun Microsystems. Java Card technology, java.sun.com/javacard

Some Interdisciplinary Observations about Getting the "Right" Specification

Cliff B. Jones

Newcastle University
Newcastle, NE1 7RU, UK
cliff.jones@ncl.ac.uk

One can use formal approaches either *post facto* to try to show that a program has desirable properties or one can aim for *verified by construction* (VxC). The former approach tends to focus on specific properties such as avoiding the de-referencing of null pointers; the latter is more likely to address the question of whether the steps of design satisfy some overall specification. I not only prefer the latter but I have also argued that this is the main way to get formal methods to pay off: there is more mileage in getting a clean architecture than in trying to debug a bad design by retrofitting a proof.

I think VxC is also a way to choose an appropriate level of formality perhaps using outline arguments and filling in details if doubt arises (see [Jon96]; Jackson and Wing made a similar point in the same journal; [Jon05] makes a similar point related to proofs).

But we must also face the crucial question "how do we know that the specification is right?". This is not a trivial question especially with the way computers are used today. As computers have become more powerful and less expensive, they have become ever more deeply embedded in the way nearly everyone works. In their short history, computers have moved from batch processors in their own buildings to work tools on every desk (or lap). They are now essential components of administration, retail trade, banking and vehicles; computers in the future will become invisible dust sprinkled on who-knows-what. This has transformed the task of understanding the *requirements* of a system. Above all, the close interaction of people with computer systems makes it essential that designers consider the *whole system* when formulating a specification of the technical parts. This larger system involves people as essential components.

Model-oriented specification techniques like VDM, Z, ASMs and B have an enormous amount in common; among other things shared by this formal methods community is the view that one can start with a formal specification and show that a design/implementation satisfies that specification. It is obvious however that, if a specification does not actually reflect the real need, proving a program correct with respect to it is somewhat pointless. Am I arguing in favour of "XP" or fluid prototyping? Certainly not — at least not for most applications. But one might have to proceed in this way if we were to decide it's impossible to get the right specification.

I strongly believe that, for a crucial set of computer uses, one can –and must– start with a careful process of establishing a good specification. Mine is not a

B. Meyer and J. Woodcock (Eds.): Verified Software, LNCS 4171, pp. 64–69, 2008.

council of despair; I want to see how we can use technical ideas to improve the process of getting to a specification. In particular, some of the ideas below relate strongly to formal methods.

The point about where effort will have the greatest effect on dependability can be made by looking at accidents: Donald MacKenzie in [Mac94, Mac01] has traced the cause of just over 1100 deaths (up to 1994) where computer systems appear to be implicated. Only three percent of the lives lost appear to be attributed to program bugs! Far more common causes of accidents appear to be situations where humans misunderstand what is going on in a control system or the object being controlled. This is a much deeper issue than the details of HCI; in many cases it is a fundamental question of the allocation of tasks between person and machine. Key questions include the visibility of the "state" of the system being controlled and the extent to which operations which the user can perform are grouped together.

Although accidents are shocking and grab attention, there is also a significant penalty in the deployment of systems which make their users' lives more difficult than they need be. The enormous cost (often to the taxpayer) of systems which are so unusable that they are not even deployed is reported all too often in newspapers.

Of course, we should use formal specification and design techniques for fault avoidance and we still need research to make them more widely usable. (I have contributed to several sets of tools in this area including [JJLM91].) But it would also appear to be worthwhile to see whether there is a *technical* response to the question of how one arrives at a specification which does reflect the needs of the environment in which a system will be embedded. Does the formal methods community have a contribution to make here? I believe so.

This paper sets out some research challenges to which we might be able to offer useful responses. The suggestions have arisen from the six year "Interdisciplinary Research Collaboration on Dependability" (DIRC) — see the WWW pages at [WWW06] for further details. DIRC is focusing its research on how to design *Dependable* computer-based systems. The phrase "computer-based systems" is intended to emphasise that most computer systems today are deeply embedded into an environment which also involves people. For example, the requirement in a hospital is for dependability of the overall system. In such domains, humans will use a computer system to achieve objectives even where they know that it delivers less than perfect information; on other occasions, computers can be programmed to warn when errors appear to be made by humans. People are less good than computers at narrowly specified repetitive tasks but are much better at recognising and reacting to exceptional situations. To achieve overall system dependability, both humans and programs must be properly deployed.

Some of the insights from the DIRC project include:

Determining specifications. An approach being worked on with Ian Hayes and Michael Jackson [HJJ03, JHJ06] looks at determining the specification of, say, a control system by first specifying a wider system including the phenomena of the physical world which are to be influenced. To avoid having to build a model of the behaviour of all physical components, assumptions about their behaviour are recorded using *rely conditions*. This leaves a clear record of assumptions which need to be considered before the control system is deployed. Development from the derived specification of the control system is conducted in the standard (formal) way. (Dines Bjørner's books [Bjø05] tackle "domain modelling".)

Limiting failure propagation. The design of boundaries that limit the *propagation of failures* is better articulated for technical systems than for the human part of computer-based systems. This is odd because the intuition about limiting, say, accounting errors by auditors is long established. Many examples can be cited to suggest that most human systems are "debugged" rather than designed. The motivation for where to place containment boundaries ought to come from an analysis of the frequency of minor faults and the danger of their affecting a wider system. This analysis ought to precede the allocation of tasks to computers which, in turn of course, must be done prior to their specifications being "signed off".

Cognitive mismatch. A major cause of near or actual accidents is a "cognitive mismatch"[1] between an operator's view of what is going on and the actual state of affairs in the system the operator is trying to control. This was a significant factor in the Three Mile Island reactor incident. John Rushby [Rus99] has looked at pilot errors on the MD-88: in simulators, they frequently breach the required altitude ceiling. Rushby's careful formal analysis builds a state model of the pilot's understanding of the system and explores its interaction with a model of the aircraft systems. (It would be informative to compare this approach with rely conditions.)

The role of procedures. The general way in which *processes* (or procedures) are used in the human parts of computer-based systems is interesting. If one contrasts a traditional car production line with the depiction in the film *Apollo 13* of the search for a solution to the need to improvise CO_2 scrubbers in the damaged capsule, one sees that processes both limit action and reduce the need for information. Designing processes which cope with all exceptions is in many cases impossible and one argument for relying on humans in computer-based systems is precisely that they notice when it is safer to violate a procedure than slavishly to follow one that does not cover an exceptional case. Clearly, either following an inappropriate process or deviating from a correct process can lead to system failure. But it is absolutely mandatory that thought is given to processes in the design of a computer-based system. Interestingly, one can spot errors in legislation where an algorithmic rule is frozen into law: there have been several cases in financial legislation where a well-intentioned trigger has had (or nearly had) counter-productive effects. A recent DIRC book [Mac06] addresses financial markets from this perspective.

---

[1] Both of James Reason's books [Rea90, Rea97] look at relevant issues: the earlier reference looks at a division of the sort of errors that humans make; the second has insightful analyses of many system failures. Perrow in [Per99] talks of "Normal accidents".

Advisory systems. Within DIRC, the role of *advisory systems* has received particular attention: [SPA03] studies a prompter used in the analysis of mammogram images. Surprising conclusions include statistically significant evidence that, under the tested conditions, the most accurate operators offered *less accurate* conclusions with the help of the advisory system than without its use. It is clear that the role of such advisory systems has to be considered far more widely than just by looking at their technical specifications. In fact, even pure safety limiters (where one would believe they can only increase safety) have been used by operators in a way which supplants their normal judgement.

Creating dependable systems. Systems can create other things whose dependability is the goal. In the simplest case, a production line might manufacture silicon chips and faults in the manufacturing process might result in faulty components for computers. A software example is a compiler that, if faulty, could translate a perfect program into machine code which does not respect the formal semantics of the source language. In many cases, the creation process is human and, for example, a designer of a bridge which fails to withstand expected forces is at fault. The creation of computer software is just such a process and is not always fault free. DIRC has provided an opportunity to look at Gerry Weinberg's conjectures in [Wei71] that different psychological types might be more or less adept at different sub-tasks within the broad area known as programming [DG06]. The implications of this research for building dependable systems might include steering people toward the tasks at which they are likely to perform best (and probably be most content).

Evolution. If the above list were not daunting enough (and it is far from complete even with respect to DIRC's findings) there is another overriding concern. The sort of computer-based system we have been studying will always *evolve*. Designing a system which can be modified in reaction to a reasonable class of evolutions in the environment is extremely challenging. One class of system which has been studied within the DIRC project is *generic systems*. The justification of this sort of system is that it can be instantiated for a range of applications: characterising this range is itself a technical problem (and a further challenges is trying to maximise the range). It is clear that issues around evolution will have a long-term impact on dependability. There are related questions about how data survives such evolution which are equally challenging.

DIRC has identified far more than the above set of issues; the selection here has been based on the ease with which this one member of a project (involving more than fifty researchers) could pull together the information.

One key experience from the project is the invaluable role of interdisciplinarity. Looking at experiments on psychological type and debugging performance required wholehearted collaboration of psychologists and computer scientists; tackling the mammography advisory system involved interaction between statisticians, sociologists and psychologists. DIRC researchers could list many more examples of how our combination of psychologists, statisticians, sociologists and computer scientists has made real progress that no one of these disciplines could have accomplished.

My own inclination is to seek technical approaches to problems and I hope that the list above indicates that this is a viable challenge. But the DIRC project has been a superb example of collaboration and if faced with a complex application area, I would now know how to call on the expertise of other disciplines. In particular, the painstaking gathering of observational data needs sociologists.

One key message from our experience is to tackle application problems together as a team. With an "Operations Research" (OR) like team representing several disciplines terminology problems disappear, contributions become understood and something is achieved which no single discipline could have envisaged.

Acknowledgements

My research acknowledgement is to the many colleagues involved in DIRC; it is a privilege to lead such an exciting project.

We are all grateful to EPSRC for the six year funding window which we feel was essential to foster such a wide interdisciplinary span.

References

[Bjø05]   Bjørner, D.: Software Engineering (3 vols.). Springer, Heidelberg (2005)

[DG06]   Da Cunha, A.D., Greathead, D.: Does personality matter? an analysis of code-review ability. In: Communications of the ACM (in press, 2006)

[HJJ03]   Hayes, I., Jackson, M., Jones, C.: Determining the specification of a control system from that of its environment. In: Araki, K., Gnesi, S., Mandrioli, D. (eds.) FME 2003. LNCS, vol. 2805, pp. 154–169. Springer, Heidelberg (2003)

[JHJ06]   Jones, C., Hayes, I., Jackson, M.: Specifying systems that connect to the physical world. Acta Informatica (submitted, 2006)

[JJLM91]   Jones, C.B., Jones, K.D., Lindsay, P.A., Moore, R.: mural: A Formal Development Support System. Springer, Heidelberg (1965)

[Jon96]   Jones, C.B.: A rigorous approach to formal methods. IEEE, Computer 29(4), 20–21 (1996)

[Jon05]   Jones, C.B.: Reasoning about the design of programs. Royal Soc. Phil. Trans. R Soc. A 363(1835), 2395–2396 (2005)

[Mac94]   MacKenzie, D.: Computer-related accidental death: an empirical exploration. Science and Public Policy 21, 233–248 (1994)

[Mac01]   MacKenzie, D.: Mechanizing Proof: Computing, Risk, and Trust. MIT Press, Cambridge (2001)

[Mac06]   MacKenzie, D.: An Engine, Not a Camera: How Financial Models Shape Markets. MIT Press, Cambridge, Mass (2006)

[Per99]   Perrow, C.: Normal Accidents. Princeton University Press, Princeton (1999)

[Rea90]   Reason, J.: Human Error. Cambridge University Press, Cambridge (1990)

[Rea97]   Reason, J.: Managing the Risks of Organisational Accidents. Ashgate Publishing Limited (1997)

[Rus99]   Rushby, J.: Using model checking to help discover mode confusions and other automation surprises. In: Proceedings of 3rd Workshop on Human Error. HESSD 1999, pp. 1–18 (1999)

[SPA03]   Strigini, L., Povyakalo, A., Alberdi, E.: Human machine diversity in the use of computerised advisory systems: A case study. In: DSN 2003-IEEE International Conference on Dependable Systems and Networks, San Francisco, USA, pp. 249–258 (2003)

[Wei71]   Weinberg, G.M.: The Psychology of Computer Programming. Van Norstrand (1971)

[WWW06]   WWW (2006), www.dirc.org.uk

Software Verification and Software Engineering
a Practitioner's Perspective

Anthony Hall

anthony@anthonyhall.org

Extended Abstract

The web page for this conference announces

> a "Grand Challenge" of crucial relevance to society: ensuring that the software of the future will be error-free.

According to the Scope and Objectives

> In the end, the conference should work towards the achievement of the long-standing challenge of the Verifying Compiler.

I want to question whether this long-standing challenge is really relevant to the greater goal of achieving trustworthy software. Instead, I suggest that research in verification needs to support a larger effort to improve the software engineering process.

I am a strong advocate – and a practitioner – of formal methods as part of a rigorous software engineering process. But formal methods are very much more than program verification. The goal of verification is to take a given program and to prove that it is correct. The goal of software engineering is quite different: it is to create a program that is verifiably correct. Program verification is neither necessary nor sufficient for software engineering. Its pursuit may even have harmful consequences.

To illustrate, let me take two examples from the field of security.

First, consider the appalling fact that most security flaws are caused by buffer overflow. Why is this appalling? Because there is absolutely no need for anyone, ever, to write a program that contains buffer overflows. That we continue to do so is a reflection our addiction to atrocious languages like C++. There are perfectly good languages around that make it simply impossible to write code that can cause buffer overflows. We should use them. No research is necessary. No proofs are necessary. It's a decidable – indeed solved – problem.

Now let me take a more sophisticated example: cryptography on smart cards. This is a field that seems to be natural for verification. Indeed we could hope to prove, for example, that a cryptographic algorithm needed exponential time to break by brute force and that it was correctly implemented on a smart card. So the smart card would be secure, right? Wrong. Along comes Paul Kocher with a watt meter and breaks the key that you have proved is secure. How did he do that? He did it by bypassing the assumptions you made in your proof. But you never even stated those assumptions: how many proofs contain the following assumption?

Ass1: No-one will measure the power used by the processor

The harmful consequence here is obvious: by doing a proof we have given ourselves a false sense of security. But I think there are more insidious dangers, exemplified even by excellent work in the field. Program verification can all too easily seem to support

B. Meyer and J. Woodcock (Eds.): Verified Software, LNCS 4171, pp. 70–73, 2008.

a process of "Ready – Fire – Aim". For example, one – rightly acclaimed – application of verification is Microsoft's Static Driver Verifier. The web page for SDV says:

> SDV ... is designed to be run near the end of the development cycle
> on drivers that build successfully and are ready for testing.

This is encouraging a wasteful process of guess and debug: one that is almost guaranteed to fail for large and complex software. We have direct experience of this with another static analysis tool, the SPARK Examiner. In principle, the Examiner can be run retrospectively over any SPARK code. In practice, we find that all this proves is that the code has lots of information flow errors.

A far more powerful approach is to design the code with correct information flow in mind, and run the analyser on your design – before you have even created all the package bodies – to eliminate design errors. This is an example of Correctness by Construction: a step-by step process starting from early requirements and progressing through formalisation of the specification, rigorous design, coding in a sound language, static analysis and specification-based testing. Every step of this process is subject to rigorous analysis and of course once one is in the formal domain that analysis can be supported by verification tools.

I suggest that the real opportunity for the verification community is to provide better support for Correctness by Construction. The real Grand Challenge for formal methods is to make Correctness by Construction the mainstream approach to software development. Proponents of this specification-oriented style of formal methods have sometimes underplayed the importance of tools, including verification tools. There is a real opportunity is to bring the specification and verification communities together and to apply the extremely sophisticated tools coming from the verification community to the systematic construction of software. Here are some of the big issues that need to be addressed.

1. Early requirements. How can we add rigour to scenarios, use cases and other techniques that are essential for communicating with stakeholders? How can we formalise domain knowledge? What about the problem of "unbounded relevance" – how do we know what assumptions to make?
2. Specification languages. How can we have rich and expressive specification languages and at the same time have tractable proofs? How can we make specification languages and reasoning about them more accessible?
3. Design notations. How can we express the multiple dimensions of design? What are the refinement rules when we are using a distributed design, working with COTS, building on a database...?
4. Concurrency. How can we express concurrency properties in a compositional way? How can we turn a black-box sequential specification into a concurrent implementation?
5. Testing. How can we develop efficient test cases from our requirements? How can we relate test effectiveness and proof coverage?
6. Proof. How can we choose what to prove? How can we make proof accessible? How can we use proof for finding errors?

This challenge is both easier and harder than pure verification. It's easier, because a step by step process reduces the semantic gap to be bridged and makes verification feasible. It's harder, because we have to face up to the difficulties of the real world, the problem of imperfect knowledge and the difficulty of reconciling rigour and creativity. The reward is that we really could turn software into engineering.

A Discussion on Anthony Hall's Presentation

Bertrand Meyer

I want to take issue with one of your slides, which, I think, detracts from the rest of your presentation. This is the one where you cited parts of the Standish report. Actually the first comment is that there have been new versions of the Standish report which give a quite different picture from the original 1994 report that everyone quotes. But more specifically the overall view that technology does not matter seems a bit weak. I think that if the time were 1820, you could make a very serious case about sailing boats not being fast and reliable enough, that it is all a managerial problem and it does not matter whether to improve the sailing technology or not. This ignores the possibility of a technology breakthrough, which redefines the problem.

Anthony Hall

I do not remember saying anything about technology not mattering, quite the contrary. What I have said was that if we wanted to attack these problems, we had better attack the problems where they are, not where we would like them to be. What I said is, technology as here is probably the one bit, by lurking in there (*pointing at a slide*), perhaps 10% of that slide is maybe errors that can be covered by proofs of correctness. This covers use of tools or people learning new methods and so on. I certainly did not mean to say technology is not important. What I mean is, technology better be applied to the 49% that matters rather than the 10% or 15% that occasionally cause failures.

Richard Bornat

I have lots of objections to what you said. I shall not object to every slide. I would just like to say that you could have given that talk 40 years ago, and indeed, talks like that were given 40 years ago, simply by replacing the words "program verification" by the word "compiling". The fact is, new program verification is but old compiling writ large. And in the old days, you would have to say: the problem is not what language you write it in, the problem is the design. And they were right, and they were wrong. The fact is, compiling has had a massive effect on all of the problems you dealt with. And compiling has meant that the problem of software evolution—although not overcome, and the proportions are still the same—is yet dented. We can more rapidly recompile our design than we could. And new program verification is just another step down the same road. Yes, it does not solve the problem, but it does help.

Now, I want to argue with you about your Lakatos thing, but I shall not do that now. I just want to point out to you that please be careful when you quote Hardy!

Hardy, you remember, was the author of your quote that "proof is just gas". Now, Hardy was a sucker for a well-turned phrase, as I am. But his other most famous quote was that "I am absolutely sure that everything I have done in my life has been completely useless." Hardy was absolutely wrong, because his work is the foundation of RSA. And he was absolutely wrong about that, and he is absolutely wrong about the gas, too. And I think, you would be very, very careful about building an argument onto Hardy, Sir, it will swallow you up!

Anthony Hall

Well, I have to say, I had some doubts about quoting Hardy. However, both of those statements, of course, are propaganda statements. His statement about that he is absolutely certain that everything is useless, was a statement of propaganda. It appears in *A Mathematician's Apology*.

It was a statement which he would *like* to be true. He would like to be pure and isolated from the real world.

Willem-Paul de Roever (*laughing*)

I would like to support the speaker after these attacks, because it is laughable. Well, the point is, we all know mathematical proofs, and I have given extremely many methodical proofs in my lifetime. But if I go to John Rushby and Shankar here, we all know that when you try to formalize any mathematical proof it is full of holes, there are all sorts of mistakes, but it is very seldom the case that the theorem is completely incorrect. So the point is that it is a sketch for communication, and the poor sucker who has to formalize it in PVS or Isabelle is very proud that he found so many errors. But at the end, he did not find an error in the theorem. So, I would like to have Rushby and Shankar cooperate on this, because I think that is relevant.

What I myself thought is, logically speaking, you do not give place to bottom-up development, and you are so much experienced in developing software, so you certainly know where to put bottom-up in this picture. That is, what I wanted to say.

Decomposing Verification Around End-User Features[*]

Kathi Fisler[1] and Shriram Krishnamurthi[2]

[1] Department of Computer Science, WPI, Worcester, MA, USA
kfisler@cs.wpi.edu
[2] Computer Science Department, Brown University, Providence, RI, USA
sk@cs.brown.edu

Abstract. Practical program verification techniques must align with the software development methodologies that produce the programs. Numerous researchers have independently proposed models of program development in which modules encapsulate units of end-user functionality known as *features*. Such encapsulation reflects user concerns into a program's modular structure, which in turn promises to simplify program maintenance in the face of requirements evolution. The interplay between feature-oriented modules and verification raises some interesting challenges and opportunities. Such modules ameliorate some difficulties with conventional modular verification, such as property decomposition, while creating others, by contradicting assumptions that underlie most modular program verification techniques. This paper motivates the decomposition of systems by features and provides an overview of the promises and challenges it poses to verification.

1 A Notion of Software Development

For program verification to thrive, verification methodologies must align with software development methodologies. This goal imposes several requirements. First, verification tools should be able to handle program fragments of the style and granularity that programmers produce. Second, the effort to verify a program increment should bear some reasonable ratio to the effort to develop that increment. Third, the effort needed to reverify a program or fragment as it evolves should be proportional to the effort required to make the modification. Today's verification techniques fail to meet these goals, partly due to a misalignment between the models of software development and programming on which the techniques are built.

Our understanding of this problem is inspired by the picture in Figure 1 which Michael Jackson used in his presentation at ESEC/FSE 2001 (following his acceptance of the SIGSOFT Outstanding Research Award).[1] The box at

---

[*] This work is partially funded by NSF grants CCR-0305834, CCR-0132659, CCR-0447509 and CCR-0305950.
[1] We have transcribed this picture from our notes; a related version is in a paper [1].

B. Meyer and J. Woodcock (Eds.): Verified Software, LNCS 4171, pp. 74–81, 2008.
© IFIP International Federation for Information Processing 2008

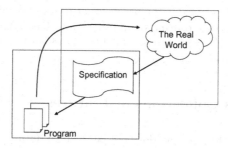

Fig. 1. The requirements-program feedback loop

the lower-left might be grossly characterized as the province of programming languages, proceeding from specifications to programs that, we hope, properly implement those specifications. Jackson calls this box the *solution space*. The box at the upper-right is the domain of requirements engineering: the collection of processes, many sociological (and imprecise!), that glean requirements for a system from its users and other stakeholders or, more broadly, from the fuzzy blob that is the "real world". In Jackson's terminology, the transactions in this world must remain in the *problem space*.

As soon as the program comes into existence, however, it itself becomes a part of the world. This invariably triggers a possibly new set of requirements. (As most requirements engineers and user interface designers will attest, a common user reaction is, "Oh, it does *that*?" followed by, "That is not what I meant at all. That is not it, at all" [2].) This cyclic dependency and directed flow of requirements is a source of many contemporary software development problems. This suggests that our techniques for software development should account for this by finding ways to be more pliable in the face of requirements and specification changes.

2   Program Development Styles and Verification

These ideas have significant implications for program verification. Research in property-based verification (which this paper considers distinct from correct-by-construction approaches) has often assumed a simplistic model of program development, in which the verifier has a complete program to analyze against established specifications. The body of work on modular verification relaxed that assumption to handle portions of programs that correspond to units of separate compilation [3]. This position paper argues that emerging forms of software development embody different assumptions from most current verification methodologies. It is therefore essential for verification to support these development techniques; better still would be if verification could *exploit* it.

Some researchers [4] believe verification should be organized around *software components*. Unfortunately, the term "component" seems to mean too many things (and often too little) in the literature. In particular, a component may or may not have a direct relationship to the specifications that inspired the program in the first place. (Sometimes it might; in other cases, it may be a generic unit of reuse, such as a sorting routine or database interface.) We therefore believe the emphasis must shift from using terms like "modules" and "components" to discussing *what the modules encapsulate*.

3   Programs as Collections of Features

An end-user of a system typically does not care which database interface or sorting routine is used in the implementation, or even whether they are used at all; rather, users describe how they would like to see the system behave (via methods such as use cases) as a collection of units of functionality that we call *features*. When requirements change, they often either add or remove features, or change a previously identified feature. Managing changes to features is therefore a key problem in software development. If each feature is implemented by a specific module, it becomes easier to identify where changes must be made. Furthermore, if these modules meet the criteria of components laid out by Szyperski [5], then creating the system is just a matter of component composition, while adding and removing features is simply a matter of writing a new composition. In other words, this style of program organization would respect the feedback loop in the Jackson figure, observing that if the program's shape mirrors the requirements and specifications, software evolution will become easier to manage.

Writing these identifiable increments in conventional programming languages is challenging because an increment may affect parts of a program across traditional module boundaries: such increments are said to be *cross-cutting*. This observation has led to a growing body of work on developing new forms of program modularity [6,7,8,9,10,11,12,13,14,15,16] that support modularization around features and composition to create a variety of individual systems (thus forming a software *product line* [17]). Some techniques are purely static, effectively manipulating the program's source, while others have dynamic elements, offering the ability to reflect on the state of the program's execution and then to modify it. There is now a growing awareness of this style of programming (especially as popularized by "aspect-oriented programming"), and several case-studies highlight its feasibility and observe its benefits.

4   Research Program on Verifying Feature Modules

This model of program organization offers a substantial benefit to verification as well. One of the main challenges in modular verification is the decomposition of properties to align with the program module's boundaries. In theory, feature-orientation should largely eliminate this hurdle. As the user's perspective frames both the features (modules) and the properties, the scope of each property largely matches the scope of some module (with the exception of global system properties). This correspondence should also make verification more scalable in the face of specification evolution, by localizing re-verification to the relevant parts of a program. In return for these benefits, feature-orientation demands new theories of modular reasoning to support feature-based decompositions.

We have been working on techniques for modular model checking of feature-based designs since 2001 [18,19,20]. At a high level, this work shares the goals of other modular verification research, namely, to verify code fragments independently and derive some properties of the composed program from the properties of the fragments. The nature of feature-based design, however, adds some nuances to this problem.

1. Since features are added to programs to provide some user-defined functionality, we may need to prove that adding a feature (a) preserves established properties of programs, or (b) establishes a *new* property of the composed program. In some models, a feature might (c) establish a property that the original program should have satisfied, but did not.

   Performing these analyses modularly is important because we could potentially add many features to an existing program, at which point the cost of analyzing each possible product (a subset of features) becomes prohibitive. Feature-based design shifts the motivation for modular reasoning from making verification tractable in terms of computational resources to making it practical across the combinatorial number of products that can be built from designer-specified program modules.

2. Features can interact, causing properties of individual components to be violated in the composed program. In a telecommunications system, for example, a voice mail feature might be required to pick up an unanswered call after 4 rings and a call forwarding feature might be required to pass an unanswered call along after 4 rings. A system with both voice mail and call forwarding will respect only one of these requirements. Other examples are far more subtle. This *feature-interaction* problem is pervasive and not always amenable to formal analysis [21]. As model checking each combination of features for interactions is infeasible, modular analysis must support detecting those interactions that can be captured formally.

To date, our work has focused on property preservation (nuance 1a) with preliminary attention to feature interaction (nuance 2). We are able to model check CTL properties against individual features and perform lighter-weight checks to confirm that a feature's properties will be preserved when composed into an existing program. We are also able to modularly detect feature interactions that manifest as violations of properties expressed in CTL. Our work has identified several ways in which feature-based designs challenge the conventional assumptions of modular model checking:

1. Most modular verification work assumes parallel composition, while feature composition is largely (though not entirely) sequential. This in turn has interesting consequences. For example, module composition can create new paths through programs (parallel composition deletes but does not add paths). Although parallel composition can simulate sequential composition, it is not clear that doing so best exploits the advantages of sequential composition.

2. Modules are not closed because data from one module may persist into another. For instance, in an email system, one feature may encrypt a message and that attribute should persist into subsequent features, even though the models of those features do not mention encryption.
3. One module may refine the interpretations of propositions in another. E.g.: An email system may classify a message as anonymous if it has passed through an anonymous remailer, but adding a digital signing feature forces the interpretation of anonymity to also require the message to be unsigned. Reinterpreted or persistent propositions often preclude lifting properties proven of an individual module to the composed program.

Even more fundamental, however, is our growing understanding that *verification may be the wrong problem to solve*. Traditional verification methods (especially model checking) are primarily designed to authoritatively determine the truth or falsity of properties over models. However, most of the property violations we observe arise only upon composition, because some compositions satisfy the properties while others fail them. Most verification runs over individual features are invariably inconclusive because there isn't enough information in the module to entirely satisfy or fail the property. This pushes the verification decision onto the composition step, which needs appropriate information that it can then use to perform a lightweight check that (a) is not too expensive, and (b) does not involve re-examining the innards of the individual modules. The appropriate analysis on individual modules is therefore some form of constraint generation, rather than outright verification. In our work on this approach [18] the constraints have been propositional and temporal, reflecting their foundation in model checking.

The need for constraint generation in practice does not contradict our earlier claim that properties align naturally with features. The truth of a property in a feature often depends on two specific pieces of information from the feature's environment: (1) whether control paths exiting the feature reach particular states in the original program, and (2) the values of persistent and reinterpreted data propositions determined in earlier features. Our proposed constraint generation is akin to generating environmental constraints; this step is feasible in our work because we generate environments specific to the program properties that a feature must preserve. The checks required to discharge these constraints at feature-composition time tend to be lightweight (simple propositional or reachability checks) because the feature that aligns with a property discharges the bulk of that property's obligations.

5   Some Challenges

Our observations leave open a large collection of interesting research problems. Some questions that need to be addressed include:

– Theoretical foundations for richer notions of composition. Most verification research is built on purely sequential composition or variations (synchronous, interleaved, etc) on parallel composition. The composition models in many feature-oriented programs lie between these extremes. We have studied programs that employ what we call *quasi-sequential composition* [19]: at the highest level, modules compose sequentially, but each module is formed of components that compose in parallel. This form of composition is interesting because it leads to states in the global state space that span different modules, but in controlled and predictable ways. Quasi-sequentiality is reminiscent of the pattern of execution in Valiant's Bulk Synchronous Parallel model [22], but that model has no notion of program modularity and does not consider verification.

– Techniques for generating temporal constraints rich enough to support modular feature verification.
– Techniques for determining whether a code fragment introduces a desirable though previously untrue property over a program.
– Theories of compositional reasoning that are tuned for predicting feature interaction errors, instead of checking success or failure of known properties.

6   Perspective

We find it telling that several researchers, working independently and in entirely distinct areas (often without any knowledge of each other), have within a few years proposed extremely similar models of software development centered around features. We believe that Jackson's picture explains why this model is not accidental, but rather fundamental to the way programs originate and evolve. Without lapsing into thoughts of silver bullets, we should take this model seriously, especially as formal programming language research is beginning to catch up with these less formal approaches (several papers [23,24,25,26] offer a representative sampling). Any attempt to lay the foundations for a practical program verifier must look ahead to how programs will be developed in the future, not only at programs written using antediluvian methods in legacy languages.

Acknowledgements. Many colleagues and students have shaped our thoughts on this problem. Matthew Flatt, Matthias Felleisen, and Robby Findler helped us understand program modularity. Don Batory taught us about scaling modularity and gave us invaluable help with examples. A series of Brown undergraduates—Harry Li, Colin Blundell, and Michael Greenberg—collaborated with us on much of the verification work, greatly enhancing both our knowledge and enjoyment.

References

1. Jackson, M.: Why software writing is difficult and will remain so. Information Processing Letters 88, 13–25 (2003)
2. Eliot, T.S.: The love song of J. Alfred Prufrock. In: Prufrock and Other Observations, The Egoist, Ltd. London (1917)
3. Abadi, M., Lamport, L.: Conjoining specifications. ACM Transactions on Programming Languages and Systems 17, 507–534 (1995)

 4. Xie, F., Browne, J.C.: Verified systems by composition from verified components. In: Joint European Software Engineering Conference and Symposium on the Foundations of Software Engineering, New York, NY, USA, pp. 277–286. ACM Press, New York (2003)
 5. Szyperski, C.: Component Software: Beyond Object-Oriented Programming. Addison-Wesley, Reading (1998)
 6. Aßmann, U.: Invasive Software Composition. Springer, Heidelberg (2003)
 7. Batory, D.: Feature-oriented programming and the AHEAD tool suite. In: International Conference on Software Engineering (2004)
 8. Batory, D., O'Malley, S.: The design and implementation of hierarchical software systems with reusable components. ACM Transactions on Software Engineering and Methodology 1, 355–398 (1992)
 9. Findler, R.B., Flatt, M.: Modular object-oriented programming with units and mixins. In: ACM SIGPLAN International Conference on Functional Programming, pp. 94–104 (1998)
10. Harrison, W., Ossher, H.: Subject-oriented programming: a critique of pure objects. In: ACM SIGPLAN Conference on Object-Oriented Programming Systems, Languages & Applications, pp. 411–428 (1993)
11. Jackson, M., Zave, P.: Distributed feature composition: A virtual architecture for telecommunications services. IEEE Transactions on Software Engineering 24, 831–847 (1998)
12. Kiczales, G., Lamping, J., Mendhekar, A., Maeda, C., Lopes, C.V., Loingtier, J.M., Irwin, J.: Aspect-oriented programming. In: European Conference on Object-Oriented Programming (1997)
13. Lieberherr, K.J.: Adaptive Object-Oriented Programming. PWS Publishing, Boston (1996)
14. Mezini, M., Lieberherr, K.: Adaptive plug-and-play components for evolutionary software development. In: ACM SIGPLAN Conference on Object-Oriented Programming Systems, Languages & Applications, pp. 97–116 (1998)
15. Smaragdakis, Y., Batory, D.: Implementing layered designs and mixin layers. In: European Conference on Object-Oriented Programming, pp. 550–570 (1998)
16. van Ommering, R.: Building Product Populations with Software Components. PhD thesis, Rijksuniversitat Groningen (2004)
17. Clements, P., Northrop, L.: Software Product Lines: Practices and Patterns. Addison-Wesley, Reading (2002)
18. Blundell, C., Fisler, K., Krishnamurthi, S., Hentenryck, P.V.: Parameterized interfaces for open system verification of product lines. In: IEEE International Conference on Automated Software Engineering (2004)
19. Fisler, K., Krishnamurthi, S.: Modular verification of collaboration-based software designs. In: Symposium on the Foundations of Software Engineering, pp. 152–163. ACM Press, New York (2001)
20. Li, H.C., Krishnamurthi, S., Fisler, K.: Modular verification of open features through three-valued model checking. Automated Software Engineering 12, 349–382 (2005)
21. Keck, D.O., Kuehn, P.J.: The feature and service interaction problem in telecommunications systems: A survey. IEEE Transactions on Software Engineering 24, 779–796 (1998)
22. Valiant, L.G.: A bridging model for parallel computation. Communications of the ACM 33, 103–111 (1990)
23. Ancona, D., Lagorio, G., Zucca, E.: Jam—designing a Java extension with mixins. ACM Transactions on Programming Languages and Systems 25, 641–712 (2003)

24. Flatt, M., Krishnamurthi, S., Felleisen, M.: Classes and mixins. In: ACM SIGPLAN-SIGACT Symposium on Principles of Programming Languages, pp. 171–183 (1998)
25. Odersky, M., Altherr, P., Cremet, V., Emir, B., Maneth, S., Micheloud, S., Mihaylov, N., Schinz, M., Stenman, E., Zenger, M.: An overview of the Scala programming language. Technical Report IC/2004/64, EPFL Lausanne, Switzerland (2004)
26. Schärli, N., Ducasse, S., Nierstrasz, O., Black, A.: Traits: Composable units of behavior. In: European Conference on Object-Oriented Programming, pp. 248–274 (2003)

A   Discussion on Kathi Fisler's Presentation

Greg Nelson

Kathi, I have a question about your "New challenges" slide. It sounds at first very daunting. But I wonder if you would agree that the fundamental problem with that multilingual issue is... (sentence left incomplete). I mean, a simple answer would be that for each language in which you program, you develop a verifier, and the problem with that simple answer is, that the interfaces between two components may not be in the language of either component. But I only see a small, bounded number of possible interfaces: There is the procedure call interface as when a Modula program calls a C program, there is the byte stream interface as when you pipe the output of grep into sort or when you open a TCP-connection to a file server, and there are the remote procedure call kinds of interfaces as in an HTTP call or a Java RMI call, where it is like a procedure call interface, but it crosses machine boundaries. And if you can handle those kinds of interfaces, then it should not matter that the components are in different languages, I hope.

Kathi Fisler

Well, it is not that you have a large number of interfaces. The problem is, you have an awful lot of interaction between the components at those interfaces, okay? So, it is fairly small to say: "I make a call to my access control policy and say: 'Is this action permitted?'" But these kinds of interactions between language do not happen in a small number of places. So that is really where this problem is that is going to be fairly challenging. I hope, this answers the question.

Automatic Verification of
Strongly Dynamic Software Systems

N. Dor[1,*], J. Field[2], D. Gopan[3], T. Lev-Ami[4], A. Loginov[2,**], R. Manevich[4],
G. Ramalingam[5,***], T. Reps[3], N. Rinetzky[4], M. Sagiv[4], R. Wilhelm[6],
E. Yahav[2], and G. Yorsh[4]

[1] Panaya Ltd.
nurit@panayainc.com
[2] IBM Research
{jfield,alexey,eyahav}@us.ibm.com
[3] University of Wisconsin
{alexey,gopan,reps}@cs.wisc.edu
[4] Tel Aviv University
{tla,rumster,maon,msagiv,gretay}@tau.ac.il
[5] Microsoft Research
grama@microsoft.com
[6] Universität des Saarlandes
wilhelm@cs.uni-sb.de

Abstract. Strongly dynamic software systems are difficult to verify. By
strongly dynamic, we mean that the actors in such systems change dynamically, that the resources used by such systems are dynamically allocated and deallocated, and that for both sets, no bounds are statically
known. In this position paper, we describe the progress we have made
in automated verification of strongly dynamic systems using abstract interpretation with three-valued logical structures. We then enumerate a
number of challenges that must be tackled in order for such techniques
to be widely adopted.

1 The Problem

We will use the term *strongly dynamic* system to refer to software in which the set
of actors in the system changes dynamically, where resources are dynamically
allocated and deallocated, and where for both sets no bounds are statically
known.

Heap allocation of data structures, which is the principal mechanism for creating structured data in modern languages, is the classical manifestation of a
strongly dynamic system. It is well known that manipulating heap-allocated
data is error-prone, due primarily to the complexity of potential aliasing relationships among pointer-valued data. However, dynamic resource manipulation

---

* Work done while the author was at Tel Aviv University.
** Work done while the author was at the University of Wisconsin.
*** Work done while the author was at IBM Research.

B. Meyer and J. Woodcock (Eds.): Verified Software, LNCS 4171, pp. 82–92, 2008.

occurs at many levels in modern software; such dynamic resources may include, e.g., persistent data in databases, language-level threads, operating system resources such as files and sockets, and web sessions.

Formally, the state of strongly dynamic systems may be viewed as a evolving universe of entities over which the program operates. Due to its evolving character, such universes are difficult to reason about, both for programmers and for automated reasoning tools. This in turn makes automated verification for such programs both important and challenging.

While automatic memory allocation and garbage collection in modern programming languages has eased the burden of correctly managing the lifetime of heap-allocated memory, reasoning about the *states* of an unbounded number of heap-allocated objects and their interrelationships remains a difficult challenge.

Frequently, strongly dynamic systems are encapsulated in abstract data types that restrict direct access to the underlying evolving universe, and hence allow the programmer to reason only about the data type's interface. In such cases, the principal verification challenge is to ensure that the implementation of the data type correctly realizes the desired abstract properties.

However, in the case of scarce high-level system resources, such as processes, sessions, and buffers, programmers do not have the luxury of automatic resource management or abstract data type encapsulation; instead, they must reason directly about resource state *and* resource lifetime. Verifying the correct usage of such resources is therefore particularly challenging.

Finally, concurrency and distribution drastically complicates the problem of program verification, since both the data *and* control structures of the program operate over unbounded universes.

This position paper sketches the state of art in automatic verification of properties of strongly dynamic systems using abstract interpretation [6] with *three-valued logical structures*.

1.1 Program Properties

Our focus is on verifying that programs satisfy certain specific (but not fixed) safety and liveness properties, such as those illustrated below, as opposed to establishing complete correctness of a program (with respect to its complete specification). The progress made in selective "property verification" in recent years makes us cautiously optimistic about its long-term prospects. It poses several challenging research problems, but promises to play an important and relevant role in industrial software-development practice within a reasonable time frame. We are in general interested in the following safety properties:

Memory Cleanness. In this case, we wish to prove that a program does not perform pointer manipulations that have unpredictable effects. We call these *cleanness* properties, since they are generic to a given programming model, rather than application-specific (although frequently, in order to show cleanness, it is necessary to prove stronger properties as well). For sequential C-like programs, such properties include: (i) absence of null dereferences, (ii) absence of memory leaks, and (iii) absence of double deallocations. The failure of these properties is frequently exploited by hackers, see, e.g., [26].

The use of garbage collection in modern languages eliminates some of the problems that occur when programmers manage memory allocation and deallocation manually. However, garbage collection does not eliminate the possibility of premature resource depletion due to delayed deallocation.

Similar resource-management problems are possible with other kinds of resources; e.g., database connections, buffers, files, and sockets. In our experience, many serious problems in large applications arise from resources that are freed too late.

Establishing Data-Structure Invariants. Data structures built using pointers can be characterized by invariants describing their "shape" at stable states, i.e., between operations defined by their external interfaces. These invariants are usually not preserved by the execution of individual program statements, and it is challenging to prove that data-structure invariants are reestablished after a sequence of statements executes [15].

Conformance of Library Specifications. In cases where a library's interface is accompanied by a formal specification of key assumptions and guarantees, it is useful to statically verify that a particular client satisfies, or *conforms* to the interface properties. One can then choose to verify that a library's implementation satisfies its interface specification (thus enabling modular reasoning and analysis of full systems), or simply treat the interface specification as presumptively correct (thus limiting the scope of verification to the client). While significant progress has been made in client-component conformance verification (e.g., see [5,8,12,11,2,25,10,7]), doing precise verification that can scale to large and complex programs is challenging.

Concurrency. Concurrent programs introduce a number of challenging verification issues, particularly when the number of concurrent threads may be unbounded. In this context, data and control are strongly related: thread-scheduling information may require an understanding of the structure of the heap (e.g., the structure of the scheduling queue). Also, heap analysis requires information about thread scheduling, because multiple threads may be manipulating the heap simultaneously. In addition to verifying the absence of "generic" concurrency anomalies, such as races and deadlocks, one often wishes to prove application-specific properties of concurrent protocols that are required to hold under arbitrary thread interleavings.

2   What Has Been Achieved So Far

This section summarizes the progress our group has made on property verification using abstract interpretation with three-valued logical structures [30] and the TVLA system [18], a general-purpose abstract-interpretation engine based on three-valued logic.

Abstract interpretation can be used for verification by generating an over-approximation to the set of states that can arise in any valid program execution; the property of interest is established if the over-approximation demonstrates that no undesirable state can be reached. Typically, problems are cast as a set of equations over a semi-lattice of program properties, and solved by means of successive approximation, possibly with extrapolation.

In [30], we showed that first-order logic can be viewed as a parametric framework for defining both the semantics of a program and for expressing a variety of properties to be verified. In this framework, concrete program states are represented by logical structures. Three-valued logic, which adds an "unknown" value to the Boolean values of ordinary two-valued logic, is a natural framework for defining sound, finitary *abstractions* of two-valued structures for the purpose of abstract interpretation.

Memory Cleanness. The first application of TVLA was to show memory cleanness of C programs [9]. The algorithm is rather precise in the sense that it yields very few false alarms but it was only applied to small programs.

Interprocedural Analysis. [27] handles procedures by explicitly representing stacks of activation records as linked lists, allowing rather precise analysis of recursive procedures. However, it does not scale very well. [17] handles procedures by summarizing their behavior. [28] presents a new concrete semantics for programs that manipulate heap-allocated storage which only passes "local" heaps to procedures. A simplified version of this semantics is used in [29] to perform more modular summarization by only representing reachable parts of the heap.

Concurrent Java Programs. [33] presents a general framework for proving safety properties of concurrent Java programs with an unbounded number of objects and threads. In [36] this approach is applied to verify partial correctness of concurrent-queue implementations.

Temporal Properties. [35] proposes a general framework for proving temporal properties of programs by representing program traces as logical structures. A more efficient technique for proving local temporal properties is presented in [31] and applied to compile-time garbage collection in JavaCard programs.

Correctness of Sorting Implementations. In [19], TVLA is applied to analyze programs that sort linked lists. It is shown that the analysis is precise enough to discover that (correct versions) of bubble-sort and insertion-sort procedures do, in fact, produce correctly sorted lists as outputs, and that the invariant "is-sorted" is maintained by list-manipulation operations such as merge. In addition, it is shown that when the analysis is applied to erroneous versions of bubble-sort and insertion-sort procedures, it is able to discover the error. In [20], abstraction refinement is used to *automatically* derive abstractions that are successfully used to prove partial correctness of several sorting algorithms. The derived abstractions are also used to prove that the algorithms possess additional properties, such as stability and anti-stability.

Conformance to API Specifications. [25] shows how to verify that client programs using a library conform to the library's API specifications. In particular, an analysis is provided for verifying the absence of concurrent-modification exceptions in Java programs that use Java collections and iterators. In [34], separation and heterogeneous abstraction are used to scale the verification algorithms and to allow verification of larger programs (several thousands lines of code) that use libraries such as JDBC.

Computing Intersections of Abstractions. [1] considers the problem of computing the intersection (meet) of heap abstractions, namely the greatest lower bound of two sets of 3-valued structures. This problem proves to have many applications in program analysis such as interpreting program conditions, refining abstract configurations, reasoning about procedures [17], and proving temporal properties of heap-manipulating programs, either via greatest-fixed-point approximation over trace semantics or in a staged manner over the collecting semantics. [1] describes a constructive formulation of meet that is based on finding certain relations between abstract heap objects. The enumeration of those relations is reduced to finding constrained matchings over bipartite graphs.

Efficient Heap Abstractions and Representations. [21] addresses the problem of space consumption in first-order state representations by describing and evaluating two new representation techniques for logical structures. One technique uses ordered binary decision diagrams (OBDDs); the other uses a variant of a functional map data structure. The results show that both the OBDD and functional implementations reduce space consumption in TVLA by a factor of 4 to 10 relative to the original TVLA state representation, without compromising analysis time.

[22] presents a new heap abstraction that works by merging shape descriptors according to a partial isomorphism similarity criterion, resulting in a partially disjunctive abstraction. This abstraction provides superior performance compared to the powerset heap abstraction, without any loss of precision, for a suite of TVLA benchmark verification problems.

[23] provides a family of simple abstractions for potentially cyclic linked lists. In particular, it provides a relatively efficient predicate abstraction that allows verification of programs that manipulate potentially cyclic linked lists.

Abstracting Numerical Values. [13] presents a generic solution for combining abstractions of numeric and heap-allocated storage. This solution has been integrated into a version of TVLA. In [14], a new abstraction of numeric values is presented, which like canonical abstraction tracks correlations between aggregates and not just indices. For example, it can identify loops that perform array-kills (i.e., assign values to a an entire array). This approach has been generalized to define a family of abstractions (for relations as well as numeric quantities) that is more precise than pure canonical abstraction and allows the basic idea from [13] to be applied more widely [16].

Assume-Guarantee Reasoning. One of the potential ways to scale up shape analysis is by applying it to smaller pieces of code using specifications. [37] presents a new algorithm that takes as input a shape descriptor (describing some set of concrete stores X) and a precondition p, and computes the most-precise shape descriptor for the stores in X that satisfy p. This combines abstract interpretation and theorem provers in a novel way. A prototype has been implemented in TVLA, using the SPASS theorem prover.

Safety Properties of Mobile Ambients. The mobile ambient calculus was introduced in [3]. In [24], TVLA was applied to prove safety properties programs in the ambient calculus. The main idea is to code the ambient calculus using two-valued logic, and then use TVLA to obtain a sound over-approximation by reinterpreting the logical formulas in Kleene's three-valued logic.

3 Some Remaining Challenges

We have found the framework of abstract interpretation based on three-valued logic to be remarkably powerful, both in its ability to provide a natural formal framework for reasoning about dynamic resource manipulation, and as a substrate for developing efficient data structures and algorithms for verification of such properties. We believe that the formal and practical strengths of this framework should provide a strong base for further research in verification of strongly dynamic systems in the future. In this section, we outline some of the remaining research challenges in this framework.

Scalability and Precision. For most of the properties discussed in prior sections, automatic verification of a software system of significant size (e.g., web servers, operating systems, or a *compiler*) remains infeasible. The main problem is the scalability of the existing techniques. We believe that we are likely to make steady advances in the scalability of our techniques by (1) exploiting locality in abstractions (e.g., for interprocedural analysis), (2) exploiting compositionality, i.e., exploiting proven properties of small components or ADTs in verification of large systems, (3) dealing with state explosion caused by interleaving of concurrent threads, and (4) developing improved algorithms for manipulating first-order structures.

Determining the properties that are relevant to the verification problem and identifying the objects that need to be reasoned about at any given program point is key to scalable verification using abstract interpretation. This fundamental problem of "choosing the right set of abstractions" appears to be shared by other verification techniques (including deductive approaches) as well. We believe that machine-learning techniques provide one promising *automated* approach to this problem [20]. We are also investigating the use of counterexample-guided abstraction refinement [4] to address this problem in an automated fashion.

Another approach to effective abstraction selection is to induce programmers to annotate programs with information about properties or abstractions relevant to the problem at hand. Currently, programmers have little incentive to add annotations defining properties or abstractions of interest, since the benefit of doing so using current verification technology is low. However, as the power of verification techniques to perform state-space exploration begins to scale to programs of realistic size, a cycle of positive reinforcement will arise: programmers will be encouraged to annotate their program with properties of utility to verifiers, because by doing so they will receive accurate and precise feedback on critical aspects of program correctness, which will in turn make them more productive programmers. Strong type systems provide a precedent: while programmers were initially skeptical of the benefits of strong typing, there is now little disagreement over its value.

Usability. Even in cases where automated verification is sufficiently scalable, there are a number of usability challenges: (1) For automatic verification to become an accepted part of everyday programming, it must provide useful feedback as quickly as current compilers generate type errors. (2) In cases where verification fails, counterexamples and error explanations must guide programmers quickly to potential sources of errors. (3) Particularly in safety-critical systems, the trusted code base used by a verifier must itself be verified.

Hybrid Verification Techniques. Theorem proving techniques, e.g., [11], have proved extremely useful for verifying properties of programs equipped with user-specified annotations (e.g., procedure pre- and post-conditions, and loop invariants). The power of such techniques derives from their ability to reason precisely about large collections of program states using symbolic techniques. However, such approaches are less successful in the absence of annotations, particularly when induction is required. Some initial steps have been taken at combining theorem proving and abstract interpretation (or model checking), e.g., [25]; further work aimed at exploiting the complementary strengths of these approaches seems desirable.

Combined Static and Dynamic Analysis. Although dynamic analysis (i.e., instrumentation of code execution to detect anomalies at runtime) cannot by itself prove a program correct, the results of dynamic analysis could be used to suggest certain properties, e.g., loop or class invariants, which would then be statically verified as a component of a larger verification problem.

Restricted Specification Formalisms. While it is tempting to allow program properties of interest to be specified using highly expressive formalisms such as first-order logic, by focusing on a more limited set of properties (e.g., *typestate* properties [32]), it is possible that more precise and scalable verification techniques could be developed for this class of properties than would be possible in the more general setting.

Other Issues. Some of the other challenges in making verification tools useful include: (1) The need to deal with missing source code (e.g., proprietary libraries) (2) Analyzing open programs and modeling the environment (3) Verifying distributed applications.

References

1. Arnold, G.: Combining heap analyses by intersecting abstractions. Master's thesis, Tel Aviv University (October 2004)
2. Ashcraft, K., Engler, D.: Using programmer-written compiler extensions to catch security holes. In: Proc. IEEE Symp. on Security and Privacy, Oakland, CA (May 2002)
3. Cardelli, L., Gordon, A.D.: Mobile ambients. In: Nivat, M. (ed.) ETAPS 1998 and FOSSACS 1998. LNCS, vol. 1378, pp. 140–155. Springer, Heidelberg (1998)
4. Clarke, E.M., Grumberg, O., Jha, S., Lu, Y., Veith, H.: Counterexample-guided abstraction refinement. In: Proc. Computer Aided Verification, pp. 154–169 (2000)
5. Corbett, J., Dwyer, M., Hatcliff, J., Pasareanu, C., R.,,, Laubach, S., Zheng, H.: Bandera: Extracting finite-state models from Java source code. In: Proc. Intl. Conf. on Software Eng, June 2000, pp. 439–448 (2000)
6. Cousot, P., Cousot, R.: Systematic design of program analysis frameworks. In: Proc. Symp. on Principles of Prog. Languages, pp. 269–282. ACM Press, New York (1979)
7. Das, M., Lerner, S., Seigle, M.: ESP: Path-sensitive program verification in polynomial time. In: Proc. Conf. on Prog. Lang. Design and Impl, pp. 57–68 (June 2002)
8. DeLine, R., Fähndrich, M.: Enforcing high-level protocols in low-level software. In: Proc. Conf. on Prog. Lang. Design and Impl. pp. 59–69 (June 2001)
9. Dor, N., Rodeh, M., Sagiv, M.: Checking cleanness in linked lists. In: Proc. Static Analysis Symp. Springer, Heidelberg (2000)
10. Field, J., Goyal, D., Ramalingam, G., Yahav, E.: Typestate verification: Abstraction techniques and complexity results. In: Cousot, R. (ed.) SAS 2003. LNCS, vol. 2694, pp. 439–462. Springer, Heidelberg (2003)
11. Flanagan, C., Leino, K.R.M., Lillibridge, M., Nelson, G., Saxe, J.B., Stata, R.: Extended static checking for java. In: Proc. Conf. on Prog. Lang. Design and Impl. Berlin, pp. 234–245 (June 2002)
12. Foster, J.S., Terauchi, T., Aiken, A.: Flow-sensitive type qualifiers. In: Proc. Conf. on Prog. Lang. Design and Impl. Berlin, pp. 1–12 (June 2002)
13. Gopan, D., DiMaio, F., Dor, N., Reps, T., Sagiv, M.: Numeric domains with summarized dimensions. In: Tools and Algs.for the Construct.and Anal.of Syst. pp. 512–529 (2004)
14. Gopan, D., Reps, T., Sagiv, M.: Numeric analysis of array operations. In: Proc. Symp. on Principles of Prog. Languages (2005)
15. Hoare, C.A.R.: Recursive data structures. Int. J. of Comp. and Inf. Sci. 4(2), 105–132 (1975)
16. Jeannet, B., Gopan, D., Reps, T.: A relational abstraction for functions. In: To appear in Proc. 12th Int. Static Analysis Symp. (September 2005) (to appear)
17. Jeannet, B., Loginov, A., Reps, T., Sagiv, M.: A relational approach to interprocedural shape analysis. In: Proc. Static Analysis Symp. Springer, Heidelberg (2004)
18. Lev-Ami, T., Sagiv, M.: TVLA: A system for implementing static analyses. In: Proc. Static Analysis Symp. pp. 280–301 (2000)
19. Lev-Ami, T., Reps, T., Sagiv, M., Wilhelm, R.: Putting static analysis to work for verification: A case study. In: Int.Symp.on Softw.Testing and Analysis, pp. 26–38 (2000)
20. Loginov, A., Reps, T., Sagiv, M.: Learning abstractions for verifying data-structure properties. In: Int.Conf.on Computer Aided Verif. (2005)

21. Manevich, R., Ramalingam, G., Field, J., Goyal, D., Sagiv, M.: Compactly representing first-order structures for static analysis. In: Proc. Static Analysis Symp. pp. 196–212 (2002)

22. Manevich, R., Sagiv, M., Ramalingam, G., Field, J.: Partially disjunctive heap abstraction. In: Giacobazzi, R. (ed.) SAS 2004. LNCS, vol. 3148, pp. 265–279. Springer, Heidelberg (2004)

23. Manevich, R., Yahav, E., Ramalingam, G., Sagiv, M.: Predicate abstraction and canonical abstraction for singly-linked lists. In: Cousot, R. (ed.) VMCAI 2005. LNCS, vol. 3385, Springer, Heidelberg (2005)

24. Nielson, F., Nielson, H.R., Sagiv, M.: A Kleene Analysis of Mobile Ambients. In: Smolka, G. (ed.) ESOP 2000 and ETAPS 2000. LNCS, vol. 1782, pp. 305–319. Springer, Heidelberg (2000)

25. Ramalingam, G., Warshavsky, A., Field, J., Goyal, D., Sagiv, M.: Deriving specialized program analyses for certifying component-client conformance. In: Proc. Conf. on Prog. Lang. Design and Impl. pp. 83–94 (2002)

26. Reig, F.: Detecting security vulnerabilities in C code with type checking (extended abstract) (2003), http://www.cs.nott.ac.uk/~fxr/

27. Rinetskey, N., Sagiv, M.: Interprocedural shape analysis for recursive programs. In: Wilhelm, R. (ed.) CC 2001 and ETAPS 2001. LNCS, vol. 2027, pp. 133–149. Springer, Heidelberg (2001)

28. Rinetzky, N., Bauer, J., Reps, T., Sagiv, M., Wilhelm, R.: A semantics for procedure local heaps and its abstractions. In: Proc. Symp. on Principles of Prog. Languages (2005)

29. Rinetzky, N., Sagiv, M., Yahav, E.: Interprocedural shape analysis for cutpoint-free programs. In: Hankin, C., Siveroni, I. (eds.) SAS 2005. LNCS, vol. 3672, Springer, Heidelberg (2005)

30. Sagiv, M., Reps, T., Wilhelm, R.: Parametric shape analysis via 3-valued logic. ACM Transactions on Programming Languages and Systems 24(3), 217–298 (2002)

31. Shaham, R., Yahav, E., Kolodner, E.K., Sagiv, M.: Establishing local temporal heap safety properties with applications to compile-time memory management. In: Cousot, R. (ed.) SAS 2003. LNCS, vol. 2694, pp. 483–503. Springer, Heidelberg (2003)

32. Strom, R.E., Yemini, S.: Typestate: A programming language concept for enhancing software reliability. IEEE Trans. Software Eng. 12(1), 157–171 (1986)

33. Yahav, E.: Verifying safety properties of concurrent Java programs using 3-valued logic. In: Proc. Symp. on Principles of Prog. Languages, pp. 27–40 (2001)

34. Yahav, E., Ramalingam, G.: Verifying safety properties using separation and heterogeneous abstractions. In: Proceedings of the ACM SIGPLAN 2004 conference on Programming language design and implementation, pp. 25–34. ACM Press, New York (2004), doi:10.1145/996841.996846

35. Yahav, E., Reps, T., Sagiv, M., Wilhelm, R.: Verifying temporal heap properties specified via evolution logic. In: Degano, P. (ed.) ESOP 2003 and ETAPS 2003. LNCS, vol. 2618, pp. 204–222. Springer, Heidelberg (2003)

36. Yahav, E., Sagiv, M.: Automatically verifying concurrent queue algorithms. In: Workshop on Software Model Checking (2003)

37. Yorsh, G., Reps, T., Sagiv, M.: Symbolically computing most-precise abstract operations for shape analysis. In: Tools and Algs.for the Construct.and Anal.of Syst. pp. 530–545 (2004)

A   Discussion on Thomas Reps's Presentation

Bertrand Meyer

In your list reversal example: the only way I know to teach this kind of algorithm, to understand it properly and (as I have tried to do in my own work) to prove it, is to have a loop invariant that basically says: If you are at a certain point in the list, halfway through the algorithm, then the first part of the list up to that point is the corresponding part in the original list, reversed, and the second part is unchanged from the original. In other words, the mirror image of the first part concatenated with the second part is, in some precise sense, equivalent to the original list.

Does this fundamental property of the algorithm follow from your description? And, if you knew that property, if the programmer had written it in the code, would it help your analysis at all?

Thomas Reps

The answer to the first part is that if we were trying to prove functional correctness of the list-reversal program, you would have to introduce not just the n-relation, but also the n0-relation. You basically want to freeze the initial n-relation on input in the n0-relation, so that you can make a comparison between the two. The property that you would want to show at the end of the program is that, for all pairs of individuals, if they were related by the n0-relation, n0 (v1, v2), you now have n (v2, v1), i.e., that you have reversed all the links.

If you were to look at the descriptors that appear at, say, the head of the loop, for each one of those you would see that in the list pointed to by y you would have that relationship, and in the list pointed to by x you would have that the n-relation would match the n0-relation - those links were not reversed. So what you stated as the property can be found by examining the structures at the head of the loop. But you don't have to state the property explicitly; it just comes out of the abstract interpretation.

Bertrand Meyer

It does not help you, if the programmer tells you.

Thomas Reps

Well, since you do not need it, I have not thought about, whether it would help you. There might be ways of allowing it to help you, but in this case, you do not need it.

Patrick Cousot

I have a semi-technical question. What is nice with TVLA is that you can find a good abstraction by experimentation, in fact: by refining the semantics, introducing relationships, and so on. The inconvenience is that it does not scale up very, very large. But maybe, there is a way. That would be to make this experiment and then to extract the abstraction function automatically. This is given to people as the specification of the algorithm that they have to write in some efficient way. You see, you can do the same when you have found the proper abstraction; you can reprogram it, using very efficient data structures, and so on. And this could be a way to add efficiency.

Thomas Reps

Well, what we are trying to do is, we are trying to allow the abstractions to follow the hierarchical decomposition of the program, so that if you prove low-level things, then you can get some abstract transformer that you can use at higher level, at higher. Bertrand Jeannet, Mooly, one of my students, and I did some work that was at SAS 2004 a couple of years ago that aims towards this, where you end up using the abstract structures themselves as characterizations of the summary transformers. And once you have that, that allows you to sort of walk up the levels of the hierarchical decomposition of the software. But, there is a problem is with nested data structures, so the problem is not solved.

Greg Nelson

[Question not recorded.]

Thomas Reps

If you have a binary search tree, you would be interested in showing that sortedness properties are maintained, and we can do that.

Let me also mention another thing that doesn't involve insertion and deletion, but it was mentioned yesterday-something about the Deutsch-Schorr-Waite algorithm for traversing a tree without the use of a stack, by temporarily stealing pointer fields of the tree's nodes to serve in place of a stack. So we have actually applied this to Deutsch-Schorr-Waite and shown that the tree that comes in is reestablished at the end. It took 40 hours of TVLA running time on a 3GHz machine. And, of course, TVLA itself is part of the trusted computing base, so I am not sure I trust this answer. But anyway we claim to have been able to handle Deutsch-Schorr-Waite, and not just to say that it is a tree that goes in and a tree that comes out, but to say that the tree that comes out is identical to the tree that went in.

Reasoning about Object Structures Using Ownership

Peter Müller

ETH Zurich, Switzerland
`Peter.Mueller@inf.ethz.ch`

Abstract. *Many well-established concepts of object-oriented programming work for individual objects, but do not support object structures. The development of a verifying compiler requires enhancements of programming theory to cope with this deficiency.*

In this paper, we support this position by showing that classical specification and verification techniques support invariants for individual objects whose fields are primitive values, but are unsound for invariants involving more complex object structures.

We have developed an ownership model, which allows one to structure the object store and to restrict reference passing and the operations that can be performed on references. We use this model to generalize classical object invariants to cover such object structures. We summarize the state of our work and identify open research challenges.

1   Introduction

Programming theory encompasses, among other fields, language semantics, program logics, and specification techniques. It provides the foundation for understanding how programs work. Together with theorem proving technology, programming theory forms the basis of program verification, in particular, of program verifiers such as the verifying compiler [17].

Programming theory has been advanced to cope with new developments in programming languages and programming practice: Interface specifications in terms of pre- and postconditions, frame axioms, and invariants describe the behavior of methods and classes [27]. Abstraction functions [16] enable implementation-independent specifications of program behavior. Subtyping and dynamic method binding are addressed by behavioral subtyping [26,20]. Program logics cover a variety of programming language features [1,31]. However, despite these achievements, programming theory still falls behind programming practice.

This position paper describes one aspect of a larger effort to advance programming theory in order to improve tool-assisted verification of realistic programs. Our work focuses on modular specification and verification of object-oriented programs. *Modular* verification means that a class can be verified based on its implementation and the specifications of all classes it uses, but without knowing its subclasses and clients. Modularity is a prerequisite for the scalability of

B. Meyer and J. Woodcock (Eds.): Verified Software, LNCS 4171, pp. 93–104, 2008.

verification techniques and tools, and for applying them to software libraries. By contrast, non-modular verification techniques require one to re-verify a class, say, a string class, in every context where it is (re-)used, which is not practical.

One of the major shortcomings of programming theory for object-oriented programming is summarized by the following position:

> Many well-established concepts of object-oriented programming work for individual objects, but do not support object structures. The development of a verifying compiler requires enhancements of programming theory to cope with this deficiency.

In this paper, we support this position by discussing one particularly important concept, namely object invariants. We illustrate the problems and present ownership as a general solution to this class of problems.

For simplicity, we consider a restricted programming language here. We use a language similar to C# and Java, but omit multi-threading, inheritance, and static class members. However, the presented techniques do not rely on these restrictions [18,23,22,28].

Overview. In Section 2 we describe the classical technique for reasoning about invariants and its limitations. Section 3 presents a modular verification technique for invariants over object structures based on an ownership model. We summarize our progress so far and identify open research challenges in Section 4.

2   Classical Invariants and Their Limitations

Invariants are predicates that specify what states of an object are consistent [16]. For example, the invariant of the List class, near the top of Fig. 1, states several such properties, including that the array field is always non-null and that the array holds non-negative numbers. Thus, when calling add, for example, the expression array.length cannot cause a null pointer exception.

The invariant semantics used by classical reasoning techniques [25,26,27] is that each object has to satisfy its invariant in the pre- and poststate of each exported method. To enforce this property, classical techniques require one to prove that each exported method preserves the invariant of its receiver object. For this proof, one may assume that in the prestate of the method execution the precondition of the method holds and that all allocated objects satisfy their invariants. For constructors, one has to show that the invariant of the new object is established.

The classical techniques assume that a method can break only the invariant of its receiver object. Therefore, they are sound for invariants of individual objects whose fields are primitive values, such as points with integer coordinates. However, since they do not impose proof obligations on the invariants of other objects, these techniques do not support invariants of more complex object structures.

Abstraction Layering is not Sound. Classical techniques do not support invariants of layers implemented on top of List. For example, the invariant of class BagWithMax in Fig. 2, which says that no element of the list is larger than a given upper bound, is generally not preserved by List's add method. That is, the classical technique's assumption that a method can break only the invariant of its receiver object is not valid for invariants that depend on the state of several objects. In particular, the call to add in BagWithMax's insert method temporarily violates the invariant of the BagWithMax object if k is greater than maxElem. The invariant is restored by the last statement of insert. Even if one would require add to preserve BagWithMax's invariant, this example would not be handled modularly, since modular verification of a class implies not considering its clients during its verification.

Invariants that depend on the state of objects of an underlying layer are common and important. They occur in three situations. The first is when invariants of the upper layer relate locations in the upper layer and the object states in

```
class List {
  private /*@ spec_public rep @*/ int[] array;
  private /*@ spec_public @*/ int n;

  /*@ public invariant array != null && 0 <= n && n <= array.length
    @                   && (\forall int i; 0<=i && i<n; array[i]>=0);    @*/

  /*@ requires k >= 0 && n < Integer.MAX_VALUE;
    @ assignable array, array[n], n;
    @ ensures n==\old(n+1) && array[\old(n)]==k
    @      && (\forall int i; 0<=i && i<\old(n);
    @                          array[i]==\old(array[i])); @*/
  public void add(int k) {
    if (n==array.length) { resize(); }
    array[n] = k; // temporary invariant violation
    n++;
  }

  //@ assignable array, n;
  public void resize()                  { /* ... */ }
  public List()                         { array = new /*@ rep @*/ int[10]; }
  public void addElems(int[] elems) { /* ... */ }
  // other methods omitted.
}
```

Fig. 1. Implementation and JML specification of an array-based list. Annotation comments start with an at-sign (@), and at-signs at the beginning of lines are ignored. The array object is part of the encapsulated internal representation of the list, indicated by the rep annotation. The spec_public annotation allows fields with any access modifier to be mentioned in public specifications.

```
class BagWithMax {
  private /*@ spec_public rep @*/ List theList;
  private /*@ spec_public @*/ int maxElem;

  /*@ public invariant theList != null
    @    && (\forall int i; 0<=i && i<theList.n;
    @                theList.array[i] <= maxElem); @*/

  //@ requires k>=0;
  public void insert(int k) {
    theList.add(k);  // temporary invariant violation if k > maxElem
    if (k > maxElem) { maxElem = k; }
  }
  // other methods and constructors omitted.
}
```

Fig. 2. Class `BagWithMax` builds an abstraction layer on top of `List`. `BagWithMax`'s invariant depends on the state of the `List` object and its array.

the underlying layers, as illustrated by `BagWithMax`. The second is when an upper layer restricts the object states of the underlying layers. For instance, a set built on top of a list might have an invariant that excludes duplicates in the list. The third is when the invariant of an upper layer relates the states of different objects of an underlying layer. This is often the case in aggregate objects. For example, consider `Family` objects that aggregate different `Person` objects. `Family`'s invariant could require that all `Persons` in a `Family` have the same street address.

Another way to view this soundness problem is that the classical invariant semantics is too strong for invariants over layered object structures. The class `List` cannot modularly know enough to establish the invariant of a class, `BagWithMax`, that it does not know about. Note that this problem is not due to aliasing. It occurs even if `BagWithMax` objects have unique references to their `List` objects.

Mutable Subobjects are not Sound. For example, the invariant in class `List` of Fig. 1 is not supported by classical techniques, because it refers to locations in the underlying array object. If a reference to the array could be exposed to other objects, then any method of the program could use such a reference to break `List`'s invariant [10,25]. Such an alias could occur by rep exposure or by capturing as illustrated by the version of `addElems` in Fig. 3. With that version, the code fragment in Fig. 4 would violate `List`'s invariant. This could happen even if the classical proof technique was used to prove the correctness of all of `List`'s methods. This example shows that a sound technique must either restrict invariants that depend on subobjects in lower abstraction layers, or it must control aliasing and, in particular, modifications of such subobjects.

```
/*@ requires elems != null
  @      && (\forall int i; 0<=i && i<elems.length; elems[i]>=0); @*/
public void addElems(int[] elems) {
  if (n==0) { array = elems; n = elems.length; }
  else       { /* ... */ }
}
```

Fig. 3. A questionable implementation of the `List` method `addElems` that stores the argument array into the `array` field

```
class Client {
  /*@ requires list.n == 0; @*/
  void violator(List list) {
    // invariant of list holds in prestate
    int[] aliasedArray = new int[10];
    list.addElems(aliasedArray);
    aliasedArray[0] = -1;
    // invariant of list is violated in poststate
  }
}
```

Fig. 4. Client code that shows the problem with aliased representations

3   Ownership-Based Invariants

Ownership allows one to structure the object store and to restrict reference passing and the operations that can be performed on references. We use ownership also to control the dependencies of invariants and to define a weaker semantics for invariants that allows layering.

3.1   Ownership Model

Ownership organizes objects into *contexts*: Each object is owned by at most one other object, called its *owner*. A context is the set of all objects with the same owner. The set of objects without owner is called the *root context*. The contexts of a program execution form a tree, where the context of all objects with owner X is a child of the context containing X. The context tree is rooted in the root context.

Our ownership model enforces the *owner-as-modifier* property: All modifications of an object, X, must be initiated by X's owner. That is, X can be referenced by any other object, but reference chains that do not pass through X's owner must not be used to modify X [22,28]. Therefore, owners can control modifications of owned objects.

The ownership relation is expressed in programs by the ownership modifier `rep`, which can be used in field declarations and object creation expressions. In class `List` (Fig. 1) the `rep` keyword indicates that the array referenced by `array` and the array created in the constructor are owned by `this`.

Ownership and the owner-as-modifier property can be enforced by type systems or by standard verification techniques [12]. For instance, our Universe type system [28] would forbid the assignment to `array` in Fig. 3 and require copying `elems` to avoid the unwanted alias.

3.2   The Ownership Technique

The ownership model allows one to generalize the classical technique to invariants over layered object structures. To avoid the soundness problems described in Sec. 2, we use the hierarchical structure of the ownership model to refine the classical invariant semantics.

Admissible Invariants. The ownership technique allows the invariant of an object, X, to depend on fields of X (like the classical technique) and on fields of objects owned by X. The invariant of class `List` is an ownership-based invariant because it depends on the fields of `this` (`array` and `n`) and on fields of the array owned by `this` (`array.length` and `array[i]`).

Ownership-based invariants can express properties of layered object structures. For instance, `BagWithMax`'s invariant is allowed to depend on fields of the associated list, because the ownership model guarantees that all modifications of the list are initiated by a method of the owning `BagWithMax` object, and this `BagWithMax` method makes sure that the invariant is preserved. In particular, invariant violations through representation exposure, as illustrated in Fig. 4, are ruled out by the ownership model.

Semantics of Invariants. In Section 2, we showed that invariants over layered object structures may not hold in the pre- and poststates of all exported methods. For example, a `BagWithMax` object needs to temporarily violate its invariant when changing its underlying `theList` object. To allow such violations, we weaken the invariant semantics from the classical technique.

The weakened semantics allows a method executed on a receiver object, X, to violate the invariants of all objects in ancestor contexts of the context containing X. In particular, the method is allowed to violate the invariants of X's transitive owner objects. For instance, method `add` executed on a `List` object is allowed to violate the invariant of the owning `BagWithMax` object.

Ownership Proof Technique. Like the classical proof technique, the ownership proof technique requires one to prove that each exported method preserves the invariant of its receiver object. For this proof, one may assume that in the prestate of the method execution (1) the precondition of the method holds and (2) those allocated objects that are in the context of the receiver object or its descendants satisfy their invariants. However, a method must not assume that the (transitive) owners of the receiver object satisfy their invariants, which corresponds to the refined invariant semantics.

To illustrate how to use the ownership proof technique, consider BagWithMax's insert method. For the call to List's add method we may assume that the method preserves the invariant of theList. However, since the BagWithMax object this is the owner of the receiver of this call to add, its invariant might be broken by the call. To show that the insert method preserves this invariant, we use the postcondition of add to derive that the list after the call contains exactly the elements before the call plus the new element k. If k happens to be a new maximum in the list, then BagWithMax's invariant is violated after the call, but reestablished by the subsequent assignment to maxElem. Therefore, the invariant of this is preserved.

As can be seen from the example above, responsibility for verifying invariants is divided. A method's implementor is responsible for the objects (transitively) owned by the method's receiver object, but its calling method is responsible for other objects.

This ownership proof technique is modular and sound [22,28,30].

4   Progress so Far and Open Research Challenges

We have developed the ownership technique for object invariants in cooperation with Gary Leavens, Rustan Leino, and Arnd Poetzsch-Heffter [22,28,30]. To handle implementations that are not supported by the ownership model such as mutually recursive data structures, we combined ownership-based invariants with so-called visibility-based invariants that gain modularity by imposing certain visibility requirements on fields [4,22,24,30]. We have also extended our methodology to static class invariants [23] and adapted it to the verification of frame properties [29]. The combination of these techniques can handle many interesting implementations.

We have developed two approaches to specifying the ownership relation and enforcing the owner-as-modifier property. The Universe type system [12,28] expresses ownership by extended type information and checks the owner-as-modifier property as part of type checking. An alternative approach [22] encodes ownership by a specification-only field that can be used in interface specifications. The owner-as-modifier property is enforced by a programming methodology that restricts how objects can be modified.

Although we have made significant progress with ownership-based verification, there are a number of open research challenges. We summarize these challenges in the following.

Ownership. Our ownership model can handle realistic applications. However, there are common implementation patterns that cannot directly be expressed, for instance, several objects sharing and modifying a common representation. We plan to generalize our ownership model to allow more implementations, in particular, multiple ownership and ownership transfer. We will also study how implementation patterns that are not directly supported can be rewritten to follow the ownership model.

To reduce the overhead of writing ownership annotations, we are working on ownership inference. Besides classical type inference techniques, we study runtime inference [13] to infer ownership relations. The results so far are promising. A major application of ownership inference will be to run case studies to investigate how common ownership relations are.

Specification Features. An important topic for future work is invariants over model (specification-only) fields [19,21], which are useful to describe properties of data structures without referring to their concrete implementation.

History constraints [26] suffer from the same problems as the classical invariant technique when applied to object structures. We plan to extend ownership-based techniques to history constraints and to more general temporal constraints.

Specification languages like Eiffel and JML allow method calls in interface specifications. Methods that can be called in specifications must be pure, that is, side-effect free. Therefore, they can be formally modeled by mathematical functions. Especially for recursive functions, ownership can help to show that the functions are well-defined [8]. We plan to support method calls in specifications in the Boogie tool [3], which is being developed at Microsoft Research.

Automation. Practical applications of program verification require a high degree of automation. Research on automated verification has mainly focused on automated verification tools [11,15] and automated theorem provers [9].

We investigate combinations of classical logic-based reasoning with extended type systems [14,28], abstract interpretation [7], and static analyses. For instance, we plan to develop static, modular analyses for purity and frame properties of methods. These analyses build on the ownership structure to simplify the pointer and escape analysis used by related approaches [32].

5   Conclusions

We have illustrated the problems of reasoning about object structures by discussing object invariants. We have summarized the ideas of ownership-based verification, which allows one to reason about layered object structures in a modular way. Details of this approach are presented in earlier papers [22,30].

Ownership allows one to structure the object store systematically. Structuring is important for many important applications. For instance, ownership has also been applied successfully to the modular verification of frame properties [29], static class invariants [23], reasoning about multi-threaded programs [5,18], confinement of internal representations of data structures [6], and proving representation independence [2]. Therefore, we believe that ownership is a fundamental principle of programming theory.

Parts of our work on the foundations of ownership and ownership-based verification have been implemented in JML [19], in the semi-automated Java Interactive Verification Environment (JIVE), and in the fully automated verification tool Boogie [3]. One important aspect of future work is to use these tools for non-trivial case studies.

References

1. Abadi, M., Leino, K.R.M.: A logic of object-oriented programs. In: Bidoit, M., Dauchet, M. (eds.) CAAP 1997, FASE 1997, and TAPSOFT 1997. LNCS, vol. 1214, pp. 682–696. Springer, Heidelberg (1997)
2. Banerjee, A., Naumann, D.: Representation independence, confinement, and access control. In: Principles of Programming Languages, pp. 166–177. ACM Press, New York (2002)
3. Barnett, M., Chang, B.-Y.E., DeLine, R., Jacobs, B., Leino, K.R.M.: Boogie: A modular reusable verifier for object-oriented programs. In: Submitted (2006), http://research.microsoft.com/~leino/papers/krml160.pdf
4. Barnett, M., Naumann, D.: Friends need a bit more: Maintaining invariants over shared state. In: Kozen, D. (ed.) MPC 2004. LNCS, vol. 3125, Springer, Heidelberg (2004)
5. Boyapati, C., Lee, R., Rinard, M.: Ownership types for safe programming: Preventing data races and deadlocks. In: Object-Oriented Programming, Systems, Languages, and Applications (OOPSLA), pp. 211–230. ACM Press, New York (2002)
6. Clarke, D.G., Potter, J.M., Noble, J.: Ownership types for flexible alias protection. In: Proceedings of Object-Oriented Programming Systems, Languages, and Applications (OOPSLA), October 1998. SIGPLAN Notices, vol. 33(10), ACM Press, New York (1998)
7. Cousot, P., Cousot, R.: Abstract interpretation: a unified lattice model for static analysis of programs by construction or approximation of fixpoints. In: Principles of programming languages (POPL), pp. 238–252. ACM Press, New York (1977)
8. Darvas, A., Müller, P.: Reasoning About Method Calls in Interface Specifications. Journal of Object Technology (JOT) (to appear, 2006)
9. Detlefs, D., Nelson, G., Saxe, J.B.: Simplify: A theorem prover for program checking. Technical Report HPL-2003-148, HP Labs (July 2003)
10. Detlefs, D.L., Leino, K.R.M., Nelson, G.: Wrestling with rep exposure. Research Report 156, Digital Systems Research Center (1998)
11. Detlefs, D.L., Leino, K.R.M., Nelson, G., Saxe, J.B.: Extended static checking. Research Report 159, Digital Systems Research Center (1998)
12. Dietl, W., Müller, P.: Universes: Lightweight ownership for JML. Journal of Object Technology (JOT) 4(8), 5–32 (2005)
13. Ernst, M.D., Cockrell, J., Griswold, W.G., Notkin, D.: Dynamically discovering likely program invariants to support program evolution. IEEE Transactions on Software Engineering 27(2), 1–25 (2001)
14. Fähndrich, M., Leino, K.R.M.: Declaring and checking non-null types in an object-oriented language. In: Object-oriented programing, systems, languages, and applications (OOPSLA), pp. 302–312. ACM Press, New York (2003)
15. Flanagan, C., Leino, K.R.M., Lillibridge, M., Nelson, G., Saxe, J.B., Stata, R.: Extended static checking for Java. In: Programming Language Design and Implementation (PLDI), pp. 234–245. ACM Press, New York (2002)
16. Hoare, C.A.R.: Proofs of correctness of data representation. Acta Informatica 1, 271–281 (1972)

17. Hoare, C.A.R.: The verifying compiler: A grand challenge for computing research. Journal of the ACM 50(1), 63–69 (2003)
18. Jacobs, B., Leino, K.R.M., Schulte, W.: Verification of multithreaded object-oriented programs with invariants. In: Specification and Verification of Component-Based Systems (SAVCBS), pp. 2–9, Technical report 04-09, Department of Computer Science, Iowa State University (2004)
19. Leavens, G.T., Baker, A.L., Ruby, C.: JML: A notation for detailed design. In: Kilov, H., Rumpe, B., Simmonds, I. (eds.) Behavioral Specifications of Businesses and Systems, pp. 175–188. Kluwer Academic Publishers, Dordrecht (1999)
20. Leavens, G.T., Weihl, W.E.: Reasoning about object-oriented programs that use subtypes (extended abstract). In: Meyrowitz, N. (ed.) OOPSLA ECOOP 1990 Proceedings. SIGPLAN, vol. 25(10), pp. 212–223. ACM Press, New York (1990)
21. Leino, K.R.M.: Toward Reliable Modular Programs. PhD thesis, California Institute of Technology (1995)
22. Leino, K.R.M., Müller, P.: Object invariants in dynamic contexts. In: Odersky, M. (ed.) ECOOP 2004. LNCS, vol. 3086, pp. 491–516. Springer, Heidelberg (2004)
23. Leino, K.R.M., Müller, P.: Modular verification of static class invariants. In: Fitzgerald, J.S., Hayes, I.J., Tarlecki, A. (eds.) FM 2005. LNCS, vol. 3582, pp. 26–42. Springer, Heidelberg (2005)
24. Leino, K.R.M., Nelson, G.: Data abstraction and information hiding. ACM Transactions on Programming Languages and Systems 24(5), 491–553 (2002)
25. Liskov, B., Guttag, J.: Abstraction and Specification in Program Development. MIT Press, Cambridge (1986)
26. Liskov, B., Wing, J.M.: A behavioral notion of subtyping. ACM Transactions on Programming Languages and Systems 16(6) (1994)
27. Meyer, B.: Object-Oriented Software Construction, 2nd edn. Prentice Hall, Englewood Cliffs (1997)
28. Müller, P.: Modular Specification and Verification of Object-Oriented Programs. LNCS, vol. 2262. Springer, Heidelberg (2002)
29. Müller, P., Poetzsch-Heffter, A., Leavens, G.T.: Modular specification of frame properties in JML. Concurrency and Computation: Practice and Experience 15, 117–154 (2003)
30. Müller, P., Poetzsch-Heffter, A., Leavens, G.T.: Modular invariants for layered object structures. In: Science of Computer Programming, ETH Zurich. Accepted for publication. Also available as TR 424 of the Department of Computer Science (2006)
31. Poetzsch-Heffter, A., Müller, P.: A programming logic for sequential Java. In: Swierstra, S.D. (ed.) ESOP 1999 and ETAPS 1999. LNCS, vol. 1576, pp. 162–176. Springer, Heidelberg (1999)
32. Salcianu, A., Rinard, M.: Purity and side effect analysis for java programs. In: Cousot, R. (ed.) VMCAI 2005. LNCS, vol. 3385, pp. 199–215. Springer, Heidelberg (2005)

A   Discussion on Peter Müller's Presentation

Greg Nelson

Peter, I was surprised to hear you say that you thought programmers would find it so burdensome to specify the ownership relations that it was important to do it by automatic inference. I would have thought that that was a small fraction of the effort in giving a functional specification for the interface, and an easy design decision to record. So, I guess that was a comment rather than a question, but I would be happy to be persuaded that you are right and I am wrong.

Peter Müller

Well, I do not think one of us is right or wrong. I think, at a certain point of the program, you make a design decision, like: the list should own the array, and somewhere record that and this should be an explicit specification. But for instance, if you use a global type system, you have to add many more types you use, to all the local variables you use, to all the parameters you use. And these additional things, which are just necessary to make type-checking work, can easily be inferred. So, I think, it is really a mixture of both.

Greg Nelson

Thank you, that actually clarifies it. But if you use the verification kinds of systems instead of the type-checking systems, then the first-step variation of ownership would be enough of an annotation?

Peter Müller: Exactly, that's enough.

Rustan Leino

Just a response also to Greg's question. Last month, I worked with one particular programmer who tried to use the ownership domains that we provide in Spec#, and we have the ownerships there so that we can provide the invariants. I have always thought that it has been the invariants that are difficult, but in fact, this particular programmer has found great difficulties with the ownership system, which has really surprised me, and I do not think it is specific to him. But it could be that our error messages are not clear enough to explain that, but I have been surprised at that, too.

Peter Müller: *(laughing)* Easy question for me.

Bertrand Meyer

You are working basically with existing languages. Is there a simple language mechanism that you could propose for a new language that would make the type ownership very visible, straightforward, and under programmer control? This is somewhat in line with Greg's question.

Peter Müller

I think, some of the ownership type systems are simple enough to actually put them in a programming language. The problem is that we still have to accept programs that do not follow these structures, because, of course, there are design patterns that do not follow the hierarchical object model. But I think there are type systems that could be actually used by mainstream programming languages.

Modular Reasoning in Object-Oriented Programming

David A. Naumann*

Department of Computer Science, Stevens Institute of Technology
naumann@cs.stevens.edu

Abstract. Difficulties in reasoning about functional correctness and relational properties of object-oriented programs are reviewed. An approach using auxiliary state is briefly described, with emphasis on the author's work. Some near term challenges are sketched.

Formal verification depends on scientific theories of programming, which answer questions such as these: What are good models of computational behavior? What behavioral properties of components are needed for modular reasoning about a composed system? How can such properties be specified and a component be verified, or even derived from its specification? How can a program and justification of its correctness be revised in accord with small revision of its specification? Such questions have well developed answers that are adequate for small programs under strong simplifying assumptions. But many useful programs are quite large and built from complicated components that violate simplifying assumptions.

The longstanding challenge of compositional reasoning remains substantially unsolved. Object-oriented programs pose several challenges that are the focus of my recent research, in which auxiliary state is being used to specify encapsulation boundaries and disciplined interdependence. Section 2, explains the approach, accomplishments, and challenges in terms of invariants for shared mutable objects. Section 3 addresses relational properties including data refinement and secure information flow. This line of research has been carried out for Java-like programming languages; I argue in Section 1 for the importance of such languages. Some additional challenges pertinent to object-oriented programming, but not tied to the main theme, are discussed in Section 4. A detailed tutorial on the state-based approach to encapsulation advocated here appears elsewhere [33].

Several near-term challenges (1–5 years) are presented here in the setting of sequential object-oriented programs. Because the approach taken here is based on the use of assertions, it is also quite relevant to verification of concurrent object-oriented programs and low level imperative code.

1 Why Java-Like Language?

In order to develop theory for modular reasoning about large programs, we need a corpus of large programs and automated support for experiments. Since I would like to do

---

* Partially supported by the National Science Foundation under grants CCR-0208984 and CCF-0429894 and by Microsoft Research.

B. Meyer and J. Woodcock (Eds.): Verified Software, LNCS 4171, pp. 105–115, 2008.

science that contributes to human good through improved engineering, the primary objects of study should be representative examples of large programs that are significantly deployed and used. This means confronting programs written in notations like C, Java, and C#—though not necessarily handling all of their features without restriction. Aside from obvious pragmatic reasons for interest in Java-like languages, there are technical reasons why such a language is a good point in the language design space.

- The language is sufficiently rich to express higher order design patterns which are needed for well structured programs and used in common practice.
- Despite the preceding item, the language is essentially "defunctionalized" [42, 4] owing to the binding of methods to classes rather than to instances. Thus relatively simple semantic models are adequate, at least for large fragments of the language. For example, my work discussed in Sections 2 and 3 has been done using a straightforward Scott-Strachey denotational semantics, for a fragment of Java including recursive types, inheritance, mutable objects, and other features without restriction; this model has been encoded in PVS [34]. Nipkow's group and others have obtained strong results using straightforward operational models [26].
- The module system (packages, generic classes, public/private/protected visibility) embodies most of what current theory offers for scope-based encapsulation.
- The Java type system is name-based; named types provide a convenient hook on which to hang specifications and encapsulation boundaries. In particular, it helps deal with inheritance, which is widely used if problemmatic.
- Pointer arithmetic is absent. Parameter passing is by value and identifiers cannot alias. Method declarations are not nested, avoiding the semantic complexity of reference to variables in enclosing scopes other than global scope.[1]

These features are not without cost. Java programs make much use of global variables ("statics")—global in that they are in outermost scopes; this is mitigated in that the scope of visibility may be a single class or package. Reflection, at least in full generality, is a feature I see as a very difficult and long-term challenge for verification. This is exacerbated in that reflection, like threads and permission-based access control, appears in the form of special libraries rather than being distinguished with separate syntax.

Perhaps the highest cost is the ubiquity of aliasing in the sense of shared references to mutable objects in the heap.

2   Heap Encapsulation Using Auxiliary State

For modular reasoning in object-oriented programming there are several challenges.

1. Non-hierarchical control flow due to callbacks leads, even in sequential programs, to interference like that in concurrent programs.
2. The conventional notion of layered abstraction is also subverted by non-hierarchical control flow due to inheritance and method overriding.

---

[1] Compare the complexity of Idealized Algol models [44] with Modula-3 and Oberon, where non-local references are restricted for those procedures that are passed as arguments or stored in variables [32].

3. Design patterns that are essentially higher order are often used, but unlike in functional programming the encapsulation aspects are not explicit in the program text, owing to data representation based on shared heap objects.

4. Functional aspects of such patterns are also not specified formally, for lack of good models (compare "map" in functional programming with the "Visitor" pattern).

The second challenge is addressed by the notion of behavioral subtyping which is well understood [29, 20] except that the extant theories do not fully deal with the first and third challenges.

For the fourth challenge, which we discuss in Section 4, one might argue that at best we should aim for verifying simple safety properties. Indeed, in his VSTTE talk Bart Jacobs said that full functional verification of nontrivial Java programs is impractical. But for realistically complex systems, attempts to verify simple safety properties lead to the need for more general properties, especially object invariants.

For the first and third challenges, progress is being made using auxiliary state to express encapsulation using assertions. That is the topic of this section, which focuses on object invariants. More extensive discussions and citations on these topics can be found in Müller's VSTTE paper [31] and my survey paper [33].

Non-hierarchical control flow. As an example of the first challenge, consider a sensor playing the role of Subject in the Subject/Observer pattern [22]. The sensor maintains a set of registered Views: when the sensor value reaches the threshhold $v.thresh$ of a given view v, the sensor invokes method $v.notify$ and removes v from the set. This description is in terms of a set, part of the abstraction offered by the Subject; the implementation might store views in an array ordered by *thresh* values. The pattern cannot be seen simply as a client using an abstraction, because *notify* is what is known as an *upcall* to the client. The difficulty is that $v.notify$ may make a *reentrant callback* to the sensor. Some callbacks are quite sensible, e.g., the view could query the sensor value. But trouble is likely if $v.notify$ invokes a method to enumerate the current set of views. While notifications are under way, the array may be in an inconsistent state—is v in the set? in the array?—yet the enumeration method may assume as precondition the sensor's invariant. Non-hierarchical control flow renders naive reasoning about object invariants unsound.

The problem is similar to interference in shared-variable concurrency, for which there are several established and well understood solutions. For the reentrant callback problem, which already occurs in sequential code, the situation is less settled, although the probem is a frequent cause of insidious bugs. Various solutions have been proposed:

– Establish caller's invariant before *every* method call. But this is impractical in many cases: most calls do not result in reentrant callbacks and good use of abstraction in design leads to many calls to substructures while a super-structure's invariant is temporarily violated.

– Use concurrency locks. But this leads to deadlocks in the sequential case.

– Use temporal specification of allowed calling sequences. This can be heavy handed and violates abstraction by making method calls visible. Moreover, verification of such properties requires the whole program in general.

A more promising approach begins by making the invariant an explicit precondition on those methods that assume it, like the enumerator in the example. This precondition cannot be established by client v attempting a reentrant callback, unless in fact the sensor restores its invariant before invoking *v.notify*.

An object invariant $\mathcal{I}$ ought not appear in the precondition of a public method, as that could expose the internal representation. Various techniques have been proposed to hide information, e.g., treating $\mathcal{I}$ in a precondition as an opaque predicate [14, 15], a typestate [19], a call to a pure method, or a model field [30, 25].

We advocate the approach of Leino *et al* [8], known as the *Boogie methodology* or the inv/own discipline. We give a simplified account sufficient for discussion. The discipline uses a *ghost* (auxiliary) field[2] inv of type boolean which represents whether the invariant of o is in force, just as a programmer might do using an ordinary field. There are several associated proof obligations; together they embody a discipline that ensures the following is a *program invariant*, i.e., it holds in all reachable states:

$$(\forall o \mid o.inv \Rightarrow \mathcal{I}(o)) \tag{1}$$

Informally: for each allocated object o, the object's invariant holds if $o.inv = true$. Thus within the body of a method with precondition inv, one can exploit the invariant $\mathcal{I}$ while exposing to clients not the predicate $\mathcal{I}$ but only the boolean field inv.

Heap encapsulation. Besides its own fields, an object may depend on some objects that serve as its internal representation. This can be represented using another auxiliary field by which an object points to its direct *owner*, if any. An object's invariant is allowed to depend only on objects it transitively owns. An associated program invariant is that $o.inv$ implies $p.inv$ for every object p owned by o. If an object is in a consistent state then so are its representation objects. This invariant is maintained owing to a proof obligation: update of a field of an object p has as precondition that $p.inv = false$. So, if an object p is susceptible to update then not only may $\mathcal{I}(p)$ be temporarily violated but also if p is part of the representation of some object o then also $o.inv = false$ and $\mathcal{I}(o)$ may be temporarily violated.

Ownership imposes a forest structure on the heap, separating encapsulated data from clients. Ownership types [18, 2] embody this idea and an account of the resulting encapsulation has been given in terms of the theory of representation independence [5]. But it has proved difficult to find an ownership type system that admits common design patterns and also enforces encapsulation sufficiently strong for modular reasoning about object invariants. In particular, many examples call for the transfer of ownership (e.g., in resource management) and this does not sit well with types.

An alternative to types is separation logic [45, 39]. In separation logic, owning an object p has been equated with having a precondition dependent on p. A modest challenge is how to scale the logic up to classes (instantiable abstractions) instead of single-instance modules. A bigger challenge is how to cope with the fact that in object-oriented languages, the object is the unit of addressability but some fields are inherited and

---

[2] For our purposes, a *model field* is an auxiliary field, the value of which is defined as a function of other state, whereas the value of a *ghost field* must be updated by explicit auxiliary assignments.

others (to be added in subclasses) are not known to the modular reasoner. Parkinson and Bierman [41, 14] have taken initial steps and their treatment of encapsulation has been given an acount in terms of higher order separation logic [13, 15]. By contrast with separation logic, the approach described here is compatibility with standard logics and specification notions, which can leverage existing tools and programmer expertise.

One advantage of encoding ownership with a ghost field is that transfer is straight-forward; the field is mutable. In combination with the invariant-tracking field inv, the discipline [8, 28] expresses very directly the flow of control in and out of hierarchical encapsulation boundaries even as those boundaries are mutated.

The most exciting advantage of the approch is that it generalizes to more elaborate patterns. Ownership is concerned with a single object and its representation. Already the pattern of iterators is problemmatic, in that an iterator needs access to the representation objects of its associated collection but a collection is not owned by its iterators. There are many situations where several publically-accessible objects cooperate to provide an abstraction, so their individual invariants need to depend on non-owned objects. Just as the $owner$ field records a dependence that can be taken into account in reasoning, one can use a ghost field to record the dependence between peer objects.

This idea has been developed in the simple case of one object's invariant depending on another: the "friendship" discipline [37, 10] imposes modular obligations on both dependee and dependant, so (1) is maintained even when an invariant $\mathcal{I}$ depends on non-owned objects. A field $deps$ is used so that $p.deps$ is a set of object references that includes all o that could have an invariant currently dependent on p that is not licensed by ownership.

The friendship discipline has been successfully applied to several design patterns including iterators [38] and Subject/View [10], but it does not seem likely that there is a single such discipline sufficiently general to handle every situation. I believe that by using auxiliary state to record encapsulation boundaries for heap structure, we can formalize a number of generally applicable *specification patterns*. Interactive theorem proving or just pencil and paper can be used to show that the associated global invariant is a consequent of the pattern's stipulated annotation discipline. Automated first-order provers may then be used to discharge the assertions in particular instances of the pattern, treating program invariants like (1) as axiom schemes.

For patterns that can be specified using just ownership, the Spec# system implements the Boogie methodology using a first-order prover as discussed in the VSTTE paper of Barnett *et al* [9]. Ownership can also be encoded in the JML specification language which is being used in a number of verification systems, as discussed in the VSTTE paper of Leavens and Clifton [27]. There is impressive agreement about syntax but the semantics is neither formalized nor entirely consistent between projects. Within a 5-year time frame it should be possible to provide a foundational logic for JML, encompassing encapsulation (via scope and via auxiliary state), reentrancy, and behavioral subtyping. This would serve to integrate and assess, in particular helping to ensure that the axiomatic semantics embodied in some tools is sound with respect to an (idealized) operational semantics. Concurrency specification is less developed but a sound treatment using strong atomicity assumptions should be within reach [46].

3   Relational Properties

By relational property I mean notions like simulation, where a pair of programs preserve some relation. The most important relational property is preservation of a simulation between implementations of an abstract data type —yielding modular proof of program equivalence or data refinement. Another is noninterference in the sense of secure information flow and dependency analyis [1, 47], which in turn can be used to justify use of impure method calls in specifications [36]. Sampaio *et al* developed a refinement calculus for a subset of Java [16] and implemented a tool that applies general refactoring transformations that are validated on the basis of a theory of data refinement [17].

The latter theory is only sound in the absence of heap sharing. Anindya Banerjee and I have adapted the *inv/own* discipline to support representation independence [7], i.e., soundness of simulations for proof of program equivalence with heap sharing. In five years it should be possible to integrate these theories to encompass refinement and shared heap objects, allowing as units of encapsulations multiple classes and more importantly small configurations of cooperating objects (e.g., a set and its enumerators). An associated milestone would be a refactoring tool, say for Java's Eclipse developments environment, that applies semantically validated transformations.

Benton [12] and Yang [50] propose relational Hoare logics in which the basic correctness condition takes the form

$$\{R\}^{S}_{S'}\{P\} \tag{2}$$

where S and S' are commands, R and Q are relations. The meaning is that running S in parallel with S' on a pair of R-related states yields P-related final states. Amtoft *et al* [3] axiomatize a relational Hoare logic for the special case of noninterference, using special syntax in assertions to specify relations between heap regions for precise reasoning about sharing. These logics merit further development and machine support.

Relational properties can be proved using extant tools for ordinary correctness. The idea is make two copies of the state space and somehow compose the related programs together in such a way that relations are predicates and the relational property is reduced to a Hoare triple [21, 43, 23, 49, 11]. Essentially, (2) is reduced to $\{R\}S; S'\{P\}$. This has been called the *auxiliary variable* technique, Reynolds' method, and *pair composition* among others. Making two copies of a state given by explicit variables is easy; just make a renamed copy of the variables. For the heap, the relevant relations typically involve a partial bijection on addresses [5, 6] and this needs to be encoded in a single heap. I have recently used ghost variables to encode heap-based relations and thereby adapt the pair composition technique to Java programs [35]. This technique can leverage existing verification tools; experiments using ESC/Java2 and Spec# have been promising.

There is a difficulty with this technique. It already appears in the special case of noninterference, where in (2) S' is a renamed copy of S. Terauchi and Aiken [49] experimented with this case, called *self composition*, and found that even when R, P are very weak, a strong assertion is needed at the semicolon in $\{R\}S; S'\{P\}$. They also show how type-based analysis that conservatively approximates noninterference can facilitate automation of self composition technique, by justifying transformation of $S; S'$ into a better, interleaved form. Similar transformations are especially useful for the ghost assignments needed to use the technique with the heap.[3] As I point out in [35], such transformations are exactly the kind Benton aims to account for [12].

It is debatable whether a specialized relational property like noninterference merits much attention in the Program Verifier project. But the importance of data refinement seems clear. While the pair composition technique is attractive in that it can encode relations in an ordinary specification logic like JML, such logics are not so expressive in terms of high level mathematical abstractions. For my small experiments [35], I used ad hoc specifications but in general what is needed is to express the pair encoding of heaps using something like friendship invariants.

Within five years we should be able to develop a theory of relational Hoare logic encompassing the heap and inheritance that is complete and which supports the noninterference transformations as derived laws. We should also be able to extend the theory and implementations of verifiers like ESC/Java2 and Spec# to support a sufficiently expressive specification language for pair composition. This would avoid the need to build tools specific to relational Hoare logic.

4   Design Patterns, Higher Order Logic, and Refinement

Regions of the heap, such as a small configuration of objects and their transitively owned representations, are often the focus of reasoning. Why are heap regions second class? In separation logic, quantification over predicates is needed for interesting specifications, in part because patterns of heap structure are expressed using separation at the level of predicates. Moreover, sound reasoning about invariants depends on them being supported by a definite region of the heap [40]. In the inv/own discipline, relevant sets of objects are determined by $owner$ paths. In neither case are regions directly manipulated. Why not expressions describing regions? Reynolds [45] mentions ghost variables ranging over heaps, but this is not available in extant work on higher order separation logic [15, 13].

Kassios introduced something akin to expressions for regions [25]. He uses model fields to express encapsulation in a way somewhat different from the Boogie approach. Whereas the latter protects $\mathcal{I}(o)$ by restricting it to depend on objects p that record the dependence in an auxiliary field of p (i.e., $p.own$ or $p.deps$), Kassios uses a field of o to hold the refs to all objects on which $\mathcal{I}(o)$ currently depends. The fact that this field conservatively approximates the current footprint of $\mathcal{I}(o)$ can itself be expressed in assertions.[4] Kassios' methodology is quite flexible, in a way reminiscent of separation logic, and it elegantly handles some of the leading examples for the Boogie/friendship discipline. But the development is at an early stage.

In five years it should be possible to specify and verify programs such as application level resource managers by directly describing the heap regions on which they act —

---

[3] A suitable type-based analysis for Java-like programs was developed in [6].

[4] The construct "$f\ frames\ E$" says that the heap objects on which expression E depends are contained in object set f. This is a second order condition, but there appear to be adequate first order laws for reasoning with this as an uninterpreted predicate.

thus making transparent their frame properties. Better still, comparative case studies would serve to assess the alernative approaches we have mentioned.

Region notation would be especially useful for describing configurations of objects in design patterns, now expressed informally with various diagrams. I am aware of no convincing functional specifications for basic design patterns such as Visitor or Observer. Are there useful first-order specifications? Higher order? Absent a general functional specification, how can an instance of the pattern be specified in order to verify "structural integrity" of a system [24] and even functional correctness of the particular instance?

In five years it should at least be possible to verify absence of runtime errors in a 10Kloc Java application making use of inheritance and design patterns such as these.

An interesting aspect of the popularity of design patterns is that software engineers are increasingly familiar with the distinction between abstraction and modular structure in design versus in coding. Java, for example, offers classes and packages but no specialized construct for the visitor pattern or for the iterator pattern. Furthermore, "model driven development" emphasizes the construction of multiple linked artifacts, where again some high level structure need not be manifest in the lower level artifacts such as source code. This trend is hardly surprising to formal methods researchers and indeed it was emphasized long ago by Parnas. It offers some hope in moving away from rigid attachment to feature-rich monolithic languages (see also Abrial's VSTTE paper).

Since object-oriented design patterns show how to embody, in a conventional language, abstractions that are not directly expressed, one can hope for formal specification of a pattern as a refinement. This could provide an alternative to annotations as means to move software engineers towards writing formal specifications.

References

[1] Abadi, M., Banerjee, A., Heintze, N., Riecke, J.G.: A core calculus of dependency. In: ACM Symp. on Princ. of Program. Lang. (POPL) (1999)

[2] Aldrich, J., Chambers, C.: Ownership Domains: Separating Aliasing Policy from Mechanism. In: Odersky, M. (ed.) ECOOP 2004. LNCS, vol. 3086, pp. 1–25. Springer, Heidelberg (2004)

[3] Amtoft, T., Bandhakavi, S., Banerjee, A.: A logic for information flow in object-oriented programs. In: POPL (2006), Extended version available as KSU CIS-TR-2005-1

[4] Banerjee, A., Heintze, N., Riecke, J.G.: Design and correctness of program transformations based on control-flow analysis. In: Kobayashi, N., Pierce, B.C. (eds.) TACS 2001. LNCS, vol. 2215, pp. 420–447. Springer, Heidelberg (2001)

[5] Banerjee, A., Naumann, D.A.: Ownership confinement ensures representation independence for object-oriented programs. Journal of the ACM 52(6), 894–960 (2005)

[6] Banerjee, A., Naumann, D.A.: Stack-based access control for secure information flow. Journal of Functional Programming 15(2), 131–177 (2005)

[7] Banerjee, A., Naumann, D.A.: State Based Ownership, Reentrance, and Encapsulation. In: Black, A.P. (ed.) ECOOP 2005. LNCS, vol. 3586, pp. 387–411. Springer, Heidelberg (2005)

[8] Barnett, M., DeLine, R., Fähndrich, M., Leino, K.R.M., Schulte, W.: Verification of object-oriented programs with invariants. In: Cardelli, L. (ed.) ECOOP 2003. LNCS, vol. 2743, pp. 27–56. Springer, Heidelberg (2003); Journal of Object Technology, 3(6), 27–56, (2004)

[9] Barnett, M., DeLine, R., Jacobs, B., Fähndrich, M., Leino, K.R.M., Schulte, W., Venter, H.: The Spec# programming system: Challenges and directions. In: Meyer, B., Woodcock, J.C.P. (eds.) Verified Software: Theories, Tools, and Experiments (VSTTE 2005). LNCS, vol. 4171, pp. 144–152. Springer, Heidelberg (2008) (this volume)

[10] Barnett, M., Naumann, D.A.: Friends Need a Bit More: Maintaining Invariants Over Shared State. In: Kozen, D. (ed.) MPC 2004. LNCS, vol. 3125, pp. 54–84. Springer, Heidelberg (2004)

[11] Barthe, G., D'Argenio, P.R., Rezk, T.: Secure information flow by self-composition. In: Proceedings of the 17th IEEE Computer Security Foundations Workshop (CSFW 2004), pp. 100–114 (2004)

[12] Benton, N.: Simple relational correctness proofs for static analyses and program transformations. In: ACM Symp. on Princ. of Program. Lang. (POPL), pp. 14–25 (2004)

[13] Biering, B., Birkedal, L., Torp-Smith, N.: BI hyperdoctrines and higher-order separation logic. In: Sagiv, M. (ed.) ESOP 2005. LNCS, vol. 3444, pp. 233–247. Springer, Heidelberg (2005)

[14] Bierman, G., Parkinson, M.: Separation logic and abstraction. In: ACM Symp. on Princ. of Program. Lang (POPL), pp. 247–258 (2005)

[15] Birkedal, L., Torp-Smith, N., Yang, H.: Semantics of separation-logic typing and higher-order frame rules. In: IEEE Symp. on Logic in Computer Science (LICS), pp. 260–269 (2005)

[16] Borba, P., Sampaio, A., Cavalcanti, A., Cornélio, M.: Algebraic reasoning for object-oriented programming. Sci. Comput. Programming 52(1-3), 53–100 (2004)

[17] Cavalcanti, A.L.C., Naumann, D.A.: Forward Simulation for Data Refinement of Classes. In: Eriksson, L.-H., Lindsay, P.A. (eds.) FME 2002. LNCS, vol. 2391, pp. 471–490. Springer, Heidelberg (2002)

[18] Clarke, D.: Object ownership and containment. In: Dissertation, Computer Science and Engineering, University of New South Wales, Australia (2001)

[19] DeLine, R., Fähndrich, M.: The Fugue protocol checker: Is your software baroque (2003), http://research.microsoft.com/~maf/papers.html

[20] Dhara, K.K., Leavens, G.T.: Forcing behavioral subtyping through specification inheritance. In: Proceedings of the 18th International Conference on Software Engineering, Berlin, Germany, March 1996, pp. 258–267. IEEE Computer Society Press, Los Alamitos (1996)

[21] Dijkstra, E.W.: A Discipline of Programming. Prentice-Hall, Englewood Cliffs (1976)

[22] Gamma, E., Helm, R., Johnson, R., Vlissides, J.: Design Patterns: Elements of Reusable Object-Oriented Software. Addison-Wesley, Reading (1995)

[23] Gries, D.: Data refinement and the tranform. In: Broy, M. (ed.) Program Design Calculi, International Summer School at Marktoberdorf, Springer, Heidelberg (1993)

[24] Hoare, T., Misra, J.: Verified software: Theories, tools, experiments. In: Meyer, B., Woodcock, J.C.P. (eds.) Verified Software: Theories, Tools, and Experiments (VSTTE) (2005)

[25] Kassios, I.T.: Dynamic Frames: Support for Framing, Dependencies and Sharing Without Restrictions. In: Misra, J., Nipkow, T., Sekerinski, E. (eds.) FM 2006. LNCS, vol. 4085, pp. 268–283. Springer, Heidelberg (2006)

[26] Klein, G., Nipkow, T.: A machine-checked model for a Java-like language, virtual machine and compiler. ACM Trans. Prog. Lang. Syst (2006)

[27] Leavens, G.T., Clifton, C.: Lessons from the JML project. In: Meyer, B., Woodcock, J.C.P. (eds.) Verified Software: Theories, Tools, and Experiments (VSTTE) (2005)

[28] Leino, K.R.M., Müller, P.: Object Invariants in Dynamic Contexts. In: Odersky, M. (ed.) ECOOP 2004. LNCS, vol. 3086, pp. 491–515. Springer, Heidelberg (2004)

[29] Liskov, B.H., Wing, J.M.: A behavioral notion of subtyping. ACM Trans. Prog. Lang. Syst. 16(6) (1994)

[30] Müller, P.: Modular Specification and Verification of Object-Oriented Programs. LNCS, vol. 2262. Springer, Heidelberg (2002)

[31] Müller, P.: Reasoning about object structures using ownership. In: Meyer, B., Woodcock, J.C.P. (eds.) Verified Software: Theories, Tools, and Experiments (VSTTE 2005) LNCS, vol. 4171, pp. 93–104. Springer, Heidelberg (2008) (this volume)

[32] Naumann, D.A.: Predicate transformer semantics of a higher order imperative language with record subtyping. Sci. Comput. Programming 41(1), 1–51 (2001)

[33] Naumann, D.A.: Assertion-Based Encapsulation, Object Invariants and Simulations. In: de Boer, F.S., Bonsangue, M.M., Graf, S., de Roever, W.-P. (eds.) FMCO 2004. LNCS, vol. 3657, pp. 251–273. Springer, Heidelberg (2005)

[34] Naumann, D.A.: Verifying a Secure Information Flow Analyzer. In: Hurd, J., Melham, T. (eds.) TPHOLs 2005. LNCS, vol. 3603, pp. 211–226. Springer, Heidelberg (2005)

[35] Naumann, D.A.: From Coupling Relations to Mated Invariants for Checking Information Flow. In: Gollmann, D., Meier, J., Sabelfeld, A. (eds.) ESORICS 2006. LNCS, vol. 4189, pp. 279–296. Springer, Heidelberg (2006)

[36] Naumann, D.A.: Observational purity and encapsulation. Theoretical Comput. Sci. (to appear, 2006)

[37] Naumann, D.A., Barnett, M.: Towards imperative modules: Reasoning about invariants and sharing of mutable state (extended abstract). In: IEEE Symp. on Logic in Computer Science (LICS), pp. 313–323 (2004)

[38] Naumann, D.A., Barnett, M.: Towards imperative modules: Reasoning about invariants and sharing of mutable state. Theoretical Comput. Sci. 365, 143–168 (2006); Extended version of [37]

[39] O'Hearn, P.: Scalable specification and reasoning: Technical challenges for program logic. In: Meyer, B., Woodcock, J.C.P. (eds.) Verified Software: Theories, Tools, and Experiments (VSTTE) (2005)

[40] O'Hearn, P., Yang, H., Reynolds, J.: Separation and information hiding. In: ACM Symp. on Princ. of Program. Lang. (POPL), pp. 268–280 (2004)

[41] Parkinson, M.J.: Local reasoning for Java. Technical Report 654, University of Cambridge Computer Laboratory, Dissertation (November 2005)

[42] Reynolds, J.C.: Definitional interpreters for higher-order programming languages. In: Proceedings of the ACM Annual Conference, vol. 2, pp. 717–740. ACM Press, New York (1972)

[43] Reynolds, J.C.: The Craft of Programming. Prentice-Hall, Englewood Cliffs (1981)

[44] Reynolds, J.C.: The essence of Algol. In: de Bakker, J.W., van Vliet, J.C. (eds.) Algorithmic Languages, North-Holland, Amsterdam (1981)

[45] Reynolds, J.C.: An overview of separation logic. In: Meyer, B., Woodcock, J.C.P. (eds.) Verified Software: Theories, Tools, and Experiments (VSTTE 2005) LNCS, vol. 4171, pp. 460–469. Springer, Heidelberg (2008) (this volume)

[46] Rodríguez, E., Dwyer, M., Flanagan, C., Hatcliff, J., Leavens, G.T., Robby, F.: Extending JML for Modular Specification and Verification of Multi-threaded Programs. In: Black, A.P. (ed.) ECOOP 2005. LNCS, vol. 3586, pp. 551–576. Springer, Heidelberg (2005)

[47] Sabelfeld, A., Myers, A.C.: Language-based information-flow security. IEEE J. Selected Areas in Communications 21(1), 5–19 (2003)

[48] Sun, Q., Banerjee, A., Naumann, D.A.: Modular and Constraint-Based Information Flow Inference for an Object-Oriented Language. In: Giacobazzi, R. (ed.) SAS 2004. LNCS, vol. 3148, pp. 84–99. Springer, Heidelberg (2004)

[49] Terauchi, T., Aiken, A.: Secure Information Flow as a Safety Problem. In: Hankin, C., Siveroni, I. (eds.) SAS 2005. LNCS, vol. 3672, pp. 352–367. Springer, Heidelberg (2005)

[50] Yang, H.: Relational separation logic. Theoretical Comput. Sci. (to appear, 2004)

A   Discussion on David Naumann's Presentation

Richard Bornat

One comment and a question, they are both short. One comment is, that you are much closer to separation logic than you realise; we are experimenting with ghost state, too...

David Naumann *(interrupting)*

Look, I am sandwiched between Peter's and Peter's talks... (Editor's note: Peter Müller and Peter O'Hearn.)

Richard Bornat *(interrupting)*

The question is this: those people, who, like me, do not really get object-oriented programming, often form the opinion that inheritance might be related to refinement. This really is a question. Is the notion of behavioral subtyping and specification inheritance a version of that idea? Is it related to that idea? Does it clarify that idea?

David Naumann

It at least ties very closely to that idea, right. The usual formulations of behavioural subtyping allow that the subclasses or subtypes can have different implementations, and then they are tied by an abstraction relationship.

Peter O'Hearn, Queen Mary, University of London

Would there be a way to define this ownership idea in a language that did not have objects, say C? I mean, is it dependent on the object-oriented point of view?

David Naumann

No, certainly not. No, the idea of ownership is being used in verifications. For example, I know someone working on verifying a separation kernel. It is written in C; you want to pay attention to ownership of individual bits in interesting words. So certainly, it is not tied to object-oriented programming. It seems to fit nicely with some existing specification languages, though.

Scalable Specification and Reasoning: Challenges for Program Logic

Peter W. O'Hearn

Queen Mary, University of London

Abstract. If program verification tools are ever to be used widely, it is essential that they work in a modular fashion. Otherwise, verification will not scale. This paper discusses the scientific challenges that this poses for research in program logic. Some recent work on separation logic is described, and test problems that would be useful in measuring advances on modular reasoning are suggested.

1 Introduction

Software verification has seen an upsurge of interest in recent years. Partly this is a result of a convergence that has resulted from maturation of proof tools and lowering of aims, from full behavioural specifications to partial (often safety) properties of a system. Prominent examples include the SLAM model checker [2] and the ESC/Java static assertion checker [19,14]. But modularity is a problem.

Modularity is essential for scalable specification and reasoning. If we find ourselves in a position where the specification of one program component must talk about all other components in a system, or the states of other components, then we will very quickly be overwhelmed by the complexity of specifications. Programming features such as pointers (in various of their guises), concurrency and reflection raise particularly challenging problems for program logic. Simple methods for achieving modularity, such as listing the variables that might change (using "modifies" clauses), are not sufficient for common programs written in widely-used languages, which feature complex and dynamically changing interconnections between program components.

The problem faced by program logic is not an in-principle one – being able to describe behaviours at all – but rather is one of tractability. For example, when one considers programs with pointers and concurrency, reasoning with traditional program logic can become so complex as to be detached from computational intuition. The best way to illustrate this claim is with examples, and I consider three, describing what the more general technical challenges are as we go along. Some relevant work on separation logic [46,26,37,47] is described, and the promise of and problems for this approach are discussed. Finally, some wholly unresolved problems are mentioned.

There are many obstacles facing any Program Verifier challenge project [24] – particularly, the strength of theorem provers – and I am not saying that full solutions to the problems I discuss are necessary for it to have some success. My

B. Meyer and J. Woodcock (Eds.): Verified Software, LNCS 4171, pp. 116–133, 2008.

aim here is just to communicate some unsolved problems in program logic which, if progress were made on them, could have a considerable positive impact.

2 Framing and Indirection

I begin with a simple program and consider how one might specify it using traditional Floyd-Hoare logic. The specification is found to be unsatisfactory, and then is amended to provide a technically correct one. It is then argued that this technically correct specification is conceptually wrong.

2.1 An Incorrect Specification

Consider a procedure for disposing a tree, held as a linked structure in memory.

```
procedure DispTree(p)
local i, j;
if  p≠nil then
    i = p→l ; j:= p→r;
    DispTree(i);
    DispTree(j);
    dispose(p)
```

This is the expected procedure that walks a tree, recursively disposing left and right subtrees and then the root pointer. It uses a representation of tree nodes with left, right and data fields, and the empty tree is represented by nil.

A first attempt at a specification might be something like

$$\{\text{tree}(p) \wedge \text{reach}(p, n)\} \ \text{DispTree}(p) \ \{\neg\texttt{allocated}(n)\}$$

assuming that we have defined the predicates that say when p points to a (binary) tree in memory, when n is reachable (following l and r links) from p, and when n is allocated. This spec says that any node n which is in the tree pointed to by p is not allocated on conclusion.

While this specification says part of what we would like to say, it leaves too much unsaid. It does not say what the procedure does to nodes that are not in the tree; we have left out the notorious *frame axioms* [33].

The result is that, while the specification is something that we would expect to be true of the procedure, it is too weak to use at many call sites. For example, consider the first recursive call, DispTree(i), to dispose the left subtree. If we use the specification (instantiating p by i) as an hypothesis, in the usual way when reasoning about recursive procedures [22], then we have a problem. For, the specification does not rule out the possibility that the procedure call alters the right subtree j, perhaps creating a cycle or even disposing some of its nodes. As a consequence, when we come to the second call DispTree(j), we will not know that the required tree(j) part of the precondition will hold. So our reasoning will get stuck.

The moral of this story is that [37]

if one does not have some way of representing or inferring frame axioms, then the proofs of even simple programs with procedure calls will not go through.

The `DispTree` program makes this point especially vivid because of its use of recursion, where the spec and the call sites have to get along:

for recursive programs attention to framing is essential if one is to obtain strong enough induction hypotheses.

The problem does not depend on having low-level operations such as pointer disposal. For example, specifying tree copying leads to similar difficulties.

2.2   An Unfortunate Fix

How can we fix the specification of `DispTree`? Here is my attempt:

$\{$tree$(p) \wedge$ reach$(p, n) \wedge \neg$reach$(p, m) \wedge$ allocated$(m) \wedge m.f = m' \wedge$
$\neg$allocated$(q)\}$
DispTree(p)
$\{\neg$allocated$(n) \wedge \neg$reach$(p, m) \wedge$ allocated$(m) \wedge m.f = m' \wedge$
$\neg$allocated$(q)\}$

This says, in addition, that any allocated cell not reachable from p has the same contents in memory and that any previously unallocated cell remains unallocated. The additional clauses are the frame axioms. (I am assuming that m, m', n and q are auxiliary variables, guaranteed not to be altered. The reason why, say, the predicate $\neg$allocated(q) could conceivably change, even if q is constant, is that the allocated predicate refers to a behind-the-scenes heap component. f is used in the spec as an arbitrary field name.)

I *believe* that this specification is strong enough to prove the procedure, but I have never attempted to carry out a proof. It would be complex. But, more importantly, I believe that the specification is badly wrong from a conceptual point of view.

The problem is not that we cannot specify `DispTree` at all, but rather is that final specification makes ugly statements about what is not reachable and what is not allocated that have, really, nothing to do with the program. Programmers *think locally*, and when reasoning about a program they concentrate on the resources that are relevant to its correct operating [37]. The need to state these frame axioms explicitly is violently at odds with programming intuition. So, even if technically alright, I view such a specification as conceptually wrong, a symptom of a problem in program logic.

2.3   The Frame Problem

The frame problem is that, traditionally, an inordinate amount of effort needs to be spent specifying what a program doesn't change, so much so that these frame axioms distract from the main concern – what changes [33]. In the absence of pointers what doesn't change can be succinctly summarized using modifies clauses, which list the program variables corresponding to locations that can be altered by a program. But, in the presence of pointers of other forms of indirect addressing the relevant locations are not always directly named by program variables, and the idea of modifies clause is then much more difficult to make work. The unhappy consequence is that sound, modular specification methods are lacking for widely-used programming languages such as C and Java.

A full solution to the frame problem would allow us to make a positive statement about what changes, like in our first, faulty, specification, with the frame axioms coming along for free. A partial solution would at least let us represent the frame axioms compactly and intuitively.

The frame problem is extremely irritating. When you see it, you expect that there should be some sort of easy solution. It should be possible for a specification to say just what is relevant, like in our first specification of DispTree, and for the rest (the frame axioms) to come along for free. I have often felt that way.

The frame problem has been intensely studied in AI, and there are too many papers to survey here; I mention only one, the extremely clear paper of Reiter [44], which can serve as a good introduction to the problem. Unfortunately, there has been little crossover work applying the techniques there to programs (a notable exception is [9]). Although the frame problem is irritating, it is genuine, and a central problem in modular reasoning. But it is not the whole story, as we shall see in later sections.

The frame problem is stated above in a decidedly negative manner. I prefer to take a more positive perspective [37]:

> When specifying a program, it should be possible to concentrate exclusively on the information (data, resources, etc) that is relevant to its correct operating. Any information it is independent of should not have to be mentioned.

3   Separation Logic

The separation logic specification of DispTree is just

$$\{\mathsf{tree}(p)\}\,\mathtt{DispTree}(p)\,\{\mathsf{empty}\}$$

which says that if you have a tree at the beginning then you end up with the empty heap at the end. And the proof is very simple. The crucial part, in the else branch, looks like this:

$$\{p\mapsto[l\colon x, r\colon y] * \mathsf{tree}(x) * \mathsf{tree}(y)\}$$
$$i := p{\to}l;\ j := p{\to}r;$$
$$\{p\mapsto[l\colon i, r\colon j] * \mathsf{tree}(i) * \mathsf{tree}(j)\}$$
$$\mathtt{DispTree}(i);$$
$$\{p\mapsto[l\colon i, r\colon j] * \mathsf{tree}(j)\}$$
$$\mathtt{DispTree}(j);$$
$$\{p\mapsto[l\colon i, r\colon j]\}$$
$$\mathtt{dispose}\ p;$$
$$\{\mathsf{empty}\}$$

After we enter the conditional statement we know that $p \neq$nil, so that p is an allocated node that points to left and right subtrees occupying separate storage. Then the roots of the two subtrees are loaded into i and j. Notice how the proof steps then follow operational intuition. The first recursive call removes the left subtree, the second call removes the right subtree, and the final instruction removes the root pointer p. This verification is carried out using the procedure specification as an assumption, as in the usual treatment of recursive procedures in Hoare logic [22].

I have just given you a proof snippet in what is probably an unfamiliar formalism, so some explanation is in order. To understand separation logic intuitively you should think in terms of *heaplets*, portions of heap, rather than the whole global heap. The separating conjunction $P * Q$ holds of a given heaplet if it can be split into two disjoint heaplets, one of which satisfies P and the other of which satisfies Q. So, the assertion $p \mapsto [l: i, r: j] * \text{tree}(i) * \text{tree}(j)$ describes a portion of heap with a pointer p that points to a record with l and r fields holding values i and j that themselves point to trees. The use of $*$ indicates that there is no overlap between p and i's tree and j's tree.

A question that often comes up is whether a pointer can go from one $*$-conjunct to another. The answer is yes. For instance, $p \mapsto [l: i, r: j]$ describes just a single cell, p, whose contents i and j point across $*$ into other heaplets in $p \mapsto [l: i, r: j] * \text{tree}(i) * \text{tree}(j)$. it helps to use a graphical intuition: take a directed graph, and then draw a line, partitioning it in two. Some of the links in the graph will go over the partition. The p to the left of $\mapsto$ corresponds to the sources of links to targets i and j.

There is a subtle point in the specification of `DispTree` that the reader might have noticed: In order to get the empty heap in the postcondition the precondition must say that "p points to a tree, *and there are no other cells in the given heaplet*". For, if there were other cells then you could not conclude `empty`, those cells that were not originally in the tree would still be around. This "no other cells" aspect is treated implicitly in separation logic. The tree predicate satisfies the recursive specification

$$\text{tree}(E) \iff (E=\text{nil} \wedge \text{ empty})$$
$$\vee\ (\exists x, y.\ E \mapsto l: x, r: y * \text{tree}(x) * \text{tree}(y))$$

where the use of `empty` when $E=$nil leads, inductively, to $\text{tree}(E)$ not having additional cells.

Finally, there is a crucial interplay between the separating conjunction and a "tight" interpretation of Hoare triples [37,51,50]. A specification $\{P\}C\{Q\}$ means that C will (if it terminates) transform a heaplet satisfying P into one satisfying Q. It does this transformation in an in-place fashion, leaving the global heap surrounding the input heaplet unchanged. This in-place aspect can be seen clearly in the proof steps. For instance, for the first recursive call to `DispTree` the precondition is $p \mapsto [l: i, r: j] * \text{tree}(i) * \text{tree}(j)$, and this does not match up with the overall specification, which would expect only $\text{tree}(i)$. What we do is use the overall specification to replace tree(i) by empty, obtaining $p \mapsto [l: i, r: j] * $ empty$*$ tree(j), and then we can take one further step using the identity empty$* P \leftrightarrow P$.

These intuitions about heaplets and in-place update are codified in an inference rule, the frame rule

$$\frac{\{P\}\, C\, \{Q\}}{\{R * P\}\, C\, \{R * Q\}} \quad \text{ModifiesOnly}(C) \cap \text{free}(R) = \emptyset$$

The R here is a frame axiom. The idea of this rule is that if C works on a portion of heap described by P, then it will not alter any additional heaplet described by R. There is also a side condition which has to do with named variables; e.g., the i and j in DispTree. (It is an embarassment that the heap is treated more cleanly than simple variables here, and we hope someday to get rid of the variable conditions altogether; see [10].)

As it is a relatively recent development, research on mechanized reasoning with separation logic is just beginning. The Smallfoot static assertion checker discovers proofs of lightweight shape specifications done using the logic [5]. And there are developing applications using interactive proof tools [32,49] and abstract interpretation [17,12,7,20,21].

4   Independence, Interference and Concurrency

Reasoning about concurrency is a subject that has received significant attention, and for good reason. The tremendous number of potential interactions between concurrent processes makes concurrent programs hard to grasp; a successful Program Verifier could provide considerable help to the concurrent programmer.

But, though it has received much attention, the difficulties that the theory meets on even simple examples are not as widely appreciated as perhaps they ought to be. To illustrate, I consider a very simple program: parallel mergesort.

```
{ array(a, i, j) }
procedure ms(a, i, j)
local m:= (i+j)/2;
if   i < j then
     (ms(a, i, m) ‖ ms(a, m+1, j));
     merge(a, i, m + 1, j);
{ sorted(a, i, j) }
```

For simplicity this specification just says that the final array is sorted, not that it is a permutation of the initial array.

Now, this program displays a trivial form of concurrency: *disjoint concurrency*. The recursive calls are completely independent, because they act on disjoint array segments. And yet, the program causes immediate difficulties for all of the best known proof methods.

Hoare had provided a beautiful rule for disjoint concurrency [23]

$$\frac{\{P\}C\{Q\} \qquad \{P'\}C'\{Q'\}}{\{P \wedge P'\}C \parallel C'\{Q \wedge Q'\}}$$

where C does not modify any variables free in P', C', Q', and conversely. Unfortunately, using this rule we cannot reason about the parallel calls in mergesort, because Hoare logic treats array-component assignment globally, where an assignment to $a[i]$ is viewed as an assignment to the entire array

$$\{P[(a \mid i\colon E)/a]\} \, a[i]\colon= E \, \{P\}$$

In this view the two parallel calls to ms are judged to be altering the *same* variable, a. So, the rule does not apply.

Cliff Jones has proposed a powerful approach to reasoning about concurrency, in his rely-guarantee formalism [27] (see also, [34]). For this example, we would add two conditions to the pre/post specification, formalizing the

- **Rely:** No other process touches my array segment $array(a, i, j)$; and
- **Guarantee:** I do not touch any storage outside my segment $array(a, i, j)$.

The Guarantee condition here is something like a frame axiom. The Rely, however, goes beyond the frame issue (one might fancifully consider it a kind of inverse frame axiom).

The point of this example is that it illustrates a breakdown of modularity. The guarantee condition (when formalized) talks about parts of the array not touched by a procedure call. In the worst case, this would have to be extended to other parts of memory than the single array given as a parameter. The issue is not just the cost for individual steps of reasoning, but rather that the rely and guarantee conditions, which are present to deal with subtle issues of interference, complicate the specification itself, even when no interference is present.

I have focussed on rely-guarantee here because is rightly lauded as providing a compositional approach to reasoning about concurrency. My point is that compositionality in program text does not guarantee locality in reasoning about resources such as program state: compositional reasoning can be extremely global. Also, I used a pre/post specification just because it is appropriate to the example, but the same modularity problem I have described here arises as well in temporal logics.

Because it is intuitively about separation, this example can be treated very easily in a concurrent extension of separation logic [39,11]. The crucial part of the proof is the following proof figure for the parallel composition.

$$\{array(a, i, m) \, * \, array(a, m+1, j)\}$$

$$
\begin{array}{ccc}
\{array(a, i, m)\} & & \{array(a, m+1, j)\} \\
\mathrm{ms}(a, i, m) & \parallel & \mathrm{ms}(a, m+1, j) \\
\{sorted(a, i, m)\} & & \{sorted(a, m+1, j)\}
\end{array}
$$

$$\{sorted(a, i, m) \, * \, sorted(a, m+1, j)\}$$

The use of the $*$ connective in $array(a, i, m) \, * \, array(a, m+1, j)\}$ implies that the array segments occupy separate memory, and we can then use a proof rule

$$\frac{\{P\}C\{Q\} \qquad \{P'\}C'\{Q'\}}{\{P * P'\}C \parallel C'\{Q * Q'\}}$$

that lets us reason independently about the two processes independently.

This rule is, of course, a descendent of Hoare's rule for disjoint concurrency. There are two reasons why we are able to treat this example where the original rule was not: (i) the assignment $a[i] := e$ is not viewed by separation logic as an assignment to a, but rather to a single cell; (ii) $*$ can be used to describe partitioning of an array that is dynamic, depending on the program state.

My remarks on the rely-guarantee method should be taken in the right spirit: Indeed, they agree with a criticism of it lodged by Jones himself [28]. What he wants, and what I want, is a way to use complex methods where necessary to deal with interference when it is present, but to contain this complexity and default to simpler specification forms for interfaces between components that do not interfere with one another. The desire is to prevent *interference flooding*, where the mere possibility of interference complicates the specification notation, even in situations where there is a great degree of independence.

I do not claim that concurrent separation logic in its current state is the answer. It is good at specifying independence, but struggles with tightly-coupled, interfering processes. In contrast, rely-guarantee is good at describing interference, but is not well oriented to specifications of independent processes. Recently, there have been attempts to marry the advantages of concurrent separation logic and rely/guarantee [41,18]; these are perhaps further steps on the way to modular reasoning about (shared variable) concurrent processes.

5   Information Hiding

Pointers can wreak havoc with data abstraction. It is difficult to keep track of aliases, different copies of the same address, and so it is difficult to know when there are no pointers into the internals of a module. This problem has received attention in the object-oriented types community in work on ownership and confinement [13,3], stemming Hogg's colorful declaration "that objects provide encapsulation is the big lie of object-oriented programming [25]". Further difficulties, beyond confinement, are caused by low-level features such as address arithmetic and storage deallocation.

A good initial challenge which illustrated many issues is a resource management module, that provides primitives for allocating and deallocating resources which are held in a local free list. A client program should not alter the free list, except through the provided primitives; for example, the client should not tie a cycle in the free list. However, it is entirely possible for a client program to hold an alias to an element of the free list, after a deallocation operation is performed.

As an example, suppose that we have written our own memory manager, with operations `alloc(x)` and `free(x)` for allocating and deallocating records, where our implementation uses a free list in the usual way. A first attempt at specification might be something like

$$\{\texttt{allocated}(y) \wedge y.f = m \wedge \neg\texttt{allocated}(z)\}$$
$$\texttt{alloc}(x)$$
$$\{\texttt{allocated}(y) \wedge y.f = m \wedge \texttt{allocated}(x) \wedge y \neq x$$
$$\wedge (z \neq x \Rightarrow \neg\texttt{allocated}(z))\}$$

$$\{\texttt{allocated}(y) \wedge y.f = m \wedge \texttt{allocated}(x) \wedge y \neq x \wedge \neg\texttt{allocated}(z)\}$$
$$\texttt{free}(x)$$
$$\{\texttt{allocated}(y) \wedge y.f = m \wedge \neg\texttt{allocated}(x) \wedge y \neq x \wedge \neg\texttt{allocated}(z)\}$$

where, in addition to saying that x is allocated or deallocated, I have included a lot of frame axioms. I admit to some unease, I am not sure I have got the frame axioms exactly right (echoing the discussion from earlier), but there is a further problem I want to show, so let us assume that these are indeed the correct frame axioms. Here, I am again assuming that all variables other than x are auxiliary variables that are guaranteed not to be changed, and that $\{x\}$ is the entire modifies set of the specs (modifies for variables, not heap cells).

The further problem is that this specification does not stop a user of the memory manager from corrupting the free list, breaking the abstraction. For example, a sequence of statements

$$\texttt{alloc}(x) \,;\;\; \texttt{free}(x) \,;\, x{\rightarrow}r{:=}\,x$$

might tie a cycle in the free list, if the implementation uses the r field to point to the next record in the free list.

We can get around this problem by adding an invariant to the specifications. To each precondition and postcondition we add a predicate $\texttt{freelist}(free)$ saying that variable $free$ used by the manager points to a linked list without cycles, and where $\neg\texttt{allocated}(n)$ holds for each element in the list.

This fix, though, has come at great cost: we have exposed the invariant describing the ostensibly private storage of the memory management module. To see the cost, suppose a program makes use of n different modules. It would be unfortunate if we had to complicate specifications of user procedures by including descriptions of the internal resources of all modules that might be accessed. A change to a module's internal representation would necessitate altering the specifications of all other procedures that use it.

Stated plainly,

> *information hiding should be the bedrock of modular reasoning, but it is difficult to support soundly*

and this presents a great challenge for research in program logic.

This sort of example has been successfully treated in separation logic [38]. The details are much more involved than the earlier examples, and I will not give the proof here. The basic idea is that the $*$ connective allows the separation of the state owned by a client and the state owned by the manager (the free list). Crucially, since $*$ is a logical connective, the partition it describes can change over time: in a sense, the logic tracks the right to dereference a cell transfers back and forth between client and module.

6   The Boogie Methodology and Relatives

Many of the issues touched on in this paper have also been approached in work on the "Boogie methodology" [30,36,4], and also in its precursors (see [29]). The basic idea of Boogie it to use certain auxiliary variables, such as ones to describe "ownership" of heap cells, to structure specifications and to constrain who can access what and when. Boogie builds on type systems for ownership [13,16], but uses assertions rather than types. Ownership gives a way to express a form of separation, and frame axioms are avoided by using general invariants which relate the states of auxiliary variables and the program state. The auxiliary variables allow fine control over when certain assertions, such as object invariants, must hold; this has allowed a novel approach to the old and vexing problem of object invariants for re-entrant modules (which allow implicit or explicit recursion).

I discussed an example similar to the first one in this paper with Peter Müller (we discussed copytree rather than disposetree). The early versions of Boogie could not handle that example due to inadequate framing properties, but a later version [31] could. Conversely, the earliest approach to information hiding using separation logic [38] could not handle re-entrant modules, but the later approach of [40] can. As shown in [8], the approach pioneered in [40] can be understood as using quantified predicates in a way that is analogous to the use of polymorphic typing to account for hiding of internal representation types [45,35]. On the other hand, Boogie has "pack" and "unpack" primitives which are intuitively similar to the corresponding primitives for existential types.

I just wanted to mention Boogie, to acknowledge (and point the reader to) the advances it and its relatives have made on difficult problems concerning modular reasoning about object-oriented programs. The exact relationship between Boogie and separation logic is not clear; there are similarities in intuition, but many differences in technique. The reader is referred to [29] for more information on this line of work, including work on ESC/Java and JML that I have not mentioned here.

7   Conclusion

In this paper I wanted to show some difficulties as regards modularity that traditional program logic has on even simple examples, and how it is not impossible to do much better, at least on those examples. In doing this I purposely started from programs rather than specifications; it is a good way to show where formalisms have difficulties. There are many other, more difficult, programs that can serve as challenging test cases.

Although I enjoy starting from programs, I would also love to be able to arrive at the kinds of program I considered by refinement, starting from a simple specification. I just don't know how to do so. The refinement formalisms that I am aware of (VDM, B, etc) are based on a static form of modularity, where the state that a program component can change is listed in a fixed collection of variables, and the frame properties used are with respect to modifies clauses for these variables. This fixed modularity does not deal well when the partitions between the state used by program components is more dynamic, as is the case in parallel mergesort, in the resource manager example, and typically in systems programs. Of course, this last point should be taken as a challenge. It seems inconceivable that the modularity issues that separation logic and Boogie attempt to address should not show up as well on a design level. Furthermore, there are all sorts of dynamic, interconnected structures other than the program heap, those obtained from networks and message passing being prime examples. One might hope for a design formalism (say, an analogue of B or Z) that goes beyond static modularity, and that has the specific heap modularity of separation logic or Boogie as an instance.

Similar remarks apply to my focus on imperative programs, and shared-variable concurrency. A good problem would be to obtain a reasoning formalism for, say, the pi-calculus or for socket programs that displays the same sort of modularity in its account of channel usage as separation logic or Boogie does for the heap.

All of the examples in this paper have concerned safety properties. Recently, there has been progress on automatic proofs of liveness properties properties of software, using novel applications of abstract interpretation [42,15,6]. The problem of modular, or local, specifications and verifications of liveness properties of concurrent processes looms as an extremely difficult one; see [48,1] for important work in this direction.

Finally, one might question whether modular reasoning methods for software are in general even possible. In temporal logic there have been negative technical results [43], and we should be on the lookout for others. But, there has been considerable progress on modular reasoning about programs and this author, for one, plans to continue searching.

References

1. Amadi, M., Lamport, L.: Composing specifications. ACM TOPLAS 15(1), 73–132 (1993)
2. Ball, T., Cook, B., Levin, V., Rajamani, S.K.: SLAM and Static Driver Verifier: Technology Transfer of Formal Methods inside Microsoft. In: Boiten, E.A., Derrick, J., Smith, G.P. (eds.) IFM 2004. LNCS, vol. 2999, pp. 1–20. Springer, Heidelberg (2004)
3. Banerjee, A., Naumann, D.A.: Ownership confinement ensures representation independence for object-oriented programs. J.ACM (to appear, 2005)
4. Barnett, M., DeLine, R., Fahndrich, M., Leino, K.R.M., Schulte, W.: Verification of object-oriented programs with invariants. Journal of Object Technology 3(6), 27–56 (2004)
5. Berdine, J., Calcagno, C., O'Hearn, P.W.: Smallfoot: Automatic modular assertion checking with separation logic. In: 4th FMCO, pp. 115–137 (2006)

6. Berdine, J., Chawdhary, A., Cook, B., Distefano, D., O'Hearn, P.W.: Variance analyses from invariance analyses. In: 34th POPL, pp. 211–224 (2007)
7. Berdine, J., Cook, B., Distefano, D., O'Hearn, P.W., Wies, T., Yang, H.: Shape Analysis for Composite Data Structures. In: Damm, W., Hermanns, H. (eds.) CAV 2007. LNCS, vol. 4590, pp. 178–192. Springer, Heidelberg (2007)
8. Biering, B., Birkedal, L., Torp-Smith, N.: BI-hyperdoctrines, higher-order separation logic, and abstraction. ACM TOPLAS (to appear, 2007)
9. Borgida, A., Mylopoulos, J., Reiter, R.: On the frame problem in procedure specifications. IEEE Transactions of Software Engineering 21, 809–838 (1995)
10. Bornat, R., Calcagno, C., Yang, H.: Variables as resources in separation logic. In: 19th MFPS (2005)
11. Brookes, S.D.: A semantics for concurrent separation logic. In: Gardner, P., Yoshida, N. (eds.) CONCUR 2004. LNCS, vol. 3170, pp. 227–270. Springer, Heidelberg (2004)
12. Calcagno, C., Distefano, D., O'Hearn, P.W., Yang, H.: Beyond reachability: Shape abstraction in the presence of pointer arithmetic. In: Yi, K. (ed.) SAS 2006. LNCS, vol. 4134, pp. 182–203. Springer, Heidelberg (2006)
13. Clarke, D., Noble, J., Potter, J.: Simple ownership types for object containment. In: Knudsen, J.L. (ed.) ECOOP 2001. LNCS, vol. 2072, pp. 53–76. Springer, Heidelberg (2001)
14. Cok, D., Kiniry, J.: ESC/Java2: Uniting ESC/Java and JML. In: CASSIS, pp. 108–128 (2004)
15. Cook, B., Podelski, A., Rybalchenko, A.: Termination proofs for systems code. In: 13th PLDI (2006)
16. Dietl, W., Müller, P.: Universes: Lightweight ownership for JML. Journal of Object Technology (JOT) (to appear, 2005)
17. Distefano, D., O'Hearn, P., Yang, H.: A local shape analysis based on separation logic. In: 12th TACAS, pp. 287–302 (2006)
18. Feng, X., Ferreira, R., Shao, Z.: On the Relationship Between Concurrent Separation Logic and Assume-Guarantee Reasoning. In: De Nicola, R. (ed.) ESOP 2007. LNCS, vol. 4421, pp. 173–188. Springer, Heidelberg (2007)
19. Flanagan, C., Leino, K.R.M., Lillibridge, M., Nelson, G., Saxe, J.B., Stata, R.: Extended static checking for Java. In: 9th PLDI (2002)
20. Gotsman, A., Berdine, J., Cook, B., Sagiv, M.: Thread-modular shape analysis. In: PLDI (to appear, 2007)
21. Guo, B., Vachharajani, N., August, D.: Shape analysis with inductive recursion synthesis. In: PLDI (to appear, 2007)
22. Hoare, C.A.R.: Procedures and parameters: An axiomatic approach. In: Engler, E. (ed.) Symposium on the Semantics of Algebraic Languages. Lecture Notes in Math. vol. 188, pp. 102–116. Springer, Heidelberg (1971)
23. Hoare, C.A.R.: Towards a theory of parallel programming. In: Hoare, Perrot (eds.) Operating Systems Techniques, Academic Press, London (1972)
24. Hoare, C.A.R.: The verifying compiler: A grand challenge for computing research. J. ACM 50(1), 63–69 (2003)
25. Hogg, J.: Islands: aliasing protection in object-oriented languages. In: 6th OOPSLA (1991)
26. Isthiaq, S., O'Hearn, P.W.: BI as an assertion language for mutable data structures. In: 28th ACM SIGPLAN-SIGACT Symposium on Principles of Programming Languages, London, January 2001, pp. 36–49 (2001)

27. Jones, C.B.: Specification and design of (parallel) programs. In: IFIP Conference (1983)

28. Jones, C.B.: Wanted: A compositional approach to concurrency. In: McIver, A., Morgan, C. (eds.) Programming Methodology, pp. 1–15. Springer, Heidelberg (2003)

29. Leavens, G.T., Leino, K.R.M., Müller, P.: Specification and verification challenges for sequential object-oriented programs. In: Formal Aspects of Computing (to appear, 2007)

30. Leino, K.R.M., Müller, P.: Object Invariants in Dynamic Contexts. In: Odersky, M. (ed.) ECOOP 2004. LNCS, vol. 3086, pp. 491–515. Springer, Heidelberg (2004)

31. Leino, K.R.M., Müller, P.: A Verification Methodology for Model Fields. In: Sestoft, P. (ed.) ESOP 2006 and ETAPS 2006. LNCS, vol. 3924, pp. 115–130. Springer, Heidelberg (2006)

32. Marti, N., Affeldt, R., Yonezawa, A.: Verification of the heap manager of an operating system using separation logic. In: Proceedings of the 3rd SPACE Workshop, Charleston (2006)

33. McCarthy, J., Hayes, P.: Some philosophical problems from the standpoint of artificial intelligence. In: Machine Intelligence, vol. 4, pp. 463–502 (1969)

34. Misra, J., Chandy, K.M.: Proofs of networks of processes. IEEE Trans. Software Eng. 7(4), 417–426 (1981)

35. Mitchell, J.C., Plotkin, G.D.: Abstract types have existential types. ACM Trans. Programming Languages and Systems 10(3), 470–502 (1988)

36. Naumann, D.A., Barnett, M.: Towards imperative modules: Reasoning about invariants and sharing of mutable state. In: 19th LICS, pp. 313–323 (2004)

37. O'Hearn, P., Reynolds, J., Yang, H.: Local reasoning about programs that alter data structures. In: Proceedings of 15th Annual Conference of the European Association for Computer Science Logic. LNCS, pp. 1–19. Springer, Heidelberg (2001)

38. O'Hearn, P.W., Yang, H., Reynolds, J.C.: Separation and information hiding. In: 31st POPL, pp. 268–280 (2004)

39. O'Hearn, P.W.: Resources, Concurrency and Local Reasoning. In: Gardner, P., Yoshida, N. (eds.) CONCUR 2004. LNCS, vol. 3170, pp. 49–67. Springer, Heidelberg (2004)

40. Parkinson, M., Bierman, G.: Separation logic and abstraction. In: Proceedings of POPL (2005)

41. Parkinson, M., Vafeiadis, V.: A Marriage of Rely/Guarantee and Separation Logic. In: Caires, L., Vasconcelos, V.T. (eds.) CONCUR. LNCS, vol. 4703, pp. 256–271. Springer, Heidelberg (2007)

42. Podelski, A., Rybalchenko, A.: Transition invariants. In: 19th LICS (2004)

43. Rabinovich, A.: On compositionality and its limitations. ACM TOCL 8(1), 73–132 (2007)

44. Reiter, R.: The frame problem in the situation calculus: a simple solution (sometimes) and a completeness result for goal regression. In: Lifschitz, V. (ed.) Artificial Intelligence and Mathematical Theory of Computation: Papers in Honor of John McCarthy, pp. 359–380. Academic Press, London (1991)

45. Reynolds, J.C.: Types, abstraction and parametric polymorphism. In: Proceedings of IFIP (1983)

46. Reynolds, J.C.: Intuitionistic reasoning about shared mutable data structure. In: Davies, J., Roscoe, B., Woodcock, J. (eds.) Millennial Perspectives in Computer Science, Houndsmill, Hampshire, Palgrave, pp. 303–321 (2000)

47. Reynolds, J.C.: Separation logic: A logic for shared mutable data structures. In: 17th LICS, pp. 55–74 (2002)
48. Stark, E.W.: A proof technique for rely/guarantee properties. In: Maheshwari, S.N. (ed.) FSTTCS 1985. LNCS, vol. 206, pp. 369–391. Springer, Heidelberg (1985)
49. Tuch, H., Klein, G., Norrish, M.: Types, bytes, and separation logic. In: 34th POPL (2007)
50. Yang, H.: Local Reasoning for Stateful Programs. Ph.D. thesis, University of Illinois, Urbana-Champaign (2001)
51. Yang, H., O'Hearn, P.W.: A Semantic Basis for Local Reasoning. In: Nielsen, M., Engberg, U. (eds.) ETAPS 2002 and FOSSACS 2002. LNCS, vol. 2303, Springer, Heidelberg (2002)

A Discussion on Peter O'Hearn's Presentation

Willem-Paul de Roever

You presented two examples explaining why concurrency and pointer manipulation are complicated. Actually, you needed only one example, the first one, because if you look at its scheme, it is part of the concurrent garbage collector of Dijkstra, Lamport and Scholten. And if you have concurrently with this a so-called mutator program, which changes the links, this marking strategy, which you give, is wrong. This was the famous error of these three persons in 1976. This is what you just took, that is the famous error.

Peter O'Hearn

No, the point I am making is that the specifications will be far more complicated. I was not trying to point out an error in a program. Perhaps I misunderstood what you said.

Willem-Paul de Roever: No, you used two examples...

Peter O'Hearn: Yes.

Willem-Paul de Roever: ...you could have used one example.

Peter O'Hearn: Oh yes, I could use a specially prepared example...

Willem-Paul de Roever: No, no, this one!

Peter O'Hearn:

I could have used a parallel-disposed tree, and that would have shown both of my points. But the other point, I wanted to make is, even with our pointers, even with simpler examples than concurrency, we still have more complex specifications than we would like.

Willem-Paul de Roever: OK.

Peter O'Hearn: Oh, but your point is taken.

Willem-Paul de Roever: Yes, OK.

Peter Schmitt

I want to come back to the frame problem. A method that turned out to work pretty well for us is to use this modifies or assignable clause from JML. So, we specify: It is only these elements, only these expressions that might change. But this [example] needs an additional twist, because here, you refer to an unbounded number of elements. But we have these star notations or reachable notations, and, including this, it turned out that it worked pretty well.

Peter O'Hearn

I believe that it works. Many things have been tried that worked pretty well. But the problem here is that the things that are changed are not named by a fixed, finite number of program identifiers, and so the simple approach to modifies clauses would not work for an example like this. There might be more subtle approaches, but I would repeat one thing: that the frame problem was set down 35 years ago or so. And I think, there is still no general solution, and so... I would love to see any approaches people have to solve these problems apart from separation logic!

Peter Schmitt

My point is, we do not need a general solution, we need a solution here in programming logic context, and you are right, we need a more subtle mechanism. So we need a way to describe: We want to address all locations that are reachable from some node by all the L- and R-operations. But the machinery is there to do this.

Peter O'Hearn

Is there to do what? Is there to specify the frame axioms? The problem is not to have to write the frame axioms, yes?

Peter Schmitt

Oh, what you have to do is to specify in the assignable clauses all the elements that get at most changed. That is what you have to do.

Egon Börger, University of Pisa

I think, you have a problem with the approach. Let us look at what people do in mathematics. They never would complicate a definition for the reason that during the attempt to prove something by induction, you need a stronger hypothesis at the inductive step. You see? So, separating definitions-that means specifications and what you need for the proofs-I think this is really crucial for being able to do challenging proofs of really relevant properties. Now, I know that this is heretical in this community for many of my colleagues, but if you mix up these two things, you will always be in full trouble.

Peter O'Hearn

I understand what you are saying. To repeat what he is saying: We might want a simpler spec for use, and a more complicated spec to have a strong enough induction hypothesis. But the problem is, the simple spec won't be usable at very many call sites, even not just these two call sites. So, I agree with what you say, but I don't agree that this impacts this problem.

Rustan Leino

I wondered what you thought of the abstraction dependencies or the data groups or the Boogie methodology for handling the frame problem.

Peter O'Hearn

I do not know the extent to which it solves it. I have seen some approaches based on type systems [that] I think definitely do now solve it.

Rustan Leino

None of which I said uses type systems. Each one of the three has been used in verification. We use the Boogie methodology right now, for example, in Spec#.

Peter O'Hearn

Yes, I am hoping that someone can explain that methodology to me, and we can go for a few examples to see if it handles, for instance, examples like dispose tree. Simple ones like that.

Wolfgang Paul

I am slightly confused, as often in my life. I have a very simple question. I have seen you had some simple programs and you have presented certain proofs, and although they were not completely trivial, I failed to see why those proofs were complicated. There are certain things you want to prove. You have to prove that things that change, change in the right way, and on the way, you have to prove that certain things do not change in undesired ways. It is completely normal.

You observe this, write down the right tools, and everything you wrote down was very nice and beautiful and the right things, but I would not call it complicated! So, as a consequence, if we call things complicated that for Russian scientists certainly are not, then we are limiting the things which we can do.

Peter O'Hearn

I only showed you the proofs that were in the formalism that at least partially solve those problems.

David Naumann

To put a slightly different twist on it... I think Wolfgang is pointing out that in large systems, there is all sorts of complexity in the interactions. And the ghost variable approach that we have been talking about a little this morning, and Rustan was just alluding to as well, is somewhat ad-hoc, but one can look for reasoning patterns particular to situations and try to formalize the dependencies there and be able to make sense of the footprints of various predicates and reason about their interferences or risks thereof or absence thereof. By contrast, separation logic has complete separation of the footprint of predicates expressed by a logical connective, and then the footprint per se does not exist. That is sort of the interpretation of these triples. It's gorgeous for small algorithms, but it poses the questions of: Will this scale to more complex interactions and overlaps between resources? And will there be further connectives needed for such?

Peter O'Hearn

I don't know. I mean, I was struck by you using the "star of heaps", because what is behind separation logic, the reason it works so well on the small examples, is the local way that programs operate, which guarantees that many frame axioms are simply true. And you might be able to, in a traditional logic, make use of that same observation. So, it is just that separation logic gives you a convenient way to do it, but there is a deeper reason for why it is working well.

Wolfgang Paul

Let me insist! Maybe this is controversial and I do not want to hurt anybody, but: I always hear "reasoning patterns". If I want to teach mathematics to somebody, I do not teach him reasoning patterns, I teach him how to find proofs. When I teach a class of retarded children in lower classes to prepare for a school examination, then I teach them reasoning patterns, but among scientists, for heaven's sake! I do not try to identify reasoning patterns; I think that is harmful!

Peter O'Hearn: To identify reasoning patterns?

Wolfgang Paul

Reasoning patterns might be good if I want to automate things, and then I say: With what reasoning pattern can I automatically kill the following problem? Then, it is great, but just for finding proofs... what's the problem? In mathematics, it is not done this way, and this is mathematics!

Peter O'Hearn

No, mathematics also, we are allowed to be scientists, and we can insist that we do not like a solution because it is complicated, and we can try for a simpler solution. And so, that is why I am insisting.

Lessons from the JML Project

Gary T. Leavens and Curtis Clifton*

Department of Computer Science, Iowa State University,
226 Atanasoff Hall, Ames, IA 50011 USA

Abstract. To have impact, a grand challenge should provide a way for diverse research to be integrated in a synergistic fashion. Synergy in the JML project comes from a shared specification language, and thus holds several lessons for the verifying compiler grand challenge. An important lesson is that the project should focus considerable resources on specification language design, which still contains many open research problems. Another important lesson is that, to support such a specification language, the project needs to involve groups doing research on extensible compilers and integrated development environments.

1 Introduction

Hoare's verifying compiler grand challenge is "the construction and application of a verifying compiler that guarantees correctness of a program before running it" [1, p. 63]. This challenge is of such a broad scope that a project meeting the challenge would involve "a significant section of the research community" that would "work together towards a common goal, agreed to be valuable and achievable by a team effort" [1, p. 63].

This position paper focuses on one way that these researchers could work together, drawing lessons from the experience of the Java Modeling Language (JML) project [2,3]. These lessons are relevant because the JML project, although smaller and less ambitious, has many parallels with the verifying compiler grand challenge.

2 What Kind of Specifications?

To verify a program, one must have a specification. The specification can be implicit, such as that the program should not encounter unexpected exceptions due to obvious program errors (such as dereferencing a null pointer or indexing an array beyond its bounds). But finding such bugs is possible with existing tools, such as ESC/Java [4]. While such tools are a subject of current research and engineering, they hardly constitute a grand challenge at this point. Therefore, implicit in the grand challenge are interesting specifications, written in some specification language. Examples of interesting specifications include specifications of functional behavior that involves data values and specifications of safety properties that describe synchronization of concurrent threads.

---

* Current address for Curtis Clifton: Dept. of Comp. Sci. and Soft. Eng., Rose-Hulman Inst. of Technology, 5500 Wabash Ave., Terre Haute, IN 47803.

B. Meyer and J. Woodcock (Eds.): Verified Software, LNCS 4171, pp. 134–143, 2008.

The main cost of such interesting specifications is that, in general, they cannot be automatically generated. Instead, they must be written, to some extent, by humans. The reason human input is needed is that only humans can judge the intent of a specification. For example, consider a square root routine. A particular implementation may produce roots with 7 decimal digits of accuracy, but only a human can decide if the intended behavior is 7 digit accuracy, rather than 5 or 10 digit accuracy. Put another way, interesting specifications describe the set of all acceptable implementations abstractly; the intent behind this description allows them to be used as contracts that govern future evolution of both implementations and clients [5]. Ultimately these contracts are a matter for human judgment and negotiation.

3   Why Design a Specification Language?

Strictly speaking, the grand challenge can proceed with only a few interesting specifications. For example, a group of experts might specify the Linux kernel or write a few other interesting specifications as tests of verification technology. If the focus of the project is solely on proving programs correct, then a small set of such specifications would be adequate, and the costs of writing the specifications and designing specification languages could be largely ignored by the project.

However, we believe that including specification language design is necessary to maximize the project's impact, and would also have several other benefits.

The relationship between the project's potential impact and including specification language design in its scope can be seen by considering the alternative. Suppose that the project only works with a small set of test specifications, and does not provide an easily-usable, well-documented specification language. Assuming that the project succeeds, then how can programmers apply its verification technology to code that does not implement the test specifications? In this scenario, such applications might still be very costly, as programmers would have to write new interesting specifications, which we are assuming would be hard. Hence many programming projects would not be able to cost-effectively use the new verification technology.

Another benefit, not to be overlooked, is that a specification language is a good way to coordinate efforts among different verification tools. This is one of the main lessons of the JML project, which has been fairly successful in coordinating the efforts of diverse research groups [2]. Having JML as a common specification language allows these groups to also share users, and thus have a larger pool of users to test their ideas and to obtain feedback. It also facilitates the exchange of ideas among research groups.

Therefore, we believe that one of the project's overall goals should be to make it easy (inexpensive) and valuable (cost-effective) for ordinary programmers to write interesting formal specifications. One milestone would be to replace most informal documentation with formal specifications, while decreasing the overall cost of program development and maintenance, since at that point formal specifications become economically attractive.

Achieving such a goal requires efforts in education, language design, and tools. The educational effort needs to address documentation and training issues. This implies that documentation of the specification language, including examples, should have a high priority. It also implies that tutorial and teaching materials should have a high priority. This also presents an opportunity include in the project people interested in computer science education, with the goal of integrating more formal methods training into the standard computer science curriculum. One promising approach to doing this would be to promote undergraduate textbooks that use formal specifications.

The specification language design and tool-building efforts should have as their overall goal making it as easy as possible for programmers to read and write interesting specifications, in order to minimize educational costs. In the rest of this position paper, we will focus on these language design and tool building problems, since they are the ones we have the most experience with in JML.

4   Nature of the Specification Language

Assuming that the project will devote some effort to specification language design, we now consider what kinds of specification languages would be suitable, and whether there should be a single specification language.

A basic decision is whether the specification languages should be tailored to some specific programming language. That is, should they be interface specification languages (like Eiffel, Larch/C++, or JML), or should they be languages that are independent of any particular programming language (as are VDM, Z, or OCL)? Perhaps the specification language could even be that of some theorem prover, such as PVS or Isabelle?

We believe that the specification languages should be interface specification languages. The great advantage of an interface specification language is that it can specify details particular to some programming model, such as exceptions, visibility restrictions, encapsulation, and typing. Furthermore, an interface specification language can be translated into the input of various theorem provers and other tools, serving as a common front end for them. From the perspective of the verification tools, it may be possible to achieve some of the benefits of an interface specification language, while being somewhat language independent, by targeting an execution platform, such as the Java Virtual Machine or Microsoft's Common Language Runtime. However, even if the language targeted such an execution platform, to have impact on programmers the project would still require user-level specification languages that map to such platform-level languages.

One of the lessons of the JML project is that focusing on just a single specification language allows that language to serve as a central coordination mechanism for diverse groups of researchers. The common language:

- gives these groups a *lingua franca* in which to present semantic issues and tool-building issues,
- provides fresh insights as various technologies can be compared and contrasted through how they deal with common language features, and
- relieves groups of some of the tedium of fine-grained language design, which frees them to innovate in specialized areas.

Therefore, for the remainder of this paper, we will assume a single specification language targeting a specific programming language. Most of the arguments we raise will also apply to a lower-level specification language that targets an execution platform.

5 Problems in Specification Language Design

A major lesson of the JML project is that, even for sequential programs, the design of interface specification languages is still an interesting and quite difficult research problem.

The overall problem for specification language design is how the language can give its users sufficient value to justify the cost of specification. This is hard because, in our experience, the costs of writing a fairly complete functional specification of program behavior is usually about the same as that of writing the code to implement it. Therefore, it is necessary to either reduce these costs or to provide a wealth of tool support to compensate.

JML's approach has been to provide a wealth of tool support. This tool support works to both decrease the cost of writing specifications (for example, by improving the reporting of errors in specifications) and increase the usefulness of specifications (by using them to derive testing oracles and to generate documentation, among other things).

In addition to this tool support, JML is also designed to be easy for Java programmers to adopt and use. The main technical ideas here are to use an extended subset of Java expressions for assertions (drawing on the Eiffel experience), provide mathematical models as Java classes (drawing on the Larch and VDM experience), and prohibit side effects in expressions used in assertions [3].

Techniques for avoiding side effects in JML assertions are rather draconian at the moment and need refinement in order to be practical. The basic problem is that in a language like JML, one must be able to call methods in specifications. For example, to specify Java collections, one must be able to call the `equals` method on `Object`s. However, because of the specification inheritance used in JML to guarantee behavioral subtyping [6,7,8,9], saying that `Object`'s `equals` method is free of side effects means that no side effects are allowed in any overriding `equals` method [3]. We are working on allowing side effects that are not observable, which would allow caches in such methods, based on work by Barnett, *et al.* [10,11].

Another area of ongoing research is how to specify frame axioms (modifies clauses) and invariants in a modular fashion. To achieve modularity for frame axioms, there are several current approaches. The Boogie method [12,13] uses new language statements (`unpack` and `pack`), a dynamically unique object owner, and explicit specification of what objects are threatened by a method. While this makes soundness clear and is very flexible, it is (at present) fairly tedious to use in practice. Like the Boogie method, other techniques [14,15] seem to involve some control of aliasing. The same seems true of a modular treatment of invariants. Again, the Boogie method is more explicit, and also uses unique ownership, and other methods [16] also rely on control of aliasing. In any case some integration with alias control is necessary to prevent representation exposure. Thus these problems and current solutions seem to lead the research into the realm of alias-controlling type systems [17,18]. However, such alias-controlling type systems and their integration with specification languages are still a very active area of research. The work on JML cited above [15,16] builds on one such research project, the Universe type system [19].

Another notable area of research is how to specify and verify callbacks. Higher-order features, and especially callbacks, are well known to cause difficulties both for practical programming [20]. In specification, the main problem is that the specifications become highly parameterized [21,22], and hence difficult to write and read. In JML we are pursuing the "grey-box approach" [23,24,25]: writing specifications in a refinement-calculus style as abstract programs, but interpreting the internal callbacks as observable.

All the above issues in specification language design apply to specification languages for sequential programs. Another host of issues enters when one tries to specify concurrent programs. The JML effort has mostly ignored these problems, because it has focused on a sequential subset of Java. However, one problem that is important for concurrent programs is also a problem for sequential programs: how to specify orderings of events. That is, the ability to specify permitted sequences of operations would be a useful adjunct to traditional Hoare-style specification languages. Some specification languages have used finite-state machine descriptions for such sequencing [26]. Temporal logic is a widely-known formalism for such sequence specifications [27], although other formalisms may be easier for ordinary programmers to write and read [28,29]. There has been some preliminary work in JML on this [30].

Beyond these issues in functional specification languages is the largely unexplored territory of specification languages that combine features for specification of both functional behavior (including data values) and concurrency control (including safety and liveness). Most specification languages and tools address only one of these areas. However, modern software requires a specification language that can help integrate techniques from these two disparate camps. A start towards this problem in JML is found in the work of Rodríguez et al. [31]. This work uses atomicity to reduce reasoning about concurrent programs to the sequential case.

6   Keeping Up with Evolution

As we argued above, to have maximal impact on practice, a specification language and its tools must be designed for practicing programmers. The problem is that widely-used languages and their programming environments evolve rapidly, and it is difficult for researchers to keep up with industrial evolution of languages and development environments. This is the case for any "standardized" language, such as C (since the standards committees issue a new standard roughly every 5 years), and perhaps more so for languages that are not standardized, such as Java.

The history of the JML project provides several lessons related to this problem. The JML project started in 1998 as an outgrowth of work on the interface specification language Larch/C++.[1] Larch/C++ was an interface specification language tailored to the specification of C++ modules. C++ was originally chosen because it was a popular

---

[1] The Larch family of interface specification languages [32], was a refinement of Hoare-style specification languages exemplified by VDM.

object-oriented language, and we believed that we could have maximum impact by working with real problems in a broadly-used language.

However, the size and complexity of C++ presented great problems for our tool building efforts. In particular, the grammatical complexity of C++ presented enormous difficulty. In practice, another large difficulty was the unsafe nature of C++, which complicated specifications in many practical ways.

Thus when Java became available, we abandoned work on Larch/C++ and started work on an interface specification language tailored to Java—JML. Java was (at the time) a much simpler language than C++, which initially seemed to solve many of the tool problems.

Unfortunately, Java has since grown much larger than it was originally; furthermore, it has grown rather quickly. Indeed, the latest release of Java (version 1.5 also known as Java 5) introduces several non-trivial features, so it is challenging for an open-source project like JML to keep up. This dilemma is likely to be faced by the verifying compiler challenge also. In short: (a) in order to have impact, it is helpful to target a popular language, (b) but one way that a language stays popular is by evolving rapidly. This puts great pressure on fundamental tool support: parsing and basic compiler infrastructure have to be frequently updated to track the language's evolution.

Another issue for practical adoption is building integrated development environments (IDEs). Few modern programmers use the traditional command line compilers and old-style text editors; instead they demand integrated support for editing, compiling, and debugging (to say nothing of version control, support for refactoring, etc.). Thus, to have an impact—indeed, just to have users—tools must fit into some IDE. Like languages, IDEs are also evolving rapidly, as evidenced by Eclipse[2]. Thus, while it is not a grand challenge to produce a state-of-the-art IDE, the project must keep up with their evolution.

The lesson we draw from this is that the project must have groups that are interested in building and maintaining basic compiler tool and IDE support. Researchers in formal methods are not interested in building basic compiler tools and IDEs; so the project must find people who are interested in these issues, in order to help the formal methods researchers stay focused. That is, formal methods researchers need help from some groups that are dedicated to providing up-to-date and extensible compiler support. These groups could track changes in programming language(s) and relieve some of the pressure in dealing with the evolution of popular languages. Similarly, formal methods researchers need help from groups that are dedicated to providing extensible IDEs.

The need to interact with researchers in extensible compilers and IDEs should be seen as an opportunity to involve more areas of computing in the grand challenge. One way to convince researchers interested in compilers to work with the grand challenge is to let them see additional opportunities for optimization and for exploring language extension techniques. Extensibility is needed not just to track evolution in the programming language, but also to allow experimentation in specification language design. Similarly, IDE researchers might be attracted to the grand challenge if they see opportunities to experiment with extensibility, or to improve the programmer's experience through improved error reporting, specification-enabled visualization, or editing mechanisms.

---

[2] Details on Eclipse's rapid evolution are available from `http://www.eclipse.org`

It is a fortunate fact that, at least in the United States, compiler research and formal methods research are housed in the same division of the National Science Foundation. It will be easier to get support for a grand challenge if we can find ways to involve compilers and other subareas of computing (such as education and human-computer interfaces).

7 Conclusions

To summarize, the grand challenge needs interesting specifications as tests of its verification technology. To have maximum impact, the grand challenge should have as a goal making it easy and cost-effective to write such interesting specifications. This necessarily involves some effort in specification language design. We listed some of the research challenges in specification language design from our experience with the JML project; the grand challenge should not assume that specification languages are completely understood and adequate.

The lessons from the JML project also indicate that the verifying compiler grand challenge should involve researchers in extensible compiler technologies and IDEs. Work in all these areas is necessary for the project to have a practical impact worthy of being a "grand challenge."

Acknowledgments

Thanks to the program committee for comments that helped clarify our arguments.

The work of Leavens and Clifton was supported in part by the US National Science Foundation through grants CCF-0428078 and CCF-0429567.

References

1. Hoare, T.: The verifying compiler: A grand challenge for computing research. Journal of the ACM 50(1), 63–69 (2003)
2. Burdy, L., Cheon, Y., Cok, D.R., Ernst, M.D., Kiniry, J.R., Leavens, G.T., Leino, K.R.M., Poll, E.: An overview of JML tools and applications. Journal on Software Tools for Technology Transfer 7(3), 212–232 (2005)
3. Leavens, G.T., Cheon, Y., Clifton, C., Ruby, C., Cok, D.R.: How the design of JML accommodates both runtime assertion checking and formal verification. Science of Computer Programming 55(1-3), 185–208 (2005)
4. Flanagan, C., Leino, K.R.M., Lillibridge, M., Nelson, G., Saxe, J.B., Stata, R.: Extended static checking for Java. In: Proceedings of the ACM SIGPLAN 2002 Conference on Programming Language Design and Implementation (PLDI 2002), June 2002. SIGPLAN, vol. 37(5), pp. 234–245. ACM Press, New York (2002)
5. Meyer, B.: Object-oriented Software Construction, 2nd edn. Prentice Hall, New York (1997)
6. Dhara, K.K., Leavens, G.T.: Forcing behavioral subtyping through specification inheritance. In: Proceedings of the 18th International Conference on Software Engineering, March 1996. A corrected version is ISU CS TR #95-20c, pp. 258–267. IEEE Computer Society Press, Berlin (1996), http://tinyurl.com/s2krg

7. Leavens, G.T.: JML's rich, inherited specifications for behavioral subtypes. In: Liu, Z., He, J. (eds.) ICFEM 2006. LNCS, vol. 4260, pp. 2–34. Springer, Heidelberg (2006)

8. Leavens, G.T., Naumann, D.A.: Behavioral subtyping, specification inheritance, and modular reasoning. Technical Report 06-20b, Department of Computer Science, Iowa State University, Ames, Iowa, 50011 (September 2006)

9. Leavens, G.T., Poll, E., Clifton, C., Cheon, Y., Ruby, C., Cok, D.R., Müller, P., Kiniry, J., Chalin, P.: JML reference manual. In: Department of Computer Science, Iowa State University (February 2007), http://www.jmlspecs.org

10. Barnett, M., Naumann, D.A., Schulte, W., Sun, Q.: Allowing state changes in specifications. In: Müller, G. (ed.) ETRICS 2006. LNCS, vol. 3995, pp. 321–336. Springer, Heidelberg (2006)

11. Naumann, D.A.: Observational Purity and Encapsulation. In: Cerioli, M. (ed.) FASE 2005. LNCS, vol. 3442, pp. 190–204. Springer, Heidelberg (2005)

12. Barnett, M., DeLine, R., Fähndrich, M., Leino, K.R.M., Schulte, W.: Verification of object-oriented programs with invariants. Journal of Object Technology 3(6), 27–56 (2004)

13. Leino, K.R.M., Müller, P.: Object invariants in dynamic contexts. In: Odersky, M. (ed.) ECOOP 2004. LNCS, vol. 3086, pp. 491–516. Springer, Heidelberg (2004)

14. Leino, K.R.M., Nelson, G.: Data abstraction and information hiding. ACM Transactions on Programming Languages and Systems 24(5), 491–553 (2002)

15. Müller, P., Poetzsch-Heffter, A., Leavens, G.T.: Modular specification of frame properties in JML. Concurrency and Computation: Practice and Experience 15(2), 117–154 (2003)

16. Müller, P., Poetzsch-Heffter, A., Leavens, G.T.: Modular invariants for layered object structures. Science of Computer Programming 62(3), 253–286 (2006)

17. Boyland, J., Noble, J., Retert, W.: Capabilities for sharing. In: Knudsen, J.L. (ed.) ECOOP 2001. LNCS, vol. 2072, pp. 1–27. Springer, Heidelberg (2001)

18. Noble, J., Vitek, J., Potter, J.: Flexible alias protection. In: Jul, E. (ed.) ECOOP 1998. LNCS, vol. 1445, pp. 158–185. Springer, Heidelberg (1998)

19. Dietl, W., Müller, P.: Universes: Lightweight ownership for JML. Journal of Object Technology 4(8), 5–32 (2005)

20. Szyperski, C., Gruntz, D., Murer, S.: Component Software: Beyond Object-Oriented Programming, 2nd edn. ACM Press and Addison-Wesley, New York (2002)

21. Ernst, G.W., Navlakha, J.K., Ogden, W.F.: Verification of programs with procedure-type parameters. Acta Informatica 18(2), 149–169 (1982)

22. Goguen, J.A.: Parameterized programming. IEEE Transactions on Software Engineering SE-10(5), 528–543 (1984)

23. Büchi, M., Weck, W.: A plea for grey-box components. Technical Report 122, Turku Center for Computer Science, Presented at the Workshop on Foundations of Component-Based Systems, Zürich (1997) (September 1997), http://tinyurl.com/2833tr

24. Büchi, M., Weck, W.: The greybox approach: When blackbox specifications hide too much. Technical Report 297, Turku Center for Computer Science (August (1999), http://tinyurl.com/ywmuzy

25. Büchi, M.: Safe language mechanisms for modularization and concurrency. Technical Report TUCS Dissertations No. 28, Turku Center for Computer Science (May 2000)

26. Ball, T., Rajamani, S.K.: The SLAM project: Debugging system software via static analysis. In: Conference Record of POPL 2002: The 29th ACM SIGPLAN-SIGACT Symposium on Principles of Programming Languages, Portland, Oregon, January 16–18, 2002, pp. 1–3 (2002)

27. Manna, Z., Pnueli, A.: The Temporal Logic of Reactive and Concurrent Systems. Springer, New York (1992)

28. Corbett, J.C., Dwyer, M.B., Hatcliff, J., Laubach, S., Pasareanu, C.S., Robby, Z.H.: Bandera: Extracting finite-state models from Java source code. In: Proceedings of the 22nd International Conference on Software Engineering, June 2000, pp. 439–448. ACM Press, New York (2000)
29. Harel, D.: Statecharts: A visual formalism for complex systems. Science of Computer Programming 8(3), 231–274 (1987)
30. Cheon, Y., Perumendla, A.: Specifying and checking method call sequences in JML. In: Arabnia, H.R., Reza, H. (eds.) Proceedings of the 2005 International Conference on Software Engineering Research and Practice (SERP 2005), June 27-29, 2005, vol. II, pp. 511–516. CSREA Press, Las Vegas, Nevada (2005)
31. Rodríguez, E., Dwyer, M.B., Flanagan, C., Hatcliff, J., Leavens, G.T.: Robby: Extending JML for modular specification and verification of multi-threaded programs. In: Black, A.P. (ed.) ECOOP 2005. LNCS, vol. 3586, pp. 551–576. Springer, Heidelberg (2005)
32. Guttag, J.V., Horning, J.J., Garland, S., Jones, K., Modet, A., Wing, J.: Larch: Languages and Tools for Formal Specification. Springer, New York (1993)

A   Discussion on Gary Leavens's Presentation

Peter Schmitt

I like JML, and it is one important part of our project, but there is one thing that worries me. There never has been a complete description. I mean, this manual is still a draft.

Gary Leavens

Right. That's my fault.

Peter Schmitt

And new features are added and added, but the manual is not updated in the same speed. So, what do you plan to do to prevent the process from getting out of hand. Do you want to submit a standard at some point? That would be an option. Or do you just say: "Let's just move along and put more effort into writing the manual?"

Gary Leavens

Yes, I think this is a problem I have obviously not been able to solve very well. I think we need more help, perhaps, working on the manual. I have been trying to get myself out of some of the more tool-building efforts, and I think that's starting to happen, so maybe I can devote some more of my effort to writing the reference manual and stuff. And I have also tried to get myself off some of the university committees that have been taking up some of my time, but that's immaterial. So, I don't have a great answer for this. I feel like, partly, it's not the best idea to formalize everything completely before we get the right language, but on the other hand, we do need to have more formalization. So one of the approaches that I think has a lot of promise is Joe Kiniry, Patrice [Chalin] and a few other people are trying to develop a semantics of a core subset of JML which is unlikely to change, and I think that effort is a really good one to pursue. And maybe the rest of the language with all its amazing amount of syntactic sugars can just be regarded as research.

Peter Schmitt

So, the natural language specification is at present the goal.

Gary Leavens: Yes, that is mostly my fault.

Peter Schmitt

I do not consider this a fault.

Gary Leavens: OK.

The Spec# Programming System: Challenges and Directions

Mike Barnett, Robert DeLine, Manuel Fähndrich, Bart Jacobs,
K. Rustan M. Leino, Wolfram Schulte, and Herman Venter

Microsoft Research, Redmond, WA, USA
{mbarnett,rdeline,maf,leino,schulte,hermanv}@microsoft.com
bart.jacobs@cs.kuleuven.be

1 Introduction

The Spec# programming system [4] is a new attempt to increase the quality of general purpose, industrial software. Using old wisdom, we propose the use of specifications to make programmer assumptions explicit. Using modern technology, we propose the use of tools to enforce the specifications. To increase its chances of having impact, we want to design the system so that it can be widely adopted.

For a programming system to be adopted widely, we think that it must:

- build on a widely used object-oriented programming language; in our case C#;
- build on existing infrastructure and allow interoperability with existing code, here the .NET runtime.
- fully integrate into an development environment; in our case the Microsoft Visual Studio environment.
- build on a teachable and sound methodology; in our case a revised design-by-contract methodology;
- include tools that enforce the methodology; in our case this includes type checking, easily usable dynamic checking, as well as high-assurance automatic static verification;
- support a smooth adoption path whereby programmers can gradually start taking advantage of the benefits of specification;
- be moderate; we added only a few constructs to C#, and soundness is guaranteed only as long as the source comes from constructs that are under our control.

In this extended abstract, we give an overview of the Spec# programming system [as of September 2005], the rationale of its design, and a sketch of some open problems. Spec# is currently under development at Microsoft Research, Redmond.

2 The Language

The Spec# language is a superset of C#, an object-oriented language targeted for the .NET Platform. C# features single inheritance whose classes can implement multiple interfaces, object references, dynamically dispatched methods, and exceptions, to mention the features most relevant to this paper.

B. Meyer and J. Woodcock (Eds.): Verified Software, LNCS 4171, pp. 144–152, 2008.

Spec# adds to C# type support for distinguishing non-null object references from possibly-null object references [14], method specifications like pre- and postconditions, a discipline for managing exceptions [22], and support for constraining the data fields of objects [2]. While conceptually simple, all have some complicated consequences. Next, we give an overview of each feature.

2.1 Non-null Types

Many errors in modern programs manifest themselves as null-dereference errors. We have opted to add type support for nullity discrimination to Spec#, because we think types offer the easiest way for programmers to take advantage of nullity distinctions. Here is a list of challenges with some solutions.

Initialization of fields and arrays. For type safety, any time a variable of a non-null type is read, the value obtained must be non-null. Without further restrictions, this is not guaranteed for instance fields, static fields, and array elements. Spec# offers a simple syntactic solution for instance fields, which ensures that they are initialized before the object being constructed can be accessed. Handling non-null static fields requires ordering restrictions on the initialization of classes. Spec# supports non-null static fields, but the initialization restrictions are checked only at run time. Supporting non-null element types of arrays is tricky, because there is no language construct that marks the end of the initialization of an array's elements.

Language interoperability. The .NET platform supports multiple languages, not all of which may be required to support non-null types. This raises many problems, like calling from such a language methods whose in-parameters have non-null types. One could disallow such calls, but we want to encourage libraries to be updated with explicit non-null information without forcing changes in the clients. A better solution is to add non-null types to the virtual machine and to adapt the just-in-time compiler, but this would greatly impact all virtual-machine implementations.
Arrays with non-null element types also require changes in the virtual machine, because of array covariance. For this reason, we do not support them in Spec#.

Stability of non-nullity. One must support some form of down-cast of an expression from a maybe-null type to a non-null type. The Spec# compiler infers the non-nullity of local variables by performing a data-flow analysis that takes into account type casts and tests for null. However, this is problematic for fields, whose values may be changed between a test and a use by calls or by other threads about which the compiler has no information.

Non-null types with various degress of type soundness have also been used in program checking systems like LCLint [13] and are being incorporated into the object-oriented language Eiffel [24]; see Fähndrich and Leino's paper [14] for more information about previous work.

2.2 Method Contracts

To allow programmers to capture more complicated properties, which may involve more than one variable, we advocate using general specifications instead of further enrichments to the type system. Like for example Eiffel [23], Spec# supports pre- and postconditions of methods; these use ordinary side-effect free boolean expressions.

Inheritance. Pre- and postconditions are inherited in method overrides. Spec# allows overrides to declare additional postconditions. However, Spec# does not allow an override to weaken the precondition, despite the fact that this would be sound. Here's our justification: There is a mindset in .NET (and in Java) that the misuse of language primitives (like indexing an array outside its bounds) and methods always be detected and reported immediately when the violation occurs at run time. It would seem to go against this mindset to allow an override to eliminate this detection. Actually, though a fine syntactic convenience, there is never a need for weakening preconditions, because a subclass can always define a new method with a weaker precondition and let the old method call the new one.

Because of interfaces, there is a limited form of multiple inheritance. In these cases, a method implementation can inherit its specification from several sources. However, to avoid weakening preconditions, Spec# allows this multiple inheritance only in certain situations where all the inherited preconditions are the same. Actually, this is not a semantic restriction in Spec#, because a class can provide different implementations for multiply inherited methods.

Frame conditions. To reason statically about a call, one needs to know what variables the callee may modify. Specifying this *frame condition* is difficult, because of information hiding: the frame condition must say that the caller's variables are unchanged and must allow the implementation's variables to be changed. But these variables are in general not visible to both the caller and the implementation. Spec# uses syntactic and semantic abstractions to address this problem, but we do not yet have enough evidence to evaluate whether or not this particular solution is the right one.

Evaluation of contracts. We take the view that contracts should contribute to the specification of programs, but not to their effects. Therefore, Spec# insists that expressions used in contracts be side-effect free. We do allow procedural abstraction in contracts, as long as any procedure (method, rather) called also is side-effect free, that is, *pure*. A syntactic notion of purity is overly restrictive, so we are exploring notions of *behavioral purity*, but don't have all the answers yet [6,26].

The fact that contracts are given by expressions of the language raises the problem that the evaluation of those expressions can fail. Spec# chooses to hold the specification writer accountable for such errors. That is, contracts are enforced to be totally defined.

2.3   Class Contracts

Invariants are key to describing the correctness of programs, and Spec# allows classes to declare invariants that describe the internal consistency of the state of their objects. However, the problem of maintaining invariants that span several objects has been under-studied. Two central problems are delineating when an object invariant holds (which is made difficult because of re-entrancy) and controlling changes to sub-objects (which is made difficult because references to these sub-objects may be leaked).

Spec# uses a sound methodology that addresses both of these central problems (and the problem of writing frame conditions) [2,18,5,19]. Spec# provides a block statement that delineates where object invariants may temporarily be violated, and it uses ownership domains to confine references.

2.4   Concurrency

Multi-threading introduces the possibility of race conditions and deadlocks. This makes data consistency even more difficult to achieve in a multi-threaded program. We feel that a programming methodology should permit extensions that cover concurrent programs, too. We have formulated an extension of our object-invariant methodology for multi-threading [15]. It ensures mutual exclusion on ownership domains and maintains data consistency. But our extension still has several shortcomings, including: it does not check for deadlocks [but see our newer work [16]] and its locking is sometimes too coarse-grained.

2.5   Data Abstraction

More elaborate specifications of programs require a way to present a view of objects that abstracts away from implementation details. We find that this form of data abstraction already exists in many .NET programs in the form of *properties* (which are essentially parameter-less methods). If a property is a pure function of the state of an object and its immediate ownership domain, then we call it a *model field* [9,17,21,25]. We are hopeful that one can formulate the definition and use of model fields in a way that is amenable to static program verification [see our newer work [20]].

3   System Architecture

Architecturally, the Spec# programming system consists of the compiler, a runtime library, and the static program verifier. Spec# has been integrated into the Microsoft Visual Studio environment. For example, violations of the non-null type system are indicated by "red squigglies", specifications of methods (including any specifications on library methods) are available in tool tips. The static program verifier runs continuously while editing the program and interactively produces red squigglies for semantic errors, but it can also be run as a standalone tool.

3.1   Levels of Checking

Spec# provides three levels of checking.

The first level of checking is provided by the type checker, which runs as part of the compiler and which must accept the program before any code is emitted. The type checker is stronger than some other traditional type checkers in that it is sometimes sensitive to data flow.

The second level of checking is provided by compiler-emitted run-time checks. These checks are always emitted, but we do provide some compiler options that disable them, because development organizations sometimes feel they have reached a point in the development cycle where they are willing to risk not having the checks and would rather gain performance. The run-time checks enforce many contracts, but do not enforce the entire Spec# programming methodology. For example, frame conditions (modifies clauses) are not checked at run time and, by default, ownership domains are not enforced at run time.

The third level of checking, which is optional, is provided by the Spec# static program verifier. It enforces all contracts and the entire Spec# programming methodology, except assume statements, which are provided for the specific purpose of introducing a run-time check for programmer assumptions that would take great effort to prove statically.

3.2 Contract Persistence

The Spec# compiler preserves the specifications as metadata in the same binary assembly as the compiled code. This enables reuse of specifications across tools.

To enable clients of a legacy library to be verified, such a library needs to be retrofitted with specifications. If the library cannot be converted into Spec#, we support the compilation and use of *out-of-band contracts* in shadow assemblies. These give the illusion that the specifications were declared in the library itself.

3.3 Static Verification

From MSIL (the .NET bytecode), Spec#'s static program verifier (whose codename is Boogie [1]) constructs a program in its own intermediate language, BoogiePL [12]. BoogiePL is a simple imperative language with procedures. BoogiePL also supports the introduction of uninterpreted function symbols and axioms, which makes it suitable as a stepping stone in program verification. In fact, all of the Spec# to be verified is translated into BoogiePL, including the axiomatization of the Spec# type system, *etc.* From the BoogiePL program, Boogie infers loop invariants using abstract interpretation [10,11,7,8] and generates verification conditions (logical formulas that are valid iff the program is correct) that it passes to an automatic theorem prover [3]. Counterexamples reported by the theorem prover are translated back into error messages about the source code, which are reported to the user.

Technology for abstract interpretation and theorem proving exist. We feel that the work in this area has reached the kind of maturity where what is needed for Spec# consists mainly in adapting and tuning existing technologies for the verification task at hand. One difference from previous work is perhaps the emphasis on the heap in Spec# programs. There is also room for improving the combination of various abstract domains as well as exploring the combination of abstract domains and decision procedures.

In the verification community, various standard or canonical formats have been useful for interoperability, substitutability, and evaluation of tools (for example, the primitive DIMAC format for SAT formulas). Our position is that BoogiePL is a good candidate for playing that same role in the space of verifying programs. Boogie can be invoked not just on MSIL assemblies, but also on BoogiePL programs directly.

This means that other researchers can reuse the abstract interpretation and verification-condition generation in Boogie.

4 Conclusion

We are excited about the Verification Grand Challenge working conference. We see the largest remaining challenge to be the formulation of programming methodology that allows modern programs to be specified and verified, as well as the serious engineering effort to build such a programming system.

The Spec# system, including the Boogie program verifier, can be downloaded from `http://research.microsoft.com/SpecSharp`.

References

1. Barnett, M., Chang, B.-Y.E., DeLine, R., Jacobs, B., Leino, K.R.M.: Boogie: A Modular Reusable Verifier for Object-Oriented Programs. In: de Boer, F.S., Bonsangue, M.M., Graf, S., de Roever, W.-P. (eds.) FMCO 2005. LNCS, vol. 4111, pp. 364–387. Springer, Heidelberg (2006)
2. Barnett, M., DeLine, R., Fähndrich, M., Leino, K.R.M., Schulte, W.: Verification of object-oriented programs with invariants. Journal of Object Technology 3(6) (2004), www.jot.fm
3. Barnett, M., Leino, K.R.M.: Weakest-precondition of unstructured programs. In: Proceedings of the 2005 ACM SIGPLAN-SIGSOFT Workshop on Program Analysis For Software Tools and Engineering, PASTE 2005, September 2005, ACM, New York (2005)
4. Mike Barnett, K., Rustan, M.: Leino, and Wolfram Schulte. In: Barthe, G., Burdy, L., Huisman, M., Lanet, J.-L., Muntean, T. (eds.) CASSIS 2004. LNCS, vol. 3362, pp. 49–69. Springer, Heidelberg (2005)
5. Barnett, M., Naumann, D.A.: Friends Need a Bit More: Maintaining Invariants Over Shared State. In: Kozen, D. (ed.) MPC 2004. LNCS, vol. 3125, pp. 54–84. Springer, Heidelberg (2004)
6. Barnett, M., Naumann, D.A., Schulte, W., Sun, Q.: 99.44% pure: Useful abstractions in specifications. In: Proceedings, 6th workshop on Formal Techniques for Java-like Programs (June 2004)
7. Chang, B.-Y.E., Leino, K.R.M.: Abstract Interpretation with Alien Expressions and Heap Structures. In: Cousot, R. (ed.) VMCAI 2005. LNCS, vol. 3385, pp. 147–163. Springer, Heidelberg (2005)
8. Chang, B.-Y.E., Leino, K.R.M.: Inferring object invariants. In: Proceedings of First International Workshop on Abstract Interpretation of Object-Oriented Languages (AIOOL 2005) (2005)
9. Cheon, Y., Leavens, G.T., Sitaraman, M., Edwards, S.: Model variables: cleanly supporting abstraction in design by contract. Software—Practice and Experience 35(6), 583–599 (2005)
10. Cousot, P., Cousot, R.: Abstract interpretation: a unified lattice model for static analysis of programs by construction or approximation of fixpoints. In: Conference Record of the Fourth Annual ACM Symposium on Principles of Programming Languages, January 1977, pp. 238–252. ACM, New York (1977)
11. Cousot, P., Halbwachs, N.: Automatic discovery of linear restraints among variables of a program. In: Conference Record of the Fifth Annual ACM Symposium on Principles of Programming Languages, January 1978, pp. 84–96 (1978)

12. DeLine, R., Rustan, K., Leino, M.: BoogiePL: A typed procedural language for checking object-oriented programs. Technical report, Microsoft Research (2005)
13. Evans, D., Guttag, J.V., Horning, J.J., Tan, Y.M.: LCLint: A tool for using specifications to check code. In: Wile, D.S. (ed.) SIGSOFT 1994, Proceedings of the Second ACM SIG-SOFT Symposium on Foundations of Software Engineering, December 1994. ACM SIG-SOFT Software Engineering Notes, vol. 19(5), pp. 87–96 (1994)
14. Fähndrich, M., Leino, K.R.M.: Declaring and checking non-null types in an object-oriented language. In: Crocker, R., Steele Jr., G.L. (eds.) Proceedings of the 2003 ACM SIGPLAN Conference on Object-Oriented Programming Systems, Languages and Applications, OOP-SLA 2003, October 2003. SIGPLAN Notices, vol. 38(11), pp. 302–312. ACM, New York (2003)
15. Jacobs, B., Leino, K.R.M., Piessens, F., Schulte, W.: Safe concurrency for aggregate objects with invariants. In: Aichernig, B.K., Beckert, B. (eds.) 3rd International Conference on Software Engineering and Formal Methods, September 2005, pp. 137–146. IEEE, Los Alamitos (2005)
16. Jacobs, B., Smans, J., Piessens, F., Schulte, W.: A statically verifiable programming model for concurrent object-oriented programs. In: Liu, Z., He, J. (eds.) ICFEM 2006. LNCS, vol. 4260, pp. 420–439. Springer, Heidelberg (2006)
17. Leavens, G.T., Baker, A.L., Ruby, C.: Preliminary design of JML: A behavioral interface specification language for Java. Technical Report 98-06-rev28, Iowa State University, Department of Computer Science, See (2003), http://www.jmlspecs.org
18. Rustan, K., Leino, M., Müller, P.: Object invariants in dynamic contexts. In Martin Odersky. In: Odersky, M. (ed.) ECOOP 2004. LNCS, vol. 3086, pp. 491–516. Springer, Heidelberg (2004)
19. Rustan, K., Leino, M., Müller, P.: Modular verification of static class invariants. In: Fitzgerald, J.S., Hayes, I.J., Tarlecki, A. (eds.) FM 2005. LNCS, vol. 3582, pp. 26–42. Springer, Heidelberg (2005)
20. Rustan, K., Leino, M., Müller, P.: A verification methodology for model fields. In: Sestoft, P. (ed.) ESOP 2006 and ETAPS 2006. LNCS, vol. 3924, pp. 115–130. Springer, Heidelberg (2006)
21. Rustan, K., Leino, M., Nelson, G.: Data abstraction and information hiding. ACM Transactions on Programming Languages and Systems 24(5), 491–553 (2002)
22. Rustan, K., Leino, M., Schulte, W.: Exception safety for C#. In: Cuellar, J.R., Liu, Z. (eds.) SEFM 2004—Second International Conference on Software Engineering and Formal Methods, September 2004, pp. 218–227. IEEE, Los Alamitos (2004)
23. Meyer, B.: Object-oriented Software Construction. Series in Computer Science. Prentice-Hall International, New York (1988)
24. Meyer, B.: Attached Types and Their Application to Three Open Problems of Object-Oriented Programming. In: Black, A.P. (ed.) ECOOP 2005. LNCS, vol. 3586, pp. 1–32. Springer, Heidelberg (2005)
25. Müller, P.: Modular Specification and Verification of Object-Oriented Programs. LNCS, vol. 2262. Springer, Heidelberg (2002)
26. Naumann, D.A.: Observational purity and encapsulation. In: Cerioli, M. (ed.) FASE 2005. LNCS, vol. 3442, pp. 190–204. Springer, Heidelberg (2005)

A   Discussion on Rustan Leino's Presentation

Roderick Chapman

I noticed, you spent a lot of time on declaring objects to be of type int, and then saying: "Oh no they're not, they're positive." You say it's an int, then you say "oh no it's not, it's greater than or equal to nought, or it's greater than nought, it's positive, blah, blah, blah..." and you seem to have to do this quite a lot.

Rustan Leino: Yes.

Roderick Chapman

Am I completely missing something about C# or does the language not have a facility to declare integer subrange types?

Rustan Leino: No integer subrange types.

Roderick Chapman

Is this not an abominable decision? It shatters me to find that that is not in the language!

Rustan Leino

It would be great to have. Of course, the type system would not do everything for you. You would get runtime checks or the static verifier would pick up where the type checker leaves off, like for so many other things. But sure, that would be great. Actually, there are a number of such things that one can imagine wanting. We've added a few things to C# to make Spec#, but not everything.

Bertrand Meyer

On that last point, I am with you, Rustan. Next, you'll be asked about even integers: Are you going to have a special type for that? But actually, I had a different question. In my experience, it is extremely common to have a postcondition that refers to a secret attribute, and there is absolutely nothing wrong with this conception. Preconditions, of course, are a different business. And the way you addressed the supposed error-which, I think, is not an error-scared me, because then you made the attribute public, and I suspect that in the C++/Java-tradition making an attribute public means making it public for write as well as read. It is not the path that I would like to follow.

Rustan Leino

Yes, thank you for that comment. I made the chunk size read-only here, if that perhaps would make you feel a little bit better. But yes, in general, we would not have to report that error message for postconditions, you are quite right. You have to be a little bit careful that it is at least protected, because if you inherit the method, then the subclass also has to live up to that postcondition. But indeed, preconditions-that's more a requirement-and invariants also help you there, because invariants can talk about the private state. And of course, you need some ways to abstract over the state in other ways, which we will support, but actually, for the moment, we don't, but we will.

Jianjun Zhao

Would you tell us some lessons learned from the design of Spec# for programming language design?

Rustan Leino

To the programming language community, for example. I think we learned many lessons and it would be nice, if the programming language community would pick up some. Let me just say something simple, since we are short on time, maybe we can take it more in discussion later. You saw me move the base class constructor call I move that from the beginning of the method to the end. Well, that is required for soundness, if you have something like non-null types. And the interesting thing is that if you go through your C# programs to convert them into Spec# and you add some non-null features and things, it turns out that almost always, you call the base class constructor last. So, if we should have any default at all, it should be to call it last. But neither C# nor Java supports that today. So, that would be one lesson, but I think, there are more lessons as well.

Integrating Static Checking and Interactive Verification: Supporting Multiple Theories and Provers in Verification

Joseph R. Kiniry[1], Patrice Chalin[2], and Clément Hurlin[3]

[1] Systems Research Group
School of Computer Science and Informatics
UCD Dublin
Belfield, Dublin 4, Ireland
[2] Dependable Software Research Group
Department of Computer Science and Software Engineering
Concordia University
Montreal, Quebec, H3G 1M8, Canada
[3] Université Henri Poincaré, Nancy 1
BP 60120, Nancy Cedex, France
with contributions from
Cees-Bart Breunesse, Julien Charles, David Cok, Bart Jacobs,
Erik Poll, Silvio Ranise, Aleksy Schubert, and Cesare Tinelli

Abstract. Automatic verification by means of extended static checking (ESC) has seen some success in industry and academia due to its lightweight and easy-to-use nature. Unfortunately, ESC comes at a cost: a host of logical and practical completeness and soundness issues. Interactive verification technology, on the other hand, is usually complete and sound, but requires a large amount of mathematical and practical expertise. Most programmers can be expected to use automatic, but not interactive, verification. The focus of this proposal is to integrate these two approaches into a single theoretical and practical framework, leveraging the benefits of each approach.

1 Introduction

Endemic in society today are problems related to the lack of software quality which, as a result, is costing governments, businesses, and nations billions of dollars annually [18]. Correctness and security issues are also directly related to some of the most important concerns of the day such as those of national security and technology-based voting. Additionally, driven by governmental regulations and market demands, businesses are now slowly beginning to assume liability for the faults exhibited by the software systems they offer to their customers. This is particularly true in safety and security critical domains.

While a variety of software engineering practices have been developed to help increase software quality (e.g., testing practices, system design, modern processes, robust operating systems and programming languages), it is widely acknowledged that a promising way to achieve highly reliable software in critical domains is to couple

B. Meyer and J. Woodcock (Eds.): Verified Software, LNCS 4171, pp. 153–160, 2008.
© IFIP International Federation for Information Processing 2008

these practices with applied formal techniques supported by powerful modern tools and technologies like those discussed in this paper.

1.1 Program Verification

Applied formal methods has turned a corner over the past few years. Various groups in the semantics, specification, and verification communities now have sufficiently developed mathematical and tool infrastructures that automatic and interactive verification of software components that are written in modern programming languages like Java has become a reality. Automatic verification by means of Extended Static Checking (ESC) has seen some success in industry and academia due to its lightweight and easy-to-use nature. Unfortunately, ESC comes at a cost: a host of logical and practical completeness and soundness issues. Interactive verification technology, on the other hand, is usually complete and sound, but requires a large amount of mathematical and practical expertise. Typical programmers can be expected to use automatic, but not interactive, verification.

In this paper we discuss work which is being undertaken to:

- integrate the ESC and interactive verification approaches into a single *theoretical framework*, thus creating a unified semantic foundation, and
- directly realize this theoretical framework in a modern software development environment (IDE) as an Open Source initiative.

Specifically, our current work is focused on the integration of the verification technologies behind two successful tools, namely ESC/Java2 [5] and the LOOP program verifier [12] (both will be described shortly). The proposed integrated environment will perform as much automated verification as possible, falling back on interactive verification only when necessary. Additionally, in those situations where developers wish to delay the completion of the interactive proofs, the tool will insert run-time assertion checking code.

2 Two Key Java Verification Tools

Next, we discuss two complementary verification tools for Java upon which we base this work. These two tools are complementary because one is an *automatic* checker and the other is an *interactive* one.

2.1 Extended Static Checking: ESC/Java2

One of the most successful automatic verification tools for Java has been ESC/Java, an extended static checker originally developed at DEC SRC [7]. The next-generation release, called "ESC/Java2", is now available as an Open Source project that is supported by academic and industrial researchers [13]. David Cok and the first author are the ESC/Java2 project administrators and have been the main contributors (until recently). ESC/Java2 is currently used as a research foundation by over a half dozen research groups and as an instructional tool in nearly two dozen software-centric courses around the world.

ESC/Java2 reasons about Java programs that are specified with annotations written in the Java Modeling Language (JML) [2,14]. ESC/Java2 automatically converts JML-annotated Java code into verification conditions that are automatically discharged by an embedded theorem prover—currently, Simplify [6]. Problems in the specifications, programs, or the checking itself are indicated to the user by means of error messages. As ESC/Java2's performance and mode of interaction are comparable to an ordinary compiler, it is quite usable by industry developers as well as computer science and software engineering students.

2.2   Interactive Verification: The LOOP Tool

The LOOP tool, developed by the SoS Group at Radboud University Nijmegen under the supervision of Prof. Bart Jacobs, is an interactive verification tool for JavaCard [3]. The LOOP tool is one of the most complete verifiers with respect to the subset of Java that it covers. LOOP compiles JML-annotated Java programs into proof obligations expressed as theories for the PVS theorem prover. By making use of PVS to interactively discharge the proof obligations, one is able to prove a program correct with respect to its JML specification.

The base Java/JML semantics of the LOOP tool essentially consists of a parameterized theory. The theory parameters are for the (sub-)theory to be used to reason about integral types. Early in the LOOP Project, Java's integral types were modeled by the mathematical integers. Later, support was added for bounded integers (with the familiar modulo arithmetic) and a bitvector representation (which facilitates reasoning about bit-wise operations—something that is common in JavaCard applications). When reasoning about Java programs, one has a choice of program logics including Hoare logics and two weakest precondition calculi. Recently, Breunesse has merged these into a single, unified theory in which different representations can be used simultaneously [1].

As these two tools represent some of the best-of-breed of applied formal methods in the Java domain, integrating their foundations and approaches has merit. To accomplish this goal, there are several theoretical and practical challenges to be faced.

3   Integration: Observations and Challenges

There is no single canonical semantics of Java.   The canonical *informal* semantics for Java is embodied in the Java Language Specification [9]. Various groups have formalized portions of this text and built complementary tools, e.g., the

- Everest Group at INRIA Sophia-Antipolis,
- SoS Group at the Radboud University Nijmegen,
- Logical Group at INRIA Futurs/Université Paris-Sud,
- SAnToS Laboratory at Kansas State University,
- KeY group, composed of researchers from the Chalmers University of Technology, the University of Koblenz, and the University of Karlsruhe,
- Software Component Technology Group at ETH Zürich, and
- now disbanded Extended Static Checking Group at Hewlett-Packard/Compaq/Digital Systems Research Center.

In all of these cases the formalizations are incomplete, either in scope or in accuracy. Also, very little is understood about how the various semantics relate to each other.

There is no single, core, canonical semantics of JML. While there are several partial informal and formal semantics for JML, there is no single, core semantics. Furthermore, the informal semantics of JML is much more transient and imprecise than that of Java, so the problems mentioned above for Java are compounded for JML. This state of affairs leads to subtle inconsistencies between the interpretation of specifications by the tools that support JML. Because of this inconsistency, relating the semantics to each other is extremely difficult. Additionally, explaining, extending, and reasoning about these artifacts (e.g., the calculi of ESC/Java2) is very difficult.

Little work has been done on meta-logical reasoning about object logics. By meta-logical reasoning we mean reasoning *about*, rather than *within*, the semantics of program and specification languages. Formal meta-mathematical proofs are rare. It is not known, for example, if ESC/Java2's object logic is sound. This is a critical issue.

4   An Integrated Verification Environment

In collaboration with others, our research groups have begun work on an integrated verification environment (IVE) and its necessary theoretical foundations. In doing so we have started to address the problems identified in the previous section.

We are (concurrently) working on the achievement of the following initial milestones:

- elaboration of a semantics for a "core" JML,
- extracting, analysing, and extending ESC/Java2's logic and calculi, and
- redesigning ESC/Java2's proof infrastructure as well as backend interfaces and adaptors with the main objective of allowing it to support new provers.

4.1   Semantics for JML

Semantics have been developed for JML within different logics, nearly all of which have been embedded in the various tools developed by the groups enumerated in Section 3. A few of these tools are publicly available, but most were never used outside the group that originally developed them.

To resolve ambiguities, disagreements, and lack of detailed formal documentation within the JML community, a *single, open* semantics of a "core" of JML (recently named JML Level 1) needs to be written. Chalin and Kiniry are currently outlining a proposed core and have begun formalizing its definition. The outcome of this effort is also a major goal of the MOBIUS project [15].

This semantics will be written in a well-understood formalism, e.g., within a modern extension to Hoare logic, a denotational semantics, and/or in an operational semantics. In our initial work we have decided to express our base, canonical semantics in PVS and Isabelle. Realizing the object logic within higher-order provers will help us characterize and compare semantics.

It is expected that multiple formalizations of the object logic will be created due to practical and theoretical reasons. E.g., most research groups have developed expertise in only one prover, and furthermore, the community can benefit from experimentation with the varying capabilities of each of these provers.

4.2   Evolving ESC/Java2's Logic and Calculi

As inherited from its predecessor, SRC's ESC/Java, ESC/Java2 makes use of an unsorted object logic and two calculi (a weakest precondition calculus and a strongest postcondition calculus). The unsorted object logic consists of approximately 80 axioms written in the language understood (only) by the Simplify prover. These axioms are highly tuned to the quirks and capabilities of Simplify. Initial logical extensions in ESC/Java2 saw the logic augmented with approximately another 20 axioms.

A transcription of this Simplify-based unsorted object logic has been written in PVS. We refer to this formalization of the logic as EJ_0. Two other logics, EJ_1 and EJ_2, have also been written; EJ_1 is merely a sorted version of EJ_0 whereas EJ_2, also a sorted logic, was written from scratch with the purpose of better representing the abstractions needed by ESC/Java2 to reason about JML annotated Java programs. Soundness proofs as well as results on the (semi-)equivalence of the EJ_i logics are underway.

We will also be "extracting" the weakest precondition and a strongest postcondition calculi of ESC/Java2, as well as at least one of the weakest precondition calculi used with the LOOP verification system. This will most likely be done in a higher-order logic or a term rewriting framework. The rewriting speed of special purpose environments like Maude [4] may be of benefit as the tool and verification efforts scale to larger problems.

4.3   Supporting Multiple Provers

As we progress in our work on the definition and proofs of soundness and completeness of the EJ_i logics, we are also progressing in our work on extending and adapting ESC/Java2 to support multiple provers. By developing a generic prover interface along with suitable adaptors, we plan on experimenting with next-generation first-order provers, and a few higher-order provers.

We anticipate the possibility of supporting the use of multiple provers, simultaneously or independently. Which prover to use might be determined automatically by ESC/Java2 based on the context of the verification and the capabilities of the provers. For example, while Simplify is a very fast predicate solver, it does not support a complete or sound (fragment of) arithmetic, thus in verification contexts where arithmetic is used, the tool should automatically avoid using Simplify.

We have chosen Sammy and haRVey as the initial provers for experimentation [8,16]. This choice was made due to our research relationship with the authors of these two tools as well as the authors' high-profile position within the SMT-LIB community [19].

As a necessary precursor to being able to support multiple provers, we are required to translate our object logic, whose current canonical representation is in PVS, into an appropriate formalism understood by each of the provers. Encoding of the ESC/Java2 object logic for these provers is being accomplished primarily by their respective research teams.

We will also be experimenting with the use of higher-order provers as backends for ESC/Java2. Our initially targeted provers are PVS, Isabelle, and Coq. Aside from the authors, Julien Charles at INRIA is working on a Coq realization of the object logic and Cesare Tinelli is contributing to the PVS realization.

5 Conclusion

One of the advantages of our project is that we have a working toolset today that supports Java and JML. These tools are actively being used by researchers and a few industry practitioners. Our goal is to help evolve these tools into their next-generation counterparts and, all the while, make sure that we take our own medicine. Thus, for example, writing JML specifications for the Java modules of our toolsets has been and is routinely done. We are also applying our tools to themselves, thus providing non-trivial case studies demonstrating the practical utility of the tools.

ESC/Java2 and LOOP have been applied to other case studies in the areas of Internet voting [11], JavaCard applications [10], and web-based enterprise applications [17], for example. Some of these case studies are already part of our GForge [20]. We will be routinely re-executing these case studies as the tools evolve so as to validate the tools and ensure that their effectiveness is, in fact, improving.

Acknowledgments

This proposal is based upon the work of many people. Our collaborators are gratefully acknowledged on the first page as well as in the various sections of the proposal. We thank the anonymous referees for their helpful comments. This work is being supported by the Ireland Canada University Foundation as well by the European Project Mobius within the frame of IST 6th Framework and national grants from the Science Foundation Ireland and Enterprise Ireland. This paper reflects only the authors' views and the Community is not liable for any use that may be made of the information contained therein.

References

1. Breunesse, C.-B.: On JML: Topics in Tool-assisted Verification of Java Programs. PhD thesis, Radboud University Nijmegen (2006)
2. Burdy, L., Cheon, Y., Cok, D., Ernst, M., Kiniry, J., Leavens, G.T., Leino, K.M., Poll, E.: An overview of JML tools and applications. International Journal on Software Tools for Technology Transfer (STTT) 7(3), 212–232 (2005)
3. Chen, Z.: Java Card Technology for Smart Cards: Architecture and Programmer's Guide (2000)
4. Clavel, M., Durán, F., Eker, S., Meseguer, J., Stehr, M.-O.: Maude as a formal meta-tool. In: Proceedings of the World Congress on Formal Methods in the Development of Computing Systems (1999)
5. Cok, D.R., Kiniry, J.R.: ESC/Java2: Uniting ESC/Java and JML. In: Barthe, G., Burdy, L., Huisman, M., Lanet, J.-L., Muntean, T. (eds.) CASSIS 2004. LNCS, vol. 3362, pp. 108–128. Springer, Heidelberg (2005)
6. Detlefs, D., Nelson, G., Saxe, J.B.: Simplify: a theorem prover for program checking. J. ACM 52(3), 365–473 (2005)

7. Flanagan, C., Leino, K.R.M., Lillibridge, M., Nelson, G., Saxe, J.B., Stata, R.: Extended static checking for Java. In: ACM SIGPLAN 2002 Conference on Programming Language Design and Implementation (PLDI 2002), pp. 234–245 (2002)

8. Ganzinger, H., Hagen, G., Nieuwenhuis, R., Oliveras, A., Tinelli, C.: DPLL(T): Fast decision procedures. In: Alur, R., Peled, D.A. (eds.) CAV 2004. LNCS, vol. 3114, pp. 175–188. Springer, Heidelberg (2004)

9. Gosling, J., Joy, B., Steele, G.: The Java Language Specification, 1st edn. (August 1996)

10. Jacobs, B.: JavaCard program verification. In: Boulton, R., Jackson, P. (eds.) Theorem Proving in Higher Order Logics TPHOL 2001, vol. 2151, pp. 1–3 (2001)

11. Jacobs, B.: Counting votes with formal methods. In: Rattray, C., Maharaj, S., Shankland, C. (eds.) AMAST 2004. LNCS, vol. 3116, pp. 21–22. Springer, Heidelberg (2004)

12. Jacobs, B., Poll, E.: Java program verification at Nijmegen: Developments and perspective. In: Futatsugi, K., Mizoguchi, F., Yonezaki, N. (eds.) ISSS 2003. LNCS, vol. 3233, pp. 134–153. Springer, Heidelberg (2004)

13. Kiniry, J.R., Cok, D.R.: ESC/Java2: Uniting ESC/Java and JML: Progress and issues in building and using ESC/Java2 and a report on a case study involving the use of ESC/Java2 to verify portions of an Internet voting tally system. In: Barthe, G., Burdy, L., Huisman, M., Lanet, J.-L., Muntean, T. (eds.) CASSIS 2004. LNCS, vol. 3362, pp. 108–128. Springer, Heidelberg (2005)

14. Leavens, G.T., Poll, E., Clifton, C., Cheon, Y., Ruby, C., Cok, D., Kiniry, J.: JML Reference Manual. Department of Computer Science, Iowa State University, 226 Atanasoff Hall, draft revision 1.94 edition (2004)

15. The MOBIUS project. http://mobius.inria.fr/

16. Ranise, S., Deharbe, D.: Light-weight theorem proving for debugging and verifying units of code. In: International Conference on Software Engineering and Formal Methods SEFM 2003, Canberra, Australia (September 2003)

17. Rioux, F., Chalin, P.: Improving the quality of web-based enterprise applications with extended static checking: A case study. Electronic Notes in Theoretical Computer Science 157(2), 119–132 (2006)

18. RTI: Health, Social, and Economics Research, Research Triangle Park, NC. The economic impacts of inadequate infrastructure for software testing. Technical Report Planning Report 02-3, NIST (May 2002)

19. SMT-LIB: The satisfiability modulo theories library. http://goedel.cs.uiowa.edu/smtlib/

20. The Systems Research Group GForge. http://sort.ucd.ie/

A   Discussion on Joseph Kiniry's Presentation

[Demo by Joseph Kiniry, requested by Eric Hehner.]

Bertrand Meyer

Don't you want your students to use some kind of specification whatsoever?

Joseph Kiniry

Oh, very much so! I teach in a style where we do Design by Contract, you know all that, Bertrand. So, we do all that. But oftentimes, you are dealing with code that has no annotations to begin with, and it is a bootstrapping problem. The students want to know what utility they get out of tools when there are no annotations at all. And that is where you start doing the game that Rustan was playing, where you have code that has no annotations and use the tool to give you feedback to make changes, and basically do what I call "contracting the design", which is unfortunately the way most people work with the tools, even when we keep educating them about the "dual". You have to be able to give them a tool where they actually can start out from nothing, in a sense. And that is what this tool lets you do, because there is a lot of implicit annotations inside here besides all these fancy ones with data refinement and data group support and heavyweight specs and all these kinds of things. So, in a sense, the only reason we do it this way is because we can, and it helps people to bootstrap and to understand, how to write specifications without forcing them to do design by contract initially, which we teach in a different course. So, this is how we gently introduce them to this sort of tool use. So, pedagogically, it might not be the right way, but it is a nice way to slip it in. I call it "Secret Ninja Formal Methods".

Bertrand Meyer *[after some silence]*

If no one else is speaking, I'll just add to what Joseph just said, just to fill the silence, that here at ETH contracts come in week two, lecture three actually, of our first-semester "Introduction to programming" course.

Automated Test Generation
and Verified Software*

John Rushby

Computer Science Laboratory
SRI International
333 Ravenswood Avenue
Menlo Park, CA 94025 USA

Abstract. Testing remains the principal means of verification in commercial practice and in many certification regimes. Formal methods of verification will coexist with testing and should be developed in ways that improve, supplement, and exploit the value of testing. I describe automated test generation, which uses technology from formal methods to mechanize the construction of test cases, and discuss some of the research challenges in this area.

1 Introduction

By *testing* I mean observation of a program in execution under controlled conditions. Observations are compared against an explicit or informal oracle to detect bugs or confirm correctness. Much of the testing process (i.e., the execution and monitoring of tests) is automated in modern development environments, but construction of test cases (i.e., the specific experiments to be performed) remains a largely manual process.

Testing is the method by which most software is verified today. This is true for safety critical software as well as the commodity variety: the highest level of flight critical software (DO-178B Level A) is required to be tested to a structural code coverage criterion known as MC/DC (Modified Condition/Decision Coverage) [1]. And although formal methods of analysis and verification are becoming sanctioned, even desired, by some certification regimes, testing continues to be required also—because it can expose different kinds of problems (e.g., compiler bugs), can examine the program in its system context, and increases the diversity of evidence available.

The weakness of testing is well-known to the formal methods and verification communities—it can only show the presence of bugs—but those communities are now beginning to recognize its strength: it *can* show the presence of bugs—often, very effectively. It is a great advantage in verification if the software to be verified is actually correct, so inexpensive methods for revealing incorrectness early in

---

* This work was partially supported by NASA Langley Research Center through contract NAS1-00079, and by NSF grant CNS-0644783.

B. Meyer and J. Woodcock (Eds.): Verified Software, LNCS 4171, pp. 161–172, 2008.

the development and verification process are necessary for verified software to be economically viable.

Thus, testing is not a rival to formal methods of verification but a valuable and complementary adjunct. It is worthwhile to study how each can support the other, both in the technology that they employ, and in their contribution to the overall goal of cost-effective verification.

In this regard, the most significant recent development in testing has been the application of technologies from verification (notably, model-checking, SAT and SMT solving, and constraint satisfaction) to automate the generation of test cases. Automated test generation poses urgent challenges and opportunities: there are many technical challenges in achieving effective automation, there is a wealth of opportunity in the different ways that automated testing can be used, and there are serious implications for traditional certification regimes—and opportunities for innovative ones; there are also opportunities for theoretical research in the relationship between testing and verification, and for empirical inquiry into their pragmatic combination.

In this paper, I briefly survey the topics mentioned above, and suggest research directions for the development and use of automated test generation in verification.

2   Technology for Automated Test Generation

Much of the process of test execution and monitoring is automated in modern software development practice. But the generation of test cases has remained a labor-intensive manual task. Methods are now becoming available that can automate this process.

A simple test-generation goal is to find an input that will drive execution of a (deterministic, loop-free) program along a particular path in its control flow graph. By performing symbolic execution along the desired path and conjoining the predicates that guard its branch points, we can calculate the condition that the desired test input must satisfy. Then, by constraint satisfaction, we can find a specific input that provides the desired test case. This method generalizes to find tests for structural coverage criteria such as statement or branch coverage, and for programs with loops and those that are reactive systems (i.e., that take an input at each step). A major impetus for practical application of this approach was the realization that (for finite state systems) it can be performed by an off-the-shelf model checker: we simply check the property "always not P," where P is a formula that specifies the desired structural criterion, and the counterexample produced by the model checker is then the test case desired [2]. Different kinds of structural or specification-based tests can be generated by choosing suitable P.

Using a model checker to generate tests in this way can be very straightforward in model-based development, where we have an executable specification for the program that is in, or is easily translated to, the language of a model checker: the tests are generated from the executable specification, which then provides the oracle when these are applied to the generated program. There are many pragmatic issues in the selection of explicit-state, symbolic, or bounded model checkers for this task [3] and it is, of course, possible to construct specialized test generators that use the technology of model checking but customize it appropriately for this application.

The test generation task becomes more challenging when tests are to be generated directly from a low-level program description, such as C code, when the path required is very long (e.g., when it is necessary to exhaust a loop counter), when the program is not finite state, and when nondeterminism is present.

When a higher-level specification is unavailable and tests must be generated directly from C code or similar low-level description, it is natural to adopt techniques from software model checking. These seldom translate the program directly into the language of a model checker but usually first abstract it in some way. Predicate abstraction [4] is the most common approach, and discovery of suitable predicates is automated very effectively in the lazy-abstraction approach [5]. Abstractions for test generation are not necessarily the same as those used for verification. For the latter, the abstraction needs to be conservative (i.e., it should have more behaviors than the concrete program), whereas in the former case we generally desire that any test generated from the abstraction should be feasible in the concrete program (i.e., the abstraction may have fewer behaviors than the concrete program) [6]. This impacts the method for constructing the abstraction, and the choice of theorem proving or constraint satisfaction methods employed [7].

When very long test sequences are needed to reach a desired test target, it is sometimes possible to generate them using specialized model checking methods (e.g., those based on an ATPG engine [8]), or by generating the test incrementally, so that each subproblem is within reach of the model checker [3]. Some of the most effective current approaches for generating long test sequences use combinations of methods. For example, random test generation rapidly produces many long paths through the program; to reach an uncovered test target, we find a location "nearby" (e.g., measured by Hamming distance on the state variables) that has been reached by random testing and then use model checking or constraint satisfaction to extend the path from that nearby location to the one desired [9]. DART [10] uses a different approach to explore all feasible execution paths: the program under test is first executed on some random input and monitored to gather constraints on inputs at conditional branches during that run; then a constraint solver is used to generate variants on the inputs to steer the next execution of the program towards different execution paths.

Traditional model checking technology must be extended or adapted when the program is not finite state. In some cases, an infinite state bounded model checker can be used (i.e., a bounded model checker that uses a decision procedure for satisfiability modulo theories (SMT) [11] rather than a Boolean SAT solver) [12]. An SMT solver can, for example, generate real-valued inputs that can be interpreted as delays to be used in testing a real-time program.

In cases where inputs to the program are not simple numerical quantities but data types such as trees or lists, a plausible approach is to fix the base type (e.g., elements of the tree are chosen from an alphabet of size 2), bound the size of the data type (e.g., trees with no more than 5 nodes), and then generate all or many instances of the data type within those constraints. This is easily automated when an axiomatic specification for the data type is available (e.g., rewrite rules specifying a tree), but straightforward approaches produce highly redundant tests (i.e., they generate many inputs that are structurally "isomorphic" to each other). Gaudel and her colleagues have developed methods for generating tests in this way while reducing redundancy using "regularity" and "uniformity" hypotheses [13, 14].

A variant is where we lack a generator for the data type but have a recognizer for it: for example, we may have a predicate that recognizes red-black trees represented as linked lists. Here, we could randomly or exhaustively generate all inputs up to some specified size and test them against the recognizing predicate, but this is very inefficient (e.g., very few randomly generated list structures represent a valid red-black tree) and also generates many "isomorphs." Hence, it is best to view the search as a constraint satisfaction problem and to use technology from that domain [15].

The test generation problem changes significantly when the program under test is nondeterministic, or when part of the testing environment is not under the control of the tester (e.g., testing an embedded system in its operational environment). In these cases, we cannot generate test sequences independently of their actual execution: it is necessary to observe the behavior of the system in response to the test generated so far and to generate the next input in a way that advances the purpose of the test (and to recognize when this cannot be achieved and the current test should be abandoned). This kind of testing can be seen as a game between the tester and the system under test: rather than passive test cases (i.e., data) we need an active tester (i.e., a program), and test generation becomes a problem of controller synthesis. Methods for solving this problem can use technology similar to model checking but can seldom use an off-the-shelf model checker [16]; SpecExplorer is a tool of this kind [17].

The problem becomes yet more difficult when the test environment includes mechanical or biological systems: for example, testing the shift controller of an automatic gearbox in its full system context with a (real or simulated) gearbox attached, or testing a pacemaker against a simulated heart. Here, the test generation problem is escalated to one of controller synthesis in a hybrid system (i.e., one whose description includes differential equations). This is a challenging problem, but a plausible approach is to replace the hybrid elements of the modeled environment by conservative discrete approximations, and then use methods for test generation in nondeterministic systems [18]. As in the case of predicate abstraction, the notion of "conservative" that is suitable for test generation may differ from that used in verification.

3   Selection of Test Targets

The previous section has sketched how test cases can be generated automatically; the next problem is to determine how to make good use of this capability.

One approach uses test generation to help developers explore their emerging designs [19]: a designer might say "show me a run that puts control at this point with $x \leq 0$." This approach is very well-suited to model-based design environments (i.e., those where the design is executable), but is less so for traditional programming. An approach that has proven useful in traditional programming is random test generation at the unit level. In some programming environments, each unit is automatically subjected to random testing against desired properties if these have been specified, or generic ones (e.g., no exceptions) as it is checked in (Haskell QuickCheck [20] is the progenitor of this approach). A similar approach can be used in theorem proving environments: before attempting to prove a putative theorem, first try to refute it by random test generation [21] (in PVS, this can also be tried during an interactive proof if the current proof goal looks intractable [22]). These simple approaches are highly effective in practice. More challenging tests can be achieved by exhaustive generation of inputs up to some bounded size [23]. In Extreme Programming, tests take on much of the rôle played by specifications in more traditional development methods [24], and automated, incremental test generation can support this approach [25].

More traditional uses of testing are for systematic debugging, and for validation and verification. In tests developed by humans, the first of these is generally driven by some explicit or implicit hypotheses about likely kinds of bugs, while the others are driven by systematic "coverage" of requirements and code.

One simple fault hypothesis is that errors are often made at the boundaries of conditions (e.g., the substitution of $<$ for $\leq$) and some automated test generators target these cases [26]. Another hypothesis is that compound decisions (e.g., $A \wedge B \vee C$) may be constructed incorrectly so tests should target the "meaningful impact" [27] of each condition within the decision (i.e., each must be shown able to independently affect the outcome).[1] It turns out that these ideas are related: boundary testing for $x \leq y$ is equivalent to rewriting the decision as $x < y \vee x = y$ and then testing for meaningful impact of the two conditions. The classes of faults detected by popular test criteria for compound decisions have been analyzed by Kuhn [28] and extended by others [29, 30].

Requirements- or specification-based testing is most easily automated when the requirements or specification are provided in executable form—as is commonly done in model based development, thereby giving rise to model-based testing [31]. Here, we can use the methods sketched in Section 2 to generate tests that systematically explore the specified behavior. The usual idea is that a good set of tests should thoroughly explore the control structure of the specification; typical criteria for such structural coverage are to reach every control state, to take every transition between control states, and more elaborate variants that explore the conditions within the decisions that control selection of transitions (as in the meaningful impact criteria mentioned earlier). Structural coverage criteria can be augmented by "test purposes" [32] that describe the kind of tests we want to generate (e.g., those in which the **gear** input to a gearbox shift se-

---

[1] This use of *decision* and *condition* is the one employed in MC/DC, which is a testing criterion of this kind.

lector changes at each step, but only to an adjacent value), by predicates that describe relationships that should be explored (e.g., a queue is empty, full, or in between) [33], or by specifications that describe the external environment [34]. Test purposes and predicates are related to predicate abstraction and can be used to reduce the statespace of the model, and thereby ease the model checking task underlying the test generation. Generating a separate test for each coverage target produces inefficient test sets that contain many short tests and much redundancy, so recent methods attempt to construct more efficient "tours" that visit many targets in each test [35, 3, 33].

Requirements-based testing is more difficult when requirements are specified by properties rather than models. One approach is to translate the properties into automata (i.e., synchronous observers), then target structural coverage in the automata. Alternatively, a direct approach is described in [36].

4   Testing for Verification

Certification regimes for which testing is an important component generally require evidence that the testing has been thorough. DO-178B Level A (which applies to the highest level of flight-critical software in civil aircraft) is typical: it requires MC/DC code coverage. The expectation is that tests are generated by consideration of requirements and their execution is monitored to measure coverage of the code. As the industry moves toward model-based development, it can be argued that the requirements are represented by the models, and hence that automated test generation from the model is a form of requirements-based testing. One way to do this is by targeting MC/DC coverage in the model. Heimdahl, George, and Weber did this for a model of a flight guidance system developed by Rockwell, and then executed the tests on implementations that had been seeded with errors [37]. They found that the autogenerated tests detected relatively few bugs, and generally performed worse than random testing. Part of the explanation for this distressing observation is that the model checking technology underpinning the test generation is "too clever": it generally finds the *shortest* test to discharge any given goal, and these short tests often exploit some special case and never reach the interesting parts of the state space. There is hope that methods that generate tours through many test goals will do better than those that target the goals individually, or that suitable test purposes may guide the test generator into more productive areas of the state space, but these ideas need to be validated in practice.

Another way in which testing has been employed for verification is in "conformance testing," which is generally applied to distributed systems and protocols (where the tester must be an active program). Given a formal specification and an implementation that purports to satisfy it, conformance testing generates a series of tests such that any departure from the specification will eventually be revealed (subject to various technical caveats) [38]. Only a relatively small number of tests can be performed in practice, so the eventuality guarantee is of mainly theoretical interest, and the more pragmatic concern is to try and arrange things so that tests generated early in the series are effective at finding bugs.

Until recently, there has been relatively little work that uses automated testing and static analysis or formal verification in combination. One idea is to reduce "false alarms" in static analysis by emitting only those errors for which a test case to manifest it can be constructed. Dually, some static analysis methods (such as slicing) can be used to ease the test generation task [39]. Rusu uses test generation to decompose the classical formal verification problem into smaller components [40], while the Synergy method [41] alternates DART-like testing and formal verification to achieve highly automated property checking.

5   Research Challenges

Testing is the dominant means of verification used today. Any research agenda in software verification must include testing as a topic, and its roadmap must suggest how the proposed research will improve testing, and how it can use it, as well as how it may replace it in selected areas.

Automated test generation is an attractive topic in this area: it can reduce the cost of testing and may improve its quality. And it is an "invisible" application of formal methods and thus provides a good opportunity to introduce this technology to new communities. Among the most eager adopters of this capability are those in regulated industries where onerous testing requirements constitute a significant part of overall development costs.[2] As mentioned above, there is some evidence that simply using the test coverage requirements as a target for automated test generation may be a flawed strategy: coverage metrics are intended to measure the thoroughness of human-generated tests, and do not necessarily lead to good test sets when used in an inverted role as a specification for the tests required.

Thus, an urgent research topic is development of techniques for specifying good test sets. There are two subtopics here: the role of the human tester will change from construction of tests to *specification* of tests (the tests will be generated automatically from the specification), so we need ideas and techniques for specifying tests (e.g., an extended notion of test purpose); second, we need empirical data on what kinds of test specification produce good tests (i.e., those that are effective in revealing errors). It is natural to assume that specifications for tests should directly correspond to a method for generating the tests, but modern automated test generation operates by constraint satisfaction (either explicitly, or implicitly via model checking) and this opens up the possibility that tests can be specified indirectly in terms of recognizers. Concretely, we can specify tests indirectly by means of synchronous observers that "recognize a good test when they see one" and raise a flag to indicate it. Then we use a model checker to find circumstances that raise the flag. This use of recognizers creates many attractive possibilities for test specification [43].

Most current methods and tools for automated test generation are limited to unit tests. A second general research area is development of methods and

---

[2] Alternatively, there has been some industrial use of formal verification as a lower-cost replacement for MC/DC testing [42].

technology for other (arguably more important) testing tasks, such as integration and system tests. At these levels, tests become interactive programs, and the formal context becomes that of controller synthesis for nondeterministic, timed, and hybrid systems. Abstraction is likely to be necessary, both for the system under test and for its environment, and there are interesting questions regarding the appropriate kinds of abstractions to use, and the theorem proving and model checking methods that are most suitable for constructing and using them. Integration testing need not be restricted to the later stages of development: much of requirements engineering is concerned with anticipation of interactions among components, and the earlier and more completely these can be understood the better. Model checking and automated integration testing during development of (model-based) requirements could reduce the well-known "explosion" of problems that traditionally arise at system integration time.

A third suggested general research area is the integration of testing with formal methods of analysis and verification. Again, there are two subtopics: one is technical integration—for example, how can testing help in formal specification and proof (cf. QuickCheck-like methods for rapid refutation)—while the other focuses on how the overall verification process can be decomposed into elements that are effectively tackled by different means. For example, formal verification not only provides guarantees, it exposes assumptions—and these assumptions can be useful targets for testing. Penetration testing for security at the highest "evaluation assurance levels" uses exactly this approach. Here, the relationship between formal verification and testing is clear, but in other contexts it can be less so. There are proposals, for example, to replace some unit test requirements in avionics by static analysis; yet testing can address some issues (such as compiler bugs, which are a genuine problem) that static analysis does not (unless applied to machine code), so the overall web of argument in support of verification may become interestingly complex.

A companion paper in these proceedings outlines some of the issues in technical integration of verification components [44], while the larger issues of "multi-legged assurance," in which the assurance case for a system is composed from different kinds of evidence, is only just beginning to receive attention [45, 46, 47] and is a worthy topic for future study.

References

1. Hayhurst, K.J., Veerhusen, D.S., Chilenski, J.J., Rierson, L.K.: A practical tutorial on modified condition/decision coverage. NASA Technical Memorandum TM-2001-210876, NASA Langley Research Center, Hampton, VA (2001), http://www.faa.gov/certification/aircraft/av-info/software/Research/MCDC%20Tutorial.pdf
2. Gargantini, A., Heitmeyer, C.: Using model checking to generate tests from requirements specifications. In: Nierstrasz, O., Lemoine, M. (eds.) ESEC 1999 and ESEC-FSE 1999. LNCS, vol. 1687, pp. 146–162. Springer, Heidelberg (1999)
3. Hamon, G., de Moura, L., Rushby, J.: Generating efficient test sets with a model checker. In: 2nd International Conference on Software Engineering and Formal Methods (SEFM), pp. 261–270. IEEE Computer Society, Beijing (2004)

4. Saïdi, H., Graf, S.: Construction of abstract state graphs with PVS. In: Grumberg, O. (ed.) CAV 1997. LNCS, vol. 1254, pp. 72–83. Springer, Heidelberg (1997)
5. Henzinger, T.A., Jhala, R., Majumdar, R., Sutre, G.: Software verification with BLAST. In: Ball, T., Rajamani, S.K. (eds.) SPIN 2003. LNCS, vol. 2648, pp. 235–239. Springer, Heidelberg (2003)
6. Ball, T., Kupferman, O., Yorsh, G.: Abstraction for falsification. In: [48], pp. 67–81
7. Xia, S., Di Vito, B., Muñoz, C.: Predicate abstraction of programs with non-linear computation. In: Graf, S., Zhang, W. (eds.) ATVA 2006. LNCS, vol. 4218, pp. 352–368. Springer, Heidelberg (2006)
8. Boppana, V., Rajan, S.P., Takayama, K., Fujita, M.: Model checking based on sequential ATPG. In: [49], pp. 418–430
9. Ho, P.H., Shiple, T., Harer, K., Kukula, J., Damiano, R., Bertacco, V., Taylor, J., Long, J.: Smart simulation using collaborative formal simulation engines. In: International Conference on Computer Aided Design (ICCAD), Jan Jose, CA, Association for Computing Machinery, pp. 120–126 (2000)
10. Godefroid, P., Klarlund, N., Sen, K.: DART: Directed automated random testing. In: Conference on Programming Language Design and Implementation: PLDI, Chicago, IL. Association for Computing Machinery, pp. 213–223 (2005)
11. Barrett, C., de Moura, L., Stump, A.: SMT-COMP: Satisfiability modulo theories competition. In: [48], pp. 20–23.
12. de Moura, L., Rueß, H., Sorea, M.: Lazy theorem proving for bounded model checking over infinite domains. In: Voronkov, A. (ed.) CADE 2002. LNCS (LNAI), vol. 2392, pp. 438–455. Springer, Heidelberg (2002)
13. Bernot, G., Gaudel, M.C., Marre, B.: Software testing based on formal specifications: A theory and a tool. IEE/BCS Software Engineering Journal 6, 387–405 (1991)
14. Gaudel, M.C.: Testing from formal specifications, a generic approach. In: Strohmeier, A., Craeynest, D. (eds.) Ada-Europe 2001. LNCS, vol. 2043, pp. 35–48. Springer, Heidelberg (2001)
15. Boyapati, C., Khurshid, S., Marinov, D.: Korat: Automated testing based on Java predicates. In: International Symposium on Software Testing and Analysis (IS-STA), Rome, Italy. Association for Computing Machinery, pp. 123–122 (2002)
16. Jéron, T., Morel, P.: Test generation derived from model-checking. In: [49], pp. 108–121
17. Veanes, M., Campbell, C., Schulte, W., Tillmann, N.: Online testing with model programs. In: Proceedings of the 13th Annual Symposium on Foundations of Software Engineering (FSE), Lisbon, Portugal. Association for Computing Machinery, pp. 273–282 (2005)
18. Tiwari, A.: Abstractions for hybrid systems. In: Formal Methods in Systems Design (to appear, 2007), http://www.csl.sri.com/~tiwari/new.pdf
19. Ben-David, S., Gringauze, A., Sterin, B., Wolfsthal, Y.: PathFinder: A tool for design exploration. In: Brinksma, E., Larsen, K.G. (eds.) CAV 2002. LNCS, vol. 2404, pp. 510–514. Springer, Heidelberg (2002)
20. Claessen, K., Hughes, J.: QuickCheck: a lightweight tool for random testing of Haskell programs. In: International Conference on Functional Programming, Montreal, Canada. Association for Computing Machinery, pp. 268–279 (2000)
21. Berghofer, S., Nipkow, T.: Random testing in Isabelle/HOL. In: 2nd International Conference on Software Engineering and Formal Methods, Beijing, China, pp. 230–239. IEEE Computer Society, Los Alamitos (2004)
22. Owre, S.: Random testing in PVS. In: Workshop on Automated Formal Methods (AFM), Seattle, WA (2006), http://fm.csl.sri.com/AFM06/papers/5-Owre.pdf

23. Sullivan, K., Yang, J., Coppit, D., Khurshid, S., Jackson, D.: Software assurance by bounded exhaustive testing. In: International Symposium on Software Testing and Analysis (ISSTA), Boston, MA. Association for Computing Machinery, pp. 133–142 (2004)

24. Beck, K.: Test Driven Development: By Example. Addison-Wesley, Reading (2002)

25. Henzinger, T.A., Jhala, R., Majumdar, R., Sanvido, M.A.: Extreme model checking. In: Dershowitz, N. (ed.) Verification: Theory and Practice. LNCS, vol. 2772, pp. 332–358. Springer, Heidelberg (2004)

26. Kosmatov, N., Legeard, B., Peureux, F., Utting, M.: Boundary coverage criteria for test generation from formal models. In: 15th International Symposium on Software Reliability Engineering (ISSRE 2004), Saint-Malo, France, pp. 139–150. IEEE Computer Society, Los Alamitos (2004)

27. Weyuker, E., Goradia, T., Singh, A.: Automatically generating test data from a Boolean specification. IEEE Transactions on Software Engineering 20, 353–363 (1994)

28. Kuhn, D.R.: Fault classes and error detection capability of specification-based testing. ACM Transactions on Software Engineering and Methodology 8, 411–424 (1999)

29. Tsuchiya, T., Kikuno, T.: On fault classes and error detection capability of specification-based testing. ACM Transactions on Software Engineering and Methodology 11, 58–62 (2002)

30. Okun, V., Black, P.E., Yesha, Y.: Comparison of fault classes in specification-based testing. Information and Software Technology 46, 525–533 (2004)

31. Utting, M., Legeard, B.: Practical Model-Based Testing. Morgan Kaufmann, San Francisco (2006)

32. Clarke, D., Jéron, T., Rusu, V., Zinovieva, E.: STG: a symbolic test generation tool. In: Katoen, J.-P., Stevens, P. (eds.) ETAPS 2002 and TACAS 2002. LNCS, vol. 2280, pp. 470–475. Springer, Heidelberg (2002)

33. Grieskamp, W., Gurevich, Y., Schulte, W., Veanes, M.: Generating finite state machines from abstract state machines. In: International Symposium on Software Testing and Analysis (ISSTA), Rome, Italy. Association for Computing Machinery, pp. 112–122 (2002)

34. du Bosquet, L., Ouabdesselam, F., Richier, J.L., Zuanon, N.: Lutess: A specification-driven testing environment for synchronous software. In: 21st International Conference on Software Engineering, pp. 267–276. IEEE Computer Society, Los Alamitos (1999)

35. Lee, D., Yannakakis, M.: Principles and methods of testing finite state machines. Proceedings of the IEEE 84, 1090–1123 (1996)

36. Whalen, M.W., Rajan, A., Heimdahl, M.P.E., Miller, S.P.: Coverage metrics for requirements-based testing. In: International Symposium on Software Testing and Analysis (ISSTA), Portland, ME. Association for Computing Machinery, pp. 25–36 (2006)

37. Heimdahl, M.P., George, D., Weber, R.: Specification test coverage adequacy criteria = specification test generation *In*adequacy criteria? In: High-Assurance Systems Engineering Symposium, Tampa, FL, pp. 178–186. IEEE Computer Society, Los Alamitos (2004)

38. Tretmans, J., Belinfante, A.: Automatic testing with formal methods. In: EuroSTAR 1999: 7th European Int. Conference on Software Testing, Analysis & Review. EuroStar Conferences, Barcelona, Spain, Galway, Ireland (1999)

39. Bozga, M., Fernandez, J.C., Ghirvu, L.: Using static analysis to improve automatic test generatin. In: Schwartzbach, M.I., Graf, S. (eds.) ETAPS 2000 and TACAS 2000. LNCS, vol. 1785, pp. 235–250. Springer, Heidelberg (2000)
40. Rusu, V.: Verification using test generation techniques. In: Eriksson, L.-H., Lindsay, P.A. (eds.) FME 2002. LNCS, vol. 2391, pp. 252–271. Springer, Heidelberg (2002)
41. Gulavani, B.S., Henzinger, T.A., Kannan, Y., Nori, A.V., Rajamani, S.K.: Synergy: A new algorithm for property checking. In: Proceedings of the 14th Annual Symposium on Foundations of Software Engineering (FSE), Portland, OR. Association for Computing Machinery, pp. 117–127 (2006)
42. Duprat, S., Souyris, J., Favre-Felix, D.: Formal verification workbench for Airbus avionics software. In: ERTS 2006: Embedded Real Time Software, Societe des Ingenieurs de l'Automobile (2006)
43. Hamon, G., de Moura, L., Rushby, J.: Automated test generation with SAL. Technical note, Computer Science Laboratory, SRI International, Menlo Park, CA (2005), http://www.csl.sri.com/users/rushby/abstracts/sal-atg
44. de Moura, L., Owre, S., Rueß, H., Rushby, J., Shankar, N.: Integrating verification components. In: These proceedings (2007)
45. Bloomfield, R., Littlewood, B.: Multi-legged arguments: The impact of diversity upon confidence in dependability arguments. In: The International Conference on Dependable Systems and Networks, pp. 25–34. IEEE Computer Society, San Francisco (2003)
46. Littlewood, B., Wright, D.: The use of multi-legged arguments to increase confidence in safety claims for software-based systems: a study based on a BBN analysis of an idealised example. IEEE Transactions on Software Engineering 33, 347–365 (2007)
47. Rushby, J.: What use is verified software? In: 12th IEEE International Conference on the Engineering of Complex Computer Systems (ICECCS), Auckland, New Zealand, IEEE Computer Society, Los Alamitos (2007), http://www.csl.sri.com/~rushby/abstracts/iceccs07-vsi
48. Etessami, K., Rajamani, S.K. (eds.): CAV 2005. LNCS, vol. 3576. Springer, Heidelberg (2005)
49. Halbwachs, N., Peled, D.A. (eds.): CAV 1999. LNCS, vol. 1633. Springer, Heidelberg (1999)

A Discussion on John Rushby's Presentation

Greg Nelson

John, I enjoyed your talk, especially the proposal part of it, and I have two amendments to suggest to your proposal. First of all, you said that you did not see any reason not to have the top-level logic to be quite comprehensive, a superset of all the logics used by the tools, and you then rapidly read a paragraph of features including, I remember, dependent typing but I heard many others. And that caused alarm bells to go off in my mind, because I found that it is easier to integrate a large number of features into a logic than into a programming language, and it is not trivial. You can't always get all the features that you want to be added. For example, it is very difficult to combine tools that assume a typed logic with an untyped logic. And if you throw in dependent subtyping, because you know that it is useful some time, you are actually excluding many tools from the tool bus.

John Rushby

Yes, that is true. So, for example, SAL has predicate subtypes like PVS, which does not have full dependent subtyping. [*Missing sentence*]. So I think there is some discussion possible here, mainly among those who can go into the highly technical details. I'd observe, some of what is going on on the bus is typing judgements. You know whether a thing is a finite state machine and that itself is a predicate subtype, whether it is dependent or not is up to the discussion.

Greg Nelson

I just was conveying my concern for what it is worth to you that I would try to make that top thing as simple as possible rather than as comprehensive as possible.

John Rushby

Okay, we got 15 years of competition to figure this out.

Greg Nelson

My second proposal is that the query language by which the front-end or top looks for tools on the tool bus to answer queries, I think, will become quite more complicated than what you are describing. Let me give you an example to explain that issue that, I think, is probably most important: Your example was: I want to know if this is a well-typed term and one of the tools that can test well-typedness comes back and returns the answer. It may very well be that no single tool can do that, but that one tool can put that query into a certain normal form and another query can find the well-typedness of that normal from, so that you really need to find sequential compositions or functional compositions of tools.

John Rushby

That is exactly right. I glossed over [*some aspects*]. But I did have a slide that talked about how you could discover that you could verify an infinite state system by making it finite state. The same chaining on queries could perhaps build those sequential compositions for tasks like type checking. So I think, your question shows that there are a lot of opportunities for spending money in this direction, and I look forward to those of us trying it.

Tony Hoare

I hope, you will accept *payment* in kind.

John Rushby

Contributions? Certainly. Of tools and code, yes.

Dependent Types, Theorem Proving, and Applications for a Verifying Compiler

Yves Bertot and Laurent Théry

INRIA Sophia Antipolis

1 Theorem Proving and Program Development

One approach to Prof. Hoare's challenge is to view the development of verified software from the perspective of interactive theorem provers. This idea is not new and many medium-scale software systems have been developed and verified in this manner. Developments based on HOL, ACL2, or PVS have already been described and advocated and our position stands on the same line: most powerful (higher-order) theorem proving systems already contain a programming language, programs can be developed and the correctness of these programs can be specified and verified, they can then be compiled into traditional executable code. In this sense, we already have a small scale example of a verification aware programming language.

We propose to take advantage of the notion of "dependent types" to ensure that this programming language combines powerful logical capabilities, reasonable expressive power, and practical linkage between computational content and logical annotations.

Almost all mathematic developments contain algorithms. This imposes that all theorem proving tools should contain a programming language. The usual approach is to restrict this programming language to make the verification of algorithms more regular. The most common kind of restriction is to consider a strongly typed side-effect free functional language, with restricted forms of recursion to ensure that all computations terminate (often boiling down to a language with algebraic data-types and a form of primitive recursion adapted to these datatypes). Apparently, this limitation on the programming language hinders the possibility to study realistic efficient programs, but this question can be circumvented to obtain the equivalent of full-fledged general purpose programming language.

The annotation mechanism found in the Floyd-Hoare approach is one of the best solutions to associate properties to programs and support mechanical verification of these properties. In a functional language programming with dependent types, this capability becomes naturally practical for functional programming languages.

2 Extension with Dependent Types

In the wide family of theorem provers for higher-order logic, we have experimented with provers based on type theory [5], where the distinguishing feature is the use

B. Meyer and J. Woodcock (Eds.): Verified Software, LNCS 4171, pp. 173–181, 2008.
© IFIP International Federation for Information Processing 2008

of dependent types and their possible interpretation as logical formulae. This feature adds expressive power to the programming language being studied inside the theorem prover. First, dependent types can be used to carry the annotations usually found in programs in the Floyd-Hoare approach. Second, the programs need not be total anymore, they can be partial because dependent types can be used to restrict the way functions are supposed to be used. Actually both points are the same: with dependent types we can assert that some function is to be used only on data that satisfies some input specification and we can also assert that the output data satisfies some property with respect to the input. In a sense, we consider that dependent types are the equivalent in the functional programming world to the Floyd-Hoare triples in the imperative programming world.

The treatment of partial functions is quite extensive. For instance, it is possible to describe functions whose termination is undecidable in general. Dependent types can be used to express that the value returned by these functions is valid only when one is able to prove that they do terminate. Dependent types are thus used to give a logical description of the domain of definition.

Translating the dependently typed programming language found in a type-theory based theorem prover to a conventional programming language is not direct. It is a more complex problem than for the recursive functional programming language found in other systems. It can be performed in a way that the computations that are relevant to the logical parts are discarded and only the relevant computations for an efficient construction of the result are present in the target program. This translation process, akin to separation between compile-time optimization run-time computation is usually known as *extraction* [9].

State-based programs from the conventional imperative programming world can also be described using monadic approaches (a big word to state that all functions take an extra argument representing the state and return a tuple as argument, where an extra component represents the modified state). Exceptions and other programming constructs can probably also be accommodated. The encoding of non-functional programming constructs needs to be taken into account in the extraction mechanism, so that efficient state-based programs are not translated to inefficient functional programming languages. This improvement of extraction is not done today, but there is no doubt it could be done satisfactorily in the foreseeable future.

The direct integration of dependent types into existing programming languages has also been studied for about 10 years. Notable results are exposed in [13] where the language ML is extended with a restricted form of dependent types, so that the conditions that need to be satisfied for type verification fall in the category of problems satisfied by some form of constraint programming. Another notable experiment is described in [1], where a subset of the Haskell language is extended with dependent types and verification relies on existence of proofs, which are simply other collections of well-typed programs. In both cases, the absence of restriction on recursion imply that well-typed programs may exhibit a behavior that is not foreseen by their types, but dependent types make it possible to perform more accurate verification of the correctness of programs.

3   Example Applications

In our team, we worked on a variety of examples, drawn from a variety of computer science domains, and often in collaboration with specialists from the addressed fields.

- Computer algebra: Buchberger's algorithm to compute Gröbner bases [11],
- Decision procedures: Stålmarck's algorithm for propositional logic [8], Presburger's procedure.
- Computer arithmetics: libraries for correct rounding in floating points, algorithms on floating point expansions (based on IEEE754 operations) [7], efficient square root computation (taken from the GMP library) [6].
- Programming language technology: Java byte-code verifier [3], compiler for a non-trivial fragment of C.
- Computational geometry: convex-hulls [10].

While many of these algorithms have been described in a purely functional language, we studied state-based encodings in a variety of manners, through abstract data-types or encodings of imperative programming languages with Floyd-Hoare like assertions. In some cases, this made it possible to prove properties about memory usage. Most of these program studies were supported by the development of important bodies of mathematical theory concerning for instance polynomials, plane geometry, real or rational numbers, programming language semantics, lattice theory.

3.1   Detailed Examples

In conventional functional programming, we write `a : b` to express that the value `a` has the type `b`. Types are constants like `int` or `bool`, sometimes parameterized constants like $list_\tau$, where τ is itself a type, and function types, written $\tau \to \tau'$. The use of parameterized constants is a precursor of using dependent types. For example the function that takes a list and returns its first element has the type $list_\tau \to \tau$, so the type of the result depends on the type of the input. So the extension is quite simple to express: with dependent types, parameterized type constants may be indexed by arbitrary values and the type of a function's result will be allowed to depend on the type of that function's argument. We need a new notation to represent this. We will use $\forall x : \tau, T\ x$ to represent the type of functions that take arguments in type τ and return a value in a type $T\ x$ that varies when the input x varies.

Meaningful dependent types and values could have the following form:

- vect x, the vectors of integers of length x, the value `vector_nil` could be a value in the type `vect 0` and the value
  `vector_app : ` $\forall$ ` n m, vect n * vect m ` $\to$ ` vect (n+m)`
  could be a dependently typed function that takes two vectors and builds an new vector by concatenation.

- lt y x, the witnesses (proofs) that $y < x$, The functions
  lt_1: $\forall$ x, lt x (x+1), and
  lt_m : $\forall$ x, lt x m $\rightarrow$ lt x (m+1)
  could be used to construct these witnesses. The type family lt is not a real type of values, but rather a type of proofs. Types of this kind are mostly understood as predicates.
- Given an arbitrary predicate P on the type τ, the {y | P y} would be a special notation to represent the elements of τ that satisfy the predicate P. Actually the elements of this type are the pair of a value y in τ and an element in the type P y.
- sorted a predicate on lists of integers,
- sorted_nil : sorted [],
  sorted_one : $\forall$ x, sorted [x], and
  sorted_cons : $\forall$ x y l,
  $\qquad\qquad$ lt x y $\rightarrow$ sorted (y::l) $\rightarrow$ sorted (x::y::l),
  theorems that can be used to build proofs that a list is sorted[1]
- {l | sorted l} could be the type of sorted list,
- permutation a 2-place predicate on lists of integers,
- permutation_refl : $\forall$ l, permutation l l,
  permutation_swap : $\forall$ x y l, permutation (x::y::l) (y::x::l),
  permutation_skip : $\forall$ x l_1 l_2,
  $\qquad$ permutation l_1 l_2 $\rightarrow$ permutation (x::l_1) (x::l_2), and
  permutation_trans : $\forall$ l_1 l_2 l_3, permutation l_1 l_2 $\rightarrow$
  $\qquad$ permutation l_2 l_3 $\rightarrow$ permutation l_1 l_3
  theorems that can be used to build proofs that a list is a permutation of another list.
- $\forall$ x, {y | sorted y /\ permutation x l}
  could be the type of a sorting function.
- mk_sorted_value : $\forall$ l x, sorted x $\rightarrow$
  $\qquad$ permutation l x $\rightarrow$ {y | sorted y /\ permutation l y}
  could be the type of the function that takes a reference list as first argument and injects a list and proofs that this list is sorted and a permutation of the reference in the type of sorted permutations of the reference.
- insert : $\forall$ x l, sorted l $\rightarrow$
  $\qquad$ {l' | sorted l' /\ permutation (x::l) l'}
  could be a function that inserts an element in a sorted list, where the type ensures that the result list is sorted and contains the elements of the initial list plus the inserted element.

Using dependent types also imposes that one adapts the constructs in the programming language. For instance, the different values returned for different patterns in a pattern-matching construct may have different types and the pattern-matching construct is adapted to let the programmer indicate how the return type varies depending on the matched pattern. The programming construct takes the following form:

---

[1] The notation a::l represents the list whose first element and tail are a and l.

```
match t₁ return T t₁ with
   p₁ => e₁
 | p₂ => e₂
end
```

This expression is only well-typed if e_i has the type p_i for the two possible values of i. The text appearing after **return** serves as an annotation of the functional program. For instance, a sorting algorithm could have the following formulation:

```
let rec sort l :
      {l' | sorted l' /\ permutation l l'} :=
match l return sorted l /\ permutation l l' with
      [] => mk_sorted_value [] sorted0 (permutation_refl l [])
 | x::l₁ => let (l₂,hyp_sorted_l₂, hyp_perm_l₁_l₂) := sort l₁ in
            let (l', hyp_sorted_l', hyp_perm_x_cons_l₂_l') :=
                 insert x l₂ hyp_sorted_l₂ in
              mk_sorted_value (x::l₁) l' hyp_sorted_l'
                 (permutation_trans (x::l₁) (x::l₂) l'
                   (permutation_skip x l₁ l₂ hyp_perm_l₁_l₂)
                   hyp_perm_x_cons_l₂_l')
end
```

This program contains computation information: the **sort** algorithm decomposes the argument list, sorts recursively the tail and then inserts the first element. The logical information given in the algorithm formulation shows how to combine hypotheses given by auxiliary functions and recursive calls to construct proofs that the result list is sorted and a permutation of the input.

This formulation of the algorithm contains both the description of what needs to be done to compute a sorted list and the justifications for these operation. If this is to be used as input to a compiler, one needs to get rid of all computations that are only relevant for the proofs. This operation is called extraction and it actually produces a new formulation of the algorithm where all logical information is discarded:

```
let rec sort l :=
match l with
      [] => []
 | (x::l₁) => let l₂ := sort l₁ in
              let l' := insert x l₂ in
              l'
end
```

The corresponding program is close to a regular program in a functional programming language and can be further compiled using a conventional compiler.

It is a matter of taste to decide how much logical information should appear inside the algorithm formulation. A conservative approach is to first describe the algorithm without using dependent types and then to prove its correction. The approach outlined in this example was to show that the logical information can appear in selected places in the algorithm formulation, using auxiliary theorems to condense all reasoning steps. When the function to be considered is partial and checking if an element belongs to the domain of definition is undecidable, there may be no other possibilities than mixing logical information inside the program.

4   Research Challenges

4.1   Libraries

The programming language supported by a verifying compiler is only likely to be adopted if it provides enough libraries so that programmers don't have to redo everything from scratch. Today, the programming languages for which complete program verification is possible suffer from the lack of companion libraries.

The work of adding libraries to a verifiable programming language can be done at two levels. The first level consists in weak specification and implementation, but no verification of the library itself. By weak specification, we mean that most of the characteristics of input and output for various procedures are left untold, but the specifications are enough to avoid most practical errors. This level is meaningful for libraries whose content is difficult to describe mathematically (think of the interface to windowing systems or networking tools, for instance).

In the second level for adding libraries to a verifiable programming language, the verifiable compiler itself is used to compile the libraries and ensure that they are correct. In this case, meaningful specifications of the procedures should be provided (for instance, the input to an integer square-root function should be a positive integer and the result is specified as the largest integer value whose square is smaller than the input).

Libraries of reusable components verified at the second level are being developed today, but true reusability has not been effectively assessed. Cases where a new software system is verified and relies on previously verified software units are rare. Intermediate objectives should be set for a variety of domains. In our case, we believe that libraries for continuous mathematics should be developed to make it possible to verify programs in domains that concern the measure and control of physical artifacts. More and more software is developed to control physical devices, in avionics, railroads, or automobiles. Some of this software may have a direct impact on human life, like for instance software used in medical robotics. We believe that this software should be verified with the utmost precision and should rely on libraries that are verified with the best available technology.

4.2   Algorithmic Structures and Programming Constructs

In our study of a wide variety of algorithms, we have found that there are several kind of algorithmic structures: simple loops, structural recursion, well-founded recursion, lazy recursion on potentially infinite data-structures. We know techniques to encode most of these algorithmic structures inside the restricted language of theorem proving systems. However, some of these techniques are especially difficult to implement and sometimes require intensive work from an expert to achieve an encoding that is amenable both to compilation (respecting the intended efficiency) and to formal verification. We believe the required level of expertise can also be lowered by providing proof toolkits that are adapted to these algorithmic structures. For instance, we are currently working on lazy evaluation on infinite data-structures [4].

In general, we believe that each specific domain requires specific methodologies. While an expert can encode most programs in a theorem prover's language by coming back to first principles, it is relevant to capitalize the expertise in a domain specific programming language. In this sense, verifying compilers are already provided in today's world, in the form of specialized programming languages with a well known formal semantics. Examples that come to the authors' mind (because of geographical proximity) are Esterel and Scade [2].

4.3 Software Reuse and Collaborative Work

Specifying the requirements and guarantees for a software component should obviously contribute to better re-usability of compiled code and promote contract-based collaboration on software development. However, our direct experience has shown that some problems need to be overcome to make software verification more productive.

The first point is that the specification of a software fragment should be interchangeable (for the same algorithmic content). Some characteristics of a given algorithm are usually left untold when writing its specification to make it easier to replace this algorithm with another. However, some untold characteristics may have a crucial importance for some larger programs. For instance, sorting algorithms work quite well if the relation with respect to which sorting occurs is not anti-symmetric. However, some algorithms are better than others (even for the same algorithmic complexity), because they may or may not provide the guarantee that an already sorted input will be left unchanged. This shows that a piece of software may have to be recompiled with respect to a modified specification. Verification re-use should be optimized in this case.

A second point concerns maintainability. When new improvements to the algorithms are designed, there is no certainty that verifying the improvement will incur only a marginal cost of verification. Systematic approaches to re-use the proof-work that was performed for a previous version of an algorithm need to be proposed.

5   The Wider Perspective

The challenge of providing a verifying compiler implies the challenge of designing a new programming language, because verification is more likely to succeed if the semantics of the language are suited for the purpose. Previous successful languages also came with a new field of application: C for system programming, Java for Internet applications, etc. It is sensible that a new important concept like verified software should justify investing in a new language. Past experiments where legacy languages were instrumented to support verification did clarify the situation, but the post-hoc verification of all legacy software is probably out of reach, and future programs should be written in a language that encourages programmers to insert meaningful logical information.

Software formal verification is gradually accepted in the industry today. If a verifying compiler has to become widely accepted, it has to prove its own relevance by bootstrapping. Verifying the compiler itself is also a keypoint for acceptance in the production of safety critical software. In this sense, it is a suitable landmark to provide a formally verified compiler. We have also worked on this topic and we believe this landmark can be reached in a few years.

Another general question is whether one should impose complete verification, as often performed in the theorem proving community, or be content with only partial verification of well-known kinds of properties, hoping to stay in a decidable logic. For instance, array bounds correctness problems are often solved easily with decision procedures for Presburger's arithmetic, and many programs will be verified completely automatically when they do not rely on advanced number theory. This characteristic will be an important one for the acceptance of this approach in a general setting. But seemingly simple programs may sometimes fall outside the area of decidable (or tractable) logic. In the example we studied in [12], array bound correctness actually relies on a complex theorem, stating that there always exists a prime number between n and $2n$. Algorithms that cannot be verified automatically should always be programmable in the language. Fully automatic and partial verification must be accommodated, but it should rather be at the choice of the programmer (for instance by choosing to admit unproven facts) than by restricting the logic.

References

1. Augustsson, L.: Cayenne - a language with dependent types. In: International Conference on Functional Programming, pp. 239–250 (1998)
2. Berry, G., Gonthier, G.: The esterel synchronous programming language: Design, semantics, implementation. Science of Computer Programming 19(2), 87–152 (1992)
3. Bertot, Y.: Formalizing a jvml verifier for initialization in a theorem prover. In: Berry, G., Comon, H., Finkel, A. (eds.) CAV 2001. LNCS, vol. 2102, pp. 14–24. Springer, Heidelberg (2001)
4. Bertot, Y.: Filters on coinductive streams, an application to Eratosthenes' sieve. In: Urzyczyn, P. (ed.) TLCA 2005. LNCS, vol. 3461, pp. 102–115. Springer, Heidelberg (2005)
5. Bertot, Y., Castéran, P.: Interactive Theorem Proving and Program Development, Coq'Art:the Calculus of Inductive Constructions. Springer, Heidelberg (2004)
6. Bertot, Y., Magaud, N., Zimmermann, P.: A proof of GMP square root. Journal of Automated Reasoning 22(3–4), 225–252 (2002)
7. Daumas, M., Rideau, L., Théry, L.: A generic library of floating-point numbers and its application to exact computing. In: Boulton, R.J., Jackson, P.B. (eds.) TPHOLs 2001. LNCS, vol. 2152, pp. 169–184. Springer, Heidelberg (2001)

8. Letouzey, P., Théry, L.: Formalizing Stålmarck's algorithm in Coq. In: Aagaard, M.D., Harrison, J. (eds.) TPHOLs 2000. LNCS, vol. 1869, pp. 387–404. Springer, Heidelberg (2000)
9. Paulin-Mohring, C., Werner, B.: Synthesis of ML programs in the system Coq. Journal of Symbolic Computation 15(5-6), 607–640 (1993)
10. Pichardie, D., Bertot, Y.: Formalizing convex hull algorithms. In: Boulton, R.J., Jackson, P.B. (eds.) TPHOLs 2001. LNCS, vol. 2152, pp. 346–361. Springer, Heidelberg (2001)
11. Théry, L.: A machine-checked implementation of Buchberger's algorithm. Journal of Automated Reasoning 26, 107–137 (2001)
12. Théry, L.: Proving pearl: Knuth's algorithm for prime numbers. In: Basin, D., Wolff, B. (eds.) TPHOLs 2003. LNCS, vol. 2758, Springer, Heidelberg (2003)
13. Xi, H., Pfenning, F.: Dependent types in practical programming. In: Conference Record of POPL 1999: The 26th ACM SIGPLAN-SIGACT Symposium on Principles of Programming Languages, San Antonio, Texas, pp. 214–227 (1999)

A Discussion on Yves Bertot's Presentation

Panagiotis Manolios

When you talked about compiler verification, you did not say anything about resource constraints. So, does your source language have unbounded memory or did you think about compiling it down to 32-bit architecture, where you also have to worry about not running out of resources?

Yves Bertot

Do you think about the square-root algorithm?

Panagiotis Manolios

No, no, about the compiler correctness.

Yves Bertot

For compiler correctness... No, it is not infinite memory. All memory can be addressed using an integer. So, we assimilated the type of pointers to the type of integers and we fixed the size for the integers. But this size does not need to be 2^{32}, it can be any fixed parameter.

Panagiotis Manolios

So, then you can have a correct C program that gets compiled down to a lower-level language, but the semantics is not preserved, because you run out of memory, say.

Yves Bertot

What we did is that at the level of C, we look at, the notion of address is already clear. So, this is an intermediate language and it would be the task of a higher-level language on top of it to take care of this distinction between conceptually infinite memory and this finite memory.

Generating Programs Plus Proofs by Refinement

Douglas R. Smith

Kestrel Institute, Palo Alto, California 94304 USA

1 Technical Approach

We advocate an automated refinement approach to developing programs and their proofs. The approach is partially embodied in the Specware system [6] which has found industrial and government applications. Our view is that the future of software engineering lies in the tight integration of synthesis and analysis processes.

1.1 Specifications

Refinement-oriented development starts with the requirements of the procuring organization. These requirements are typically a mixture of informal and semi-formal notations that reflect the needs of various stakeholders. To provide the basis for a clear contract, the requirements must be formalized into specifications that both the procuring organization (the buyer) and the developer (the seller) can agree to. Specifications can be expressed at a variety of the levels of abstraction. At one extreme a suitable high-level programming language can sometimes serve to express executable specifications. However, an executable specification requires the inclusion of implementation detail that (1) is time-consuming to develop and get right, and (2) might be better left to the developer's discretion. At the other extreme, a property-oriented language (such as a higher-order logic) can be used to prescribe the properties of the intended software with minimal prescription of implementation detail. The solution in Specware is a mixture of logic and high-level programming constructs that provides a wide-spectrum approach, allowing specification writers to choose an appropriate level of abstraction from implementation detail.

1.2 Refinement

A formal specification serves as the central document of the development and evolution process. It is incrementally refined to executable code. A refinement typically embodies a well-defined unit of programming knowledge. Refinements can range from situation-specific/ad-hoc rules, to domain-specific transformations, to domain-independent theories/representations of abstract algorithms, data structures, optimization techniques, software architectures, design patterns, protocol abstractions, and so on. KIDS [9] and Designware [12] are examples of systems that automate the construction of refinements from reusable/abstract

B. Meyer and J. Woodcock (Eds.): Verified Software, LNCS 4171, pp. 182–188, 2008.

design theories. A crucial feature of a refinement from specification A to specification B is that it preserves the properties and behaviors of A in B, while typically adding more detail in B. This preservation property allows us to compose refinements, meaning that a chain of refinements from an initial specification to a low-level executable specification can be treated as a single property- and behavior-preserving refinement, thereby establishing that the generated code satisfies the initial specification. An intrinsic capability of a refinement process is that proofs of consistency between the source and target of a refinement can be composed in a similar way. While this capability has not been implemented for general-purpose design (to our knowledge), it paves the way for refinement machinery that produces programs and proofs at the same time. Evidence for the feasibility of this capability may be found in several recent domain-specific code generators that generate programs, proofs, and other certification documentation automatically from specifications; e.g. the Specware-based JavaCard Applet generator from Kestrel [3], and the AutoBayes and AutoFilter projects at NASA Ames [14,15].

Why take a refinement approach to developing programs plus proofs? We can look at this question from several points of view.

1. *Software Lifecycle View* – Boehm observed many years ago that it is exponentially less expensive to fix an error in the requirements phase than to fix it in subsequent design, maintenance, and evolution phases [2]. The lesson is to focus attention on the requirements up-front and to rigorously maintain consistency during development and evolution (for a comparative experiment along these lines see [16]). This is the essence of refinement-oriented development. Boehm also estimated that many measures of software cost (including cost, schedule, and errors) increase superlinearly in code size (approximately to the 1.2 power). By focusing on specifications that omit implementation detail, the developer gains a quantitative advantage in managing this intrinsic complexity during design and evolution. In a simple experiment at Kestrel, Green and Westfold [5] show a 2-5x increase in dependencies when moving from specs to code. Since dependencies seem to be closely related to the inertia of complex systems, again the advantage accrues to a development process that focuses development effort on specifications and early designs.

2. *Language View* – Progress in Computer Science is often measured by progress in the the abstraction levels provided by programming and modeling languages. The natural continuation is towards languages that abstract away increasing amounts of implementation detail, together with the generative mechanisms for adding the missing detail. Compilers and automatic program generators typically work by supplying fixed implementations for the constructs of the source language. Clearly, for general-purpose design there will not be unique ways to implement property-oriented specifications, but instead there will be a choice of design abstractions that may apply. Therefore, a general-purpose refinement environment will be interactive, in much the same way that many successful theorem-provers are currently driven by user-guidance and automated tactics (e.g. PVS, HOL, Isabelle). However, by narrowing the scope to domain-specific

specification languages, the refinement process can again be fully automatic; e.g. Planware [1], JavaCard, AutoBayes, AutoFilter, and others).

3. *Cost of Assurance View* – A refinement-oriented development process has a different cost structure than traditional development. There is a capital investment in building domain models and machine-usable design knowledge, but these costs are amortized through reuse. Thus the cost of producing the first program in a domain may be higher, but the incremental cost of producing subsequent versions and other programs in the domain should decrease below the level of conventional programming. The cost of handling of proof obligations of specs and refinements should be less than the cost of analyzing the final product. Moreover, the incremental cost of (re)assurance under evolutionary steps is dramatically reduced under refinement when compared with post-hoc verification. The key lies in the reuse of the refinements. In a domain-specific setting, an evolution step is performed by modifying the initial specification or model, and then automatically generating a new program, plus its proof and certificates. In a general-purpose setting, the refinement structure may be at least partially replayed. If the refinements are generic and derived from reusable design knowledge, then the refinements may often still apply and absorb the changes. The assurance costs are mainly borne at library-development time when the generic/reusable refinements are verified (or generated correctly).

2   Progress – Specware Foundations

Specware [6] provides a mechanized framework for the composition of specifications and their refinement to codes in several programming languages. The framework is founded on a cocomplete category of specifications. The specification language, called MetaSlang, is based on a higher-order logic with predicate subtypes and extended with a variety of ML-like programming constructs. MetaSlang supports pure property-oriented specifications, as well as executable specifications and mixtures of these two styles. Specification morphisms are used to structure and parameterize specifications, and to refine them. Colimits are used to compose specifications, instantiate parameterized specifications, and construct refinements. Diagrams are used to express the structure of large specifications, the refinement of specifications to code, and the application of design knowledge to a specification. A recent extension of Specware supports the specification, composition and refinement of behavior through a category of abstract state machines [8].

The framework features a collection of techniques for constructing refinements based on formal representations of programming knowledge. Abstract algorithmic concepts, datatype refinements, program optimization rules, software architectures, abstract user interfaces, and so on, are represented as diagrams of specifications and morphisms. We arrange these diagrams into taxonomies, which allow incremental access to and construction of refinements for particular requirement specifications [11].

The framework is partially implemented in the research systems Specware, Accord, and Planware. Specware provides basic support for composing specifications and refinements, and generating code. Code generation in Specware is supported by inter-logic morphisms that translate between the specification language/logic and the logic of a particular programming language (e.g. CommonLisp, C, and Java). It is intended to be general-purpose and has found use in industrial settings. Accord extends Specware to support the specification and refinement of behavior and the generation of imperative code [8]. Planware transforms behavioral models of tasks and resources into high-performance scheduling algorithms [1].

A key feature of Kestrel's approach is the automated application of reusable refinements and the automated generation of refinements by instantiation. Previous experience with manually constructed and verified refinement (e.g. in VDM or B) has resulted in small-scale developments and costly rework when requirements change. In contrast, automated construction of refinements allows larger-scale applications and a more rapid evolution process. For example, in the 1990's Kestrel developed a strategic airlift scheduler for the US Air Force that was entirely evolved at the specification level. The application had about 24000 lines of generated code from a first-order logic specification. Over 100 evolutionary derivations were carried out over a period of several years using the KIDS system [9], each derivation consisting of approximately a dozen user design decisions. Current scheduling applications being developed using the newer Planware system consist of over 100k lines of generated code from less than 1000 lines of source specification. Code generation is completely automatic and takes a few minutes.

3   Research Challenges

Although we have emphasized a synthetic approach to program assurance, our view is that the future of software engineering lies in the integration of synthesis and analysis processes. By way of analogy, conventional programming relies on a tight integration of synthesis and analysis – compilers and their type analyzers work together to check the programmer's work and generate executables; and inside the compiler, flow analysis is used to inform various optimizations that transform and speed up the executable.

Similarly, we see an opportunity for a tight integration between the refinement process and the assurance generation process. At the spec level, there are proof obligations on the static consistency that can be verified (this is essentially an extended type analysis that includes for example, checking that predicate subtype properties hold). We would like to record such proofs together with the specification. When we compose specs, we would like to reuse those proofs to obtain necessary proofs of consistency of the composite specification.

Refinements also have proof obligations, which can be handled in a post-hoc verification style, or in a correct-by-construction style (which we prefer). Constructive theorem-proving (e.g. [4,7]) in the correct-by-construction generation of refinements provides a clear example of integrated, automated analysis and synthesis. In order to construct an expression to serve as the translation of a domain symbol in a specification morphism, we set up the problem of finding a constructive proof for a forall-exist formula [10]. A witness for the existential may be found by a saturation procedure in general logics or algorithmically by constraint solving in special theories.

One example of refinement construction involves the use of constructive theorem proving and reuse of code templates – code fragments for instantiating a code template can be generated as witnesses to existentially quantified variables in the correctness formula for the template, resulting in a correct-by-construction instantiation of the template [10,13]. The proving should be more robust and informed because it is taking place in a context where both intent (the specification) and design knowledge (the template and code context) are explicit.

Another point of connection lies in refinement generators. Some optimization techniques, such as simplification, partial evaluation, and finite differencing, are written as metaprograms that use a constructive prover and generate refinements [9]. To support the construction of both code and proofs, the metaprogram must produce also a proof for the obligations of the refinement and appropriately transform the proofs in the source specification.

One general need is for mechanisms to carry proofs along with specs as they undergo refinement. With such mechanisms, the definitions and proofs at one level are refined to definitions and proofs at the next level, so that proofs are integral to design, rather than a side activity. Proofs must also be composed under colimit, so that again, all composition and refinement activities produce both code and proofs.

The discussion above focuses on technical approaches to developing program and proof together during a refinement process. An orthogonal issue is the control of such a refinement process. As noted earlier, for general-purpose design it unlikely that there can be a tractable automatic procedure for translating requirement-level specifications to correct and efficient code. Our research prototypes KIDS [9] and Designware [12] support an interactive interface in which users select which form of design knowledge to apply next (design knowledge is embodied in metaprograms that may invoke constructive inference for subtasks). The Specware system [6] supports user-written metaprograms which, at compile time, have the effect of generating implementations from specifications in higher-order logic. Our experience with developing a variety of medium-scale applications with these systems is that, because of the granularity of the knowledge representations that we use, relatively few user decisions (a dozen or two) are needed to generate fairly complex, but correct, code.

However, the sweet spot for automated code generation lies in narrowing down the specification language and design knowledge to specific application domains. Planware [1] and JavaCard [3] are two domain-specific fully automatic code generators built in Specware. Planware defines a domain-specific requirement language for modeling planning and scheduling problems. From such a problem model (typically 100 to 1000 lines of text derived from mixed text and graphical input), it automatically generates a complex planner/scheduler together with editors and visual display code (over 100,000 lines of code for some applications).

By narrowing the specification language, the generator developers can effectively hard-wire a fixed sequence of design choices (of algorithms, datatype refinements, optimizations) into an automatic design tactic. The JavaCard generator (see paper in this issue) furthermore also generates proof of consistency between specification and code as a by-product of refinement.

4   Concluding Remarks

In light of the above discussion, we see the following activities as key aspects of an effective and scalable technology for generating programs and proofs of their consistency with specifications.

- Developing libraries of design theories and refinement generators – e.g. theories and application mechanisms for generating refinements that embody knowledge of architectures, formalized design patterns, policy classes, algorithm theories, datatype refinements, optimization transforms, and so on.
- An elaborated refinement process that tightly integrates the generation of refinements with recording, composition, and refinement of proofs.
- Experiments in the rational reconstruction of benchmarks – develop formal specifications for various benchmarks, as well as relevant domain theories and design theories, followed by a rational reconstruction of the design by refinement of similar code from the specifications.

References

1. Becker, M., Gilham, L., Smith, D. R. Planware II: Synthesis of schedulers for complex resource systems. Tech. rep. Kestrel Technology (2003)
2. Boehm, B.: Software Engineering Economics. Prentice-Hall, Englewood Cliffs (1981)
3. Coglio, A.: Toward automatic generation of provably correct Java Card applets. In: Proc. 5th ECOOP Workshop on Formal Techniques for Java-like Programs (July 2003)
4. Green, C.: Application of theorem proving to problem solving. In: Proceedings of the First International Joint Conference on Artificial Intelligence, pp. 219–239 (1969)
5. Green, C., Westfold, S.: Experiments suggest high level formal models and automated code synthesis significantly increase dependability. Tech. Rep. KES.U.00.8, Kestrel Institute (January 2001)
6. Kestrel Institute. Specware System and documentation (2003), http://www.specware.org/
7. Manna, Z., Waldinger, R.: A deductive approach to program synthesis. ACM Transactions on Programming Languages and Systems 2(1), 90–121 (1980)
8. Pavlovic, D., Smith, D.R.: Composition and refinement of behavioral specifications. In: Proceedings of Sixteenth International Conference on Automated Software Engineering, pp. 157–165. IEEE Computer Society Press, Los Alamitos (2001)
9. Smith, D.R.: KIDS – a semi-automatic program development system. IEEE Transactions on Software Engineering Special Issue on Formal Methods in Software Engineering 16(9), 1024–1043 (1990)

10. Smith, D.R.: Constructing specification morphisms. Journal of Symbolic Computation, Special Issue on Automatic Programming 15(5-6), 571–606 (1993)
11. Smith, D.R.: Toward a classification approach to design. In: Nivat, M., Wirsing, M. (eds.) AMAST 1996. LNCS, vol. 1101, pp. 62–84. Springer, Heidelberg (1996)
12. Smith, D.R.: Mechanizing the development of software. In: Broy, M., Steinbrueggen, R. (eds.) Calculational System Design, Proceedings of the NATO Advanced Study Institute, pp. 251–292. IOS Press, Amsterdam (1999)
13. Smith, D.R., Lowry, M.R.: Algorithm theories and design tactics. Science of Computer Programming 14(2-3), 305–321 (1990)
14. Whalen, M., Schumann, J., Fischer, B.: Synthesizing certified code. In: Eriksson, L.-H., Lindsay, P.A. (eds.) FME 2002. LNCS, vol. 2391, pp. 431–450. Springer, Heidelberg (2002)
15. Whittle, J., Schumann, J. Automating the implementation of Kalman filter algorithms. Tech. rep. NASA Ames Automated Software Engineering Group(submitted, 2004)
16. Widmaier, J., Schmidts, C., Huang, X.: Producing more reliable software: Mature software engineering process vs. state-of-the-art technology? In: Proceedings of the International Conference on Software Engineering 2000, Limerick, Ireland, pp. 87–92. ACM Press, New York (2000)

A Discussion on Douglas Smith's Presentation

Anthony Hall

You showed a very general notion of morphism where all theories from the higher level were preserved under the morphism. Now, in general, there are properties that are not preserved by refinement. So, is there somewhere a characterization of the theories that are preserved by your refinement steps?

Douglas Smith

The mathematical definition of morphism and interpretation between is that it preserves of theorems, not a theory. What the notion of theory is, what category you are in, or what logic you are in, is... [*sentence left incomplete*]. Maybe that is part of your question. Do we have logics that are rich enough to encapsulate the properties that are much more difficult to manage, like security properties or non-functional sorts of properties? And I think, that is a great avenue of research. We have looked at timed or hybrid automata with which a much richer collection of properties are representable. So, the question is, what are the morphisms and categories of timed automata? So, you are able to talk about the preservation of timing properties. I think, that is the game to play. Not to say that there is something that you cannot do, it is the question of, what is the right category that captures more and more the properties that we really want to have, and then get this nice, clean mathematical basis for doing refinement. I certainly do not have the full answer quite yet.

The Verification Grand Challenge
and Abstract Interpretation

Patrick Cousot

École normale supérieure
45 rue d'Ulm
75230 Paris cedex 05
France
Patrick.Cousot@ens.fr

1 Introduction

Abstract Interpretation is a theory of approximation of mathematical structures, in particular those involved in the semantic models of computer systems [4,10,11]. Abstract interpretation can be applied to the systematic construction of methods and effective algorithms to approximate undecidable or very complex problems in computer science. The scope of application is rather large e.g. from type inference [5], model-checking [13], program transformation [14], watermarking [15] to context-free grammar parser generation [16].

In particular, abstract interpretation-based static analysis, which automatically infers dynamic properties of computer systems, has been very successful these last years to automatically verify complex properties of real-time, safety critical, embedded systems.

For example, ASTRÉE [1,2,3,17,18,25] can analyze mechanically and verify formally the absence of runtime errors in industrial safety-critical embedded synchronous control/command codes of several hundred thousand to one million of lines C.

We summarize the main reasons for the technical success of ASTRÉE, which provides directions for application of abstract interpretation to the Verification Grand Challenge [22,23].

2 The Static Analyzer ASTRÉE

2.1 Programs Analyzed by ASTRÉE

ASTRÉE [1,2,3,17,18,25] is a static program analyzer aiming at proving the absence of Run Time Errors (RTE) in programs written in the C programming language[1].

ASTRÉE analyzes structured C programs, without side effects in expressions, dynamic memory allocation and recursion. All other features of C are handled including arrays, structures, union types, pointers, pointer arithmetics, etc [31].

---

[1] C programs are analyzed after macro-expansion.

B. Meyer and J. Woodcock (Eds.): Verified Software, LNCS 4171, pp. 189–201, 2008.
© IFIP International Federation for Information Processing 2008

These restrictions encompass many synchronous, time-triggered, real-time, safety critical, embedded software programs as found in aerospace, automotive, customer electronics, defense, energy, industrial automation, medical device, rail transportation and telecommunications applications.

2.2   Specifications Checked by ASTRÉE

ASTRÉE aims at proving that the C programming language is correctly used and that there can be no Run-Time Errors (RTE) during any execution in any environment. This covers:

- Any use of C defined by the international norm governing the C programming language (ISO/IEC 9899:1999) as having an undefined behavior (such as division by zero or out of bounds array indexing);
- Any use of C violating the implementation-specific behavior of the aspects defined by ISO/IEC 9899:1999 as being specific to an implementation of the program on a given machine (such as the size of integers and arithmetic overflow);
- Any potentially harmful or incorrect use of C violating optional user-defined programming guidelines (such as no modular arithmetic for signed integers, even though this might be the hardware choice);
- Any violation of optional, user-provided assertions (similar to assert diagnostics for example), to prove user-defined run-time properties.

2.3   Characteristics of ASTRÉE

ASTRÉE is sound, exhaustive, automatic, infinitary, efficient, trace-based, relational, specialized, domain-aware, parametric, modular and precise. More precisely:

- ASTRÉE is *sound* in that it always considers an over-approximation of all possible executions (for example with respect to the rounding of floating-point computations [33]). Since execution is undefined after some runtime errors and may have an unpredictable, implementation dependent effect (e.g. an array bound overflow might destroy code), ASTRÉE may have to assume that execution stops in case of definite runtime error (although in practice it may go on with an "undefined" behavior). If ASTRÉE can prove the absence of any runtime error, the program semantics is well-defined and the analysis is perfectly sound. Otherwise, the results produced by ASTRÉE describe correctly all executions before the first runtime error, if any;
- ASTRÉE is *exhaustive* and considers all possible run-time errors in all possible program executions. Hence ASTRÉE *never* omits to signal a potential run-time error, a minimal requirement for safety critical software;
- ASTRÉE is fully *automatic*, that is never needs to rely on the user's help such as program decoration with inductive invariants. It may only happen that a few hypotheses on the range of variation of some inputs or the clock rate and maximal execution time may have to be specified in a separate configuration file to exclude e.g. impossible behaviors of the execution environment;

- ASTRÉE is *infinitary*, that is uses infinite abstractions which are provably more powerful than finite abstract models [12]. This implies that convergence acceleration techniques such as widening/narrowing [10] must be used to enforce termination of fixpoint iterations. Simultaneous widenings in several separate, independently designed, abstract domains are ensured to enforce convergence thanks to an appropriate cooperation between abstract domains [18];
- ASTRÉE always terminates and has shown to be *efficient* and to scale up to real size programs as found in the advanced industrial practice. Observed typical figures are about 1 to 2 hours of computation per hundred thousands lines (although the program size only is not an appropriate measure of the program analysis complexity);
- ASTRÉE is *trace-based*, that is abstracts sets of execution traces as opposed to invariance involving only sets of states. This refined abstraction considerably enhances the precision of the analysis, in particular for functions and procedures [26];
- ASTRÉE is *relational* that is keeps track of relations between the values of program data (variables, fields of structures, array elements, etc). Examples are the octagon abstract domain [28,29,30,32,27] or binary decision trees [3,17]. Contrary to attribute-independent abstract domains (such as intervals [9]), relational abstract domains are expensive (with a polynomial behavior with high degrees, if not exponential [19], in the number of abstract variables). To scale up, ASTRÉE uses program analysis directives (which insertion in the program can be automated by preliminary phases of the analysis) to determine which candidate packs of variables should be separately considered in relational abstractions [3,17].
- Like *general-purpose static analyzers*, ASTRÉE relies on programming language-related properties to point at potential run-time errors. Like *specialized static analyzers*, ASTRÉE puts additional restrictions on considered program (e.g. no recursion, no side-effect in expressions, no forward go to) and so can take specific program structures into account. For example function and pointer analysis involves no approximation at all, which would not be possible with dynamic memory allocation and recursion;
- Moreover, ASTRÉE is *domain-aware* and so knows facts about application domains that are indispensable to make sophisticated proofs. For example, ASTRÉE takes the logic and functional properties of control/command theory into account as implemented in embedded programs [3,20,21];
- ASTRÉE is *parametric* in that the degree of precision of the analysis can be adjusted either manually (through parameters or directives in the program text) or mechanically (by automatic insertion of the directives by preliminary analysis phases). This means that the performance rate (cost of the analysis/precision of the analysis) can be fully adapted to the needs of its end-users;
- ASTRÉE is *modular*. It is made of separate parts (so called *abstract domains*) that can be assembled and parameterized to build application specific analyzers, fully adapted to a domain of application or to end-user needs. Written

in OCaml, the modularization of ASTRÉE is made easy thanks to OCaml's modules and functors;

- A consequence of undecidability in fully automatic static analysis is false alarms. Even a high selectivity rate of 1 false alarm over 100 operations with potential run-time errors leaves a number of doubtful cases which may be unacceptable for very large safety-critical or mission-critical software (for example, a selectivity rate of 1% yields 1000 false alarms on a program with 100 000 operations);

In contrast ASTRÉE, being modular, parametric and domain-aware can be made very *precise* and has shown to be able to produce *no false alarm* (and even *no alarm* after minor modifications for some critical programs), that is fully automated correctness proofs.

2.4   Program Verification with ASTRÉE

The strength of ASTRÉE is that, despite fundamental undecidability limitations, it scales up and can automatically do (or has shown to be easily adaptable by specialists to do) complex proofs of absence of RTE for the considered family of synchronous control/command software. Such proofs are large, complex and subtle, even more than the program itself, whence well beyond human capacity, even using provers or proof assistants.

This strength comes from a careful, domain-specific design of the abstract interpretation. Any imprecise abstraction that would not be able to express and automatically infer, without loss of information, an *inductive* invariant which is necessary to prove absence of RTE for any program in the considered family would inexorably produce false alarms and in practice many, because of cascaded dependencies. On the other hand, an abstraction that would be too precise for the objective of proving absence of RTE in the considered family of programs would lead to excessive computational and memory costs. Essentially ASTRÉE has demonstrated in practice that for a specific program property (absence of RTE) and a specific family of programs (synchronous control/command C programs) it is possible to find an abstract interpretation of the program which encompasses all necessary inductive proofs at reasonable costs.

This strength is also the weakness of ASTRÉE. Since ASTRÉE produces "miracles" on the considered family of properties and programs, end-users would like it to produce very good results on any C program. Obviously this is impossible since the abstractions considered in ASTRÉE will miss the inductive invariants which are out of its precisely defined scope. However, new abstractions can be explored outside the current scope of ASTRÉE and easily incorporated in the static analyzer.

3   Directions for Application of Abstract Interpretation to the Verification Grand Challenge

In light of the ASTRÉE, we propose a few directions for application of abstract interpretation to verification.

3.1   Program Verification

"A program verifier uses automated mathematical and logical reasoning to check the consistency of programs with their internal and external specifications" [23]. Following E.W.D. Dijkstra, there is a clear distinction between the verification or proof of the presence of bugs (that is "testing" or "debugging") from the verification or proof of the absence of bugs (that is "correctness verification" or "verification" for short). Of course the Verification Grand Challenge addresses the *correctness verification* only since the real challenge should be to find the *last* bug.

3.2   Error Tracing

Nevertheless, bugs have to be considered in the development process. When an automatic verification system signals an error, it is important to be able to trace the origin of the error, in particular to determine whether it is a bug or a false alarm. Abstract slicing may be useful to trace back the part of the computation which is involved in the bug/false alarm [38,39]. Then constraint solving techniques can help finding an actual counter-example. However, finding counter-examples can be extremely difficult, if not impossible, e.g. when tracking the consequences of accumulating rounding errors after hours of floating point computations.

3.3   Program Semantics

A program is checked with respect to a semantics that is a formal description of its computations. Numerous semantics have been proposed which differ in the level of abstraction at which they describe computations (e.g. sets of reachable states versus computation histories) and in the method for associating computations to programs (e.g. by induction on an abstract syntax using fixpoints versus using rule-based formal systems). These semantics can be organized in a hierarchy by abstract interpretation [7] so that different analyzers can rely on different semantics which can be formally guaranteed to be coherent, at various levels of abstractions.

In practice, although norms do exist for programming languages like C, they are of little help because too many program behaviors are left unspecified. So one must rely on compilers, linkers, loaders and machines to know, e.g. the exact effect of evaluating an arithmetic expressions. Since the Verification Grand Challenge addresses "significant software products", it is clear that methods for defining the semantics of programs are needed, at a level of precision which is compatible with the implementation.

An approach could be, like in ASTRÉE for absence of side effects in expressions, to reject programs for which this compatibility cannot be formally guaranteed. The abstraction methods to do so, might then be part of the programming language semantics, the restricted language being a subset of a larger existing language where undefined behaviors have been excluded. Such programming norms limiting the use of obscure, error-prone and/or non-portable features of programming languages tend to be more widely accepted in practice.

3.4   Compilation

That the semantics of a programming language precisely reflects program executions depends upon the correctness of the translation into machine code. So that verification of the compiler [24], of the object code [35,36] or of the translation [37] must be part of the complete verification process.

3.5   Specification

The program semantics restricts the verification to properties that can be expressed in terms of this semantics. The specifications (such as invariance, safety, security, liveness) further restricts the verification process to specific properties. Specifications themselves translate external requirements in terms of program computations. Thus it is necessary to define adequate specification languages, their semantics with respect to that of the programming language. This ranges from implicit internal specifications (like absence of runtime errors as defined by the semantics of the programming language) to arbitrary complex specification languages.

Specifications cannot be simply be considered as correct, since in practice they are not or e.g. only one side of interfaces satisfies the given specifications. Abstract interpretation techniques could be used both to analyze specifications and to check programs for resistance to specification unsatisfaction.

Finally, the analysis of the specification, should be checked to remain valid in the implementation, e.g. by reanalysis of the program or by translation validation.

3.6   Specification and Verification of Complex Systems

More generally, specifications refer, especially in the case of embedded systems, to an external world which should be taken into account to prove the correctness of a whole system, not only the program component. Progress has to be made on the abstraction of this external, often physical world, to be compatible with the program interfaces. We envision that abstraction can be applied to the full system (program + reactive environment) although the descriptions of the program and physical part of the system are a quite different nature (e.g. continuous versus discrete). A unification of abstraction in computer science and engineering sciences must be considered to achieve the goal of full system verification [8].

3.7   Verification of Program Families

The considered programs to be verified may range from one program (with a finite specific abstraction), to a family of programs with specific characteristics, to a programming language or even a family of programming languages. A broad spectrum verifier is likely to have many customers but also to produce too many false alarms, a recurrent complain of end-users of static analyzers. A finite abstraction can always be found for a given program and specification but discovering this abstraction amounts to making the proof [6], i.e. iteratively computing the weakest inductive argument. To get no false alarm, the consideration of families of programs for which generic, precise and efficient abstractions can be found might be a useful alternative, as was the case in ASTRÉE.

3.8   Required Precision of Verifiers

Automatic program verification requires the discovery of inductive arguments (for loops, recursion, etc). Proceeding by direct reference to the program semantics (as in refinement-based methods) amounts to the computation of the program semantics restricted to the program specification, which is not a finitary process. Abstraction is therefore necessary but leads to false alarms. The condition for absence of false alarm is that the weakest inductive argument suitable for the proof be expressible without loss of precision in the abstract (including for its transformers in the induction step) [6]. There is obviously no hope to find an abstract domain containing all of such inductive arguments, since this will ultimately amount to include e.g. all first-order predicates with arithmetic and one is back to undecidability.

3.9   Abstract Assertions

The choice of the form of the abstract assertions depends on the considered family of programs, the nature of the considered specifications and the corresponding necessary inductive arguments. Universal representations (as terms or specific encodings of sets of states), to be used in all circumstances, are likely to be very inefficient. The specific abstract assertions are implemented as abstract domains in ASTRÉE using specific encoding and computer representations that lead to efficient manipulation algorithms. The study of efficient implementation of abstract assertions and efficient algorithms in abstract domains can certainly make significant progress, in particular by considering the domains of applications of programs.

3.10   Application-Aware Verifiers

ASTRÉE is a program verifier with a very precise scope of application that is of synchronous, real-time control command systems. It can therefore incorporate knowledge about such programs, looking e.g. for ellipsoidal assertions when encountering digital filters [20]. In absence of such domain specific knowledge, a verifier might have to look for costly nonlinear invariants.

Among the application domains that have been largely neglected by the verification community are the numerical applications involving intensive floating point computations. To be sound ASTRÉE must perform a rigorous analysis of floating point computations [30]. Further abstractions of this complex semantics are needed.

3.11   Abstract Solvers

ASTRÉE uses sophisticated iteration techniques to propagate assertions and perform inductive steps by widening in solvers (see e.g. trace partitioning [26]). A lot of progress can still be done on abstract solvers, in particular for generic, parametric, modular and parallel [34] ones.

3.12   Combination of Abstractions

A verification in ASTRÉE is done by parts, each part corresponding to a separate abstract domain handling specific abstract assertions, with an interaction between the parts, formalized by the reduced product [11]. So a specific version of ASTRÉE is built by incorporating a choice of abstract domains, which can be program specific, and of the corresponding interactions [18].

3.13   Modular Analyzers

The modular design of ASTRÉE might be a useful approach to the necessity to have specific analyzers adapted to domains of applications and the need for general tools for program verification. One can imagine a large collections of abstract domains and solvers that can be combined on demand to adjust the cost/precision ratio, depending upon the proposed application of the verifier.

3.14   User Interface

Static analyzers like ASTRÉE yield extremely complex informations on program executions that the end-user may want to understand. For that purpose, a user-interface is needed to present internal information in understandable form, at different levels of abstractions.

3.15   Verifier Infrastructure

Once a programming, a specification and a user-interface language have been chosen, and their semantics defined, a static analyzer has to provide computer representations of these languages for the purpose of the program analysis, the specification checking and the report of the results to the end-user. Despite the difficulty to design such a general-purpose infrastructure, it should be sharable between different verifiers to accelerate experimentations and developments.

3.16   The Verified Verifier

A recurrent question about ASTRÉE is whether it has been verified and this question is likely to appear for any verifier. A verification has three phases,

1. the computation of an inductive assertion implied by the semantics and the specification which involves resolution of fixpoint inequations,
2. the verification that the assertion is indeed inductive, and
3. finally the proof that the inductive assertion implies the specification.

All phases are formally specified by abstract interpretation theory. The first phase is indeed the more complex but, from a strict soundness point of view, it does not need to be formally verified. Only the second and third phases of the verifier must be verified, which is simpler. Preliminary work on ASTRÉE shows that this is indeed possible. The verified verifier is indeed part of the Verification Grand Challenge.

3.17   Acceptance and Dissemination of Static Analysis

The dissemination and widespread adoption of formal methods is confronted with economic payoff criteria. Not doing any correctness proof is, at first sight, easier and less expensive.

Regulation might be necessary to enforce the adoption of formal methods to produce safer software (e.g. in industrial norms). Static analysis, which has shown to scale up in an industrial context, is a very good candidate.

End-users might also be willing to enforce their right for verified software products. The ability to perform automatically static analyzes showing that products are not state of the art might even be a decisive argument to change present-day permissive laws regarding software reliability.

4   Conclusion

Abstraction, as formalized by Abstract Interpretation, is certainly central in the Verification Grand Challenge, as shown by its recent applications, that do scale up for real-life safety critical industrial applications. A Grand Challenge for abstract interpretation is to extend its scope to complex systems, from design to implementation.

References

1. Blanchet, B., Cousot, P., Cousot, R., Feret, J., Mauborgne, L., Miné, A., Monniaux, D., Rival, X.: The ASTRÉE Static Analyzer, http://www.astree.ens.fr/
2. Blanchet, B., Cousot, P., Cousot, R., Feret, J., Mauborgne, L., Miné, A., Monniaux, D., Rival, X.: Design and implementation of a special-purpose static program analyzer for safety-critical real-time embedded software. In: Mogensen, T.Æ., Schmidt, D.A., Sudborough, I.H. (eds.) The Essence of Computation. LNCS, vol. 2566, pp. 85–108. Springer, Heidelberg (2002)
3. Blanchet, B., Cousot, P., Cousot, R., Feret, J., Mauborgne, L., Miné, A., Monniaux, D., Rival, X.: A static analyzer for large safety-critical software. In: Proceedings of the ACM SIGPLAN '2003 Conference on Programming Language Design and Implementation (PLDI), San Diego, California, United States, June 7-14, 2003, pp. 196–207. ACM Press, New York (2003)
4. Cousot, P.: Méthodes itératives de construction et d'approximation de points fixes d'opérateurs monotones sur un treillis, analyse sémantique de programmes (in French). In: Thèse d'État ès sciences mathématiques, Université scientifique et médicale de Grenoble, Grenoble, France, March 21, (1978)
5. Cousot, P.: Types as abstract interpretations. In: Conference Record of the Twentyfourth Annual ACM SIGPLAN--SIGACT Symposium on Principles of Programming Languages, Paris, France, January 1997, pp. 316–331. ACM Press, New York (1997)
6. Cousot, P.: Partial completeness of abstract fixpoint checking. In: Choueiry, B.Y., Walsh, T. (eds.) SARA 2000. LNCS (LNAI), vol. 1864, pp. 1–25. Springer, Heidelberg (2000)

7. Cousot, P.: Constructive design of a hierarchy of semantics of a transition system by abstract interpretation. Theoretical Computer Science 277(1—2), 47–103 (2002)
8. Cousot, P.: Integrating physical systems in the static analysis of embedded control software. In: Yi, K. (ed.) APLAS 2005. LNCS, vol. 3780, pp. 135–138. Springer, Heidelberg (2005)
9. Cousot, P., Cousot, R.: Static determination of dynamic properties of programs. In: Proceedings of the Second International Symposium on Programming, Paris, France, pp. 106–130. Dunod, Paris, France (1976)
10. Cousot, P., Cousot, R.: Abstract interpretation: a unified lattice model for static analysis of programs by construction or approximation of fixpoints. In: Conference Record of the Fourth Annual ACM SIGPLAN--SIGACT Symposium on Principles of Programming Languages, Los Angeles, California. United States, pp. 238–252. ACM Press, New York (1977)
11. Cousot, P., Cousot, R.: Systematic design of program analysis frameworks. In: Conference Record of the Sixth Annual ACM SIGPLAN--SIGACT Symposium on Principles of Programming Languages, San Antonio, Texas, pp. 269–282. ACM Press, New York (1979)
12. Cousot, P., Cousot, R.: Comparing the Galois connection and widening/narrowing approaches to abstract interpretation. In: Bruynooghe, M., Wirsing, M. (eds.) PLILP 1992. LNCS, vol. 631, pp. 269–295. Springer, Heidelberg (1992)
13. Cousot, P., Cousot, R.: Temporal abstract interpretation. In: Conference Record of the Twentyseventh Annual ACM SIGPLAN--SIGACT Symposium on Principles of Programming Languages, Boston, Massachusetts, United States, January 2000, pp. 12–25. ACM Press, New York (2000)
14. Cousot, P., Cousot, R.: Systematic design of program transformation frameworks by abstract interrpetation. In: Conference Record of the Twentyninth Annual ACM SIGPLAN--SIGACT Symposium on Principles of Programming Languages, Portland, Oregon, United States, January 2002, pp. 178–190. ACM Press, New York (2002)
15. Cousot, P., Cousot, R.: An abstract interpretation-based framework for software watermarking. In: Conference Record of the Thirtyfirst Annual ACM SIGPLAN--SIGACT Symposium on Principles of Programming Languages, Venice, Italy, January 14–16, 2004, pp. 173–185. ACM Press, New York (2004)
16. Cousot, P., Cousot, R.: Grammar analysis and parsing by abstract interpretation. In: Reps, T., Sagiv, M., Bauer, J. (eds.) Program Analysis and Compilation, Theory and Practice. LNCS, vol. 4444, pp. 175–200. Springer, Heidelberg (2007)
17. Cousot, P., Cousot, R., Feret, J., Mauborgne, L., Miné, A., Monniaux, D., Rival, X.: The ASTRÉE analyser. In: Sagiv, M. (ed.) ESOP 2005. LNCS, vol. 3444, pp. 21–30. Springer, Heidelberg (2005)
18. Cousot, P., Cousot, R., Feret, J., Mauborgne, L., Miné, A., Monniaux, D., Rival, X.: Combination of abstractions in the ASTRÉE static analyzer. In: Okada, M., Satoh, I. (eds.) Eleventh Annual Asian Computing Science Conference, ASIAN 06, LNCS, Tokyo, Japan, December 6–8, 2006. pp. 6–8. Springer, Berlin (to appear, 2006)
19. Cousot, P., Halbwachs, N.: Automatic discovery of linear restraints among variables of a program. In: Conference Record of the Fifth Annual ACM SIGPLAN-SIGACT Symposium on Principles of Programming Languages, Tucson, Arizona, pp. 84–97. ACM Press, New York (1978)
20. Feret, J.: Static analysis of digital filters. In: Schmidt, D. (ed.) ESOP 2004. LNCS, vol. 2986, pp. 33–48. Springer, Heidelberg (2004)
21. Feret, J.: The arithmetic-geometric progression abstract domain. In: Cousot, R. (ed.) VMCAI 2005. LNCS, vol. 3385, pp. 42–58. Springer, Heidelberg (2005)

22. Hoare, C.A.R.: The verifying compiler, a grand challenge for computing research. Journal of the Association for Computing Machinary 50(1), 63–69 (2003)
23. Hoare, C.A.R.: The verifying compiler, a grand challenge for computing research. In: Cousot, R. (ed.) VMCAI 2005. LNCS, vol. 3385, p. 78. Springer, Heidelberg (2005)
24. Leroy, X.: Formal certification of a compiler back-end or: programming a compiler with a proof assistant. In: Conference Record of the Thirtythird Annual ACM SIGPLAN-SIGACT Symposium on Principles of Programming Languages, Charleston, South Carolina, pp. 42–54. ACM Press, New York (2006)
25. Mauborgne, L.: ASTRÉE: Verification of absence of run-time error. In: Jacquart, P. (ed.) Building the Information Society, ch. 4, pp. 385–392. Kluwer Academic Publishers, Dordrecht (2004)
26. Mauborgne, L., Rival, X.: Trace partitioning in abstract interpretation based static analyzer. In: Sagiv, M. (ed.) ESOP 2005. LNCS, vol. 3444, pp. 5–20. Springer, Heidelberg (2005)
27. Miné, A.: The Octagon abstract domain library. http://www.di.ens.fr/~mine/oct/
28. Miné, A.: A new numerical abstract domain based on difference-bound matrices. In: Danvy, O., Filinski, A. (eds.) PADO 2001. LNCS, vol. 2053, pp. 155–172. Springer, Heidelberg (2001)
29. Miné, A.: A few graph-based relational numerical abstract domains. In: Hermenegildo, M.V., Puebla, G. (eds.) SAS 2002. LNCS, vol. 2477, pp. 117–132. Springer, Heidelberg (2002)
30. Miné, A.: Relational abstract domains for the detection of floating-point run-time errors. In: Schmidt, D. (ed.) ESOP 2004. LNCS, vol. 2986, pp. 3–17. Springer, Heidelberg (2004)
31. Miné, A.: Field-sensitive value analysis of embedded C programs with union types and pointer arithmetics. In: Proceedings of the ACM SIGPLAN/SIGBED Conference on Languages, Compilers, and Tools for Embedded Systems, LCTES '2006, June 2006, pp. 54–63. ACM Press, New York (2006)
32. Miné, A.: The octagon abstract domain. Higher-Order and Symbolic Computation 19, 31–100 (2006)
33. Miné, A.: Symbolic methods to enhance the precision of numerical abstract domains. In: Emerson, E.A., Namjoshi, K.S. (eds.) VMCAI 2006. LNCS, vol. 3855, pp. 348–363. Springer, Heidelberg (2005)
34. Monniaux, D.: The parallel implementation of the ASTRÉE static analyzer. In: Yi, K. (ed.) APLAS 2005. LNCS, vol. 3780, pp. 86–96. Springer, Heidelberg (2005)
35. Rival, X.: Abstract interpretation based certification of assembly code. In: Zuck, L.D., Attie, P.C., Cortesi, A., Mukhopadhyay, S. (eds.) VMCAI 2003. LNCS, vol. 2575, pp. 41–55. Springer, Heidelberg (2002)
36. Rival, X.: Invariant translation-based certification of assembly code. International Journal on Software and Tools for Technology Transfer 6(1), 15–37 (2004)
37. Rival, X.: Symbolic transfer functions-based approaches to certified compilation. In: Conference Record of the Thirtyfirst Annual ACM SIGPLAN-SIGACT Symposium on Principles of Programming Languages, Venice, Italy, pp. 1–13. ACM Press, New York (2004)
38. Rival, X.: Abstract dependences for alarm diagnosis. In: Yi, K. (ed.) APLAS 2005. LNCS, vol. 3780, pp. 347–363. Springer, Heidelberg (2005)
39. Rival, X.: Understanding the origin of alarms in ASTRÉE. In: Hankin, C., Siveroni, I. (eds.) SAS 2005. LNCS, vol. 3672, pp. 303–319. Springer, Heidelberg (2005)

A Discussion after Patrick Cousot's Presentation

Wolfgang Paul

You said that we couldn't make a formal semantics of a real programming language. If we would believe this, I would suggest we go home immediately, because then the thing has failed. Your example was IEEE floating-point arithmetic incorporated into C or a suitable subset, which is the only thing that is used in industry. And incorporating a floating-point arithmetic definition into a C semantics is no problem whatsoever, and I point you to people in France who can do it easily for you.

Patrick Cousot

No, my point was correct. There is no semantics of C, because the semantics says: If there is something going wrong, the behavior is undefined. But the program behavior is not undefined. It does something; it goes on after the error. If you make an overflow, it will do something, and maybe destroy the program. So, if you make an analysis, you have two things: Either you take the semantics where it can do anything and you get no information, or you make an hypothesis that it stops when it is undefined. But then, the result of your analysis that says that you have one error is not true. It is: one error, if you stop the program at the first error. So, when there is zero error, you can prove that the two things are well defined. But, for example, for the floating-point, if you run the program on an Intel and on a Macintosh, the result is completely different, even if it is always correct in the analyzer, but it is different. And one reason is, Intel computes 80 bits [within the processor] and the IEEE [standard] is 64 [bits]. So, if you have 80 bits in the register and you put it [somewhere] in memory, it will become 64 bits, but if you do not put it in memory, it is all done in 80 bits. The result is different and maybe incorrect.

Wolfgang Paul

You are completely right that things are not the way, they should be, and I am aware of all these things. But it does not mean that they cannot be fixed. If you say, they cannot be fixed inherently, then we must go home, and therefore, you should not say this.

Patrick Cousot

We fix it by checking that the assembler satisfies these bit things *[end of sentence missing]*.

[Session chair Ganesan Ramalingam asks to postpone further discussion to the discussion session, and notes that Roderick Chapman had raised his hand for quite some time.]

Roderick Chapman, Praxis High Integrity Systems

My hand is nearly hitting the ceiling. Three things. Firstly, this is incredibly impressive work, and as an industrial application it's brilliant.

Secondly, in the discussion here, we must distinguish between the semantics of a programming language as is defined by ISO in the standard language definition in all their glory and the semantics of a programming language as implemented by one compiler, that is what you call a dialect of a language, and it's a completely different beast.

Thirdly, the formal semantics of SPARK, which are precise and very nearly complete, were constructed and written down by my colleagues almost ten years ago. And it is done, we did it, and you can have it, it is publicly available. So, there is an industrially available, used, formally defined programming language, and some people in this room, including Jim [Woodcock], reviewed those semantics, and they are available. Thank you.

Patrick Cousot

This was a comment [rather than a question]. I agree.

WYSINWYX: What You See Is Not What You eXecute

G. Balakrishnan[1], T. Reps[1,2], D. Melski[2], and T. Teitelbaum[2]

[1] Comp. Sci. Dept., University of Wisconsin
{bgogul,reps}@cs.wisc.edu
[2] GrammaTech, Inc.
{melski,tt}@grammatech.com

Abstract. What You See Is Not What You eXecute: computers do not execute source-code programs; they execute machine-code programs that are generated from source code. Not only can the WYSINWYX phenomenon create a mismatch between what a programmer intends and what is actually executed by the processor, it can cause analyses that are performed on source code to fail to detect certain bugs and vulnerabilities. This issue arises regardless of whether one's favorite approach to assuring that programs behave as desired is based on theorem proving, model checking, or abstract interpretation.

1 Introduction

Recent research in programming languages, software engineering, and computer security has led to new kinds of tools for analyzing code for bugs and security vulnerabilities [23,41,18,12,8,4,9,25,15]. In these tools, static analysis is used to determine a conservative answer to the question "Can the program reach a bad state?"[1] However, these tools all focus on analyzing *source code* written in a high-level language, which has certain drawbacks. In particular, there can be a mismatch between what a programmer intends and what is actually executed by the processor. Consequently, analyses that are performed on source code can fail to detect certain bugs and vulnerabilities due to the WYSINWYX phenomenon: "What You See Is Not What You eXecute". The following source-code fragment, taken from a login program, illustrates the issue [27]:

```
memset(password, '\0', len);
free(password);
```

The login program temporarily stores the user's password—in clear text—in a dynamically allocated buffer pointed to by the pointer variable password. To minimize the lifetime of the password, which is sensitive information, the code fragment shown above zeroes-out the buffer pointed to by password before returning it to the heap. Unfortunately, a compiler that performs useless-code elimination may reason that the program never uses the values written by the call on memset, and therefore the call on memset

---

[1] Static analysis provides a way to obtain information about the possible states that a program reaches during execution, but without actually running the program on specific inputs. Static-analysis techniques explore the program's behavior for *all* possible inputs and *all* possible states that the program can reach. To make this feasible, the program is "run in the aggregate"—i.e., on descriptors that represent *collections* of memory configurations [13].

B. Meyer and J. Woodcock (Eds.): Verified Software, LNCS 4171, pp. 202–213, 2008.

can be removed—thereby leaving sensitive information exposed in the heap. This is not just hypothetical; a similar vulnerability was discovered during the Windows security push in 2002 [27]. This vulnerability is invisible in the source code; it can only be detected by examining the low-level code emitted by the optimizing compiler.

The WYSINWYX phenomenon is not restricted to the presence or absence of procedure calls; on the contrary, it is pervasive:

- Bugs and security vulnerabilities can exist because of a myriad of platform-specific details due to features (and idiosyncrasies) of compilers and optimizers, including
  - memory-layout details, such as (i) the positions (i.e., offsets) of variables in the runtime stack's activation records, and (ii) padding between structure fields.
  - register usage
  - execution order (e.g., of actual parameters)
  - optimizations performed
  - artifacts of compiler bugs

  Access to such information can be crucial; for instance, many security exploits depend on platform-specific features, such as the structure of activation records. Vulnerabilities can escape notice when a tool does not have information about adjacency relationships among variables.
- Analyses based on source code[2] typically make (unchecked) assumptions, e.g., that the program is ANSI-C compliant. This often means that an analysis does not account for behaviors that are allowed by the compiler (e.g., arithmetic is performed on pointers that are subsequently used for indirect function calls; pointers move off the ends of arrays and are subsequently dereferenced; etc.)
- Programs typically make extensive use of libraries, including dynamically linked libraries (DLLs), which may not be available in source-code form. Typically, analyses are performed using code stubs that model the effects of library calls. Because these are created by hand they are likely to contain errors, which may cause an analysis to return incorrect results.
- Programs are sometimes modified subsequent to compilation, e.g., to perform optimizations or insert instrumentation code [42]. (They may also be modified to insert malicious code.) Such modifications are not visible to tools that analyze source.
- The source code may have been written in more than one language. This complicates the life of designers of tools that analyze source code because multiple languages must be supported, each with its own quirks.
- Even if the source code is primarily written in one high-level language, it may contain inlined assembly code in selected places. Source-level tools typically either skip over inlined assembly code [11] or do not push the analysis beyond sites of inlined assembly code [1].

In short, there are a number of reasons why analyses based on source code do not provide the right level of detail for checking certain kinds of properties:

- Source-level tools are only applicable when source is available, which limits their usefulness in security applications (e.g., to analyzing code from open-source projects).

---

[2] Terms like "analyses based on source code" and "source-level analyses" are used as a shorthand for "analyses that work on intermediate representations (IRs) built from the source code."

– Even if source code is available, a substantial amount of information is hidden from analyses that start from source code, which can cause bugs, security vulnerabilities, and malicious behavior to be invisible to such tools. Moreover, a source-code tool that strives to have greater fidelity to the program that is actually executed would have to duplicate all of the choices made by the compiler and optimizer; such an approach is doomed to failure.

The issue of whether source code is the appropriate level for verifying program properties is one that should concern all who are interested in assuring that programs behave as desired. The issues discussed above arise regardless of whether one's favorite approach is based on theorem proving, model checking, or abstract interpretation.

The remainder of the paper is organized as follows: §2 presents some examples that show why analysis of an executable can provide more accurate information than a source-level analysis. §3 discusses different approaches to analyzing executables. §4 describes our work on CodeSurfer/x86, as an example of how it is possible to analyze executables in the absence of source code.

2   Advantages of Analyzing Executables

The example presented in §1 showed that an overzealous optimizer can cause there to be a mismatch between what a programmer intends and what is actually executed by the processor. Additional examples of this sort have been discussed by Boehm [5]. He points out that when threads are implemented as a library (e.g., for use in languages such as C and C++, where threads are not part of the language specification), compiler transformations that are reasonable in the absence of threads can cause multi-threaded code to fail—or exhibit unexpected behavior—for subtle reasons that are not visible to tools that analyze source code.

A second class of examples for which analysis of an executable can provide more accurate information than a source-level analysis arises because, for many programming languages, certain behaviors are left unspecified by the semantics. In such cases, a source-level analysis must account for all possible behaviors, whereas an analysis of an executable generally only has to deal with *one* possible behavior—namely, the one for the code sequence chosen by the compiler. For instance, in C and C++ the order in which actual parameters are evaluated is not specified: actuals may be evaluated left-to-right, right-to-left, or in some other order; a compiler could even use different evaluation orders for different functions. Different evaluation orders can give rise to different behaviors when actual parameters are expressions that contain side effects. For a source-level analysis to be sound, at each call site it must take the join of the abstract descriptors that result from analyzing each permutation of the actuals. In contrast, an analysis of an executable only needs to analyze the particular sequence of instructions that lead up to the call.

A second example in this class involves pointer arithmetic and an indirect call:

```
int (*f)(void);
int diff = (char*)&f2 - (char*)&f1; // The offset between f1 and f2
f = &f1;
f = (int (*)())((char*)f + diff); // f now points to f2
(*f)(); // indirect call;
```

Existing source-level analyses (that we know of) are ill-prepared to handle the above code. The conventional assumption is that arithmetic on function pointers leads to undefined behavior, so source-level analyses either (a) assume that the indirect function call might call any function, or (b) ignore the arithmetic operations and assume that the indirect function call calls f1 (on the assumption that the code is ANSI-C compliant). In contrast, the analysis described by Balakrishnan and Reps [3,34] correctly identifies f2 as the invoked function. Furthermore, the analysis can detect when arithmetic on addresses creates an address that does not point to the beginning of a function; the use of such an address to perform a function "call" is likely to be a bug (or else a very subtle, deliberately introduced security vulnerability).

A third example related to unspecified behavior is shown in Fig. 1. The C code on the left uses an uninitialized variable (which triggers a compiler warning, but compiles successfully). A source-code analyzer must assume that local can have any value, and therefore the value of v in main is either 1 or 2. The assembly listings on the right show how the C code could be compiled, including two variants for the prolog of function callee. The Microsoft compiler (cl) uses the second variant, which includes the following strength reduction:

The instruction sub esp, 4 *that allocates space for* local *is replaced by a* push *instruction of an arbitrary register (in this case,* ecx*).*

In contrast to an analysis based on source code, an analysis of an executable can determine that this optimization results in local being initialized to 5, and therefore v in main can only have the value 1.

A fourth example related to unspecified behavior involves a function call that passes fewer arguments than the procedure expects as parameters. (Many compilers accept such (unsafe) code as an easy way to implement functions that take a variable number of parameters.) With most compilers, this effectively means that the call-site passes some parts of one or more local variables of the calling procedure as the remaining parameters (and, in effect, these are passed by reference—

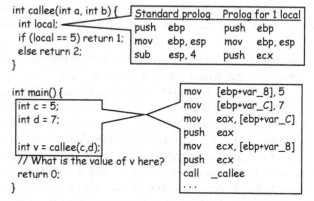

Fig. 1. Example of unexpected behavior due to compiler optimization. The box at the top right shows two variants of code generated by an optimizing compiler for the prolog of callee. Analysis of the second of these reveals that the variable local necessarily contains the value 5.

an assignment to such a parameter in the callee will overwrite the value of the corresponding local in the caller.) An analysis that works on executables can be created that is capable of determining what the extra parameters are [3,34], whereas a source-level analysis must either make a cruder over-approximation or an unsound under-approximation.

3 Approaches to Analyzing Executables

The examples in §2 illustrate some of the advantages of analyzing executables instead of source code: an executable contains the actual instructions that will be executed, and hence reveals more accurate information about the behaviors that might occur during execution; an analysis can incorporate platform-specific details, including memory layout, register usage, execution order, optimizations, and artifacts of compiler bugs.

Moreover, many of the issues that arise when analyzing source code disappear when analyzing executables:

- The entire program can be analyzed—including libraries that are linked to the program. Because library code can be analyzed directly, it is not necessary to rely on potentially unsound models of library functions.
- If an executable has been modified subsequent to compilation, such modifications are visible to the analysis tool.
- Source code does not have to be available.
- Even if the source code was written in more than one language, a tool that analyzes executables only needs to support one language.
- Instructions inserted because of inlined assembly directives in the source code are visible, and do not need to be treated any differently than other instructions.

The challenge is to build tools that can benefit from these advantages to provide a level of precision that would not otherwise be possible.

One dichotomy for classifying approaches is whether the tool assumes that information is available in addition to the executable itself—such as the source code, symbol-table information, and debugging information. For instance, the aim of *translation validation* [33,32] is to verify that compilation does not change the semantics of a program. A translation-validation system receives the source code and target code as input, and attempts to verify that the target code is a correct implementation (i.e., a refinement) of the source code. Rival [37] presents an analysis that uses abstract interpretation to check whether the assembly code produced by a compiler possesses the same safety properties as the original source code. The analysis assumes that both source code and debugging information is available. First, the source code and the assembly code of the program are analyzed. Next, the debugging information is used to map the results of assembly-code analysis back to the source code. If the results for the corresponding program points in the source code and the assembly code are compatible, then the assembly code possesses the same safety properties as the source code.

4   Analyzing Executables in the Absence of Source Code

For the past few years, we have been working to create a platform to support the analysis of executables in the absence of source code. The goal of the work is to extend static vulnerability-analysis techniques to work directly on stripped executables. We have developed a prototype tool set for analyzing x86 executables. The

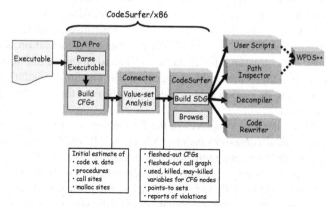

Fig. 2. Organization of CodeSurfer/x86 and companion tools

members of the tool set are: *CodeSurfer/x86*, *WPDS++*, and the *Path Inspector*. Fig. 2 shows how the components of CodeSurfer/x86 fit together.

Recovering IRs from x86 executables. To be able to apply analysis techniques like the ones used in [23,41,18,12,8,4,9,25,15], one already encounters a challenging program-analysis problem. From the perspective of the model-checking community, one would consider the problem to be that of "model extraction": one needs to extract a suitable *model* from the executable. From the perspective of the compiler community, one would consider the problem to be "IR recovery": one needs to recover *intermediate representations* from the executable that are similar to those that would be available had one started from source code.

To solve the IR-recovery problem, several obstacles must be overcome:

- For many kinds of potentially malicious programs, symbol-table and debugging information is entirely absent. Even if it is present, it cannot be relied upon.
- To understand memory-access operations, it is necessary to determine the set of addresses accessed by each operation. This is difficult because
  - While some memory operations use explicit memory addresses in the instruction (easy), others use indirect addressing via address expressions (difficult).
  - Arithmetic on addresses is pervasive. For instance, even when the value of a local variable is loaded from its slot in an activation record, address arithmetic is performed.
  - There is no notion of type at the hardware level, so address values cannot be distinguished from integer values.

To recover IRs from x86 executables, CodeSurfer/x86 makes use of both IDAPro [28], a disassembly toolkit, and GrammaTech's CodeSurfer system [11], a toolkit for building program-analysis and inspection tools.

An x86 executable is first disassembled using IDAPro. In addition to the disassembly listing, IDAPro also provides access to the following information: (1) procedure boundaries, (2) calls to library functions, and (3) statically known memory addresses and offsets. IDAPro provides access to its internal resources via an API that allows users to create plug-ins to be executed by IDAPro. We created a plug-in to IDAPro, called the Connector, that creates data structures to represent the information that it obtains from IDAPro. The IDAPro/Connector combination is also able to create the same data structures for dynamically linked libraries, and to link them into the data structures that represent the program itself. This infrastructure permits whole-program analysis to be carried out—including analysis of the code for all library functions that are called.

Using the data structures in the Connector, we implemented a static-analysis algorithm called *value-set analysis* (VSA) [3,34]. VSA does not assume the presence of symbol-table or debugging information. Hence, as a first step, a set of data objects called a-locs (for "abstract locations") is determined based on the static memory addresses and offsets provided by IDAPro. VSA is a combined numeric and pointer-analysis algorithm that determines an over-approximation of the set of numeric values and addresses (or *value-set*) that each a-loc holds at each program point.[3] A key feature of VSA is that it tracks integer-valued and address-valued quantities simultaneously. This is crucial for analyzing executables because numeric values and addresses are indistinguishable at execution time.

IDAPro does not identify the targets of all indirect jumps and indirect calls, and therefore the call graph and control-flow graphs that it constructs are not complete. However, the information computed during VSA can be used to augment the call graph and control-flow graphs on-the-fly to account for indirect jumps and indirect calls.

VSA also checks whether the executable conforms to a "standard" compilation model—i.e., a runtime stack is maintained; activation records are pushed onto the stack on procedure entry and popped from the stack on procedure exit; a procedure does not modify the return address on stack; the program's instructions occupy a fixed area of memory, are not self-modifying, and are separate from the program's data. If it cannot be confirmed that the executable conforms to the model, then the IR is possibly incorrect. For example, the call-graph can be incorrect if a procedure modifies the return address on the stack. Consequently, VSA issues an error report whenever it finds a possible violation of the standard compilation model; these represent possible memory-safety violations. The analyst can go over these reports and determine whether they are false alarms or real violations.

Once VSA completes, the value-sets for the a-locs at each program point are used to determine each point's sets of used, killed, and possibly-killed a-locs; these are emitted in a format that is suitable for input to CodeSurfer. CodeSurfer then builds a collection of IRs, consisting of abstract-syntax trees, control-flow graphs (CFGs), a call graph, a system dependence graph (SDG) [26], VSA results, the sets of used, killed, and possibly killed a-locs at each instruction, and information about the structure and layout of global memory, activation records, and dynamically allocated storage. CodeSurfer supports both a graphical user interface (GUI) and an API (as well as a scripting language) to provide access to these structures.

---

[3] VSA is a flow-sensitive, interprocedural dataflow-analysis algorithm that uses the "call-strings" approach [40] to obtain a degree of context sensitivity.

Model-checking facilities. For model checking, the CodeSurfer/x86 IRs are used to build a *weighted pushdown system* (WPDS) [7,35,36,31,30] that models possible program behaviors. Weighted pushdown systems generalize a model-checking technology known as *pushdown systems* (PDSs) [6,19], which have been used for software model checking in the Moped [39,38] and MOPS [9] systems. Compared to ordinary (unweighted) PDSs, WPDSs are capable of representing more powerful kinds of abstractions of runtime states [36,31], and hence go beyond the capabilities of PDSs. For instance, the use of WPDSs provides a way to address certain kinds of security-related queries that cannot be answered by MOPS.

WPDS++ [29] is a library that implements the symbolic reachability algorithms from [36,31,30] on weighted pushdown systems. We follow the standard approach of using a pushdown system (PDS) to model the interprocedural control-flow graph (one of CodeSurfer/x86's IRs). The stack symbols correspond to program locations; there is only a single PDS state; and PDS rules encode control flow as follows:

Rule	Control flow modeled
$q\langle u \rangle \hookrightarrow q\langle v \rangle$	Intraprocedural CFG edge $u \to v$
$q\langle c \rangle \hookrightarrow q\langle entry_P\ r \rangle$	Call to P from c that returns to r
$q\langle x \rangle \hookrightarrow q\langle\rangle$	Return from a procedure at exit node x

In a configuration of the PDS, the symbol at the top of the stack corresponds to the current program location, and the rest of the stack holds return-site locations—this allows the PDS to model the behavior of the program's runtime execution stack.

An encoding of the interprocedural control-flow as a pushdown system is sufficient for answering queries about reachable control states (as the Path Inspector does; see below): the reachability algorithms of WPDS++ can determine if an undesirable PDS configuration is reachable. However, WPDS++ also supports *weighted* PDSs, which are PDSs in which each rule is weighted with an element of a (user-defined) semiring. The use of weights allows WPDS++ to perform interprocedural dataflow analysis by using the semiring's *extend* operator to compute weights for sequences of rule firings and using the semiring's *combine* operator to take the meet of weights generated by different paths [36,31,30]. (When the weights on rules are conservative abstract data transformers, an over-approximation to the set of reachable concrete configurations is obtained, which means that counterexamples reported by WPDS++ may actually be infeasible.)

The advantage of answering reachability queries on WPDSs over conventional dataflow-analysis methods is that the latter merge together the values for all states associated with the same program point, regardless of the states' calling context. With WPDSs, queries can be posed with respect to a regular language of stack configurations [7,35,36,31,30]. (Conventional merged dataflow information can also be obtained [36].)

The Path Inspector provides a user interface for automating safety queries that are only concerned with the possible control configurations that an executable can reach. It uses an automaton-based approach to model checking: the query is specified as a finite automaton that captures forbidden sequences of program locations. This "query automaton" is combined with the program model (a WPDS) using a cross-product construction, and the reachability algorithms of WPDS++ are used to determine if an error configuration is reachable. If an error configuration is reachable, then *witnesses* (see

[36]) can be used to produce a program path that drives the query automaton to an error state.

The Path Inspector includes a GUI for instantiating many common reachability queries [17], and for displaying counterexample paths in the disassembly listing.[4] In the current implementation, transitions in the query automaton are triggered by program points that the user specifies either manually, or using result sets from CodeSurfer queries. Future versions of the Path Inspector will support more sophisticated queries in which transitions are triggered by matching an AST pattern against a program location, and query states can be instantiated based on pattern bindings.

Related work. Previous work on analyzing memory accesses in executables has dealt with memory accesses very conservatively: generally, if a register is assigned a value from memory, it is assumed to take on any value. VSA does a much better job than previous work because it tracks the integer-valued and address-valued quantities that the program's data objects can hold; in particular, VSA tracks the values of data objects other than just the hardware registers, and thus is not forced to give up all precision when a load from memory is encountered.

The basic goal of the algorithm proposed by Debray et al. [16] is similar to that of VSA: for them, it is to find an over-approximation of the set of values that each *register* can hold at each program point; for us, it is to find an over-approximation of the set of values that each (abstract) data object can hold at each program point, where data objects include *memory locations* in addition to registers. In their analysis, a set of addresses is approximated by a set of congruence values: they keep track of only the low-order bits of addresses. However, unlike VSA, their algorithm does not make any effort to track values that are not in registers. Consequently, they lose a great deal of precision whenever there is a load from memory.

Cifuentes and Fraboulet [10] give an algorithm to identify an intraprocedural slice of an executable by following the program's use-def chains. However, their algorithm also makes no attempt to track values that are not in registers, and hence cuts short the slice when a load from memory is encountered.

The two pieces of work that are most closely related to VSA are the algorithm for data-dependence analysis of assembly code of Amme et al. [2] and the algorithm for pointer analysis on a low-level intermediate representation of Guo et al. [22]. The algorithm of Amme et al. performs only an *intra*procedural analysis, and it is not clear whether the algorithm fully accounts for dependences between memory locations. The algorithm of Guo et al. [22] is only partially flow-sensitive: it tracks registers in a flow-sensitive manner, but treats memory locations in a flow-insensitive manner. The algorithm uses partial transfer functions [43] to achieve context-sensitivity. The transfer functions are parameterized by "unknown initial values" (UIVs); however, it is not clear whether the the algorithm accounts for the possibility of called procedures corrupting the memory locations that the UIVs represent.

---

[4] We assume that source code is not available, but the techniques extend naturally if it is: one can treat the executable code as just another IR in the collection of IRs obtainable from source code. The mapping of information back to the source code would be similar to what C source-code tools already have to perform because of the use of the C preprocessor (although the kind of issues that arise when debugging optimized code [24,44,14] complicate matters).

Challenges for the future. There are a number of challenging problems for which additional research is needed. Most of these are similar to the challenges one faces when analyzing source code:

- efficiency and scalability of analysis algorithms, including how to create summary transformers for procedures
- accounting for non-local transfers of control (e.g., `setjmp/longjmp` and C++ exception handling)
- analysis of variable-argument functions
- analysis of multi-threaded code
- analysis of heap-allocated data structures

As with source-code analysis, it would be useful to develop specialized analyses for particular kinds of data or particular programming idioms, including

- how strings are used in the program
- the "macro-level" effects of loops that perform array operations (e.g., that an array-initialization loop initializes all elements of an array [21])
- the effects of loops that perform sentinel search
- analysis of self-modifying code [20]

References

1. PREfast with driver-specific rules, Windows Hardware and Driver Central (WHDC) (October, 2004),http://www.microsoft.com/whdc/devtools/tools/PREfast-drv.mspx
2. Amme, W., Braun, P., Zehendner, E., Thomasset, F.: Data dependence analysis of assembly code. Int. J. Parallel Proc (2000)
3. Balakrishnan, G., Reps, T.: Analyzing memory accesses in x86 executables. In: Comp. Construct. pp. 5–23 (2004)
4. Ball, T., Rajamani, S.K.: The SLAM toolkit. In: Berry, G., Comon, H., Finkel, A. (eds.) CAV 2001. LNCS, vol. 2102, pp. 260–264. Springer, Heidelberg (2001)
5. Boehm, H.-J.: Threads cannot be implemented as a library. In: PLDI, pp. 261–268 (2005)
6. Bouajjani, A., Esparza, J., Maler, O.: Reachability analysis of pushdown automata: Application to model checking. In: Mazurkiewicz, A., Winkowski, J. (eds.) CONCUR 1997. LNCS, vol. 1243, Springer, Heidelberg (1997)
7. Bouajjani, A., Esparza, J., Touili, T.: A generic approach to the static analysis of concurrent programs with procedures. In: POPL, pp. 62–73 (2003)
8. Bush, W., Pincus, J., Sielaff, D.: A static analyzer for finding dynamic programming errors. Software–Practice&Experience 30, 775–802 (2000)
9. Chen, H., Wagner, D.: MOPS: An infrastructure for examining security properties of software. In: Conf. on Comp. and Commun. Sec, November 2002, pp. 235–244 (2002)
10. Cifuentes, C., Fraboulet, A.: Intraprocedural static slicing of binary executables. Int. Conf. on Softw. Maint. 188–195 (1997)
11. CodeSurfer, GrammaTech, Inc.
http://www.grammatech.com/products/codesurfer/
12. Corbett, J.C., Dwyer, M.B., Hatcliff, J., Laubach, S., Pasareanu, C.S.: Bandera: Extracting finite-state models from Java source code. In: ICSE (2000)
13. Cousot, P., Cousot, R.: Abstract interpretation: A unified lattice model for static analysis of programs by construction of approximation of fixed points. In: POPL (1977)

14. Coutant, D.S., Meloy, S., Ruscetta, M.: DOC: A practical approach to source-level debugging of globally optimized code. In: PLDI (1988)
15. Das, M., Lerner, S., Seigle, M.: ESP: Path-sensitive program verification in polynomial time. In: PLDI (2002)
16. Debray, S.K., Muth, R., Weippert, M.: Alias analysis of executable code. In: POPL (1998)
17. Dwyer, M., Avrunin, G., Corbett, J.: Patterns in property specifications for finite-state verification. In: ICSE (1999)
18. Engler, D.R., Chelf, B., Chou, A., Hallem, S.: Checking system rules using system-specific, programmer-written compiler extensions. In: Op. Syst. Design and Impl. pp. 1–16 (2000)
19. Finkel, A., Willems, B., Wolper, P.: A direct symbolic approach to model checking pushdown systems. Elec. Notes in Theor. Comp. Sci. 9 (1997)
20. Gerth, R.: Formal verification of self modifying code. In: Proc. Int. Conf. for Young Computer Scientists, pp. 305–313 (1991)
21. Gopan, D., Reps, T., Sagiv, M.: A framework for numeric analysis of array operations. In: POPL, pp. 338–350 (2005)
22. Guo, B., Bridges, M.J., Triantafyllis, S., Ottoni, G., Raman, E., August, D.I.: Practical and accurate low-level pointer analysis. In: 3nd Int. Symp. on Code Gen. and Opt (2005)
23. Havelund, K., Pressburger, T.: Model checking Java programs using Java PathFinder. Softw. Tools for Tech. Transfer 2(4) (2000)
24. Hennessy, J.L.: Symbolic debugging of optimized code. Trans. on Prog. Lang. and Syst. 4(3), 323–344 (1982)
25. Henzinger, T.A., Jhala, R., Majumdar, R., Sutre, G.: Lazy abstraction. In: POPL, pp. 58–70 (2002)
26. Horwitz, S., Reps, T., Binkley, D.: Interprocedural slicing using dependence graphs. Trans. on Prog. Lang. and Syst. 12(1), 26–60 (1990)
27. Howard, M.: Some bad news and some good news. In: MSDN (October, 2002), http://msdn.microsoft.com/library/default.asp?url=/library/en-us/dncode/html/secure10102002.asp
28. IDAPro disassembler, http://www.datarescue.com/idabase/
29. Kidd, N., Reps, T., Melski, D., Lal, A.: WPDS++: A C++ library for weighted pushdown systems (2004), http://www.cs.wisc.edu/wpis/wpds++/
30. Lal, A., Reps, T.: Improving pushdown system model checking. In: Ball, T., Jones, R.B. (eds.) CAV 2006. LNCS, vol. 4144, pp. 343–357. Springer, Heidelberg (2006)
31. Lal, A., Reps, T., Balakrishnan, G.: Extended weighted pushdown systems. In: Etessami, K., Rajamani, S.K. (eds.) CAV 2005. LNCS, vol. 3576, pp. 434–448. Springer, Heidelberg (2005)
32. Necula, G.: Translation validation for an optimizing compiler. In: PLDI (2000)
33. Pnueli, A., Siegel, M., Singerman, E.: Translation validation. In: Steffen, B. (ed.) ETAPS 1998 and TACAS 1998. LNCS, vol. 1384, Springer, Heidelberg (1998)
34. Reps, T., Balakrishnan, G., Lim, J.: Intermediate-representation recovery from low-level code. In: Part. Eval. and Semantics-Based Prog. Manip (2006)
35. Reps, T., Schwoon, S., Jha, S.: Weighted pushdown systems and their application to interprocedural dataflow analysis. In: Cousot, R. (ed.) SAS 2003. LNCS, vol. 2694, Springer, Heidelberg (2003)
36. Reps, T., Schwoon, S., Jha, S., Melski, D.: Weighted pushdown systems and their application to interprocedural dataflow analysis. Sci. of Comp. Prog. 58(1–2), 206–263 (2005)
37. Rival, X.: Abstract interpretation based certification of assembly code. In: Zuck, L.D., Attie, P.C., Cortesi, A., Mukhopadhyay, S. (eds.) VMCAI 2003. LNCS, vol. 2575, pp. 41–55. Springer, Heidelberg (2002)
38. Schwoon, S.: Moped system, http://www.fmi.uni-stuttgart.de/szs/tools/moped/

39. Schwoon, S.: Model-Checking Pushdown Systems. PhD thesis, Technical Univ. of Munich, Munich, Germany (July, 2002)
40. Sharir, M., Pnueli, A.: Two approaches to interprocedural data flow analysis. In: Muchnick, S.S., Jones, N.D. (eds.) Program Flow Analysis: Theory and Applications, ch. 7, pp. 189–234. Prentice-Hall, Englewood Cliffs (1981)
41. Wagner, D., Foster, J., Brewer, E., Aiken, A.: A first step towards automated detection of buffer overrun vulnerabilities. In: Network and Dist. Syst. Security (February, 2000)
42. Wall, D.W.: Systems for late code modification. In: Giegerich, R., Graham, S.L. (eds.) Code Generation – Concepts, Tools, Techniques, pp. 275–293. Springer, Heidelberg (1992)
43. Wilson, R.P., Lam, M.S.: Efficient context-sensitive pointer analysis for C programs. In: PLDI, pp. 1–12 (1995)
44. Zellweger, P.T.: Interactive Source-Level Debugging of Optimized Programs. PhD thesis, Univ. of California, Berkeley (1984)

A Discussion on Thomas Reps's Presentation

Egon Börger

It is more a remark on the first part of your talk. I think you are essentially saying that we need to take some notion of correctness of our compilers into account, assuming that at the semantical level, we have solved all our problems.

Thomas Reps

So, there are actually two points. One point is that you need to take that into account. And the second point is, I agree with Patrick [Cousot] that static analysis has much to offer. But the problem is, static analysis is the potential loss of precision that you can have by taking into account all possible paths. But some choices are fixed, when the code has been compiled. What we saw in the second example, was: You did not have to take into account two paths in that call procedure, because it was only possible for that program, as it had been compiled, to take one of those paths. So, it actually sharpens the results that you can get from static analysis. And if you are worried about security vulnerabilities or bugs, that helps you, that is just going to give us better answers.

Greg Nelson

Tom, how much effort would be required to port your tool to a platform other than Wintel?

Thomas Reps

It is based on abstract domains that can be applied to other machines. So, for example, there is an abstract domain that tracks integer arithmetic. That is actually a template; we did it as a template, because we have to deal with 16-bit and 8-bit instructions. You can instantiate it for 64-bit arithmetic, as well. So, most of it is language-independent, and of course, there is a lot of plumbing that you have to do, in order to move things to another platform.

My birthday is in seven months, and what I am hoping for is funds that would allow us to pursue some of these things like moving to other platforms, so we could examine the code that is running on your cell-phone, perhaps, or something like that. Thank you.

Implications of a Data Structure Consistency Checking System

Viktor Kuncak, Patrick Lam, Karen Zee, and Martin Rinard

MIT Computer Science and Artificial Intelligence Laboratory
32 Vassar Street, Cambridge, MA 02139, USA
{vkuncak,plam,kkz,rinard}@csail.mit.edu

Abstract. We present a framework for verifying that programs correctly preserve important data structure consistency properties. Results from our implemented system indicate that our system can effectively enable the scalable verification of very precise data structure consistency properties within complete programs. Our system treats both *internal* properties, which deal with a single data structure implementation, and *external* properties, which deal with properties that involve multiple data structures. A key aspect of our system is that it enables multiple analysis and verification packages to productively interoperate to analyze a single program. In particular, it supports the targeted use of very precise, unscalable analyses in the context of a larger analysis and verification system. The integration of different analyses in our system is based on a common set-based specification language: precise analyses verify that data structures conform to set specifications, whereas scalable analyses verify relationships between data structures and preconditions of data structure operations.

There are several reasons why our system may be of interest in a broader program analysis and verification effort. First, it can ensure that the program satisfies important data structure consistency properties, which is an important goal in and of itself. Second, it can provide information that insulates other analysis and verification tools from having to deal directly with pointers and data structure implementations, thereby enabling these tools to focus on the key properties that they are designed to analyze. Finally, we expect other developers to be able to leverage its basic structuring concepts to enable the scalable verification of other program safety and correctness properties.

1 Introduction

This paper discusses a set of issues that arise in the verification of sophisticated program correctness and consistency properties. The backdrop for this discussion is our experience building the Hob program analysis and verification system, which verifies that programs correctly preserve detailed data structure consistency properties. There are several reasons that this experience is relevant to a larger program analysis and verification effort. Data structures usually play a central role in the program. Other kinds of program correctness properties often depend on the data structure consistency properties. Analyses that are designed to verify other program correctness properties must therefore incorporate (and in some cases interact with) the analyses that verify data structure consistency properties. Failure to either verify data structure consistency

B. Meyer and J. Woodcock (Eds.): Verified Software, LNCS 4171, pp. 214–226, 2008.

properties or to present these properties in a form that supports further analysis can therefore threaten the entire program verification effort.

Data structure consistency properties are also some of the most challenging program properties to analyze and verify. Data structure consistency properties often involve complex relationships between pointers, arrays, and unbounded numbers of data objects. There is no consensus on an abstraction or analysis that would be suitable for effectively reasoning about such properties. Indeed, recent years have seen a proliferation of abstractions and analyses, each with an ability to support the verification of a particular class of data structure consistency properties [15, 2, 8, 25, 27]. It currently seems unlikely that any single approach will prove to be successful for the full range of data structures that developers will legitimately desire to use. Any system that overcomes these substantial difficulties to successfully verify detailed data structure consistency properties in non-trivial programs is therefore likely to provide concepts and approaches that will be relevant to other analysis and verification efforts. We see several specific contributions that our concepts, system, and overall approach can make to a broad program analysis and verification effort.

Data Structure Consistency Properties. Data structure consistency properties are important in and of themselves. Our system shows how to automatically verify detailed data structure consistency properties in complete programs. In particular, it shows how multiple analysis and verification systems can cooperate to verify a diverse range of properties.

Foundational System. Pointers and the data structures that they implement are a key complication that any analysis or verification system must somehow deal with. In many cases pointers are tangential to the primary focus, but if the analysis or verification system does not treat them soundly, the system can deliver incorrect results. One contribution of our system is that it provides a layer that encapsulates the pointers behind data structure interfaces and provides a characterization of the properties that objects accessed via pointers or retrieved from data structures satisfy. Our system builds on this layer, as can other systems, to obtain the data structure and pointer information needed to provide correct results.

Transferable Concepts and Approaches. Our framework provides several concepts and approaches that developers ought to be able to leverage when they build their analysis and verification tools. Approaches that we think will be relevant in other areas include 1) our approach for applying very precise, unscalable analyses to targeted sections of the program as part of a broader scalable analysis and verification effort and 2) our technique for eliminating specification aggregation (Section 2.3), which occurs when procedure preconditions propagate up the procedure call hierarchy to complicate the specifications of high-level procedures.

Multiple Interoperating Analyses. One of the major themes of this paper is the need for multiple analysis and verification systems to interoperate to analyze the same program. Attempting to build a single general system that treats all analysis and verification problems in a uniform way is counterproductive—it forces every potential developer to understand the system and work within it if they are to contribute and makes it difficult to combine results from different, potentially independently developed, program analysis and verification systems.

2 The Hob System

The Hob system is based on several observations about data structures and how systems use them.

Encapsulated Complexity.   Many data structures are designed to provide efficient implementations of relatively simple mathematical abstractions such as sets, relations, and functions. Appropriately encapsulating the data structure implementation behind an abstraction boundary (as in an abstract data type) can effectively encapsulate this implementation complexity. The complexity of the data structure (and therefore the complexity of reasoning about its consistency properties) is substantially larger inside the implementation than outside the implementation. In particular, it is usually possible to completely encapsulate any use of pointers within the data structure implementation. This encapsulation eliminates the need for analyses of data structure clients to reason about pointers—they can instead simply reason about the mathematical abstraction that the data structure implements.

Internal and External Consistency Constraints.   Most programs contain two kinds of data structure consistency constraints. *Internal constraints* identify properties of a single encapsulated data structure. These constraints typically deal with elements of the low-level representation of the data structure such as relationships between pointers and array indices. *External constraints*, on the other hand, involve multiple data structures and typically deal with individual data structures at the level of the mathematical abstraction that the data structure implements. A typical external constraint might, for example, state that one data structure contains a subset of the objects in another data structure.

Client Dependence.   Many data structure implementations will violate their internal consistency constraints if their clients use them incorrectly. For example, a linked list implementation may corrupt its internal representation if asked to insert an object into the list that is already present. Any practical data structure consistency analysis must therefore analyze both data structure implementations and clients.

Diversity.   Known data structures have a diverse range of internal consistency properties. Moreover, new data structures may very well come with new and unanticipated kinds of properties.

The overall design and approach of the Hob system takes these observerations into account and differs substantially from previous data structure analysis systems.

2.1 Decoupled Approach with Multiple Cooperating Analyses

In our approach, each data structure is encapsulated in a module, which consists of three sections: an implementation section, a specification section, and an abstraction section (which provides definitions for abstract specification variables). The *implementation*

```
spec module DLLIter {
  format Node;
  specvar Content, Iter : Node set;
  invariant Iter in Content;

  proc isEmpty() returns e:bool
    ensures not e <=> (card(Content') >= 1);
  proc add(n : Node)
    requires card(n)=1 & not (n in Content)
    modifies Content
    ensures (Content' = Content + n);
  proc remove(n : Node)
    requires card(n)=1 & (n in Content)
    modifies Content, Iter
    ensures (Content' = Content - n) & (Iter' = Iter - n);

  proc initIter()
    requires card(Iter) = 0
    modifies Iter
    ensures (Iter' = Content);
  proc nextIter() returns n : Node
    requires card(Iter)>=1
    modifies Iter
    ensures card(n')=1 & (n' in Iter) & (Iter' = Iter - n');
  proc isLastIter() returns e:bool
    ensures not e <=> (card(Iter') >= 1);
  proc closeIter()
    modifies Iter
    ensures card(Iter') = 0;
}
```

Fig. 1. Specification Section of a Doubly Linked List with an Iterator

section of a Hob module is written in a standard imperative language. The *specification section* of a module is written in terms of standard mathematical abstractions such as sets of objects. Each exported procedure has a precondition and postcondition expressed as first-order logic formulas in the language of sets. To illustrate the benefits of set interfaces, Figure 1 presents the specification section of a module implementing a doubly-linked list with an iterator. Note how complex manipulations of a list data structure are replaced by a relationship between the values of sets before and after procedure execution. The *abstraction section* is written in whatever language is appropriate for the analysis that will analyze the implementation. This section indicates a representation invariant that holds whenever control is outside of the data structure implementation, and provides the values of abstract variables (sets) in terms of the concrete variables (the values of fields of a linked data structure or expressions involving global arrays).

While this design adopts several standard techniques (invariants, the use of preconditions and postconditions to support assume/guarantee reasoning), it deploys these techniques in the context of very strong modularity boundaries that fully decouple the analyses. In particular, it is possible to apply different analyses to verify different data structure implementations and clients. Moreover, the complexity of each individual data structure implementation is encapsulated behind the data structure's interface. Here is how this design has worked out in practice.

Multiple Targeted Analyses. We have developed a variety of analyses, with each specific analysis structured to verify a specific, fairly narrow class of data structures. The ability to target each analysis to a specific class of data structures has provided substantial benefits. Eliminating the burden of building a single general analysis has reduced the overall development overhead and enabled us to produce very narrow but very sophisticated analyses with relatively little engineering effort. It has also reduced the amount of broad expertise any one person needs to acquire to develop an analysis. Finally, it has enabled us to simply decline to implement problematic special cases. These properties have made it much easier for us to bring people together to work on the system since the barrier to entry (in terms of required program analysis and verification expertise) to development effort for any one analysis are so much smaller.

Interoperating Analyses. We have been able to productively apply multiple cooperating analyses to the same program. This property has been absolutely crucial to developing a reasonable system in a reasonable amount of time—it has given us effective abstraction barriers that have allowed us to decouple individual development tasks and farm these tasks out to different people. This development strategy has had two key benefits: first, it has allowed us to parallelize the work, and second, it has allowed us to bring the strengths of multiple people to bear on the project, with each person given a task best suited to his or her capabilities.

Relief from Onerous Scalability Requirements. Because the data structure interfaces are written in terms of high-level mathematical abstractions (rather than implementation-level concepts such as pointers), the data structure implementation complexity remains encapsulated inside the implementation and is not exposed to the client. Of course, a data structure's implementation must be analyzed using some analysis technique. Because implementations may be arbitrarily complicated, and because our system aims to verify sophisticated data structure consistency properties, it is difficult to imagine any suitable analysis which could scale to sizable programs. However, our design eliminates any need for any single data structure analysis to scale—an analysis needs only analyze the data structure implementation, leaving the analysis of the clients to simpler and more scalable analyses.

Consider the implications of this approach. Roughly speaking, much of the history of program analysis deals with managing the trade-off between scalability and precision. To a first approximation, it is relatively straightforward to build an analysis or verification strategy for almost any property of interest if scalability is not a concern. It has also proved to be possible to build analyses of almost arbitrary scalability [26, 24] as long as precision is not a concern. Building scalable, precise analyses has, however, eluded the field despite years of effort. Our approach averts this problem by 1) limiting the amount of code that any one internal data structure consistency analysis is responsible for processing to the data structure implementation code, and 2) enabling the use of less precise, more scalable analyses outside of the data structure implementations.

The result is that we have been able to effectively use analyses whose scalability limitations would be prohibitive in any other context. Specifically, we have used analyses with exponential and super-exponential complexity [10] and even made good use of interactive theorem proving [30].

2.2 Clean Analysis Problems

One of the key problems that program analysis and verification researchers have struggled with is what abstraction to use for programs with pointers [5, 20, 15]. Indeed, this question is still open today and is the subject of much ongoing research. Standard approaches have used either special-purpose logics [18] or implementation-oriented ad-hoc formalisms such as graphs [23]. The result is that the field has been effectively estranged from many years of research into more standard mathematical foundations, which have provided a significant body of potentially useful results in areas such as set theory and more standard logics.

Our elimination of pointers as a concept outside of data structure implementations has enabled us to use more standard mathematical abstractions (sets and relations) for the majority of the program. This has, in turn, allowed us to effectively draw on the large body of research on the properties of these standard mathematical abstractions.

2.3 Specification Aggregation

During our development of the system we encountered a problem that, as far as we can tell, will complicate all attempts to use assume/guarantee reasoning to achieve modular program verification. Assume/guarantee reasoning starts with procedure preconditions and postconditions. To verify a procedure call, it translates the precondition into the caller's context, verifies that the analyses or verification fact at the point before the procedure call implies the translated precondition, then translates the postcondition into the caller context to obtain the analysis or verification fact at the point after the procedure call. It can verify that the procedure correctly implements its precondition and postcondition independently. In this way, assume/guarantee reasoning enables modular program analysis and verification.

If we attempt to apply this reasoning approach, however, we soon run into *specification aggregation*. To verify the precondition of the invoked procedure at a procedure call site, we typically have to include some form of the precondition in the precondition of the calling procedure. The preconditions therefore aggregate as we move up the procedure call hierarchy. At the top of the hierarchy the procedure preconditions and postconditions can become unmanageably complex. Moreover, the need to aggregate preconditions and postconditions violates the modularity of the program, as the preconditions of leaf procedures inappropriately appear in the preconditions of transitive callers; in principle, these transitive callers should be unaware of the low-level implementation details of the procedures that they invoke.

Our solution is to use aspect-oriented concepts to pull invariants out into specifications which exist on-the-side; such invariants live in *scopes* [11]. A scope identifies an invariant and the part of the program that may update the invariant. Because these invariants do not appear in procedure preconditions or postconditions, they do not cause specification aggregation. The analysis or verification algorithm does, however, have access to the invariant and can use it to prove properties anywhere except in the region of the program that may update the involved state. Scopes differ from hierarchical structuring mechanisms in that they can contain arbitrarily overlapping modules and avoid the dominant program decomposition problem. The scope construct works well with data structure consistency properties, since they tend to be true throughout most of the program and updated only in relatively small portions. The end result is a substantial simplification of the specification of the program.

2.4 Experience

We have built a prototype system and used this system to verify a range of data structure consistency properties [10,30,11,12]. As expected, we have been able to use unscalable analyses to verify very detailed internal data structure consistency properties. Specific properties include the consistency of linked data structures such as linked lists (both singly and doubly linked lists), trees, and array-based data structures. Our system is the first to verify such properties in the context of complete programs.

Our system has also been able to use the results of the analysis outside the data structure implementation to verify that the program uses the data structure correctly. In particular, we have also been able to use multiple analyses on the same program, then combine the analysis results to verify higher-level consistency properties that involve multiple data structures. These properties include correlations between data structures, for example that two data structures contain disjoint sets of objects. These properties often capture application-level constraints; for instance, in our Minesweeper program [10], we verify that the set of revealed cells is disjoint from the set of hidden cells.

Our system, perhaps surprisingly, enables developers to verify program correctness properties that may not appear, at first, to be data structure consistency properties. Specifically, we have been able to express typestate properties of objects and verify that programs do not invoke operations on objects when they are in the wrong typestate.

We have verified programs that are roughly one to two thousand lines long and contain multiple data structures analyzed by different analyses. Moreover, these programs implement complete computations such as the popular Minesweeper game, Water (a scientific computation that simulates liquid water) [3], and a web server. Our ability to demonstrate that our system is capable of verifying larger programs is limited largely by our ability to develop or port these programs.

3   Comparison to Some Related Approaches

Frameworks for formal software development use the idea of data refinement [7, Chapter 8] but achieve levels of automation similar to the use of our system with an interactive theorem prover alone [30]. The use of the full strength of our system provides a greater degree of automation compared to approaches based purely on verification condition generation and interactive theorem proving, thanks to the use of decision procedures and techniques for loop invariant inference. Like [7], our system acknowledges the importance of both aspects of the verification: the verification of data structure implementations and the verification of data structure clients. In contrast, most existing static analysis approaches verify only the clients of interfaces, typically expressed as finite state machines [1, 6], [22, Chapter 6]. The interfaces in Hob are more expressive than finite state machines, because they can express finite-state properties of an unbounded number of objects, and because they can express cardinality constraints on the number of objects that satisfy a given property. Researchers have also explored the verification of the usage of interfaces that are based on first-order logic [19]. Implementations of abstract data types have also been verified using TVLA [14]. Integration of these two sides—implementatations and interfaces—of verification in TVLA using assume/guarantee reasoning is the subject of ongoing research [29, 28]. Our approach in Hob was to single out the simple, yet powerful abstraction of global sets and explore the range of properties that such interfaces support [12]. Hob and the Spec# verifier [2] address different points in the design space. Whereas Hob adopts a simple model of encapsulation using modules and introduces new constructs for exploring novel overlapping inter-module grouping mechanisms such as scopes, Spec# uses instantiatable classes as the main unit of encapsulation and remains close to its starting point, the programming language C#. Regarding the level of automation, Hob appears to provide more automated handling of reachability properties in tree-like data structures, whereas Spec# has more support for arithmetic; these differences are partly a consequence of design decisions and partly a conequence of the decision procedures employed in these two systems. Finally, there is currently little emphasis on abstract specification variables in Spec#, whereas Hob uses them as the starting point for scalable analysis of the largest parts of the program.

4   Implications for Other Efforts

We see our system as relevant to other analysis and verification efforts in two ways. First, our treatment of pointers and data structures can serve as a foundation for other analysis or verification efforts that must deal somehow with programs that contain pointers and data structures. We envision analyses whose primary focus is not to verify detailed properties involving data structures or pointers, but that rely on the truth of some incidental data structure properties for the analysis to succeed. We envision our analysis providing these other analyses with a relatively abstract, tractable, and verified view of the data structures and pointers. Ideally, our system would give the developers of the new analysis or verification system the information they need quickly and easily, enabling them to productively focus their efforts on the problem of interest.

Second, we believe that the developers of other analyses may be able to use several of the concepts from our system to build analysis frameworks for their analysis problems. By building on these concepts, these analysis frameworks would be able to support the targeted application of multiple very precise, interoperating, unscalable analyses in a scalable way to a single program. We view our ideas as likely to be particularly useful when there is some relatively small part of the program that manipulates, in a fairly complex way, a clearly delineable part of the state (either of the program itself or of some system that it interacts with). Outside this small part of the program the state may be of interest but there is nothing complex going on. While data structures provide a canonical example of such a situation, we believe that this basic pattern is pervasive in modern software.

5   Future Work

We have implemented a prototype system Hob [13] for verifying data structure consistency and successfully applied it to a range of programs. Several further problems are worth exploring as we move forward; many of these problems are not specific to the domain of data structure consistency properties.

Specialized analyses and libraries of verified data structures. Among the strengths of our approach is the ability to verify a wide range of properties for a variety of data structures. This strength comes from the availability of specialized analyses for common data structures. Researchers have successfully verified many properties of tree-like data structures; on the other hand, there are fewer extant results on data structures that use arrays and non-tree-like data structures. Many ubiquitous data structures still lack verified implementations; we envision verifying them using techniques with varying levels of automation and building a library of verified data structures. We expect that, as such libraries grow, there will be many common reasoning patterns that will allow the results of verification to be extrapolated into fully automated analyses. Our approach supports such incremental development because it supports both interactive theorem proving and analyses with an increasing degree of automation.

Relevant tractable fragments of general-purpose logics. By using logical formulas to communicate analysis results, our system makes it convenient to build analyses that themselves use logic to encode dataflow information inside the implementations of modules. Such analyses are often precise and predictable because it is possible to describe the class of properties to which they apply. It is therefore useful to explore new classes of computationally tractable fragments of logics and constraints that can be used as a basis for analyses. We suggest defining these logics as fragments of general logics such as typed set theory, which have proven successful in formalizing a wide range of properties. The study of logical fragments allows us to deploy specialized algorithms while retaining simple semantics and the ability to communicate between different analyses. Our experience suggests that, although traditional classifications based on simple syntactic criteria are still useful [4, 9], data structure consistency constraints are likely to yield new kinds of classifications and new ways of defining subclasses of logics [17].

Experience from larger applications. Experience from using our techniques in the context of larger applications would further contribute to understanding the data structure consistency problem. We expect that the problem of internal data structure consistency is essentially the same in both large and small applications, with larger applications having greater diversity and wider data structure interfaces (to support many usage scenarios). We also believe that we have identified some of the high-level data structure consistency properties (such as disjointness and inclusion) that are likely to be generally useful. It remains to investigate classes of more complex high-level properties. It is possible that most of these properties will be domain-specific, with different kinds of useful and tractable constraints applicable to different domains.

Supporting common language features. To obtain experience with larger applications, it is important to support the features of commonly used programming languages. The evolution of languages has simultaneously contributed 1) features that simplify program semantics (such as memory safety and the ability to encode simple invariants using types) and 2) features that complicate reasoning (such as higher-order functions, continuations, dynamic dispatch, exceptions, reflection, and concurrency). An attempt to handle the worst-case scenario arising from the use of these features is not likely to be fruitful; it is instead important to consider the patterns in which these features are used and adapt the analyses to work reasonably well in these cases. In addition to making the automated analysis of these features practical, the study of these patterns is likely to yield important results in programming methodology and programming language design.

Correctness of analysis results. One of the major themes of this paper is the need for multiple analyses to interoperate on the same program. Ideally, implementors will have maximum flexibility in the implementation of these analyses, enabling the full range of implementors to bring their skills effectively to bear and make a contribution. In particular, we envision developers with varying areas of expertise, levels of competence, and programming styles and inclinations. Any time one combines the work of multiple people, questions of competence and trust arise. An error in one analysis or verification can call the entire result into question. We therefore believe that it is important to build a system that can verify the results of the various analyses and verifications. Such a system would accept and verify proofs of correctness of the results. We envision a system similar to Credible Compilation [16, 21] in which each analysis or verification system would generate, for each part of the program it processed, a proof that the specific result it generated on that analysis or verification is correct.

6   Conclusion

We are becoming ever closer to having the basic requirements in place for a successful and ambitious program analysis and verification project—a recognized and growing acknowledgement of the need for more reliable software, the raw computing power necessary to support the required reasoning, and a community of program analysis and verification researchers that, given an appropriate time and space budget, is able to deliver algorithms that extract or check virtually any well-defined property of interest.

Important remaining barriers include techniques that deal effectively with pointers and data structures and, especially, ways to bring multiple analyses together to interoperate during the analysis of a single program. It is especially important to support the targeted application of unscalable approaches in the context of a larger scalable analysis effort—these unscalable analysis and verification algorithms are the only way to verify the precise, detailed properties to which any successful analysis and verification effort must aspire.

We have addressed all of these issues in the context of the Hob system for verifying data structure consistency. This system provides an effective analysis interface for providing other analyses with pointer and data structure information. It has also employed a range of techniques that have enabled the successful coordinated application of a range of unscalable analyses to complete programs. These techniques, and especially the concepts behind them, should generalize to enable the construction of other systems for scalably verifying very precise program safety and correctness properties.

References

1. Ball, T., Majumdar, R., Millstein, T., Rajamani, S.K.: Automatic predicate abstraction of C programs. In: Proc. ACM PLDI (2001)
2. Barnett, M., Leino, K.R.M., Schulte, W.: The Spec# Programming System: An Overview. In: Barthe, G., Burdy, L., Huisman, M., Lanet, J.-L., Muntean, T. (eds.) CASSIS 2004, vol. 3362, pp. 49–69. Springer, Heidelberg (2005)
3. Blume, W., Eigenmann, R.: Performance analysis of parallelizing compilers on the Perfect Benchmarks programs. IEEE Transactions on Parallel and Distributed Systems 3(6), 643–656 (1992)
4. Börger, E., Grädel, E., Gurevich, Y.: The Classical Decision Problem. Springer, Heidelberg (1997)
5. Chase, D.R., Wegman, M., Zadeck, F.K.: Analysis of pointers and structures. In: Proc. ACM PLDI (1990)
6. Das, M., Lerner, S., Seigle, M.: ESP: Path-sensitive program verification in polynomial time. In: Proc. ACM PLDI (2002)
7. Jones, C.B.: Systematic Software Development using VDM. Prentice Hall International, UK (1986)
8. Kuncak, V., Lam, P., Rinard, M.: Role analysis. In: Annual ACM Symp. on Principles of Programming Languages (POPL) (2002)
9. Kuncak, V., Rinard, M.: Decision procedures for set-valued fields. In: 1st International Workshop on Abstract Interpretation of Object-Oriented Languages (AIOOL 2005) (2005)
10. Lam, P., Kuncak, V., Rinard, M.: On our experience with modular pluggable analyses. Technical Report 965, MIT CSAIL (September, 2004)
11. Lam, P., Kuncak, V., Rinard, M.: Cross-cutting techniques in program specification and analysis. In: 4th International Conference on Aspect-Oriented Software Development (AOSD 2005) (2005)
12. Lam, P., Kuncak, V., Rinard, M.: Generalized Typestate Checking for Data Structure Consistency. In: Cousot, R. (ed.) VMCAI 2005. LNCS, vol. 3385, pp. 430–447. Springer, Heidelberg (2005)
13. Lam, P., Kuncak, V., Rinard, M.: Hob: A tool for verifying data structure consistency. In: 14th International Conference on Compiler Construction (tool demo) (April, 2005)
14. Lev-Ami, T., Reps, T., Sagiv, M., Wilhelm, R.: Putting static analysis to work for verification: A case study. In: International Symposium on Software Testing and Analysis (2000)
15. Lev-Ami, T., Sagiv, M.: TVLA: A system for implementing static analyses. In: Proc. 7th International Static Analysis Symposium (2000)
16. Marinov, D.: Credible compilation. Master's thesis, Massachusetts Institute of Technology (2000)
17. Marnette, B., Kuncak, V., Rinard, M.: On algorithms and complexity for sets with cardinality constraints. Technical report, MIT CSAIL (August, 2005)
18. O'Hearn, P., Reynolds, J., Yang, H.: Local reasoning about programs that alter data structures. In: Fribourg, L. (ed.) CSL 2001 and EACSL 2001. LNCS, vol. 2142, Springer, Heidelberg (2001)
19. Ramalingam, G., Warshavsky, A., Field, J., Goyal, D., Sagiv, M.: Deriving specialized program analyses for certifying component-client conformance. In: PLDI (2002)
20. Reynolds, J.C.: Separation logic: A logic for shared mutable data structures. In: 17th LICS, pp. 55–74 (2002)
21. Rinard, M., Marinov, D.: Credible compilation with pointers. In: Proceedings of the Workshop on Run-Time Result Verification (1999)

22. Rinetzky, N.: Interprocedural shape analysis. Master's thesis, Technion - Israel Institute of Technology (2000)
23. Sagiv, M., Reps, T., Wilhelm, R.: Solving shape-analysis problems in languages with destructive updating. ACM TOPLAS 20(1), 1–50 (1998)
24. Steensgaard, B.: Points-to analysis in almost linear time. In: Proc. 23rd ACM POPL, Petersburg Beach, FL (January, 1996)
25. Sălcianu, A.D., Rinard, M.: Purity and side-effect analysis for java programs. In: Proc. 6th International Conference on Verification, Model Checking and Abstract Interpretation (to appear, January 2005)
26. Xie, Y., Aiken, A.: Scalable error detection using boolean satisfiability. In: POPL 2005 (2005)
27. Yang, J., Twohey, P., Engler, D., Musuvathi, M.: Using model checking to find serious file system errors. In: OSDI 2004 (2004)
28. Yorsh, G., Reps, T., Sagiv, M.: Symbolically computing most-precise abstract operations for shape analysis. In: Jensen, K., Podelski, A. (eds.) TACAS 2004. LNCS, vol. 2988, pp. 530–545. Springer, Heidelberg (2004)
29. Yorsh, G., Skidanov, A., Reps, T., Sagiv, M.: Automatic assume/guarantee reasoning for heap-manupilating programs. In: 1st AIOOL Workshop (2005)
30. Zee, K., Lam, P., Kuncak, V., Rinard, M.: Combining theorem proving with static analysis for data structure consistency. In: International Workshop on Software Verification and Validation (SVV 2004), Seattle (November, 2004)

A   Discussion on Patrick Lam's Presentation

Willem-Paul de Roever

I try to understand what you are doing, and you use a sequential setting, according to me.

Patrick Lam

Yes, that is right.

Willem-Paul de Roever

But then, can you explain, what the heck the assume-guarantee paradigm has to do with it, if you do everything sequentially?

Patrick Lam

What we mean by assume-guarantee is that we assume that the precondition holds, and then we show the postcondition. We are not talking about assume-guarantee as you usually talk about it in concurrent programs.

Willem-Paul de Roever

So, you have an individual interpretation. Thank you.

Richard Bornat

A comment rather than a question. You had a sentence that was approximately: Sets are intuitive for programmers. I say this with some trepidation in front of you [addressing Jean-Raymond Abrial] now: But there are only two people I know who are programmers and find sets intuitive. The other one is Bernard Sufrin, who developed Z with you [Abrial]. For the rest of us, sets are seductive, and we make the kind of nave errors that have caused so many problems historically in mathematics, that is, we mis-specify our programs, because we think sets are one thing, and they are in fact another. So, I plead with you: Please replace the word "intuitive" with "seductive", and consider the consequences. Thank you.

Patrick Lam: OK.

Towards the Integration of Symbolic and Numerical Static Analysis

Arnaud Venet

Kestrel Technology
4984 El Camino Real #230
Los Altos, CA 94022
arnaud@kestreltechnology.com

1 Introduction

Verifying properties of large real-world programs requires vast quantities of information on aspects such as procedural contexts, loop invariants or pointer aliasing. It is unimaginable to have all these properties provided to a verification tool by annotations from the user. Static analysis will clearly play a key role in the design of future verification engines by automatically discovering the bulk of this information. The body of research in static program analysis can be split up in two major areas: one–probably the larger in terms of publications–is concerned with discovering properties of data structures (shape analysis, pointer analysis); the other addresses the inference of numerical invariants for integer or floating-point algorithms (range analysis, propagation of round-off errors in numerical algorithms). We will call the former "symbolic static analysis" and the latter "numerical static analysis". Both areas were successful in effectively analyzing large applications [16,6,11,2,4]. However, symbolic and numerical static analysis are commonly regarded as entirely orthogonal problems. For example, a pointer analysis usually abstracts away all numerical values that appear in the program, whereas the floating-point analysis tool ASTREE [2,4] does not abstract memory at all.

If one wants to use static analysis to support or achieve verification of real programs, we believe that symbolic and numerical static analysis must be tightly integrated. Consider the two code snippets in Fig. 1. If one wants to check that the assignment operation in the first example is performed within the bounds of the array, one needs a numerical property relating the sizes of the objects pointed to by p and q and the parameter n. The second example constructs a two-dimensional array of semaphores using VxWorks' semCreate library function. If one wants to verify concurrency properties of the program, like the absence of deadlocks, one must be able to distinguish between the elements of the sems array. In the first case, a static analyzer would have to construct an abstract memory graph labeled with metavariables denoting the size of objects and relate these metavariables with the program variables. The second case is more complex, in the sense that the points-to relation itself has to be parameterized by array indices. These two examples are not artificial: the first one is

B. Meyer and J. Woodcock (Eds.): Verified Software, LNCS 4171, pp. 227–236, 2008.

```
void equate (int *p, int *q, int n) {        for(i=0; i<10; i++)
    int i;                                       for(j=0; j<8; j++)
    for(i=0; i<n; i++)                               sems[i][j] = semCreate();
        p[i] = q[i];
}
```

Fig. 1. Code samples illustrating the interaction of symbolic and numerical properties

characteristic of the object-oriented programming style used in the flight mission software developed at NASA for the Mars Exploration Program [23,3]; the second one comes from the controller of a science payload developed at NASA for the International Space Station [22].

Our research work has been mostly concerned with the design of techniques for combining symbolic and numerical static analysis in order to discover the kind of properties described above. We came up with a number of static analysis algorithms [20,19,21,22,23] aimed at various categories of properties and programs. This approach proved to be successful in achieving the large-scale verification of pointer-intensive NASA flight software [23,3]. The major difficulty in developing those kind of analyses lies in the absence of a general framework for guiding the design. Except for the base idea of blending symbolic and numerical structures together, these analyses have little commonalities. Since their architecture is quite complex and is tailored towards a specific class of applications, one may cast doubts on the viability of this approach for the development of production-level verification tools. This paper proposes a research agenda aimed at making this technology mainstream and easily applicable to a broad spectrum of verification problems. In Sect. 2 we will review the major achievements in the design of mixed symbolic and numerical static analysis tools. Section 3 gives an informal description of the technical challenges of designing such analyses. In Sect. 4 we will sketch the bases of a general abstract interpretation framework for automating the implementation of static analyzers. This framework is the formal foundation for an effort underway at Kestrel Technology to industrialize this static analysis technology.

2   Achievements

The first occurrence in the literature of a static analysis that mixes symbolic and numerical approximations is an alias analysis for strongly typed languages [8,9] that is able to discover properties such as "two lists of arbitray length share their elements pairwise". In that model, pointer aliasing is represented by an equivalence relation over access paths into data structures. The abstraction is based on a finite partitioning of the set of access paths by monomial unitary-prefix path expressions, which are given by the Eilenberg decomposition of a rational language [10]. Monomial unitary-prefix path expressions have the form $\pi_1 B_1^* \pi_2 B_2^* \ldots \pi_n B_n^* \pi_{n+1}$ where the π_i are sequences of data selectors and the B_i are rational languages, called the bases of the decomposition. The key idea consists of assigning a counter variable to each base and use standard numerical lattices to set constraints between these counters. For example, two lists x and y that share their elements pairwise can be described as follows:

$$\texttt{x.(tl)}^i\texttt{.hd} \equiv \texttt{y.(tl)}^j\texttt{.hd} \iff i = j$$

by using the numerical lattice of affine equalities [12]. The pointer aliasing relation is thus completely abstracted by a finite number of numerical relations. We have designed an abstraction of relations over free monoids inspired by this model that did not require any type annotation and did not incur the possible exponential cost of the Eilenberg decomposition [17]. The main idea was to use a regular automaton as the base symbolic structure and assign a numerical counter to each transition of the automaton. The automaton describes the access paths within data structures and is constructed jointly with the aliasing relation. Since the aliasing relation is based on this structure, changing the automaton requires to modify the representation of the aliasing relation accordingly. This operation was carried out by endowing the abstract domain with the structure of a cofibered domain [17]. This allowed us to construct a pointer analysis of similar power for dynamically typed languages like Java [20], as well as a communication analysis for systems of concurrent processes based on the π-calculus [18]. However, this numerical model has two important drawbacks: the operations on aliasing relations are costly and arrays cannot be represented precisely.

In order to lift these limitations we built a new numerical model based on a different interpretation of the semantics of memory allocation. Each object allocated in memory is assigned a timestamp, which is a numerical abstraction of the execution trace that led to the object creation. The memory is represented by a graph whose vertices are labels of allocation statements together with a timestamp, and whose edges represent the points-to relation. Arrays can naturally be integrated into this scheme by simply adding a numerical index to edges. This new model allowed us to build a flow-sensitive pointer analysis for Java-like languages [21] and a considerably simpler communication analysis for the π-calculus [19]. It also allowed us to tackle the analysis of multithreaded programs. Flow-sensitive analyses are impractical in the presence of threads due to the combinatorial blowup of interleaving. We have developed a pointer analysis for the C language that lies between flow-sensitive and flow-insensitive analyses [22]. An inexpensive flow-sensitive analysis is first run on each function in order to build flow-insensitive points-to equations that incorporate all local loop invariants. Then, these equations are solved using a constraint resolution algorithm. This analysis can be seen as an homeomorphic extension of Andersen's analysis scheme [1] in which inclusion constraints are annotated by numerical invariants. The constraint resolution algorithm is similar to Andersen's except that numerical operations are performed at each elementary step. The analysis scales well and has been successfully applied to the control software of a science payload for the International Space Station [22].

These encouraging results motivated us to apply these techniques to the large mission-critical programs developed at NASA for the Mars Exploration Program. We have developed a static array-bound checker for NASA flight software, called C Global Surveyor, which is based on a numerical abstraction of the heap [23]. The focus of this tool was not so much on memory allocation, which is scarcely used in mission-critical software, but on pointer arithmetic. In the family of programs considered, data are organized in large structures and manipulated by transmitting their address to generic functions. We designed a model in which all data are referenced using a byte-based offset within the memory block where they belong. The abstract heap is a points-to graph labeled with numerical intervals representing offset ranges. This graph is iteratively refined by narrowing intervals and pruning edges. The process is bootstrapped by using the memory graph produced by Steensgaard's analysis [16], and subsequent phases essentially consist of arithmetic manipulations on the labels of the graph. We have applied this static checker to codes ranging from 140 KLOC to 550 KLOC (the flight software of the current mission Mars Exploration Rovers). On average, 80% of all array accesses could be decided by the verifier, with the analysis speed peaking at 100 KLOC/hour [3]. The only limiting factor was the enormous amount of artifacts produced by the analyzer, which forced us to use an external storage management that degraded the performances.

3   Technical Challenges

Anyone reading the literature on mixed symbolic and numerical static analysis will likely be struck by the conceptual complexity of the algorithms. However sophisticated it may be, a pointer analysis relies on few simple concepts that can be clearly stated (unification-based/inclusion-based, flow-sensitive/flow-insensitive, store-based/storeless, etc.). Similarly, a numerical static analysis framework is acutely described by the family of geometric shapes used to approximate point clouds: linear affine spaces (linear equalities), higher-dimensional rectangles (intervals), convex polyhedra (linear inequalities), etc. In both cases, the technical description essentially consists of carrying out the formalization of these basic concepts in details. In a mixed symbolic and numerical analysis, the complexity stems from the association between symbolic values (object addres, channel name, etc.) and numerical components (index in an array, loop iteration counter, index in a list, etc.). This association seems completely arbitrary and is not supported by any general underlying concept. One could naturally question the need of building such complex analyses and suggest instead making pointer and numerical analyses cooperate. Such an approach has become quite popular in the theorem proving community [7]. In some sense, this is exactly what a mixed symbolic-numerical static analysis does. However, there is no *canonical* way of combining the symbolic and numerical components so that the resulting analysis scales well and gives precise results. The rest of this section will be devoted to discussing these points.

As a basis for our discussion we consider the pointer analysis of C with a byte-based representation of memory blocks [22]. For the sake of clarity, we ignore dynamic memory allocation. In such a model, a pointer is given by a symbolic address a and an offset o in bytes from the beginning of the block referenced by a. This low-level representation greatly simplifies the analysis of union types and casts. A program configuration is made of an environment E and a heap H. The environment maps scalar variables i to integer values and pointers p to pairs of address and offset as follows:

$$E = \langle i_1 \mapsto n_1, \ldots, i_k \mapsto n_k, p_1 \mapsto (a_1, o_1), \ldots, p_m \mapsto (a_m, o_m) \rangle$$

The heap H is a graph (V, E), such that the set of vertices V contains addresses and an edge (a_s, o_s, a_t, o_t) of E denotes the existence of a pointer in memory block a_s at offset o_s referencing the memory cell in a_t located at offset o_t. For simplicity, we ignore scalar data stored in the heap. The role of a pointer analysis consists of abstracting sets of configurations (E, H).

First, we need to recall briefly how numerical abstract interpretation works. Given a finite set of integer-valued variables $U = \{v_1, \ldots, v_n\}$, a numerical abstract domain $\mathcal{N}U$ provides a computable approximation of point clouds in $\wp(\mathbb{Z}^U)$. The precision of the approximation is determined by the class of numerical relationships between variables of U that can be expressed in the abstract numerical domain. The domain of intervals is one of the least expressive domains, since no relationship between variables can be expressed. The domain of convex polyhedra [5] can describe arbitray systems of linear inequalities over variables of U, Karr's domain [12] can describe systems of linear equalities whereas the domain of difference-bound matrices [15] can only express inequalities of the form $x - y \leq c$. Expressiveness comes with a price, and the maximum number of variables that can be handled by an abstract numerical domain in practice ranges from about a dozen for convex polyhedra, to a few tens for difference-bound matrices, to tens of thousands for intervals.

In the case of pointer analysis, it appears in many practical situations that the approximation of environments and heaps can be carried out independenlty without incurring a significant loss of accuracy. For example, in embedded applications the pointer structure in global memory is typically set up during the initialization phase and remains stable at mission time [3]. One can use a graph-based abstraction such that an edge (a_s, o_s, a_t, o_t) is abstracted by a triple (a_s, a_t, ν), where $\nu \in \mathcal{N}\{o_s, o_t\}$ describes numerical relationships between the source and target offsets. This clear separation between environment and heap abstractions enables the use of modified versions of existing pointer algorithms [22], so that the computation of numerical invariants can be carried out independently from that of the points-to graph [22], or both can be interleaved [23]. At this level, the numerical and symbolic algorithms do really work in cooperation. Experiments on aerospace code have shown that simple choices for the abstract domain yield good results in practice [23,22].

As for environments, there is a very natural abstraction. Given an environment structure with k scalar variables and m pointer variables as described above, we have to abstract a set of $k + m$ integer variables (scalar variables plus offsets) and m symbolic variables. Assuming that the set A of addresses is finite, we are left with approximating an element of $\wp(A^m \times \mathbb{Z}^{m+k})$. This is isomorphically equivalent to approximating a mapping of $A^m \to \wp(\mathbb{Z}^{m+k})$. If we denote by N the set of numerical variables $\{i_1, \ldots, i_k, o_1, \ldots, o_m\}$, a natural abstract domain for the analysis is $A^m \to \mathcal{N}N$. This can be regarded as a canonical abstraction of a set of environments. However, it poses two major scalability issues:

- since A can be large, the mapping from A^m may cause a combinatorial explosion,
- the size of N may preclude the use of expressive numerical abstract domains.

This is a major problem, since we do need epxressive numerical abstract domains in order to infer e.g., that i $\leq$ n in the first example of Fig. 1. The problem is actually much deeper than achieving good precision, since computing numerical relationships between variables is precisely what enables us to keep the construction of the abstract heap as a separate phase [23,22].

A solution to this problem consists of breaking down the "big" abstract domain $A^m \to \mathcal{N}N$ into a collection of smaller, more manageable domains. This essentially amounts to grouping variables into small clusters and applying the same reasoning for each cluster individually. For example, one can group variables in clusters of the form $C_j = \{a_j, o_j, i_1, \ldots, i_k\}$. Each cluster C_j yields an abstract domain $A \to \mathcal{N}\{o_j, i_1, \ldots, i_k\}$. With this collection of abstract domains the analysis can infer relationships between each pointer offset and all the integer variables. These relationships are parameterized by the address of the memory block that may be referenced by the pointer. However, relationships between pointers that are simultaneously manipulated within a loop (like in the statement *p++ = *q++) are lost. This is an example of clustering using a static criterion. Clustering can also be performed dynamically during the analysis as done in C Global Surveyor [23]. Using variable clusters is what makes the design of the analysis complex and intricate, mostly because a semantic operation on a variable does not only affect this variable but also all the clusters in which it appears. The choice of a particular clustering sets a certain tradeoff between precision and efficiency, and depends on the characteristics of the program or family of programs considered. This implies that clustering has to be empirically validated on the target applications.

In conclusion, combining symbolic and numerical analyses allows us to achieve the high level of precision required to perform automatic verification of pointer-intensive programs. The architecture of these static analyzers enables the integration of numerical and symbolic algorithms that work in cooperation. However, in order to achieve scalability we must introduce a layer of complexity in the structure of the analyzer. One may question the relevance of this approach to program verification if a complex analyzer has to be constructed for each application. The situation is aggravated by the absence of any methodology for designing these analyzers. We will present perspectives for addressing these issues in the next section.

4   Perspectives

4.1   Towards a General Framework

The clustering technique exposed in the previous section basically consists of *covering* the abstract domain $A^m \to \mathcal{N}N$ using smaller domains $A^n \to \mathcal{N}M$ where $n \leq m$ and $M \subseteq N$. The semantic operations on this collection of abstract domains are carried out by "patching" elements belonging to overlapping clusters, without ever using the larger domain $A^m \to \mathcal{N}N$. This computational scheme bears a striking analogy with the techniques provided by the theory of fiber bundles and sheaves [14] for studying global properties of complex topological spaces that possess a regular structure locally. Actually, there is more than a simple analogy, and we are currently investigating the transposition of these topological constructs into the theory of Abstract Interpretation. We have already come up with a framework that is able to express existing mixed symbolic-numerical pointer analyses. The major benefit of the framework is that it provides a systematic construction of the semantic operations from an arbitrary clustering of variables. This means that the complexity of designing such analyses can be encapsulated in a small set of semantic operators that are used to systematically derive the analysis algorithms from a simple specification of the concrete semantics.

4.2   Automated Generation of Static Analyzers

The implementation of this framework is underway, based on the formal specification environment SpecWare [13]. Our first objective is to be able to re-implement existing analyses with much lesser effort. In particular, we aim at achieving the same level of scalability. This is probably the main characteristic of our approach: unifying the construction of semantic transformers and the definition of optimizations (variable clustering) within a single formal framework. This comes in sharp contrast with three-valued logic for example, where there is no handle for controlling the scalability. Our experience with C Global Surveyor [23] showed that there is no universal strategy for achieving scalability. This is based on a "try and fix" process, driven by empirical data and dependent on the family of applications considered. Therefore, we believe that there is no point in trying to build a sophisticated "push button" tool that will work well on a broad spectrum of applications. It is more important to allow the developers to customize the analysis rapidly and find the best blend of semantic approximation and optimization. In our opinion, this quick turnaround is the key to a successful industrialization of the technology and its widespread use.

4.3   Spectrum of Applications

If pointer or communication analyses were the only applications of a mixed symbolic-numerical static analysis framework, however important they are, there would not be much interest in pursuing long-term research in this direction. We believe that this class of static analysis has a broader range of applications for it basically permits to attach numerical invariants to discrete structures. Numerical computations form the basis of the control structure for the vast majority of applications, and numerical properties naturally appear in resource analysis (cpu, memory, network) and the statement of some security properties (number of times a cryptographic object is used, number of channels open simultaneously, etc.). In order to analyze real code the analysis must be able to attach numerical properties to objects of the program, for example:

- the number of bytes transmitted through a channel to the channel descriptor,
- the number of times cryptographic data are used to the corresponding objects in memory.

The properties to analyze should be expressed in the semantics of the program and interpreted by the static analyzer generator with little intervention of the user. It means that the property to be analyzed should be part of the specification that forms the input of the static analyzer generator. This opens the way to the automated generation of custom static analyzers that verify properties defined by users who are not experts in the field, like software developers.

References

1. Andersen, L.: Program Analysis and Specialization for the C Programming Language. PhD thesis, DIKU, University of Copenhagen (1994)
2. Blanchet, B., Cousot, P., Cousot, R., Feret, J., Mauborgne, L., Miné, A., Monniaux, D., Rival, X.: A static analyzer for large safety-critical software. In: Proceedings of the ACM SIGPLAN 2003 Conference on Programming Language Design and Implementation (PLDI 2003), June 7–14, 2003, pp. 196–207. ACM Press, New York (2003)
3. Brat, G., Venet, A.: Precise and scalable static program analysis of NASA flight software. In: Proceedings of the 2005 IEEE Aerospace Conference (2005)
4. Cousot, P., Cousot, R., Feret, J., Mauborgne, L., Miné, A., Monniaux, D., Rival, X.: The ASTRÉE Analyser. In: Sagiv, M. (ed.) ESOP 2005. LNCS, vol. 3444, pp. 21–30. Springer, Heidelberg (2005)
5. Cousot, P., Halbwachs, N.: Automatic discovery of linear restraints among variables of a program. In: Proceedings of the Fifth Conference on Principles of Programming Languages, ACM Press, New York (1978)
6. Das, M.: Unification-based pointer analysis with directional assignments. ACM SIGPLAN Notices 35(5), 35–46 (2000)
7. de Moura, L., Owre, S., Ruess, H., Rushby, J., Shankar, N.: Integrating verification components. In: Verified Software: Theories, Tools, Experiments, Zrich, Switzerland (October, 2005)
8. Deutsch, A.: A storeless model of aliasing and its abstraction using finite representations of right-regular equivalence relations. In: Proceedings of the 1992 International Conference on Computer Languages, pp. 2–13. IEEE Computer Society Press, Los Alamitos (1992)
9. Deutsch, A.: Interprocedural alias analysis for pointers: beyond k-limiting. In: ACM SIGPLAN 1994 Conference on Programming Language Design and Implementation, ACM Press, New York (1994)

10. Eilenberg, S.: Automata, Languages and Machines, vol. A. Academic Press, London (1974)
11. Heintze, N., Tardieu, O.: Ultra-fast aliasing analysis using CLA: A million lines of C code in a second. In: SIGPLAN Conference on Programming Language Design and Implementation, pp. 254–263 (2001)
12. Karr, M.: Affine relationships among variables of a program. Acta Informatica, 133–151 (1976)
13. Kestrel,: Specware System and documentation (2003), http://www.specware.org/
14. Mac Lane, S., Moerdijk, I.: Sheaves in Geometry and Logic. Springer, Heidelberg (1992)
15. Miné, A.: A new numerical abstract domain based on difference-bound matrices. In: Danvy, O., Filinski, A. (eds.) PADO 2001. LNCS, vol. 2053, pp. 155–172. Springer, Heidelberg (2001)
16. Steensgaard, B.: Points-to analysis by type inference of programs with structures and unions. In: Computational Complexity, pp. 136–150 (1996)
17. Venet, A.: Abstract cofibered domains: Application to the alias analysis of untyped programs. In: Cousot, R., Schmidt, D.A. (eds.) SAS 1996. LNCS, vol. 1145, pp. 266–382. Springer, Heidelberg (1996)
18. Venet, A.: Abstract interpretation of the π-calculus. In: Dam, M. (ed.) LOMAPS-WS 1996. LNCS, vol. 1192, pp. 51–75. Springer, Heidelberg (1997)
19. Venet, A.: Automatic determination of communication topologies in mobile systems. In: Levi, G. (ed.) SAS 1998. LNCS, vol. 1503, pp. 152–167. Springer, Heidelberg (1998)
20. Venet, A.: Automatic analysis of pointer aliasing for untyped programs. Science of Computer Programming 35(2), 223–248 (1999)
21. Venet, A.: Nonuniform alias analysis of recursive data structures and arrays. In: Hermenegildo, M.V., Puebla, G. (eds.) SAS 2002. LNCS, vol. 2477, pp. 36–51. Springer, Heidelberg (2002)
22. Venet, A.: A scalable nonuniform pointer analysis for embedded programs. In: Giacobazzi, R. (ed.) SAS 2004. LNCS, vol. 3148, pp. 149–164. Springer, Heidelberg (2004)
23. Venet, A., Brat, G.: Precise and efficient static array bound checking for large embedded C programs. In: Proceedings of the International Conference on Programming Language Design and Implementation, pp. 231–242 (2004)

A Discussion on Arnaud Venet's Presentation

Willem-Paul de Roever

I can try to recall my algebraic topology course. What I recall from this is that you have to get change of groups to get homology theory. So, this is what homology, as I knew, is about: a classification of topological spaces. So, the mathematical analysis technique is that of groups, where you compute homology groups. What is the analogy of a homology group here?

Arnaud Venet

The use of the term "homology" stems from the striking analogy between the algebraic structures underlying this class of static analysis and those appearing in algebraic topology in the context of homology theory, or more exactly cohomology. At this point this is nothing more than an analogy, but the connection between these two fields are intriguing enough to motivate a deeper investigation. In standard algebraic topology, the cohomology groups define an equivalence relation on cochains that define the same covering. In our case, the analogue of a cochain is the definition of a semantic transformer as the gluing of numerical relations over several sets of symbolic variables that overlap. We are working on pushing this analogy further toward a more formal connection between both fields.

Reliable Software Systems Design: Defect Prevention, Detection, and Containment

Gerard J. Holzmann and Rajeev Joshi

Laboratory for Reliable Software (LaRS)
Jet Propulsion Laboratory, California Institute of Technology
Pasadena, CA 91109, USA

Abstract. The grand challenge that is the focus of this conference targets the development of a practical methodology for software verification: a methodology that can help us to reduce the number of residual defects in software products. Reducing residual defects is of course not in itself the objective of this exercise; the true objective is to reduce the number of *failures* in the use of software products. Or in other words: the objective is the development of a methodology for "reliable software systems design."

1 Introduction

It has often been argued that with the right training, discipline, and tools it should be possible to produce zero-defect code. Very few things in life, though, are zero-defect – not even the things that can be considered life critical. If you practice sky-diving, you are probably acutely aware that your main parachute could fail to open, no matter how carefully you check it before each jump. The parachutist would also be wise not to trust a company that tries to sell him a zero-defect parachute. He is more likely to avoid disaster by bringing a spare chute on every jump. That is: the seasoned parachutist takes the possibility of *component* failure into account to achieve a lowered probability of *system* failure. Elevators are another good example. Of course, any elevator component can fail, including the cable from which the elevator cab is suspended. But, the elevator system as a whole is designed in such a way that even when the cable breaks, the car will not come crashing down. We trust the system, even though we know that none of its components are zero-defect. For the parachute redundancy can trivially be used, but in the case of the elevator redundancy does not necessarily solve the problem. Multiple cables may help address one specific form of component failure, but operating multiple elevators in parallel would not address the real safety issue that is at stake here.

Reliable systems are always designed with the possibility of *component* failure in mind, and with remedies in place to significantly reduce the odds of *system* failure.

It is worth contemplating how deeply engrained the discipline of reliable system design is, outside software engineering. If your kitchen-sink leaks, you can close a valve that stops the flow of water to that sink. The valve is there because experience has shown that sinks do occasionally leak, no matter how carefully they are constructed to prevent just that. If you short-circuit an electrical outlet in your home, a

B. Meyer and J. Woodcock (Eds.): Verified Software, LNCS 4171, pp. 237–244, 2008.

fuse will blow. The fuse is there to prevent greater disaster in case the unimaginable happens. The presence of the fuse and the valve do not signify an implicit acceptance of sloppy workmanship; they are an essential part of reliable *system* design.

In contrast, most software today is build without valves and fuses. We try to build perfect parachutes that do not need a backup. When software fails, we blame the developer for failing to be perfect. Would it not be wiser to assume from the start that even carefully constructed and verified software components, like all other things in life, may fail in unexpected ways, and use this knowledge to construct assemblies of software components that provide independently *verifiable* system reliability?

2 Building Reliable Systems from Unreliable Parts

Hardware designers already know how to construct reliable systems from unreliable parts. In building these systems, the designer starts from the knowledge that any component in the system might fail, while securing that such failures can not cause the failure of the system as a whole. We have yet to learn how to apply similar principles in the construction of reliable *software* systems.

Any improvement in this domain will have to be grounded firmly in strong software verification techniques, some of which exist and some of which remain to be developed. The purpose of this position paper, though, is to point out that the development of those techniques alone will not suffice. Our ultimate objective, after all, is not necessarily to produce zero-defect software, but to produce ultra-reliable software *systems*. This position has implications for the type of work we need to do, as we will outline in more detail in the remainder of this paper.

2.1 Blue Screens of Death

Non-critical software applications are often designed in a monolithic fashion. When the application crashes, e.g. when it hits a divide by zero error, the only recourse one then has is to restart the application from scratch. This approach is, of course, not adequate to use in the construction of systems that are safety critical, for instance because human life depends on its correct and continued functioning. When, for instance, a spacecraft experiences an unexpected failure of one of its components during a launch or landing procedure, a complete restart of the software may in itself cost the loss of the mission. In manned space flight, a few minutes spent in rebooting the crew's life support system may have unintended and unacceptable consequences. Systems like this have to be ultra-reliable, even if some of their software parts are not. The wise thing to assume in these cases is that no software part is fail-proof, not even those that have been verified exhaustively.

2.2 Simplicity and Redundancy

There are two primary strategies for achieving system reliability. The first strategy is to use a design that emphasizes *simplicity and robustness*. A simple design is easier to understand, easier to test or verify, and easier to operate. The second strategy is to exploit *redundancy*. If the probability of failure of individual components is statistically independent, the chance of having both a prime and a backup component fail at the same time can be made very small. If, for instance, all components have the same probability p of failure, then the probability that all N components fail in an N-redundant system would be p^N. In a nutshell, simplicity seeks to reduce the value of p, while redundancy seeks to increase the value of N. Trivially, for all values of $N \geq 1$ and $0 < p < 1$ both techniques can lower the probability of failure p^N for the system.

Unfortunately, one of the basic premises used in the redundancy argument that we used above, the statistical independence of the failure probabilities of components, can be very hard to achieve for software. Well-known are the experiments performed in the eighties by Knight and Leveson with N-version programming techniques, which demonstrated that different programming teams tend to make the same types of design errors when working from a common set of (often flawed) design requirements. [KL86] Independently, Sha also pointed out that a decision to apply N-version programming cannot be made independently of budget and schedule decisions. With a fixed budget, each of N independent development efforts will inevitably receive only $1/N$-th of the total project resources. If we compare the expected reliability of N development efforts, each pursued with $1/N$-th of the project resources, with one targeted effort that can consume all available resources, the tradeoffs become very different. [S01]

Redundancy in the traditional sense, in the way that has proven to work well with hardware systems, therefore cannot be duplicated easily in software systems. By combining the strategies of simplicity and redundancy in a different way, though, we may be able to build larger software systems that are indeed significantly more reliable than any of their individual parts.

3 Software Architectures for Fault Containment

Consider a standard software architecture consisting of software modules with well-defined interfaces. Each module performs a separate function. The modules are defined in such a way that information flow across module boundaries is minimized. We will assume here, primarily for simplicity but without loss of generality, that the only way for modules to interact is through message passing over trusted channels. Modules execute (at least logically) on independent hardware, to secure that the crash of one module cannot affect other modules in any other way than across its module interface. A failed module may stop responding, or fail to comply with the interface protocols by sending erroneous requests or responses. We will make a further assumption that module failures can be detected either through consistency checks that are performed inside a module, or by peer modules that check the validity of messages that cross module boundaries.

One could make the argument that a failure that cannot be detected at runtime is not a failure that can be remedied. We will have to accept that not all conceivable types of failures can be defended against with this or any other fault containment discipline. We restrict our attention to those cases where a remedy is at least in principle possible.

In our proposed software architecture, each software module is provided with a simplified backup. During normal system operations, this backup module is idle. When a fault is detected, though, the faulty module is switched offline and the backup module replaces it. (Naturally, the backup module can have its own backup, and so on, but we will not pursue this generalization here.) The backup, due to the fact that it is a simplified version of the prime module, may offer fewer services, or it may offer them less efficiently. The purpose of the backup, though, is to provide a survival and recovery option to a partially failed system. It should provide the minimally necessary functionality that is required to "stay alive."

Note that in a traditional system the failing module *is* its own backup. Upon a failure one simply restarts the module that failed and hopes that the cause for failure was transient. We suggest that we can defend against a substantially larger class of defects if the backup module is *distinct* from the primary module and deliberately constructed to be significantly *simpler* than the primary module.

As indicated earlier, if the primary and backup modules are constructed within an *N*-version programming paradigm, we do not necessarily gain additional reliability from this type of system structure. This system structure will not adequately defend against design and coding errors. Some of the same design errors may be made in the construction of both modules, and if the two modules are of similar size and complexity, they should be expected to contain a similar number of residual coding defects (i.e., coding defects that escape code testing and verification). Our proposal is therefore to make the backup modules significantly simpler than the primary modules.

3.1 Simplified Redundancy

The backup modules in our proposed architecture are constructed as *simplified* versions of the primary modules. Specifically, these backup modules can be designed and build by the same developer(s) that design and build the primary modules. The primary module is build for *performance*; the backup module is build for *correctness*. The main purpose for a system architecture of this type is that the backup modules are easier to *verify* thoroughly. The *statistically expected* number of residual defects in a backup module should be significantly lower than that of the primary module, if they contain significantly less code that can be checked thoroughly.

The backup module is used to guarantee continuity of operation, though in a possibly degraded state of operation (e.g., slower and likely with reduced functionality). The backup gives the system the opportunity to recover from unexpected failures: the primary module is offline and can be diagnosed and possibly restarted, while the backup module takes care of the most urgent of tasks in the most basic of ways. If code is developed in a hierarchical fashion, using a standardized software refinement approach, the backup module could encapsulate an earlier level in the refinement of the final module: a simpler version of the code that is not yet burdened with all features, extensions, and optimizations that will support the final version, but that does perform the most critical and basic duties in the most straightforward way.

If this approach can be made to work (at the time of writing we not yet completed a realistic case study) we would expect the backup modules to be significantly smaller in size (e.g., in lines of code) than the primary modules. By virtue of being smaller and simpler, the expected number of residual defects in this code should also be smaller. We will tacitly assume here that the number of design and coding defects is proportional to the size of a module, just like the number of syntax and grammar mistakes in English prose is proportional to the length of that prose. If the primary module has a probability of failure due to residual defects p and for the backup module the probability of failure is q, we would expect to have $1 > p > q > 0$ (ignoring the boundary cases where we have either certainty of failure or absolute perfection). Because the backup module contains less code, and implements less functionality, it offers fewer opportunities for design and coding defects. The module with its backup now fails with probability $(p.q)$ which should be smaller than the probability p for the same module without the backup.

3.2 Fault Detection and Secure Fall-Back

We have assumed that we can tell, in a sufficient number of cases, when a software module fails to perform its intended function due to a design or coding error. There are several ways in which this could work, at least in principle, but none are truly satisfactory. The module code can contain assertions that check for the validity of inputs and outputs (standard pre and post-condition checks), and they can verify that essential invariants are maintained in the module code. But if we assume that the nature of the residual software defects is unpredictable and to first approximation will exhibit itself as a random divergence of the intended or desired behavior, the conclusion will be inevitable that a module cannot reliably detect all occurrences of defects in its own code. Modules can, however, be reasonably expected to check each other. If a module, for instance, detects that faulty input is provided to it across its module interface, the module could declare the peer module that provided the input to be faulty, reject the input, and command the suspect module to be switched over to its backup. There is a close correspondence here to security related problems in mainstream software design: how can a module trust that its peer is reliable? [R98, W89]

There is also another problem that has to be addressed. Even supposing that we would have, or will be able to develop, a reliable defect detection discipline, how precisely can we arrange things in such a way that the switch-over from a primary module to its backup (or vice versa) does not itself introduce a system failure? cf. [AB85, RL81] We do not have answers to these questions, but suggest them as a potentially fruitful area of research in reliable software systems design.

4 Synopsis

The goal of this position paper is to suggest that to achieve software reliability we should not restrict ourselves solely to the investigation of ways to achieve zero-defect code, but also more broadly to new methods to produce fail-proof systems. We would like to develop the art of building reliable systems from unreliable parts into a mature software engineering discipline.

The principal method of structuring code we propose to investigate is fairly simple. The code is structured into modules that can fail largely independently. Modules communicate only via well-defined interfaces. Each module is provided with at least one backup that can take over basic operations when the primary module fails. The backup module is constructed to be significantly simpler, smaller, and more reliable than the primary that it supports, possibly performing less efficiently and providing less functionality.

This basic mode of operation is already used today in the hardware design of spacecraft. Spacecraft typically do not just have redundant components on board, but also components of different types and designs, providing different grades of service. Most spacecraft, for instance, have both a high-gain and a low-gain antenna. When the high-gain antenna becomes unusable, the more reliable low-gain antenna is used, be it at a significantly reduced bit-rate. Perhaps not surprisingly, this same principle has also been applied on a modest scale in the design of mission critical software, though not always systematically. The MER rover software, for instance, was designed to support two main modes of operations: the fully functional mode with all its features and functions enabled and a minimal basic mode of operation that has been referred to as the "crippled mode." It was precisely this "crippled mode" that made it possible for the software engineers to recover from a serious software anomaly that struck one of the rovers early in its mission. [RN05] Our proposal is to use these principles more systematically, throughout the design of safety and mission critical software components.

Acknowledgement

The work described in this paper was carried out at the Jet Propulsion Laboratory, California Institute of Technology, under a contract with the National Aeronautics and Space Administration. Specifically, this work is part of a NASA funded project SISM-160, titled *Reliable Software Systems Development (RSSD)*, which targets the development of new tool-based methodologies for reliable software development.

References

[AB85] Anderson, T., Barrett, P.A., Halliwell, D.N., Moudling, M.L.: An evaluation of software fault tolerance in a practical system. In: Proc. Fault Tolerant Computing Symposium, pp. 140–145 (1985)

[KL86] Knight, J.C., Leveson, N.G.: An Experimental Evaluation of the Assumption of Independence in Multi-version Programming. IEEE Transactions on SoftwareEngineering SE-12(1), 96–109 (1986)

[RN05] Reeves, G., Neilson, T.: The Mars Rover Spirit Flash Anomaly. In: IEEE Aerospace Conference, Big Sky, MT (March, 2005)

[RL81] Rasmussen, R.D., Litty, E.C.: A Voyager attitude control perspective on fault toler-ant systems. In: Proc. AIAA Conf. Alburquerque, NM, August 1981, pp. 241–248 (1981)

[R98] Rushby, J.: Partitioning in Avionics Architectures: Requirements, Mechanisms, and Assurance. Draft technical report, Computer Science Laboratory, SRI (1998)

[S01] Sha, L.: Using Simplicity to Control Complexity. IEEE Software, 20–28 (July-August, 2001)

[W89] Weber, D.G.: Formal specification of fault-tolerance and its relation to computer security. In: Proc. 5th Int. Workshop on Software Spec. and Design, Pittsburgh, PA, May 1989, pp. 273–277 (1989)

A Discussion on Gerard Holzmann's Presentation

John Rushby

I am generally supportive of your proposal, but there is a lot of data from aircraft and rather less so from spacecraft. But most of the serious faults with redundancy management is to say: "When the staff switches over from primaries to backups..." So, aren't you potentially introducing the most dangerous of all mechanisms into your software system?

Gerard Holzmann

Yes, this is an excellent question. This was one of the bullets on my details. The one thing that I can say about it is that redundancy on spacecraft, currently—I do not know about aircraft and so on, but for spacecraft, I know very precisely—is only used for hardware. So, you can provide a redundant main engine or a redundant antenna. It is never used for software. So this is a different way to apply this technique, and the fact that the redundancy is highly simplified and thoroughly checkable is essential to this. So now, all those issues that you mentioned: "How do you make sure that you do not accidentally switch off for the wrong reason?" all those are valid. But if you do, then basically, you do not suffer major consequences, where normally, in a traditional redundant system, you might.

John Rushby

Be sure that your state is synchronized, for example. So, the backup has got the same state as the primary, otherwise, you get a [*missing word*].

Gerard Holzmann

Yes, so the "hand off" policy is one of those issues about how we do restore states, and that are methods for achieving a [*missing word*]. So, there is a demo, which I am not going to show now but can show you afterwards, that shows how you can do some of these "hand off" policies.

Tony Hoare

Thank you for a very interesting talk, and congratulations on your appointment as an engineer. We could have easily seen that you are an engineer by the contents of your talk, of course. It is a lovely example, because the only way to have more faith in your backup than your main source is by proving it. Testing it gives you no more confidence than testing the original. So, it is either prove or nothing. Wonderful! Thank you!

Patrick Cousot

The architecture that you describe, more or less exists already in aircraft, and it works, but it has a huge cost, and in particular a huge testing cost, because you have to test all the combinations of all the generated modes. Because you do less in those simplify things, it may interact with things that do more or less, and these interactions have to be checked, and this is extremely costly. You will pay by a factor of ten for coding and about factor 1,000 for testing. So, what are you going to do about that?

Gerard Holzmann

Prove you wrong?

Trends and Challenges in Algorithmic Software Verification

Rajeev Alur

Department of Computer and Information Science
University of Pennsylvania
alur@cis.upenn.edu

Recent years have witnessed remarkable progress in principles and tools for automated software verification. In this position paper, I briefly discuss the relevant projects in my group, and outline some near-term challenges for the community as concrete milestones for measuring progress.

1   Research Directions

In this section, I will briefly describe some directions we are currently pursuing that can enhance the scope and scalability of software verification tools. More information about these projects can be obtained from my homepage http://www.cis.upenn.edu/~alur.

1.1   Model Checking Structured Programs

Classical program verification focussed on correctness of structured procedural programs, while typical model checkers are aimed at concurrent finite-state reactive systems. Recent progress in software model checking allows checking temporal logic requirements of code via abstraction and symbolic state-space exploration. Standard temporal logics such as LTL and CTL employed by current model checkers, however, can specify only regular properties, and properties such as correctness of procedures with respect to pre and post conditions, that require matching of calls and returns, are not regular. Recently, we have introduced a *temporal logic of calls and returns* (CaRet) for specification and algorithmic verification of correctness requirements of structured programs. CaRet can specify a variety of non-regular properties such as partial and total correctness of program blocks and access control properties that involve inspection of the call-stack. Even though verifying context-free properties of pushdown systems is undecidable, we show that model checking CaRet formulas against a pushdown model is decidable. This result allows us to combine the classical Hoare-style reasoning about structured programs, Pnueli-style temporal specifications of reactive programs, and automated reasoning as in model checking. The decidability of CaRet against pushdown automata is not ad-hoc, and we have developed a theory of *visibly pushdown languages* that is rich enough to model interprocedural program analysis questions and yet is tractable and robust like the class of regular languages. Current efforts include extending these results to branching-time logics and tree automata.

B. Meyer and J. Woodcock (Eds.): Verified Software, LNCS 4171, pp. 245–250, 2008.

1.2   Games and Interfaces

While a typical software component has a clearly specified (static) interface in terms of the methods it supports, the information about the correct sequencing of method calls is usually undocumented. For example, for a file system, the method *open* should be invoked before the method *read*, without an intervening call to *close*. While such interfaces can be made precise using, for instance, regular expressions as types, these kinds of precise specifications are typically missing. Such dynamic interfaces for components can help applications programmers, and can possibly be used by program analysis tools to check automatically whether the component is being correctly invoked. In the JIST project, we are developing a novel solution for automatically extracting such temporal specifications for Java classes. Given a Java class, and a safety property such as "the exception E should not be raised", the corresponding *(dynamic) interface* is the most general way of invoking the methods so that the safety property is not violated. Our synthesis method first constructs a symbolic representation of the finite state-transition system obtained from the class using *predicate abstraction*. Constructing the interface then corresponds to solving a *partial-information two-player game* on this symbolic graph. We have developed a sound approach to solve this computationally-hard problem approximately using algorithms for learning finite automata and symbolic model checking for branching-time logics. A preliminary implementation of the proposed techniques has succeeded in constructing interfaces, accurately and efficiently, for sample Java2SDK library classes.

1.3   Real-Time and Hybrid Systems

Embedded systems, such as controllers in automotive, medical, and avionic systems, consist of a collection of interacting software modules reacting to a continuously evolving environment. Despite the proliferation of embedded devices in almost every engineered product, development of embedded software remains a low level, time consuming and error prone process. This is due to the fact that modern programming languages abstract away from time and platform constraints, while correctness of embedded software relies crucially on hard deadlines. The CHARON project at Penn aims at developing novel model-based design and implementation methodology for synthesizing reliable embedded software using the foundations of *hybrid systems*. Hybrid systems models allow mixing state-machine based discrete control with differential-equation based continuous dynamics. In the past, we have developed algorithms and tools for model checking of timed and hybrid systems. More recently, we are developing a programming environment using hybrid models with constructs such as hierarchy, concurrency with synchronous continuous interaction, and preemption. A key technical challenge in this work is bridging the gap between the platform-independent and timed semantics of the hybrid models and the executable software generated from it. This is crucial to be able to infer properties of software from properties of models. We are also exploring ways of integrating generation of control tasks with scheduling.

2   Challenge Projects

Research in formal methods has typically focussed on questions such as "what is the most expressive temporal logic that can be algorithmically verified," "what is the most effective way of pruning the search for a satisfying assignment for a propositional formula in clausal form," and "what are all the errors that can be found in existing code using this highly optimized tool for pointer analysis?" Such questions have led to improved understanding and technology, and are clearly essential for progress. At the other extreme, one can speculate about "grand" challenges such as developing a verifying compiler, or certified software, or new design paradigms. Instead, I have tried to articulate some concrete suggestions regarding some sample projects that are feasible within the next five years. I believe that they all share the following characteristics. First, each project is beyond the ability of individual researchers as well as current technology. Second, with sustained commitment and collaboration among a group of researchers, the project seems feasible. Third, the progress on each challenge can be measured and evaluated, and the goal of the project is clearly articulated. Finally, success in these projects will have notable impact in terms of addressing the skepticism among computer scientists concerning viability of formal methods, and in education and dissemination of our tools.

2.1   Automatic Graders for Classical Programming Assignments

Typical programming assignments in undergraduate courses include writing recursive programs such as *Quicksort*, and writing multi-threaded programs with synchronization such as *Dining Philosophers*. Typically, the submitted code is checked in an automated manner by executing it on sample tests. The goal of this challenge is to develop automatic grading programs that can *verify* the submitted code.

While formal methods tools have reported amazing successes, the heuristics underlying the decision procedures employed by the tools tend to be very fragile, and using these tools is always a frustrating experience for the novice users. To develop automatic grading programs, we need to focus on the *robustness* and *usability* of the tool rather than performance measures such as the number of lines of code analyzed by the tool or the time taken to analyze published benchmarks. Consequently, developing such automatic graders is an interesting challenge for the verification technology. Software model checking is not yet a scalable technology, but I believe with some effort, it is possible to develop a robust grading tool for analyzing the submitted code by exploiting the knowledge of the problem being solved during the abstraction phase.

The criteria for evaluating progress and success in this project are clear: with some training, the students who have correct solutions should be able to get their code verified by the tool, and the instructor should find the tool valuable enough so that (s)he recommends the tool to other instructors for use. If successful, this will make educators around the world, and the undergraduate students, aware of the promise and utility of formal methods and program analysis.

2.2   Conformance Checkers for Network Protocols

Network protocols has been a fruitful domain for application of formal methods. Existing efforts in formal analysis of network protocols are usually aimed at formalizing the specification of the protocol and proving that it has desirable properties. There have been some efforts in constructing executable code from such rigorous specifications. A complementary effort that can serve as a challenge to automated tools will be to establish that existing code for a protocol such as tcp or dhcp conforms to the published RFC specification. The RFC specification is partially in the form of state machines, and can possibly be extracted using automated tools. To demonstrate that C code implementing such a protocol in, say Linux, is a refinement of the RFC specification in a formal sense, is a nontrivial task that would require combination of several abstraction and analysis technologies. Again, I feel that this is something that is beyond the abilities of the existing tools, but can be achieved with domain-specific focus and efforts.

The success in this project should eventually lead to a scenario in which regulatory agencies will publish new RFCs in a form which can be analyzed by the tool, and the industries will be compelled to publish evidence of the conformance of their implementations with respect to the RFC specifications. Such success will result in improved reliability of widely used network protocols, and also adoption of formal methods by the industry.

2.3   Code Generator for Simulink

Contemporary industrial control design already relies heavily on tools for mathematical modeling and simulation. The most popular of such tools is Simulink developed by Mathworks. While commercial tools for compiling Simulink models into executable software exist, they do not offer any verification guarantees for the generated code. Programming languages community has largely ignored this domain, but as embedded devices become more ubiquitous, the importance of embedded systems programming will increase. When embedded software is employed in safety-critical applications such as automobiles and autonomous medical devices, the need for high assurance is obvious. Consequently, the current state of poorly understood relationship between the models and the code is not satisfactory. This creates an opportunity and a challenge problem for the formal methods community. Applying formal methods to introduce rigor into the code generation step is an interesting research challenge that can have a significant impact on reliability of control software. The semantic gap between the model and the code is large: the semantics of the model is typically defined as a solution to differential or difference equations, while the software consists of periodic tasks. This gap makes the code generation problem particularly challenging. Research in synchronous languages, time-triggered architectures, real-time scheduling, control theory, and hybrid systems offers insights into this problem, and can be exploited to build a semantics-preserving code generator for Simulink-like models.

2.4   Stateful Specifications for Java Libraries

As explained in Section 1.2, *behavioral interfaces* can capture temporal constraints such as the method `initSign` must be invoked before calling the method `sign`, without an intervening call to the method `initVerify`. Rigorously specified behavioral interfaces can play a critical role in documentation, maintenance, testing, verification and ultimately, in ensuring provable security properties of the system. Researchers in programming languages and software engineering have made a variety of proposals for notations for specifying interfaces (a prominent effort in this direction is the Java Modeling Language), automatic extraction of such interfaces, and for enforcement or verification of conformance of usage. A unified effort to annotate all the classes in public Java libraries and open source applications with stateful interfaces in machine readable and formal notation will be a worthy project.

To make this project a reality, first we need to agree on the notion of a stateful interface and a formal notation for expressing it. Second, we need to develop tools that can either extract such interfaces automatically from existing libraries, or find ways that will facilitate people to add these annotations. Finally, the interfaces will be useless unless we have effective analysis tools that will check client code against the interfaces or check conformance of newer versions of libraries with respect to interfaces for older versions. The combination of these activities make this an interesting project requiring collaboration and commitment from a team of researchers. Given the wide-spread use of Java, and the enthusiasm for open source projects, I believe that such interfaces will find expected as well as unexpected use.

A Discussion on Rajeev Alur's Presentation

Greg Nelson

Rajeev, I am afraid that I am appalled by the idea of the automatic grader for programming assignments. And I think we should be grading examples by reading them and not by running them, and that the students should be told that a programming exercise is an exercise in expository writing and that if it does not persuade the professor that it is correct, they will get a poor mark, even if there is no bug in the program.

Rajeev Alur

Well, I guess you haven't taught a course with two hundred students.

Greg Nelson

No, but I taught a course with twenty students where they wrote compilers. And I graded their compilers this way.

Rustan Leino

Do you use Java, for example? I am not expecting you to use Spec# in previous Masters, but maybe in future Masters. But if you use Java, you could use ESC/Java to require the students to turn in programs that have been checked with it. Have you done that?

Rajeev Alur

Actually, I think probably people have confused [something] about this challenge. So, if I am to teach an operating systems course, I think I can definitely convince my students to write proofs, and we can use different methods. The problem is with the people who are currently teaching operating system courses, which are mostly systems people. The interesting thing is that over the [last] twenty years, there has been a regression and a move away from logic. So, if you look at textbooks on operating systems and algorithms that were written thirty years ago, they would mention the concepts of invariants and proofs to some extent, and the people who were teaching them required them to write some kind of proofs. And over the last thirty years, this community has made tremendous progress, and the tools have improved so much, but if you look at the current operating systems textbooks, there is no mention of this. So I think, these tools are to be used by a generic instructor, who has no connection to formal methods, teaching an operating systems course.

Model Checking: Back and Forth between Hardware and Software

Edmund Clarke[1], Anubhav Gupta[1], Himanshu Jain[1], and Helmut Veith[2]

[1] School of Computer Science, Carnegie Mellon University
{emc,anubhav,hjain}@cs.cmu.edu
[2] Institut für Informatik (I-7), Technische Universität München, Germany
veith@in.tum.de

Abstract. The interplay back and forth between software model checking and hardware model checking has been fruitful for both. Originally intended for the analysis of concurrent software, model checking was first used in hardware verification. The abstraction methods developed for hardware verification however have been a stepping stone for the new generation of software verification tools including SLAM, BLAST, and MAGIC which focus on control-intensive software in C. Most recently, the experience with software verification is providing new leverage for verifying hardware designs in high level languages.

1 From Software Verification to Hardware Verification

The origins of model checking date back to the early 1980s, when Clarke and Emerson [5] and, independently, Queille and Sifakis [19] introduced a new algorithmic approach for the verification of computer systems. Their approach amounts to checking the satisfaction of a logical specification over a system model which is represented by an annotated directed graph; hence, the term *model checking*. Prior to that, the use of temporal logic for the analysis and specification of computer systems had been advocated by Pnueli [18], and model checking has in fact been employing variants of temporal logic as the predominant specification language ever since.

Experiments with early model checkers however quickly made clear that the size of the model represents the crucial technical barrier for realizing the full potential of model checking. In fact, the progress on the state explosion problem is the key to appreciating the technical achievements in model checking during the last decades. The development of *symbolic model checking* [3,17] was arguably a turning point in the formal methods field. Employing a combination of binary decision diagrams and fixed-point algorithms, the symbolic model verifier (SMV) became the first model checker to verify models with hundreds of Boolean variables and a tool to benchmark new ideas for more than a decade.

Model checking was originally designed for the verification of finite state systems. Although the first practically useful applications of model checking were oriented towards hardware verification, where the finite state restriction comes naturally, the method was originally conceived of as an approach to software verification. The early papers on model checking clearly drew their motivations from the software area,

B. Meyer and J. Woodcock (Eds.): Verified Software, LNCS 4171, pp. 251–255, 2008.

focusing in particular on concurrency properties to be verified over the synchronization skeleton of a program, i.e., a finite abstract model which preserves the relevant behavior for interprocess communication [6]. This setting reflects three major principles in successful model checking applications:

1. The separation of control flow and data flow in the system.
2. Abstraction techniques which enable us to remove significant parts of the data flow from the system.
3. Efficient tools to check properties on the abstracted systems.

Since hardware designs typically have a relatively clear separation of data and control, and are finite state, it was very natural to apply model checking to verify hardware systems [11]. In combination with symbolic model checking, this resulted in making hardware model checking a success.

Starting with [8], there has been a lot of work in devising systematic approaches to abstraction. Abstraction techniques reduce the program state space by mapping the set of states of the actual system to an abstract, and smaller, set of states in a way that preserves the actual behaviors of the system. In systems where there is no clear distinction between the control flow and data flow, it may be necessary to refine the abstraction. This abstraction refinement process has been automated by the counterexample-guided abstraction refinement paradigm [16,7,1], or CEGAR for short. In the CEGAR approach, the model checker initially works on a coarse abstraction. If the model checker finds a "spurious" abstract error trace which does not occur in the original program, it analyzes the error trace to refine the abstraction. This process is repeated until the property is either verified or disproved. Note that model checking and abstract interpretation [12] share many common techniques which deserve further exploration.

2   From Hardware Verification to Software Verification

The last several years have seen the development of a new generation of software model checkers such as SLAM, BLAST and MAGIC [1,14,4] which are based on predicate abstraction [13] and counterexample-guided abstraction refinement (CEGAR). Note that the CEGAR approach, first proposed for hardware verification [16,7], lends itself equally naturally for software [1]. Figure 1 illustrates the application of CEGAR to software. This new generation of software model checkers has been quite successful for specific classes of software, most notably device drivers, embedded software, and system software whose specifications are closely related to the control flow. While predicate abstraction is highly versatile in expressing the control flow conditions of a program, it is apparently much harder to reason about data, in particular dynamic data structures.

An alternative approach is taken by the CBMC model checker [10]. CBMC is based on bounded model checking [2], i.e., counterexample search using a SAT procedure. CBMC exploits the relatively simple semantics of the C language by describing a SAT formula which amounts to a symbolic unwinding of the C program. While this approach in principle allows to account for complicated dynamic data structures, current SAT solvers enable us only to perform a relatively small number of unwindings.

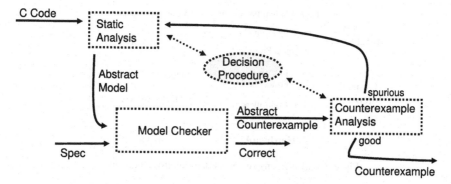

Fig. 1. Counterexample-Guided Abstraction Refinement for Software

3   Back to Hardware

Most model-checkers used in the hardware industry use a very low level design, usually a netlist, but time-to-market requirements have rushed the Electronic Design and Automation (EDA) industry towards design paradigms that offer a very high level of abstraction. This high level can shorten the design time by hiding implementation details and by merging design layers. As part of this process, an abundance of C-like system design languages like SystemC, SpecC has emerged. They promise to allow joint modelling of both the hardware and software component of a system using a language that is well-known to engineers.

Some fragments of these languages are synthesizable, and thus allow the application of netlist or RTL-based formal verification tools. However, the higher abstraction levels offered by most of these languages are not yet amenable to rigorous, formal verification. This is caused by the high degree of asynchronous concurrency used by the models, which requires thread interleaving semantics. Since languages like SystemC are closer to concurrent software than to a traditional hardware description, one needs techniques from software verification to verify programs written in these languages [15].

4   Conclusion

Control-Intensive versus Data-Intensive Systems

We have argued that the success of model checking in hardware is closely related to the relatively clear separation between the control flow and the data flow. As illustrated in Figure 2, this phenomenon occurs for both hardware and software, and explains why model checking is particularly useful for control-intensive software e.g. in embedded systems, device drivers etc.

Perspectives

Going back and forth between hardware and software, the research in model checking is gradually pushing the limits of the method by means of automated or manually

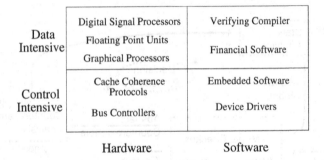

	Hardware	Software
Data Intensive	Digital Signal Processors Floating Point Units Graphical Processors	Verifying Compiler Financial Software
Control Intensive	Cache Coherence Protocols Bus Controllers	Embedded Software Device Drivers

Fig. 2. Control-intensive versus data-intensive systems

assisted abstraction, and has extended the reach of model checking quite significantly. As expressed in Rushby's notion of "disappearing formal methods", our goal is for model checking to finally become a push-button technology for certain classes of software such that the trade-off between the preciseness and the computational cost of the correctness analysis can be controlled by a few simple parameters. Generally though, the principal undecidability of virtually all questions in software verification makes clear that there is no silver bullet for verification, and there will always be a need to design model checking methods specific to problem classes.

References

1. Ball, T., Rajamani, S.K.: Automatically Validating Temporal Safety Properties of Interfaces. In: Dwyer, M.B. (ed.) SPIN 2001. LNCS, vol. 2057, pp. 103–122. Springer, Heidelberg (2001)
2. Biere, A., Cimatti, A., Clarke, E., Fujita, M., Zhu, Y.: Symbolic model checking using SAT procedures instead of BDDs. In: Proc. 36th Conference on Design Automation (DAC), pp. 317–320 (1999)
3. Burch, J.R., Clarke, E.M., McMillan, K.L., Dill, D.L., Hwang, L.J.: Symbolic Model Checking: 10^{20} States and Beyond. In: Proceedings of the Fifth Annual IEEE Symposium on Logic in Computer Science (1990)
4. Chaki, S., Clarke, E., Groce, A., Jha, S., Veith, H.: Modular Verification of Software Components in C. In: Proc. 25th Int. Conference on Software Engineering (ICSE). pp. 385–395 (2003), Extended version in IEEE Transactions on Software Engineering, 2004
5. Clarke, E., Emerson, E.A.: Design and synthesis of synchronization skeletons using branching time temporal logic. In: Kozen, D. (ed.) Logic of Programs 1981. LNCS, vol. 131, pp. 52–71. Springer, Heidelberg (1982)
6. Clarke, E., Emerson, E.A., Sistla, A.P.: Automatic Verification of Finite State Concurrent Systems Using Temporal Logic Specifications: A Practical Approach. In: Proc. POPL, pp. 117–126 (1983)
7. Clarke, E., Grumberg, O., Jha, S., Lu, Y., Veith, H.: Counterexample-guided abstraction refinement. In: Emerson, E.A., Sistla, A.P. (eds.) CAV 2000. LNCS, vol. 1855, pp. 154–169. Springer, Heidelberg (2000), Extended version in J. ACM 50(5): 752–794, 2003.
8. Clarke, E., Grumberg, O., Long, D.: Model checking and abstraction. ACM Transactions on Programming Languages and Systems 16(5), 1512–1542 (1994)
9. Clarke, E., Grumberg, O., Peled, D.: Model Checking. MIT Press, Cambridge (1999)

10. Clarke, E., Kroening, D., Lerda, F.: A Tool for Checking ANSI-C Programs. In: Jensen, K., Podelski, A. (eds.) TACAS 2004. LNCS, vol. 2988, pp. 168–176. Springer, Heidelberg (2004)
11. Clarke, E., Mishra, B.: Automatic Verification of Asynchronous Circuits. In: Proc. Logic of Programs, pp. 101–115 (1983)
12. Cousot, P., Cousot, R.: Abstract interpretation: A unified lattice model for static analysis of programs by construction or approximation of fixpoints. In: Proc. Symposium on Principles of Programming Languages (POPL), pp. 238–252 (1977)
13. Graf, S., Saidi, H.: Construction of Abstract State Graphs with PVS. In: Grumberg, O. (ed.) CAV 1997. LNCS, vol. 1254, pp. 72–83. Springer, Heidelberg (1997)
14. Henzinger, T.A., Jhala, R., Majumdar, R., Sutre, G.: Lazy Abstraction. In: Proc. ACM SIGPLAN-SIGACT Conference on Principles of Programming Languages, pp. 58–70 (2002)
15. Jain, H., Kroening, D., Clarke, E.: Verification of SpecC using predicate abstraction. In: MEMOCODE 2004, pp. 7–16. IEEE, Los Alamitos (2004)
16. Kurshan, R.P.: Computer-Aided Verification of Coordinating Processes. Princeton University Press, Princeton (1994)
17. McMillan, K.: Symbolic Model Checking: An Approach to the State Explosion Problem. Kluwer Academic Publishers, Dordrecht (1993)
18. Pnueli, A.: The temporal logic of programs. In: Proc. 18th Symposium on Foundations of Computer Science (FOCS), pp. 46–67 (1977)
19. Queille, J., Sifakis, J.: Specification and verification of concurrent systems in CESAR. In: Dezani-Ciancaglini, M., Montanari, U. (eds.) Programming 1982. LNCS, vol. 137, pp. 337–351. Springer, Heidelberg (1982)

Computational Logical Frameworks and Generic Program Analysis Technologies

José Meseguer and Grigore Roşu

Department of Computer Science,
University of Illinois at Urbana-Champaign, USA
{meseguer,grosu}@cs.uiuc.edu

1 Motivation

The technologies developed to solve the verifying compiler grand challenge should be *generic*, that is, not tied to a particular language but widely applicable to many languages. Such technologies should also be *semantics-based*, that is, based on a rigorous formal semantics of the languages.

For this, a *computational logical framework* with efficient executability and a spectrum of *meta-tools* can serve as a basis on which to: (1) define the formal semantics of any programming language; and (2) develop *generic program analysis techniques and tools* that can be instantiated to generate powerful analysis tools for each language of interest.

Not all logical frameworks can serve such purposes well. We first list some specific requirements that we think are important to properly address the grand challenge. Then we present our experience with rewriting logic as supported by the Maude system and its formal tool environment. Finally, we discuss some future directions of research.

2 Logical Framework Requirements

Based on experience, current trends, and the basic requirements of the grand challenge problem, we believe that any logical framework serving as a computational infrastructure for the various technologies for solving the grand challenge should have *at least* the following features:

1. good *data representation* capabilities,
2. support for *concurrency and nondeterminism*,
3. *simplicity* of the formalism,
4. *efficient* implementability, and efficient *meta-tools*,
5. support for *reflection*,
6. support for inductive reasoning, preferably with *initial model* semantics,
7. support for generation of *proof objects*, acting as correctness certificates.

While proponents of a framework may claim that it has all these features, in some cases further analysis can show that it either lacks some of them, or can only "simulate" certain features in a quite artificial way. A good example is the

B. Meyer and J. Woodcock (Eds.): Verified Software, LNCS 4171, pp. 256–267, 2008.

simulation/elimination of concurrency in inherently deterministic formalisms by implementing or defining thread/process scheduling algorithms. Another example might be the claim that the lambda calculus has good data representation capabilities because one can encode numbers as Church numerals.

3   The Rewriting Logic/Maude Experience

At UIUC, together with several students, we are developing semantic definitions of programming languages based on *rewriting logic* (RWL) [27]. Rewriting logic meets the requirements mentioned above, and supports semantic definitions of programming languages that combine *algebraic denotational semantics* and *SOS* semantics in a seamless way [29]. Given a language L, its rewriting logic semantics is a rewrite theory

$$\mathcal{R}_L = (\Sigma_L, E_L, R_L),$$

where Σ_L is a *signature* expressing the syntax of L, E_L is a set of *equations* defining the meaning of the sequential features of L together with that of the various state infrastructure operations, and R_L is a set of *rewrite rules* defining the semantics of the concurrent features of L.

3.1   Maude and Its Formal Tools

Rewrite theories are triples (Σ, E, R), with (Σ, E) an equational theory and R a set of rewrite rules. Intuitively, (Σ, E, R) specifies a computational system in which the *states* are specified as elements of the algebraic data type defined by (Σ, E), and the system's *concurrent transitions* are specified by the rewrite rules R. Rewrite theories can be executed in different languages such as CafeOBJ [22], and ELAN [1]. The most general support for the execution of rewrite theories is currently provided by the Maude language [6,7], in which rewrite theories with very general conditional rules, and whose underlying equational theories can be membership equational theories [28], can be specified and can be executed, provided they satisfy some basic executability requirements. Furthermore, Maude provides very efficient support for rewriting *modulo* any combination of associativity, commutativity, and identity axioms. Since an equational theory (Σ, E) can be regarded as a degenerate rewrite theory of the form $(\Sigma, E, \emptyset)$, equational logic is naturally a sublogic of rewriting logic. In Maude this sublogic is supported by *functional modules* [6], which are theories in membership equational logic. When executed in Maude, the RWL formal semantics $\mathcal{R}_L$ of language L automatically becomes an *efficient interpreter* for L: for example, faster than the Linux bc interpreter, and half the speed of the Scheme interpreter.

Besides supporting efficient execution, often in the order of several million rewrites per second, Maude also provides a range of formal tools and algorithms to analyze rewrite theories and verify their properties. These tools can be used almost directly to provide corresponding analysis tools for languages defined as rewrite logic theories. A first useful formal analysis feature is its *breadth-first search* command. Given an initial state of a system (a term), we can search for all reachable states matching a certain pattern and satisfying an equationally-defined semantic condition P. By making $P = \neg Q$, where Q is an invariant, we get in this way a *semi-decision procedure* for finding failures of invariant safety properties. Note that there is no finite-state assumption involved here: any executable rewrite theory can thus be analyzed. For systems where the set of states reachable from an initial state are finite, Maude also provides a linear time temporal logic (LTL) model checker. Maude's is an explicit-state LTL model checker, with performance comparable to that of the SPIN model checker [24] for the benchmarks that we have analyzed [17,18].

Reflection is a key feature of rewriting logic, and is efficiently supported in the Maude implementation through its `META-LEVEL` module. One important fruit of this is that it becomes quite easy to build new formal tools and to add them to the Maude environment. Indeed, such tools by their very nature manipulate and analyze rewrite theories. By reflection, a rewrite theory $\mathcal{R}$ becomes a *term* $\overline{\mathcal{R}}$ in the universal theory, which can be efficiently manipulated by the descent functions in the `META-LEVEL` module. As a consequence, Maude formal tools have a reflective design and are built in Maude as suitable extensions of the `META-LEVEL` module. They include the following:

- the Maude Church-Rosser Checker, and Knuth-Bendix and Coherence Completion tools [8,15,13,12]
- the Full Maude module composition tool [11,16]
- the Maude Predicate Abstraction tool [34]
- the Maude Inductive Theorem Prover (ITP) [5,8,9]
- the Real-Time Maude tool [33];
- the Maude Sufficient Completeness Checker (SCC) [23]
- the Maude Termination Tool (MTT) [14].

3.2 Unifying SOS and Equational Semantics

For the most part, equational semantics[1] and SOS have lived separate lives. Pragmatic considerations and differences in taste tend to dictate which framework is adopted in each particular case. For concurrent languages SOS is clearly superior and tends to prevail as the formalism of choice, but for deterministic languages equational approaches are also widely used. Of course there are also practical considerations of tool support for both execution and formal reasoning.

In the end, equational semantics and SOS, although each very valuable in its own way, are "single hammer" approaches. Would it be possible to seamlessly *unify* them within a more flexible and general framework? Could their respective limitations be overcome when they are thus unified? Our proposal is that

---

[1] In equational semantics, formal definitions take the form of *semantic equations*, typically satisfying the *Church-Rosser* property. Both higher-order (denotational semantics) and first-order (algebraic semantics) versions have been shown to be useful formalisms. We use the more neutral term *equational semantics* to emphasize the fact that denotational and algebraic semantics have many common features and can both be viewed as instances of a common equational framework.

rewriting logic does indeed provide one such unifying framework. The key to this unification is what we call rewriting logic's *abstraction knob*. The point is that in equational semantics' model-theoretic approach entities are *identified by the semantic equations*, and have unique *abstract denotations* in the corresponding models. In our knob metaphor this means that in equational semantics the abstraction knob is *always turned all the way up to its maximum position*. By contrast, one of the key features of SOS is providing a very detailed, step-by-step formal description of a language's evaluation mechanisms. As a consequence, most entities —except perhaps for built-in data, stores, and environments, which are typically treated on the side— are *primarily syntactic*, and computations are described in full detail. In our metaphor this means that in SOS the abstraction knob is *always turned down to its minimum position*.

How is the unification and corresponding availability of an abstraction knob achieved? Since a rewrite theory is a triple (Σ, E, R), with (Σ, E) an equational theory with Σ a signature of operations and sorts, and E a set of (possibly conditional) equations, and with R a set of (possibly conditional) rewrite rules, equational semantics is obtained as the special case in which $R = \emptyset$, so we only have the semantic equations E and the abstraction knob is turned up to its maximum position. SOS is obtained as the special case in which $E = \emptyset$, and we only have (possibly conditional) rules R rewriting purely syntactic entities (terms), so that the abstraction knob is turned down to the minimum position.

Rewriting logic's "abstraction knob" is precisely its crucial distinction between equations E and rules R in a rewrite theory (Σ, E, R). *States of the computation* are then E-equivalence classes, that is, *abstract elements* in the initial algebra $T_{\Sigma/E}$. A rewrite with a rule in R is understood as a transition $[t] \longrightarrow [t']$ between such abstract states. The knob, however, can be turned up or down. We can turn it *all the way down to its minimum* by converting all equations into rules, transforming (Σ, E, R) into $(\Sigma, \emptyset, R \cup E)$. This gives us the most concrete, SOS-like semantic description possible. Can we turn the knob "all the way up," in the sense of converting all rules into equations? Only if the system we are describing is *deterministic* (for example, the semantic definition of a sequential language) is this a sound procedure. In that case, the equational theory $(\Sigma, R \cup E)$ should be Church-Rosser, and we do indeed obtain a most-abstract-possible, purely equational semantics out of the less abstract specification (Σ, E, R), or even out of the most concrete possible specification $(\Sigma, \emptyset, R \cup E)$. What can we do in general to make a specification *as abstract as possible*? We can identify a subset $R_0 \subseteq R$ such that: (1) $R_0 \cup E$ is Church-Rosser; and (2) R_0 is biggest possible with this property. In actual language specification practice this is not hard to do. Essentially, we can use semantic equations for most of the sequential features of a programming language: only when interactions with memory could lead to nondeterminism (particularly if the language has threads, or they could later be added to the language in an extension) or for intrinsically concurrent features, are rules (as opposed to equations) really needed. In our experience, it is often possible to specify most of the semantic axioms with equations, with relatively few rules needed for truly concurrent or nondeterministic features. For example, the semantics of the JVM described in [21,19] has about 300 equations and 40 rules; and that of Java described in [19] has about 600 equations but only 15 rules. A semantics for an ML-like language with threads given in [30] has only two rules.

This distinction between equations and rules, besides giving to equational semantics and SOS their due in a way not possible for the other alternative if we were to remain within each of these formalisms, has also important practical consequences for *program analysis*; because it affords a massive *state space reduction* which can make formal analyses such as breadth-first search and model checking enormously more efficient. Because of state-space explosion, such analyses could easily become infeasible if we were to use an SOS-like specification in which all computation steps are described with rules. This capacity of dealing with abstract states is a crucial reason why our generic tools, when instantiated to a given programming language definition, tend to result in program analysis tools of competitive performance. Of course, the price to pay in exchange for abstraction is a *coarser level of granularity* in respect to what aspects of a computation are *observable* at that abstraction level. For example, when analyzing a sequential program using a semantics in which most sequential features have been specified with equations, all sequential subcomputations will be abstracted away, and the analysis will focus on memory and thread interactions. If a finer analysis is needed, we can always obtain it by "turning down the abstraction knob" to the right observability level by *converting some equations into rules*. That is, we can regulate the knob to find for each kind of analysis the best possible balance between abstraction and observability.

3.3 Languages Defined in Rewriting Logic

Many languages have already been given semantics in this way using Maude. The language definitions can then be used as interpreters, and —in conjunction with Maude's search command and its LTL model checker— to formally analyze programs in those languages. For example, large fragments of Java and the JVM have been specified in Maude this way, with the Maude rewriting logic semantics being used as the basis of Java and JVM program analysis tools that for some examples outperform well-known Java analysis tools [21,19]. A similar Maude specification of the semantics of Scheme at UIUC yields an interpreter with .75 the speed of the standard Scheme interpreter on average for the benchmarks tested. The specification of a C-like language and the corresponding formal analyses are discussed in detail in [31]. A semantics of an ML-like language with threads was discussed in detail in [30], a modular rewriting logic semantics of CML has been given in [4], and a definition of the Scheme language has been given in [10]. Other language case studies, all specified in Maude, include: BC [2], CCS [43,44,2], CIAO [40], Creol [25], ELOTOS [42], MSR [3,38], PLAN [39,40], and the pi-calculus [41]. In fact, the semantics of large fragments of conventional languages are by now routinely developed by UIUC graduate students as course projects [36] in a few weeks, including, besides the languages already mentioned: Beta, Haskell, Lisp, LLVM, Pict, Python, Ruby, and Smalltalk.

3.4   Formal Analysis

Furthermore, Maude's formal tools, such as its inductive theorem prover, linear temporal logic (LTL) model-checker, and breadth-first search (BFS) capability then become *meta-tools* from which we derive useful program analysis tools for L using $\mathcal{R}_L$.

We are furthermore developing new *generic program analysis technologies* such as, for example, a *generic partial-order reduction* technique [20] than can apply to any language L with threads, and does not require any changes to an underlying model checker.

Correctness of a compiler can and should mean more than just correctness with respect to functional behavior. Depending upon particular applications of interest, certain important safety policies that transcend the basic semantics of the language under consideration may need to be preserved. For example, in an application referring to physical objects, consistency with respect to units of measurement or coordinate systems needs to be assured. We are also developing *domain-specific certifiers*, which are static analysis tools that check conformance of computation with respect to particular but important domains of interest. For example, we developed RWL-based certifiers for conformance with units of measurement [37], and with coordinate frames [26].

The *cost* of generating tools for a language L this way using its formal semantic definition $\mathcal{R}_L$ is *much lower* (in the order of weeks) than that of building similar language specific analysis tools (man years). For example, it took Feng Chen at UIUC only a few weeks to develop the formal semantics of Java 1.4 (except for its libraries) as a RWL theory $\mathcal{R}_{Java}$ specified in Maude.

Furthermore, the *formal analysis tools* obtained for free from $\mathcal{R}_{Java}$ and $\mathcal{R}_{JVM}$ are *competitive* for some applications with similar language-specific tools such a NASA-Ames' Java Path Finder [45] and Stanford's Java model checker [35]. Similarly, our experiments with the generic partial order reduction technique indicate that it can achieve rates of space and time reduction similar to those of language-specific tools such as SPIN [24].

4   Future Directions Related to the Grand Challenge

Our main point has been to emphasize the need for genericity in approaching the grand challenge; otherwise, an answer to the challenge would have a limited applicability to other languages besides those chosen in the challenge project. For this, we have argued that both a computational logical framework in which to give a precise formal semantics to programming languages, and on which to base generic program analysis tools, would be very useful.

We have also summarized our experience so far with one such logical framework, namely rewriting logic, and for applying the Maude RWL language and its generic tools to formally analyze programs in different programming languages. Our results, although encouraging, are very much *work in progress*; we would like to advance in addition the following directions:

1. Modular programming language definitions in the spirit of MSOS [32]. The goal is to build a database of reusable semantic definitions, with the semantics of each language feature defined in a separate module. It should then be possible to define the semantics of a whole language by just combining the modules for the language features, renaming the syntax of each module to the chosen concrete syntax.

2. Developing various language-generic program analysis tools; we have already mentioned the ongoing work on partial order reduction, which should be further advanced; but generic abstraction tools, and also generic tools for static analysis are two other important areas to advance.

3. Language-generic theorem proving environments, based on an axiomatic semantics that uses the language rewriting semantics as its foundation are also an important direction to investigate.

4. Finally, it would be useful to investigate semantics-preserving translations between languages, in particular the generation of provably correct compilers from the formal semantics $\mathcal{R}_L$ of a language L.

References

1. Borovanský, P., Kirchner, C., Kirchner, H., Moreau, P.-E.: ELAN from a rewriting logic point of view. Theoretical Computer Science 285, 155–185 (2002)

2. Braga, C., Meseguer, J.: Modular rewriting semantics in practice. In: Proc. WRLA 2004, ENTCS

3. Cervesato, I., Stehr, M.-O.: Representing the msr cryptoprotocol specification language in an extension of rewriting logic with dependent types. In: Degano, P. (ed.) Proc. Fifth International Workshop on Rewriting Logic and its Applications (WRLA 2004), Barcelona, Spain, March 27 - 28, 2004, Elsevier ENTCS, Amsterdam (2004)

4. Chalub, F., Braga, C.: A Modular Rewriting Semantics for CML. Journal of Universal Computer Science 10(7), 789–807 (2004),
   http://www.jucs.org/jucs_10_7/a_modular_rewriting_semantics

5. Clavel, M.: Reflection in Rewriting Logic: Metalogical Foundations and Metaprogramming Applications. In: CSLI Publications (2000)

6. Clavel, M., Durán, F., Eker, S., Lincoln, P., Martí-Oliet, N., Meseguer, J., Quesada, J.: Maude: specification and programming in rewriting logic. Theoretical Computer Science 285, 187–243 (2002)

7. Clavel, M., Durán, F., Eker, S., Lincoln, P., Martí-Oliet, N., Meseguer, J., Talcott, C.: Maude 2.0 Manual (June 2003), http://maude.cs.uiuc.edu

8. Clavel, M., Durán, F., Eker, S., Meseguer, J.: Building equational proving tools by reflection in rewriting logic. In: CAFE: An Industrial-Strength Algebraic Formal Method, Elsevier, Amsterdam (2000), http://maude.cs.uiuc.edu

9. Clavel, M., Palomino, M.: The ITP tool's manual. Universidad Complutense, Madrid (April 2005), http://maude.sip.ucm.es/itp/

10. d'Amorim, M., Roşu, G.: An Equational Specification for the Scheme Language. In: Proceedings of the 9th Brazilian Symposium on Programming Languages (SBLP 2005), 2005. Also Technical Report No. UIUCDCS-R-2005-2567 (April 2005) (to appear)

11. Durán, F.: A reflective module algebra with applications to the Maude language. Ph.D. Thesis, University of Málaga (1999)
12. Durán, F.: Coherence checker and completion tools for Maude specifications. Manuscript, Computer Science Laboratory, SRI International (2000), http://maude.cs.uiuc.edu/papers
13. Durán, F.: Termination checker and Knuth-Bendix completion tools for Maude equational specifications. Manuscript, Computer Science Laboratory, SRI International (2000), http://maude.cs.uiuc.edu/papers
14. Durán, F., Lucas, S., Meseguer, J., Marché, C., Urbain, X.: Proving termination of membership equational programs. In: Sestoft, P., Heintze, N. (eds.) Proc. of ACM SIGPLAN 2004 Symposium on Partial Evaluation and Program Manipulation, PEPM 2004, pp. 147–158. ACM Press, New York (2004)
15. Durán, F., Meseguer, J.: A Church-Rosser checker tool for Maude equational specifications. Manuscript, Computer Science Laboratory, SRI International (2000), http://maude.cs.uiuc.edu/papers
16. Durán, F., Meseguer, J.: On parameterized theories and views in Full Maude 2.0. In: Futatsugi, K. (ed.) Futatsugi, editor, Proc. 3rd. Intl. Workshop on Rewriting Logic and its Applications. ENTCS, Elsevier, Amsterdam (2000)
17. Eker, S., Meseguer, J., Sridharanarayanan, A.: The Maude LTL model checker. In: Gadducci, F., Montanari, U. (eds.) Proc. 4th. Intl. Workshop on Rewriting Logic and its Applications, ENTCS, Elsevier, Amsterdam (2002)
18. Eker, S., Meseguer, J., Sridharanarayanan, A.: The Maude LTL model checker and its implementation. In: Ball, T., Rajamani, S.K. (eds.) SPIN 2003. LNCS, vol. 2648, pp. 230–234. Springer, Heidelberg (2003)
19. Farzan, A., Cheng, F., Meseguer, J., Roşu, G.: Formal analysis of Java programs in JavaFAN. In: Alur, R., Peled, D.A. (eds.) CAV 2004. LNCS, vol. 3114, pp. 501–505. Springer, Heidelberg (2004)
20. Farzan, A., Meseguer, J.: Partial order reduction for rewriting semantics of programming languages, Manuscript, submitted for publication (2005)
21. Farzan, A., Meseguer, J., Roşu, G.: Formal JVM code analysis in JavaFAN. In: Rattray, C., Maharaj, S., Shankland, C. (eds.) AMAST 2004. LNCS, vol. 3116, pp. 132–147. Springer, Heidelberg (2004)
22. Futatsugi, K., Diaconescu, R.: CafeOBJ Report. World Scientific, AMAST Series (1998)
23. Hendrix, J., Meseguer, J., Clavel, M.: A sufficient completeness reasoning tool for partial specifications. In: Giesl, J. (ed.) RTA 2005. LNCS, vol. 3467, pp. 165–174. Springer, Heidelberg (2005)
24. Holzmann, G.: The Spin Model Checker - Primer and Reference Manual. Addison-Wesley, Reading (2003)
25. Johnsen, E.B., Owe, O., Axelsen, E.W.: A runtime environment for concurrent objects with asynchronous method calls. In: Martí-Oliet, N. (ed.) Proc. 5th. Intl. Workshop on Rewriting Logic and its Applications, ENTCS, Elsevier, Amsterdam (2004)
26. Lowry, M., Pressburger, T., Roşu, G.: Certifying domain-specific policies. In: Proceedings, International Conference on Automated Software Engineering (ASE 2001), pp. 81–90. IEEE, Los Alamitos, San Diego, California (2001)
27. Meseguer, J.: Conditional rewriting logic as a unified model of concurrency. Theoretical Computer Science 96(1), 73–155 (1992)
28. Meseguer, J.: Membership algebra as a logical framework for equational specification. In: Parisi-Presicce, F. (ed.) WADT 1997. LNCS, vol. 1376, pp. 18–61. Springer, Heidelberg (1998)

29. Meseguer, J., Roşu, G.: Rewriting logic semantics: From language specifications to formal analysis tools. In: Basin, D., Rusinowitch, M. (eds.) IJCAR 2004. LNCS (LNAI), vol. 3097, pp. 1–44. Springer, Heidelberg (2004)

30. Meseguer, J., Roşu, G.: Rewriting logic semantics: From language specifications to formal analysis tools. In: Basin, D., Rusinowitch, M. (eds.) IJCAR 2004. LNCS (LNAI), vol. 3097, pp. 1–44. Springer, Heidelberg (2004)

31. Meseguer, J., Roşu, G.: The rewriting logic semantics project. In: Proc. of SOS 2005, ENTCS, Elsevier, Amsterdam (to appear, 2005)

32. Mosses, P.D.: Foundations of modular SOS. In: Kutyłowski, M., Wierzbicki, T., Pacholski, L. (eds.) MFCS 1999. LNCS, vol. 1672, pp. 70–80. Springer, Heidelberg (1999)

33. Ölveczky, P.C., Meseguer, J.: Real-Time Maude 2.1. In: Martí-Oliet, N. (ed.) Proc. 5th Intl. Workshop on Rewriting Logic and its Applications, ENTCS, Elsevier, Amsterdam (2004)

34. Palomino, M.: A predicate abstraction tool for Maude. Documentation and tool, http://maude.sip.ucm.es/~miguelpt/bibliography.html

35. Park, D.Y.W., Stern, U., Skakkebæk, J.U., Dill, D.L.: Java model checking. In: ASE 2001, pp. 253–256 (2000)

36. Roşu, G.: Programming language classes. Department of Computer Science, University of Illinois at Urbana-Champaign, http://fsl.cs.uiuc.edu/~grosu/classes/

37. Roşu, G., Chen, F.: Certifying measurement unit safety policy. In: Automated Software Engineering, 2003. Proc. 18th IEEE Intl. Conference, pp. 304–309 (2003)

38. Stehr, M.-O., Cervesato, I., Reich, S.: An execution environment for the MSR cryptoprotocol specification language, http://formal.cs.uiuc.edu/stehr/msr.html

39. Stehr, M.-O., Talcott, C.: PLAN in Maude: Specifying an active network programming language. In: Gadducci, F., Montanari, U. (eds.) Proc. 4th. Intl. Workshop on Rewriting Logic and its Applications, ENTCS, Elsevier, Amsterdam (2002)

40. Stehr, M.-O., Talcott, C.L.: Practical techniques for language design and prototyping. In: Fiadeiro, J.L., Montanari, U., Wirsing, M. (eds.) Abstracts Collection of the Dagstuhl Seminar 05081 on Foundations of Global Computing. 2005, Schloss Dagstuhl, Wadern, Germany (February 20–25, 2005)

41. Thati, P., Sen, K., Martí-Oliet, N.: An executable specification of asynchronous Pi-Calculus semantics and may testing in Maude 2.0. In: Gadducci, F., Montanari, U. (eds.) Proc. 4th. Intl. Workshop on Rewriting Logic and its Applications, ENTCS, Elsevier, Amsterdam (2002)

42. Verdejo, A.: Maude como marco semántico ejecutable. PhD thesis, Facultad de Informática, Universidad Complutense, Madrid, Spain (2003)

43. Verdejo, A., Martí-Oliet, N.: Implementing CCS in Maude. In: In Proc. FORTE/PSTV 2000, vol. 183, pp. 351–366 (2000)

44. Verdejo, A., Martí-Oliet, N.: Implementing CCS in Maude 2. In: Gadducci, F., Montanari, U. (eds.) Proc. 4th. Intl. Workshop on Rewriting Logic and its Applications, ENTCS, Elsevier, Amsterdam (2002)

45. Visser, W., Havelund, K., Brat, G., Park, S.: Java PathFinder - second generation of a Java model checker. In: Proceedings of Post-CAV Workshop on Advances in Verification (2000)

A Discussion on Grigore Rosu's Presentation

Peter Schmitt

I do not want to belittle your work, but the information you gave on formalizing semantics of programming languages in Maude, should be taken with a little grain of salt. We have looked at your Java semantics, the one that your grad students did in three weeks; it is very preliminary. There are lots of Java features that are not covered. There are no exceptions, there is no abrupt program termination. So, it covers some parts, but not too much.

Grigore Rosu

I said fragments of languages, and, actually, we have exceptions defined in other languages. We teach exceptions in that way, which I didn't put in the definition of Java. And this is not about Maude. This is about the methodology to define languages in rewriting logic; you can use another language instead of Maude if you want to. But I think that the methodology is viable, with Maude or without it; that is our point.

Patrick Cousot

I had a comment similar to this one but in a different form. You should wish to have end-users for your tool at the end, because it must correspond to something real, not an approximation of the language and things like that. That was my negative comment. My positive one is: I see a great analogy with the TVLA approach. Have you tried some universal abstractions like in TVLA?

Grigore Rosu

No. So, what was your negative comment?

Patrick Cousot

If you have a definition that is 95% complete, and the 5% that are missing that all the [difficult] problems, then it's vain. And so, you do not have end-users, because it is not real, and that is...

Grigore Rosu (*interrupts*)

Right. So, the aim would be to have complete definitions. We are working with these libraries of features, and we like to have full definitions of the language by putting all these features together. So, not 95% but full definitions, that is our purpose, and that is the language. The definition of the language, that's what the language is.

Kathi Fisler

To what extent are you trying to get interoperability between all those languages that you are defining? Is that at all an advantage you are going to get out of this framework?

Grigore Rosu

We would like to. We have not thought of that. We have not tried anything along those lines, but I think, we should be able to.

Kathi Fisler

But that is not a thing that you could get for free just because you would like it. Wouldn't you have to design that in at the beginning to get this kind of interoperation?

Grigore Rosu

I have to understand what you mean by interoperation. I mean, just to call functions from another language?

Kathi Fisler

To have a program that got fragments written in multiple languages.

Grigore Rosu

I think, that should be quite easy to do. I cannot say "100%, absolutely sure", but my feeling is that this should not be a big problem. We should keep the things disjoint somehow, yes.

Thomas Reps

Because Patrick [Cousot] mentioned TVLA, that prompted me to comment-because actually I wanted to make a negative comment that says something bad about TVLA. I think you're making the same mistake that was made in TVLA, which was to try and be all things to all people. It's a big mistake you've got to accept our transition systems, our transition-system definitions, our logic, etc., as well as our abstractions.

The alternative model is to have well-defined fragments that can be picked up by people who can drop them into Java programs or C++ programs. So, for example, the Parma Polyhedra library is an excellent example of that. There is a well-defined interface based on the primitives that one needs in abstract interpretation, plus mechanisms for defining transformers. I think that is a much better mechanism, and I think that we would do much better in TVLA by packaging up the basic programming abstraction of logical structures, together with a mechanism for defining abstract transformers, and then you do what you want with it in your programs.

There is also another layer at which to consider the issue; let me put in a plug for Stefan Schwoon's Weighted Pushdown System library and the Wisconsin system WPDS++. These are things that handle the question of reachability in weighted pushdown systems: you drop ... different weight domains into them, and then you get static analyzers from them. So, both of these systems are examples of a well-defined fragment with well-defined interfaces to little pieces that can come from others. If you try and be all things to all people, you limit your adoptability.

Grigore Rosu

First of all, I do not think we are making a mistake with what we started. Keep in mind that we keep the syntax separate; we only focus on the semantic definition of the particular features of languages. And, if I can get a chance to show you some definitions, you can see that basically, there is one rule or two at most per language feature. So, if your particular language does not have that, the methodology can do it, if you want to. And here, we are focusing on defining languages, what a language is. It is this logical specification. That is a definition of the language that I am going to use. Otherwise, what is a language? What can I start with? Well, how can I say what it means to verify a program, if I do not have a definition? So, we accept specification languages for requirements, but what is a language to start with? So here, we have a description of the language, it is executable, efficiently executable, and easy to read. So, what else do you want?

A Mechanized Program Verifier

J. Strother Moore

Department of Computer Sciences, University of Texas at Austin, Austin,
Texas 78712, USA
moore@cs.utexas.edu,
http://cs.utexas.edu/users/moore

Abstract. In my view, the "verification problem" is the theorem proving problem, restricted to a computational logic. My approach is: adopt a functional programming language, build a general purpose formal reasoning engine around it, integrate it into a program and proof development environment, and apply it to model and verify a wide variety of computing artifacts, usually modeled operationally within the functional programming language. Everything done in this approach is software verification since the models are runnable programs in a subset of an ANSI standard programming language (Common Lisp). But this approach is of interest to proponents of other approaches (e.g., verification of procedural programs or synthesis) because of the nature of the mathematics of computing. I summarize the progress so far using this approach, sketch the key research challenges ahead and describe my vision of the role and shape of a useful verification system.

1 Approach

The verification community seeks to build a system that can follow the reasoning of an average human engaged in a creative, computational, problem solving task lasting months or years and spanning an arbitrary set of application domains.

Now step back and reconsider what was just said: we seek to build a system that follows – if not reconstructs or anticipates – the reasoning of an average human in an arbitrary, creative, computational, problem solving task. This is the theorem proving problem, perhaps restricted to a computational logic. We seek to build a system that reasons about computation.

I believe one is not likely to achieve a goal unless one identifies precisely what the goal is. My goal is build a practical theorem prover for a computational logic. I believe that any attack on the verification problem will fail unless theorem proving – machine assisted reasoning – is at its heart.

My[1] approach to the "verification problem" is thus:

---

[1] This vision is consistent with McCarthy's, was developed by Boyer and me and then Kaufmann and me, and probably describes the vision of verification as seen by most of the "Boyer-Moore" community. But the community has not been consulted. So I use the first person pronoun here.

B. Meyer and J. Woodcock (Eds.): Verified Software, LNCS 4171, pp. 268–276, 2008.

- Adopt a functional programming language so that programs are functions in a mathematical theory. The particular language I use is the functional subset of the ANSI standard programming language Common Lisp.
- The theory is described by a set of axioms and rules of inference, including well-founded induction and a definitional principle that allows conservative introduction of new concepts.
- The theory is directly supported by an interactive theorem prover.
- The theorem prover employs heuristics and various decision procedures so that many "simple" proofs can be found completely automatically.
- The theorem prover is designed to operate automatically once a conjecture is posed to it. Its behavior is determined by previously proved theorems residing in its database. This addresses three key problems:

  - Since verifying functional correctness of interesting programs requires operation in an undecidable domain, provision for some user guidance is unavoidable. It should not be an after-thought, nor should it force the user to eschew powerful automatic features.
  - Using previously proved lemmas to guide the system encourages the user to think at the high level, i.e., about concepts involved in the specification and their relationships. This also encourages the creation of libraries of general concepts and lemmas.
  - Automatic operation (with respect to previously proved theorems) facilitates *proof maintenance*: the task of verifying a system produced by making incremental modifications to a previously verified one.

- The programming language and theorem prover are embedded in a program/proof development environment in which prototyping, testing, and proving are seamlessly integrated. Like any good programming environment, ours supports a rich collection of code/proof structuring tools including name scopes, modules, libraries, etc., in which the work of many other developers can be made available. The theory must support such tools formally.
- While everything proved in this system exemplifies software verification – the mathematical language is an ANSI standard programming language – systems written in other languages may be modeled and verified by using the system as a formal meta-language. This allows many different languages to be related within a common framework.
- To demonstrate the practicality of a functional programming language the system should be implemented in it.
- To keep the work focused on the goal, every opportunity should be taken to verify systems of commercial (or at least, outside) interest.

A prototype of this vision of mechanized verification was first demonstrated by Boyer and Moore in 1973 in what was called "The Edinburgh Pure Lisp Theorem Prover." The demonstration has been continuously improved and elaborated through a series of so-called "Boyer-Moore theorem provers," including Nqthm [8] and ACL2 (by Kaufmann and Moore, with early contributions by Boyer) [21].

2 Progress So Far

Here is a chronology of work done by the Boyer-Moore community. This represents 35 years of unbroken pursuit of the software verification grand challenge. This litany makes plausible the vision I describe later.

- **1970–1979.** Fully automatic proof of insertion sort, including the permutation property, and fully automatic proofs of many other theorems about Pure Lisp programs [3]; the correctness of a McCarthy-Painter-like expression compiler, the soundness and completeness of a propositional tautology checker, and the correctness of the Boyer-Moore fast string searching algorithm in FORTRAN 77 [4]; proof of the correctness of a linear-time majority vote program written in FORTRAN 77 [7]; proof that a "cruise control" program keeps a vehicle on course in a smoothly varying cross-wind and homes to the course if the wind becomes steady [10]. During this period, Boyer and Moore worked on the Software Implemented Fault Tolerance (SIFT) project [15] and our attempts to formalize the BDX 930 to explain the mix of Pascal and machine code in that system drove much of the subsequent improvement to the theorem prover.

- **1980–1989.** The invertibility of the RSA encryption algorithm [6]; the unsolvability of the halting problem [5]; Gödel's First Incompleteness Theorem [34]; the correctness of a gate-level microprocessor design [19]; the correctness of an operating system kernel [1]; the correctness of an assembler, linker and loader for a stack based relocatable symbolic assembly language supporting Booleans, integer arithmetic, bit vectors, arrays, and recursive subroutine calls – the system produced binary images for the microprocessor mentioned earlier and the proof guaranteed functional correctness of the binary images with respect to the machine code ISA [2]; the correctness of a compiler from a subset of Pascal to the assembly code above and the verification of some simple applications written in that language [38]; the correctness of a compiler from a subset of Pure Lisp to the assembly code [14]; the composition of many of the above theorems to make it possible to prove an application program correct with the high-level language semantics and then derive in one step the correctness of its binary image under the gate-level semantics of the microprocessor – – this is known as the *verified stack* of Computational Logic, Inc., and it was completed and published in a special issue of the *Journal of Automated Reasoning* in 1989.

- **1990–1999.** Proof that an NDL netlist implements the machine code ISA of a 32-bit microprocessor and the fabrication of the microprocessor by LSI Logic [20]; porting the verified stack to the fabricated machine by re-targeting and re-verifying the assembler [27]; verification that a Nim-playing program plays winning Nim and the demonstration of this program on a fabricated, verified microprocessor using the verified stack [37]; verification of 21 of the 22 routines in the Berkeley Unix C String Library – performed by compiling the library with gcc -o to obtain binary machine code for the Motorola 68020 and then verifying that with respect to a formal operational semantics capturing 80% of the user-level 68020 instructions [11]; proof by the same technique of a variety of other C programs, including the C code for binary search and Hoare's *in situ* Quick Sort from [24]; proof that the microarchitectural design of the Motorola CAP digital signal processor (dsp) implements a certain microcode engine, including the verification that a pipeline hazard detection algorithm was sufficient to insure bit- and cycle-accurate equivalence of the two models [12]; use of the formal dsp microcode engine as a simulator for the microarchitecture, because the formal microcode model was three times faster than Motorola's SPW model of the microarchitecture [12]; proof of several dsp microcode programs written by Motorola [12,13]; proof that the microcode for the AMD K5 correctly implemented IEEE floating point division – carried out *before* the K5 was fabricated [29]; proof that all elementary floating point on the AMD Athlon was correctly implemented in RTL (a variant of Verilog)[32]; proof of the soundness of a Lisp program that checks the proofs produced by the Ivy theorem prover from Argonne National Labs – Ivy proofs may thus be generated by unverified code but confirmed to be proofs by a verified Lisp function [26]; proof that a security model of the IBM 4758 secure co-processor satisfied properties required for FIPS 140-1 Level Four certification [35]; development and production use of a formal model at Rockwell Collins as the microarchitectural simulator for the first silicon-implemented JVM (the design became the JEM1 of aJile Systems, Inc.) [18] – the formal simulator runs at 90% of the speed of a comparable simulator written in C.

– **2000–2005.** Proofs of properties of components of the AMD Opteron and other processors [private communication]; proof of the soundness and completeness of a Lisp implementation of a BDD package that achieves runtime speeds of about 60% those of the CUDD package (however, unlike CUDD, the verified package does not support dynamic variable reordering and is thus more limited in scope) [36]; proof of correctness of the algorithms used for floating point division and square root on the IBM Power 4 [33]; proof of instruction equivalence between different implementations of a commercial microprocessor [16]; proof that microcode for the Rockwell Collins AAMP7 implements a given security policy having to do with process separation [17]; verification that the JVM bytecode produced by the Sun compiler `javac` on certain simple Java classes implements the claimed functionality [28], including verification of a small class file that spawns an unbounded number of non-terminating threads in contention for a common data structure [30]; verification of certain properties of the Sun bytecode verifier as described in JSR-139 for J2ME JVMs [25] (part of an ongoing effort to verify the runtime safety of the JVM).

Many other applications are available at [23].

3   Research Challenges and Milestones

Kaufmann and I describe the our research challenges in [22]. These include the mechanized invention of lemmas and new concepts, including the discovery of inductive invariants (perhaps by augmenting a user supplied core invariant); the use of examples and counterexamples to guide search and concept and conjecture formation; analogy, learning and data mining in theorem proving; the adoption of an open architecture for a theorem prover allowing it to build on other work and to be tailored by the user in a sound way; support for parallel and collaborative theorem proving projects; an empowering interactive user interface supporting, among other things, interactive steering of an ongoing proof attempt; training people to use these tools; the construction of a useful and verified theorem prover hosted on a verified platform.

4   Discussion and Speculation

While I strongly advocate and actively work on the integration of decision procedures and static analyzers into mechanized theorem provers to ease the burden of proof, I do not believe they are the breakthroughs needed to make software verification palatable to the masses. I do not believe software verification will ever be palatable to the masses (until the AI challenge is solved).

I believe that mechanized verification of the functional correctness of software crucially depends upon the designer or some other human annotating the code to explain the intention of important routines or blocks. This will not happen until programmers and their masters stop measuring productivity in lines-of-code per day and start insisting on functional correctness as a deliverable. This will probably never be commonplace because most software is non-critical.

Nevertheless, for critical applications the software industry ought to have a way to check the correctness of its products.

What follows is my own speculation as to the verification system of the future. The references below point to closely related work mentioned above. Scrutiny of those references will support my conviction that this proposal is plausible.

The necessary tool suite will have to be tightly integrated with several programming languages to provide the necessary assurance, runtime efficiency and proof power. Code portability will be provided by a virtual machine (VM). Two levels of programming language are provided. The high-level language will be a functional one – and that same language will be the mathematical language in which proofs are conducted. [The entire Boyer-Moore project supports the conclusion that adequate speed can be obtained via a functional language while providing a unified framework for machine-aided reasoning.] A verified compiler will map that language into the low level language, which will be the assembly code of the VM [27,14]. The formal semantics of the VM are given operationally in the logic [25]. Thus, VM code can be verified, using the techniques of [31] to mix inductive assertion-style proofs with direct proofs. Special static analyzers, especially something akin to escape analysis or the restrictions enforced by ACL2 on single-threaded objects [9] (ACL2's version of monads), will allow the mixture of functional high-level programs with occasional calls to VM code for efficiency.

The entire programming environment is integrated into a theorem proving environment [21]. This keeps the user focused on the obligation to deliver correct code and eliminates cognitive dissonance. The theorem prover will make our current systems seem weak and rigid. It will: be fully automatic but steered by context; provide visualization and animation of the proof search process so the user understands what is happening; be capable of using a vast database of examples to guide search, concept formation, and conjecturing; and be parallelized so that multiple strategies can be pursued simultaneously.

5 Summary

I believe the "verification problem" is the theorem proving problem, restricted to a computational logic. Are we likely to build a system that follows and reconstructs human reasoning if we adopt a lesser goal?

References

1. Bevier, W.R.: A verified operating system kernel. Ph.d. dissertation, University of Texas at Austin (1987)
2. Bevier, W.R., Hunt, W.A., Moore, J.S., Young, W.D.: Special issue on system verification. Journal of Automated Reasoning 5(4), 409–530 (1989)
3. Boyer, R.S., Moore, J.S.: Proving theorems about pure lisp functions. J. ACM 22(1), 129–144 (1975)
4. Boyer, R.S., Moore, J.S.: A Computational Logic. Academic Press, New York (1979)
5. Boyer, R.S., Moore, J.S.: A mechanical proof of the unsolvability of the halting problem. Journal of the Association for Computing Machinery 31(3), 441–458 (1984)
6. Boyer, R.S., Moore, J.S.: Proof checking the rsa public key encryption algorithm. American Mathematical Monthly 91(3), 181–189 (1984)
7. Boyer, R.S., Moore, J.S.: Mjrty – a fast majority vote algorithm. In: Boyer, R.S. (ed.) Automated Reasoning: Essays in Honor of Woody Bledsoe, pp. 105–117. Kluwer Academic Publishers, Automated Reasoning Series, Dordrecht (1991)
8. Boyer, R.S., Moore, J.S.: A Computational Logic Handbook, Second Edition. Academic Press, New York (1997)
9. Boyer, R.S., Moore, J.S.: Single-threaded objects in ACL2. In: Krishnamurthi, S., Ramakrishnan, C.R. (eds.) PADL 2002. LNCS, vol. 2257, Springer, Heidelberg (2002),
http://www.cs.utexas.edu/users/moore/publications/stobj/main.ps.gz
10. Boyer, R.S., Moore, J.S., Green, M.W.: The use of a formal simulator to verify a simple real time control program. In: Beauty is Our Business: A Birthday Salute to Edsger W. Dijkstra, pp. 54–66. Springer, Heidelberg (1990) (Texts and Monographs in Computer Science)
11. Boyer, R.S., Yu, Y.: Automated proofs of object code for a widely used microprocessor. Journal of the ACM 43(1), 166–192 (1996)
12. Brock, B., Hunt Jr., W.A.: Formal analysis of the motorola CAP DSP. In: Industrial-Strength Formal Methods, Springer, Heidelberg (1999)
13. Brock, B., Moore, J.S.: A mechanically checked proof of a comparator sort algorithm. In: Engineering Theories of Software Intensive Systems, IOS Press, Amsterdam (to appear, 2005)

14. Flatau, A.D.: A verified implementation of an applicative language with dynamic storage allocation. Ph.d. thesis, University of Texas at Austin (1992)
15. Goldberg, J., Kautz, W., Mellear-Smith, P.M., Green, M., Levitt, K., Schwartz, R., Weinstock, C.: Development and analysis of the software implemented fault-tolerance (sift) computer. Technical Report NASA Contractor Report 172146, NASA Langley Research Center, Hampton, VA (1984)
16. Greve, D., Wilding, M.: Evaluatable, high-assurance microprocessors. In: NSA High-Confidence Systems and Software Conference (HCSS), Linthicum, MD (March 2002), http://hokiepokie.org/docs/hcss02/proceedings.pdf
17. Greve, D., Wilding, M.: A separation kernel formal security policy (2003)
18. Greve, D.A.: Symbolic simulation of the JEM1 microprocessor. In: Gopalakrishnan, G.C., Windley, P. (eds.) FMCAD 1998. LNCS, vol. 1522, pp. 203–203. Springer, Heidelberg (1998)
19. Hunt, W.A.: FM8501: A Verified Microprocessor. LNCS, vol. 795. Springer, Heidelberg (1994)
20. Hunt, W.A., Brock, B.: A formal HDL and its use in the FM9001 verification. In: Proceedings of the Royal Society (April 1992)
21. Kaufmann, M., Manolios, P., Moore, J.S.: Computer-Aided Reasoning: An Approach. Kluwer Academic Press, Boston (2000)
22. Kaufmann, M., Moore, J.S.: Some key research problems in automated theorem proving for hardware and software verification. Revista de la Real Academia de Ciencias (RACSAM) 98(1), 181–196 (2004)
23. Kaufmann, M., Moore, J.S.: The ACL2 home page. In: Dept. of Computer Sciences, University of Texas at Austin (2006),
    http://www.cs.utexas.edu/users/moore/acl2/
24. Kernighan, B.W., Ritchie, D.M.: The C Programming Language, Second Edition. Prentice Hall, Englewood Cliff (1988)
25. Liu, H., Moore, J.S.: Executable JVM model for analytical reasoning: A study. In: Workshop on Interpreters, Virtual Machines and Emulators 2003 (IVME 2003), San Diego, CA, ACM SIGPLAN, New York (2003)
26. McCune, W., Shumsky, O.: Ivy: A preprocessor and proof checker for first-order logic. In: Kaufmann, M., Manolios, P., Moore, J.S. (eds.) Computer-Aided Reasoning: ACL2 Case Studies, Boston, MA, pp. 265–282. Kluwer Academic Press, Dordrecht (2000)
27. Moore, J.S.: Piton: A Mechanically Verified Assembly-Level Language. In: Automated Reasoning Series, Kluwer Academic Publishers, Dordrecht (1996)
28. Moore, J.S.: Proving theorems about Java and the JVM with ACL2. In: Broy, M., Pizka, M. (eds.) Models, Algebras and Logic of Engineering Software, pp. 227–290. IOS Press, Amsterdam (2003),
    http://www.cs.utexas.edu/users/moore/publications/marktoberdorf-03
29. Moore, J.S., Lynch, T., Kaufmann, M.: A mechanically checked proof of the correctness of the kernel of the AMD5K86 floating point division algorithm. IEEE Transactions on Computers 47(9), 913–926 (1998)
30. Moore, J.S., Porter, G.: The Apprentice challenge. ACM TOPLAS 24(3), 1–24 (2002)
31. Ray, S., Moore, J.S.: Proof styles in operational semantics. In: Hu, A.J., Martin, A.K. (eds.) FMCAD 2004. LNCS, vol. 3312, pp. 67–81. Springer, Heidelberg (2004)

32. Russinoff, D.: A mechanically checked proof of IEEE compliance of a register-transfer-level specification of the AMD-K7 floating-point multiplication, division, and square root instructions. London Mathematical Society Journal of Computation and Mathematics 1, 148–200 (1998),
    http://www.onr.com/user/russ/david/k7-div-sqrt.html
33. Sawada, J.: Formal verification of divide and square root algorithms using series calculation. In: Proceedings of the ACL2 Workshop, 2002 (April 2002),
    http://www.cs.utexas.edu/users/moore/acl2/workshop-2002
34. Shankar, N.: Metamathematics, Machines, and Godel's Proof. Cambridge University Press, Cambridge (1994)
35. Smith, S.W., Austel, V.: Trusting trusted hardware: Towards a formal model for programmable secure coprocessors. In: The Third USENIX Workshop on Electronic Commerce (September 1998)
36. Sumners, R.: Correctness proof of a BDD manager in the context of satisfiability checking. In: Proceedings of ACL2 Workshop 2000. Department of Computer Sciences, Technical Report TR-00-29 (November 2000),
    http://www.cs.utexas.edu/users/moore/acl2/workshop-2000/final/
    sumners2/paper.ps
37. Wilding, M.: Nim game proof. Technical Report CLI Tech Report 249, Computational Logic, Inc. (November 1991),
    http://www.cs.utexas.edu/users/boyer/ftp/nqthm/nqthm-1992/examples/
    numbers/nim.eventsq
38. Young, W.D.: A verified code generator for a subset of Gypsy. Technical Report 33, Comp. Logic. Inc. Austin, Texas (1988)

A Discussion on J. Strother Moore's Presentation

Kathi Fisler

In both the introduction to your talk and your list of open problems, there are suggestions of strong connections to artificial intelligence. The AI researchers that I know, all believe that the foundations of AI are now statistical more than logical. Are we being short-sighted, if we look at this as a logical problem?

J Moore

I do not think so, because of the constraint I have posited, which was: We are trying to reason about programs. I agree that trying to reason about the world in general is beyond the scope of that book; but I believe trying to reason about programs is within the scope. I could not agree more with John Rushby about the fact that in the end, system verification requires arguing about the physical world, and I am explicitly not trying to do that. I am trying to stay focused on something that I believe is achievable and is amenable to a formal approach.

Greg Nelson

Jay, in discussing the *Clink* stack, you commented that you believe that software verification inherently has to handle multiple levels of abstraction. A comment with which I deeply agree. In my work, I have aimed at different kinds of abstraction layers. There are a lot of abstractions, of course, between a *while*-loop and the RTL [register transfer level], and it is enormously impressive you are able to do that stuff. But there are equally many layers of abstraction between the *print()* of "Hello world" and the bitmap that finally actually puts the bits into the window. And most of my work has been on building verification tools that can properly and with modular soundness reason about the abstraction layers in object-oriented systems in higher levels of the software. They definitely spin abstraction layers. And I guess my question is, whether you think that I am missing anything in working at multiple abstraction layers, but the higher layers?

J Moore

No, I agree. I feel, it is almost about abstraction, and we should recognize that. But unfortunately, a lot of work on abstraction recognizes it by dealing what I would guard as toy abstractions, and not actually the practical abstractions we use, like compilers and the semantics of languages like Java, which are powerful abstractions in themselves. And the whole idea of *print()*. One of the interesting things that I did at computational logic was actually implementing a printer that puts out a bitmap, and spend some time thinking about the question: How do I know, that bitmap has got an "A" in it? So, yes, I believe that that level of abstraction is just as important as the ones that we explicitly dealt with in the stack. And all of them have to be dealt with in order to follow the kind of reasoning, a programmer engages in constantly. And that is the real challenge in my view.

Verifying Design with Proof Scores

Kokichi Futatsugi[1], Joseph A. Goguen[2], and Kazuhiro Ogata[3]

[1] Japan Advanced Institute of Science and Technology (JAIST)
futatsugi@jaist.ac.jp
[2] University of California at San Diego
goguen@cs.ucsd.edu
[3] NEC Software Hokuriku, Ltd. and JAIST
ogata@jaist.ac.jp

Abstract. Verifying design instead of code can be an effective and practical approach to obtaining verified software. This paper argues that
proof scores are an attractive method for verifying design, in that they
achieve a balance in which the respective capabilities of humans and
machines are utilized optimally.

1 Verifying Code or Design

Although creation of a verifying compiler is a difficult challenge, recent developments suggest that there are ways to make it easier. Systems that generate
lexical analyzers and parsers already have a long history (e.g. Lex and Yacc),
and recent work of Sorin Lerner [23] shows that the same can be done for compiler backends; there is also work suggesting that code generation modules can
be automatically generated (e.g. using intermediate languages). Unfortunately, a
great number of different compilers are needed in today's software world, and the
underlying machine architectures are evolving, as are the languages, so it would
be difficult to create verifying compilers for all useful combinations of language
and platform, and code verification for such tools still remains very difficult.
Major impediments include the unsolvability of discovering loop invariants, the
potential unsolvability of loop once they are found, and the further difficulties
raised by interactivity, nondeterminism, concurrency, distribution, active agents,
and unreliable communication.

A long term approach is to use high level, application specific source languages, in order to greatly simplify source program verification by eliminating
many obscure features of current languages. In the meantime, a currently feasible approach is to *verify the design* of software, instead of its code; experience
shows that design verification often leads to better design, and nearly always
leads to greater conceptual clarity. An additional motivation is that the main
sources of errors in software are in areas other than code, namely, requirements,
specification, and design.

2 The Proof Score Approach

The goal of verification in software engineering is to increase confidence in the
correctness of computer-based systems. For software verification to be genuinely

B. Meyer and J. Woodcock (Eds.): Verified Software, LNCS 4171, pp. 277–290, 2008.
© IFIP International Federation for Information Processing 2008

useful, careful account must be taken of the context of actual use, including the goals of the system, the underlying hardware, and the capabilities and culture of users. Absolute certainty is not achievable in real applications, due to the uncertainties inherent in implementation and use, e.g., breakdowns in physical infrastructure (such as cables and computers), errors by human operators, and flaws in connected systems (e.g., operating systems and databases).

Fully automatic theorem provers often fail to convey an understanding of their proofs, and they are generally unhelpful when they fail because of user errors in specifications or goals, or due to the lack of a necessary lemma or case split (both of which are very common in practice). It follows that one should seek to make optimal use of the respective abilities of humans and computers, so that computers do the tedious formal calculations, and humans do the high level planning; the tradeoff between detail and comprehension should also be carefully balanced.

Proof scores are a central concept in our approach to meeting these goals; proof scores are instructions to a proof engine, such that when they are executed (or "played"), if everything evaluates as expected, then a desired theorem is proved. Proof scores hide the detailed calculations done by machines, while revealing the proof plan created by humans. Although proof scores can be used to verify code in an imperative language (e.g., as in [20]), it generally makes more sense to verify design rather than code. These techniques differ from model checking [5] in their emphasis on re-usable designs (e.g., for protocols and other algorithms), which may be instantiated in code in many different ways, as well as in their ability to deal with systems that have an infinite number of states, and their natural affinity for abstraction.

We have recognized that many attempts are done to use model checking techniques to prove designs or algorithms which are expressed as, for example, finite state transition systems. But they are usually expressed only using low-level data types and very close to program code. Besides, model checking only gives "yes" or "no with counter example", and does not support interactive analyses or understandings of designs.

Many proof scores have been written in CafeOBJ [6,9] for verifying properties of distributed systems, especially distributed algorithms, component-based software, and security protocols [8,27,31,32,34]. Several auxiliary tools have been also been built to support this progress, including PigNose [25], Gateaux, Crème [26], and Kumo [19]. The facilities for behavioral (or observational) proof in CafeOBJ are important for verifying distributed systems, and its advanced module system can be used to express the structure of proofs as well as specifications. In addition, it provides a stable, portable, and reasonably efficient platform for the execution of proof scores, supporting not only term rewriting, but also reasoning in equational logic, rewriting logic, and basic hidden algebra [3]. BOBJ [17] has similar capabilities, featuring a powerful coinduction algorithm that has also been used to verify distributed systems [14].

The following principles can be seen as a requirements analysis for the proof score approach, based on the authors' extensive experience using OBJ [10,18], BOBJ, and CafeOBJ.

Human Computer Interaction. Since fully automatic theorem proving is often infeasible for system verification, it is desirable to integrate the human user in the best possible way: in particular, the proof plans or "scores" should be as readable as possible, and helpful feedback should be provided by machines to humans, in order to maximize their ability to contribute.

Flexible but Clear Structure. It is often desirable to arrange the parts of a verification so as to facilitate comprehension. For example, it is often helpful to state and use a result before it is proved, or even (during proof the planning process) before it is known to be true. Long sequences of proof parts can be difficult to understand, especially when there is no obvious immediate connection between two adjacent parts. But such discontinuities are rather common in published proofs, e.g., when a series of lemmas is proved before they are used in proving a main result. This implies that both subgoals and goal/subgoal relations should be very clear.

Flexible Logic. Although first order predicate logic is the dominant modern logical system, many other logics are used, and in particular, computer scientists have developed many new logics, e.g., for database systems, knowledge representation, and the semantic web; these include variants of propositional logic, modal logic, intuitionistic logic, higher order logic, and equational logic. It is desirable to be able to support as many of these as possible, as well as their combinations, within a single tool. Moreover, the necessary incompleteness of formal logics that have sufficient expressive power, means that users may want to incorporate new rules of inference "on the fly," for example, to take advantage of a symmetry at the meta level to reduce the cases that need to be considered in a proof.

It is often possible to simulate one logic within another, by imposing a suitable discipline on how its rules are used; in fact, this is precisely what proof scores accomplish. The choice of underlying basic logics for such a purpose is important in at least three dimensions: its efficiency, its simplicity and ease of use, and its ability to support other logics. We believe that equational logic and its variants are the most suitable for this purpose: Equational logics are relatively simple, have many decidable properties with associated efficient algorithms, are relatively easy to read and write, and can support reasoning in most other logics, e.g., by supplying appropriate definitions to an engine that can apply them by as rewrite rules. By contrast, higher order logic and type theory are much more complex, harder to read and write, harder to mechanize, and harder to reason with, for both humans and machines.

Behavioral Logic. Distributed systems consist of abstract machines in which states are hidden, but can be "observed" by certain "attribute" functions with values in basic data types (such as integer or boolean). Behavioral (also called observational) logic is a natural approach to verifying such systems. Three major approaches in this area are: coalgebra (e.g., see the overview [22]); the "observational logic" of Bidoit and Henniker [2,21]; and hidden algebra [15,7], on which our own work is based.

CafeOBJ mechanizes the special (but common) case of coinduction in which the effects of methods (or actions) need not be considered for behavioral equivalence, i.e., for which s, s' are behaviorally equivalent if $a(s) = a(s')$ for all applicable attributes a. More sophisticated models can be embedded within this framework, particularly the OTS (Obsevational Transition Systems) model [27] (the power of which is similar to that of UNITY [4]), and the TOTS (timed OTS) model [28], which provides a logical basis for verifying real time concurrent systems with CafeOBJ.

3   Development of Proof Scores

If a specification is expressed as a set of equations and if the equations can be used as rewriting rules for getting a simplest form of a given expression, then the validity of a statement about the specification can be checked by getting a simplest form of a boolean expression for the statement. The word *reduction* is used for simplifying an expression by rewriting rules. If a reasoning process can be designed in such a way that all the tedious calculations are done by reductions, and all rules of inference are applied by setting up special contexts for such reductions, and if every reduction gives the expected result, then the desired theorm is proved.

Several well polished small proof scores for data types appeared in OBJ already in 80's, e.g., see [18]. For example, they use reductions to prove induction steps and bases, based on the structure of initial term algebras. Typical examples are proofs of associativity and commutativity of addition for Peano natural numbers, and the identity $n \times (n + 1) = 2 \times (1 + 2 + \cdots + n)$ for any natural number n.

¿From around 1997, the CafeOBJ group at JAIST [3] started to extend the proof score method (1) to apply to distributed and real-time systems, such as classical distributed (and/or real-time) algorithms, component-based software, railway signal systems, secure protocols, etc., (2) to make the method applicable to practical size problems, and (3) to automate the method. As a result, the proof score method using reduction (rewriting) has become a promising way to do serious proofs.

From Static to Dynamic Systems. Early proof scores in CafeOBJ included (1) equivalences of functions over natural numbers, (2) equivalences of functions over lists, (3) correctness of simple compilers from expressions to machine code for stack machines, etc. These small proof scores realized an almost ideal combination of high level planning and mechanical reduction. However, even for this class of problems, some non-trivial lemma discovery and/or case splitting is required.

Dynamic systems (i.e. systems with changing states) are common in network/computer based systems, but there is no established methodology in algebraic specification for coping with this class of problems. The CafeOBJ language is designed for writing formal specifications of dynamic systems based on hidden algebra [6,12,9]. Many specifications and proof scores for dynamic systems have been done based on hidden algebra semantics, and OTS has been selected as a most promising model. OTS corresponds to a restricted class of hidden algebras, such that it is possible to write specifications for OTS in a fixed standard style that facilitates the development of specifications, and also helps in writing proof scores, since case splits can be suggested by the specifications. The followings publications show stages in the evolution of proof scores for dynamic systems:

- Specifying and verifying mutual exclusion algorithms by incorporating the UNITY model [27].
- Introduction of a primitive version of OTS [29].
- Introduction of real-time features into OTS/CafeOBJ, and accompanying development of proof scores methodology [28,11].
- A proper introduction of OTS/CafeOBJ and the related proof score writing method [30,33].
- Examples of verifications with proof scores in OTS/CafeOBJ [31,32,34] (among others).

From Explaining to Doing Proofs. A major factor distinguishing the stages of evolution of proof scores is the extent of automation. This is a most important direction of evolution for proof scores, although full automation is not a goal. Automation by reduction is suitable for a mechanical calculation with a focused role and a clear meaning in the context of a larger reasoning process. Early proof scores assisted verification by doing reductions to prove necessary logical statements for a specification. It is intended to gradually codify as many kinds of logical statements as possible into reductions in CafeOBJ. Recently, a fully automatic verification method for a subset of OTS has been developed. This algorithm can be seen as an unification of several techniques for proof scores in OTS/CafeOBJ. The following publications show the stages of automation of proof scores:

- Mainly used for writing formal specifications, but also for proof scores [27].
- Examples with sufficiently complete proof scores [31,32,34] (among others).
- A different attempt for automatiing proof scores [25].
- A fully automatic (algorithmic) method of verification for OTS [26][1].

Environment for Proof Score Development. The Kumo system [19,13] provides the proof score approach with greater rigor and better support for proof debugging, although at the cost of learning to use an additional tool. Kumo generates a website, called a *proofweb*, for each proof attempt that it executes. This website has links to background tutorial material, including tutorial pages for each major proof method used, and for the less familiar mathematical theories used, such as hidden algebra. A somewhat similar experimental tool has been developed for generating and displaying proof scores [36].

---

[1] This work used the Maude rewriting engine [24] because it provides faster associative and commutative rewriting.

4   An Example of Proof Score in CafeOBJ: An Identify-Friend-or-Foe (IFF) Protocol

This section gives a simple but non-trivial example of proof score in CafeOBJ to help readers get a more concrete idea of what proof score is.

Let us consider an Identify-Friend-or-Foe (IFF) protocol[2], which is supposedly used to check if an agent is a member of a group. The IFF protocol can be described as follows:

> 1. Check $p \rightarrow q : r$
> 2. Reply $q \rightarrow p : \mathcal{E}_K(r, q)$

We suppose that an agent belongs to only one group, a symmetric key is given to each group, whose members share the key, and keys are different from group to group. If an agent p wants to check if an agent q is a member of the p's group, p generates a fresh random number r and sends it to q as a Check message. On receipt of the message, q replies to the message by sending the random number r received and the ID q, which are encrypted with the symmetric key K of the q's group, to p as a Reply message. On receipt of the message, p tries to decrypt the ciphertext received with the symmetric key of the p's group. If the decryption succeeds and the plaintext consists of r and q, then p concludes that q is a member of the p's group. The protocol is supposed to have the property that if p receives a valid Reply message from q, q is always a member of the p's group. The property is called the IFF property in this paper.

4.1   Modeling and Specification of the Protocol

We suppose that the cryptosystem used is perfect, there is only one legitimate group, all members of the group are trustable, and there are also untrustable agents who are not members. Trustable agents exactly follow the protocol, but untrustable ones may do something against the protocol as well. The combination and cooperation of untrustable agents is modeled as the most general intruder (or enemy). The enemy gleans as much information as possible from messages flowing in the network and fakes messages based on the gleaned information, provided that the enemy cannot break the perfect cryptosystem.

We first describe the basic data types used to model the protocol. The visible sorts corresponding to the basic data types and the related operators (if any) are as follows:

- sort **Agent** denotes agents; constant **enemy** denotes the enemy,
- sort **Key** denotes symmetric keys; given an agent p, $k(p)$ denotes the key of the p's group; operator **p** returns the argument of $k(p)$,
- sort **Rand** denotes random numbers, and

---

[2] The IFF protocol used in this paper is a modified version of the IFF system described in Subsect. 2.2.2 of [1].

– sort `Cipher` denotes ciphertexts used in the protocol; given a key k, a random number r and an agent p, $\mathrm{enc}(k, r, p)$ denotes the ciphertext obtained by encrypting r and p with k; operators k, r and p return the first, second and third arguments of $\mathrm{enc}(k, r, p)$.

In addition to those visible sorts, the built-in sort `Bool` denoting truth values is used.

The two operators to denote the two kinds of messages are cm and rm, which are declared as

```
op cm : Agent Agent Agent Rand -> Msg
```
and
```
op rm : Agent Agent Agent Cipher -> Msg,
```

where `Msg` is the visible sort denoting messages. Operators crt, src and dst return the first, second and third arguments of each message; operator r returns the fourth argument of a Check message; operator c returns the fourth argument of a Reply message. Operators cm? and rm? check if a given message is a Check message and a Reply message, respectively. The first, second and third arguments of each of cm and rm mean the actual creator, the seeming sender and the receiver of the corresponding message. The first argument is meta-information that is only available to the outside observer and the agent that has sent the corresponding message, and that cannot be forged by the enemy, while the remaining arguments may be forged by the enemy. The network is modeled as a multiset of messages, which is used as the storage that the intruder can use. The network is also used as each agent's private memory that reminds the agent to send messages, whose first arguments are the agent. Any message that has been sent or put once into the network is supposed to be never deleted from the network. Consequently, the emptiness of the network means that no messages have been sent.

The enemy tries to glean two kinds of values from the network, which are random numbers and ciphertexts. The collections of these values gleaned by the intruder are denoted by operators **rands** and **ciphers**, which are declared as

```
op rands : Network -> ColRands
```
and
```
op ciphers : Network -> ColCiphers,
```

where `Network` is the visible sort denoting networks, `ColRands` is the visible sort denoting collections of random numbers, and `ColCiphers` is the visible sort denoting collections of ciphertexts. The two operators are defined in equations. `ciphers` is defined as follows:

```
eq  C \in ciphers(void) = false .
ceq C \in ciphers(M,NW) = true if rm?(M) and C = c(M) .
ceq C \in ciphers(M,NW) = C \in ciphers(NW) if not(rm?(M) and C = c(M)) .
```

Constant void denotes the empty multiset and operator ',' in M,NW denotes the data constructor of nonempty multisets. The equations say that a ciphertext C is available to the enemy iff there exists a Reply message, which includes C. rands is defined likewise.

We describe the OTS S_{IFF} modeling the protocol. The foundation behind the modeling is basically *behavioral logic* (precisely a restricted class of hidden algebras), but other logics such as the UNITY logic can be incorporated into the proof score approach flexibly and faithfully such as [35] thanks to the *flexible logic* capability of the CafeOBJ system. Two observations and five parametrized transitions are used. The two observations are denoted by observation operators nw and ur, which are declared as

```
bop nw : Field -> Network
```
and
```
bop ur : Field -> URands,
```

where Field is the hidden sort denoting the state space and URands is the visible sort denoting sets of random numbers. nw and ur are used to observe the network and the set of used random numbers. The five transitions are denoted by action operators sdcm, sdrm, fkcm1, fkrm1 and fkrm2, which are declared as follows:

```
bop sdcm  : Field Agent Agent Rand -> Field
bop sdrm  : Field Agent Msg -> Field
bop fkcm1 : Field Agent Agent Rand -> Field
bop fkrm1 : Field Agent Agent Cipher -> Field
bop fkrm2 : Field Agent Agent Rand -> Field.
```

The first two action operators formalize sending messages exactly following the protocol and the remaining the enemy's faking messages.

The action operators are defined in equations. sdrm is defined as follows:

```
ceq nw(sdrm(F,P1,M1)) = rm(P1,P1,src(M1),enc(k(P1),r(M1),P1)) , nw(F)
      if c-sdrm(F,P1,M1) .
eq ur(sdrm(F,P1,M1))   = ur(F) .
ceq sdrm(F,P1,M1)      = F if not c-sdrm(F,P1,M1) .
```

c-sdrm(F,P1,M1) equals M1 \in nw(F) and cm?(M1) and P1 = dst(M1), which means that in state F, there exists a Check message M1 in the network, which is addressed to P1. If this condition holds, the Reply message denoted by rm(...) is put into the network nw(F). fkrm1 is defined as follows:

```
ceq nw(fkrm1(F,P1,P2,C)) = rm(enemy,P1,P2,C) , nw(F)
      if c-fkrm1(F,P1,P2,C) .
eq ur(fkrm1(F,P1,P2,C))  = ur(F) .
ceq fkrm1(F,P1,P2,C)     = F if not c-fkrm1(F,P1,P2,C) .
```

c-fkrm1(F,P1,P2,C) equals C \in ciphers(nw(F)), which means that in state F, a ciphertext C is available to the enemy. The equations say that if a ciphertext C is available to the enemy, the enemy can fake and send a Reply message using C.

The remaining three action operators are defined as follows:

```
-- for action sdcm
  op c-sdcm : Field Agent Agent Rand -> Bool
  eq c-sdcm(F,P1,P2,R) = not(R \in ur(F)) .
```

```
ceq nw(sdcm(F,P1,P2,R)) = cm(P1,P1,P2,R) , nw(F) if c-sdcm(F,P1,P2,R) .
ceq ur(sdcm(F,P1,P2,R)) = R ur(F)                if c-sdcm(F,P1,P2,R) .
ceq sdcm(F,P1,P2,R)     = F                       if not c-sdcm(F,P1,P2,R) .

-- for action fkcm1
   op c-fkcm1 : Field Agent Agent Rand -> Bool
   eq c-fkcm1(F,P1,P2,R) = R \in rands(nw(F)) .
   --
   ceq nw(fkcm1(F,P1,P2,R)) = cm(enemy,P1,P2,R) , nw(F) if c-fkcm1(F,P1,P2,R) .
   eq ur(fkcm1(F,P1,P2,R))  = ur(F) .
   ceq fkcm1(F,P1,P2,R)     = F                         if not c-fkcm1(F,P1,P2,R) .

-- for action fkrm2
   op c-fkrm2 : Field Agent Agent Rand -> Bool
   eq c-fkrm2(F,P1,P2,R) = R \in rands(nw(F)) .
   --
   ceq nw(fkrm2(F,P1,P2,R)) = rm(enemy,P1,P2,enc(k(enemy),R,P1)) , nw(F)
                              if c-fkrm2(F,P1,P2,R) .
   eq ur(fkrm2(F,P1,P2,R))  = ur(F) .
   ceq fkrm2(F,P1,P2,R)     = F
                              if not c-fkrm2(F,P1,P2,R) .
```

4.2   Proof Score of the IFF Property

The IFF property is denoted by operator inv1. inv1(F,P1,P2,P3,K,R) equals (not(K = k(enemy)) and rm(P1,P2,P3,enc(K,R,P2)) \in nw(F)) implies not(P2 = enemy). We describe a proof score to prove inv1(F,P1,P2,P3,K,R) invariant wrt S_{IFF}. The proof is done by induction on the number of transitions (or action operators) applied. As described, a proof score is a proof plan to prove that a property holds for a specification. Figure 1 shows the proof plan used to prove inv1(F,P1,P2,P3,K,R) invariant wrt S_{IFF}. In the figure, edges mean case splits, ovals represent intermediate nodes, which mean case splitting in progress, and rectangles represent leaves, which mean results of case splitting. For each rectangle, a fragment of a proof score is written; such a fragment is called a proof passage. For case II.4.d, we use inv2(f,k,r) as lemma. inv2(F,K,R) equals enc(K,R,enemy) \in ciphers(nw(F)) implies (K = k(enemy)).

The proof score to prove inv1(F,P1,P2,P3,K,R) invariant wrt S_{IFF} corresponds to the proof plan shown in Fig. 1 faithfully, namely that the proof score has *clear structure*. Therefore, the proof score helps human users comprehend the proof. When writing such a proof score, what you are required to do is mainly case analyses and necessary lemma discoveries. For each case analysis, you write a proof passage for each case obtained by the case analysis. By having the CafeOBJ system execute the proof passage and examining the result returned by the CafeOBJ system, you can judge that the proof is successful in the case, a further case analysis is needed, or a lemma is needed. This is because the proof score approach and the CafeOBJ system provide a flexible *human computer interaction* mechanism in good balance such that humans make proof plans and machines conduct tedious and detailed computations, and proof scores have *flexible structure*. In the proof score approach, lemmas have not necessarily

Proof Plan

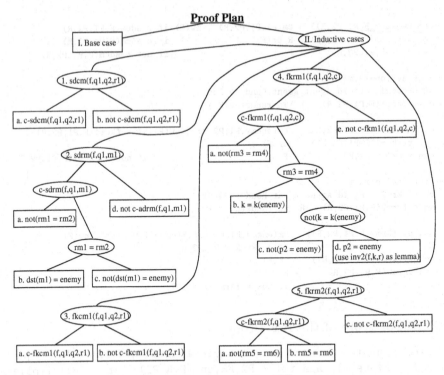

Fig. 1. Proof plan to prove the IFF property

to be proved in advance thanks to *flexible structure* of proof scores. In the proof of inv1(F,P1,P2,P3,K,R), inv2(f,k,r) is used before it is proved.

In this paper, we show the proof passage for case II.4.d, which is as follows:

```
open ISTEP
-- arbitrary objects
  ops q1 q2 : -> Agent .
  op c : -> Cipher .
-- assumptions
  -- eq c-fkrm1(f,q1,q2,c) = true .
  eq enc(k,r,enemy) \in ciphers(nw(f)) = true .
  --
  -- eq rm(enemy,q1,q2,c) = rm(p1,p2,p3,enc(k,r,p2)) .
  eq p1 = enemy .  eq q1 = p2 .  eq q2 = p3 .  eq c = enc(k,r,p2).
  --
  eq (k = k(enemy)) = false .
  eq p2 = enemy .
-- successor state
  eq f' = fkrm1(f,q1,q2,c) .
-- check if the predicate is true.
  red inv2(f,k,r) implies istep1(p1,p2,p3,k,r) .
close
```

Command **open** makes a temporary module, which imports a given module (ISTEP in this case), and command **close** destroys such a temporary module. Necessary operators and equations are declared in ISTEP. A comment starts with a double hyphen and terminates at the end of the line. Constants q1 and q2 denote arbitrary agents and constant c an arbitrary ciphertext. Constants p1, p2 and p3 denote arbitrary agents, constant k an arbitrary key, and constant r an arbitrary random number; those constants are declared in ISTEP (precisely module INV imported by ISTEP). Constant f denotes an arbitrary state and constant f' a successor state of the state; those constants are declared in ISTEP. Operator istep1 denotes a basic formula to prove in each inductive case; istep1(P1,P2,P3,K,R) equals inv1(f,P1,P2,P3,K,R) implies inv1(f',P1,P2,P3,K,R). rm3 and rm4 in Fig. 1 correspond to rm(enemy,q1, q2,c) and rm(p1,p2,p3, enc(k,r,p2)) in the proof passage. Instead of rm(enemy,q1,q2,c) = rm(p1,p2,p3,enc(k,r,p2)), the four equations p1 = enemy, q1 = p2, q2 = p3 and c = enc(k,r,p2) are declared because the former can be deduced from the latter with rewriting only, but not vice versa. Instead of c-fkrm1(f,q1,q2,c) = true, the equation enc(k,r,enemy) \in ciphers(nw(f)) = true is declared because the left-hand side of an equation should be in normal form so as to use the equation effectively as a rewrite rule. Feeding the proof passage into the CafeOBJ system, the CafeOBJ system returns true as expected, which means that the proof is successful in this case.

For the remaining cases shown in Fig. 1, similar proof passages are written. The CafeOBJ system also returns true's for those cases. To prove inv2(F,K,R) invariant wrt S_{IFF}, a similar proof score is written, but the proof does not need any lemmas.

5   Conclusions and Future Issues

Promising features and points to be improved of the current proof score method can be summarized as follows:

- Specifications in CafeOBJ can be expressed in relatively high level of abstraction thanks to facilities of user defined data types, OTS (observational transition systems in behavioral logics), and powerful module systems, etc. Proof scores enjoy the same merit and can make it possible to analyze or verify the specifications or designs in a more higher level of abstraction than other automatic theorem provers or model checkers.
- Proof scores have a high potential for providing a practical new way of doing proofs for designs or specifications, and in particular for providing a relatively low cost approach to compiler verification, and more generally, to verified code produced by application generators.
- Correctness of proof scores is relatively clear but theory for rigid correctness argument needs to be provided.
- Case analyses and lemma discoveries in proof scores can be tedious and difficult, but the current support for systematic management of case splittings and lemma discoveries are not sufficient for large scale and practical problems.

The following are important issues for future research on the proof score method:

- Introducing interactions into the Crème algorithm [26] for guiding high level planning by users while keeping other parts including reductions automatic.
- Farther development of the Kumo/Tatami project (done at UCSD as a subproject of CAFE project) [19] to realize a web (or hypertext) based proof score writing environment.
- Explore institution morphisms [16] as a formal formalization for proof scores.
- Incorporate specific decision procedures like Presburger arithmetic into reductions or as basic units of proof scores other than ordinary reductions.

References

1. Anderson, R.: Security Engineering: A Guide to Building Dependable Distributed Systems. John Wiley & Sons, Inc. NY (2001)
2. Bidoit, M., Hennicker, R.: Behavioural theories and the proof of behavioural properties. Theoretical Computer Science 165(1), 3–55 (1996)
3. CafeOBJ. CafeOBJ web page (2005), http://www.ldl.jaist.ac.jp/cafeobj/
4. Chandy, K.M., Misra, J.: Parallel Program Design: A Foundation. Addison-Wesley, Reading (1988)
5. Clarke, E.M., Grumberg, O., Peled, D.A.: Model Checking. MIT Press, Cambridge (2000)
6. Diaconescu, R., Futatsugi, K.: CafeOBJ report: The Language, Proof Techniques, and Methodologies for Object-Oriented Algebraic Specification. In: AMAST Series in Computing, 6, World Scientific, Singapore (1998)
7. Diaconescu, R., Futatsugi, K.: Behavioural coherence in object-oriented algebraic specification. J. UCS 6(1), 74–96 (2000)
8. Diaconescu, R., Futatsugi, K., Iida, S.: Component-based algebraic specification and verification in CafeOBJ. In: Woodcock, J.C.P., Davies, J., Wing, J.M. (eds.) FM 1999. LNCS, vol. 1709, pp. 1644–1663. Springer, Heidelberg (1999)
9. Futatsugi, K.: Formal methods in CafeOBJ. In: Hu, Z., Rodríguez-Artalejo, M. (eds.) FLOPS 2002. LNCS, vol. 2441, pp. 1–20. Springer, Heidelberg (2002)
10. Futatsugi, K., Goguen, J.A., Jouannaud, J.-P., Meseguer, J.: Principles of OBJ2. In: Conference Record of the Twelfth Annual ACM Symposium on Principles of Programming Languages, New Orleans, Louisiana (POPL 1985), pp. 52–66. ACM, New York (1985)
11. Futatsugi, K., Ogata, K.: Rewriting can verify distributed real-time systems. In: Proc. of International Symposium on Rewriting, Proof, and Computation (PRC2001), Tohoku Univ, pp. 60–79 (2001)
12. Goguen, J.: Hidden algebraic engineering. In: Chrystopher Nehaniv and Masami Ito, editors, Algebraic Engineering, pp. 17–36. World Scientific, 1998. Papers from a conference at the University of Aizu, Japan, 24–26 March 1997; also UCSD Technical Report CS97-569 (December 1997)
13. Goguen, J., Lin, K.: Web-based multimedia support for distributed cooperative software engineering. In: Proceedings, International Symposium on Multimedia Software Engineering, Papers from a conference Held in Taipei, Taiwan, pp. 25–32. IEEE Press, Los Alamitos (2000)
14. Goguen, J., Lin, K.: Behavioral verification of distributed concurrent systems with BOBJ. In: Ehrich, H.-D., Tse, T.H. (eds.) Proceedings of Conference on Quality Software, pp. 216–235. IEEE Press, Los Alamitos (2003)

15. Goguen, J., Malcolm, G.: A hidden agenda. Theoretical Computer Science 245(1), 55–101 (2000)
16. Goguen, J., Roşu, G.: Institution morphisms. Formal Aspects of Computing 13, 274–307 (2002)
17. Goguen, J.A., Roşu, G., Lin, K.: Conditional Circular Coinductive Rewriting with Case Analysis. In: Wirsing, M., Pattinson, D., Hennicker, R. (eds.) WADT 2003. LNCS, vol. 2755, pp. 216–232. Springer, Heidelberg (2003)
18. Goguen, J., Winkler, T., Meseguer, J., Futatsugi, K., Jouannaud, J.-P.: Introducing OBJ. Technical Report SRI-CSL-92-03, SRI International, Computer Science Laboratory (1992)
19. Goguen, J.A., Lin, K., Mori, A., Rosu, G., Sato, A.: Distributed cooperative formal methods tools. In: Proc. of 1997 International Conference on Automated Software Engineering (ASE 1997), Lake Tahoe, CA, November 02-05, 1997, pp. 55–62. IEEE, Los Alamitos (1997)
20. Goguen, J.A., Malcolm, G.: Algebraic Semantics of Imperative Programs. MIT Press, Cambridge (1996)
21. Bidoit, M., Hennicker, R.: Observational logic. In: Haeberer, A.M. (ed.) AMAST 1998. LNCS, vol. 1548, pp. 263–277. Springer, Heidelberg (1998)
22. Jacobs, B., Rutten, J.: A tutorial on (co)algebras and (co)induction. Bulletin of the European Association for Theoretical Computer Science 62, 222–259 (1997)
23. Lerner, S., Millstein, T.D., Chambers, C.: Automatically proving the correctness of compiler optimizations. In: PLDI, pp. 220–231. ACM, New York (2003)
24. Maude. Maude web page (2005), http://maude.cs.uiuc.edu/
25. Mori, A., Futatsugi, K.: CafeOBJ as a tool for behavioral system verification. In: Okada, M., Pierce, B.C., Scedrov, A., Tokuda, H., Yonezawa, A. (eds.) ISSS 2002. LNCS, vol. 2609, pp. 461–470. Springer, Heidelberg (2003)
26. Nakano, M., Ogata, K., Nakamura, M., Futatsugi, K.: Automating invariant verification of behavioral specifications (2005) (to be published)
27. Ogata, K., Futatsugi, K.: Specification and verification of some classical mutual exclusion algorithms with CafeOBJ. In: Proceedings of OBJ/CafeOBJ/Maude Workshop at Formal Methods 1999, Theta, pp. 159–177 (1999)
28. Ogata, K., Futatsugi, K.: Modeling and verification of distributed real-time systems based on CafeOBJ. In: Proceedings of the 16th International Conference on Automated Software Engineering (16th ASE), pp. 185–192. IEEE Computer Society Press, Los Alamitos (2001)
29. Ogata, K., Futatsugi, K.: Specifying and verifying a railroad crossing with CafeOBJ. In: Proceedings of the 6th International Workshop on Formal Methods for Parallel Programming: Theory and Applications (6th FMPPTA); Part of Proceedings of the 15th IPDPS, p. 150. IEEE Computer Society Press, Los Alamitos (2001)
30. Ogata, K., Futatsugi, K.: Rewriting-based verification of authentication protocols. In: Proceedings of the 4th International Workshop on Rewriting Logic and its Applications (4th WRLA), ENTCS 71, Elsevier, Amsterdam (2002)
31. Ogata, K., Futatsugi, K.: Formal analysis of the iKP electronic payment protocols. In: Okada, M., Pierce, B.C., Scedrov, A., Tokuda, H., Yonezawa, A. (eds.) ISSS 2002. LNCS, vol. 2609, pp. 441–460. Springer, Heidelberg (2003)
32. Ogata, K., Futatsugi, K.: Formal verification of the Horn-Preneel micropayment protocol. In: Zuck, L.D., Attie, P.C., Cortesi, A., Mukhopadhyay, S. (eds.) VMCAI 2003. LNCS, vol. 2575, pp. 238–252. Springer, Heidelberg (2002)

33. Ogata, K., Futatsugi, K.: Proof scores in the OTS/CafeOBJ method. In: Najm, E., Nestmann, U., Stevens, P. (eds.) FMOODS 2003. LNCS, vol. 2884, pp. 170–184. Springer, Heidelberg (2003)
34. Ogata, K., Futatsugi, K.: Equational approach to formal verification of SET. In: Proceedings of the 4th International Conference on Quality Software (4th QSIC), pp. 50–59. IEEE Computer Society Press, Los Alamitos (2004)
35. Ogata, K., Futatsugi, K.: Proof score approach to verification of liveness properties. In: 17th International Conference on Software Engineering and Knowledge Engineering (17th SEKE), pp. 608–613 (2005)
36. Seino, T., Ogata, K., Futatsugi, K.: A toolkit for generating and displaying proof scores in the OTS/CafeOBJ method. In: Proceedings of the 6th International Workshop on Rule-Based Programming (RULE'05), Electronic Notes in Theoretical Computer Science (ENTCS), Elsevier, Amsterdam (2005)

A Discussion on Kokichi Futatsugi's Presentation

Mark Utting

So just, could you explain a little bit more how you use the proof scores? It looks like it is a series of boolean propositions. Are they actually testing the definition to see if they evaluate to true? Or are they proving properties about them? Or do you do both?

Kokichi Futatsugi

It is a sort of proving theorem. Usually, it is an induction. The induction step is expressed by the boolean expression. And that step is justified by using the original specification to write rules. We write rules [and] try to find simplified forms of the boolean expressions. And if that boolean expression comes out to be true, you win. That is the main level. Of course, it is a typical domain: you can use it in many other ways. It is a proof. [*Remaining comments not recorded.*]

Integrating Theories and Techniques
for Program Modelling, Design and Verification
Positioning the Research at UNU-IIST in Collaborative Research on the Verified Software Challenge

Bernard K. Aichernig, He Jifeng, Zhiming Liu*, and Mike Reed

International Institute for Software Technology
United Nations University, Macao SAR, China
{bka,hjf,lzm,mike}@iist.unu.edu

Abstract. This submission presents our understanding of the Grand Challenge and propose an agenda on how we will position our research to contribute to this world-wide collaborative research project.

1 Introduction

The goal of the Verifying Compiler Grand Challenge [17] is very easy to understand. It is to build a verifying compiler that

> "uses mathematical and logical reasoning to check the programs that it compiles."

The fundamental problems are how to obtain and document the correctness specification of a program and how to fully automate the verification/checking of the documented aspects correctness. While accomplishing this goal now requires effort from "(almost) the entire research community" including theoretical researchers, compiler writers, tool builders, software developers and users, these two interrelated problems have been the major concern of the formal methods research community in the past several decades. Each of these two problems is and will continue to be a focus in the research on the challenge.

For a certain kind of programs, some correctness properties, such as termination of sequential programs, mutual exclusion, divergence and deadlock freedom of concurrent systems, are common and have a uniformed specification for all reasonable models and codes. They can be generated from the specification and the code and there is no need to document them. Theories and techniques for verifying these kinds of properties are nearly mature, though a lot of work may still be required in the areas of efficient and effective decision procedure design.

---

* This work is partially supported by the project HighQSofD funded by Macao Science and Technology Development Fund, the NSFC projects 60673114 and 863 of China 2006AA01Z165.

B. Meyer and J. Woodcock (Eds.): Verified Software, LNCS 4171, pp. 291–300, 2008.

These techniques are readily applicable to analysis and verification of these properties of legacy code and open source. This is also the case for typing correctness for programs written in typed languages.

However, for general correctness properties, the problem of how to specify and document them is far more challenging. The techniques for their verification depend on the model that is used for the specification. In some frameworks, one may translate the code into a specification notation or model and then use the techniques and tools developed for that notation or model to analyse the translated code. The model checking tools are based on this approach. With an approach of this kind, the main difficulties lie in

1. the automated, or even manual, procedure of abstraction in the translation is difficult, especially with the constraints that the resulting abstract model can be used for efficient checking,
2. one has to study what, where, when and how the correctness properties, i.e. "assertions and annotations", are produced and documented,
3. it is still challenging to identify properties that can be verified compositionally, and to make the specification notation and model to support more compositional analysis and verification,
4. there is a need of great of research to make the tools effective and efficient even with specified correctness criterion.

In our view, there is quite a long way for theories and techniques to be mature for solving the first three problems, and solutions to these problems will be useful for dealing with the fourth problem.

Some other paradigms have been developed from the idea of *proof outlines* based on Hoare Logic. There, correctness properties are documented as assertions and annotations at certain points of a program. These approaches to some extent avoid the first problem described above, and either a deductive proof (e.g. with a theorem prover) or a simulation proof (e.g. by a model checker) can be applied. It also allows a combination of these two verification techniques. However, the other three problems remain.

A conclusion that we can draw from the above discussion is that working towards a Verifying Compiler still needs a great amount of investigation in, among other areas discussed in the description of the Grand Challenge [17], new ways of modelling to provide better support to

1. separation of concerns, specification and analysis at different levels of abstraction and better compositionality,
2. integration of formal methods with the effective practical engineering methods,
3. unifying different formal theories of programming and verification to make it possible for the verifying compiler to "work in combination with other program development and testing tools" [17],
4. development of design techniques to ease the difficulties in identification and generation of correctness criterion and the analysis and verification procedures.

This in fact has been the main theme of the research at UNU-IIST, and we can now focus on this even better directed goal of the Grand Challenge.

2   The Grand Challenge Related Research at UNU-IIST

We outline in this section our approach to the challenge with a discussion on the research problems, and a summary of progress we have made so far.

Our overall research will be centered on the issues listed at the end of the previous section in the conclusion of our understanding about the challenge. However, we will organise the research within the UNU-IIST project on Component-Based Modelling and Design.

2.1   The Theme

We are developing an approach that allows a system to be designed by composing *components*. The aim is compositional design, analysis and verification. To achieve this aim, it is essential that the approach supports multi-view modelling, and allows separation of concerns. Different concerns are described in different viewpoints of a system at different levels of abstraction, including interfaces, functional services, synchronization behaviour, interaction protocols, resource and timing constraints. Our approach integrates a state-based model of functional behaviour and an event-based model of inter-component interaction [15,14]. The state-based model is for white-box specification in support of component design, and the event-based model is for black-box specification used when composing components [15].

Multi-View Modelling. It is crucial that the model supports abstraction with information hiding so that we can develop refinement and transformation based design techniques. This will provide theoretical foundation for integration of the formal design techniques with practical engineering development methods. Design in this way can preserve correctness to a certain level of abstraction, and good design techniques and models even support code generation that ensures certain correctness properties (i.e. being correct by construction [28]) and helps in generation and documentation of assertions and annotations. Refinement in this framework characterises the *substitutability* of one component for another. It involves all the substitutability of all the aspects, but we should be able to define and carry out refinement for different features separately, without violating the correctness of the other aspects. We are investigating different design techniques for different correctness aspects supported by the refined calculus. We hope that the refinement calculus permits *incremental and iterative* design, analysis and verification. This is obviously important for scaling up the application of the method to large scale software development, and for the development of efficient tool support. We believe being incremental and iterative is closely related and complementary to being compositional, and important for lowering the amount of specification and verification and the degree of automation.

However, the different aspects of correctness are often related. A big challenge is to solve the problems of consistency among the specifications of the different views, and provide solutions for their consistent integration and transformation. The solutions to these problems are needed to provide theoretical support to development of tools for checking the consistency and carrying out the transformation and reasoning about the correctness of the transformation. Formal specifications of different aspects and their conditions of consistency are give in our papers [15,14].

Multi-View Analysis and Verification Techniques. Analysis and verification of different aspects of correctness and substitutability have to be carried out with different techniques and tools. Operational simulation techniques and model checking tools are believed to be effective for checking correctness, consistency and refinement of interaction protocols, while deductive verification and theorem provers are found better suited for reasoning about denotational (or pre and postcondition based) functionality specification. Where fully automated verification is not possible one has to rely on approximated results. Here, testing can play a role to confirm the approximately verified property. Another important aspects of testing is the validation of the abstract properties to be verified. Fault-based testing adds an additional dimension to verification. Here, test cases are designed by mutating the specification to detect faults that violate the specification [2]. Also, different modelling notations will affect the way of test case generation. Therefore, The combination of verification, testing and design needs further exploration.

Integrating Component-Based and Object-Oriented Techniques. A component may not have to be designed and implemented in an object-oriented framework. However, the current component technologies such as COM, CORBA, and Enterprise JavaBeans are all built upon object-oriented programming. Object programs are now widely used in applications and many of them safety critical. This project also studies the techniques of modelling, design and verification of object systems and the construction of component systems on underlying object systems [15,23].

2.2   Initial Progress

A number of formal notations and theories have been well-established and proved themselves effective as tools in dealing with different aspects of computing systems. For component-based systems, analysis, design and verification can thus be carried with different techniques and tools. However, integration of components requires the integration of the theories for ensuring correctness and substitutability. In particular, we need an underlying execution model of component systems. UNU-IIST has developed a model and calculus, called **rCOS** [12], for component systems [31], The calculus is applied to formal use of UML in requirement analysis [22,20], design [33], and consistent code generation [25]. In **rCOS**, we define a component with provided and required interfaces and their functional specifications [21,15]. Composition and refinement of these kinds of components are also defined. The research is based on Hoare and He's Unifying Theories of Programming (UTP) [18] and aim to advance UTP to for analysis of object-oriented programs and component systems. Challenging as it is, the initial results show that it is promising that "many aspects of correctness of concurrent and object-oriented programs can be expressed by assertions" [17].

Our approach facilitates assurance of global refinement by local refinement via integration of the event-based simulation and the state-based refinement. Global refinement is usually defined as a set containment of system behaviours [14], and can be verified deductively within a theorem prover. Local refinement is based on specification of individual operations [15,14], and can be established by simulation techniques using a model checker. Promising results have also been achieved in unifying different verification methods [1,10,24].

The research also indicates what kind of language mechanisms, such as inheritance with attribute hiding, method overwriting and method reentry calls, are likely to cause bugs in a program. They should be avoided if possible and when they are used assertions should be inserted and verification effort should be concentrated on these assertions. To fully verify different kinds of correctness aspects, we require different verification methods (simulation, deduction and testing) and tools (model checkers, theorem provers and test case generators).

Component-Based Systems. When we specify a component, it is important to separate different views about the component [21,15,14]. From its user's (i.e. external) point of view, a component C consists a set of *provided services* [31]. The syntactic specification of the provided services is described by an interface, defining the operations that the component provides with their signatures. This is also called the *syntactic specification* of a component. Such a syntactic specification of a component does not provide any information about the effect, e.g. the *functionality* of invoking an operation of a component or the *behavior*, i.e. the temporal order of the interface operations, of the component. However, it describes the syntactic dependency on other components.

rCOS contains notations for the description of the following notions for component-based systems, which serve different purposes for different people at different stages of a system development:

- Interfaces: describe the structure nature of a component and are only used for checking syntactic dependency and compositionality.
- Guarded Designs: specify the behaviours of service operations of an interface. It describes both the condition 9as the guard) imposed on the environment for use of a service operation (the design), and the behaviours of execution of a service once invoked.
- Protocols: impose the order on use of services of an interface. They describe the way by which clients can interact with an interface, and are used to avoid deadlock when putting components together.
- Contracts: are specifications of interfaces. A contract associates an interface to an abstract data model plus a set of functional of its services specified as guarded designs, and as well as an interaction protocol.
- Components: are implementations of contracts. The designer of a component has to ensure that it satisfies its contract. Its code is used by the verifier to establish this satisfaction relation.

- Combinators: are defined for interfaces, contracts and components so that they can be composed in different ways. Their algebraic properties are used to verify design of middlewares (such as CORBA) and design patterns.
- Substitutivity: is defined in terms of refinement that integrates both state-based refinement and event-based simulation.
- Coordinators: are modelled as *processes* and used to coordinate the activities and interactions of a group of components [7].

The model provides a definition of consistency among the elements of a contract and a method for consistency checking. It also allows to extend a contract by adding more services and imposing more constraints on use of services.

Component are *passive* entities that provide functional services to be invoked. Active entities are modelled as processes that are to coordinate (schedule and glue) components. We have proven that components composed with processes that coordinating them form another component. For details, we refer the reader to the technical report [7].

Design and Verification of Object-Oriented Programs. We use **rCOS** to define an object-oriented language with subtypes, visibility, reference types, inheritance, type casting, dynamic binding and polymorphism. The language is sufficiently similar to Java and C++ and can be used in meaningful case studies and to capture certain difficulties in modelling object-oriented designs and programs.

Our semantic framework is *class-based* and refinement is about *correct* changes in structure and methods of classes. The logic is a *conservative extension* of the standard predicate logic. We define the traditional programming constructs, such as conditional, sequential composition and recursion, in the exactly same way as their counterparts in the imperative programming languages without reference types. This makes our approaches more accessible to users who are already familiar with the existing imperative languages. Also, all the laws about imperative commands remain valid without the need of reproving.

The calculus relates the classic notions of refinement and data refinement [3,16,27] in imperative languages to refactoring and object-oriented design patterns for responsibility assignments [9,19] This takes the initial attempts in formalisation of refactoring in [29,32] a step forward by providing a formal semantic justification of the soundness of the refactoring rules, and advance the theories in [4,5,6,30] on object-oriented refinement to deal with large scale object-oriented program refinement with refactoring, functionality delegation, data encapsulation and class decomposition. Within the calculus, we have already proved the soundness of several design patterns, including Expert pattern, Low Coupling pattern, and High Cohesion pattern [12].

Object-Oriented Models of Requirement and Design. **rCOS** is also applied to formal use of UML in requirement analysis [22,20], design [33], and consistent code generation [25]. We have provided a unified semantic definition for UML models of requirement and design. This semantics framework covers

- Use case model
- Class model
- Object diagram
- Interaction diagram

The unification is important and useful in dealing with consistency between different models. It in fact deals with the most informal aspects of UML, including description of use cases and the links between different UML diagrams in system development. On the other hand, the formalism still keeps the roles and views of these models clearly separate: class models correspond the program state, while the use case model describes the required services and external behaviour and the sequence diagram realise the external behaviour with internal object interactions.

The refinement calculus developed in **rCOS** is used for transformation of models that preserve certain properties. The calculus deals with refinement of class diagrams to increase its capacity in supporting more use cases. This implies the support to an incremental system development such as the Rational Unified Process. The formalisation of UML in our notation allows us to transform UML diagrams consistently and to formally define and reason about transformations of UML diagrams, such as decomposing a class into several classes, adding classes, associations, changing multiplicites of associations, etc. Moreover, **rCOS** also supports the following refinements to a class diagram:

- adding a new class
- introducing inheritance
- moving an attribute or a method from a class to its direct superclass
- introducing a fresh superclass to an existing class
- copying a method of a class to its direct subclass

Combination of the Object-Oriented and Component-Based Methods.
rCOS [12,13,14,23] also provides a consistent combination of the object-oriented and component-based methods. In general, a component in our proposed model can be realized by a family of collaborating classes. Therefore, for a component C, we treat the interface methods of C and the protocol as the specification of the use cases of the component and the components in environment of C as the actors of these use cases. The design and implementation of this component can then be carried out in a UML-based object-oriented framework.

The types of the fields (or attributes) of components can be classes. The classes and their associations form the information (data) model. This model can be represented as a UML class diagram and formalized as class declaration in **rCOS** [12,13,14,23]. The implementation of a component is based on the implementation of the class model. For example, in UML2.0, a port of a component is realized by a class too.

2.3   The Research Problems and Program

The research program of the project is also incremental and iterative and it is roughly outlined below:

1. start with modelling, design and verification of sequential object systems,
2. deal with components with only interfaces and specification functional services
3. add synchronous interactions
4. add asynchronous interactions
5. add coordinators and containers to manage interaction among components
6. deal with resource and timing constraints of embedded systems
7. add features of fault-tolerance, security and survivability
8. extend it to internet-based programming
9. test the techniques with case studies (including analysis of middlewares and design patterns), and evaluate the results by looking at how it can support tool development
10. more foundational research include a logic for object-oriented reasoning and component-based reasoning

In fact the project started two years ago and it will be a long lasting project. The aims and focus may be adjusted along the progress of the research.

3 International Collaboration

The research will be conducted in a close collaboration with Tata Research Development and Design Centre, the largest industry research development and design centre in India. They have a great interest in applying formal methods in their tool development. UNU-IIST is now establishing a collaboration project on Scaling up Formal Methods for Large Software Development. We will investigate how the research results at UNU-IIST in theories and techniques of program modelling, design and verification can be used in the design of software development tools at TRDDC. A separate submission focusing on tool support is also accepted for presentation at this working conference to be considered for a presentation about the collaboration [26].

UNU-IIST has recently joined the NoE of ARTIST II and the collaboration with the other partners, such as Aalborg University (Denmark) and Uppsala University (Sweden) on component-based development and verification will become closer.

We have also a long tradition of collaboration with the University of Macau, Peking University, Nanjing University and Software Institute of the Chinese Academy of Sciences, Oxford University, University of Minho (Portugal) and the University of Leicester (UK).

Acknowledgement. This proposal is made on behalf of all members of the academic staff at UNU-IIST. We would like to thank our colleagues, Chris George, Dang Van Hung and Tomasz Janowski for the discussions.

References

1. Aichernig, B., He, J.: Testing for design faults. Submitted to Formal Aspect of Computing (2005)
2. Aichernig, B.K.: Mutation Testing in the Refinement Calculus. Formal Aspect of Computing (2003)

3. Back, R., von Wright, L.J.: Refinement Calculus. Springer, Heidelberg (1998)
4. Back, R., et al.: Class refinement as semantics of correct object substitutability. Formal Aspect of Computing 2, 18–40 (2000)
5. Borba, P., Sampaio, A., Cornelio, M.: A refinement algebra for object-oriented programming. In: Cardelli, L. (ed.) ECOOP 2003. LNCS, vol. 2743, pp. 457–482. Springer, Heidelberg (2003)
6. Cavalcanti, A., Naumann, D.: A weakest precondition semantics for an object-oriented language. In: Woodcock, J.C.P., Davies, J., Wing, J.M. (eds.) FM 1999. LNCS, vol. 1709, Springer, Heidelberg (1999)
7. Chen, X., Liu, Z., He, J.: A theory of contracts. Technical Report UNU-IIST Report No 335, UNU-IIST, P.O. Box 3058, Macao (May 2006)
8. Fowler, M.: Refactoring, Improving the Design of Existing Code. Addison-Wesley, Reading (2000)
9. Gamma, E., et al.: Design Patterns, Elements of Reusable Object-Oriented Software. Addison-Wesley, Reading (1994)
10. He, J.: Linking simulation with refinement. In: Abdallah, A.E., Jones, C.B., Sanders, J.W. (eds.) Communicating Sequential Processes. LNCS, vol. 3525, pp. 61–75. Springer, Heidelberg (2005)
11. He, J., Hoare, C.A.R.: Unifying theories of concurrency. In: Van Hung, D., Wirsing, M. (eds.) ICTAC 2005. LNCS, vol. 3722, Springer, Heidelberg (2005)
12. He, J., Liu, Z., Li, X., Qin, S.: A relational model of object oriented programs. In: Chin, W.-N. (ed.) APLAS 2004. LNCS, vol. 3302, pp. 415–437. Springer, Heidelberg (2004)
13. He, J., Liu, Z., Li, X.: rCOS: A refinement calculus for object systems. Technical Report UNU-IIST Report No. 322, UNU-IIST, P.O. Box 3058, Macau (March 2005)
14. He, J., Liu, Z., Li, X.: A theory of contracts. Technical Report UNU-IIST Report No 327, UNU-IIST, P.O. Box 3058, Macau (July 2005)
15. He, J., Liu, Z., Li, X.: Component-based software engineering – the Need to Link Methods and their Theories. In: Van Hung, D., Wirsing, M. (eds.) ICTAC 2005. LNCS, vol. 3722, pp. 72–97. Springer, Heidelberg (2005)
16. Hoare, C.A.R., et al. : Laws of Programming. Communications of the ACM 30, 672–686 (1987)
17. Hoare, C.A.R.: The verifying compiler. Journal of ACM 50(1), 63–69 (2003)
18. Hoare, C.A.R., He, J.: Unifying theories of programming. Prentice-Hall, Englewood Cliffs (1998)
19. Larman, C.: Applying UML and Patterns. Prentice-Hall International, Englewood Cliffs (2001)
20. Li, X., Liu, Z., He, J., Long, Q.: Generating prototypes from a UML model of requirements. In: Ghosh, R.K., Mohanty, H. (eds.) ICDCIT 2004. LNCS, vol. 3347, pp. 255–265. Springer, Heidelberg (2004)
21. Liu, Z., He, J., Li, X.: Contract-oriented development of component systems. In: Proc. of IFIP WCC-TCS 2004, pp. 349–366 (2004)
22. Liu, Z., He, J., Li, X., Chen, Y.: A relational model for object-oriented requirements in UML. In: Dong, J.S., Woodcock, J. (eds.) ICFEM 2003. LNCS, vol. 2885, pp. 641–665. Springer, Heidelberg (2003)
23. Liu, Z., He, J., Li, X.: rCOS: A refinement calculus for object systems. In: de Boer, F.S., Bonsangue, M.M., Graf, S., de Roever, W.-P. (eds.) FMCO 2004. LNCS, vol. 3657, pp. 183–221. Springer, Heidelberg (2005)
24. Liu, Z., Ravn, A., Li, X.: Unifying proof methodologies of Duration Calculus and Linear Temporal Logic. Formal Aspect of Computing 16(2), 140–154 (2004)

25. Long, Q., Liu, Z., He, J., Li, X.: Consistent code generation from UML model. In: Proc. of ASWEC 2005, IEEE Computer Press, Los Alamitos (2005)

26. Liu, Z., Venky, R.: Tools for formal software engineering. In: Proc. of IFIP Working Conference on Program Verifier Challenge (2005)

27. Morgan, C.C.: Programming from Specifications. Prentice-Hall, Englewood Cliffs (1994)

28. Pnueli, A.: Looking ahead. Workshop on the Verification Grand Challenge, SRI International (2005)

29. Roberts, D.B.: Practical Analysis for Refactoring. PhD thesis, University of Illinois at Urbana Champain (1999)

30. Hankin, C. (ed.): ESOP 1998 and ETAPS 1998. LNCS, vol. 1381. Springer, Heidelberg (1998)

31. Szyperski, C.: Component Software. Addison-Wesley, Reading (1998)

32. Tokuda, L.A.: Evolving Object-Oriented Designs with Refactoring. PhD thesis, University of Texas at Austin (1999)

33. Yang, J., Long, Q., Liu, Z., Liu, X.: A predicative semantic model for integrating UML models. In: Liu, Z., Araki, K. (eds.) ICTAC 2004. LNCS, vol. 3407, pp. 170–186. Springer, Heidelberg (2005)

A Discussion After He Jifeng's Presentation

Jim Woodcock

You mention that the aim is to test your ideas on some case studies. From the point of view of the repository, I'd like to know what challenges you will eventually try.

He Jifeng

We are formalizing CORBA as simple example, because we think CORBA is a well-accepted standard middleware by many communities. We have formalized the specification at the top level, and we are going to show how to justify the refinement step by step. We will have three steps of refinement for CORBA. This is one of our case studies. We will also do some verification of CORBA design patterns. This would be a teststone for the refinement calculus.

Eiffel as a Framework for Verification

Bertrand Meyer

ETH Zurich
http://se.inf.ethz.ch
Eiffel Software
www.eiffel.com

Abstract. The Eiffel method and language integrate a number of ideas originating from work on program verification. This position paper describes the goals of the Eiffel approach, presents current Eiffel-based verification techniques using contracts for run-time checks for testing and debugging, and outlines ongoing work on static verification.

1 Application Areas

Advances in programming languages, especially object-oriented principles and techniques, have profoundly influenced the production of software. Most development teams are not ready to renounce these gains in expressive power, including both:

- Static mechanisms: classes, information hiding, genericity, inheritance (including multiple and repeated), polymorphism, smart type systems, conversions, once features, contracts.
- Dynamic mechanisms: objects, references (type-safe pointers), exception handling, dynamic object creation, automatic garbage collection.

Much of the work towards verified software explicitly gives up on these facilities, preferring to use minimal programming languages; the goal is to remove as many obstacles as possible in the quest for full verification, in particular proofs.

While this approach has been successfully applied to certain areas, in particular life-critical systems for which the goal of verification overrides all other concerns, it is not realistic for the vast majority of industry applications. This is not just a matter of programmer comfort. Modern programming constructs are there for a reason: they make it possible to turn out systems faster and at lesser cost; they favor extendibility (ease of change) and reuse, both essential in industry practice; they also provide a decisive boost to software quality, by eliminating whole classes of errors — type errors in the case of static typing, memory errors in the case of garbage collection — hence easing the task of verification.

Such software engineering concerns are crucial to many industries. A typical example is financial software. A development model that freezes the specification and then devotes two years to producing a program guaranteed to meet that specification, using a low-level language and extensive verification techniques, would just not work in the world of financial systems: specifications change frequently and new ideas for products or strategies, critical to a company's survival, need to be implemented in a

B. Meyer and J. Woodcock (Eds.): Verified Software, LNCS 4171, pp. 301--307, 2008.

matter of weeks or days. It is for this kind of environment, overwhelmingly dominant in industry, that modern development techniques and languages have been devised; managers and developers understand their benefits and will not forgo them.

This does not mean that they ignore other aspects of verification. In fact verification is almost as desirable for mainstream applications as it is — for example — for in-flight software. A software error in a financial system can cause loss of enormous amounts of money; bad investments, whether or not on the advice of a computer program, can land the company's CEO in jail for breach of fiduciary duty.

Our Eiffel-related work attempts to address the challenge of verifying software that takes advantage of the best programming language ideas and meets the software engineering constraints on mainstream industry projects.

2   Eiffel Goals

One of the distinctive features of the Eiffel approach is its effort to encompass the software engineering process as a whole, not just implementation. While also a language, Eiffel is more than anything else a method, covering the entire lifecycle. That method rejects the traditional separation of notations used at different stages: an analysis notation (usually graphical), perhaps a design notation, a programming language. Instead it uses the same formalism — the Eiffel language — for all tasks, from the most abstract and user-oriented stages of analysis and specification down to implementation, testing and maintenance. The use of a programming-like notation for analysis goes back to the advice of Kristen Nygaard, one of the inventors of object-oriented programming, who stated that "*to program is to understand*"; it is served in Eiffel by high-level modeling constructs such as deferred classes and contracts; see [13] for examples of such uses of the notation for purely modeling purposes, such as the specification of a TV station's scheduling, independently of any implementation concerns and in fact of any software aspects. This means that as a language Eiffel attempts to cover not only the traditional applications of programming languages but also the realm of analysis notations, specification languages and design tools. One of the advantages of such an integrated, seamless approach, where the software in all its aspects — description as well as implementation — is considered a single product, is to facilitate change, as there is only this one product to update. While retaining the attraction of "model-driven" approaches and their use of a high-level formalism, this technique avoids their separation between expression of intent and expression of realization. Suchg a gap can be, for large programs developed over a long period by many people and with many evolutions, detrimental to quality.

Another aspect relevant to verification work is that the very design of Eiffel was a direct result of verification concerns. In this respect Eiffel occupies a special place among mainstream tools; one has to go back to research languages such as Euclid to find the influence of similar concerns. In particular:

- Eiffel puts the notion of contract (specification of routines and classes in terms of preconditions, postconditions and class invariants) at the center of the method and notation. This idea, which of course follows directly from verification work

(Hoare semantics, Z and other specification languages) has a profound effect on how software is developed. The most important practical observation here is that Eiffel users do not view these techniques as "formal" (and hence to many people formidable) methods, simply as good analysis, design and programming practices closely integrated with the development process, and no more difficult to use than standard programming constructs such as conditionals.

- The contract mechanism is closely integrated with the object-oriented fabric of the language and in particular with inheritance and associated techniques of polymorphism and dynamic binding, through rules of invariant accumulation, precondition weakening and postcondition strengthening [13], variants of which are also present in other approaches using contracts such as JML [8] [9] and Spec# A. This makes it possible to harness advanced and potentially unsafe O-O techniques, in particular redefinition.
- Contracts are not a theoretical possibility but heavily used by Eiffel users in practice, as attested by studies of the actual code base [2].
- The exception mechanism of Eiffel differs from standard "try...catch" mechanisms by relying on the contract concept: an exception is not just some event that will be handled by a special control structure, but the indication that some operation failed to fulfill its contract; the task of exception handling is rigorously defined as an attempt to achieve the contract through another strategy or, if this is impossible, to pass on the issue to an agent higher up in the call chain, which might succeed in such a replacement strategy [13]. This gives a more systematic way of handling erroneous and special cases, a delicate component of software correctness (as attested for example by the famous Ariane 5 failure [7]).
- Eiffel development is supported by libraries of reusable software elements such as EiffelBase [12], refined over two decades, and extensively specified through contracts. The MML (Mathematical Model Library) provides a technique for completely specifying classes through models [16], and has been used to define a fully formally specified subset of EiffelBase. The advantage here is to allow complete specifications within the framework of the language, without adding higher-level, non-executable constructs such as first-order quantifiers.
- The type system includes powerful mechanisms of constrained and unconstrained genericity, multiple and repeated inheritance, tuples and agents. This enables Eiffel users to construct sophisticated models and rely on the compiler to perform advanced checks that amount to proofs of consistency. A recent addition to the type system takes these ideas further by sttically removing from the language the possibility of void calls (attempts to dereference null pointers) through a compile-time check [14].
- A concurrency mechanism, SCOOP, extends the notion of contract to concurrent programs of widely different kinds — multi-threading, multitasking, Web services, distribution —, with a precisely defined semantics [15].
- The language specification [4], while not formal, is strongly influenced by formal techniques; in particular it gives all static semantic rules in "if and only if" form, guaranteeing the validity of a construct if it satisfies certain properties. This provides programmers with an increased confidence in their basic tool

The next two sections describe benefits that can be derived from Eiffel's contract techniques today, and new developments currently in progress to meet the objectives of the verification Grand Challenge.

3   Current Applications of Contracts

The traditional applications of contracts available in Eiffel include [13]: better analysis and specification (as compared for example to purely graphical notations) through an encouragement to describe the precise semantics of system elements; guidance for the design and implementation process through encouragement to state not only how the software works but what it is supposed to achieve; automatic documentation, as offered in the EiffelStudio environment [5]; support for project management, by enabling managers to understand the essentials of a system without having to read the detailed code; support for evolution, by leaving a clear trace of key design decisions independently of implementation, and retaining the work of the best designers even when they have left; support for reuse; safe use of inheritance, as noted above; support for debugging and testing, through run-time monitoring of assertions.

Recent developments have extended these techniques, in particular the last application mentioned. For a long time Eiffel developers have been accustomed to the benefit of having bugs detected through run-time contract violations during debugging and testing. This is a much more effective way than having to prepare test oracles manually. Two important tasks, however, have so far remained manual: test case preparation, and integration of failed tests in the regression testing database.

For the first task, we have developed the AutoTest framework for automatic testing [3], which provides push-button testing of classes, without any human intervention such as preparing test cases. The basic idea is simple: AutoTest takes a set of classes and automatically produces numerous valid instances of these classes, then executes numerous calls to all their routines with arguments selected through various strategies, waiting for a postcondition or invariant to be broken. This always signals a bug. While the approach may at seem naïve, it is actually effective by the only criterion that counts: it finds real bugs (not artificially seeded ones) in actual software, including released libraries and production applications. Work is proceeding to integrate AutoTest in the EiffelStudio environment and ensure automatic, continuous background testing of software as it is being developed. What makes a fully automatic process possible is the presence of contracts, which provide the test oracles. Contracts are, as noted, a natural component of software for Eiffel programmers, allowing AutoTest to work effectively on software as it is written, rather than software that has to be instrumented for verification purposes. Here the approach benefits from *not* being a fully formal method: while proofs require complete specifications, tests as performed by AutoTest (and more classically by monitoring contracts at execution) can take advantage of any contract elements, however partial, which the programmers have cared to write.

Building on some of the same ideas, the CDD tool (Contract-Driven Development [10]) integrates failures found during development, typically through contract violations, into regression testing. The idea is that any failed test is precious information about the project and should forever become part of its test base, automatically replayed

— without explicit requests by the programmer — after any new compilation or release. It is a common phenomenon of software development that bugs have many lives; they will pop back even when thought to have died once or more. CDD, integrated in an experimental version of EiffelStudio, makes sure to reëxecute in the background every test that ever failed.

For both AutoTest and CDD, a necessary task is *test case minimization* [10], which for any execution sequence that led to a failure produces another sequence, usually much shorter, producing the same effect. This is essential if these execution sequences are to become part of the regression test database and hence be reëxecuted frequently.

4   Proofs

Eiffel's contracts have so far been applied mostly to dynamic checks, because the benefits are so clear and immediate. With improvements in proof technology — including semantic modeling, theorem provers, abstract interpretation and model checking — it becomes attractive to support proofs, as has already been the plan behind Eiffel. Several efforts are in progress at ETH and elsewhere, in particular the Ballet proof environment based on BoogiePL, the development of a full formal semantics for Eiffel including its most advanced constructs (by Martin Nordio, in collaboration with Peter Müller), and the formalization of SCOOP semantics [15]. We hope in the future to follow the lead of such developments as the Spec# framework and integrate proof technology, as unobtrusive as possible, into the EiffelStudio environment.

This will not remove the need for other approaches, in particular support for automatic testing and debugging. Proofs and tests, long considered rivals, are in fact complementary, if only because not all proofs can succeed and a failed proof can help narrow down the issues and devise better tests. The Tests And Proofs conference organized at ETH after VSTTE [6] has explored that complementarity.

Eiffel, as noted, was designed from the start with a central concern for verifiability. The long experience of designing Eiffel software — including some very large systems driving stock exchanges, simulating complex environmental or defense problems, managing billions of investment dollars, handling complex health care needs — with contracts and a constant search for quality provides the verification community with useful lessons; by contributing Eiffel concepts, tools such as the open-source EiffelStudio, carefully crafted component libraries such as EiffelBase, specification libraries such as MML, as well as books and teaching materials to the Grand Challenge effort, we hope to help in the search for fully verified software.

References

[1]   Barnett, M., Leino, R., Schulte, W.: The Spec# Programming System: An Overview. In: Barthe, G., Burdy, L., Huisman, M., Lanet, J.-L., Muntean, T. (eds.) CASSIS 2004. LNCS, vol. 3362, pp. 49–69. Springer, Heidelberg (2005)

[2]   Chalin, P.: Logical Foundations of Program Assertions: What do Practitioners Want? ENCS-CSE Technical Report 2005-05, revision 02, Concordia University (June 2005)

[3] Ciupa, I., Leitner, A., Liu, L(L.)., Meyer, B.: Automatic testing of object-oriented software. In: van Leeuwen, J., Italiano, G.F., van der Hoek, W., Meinel, C., Sack, H., Plášil, F. (eds.) SOFSEM 2007. LNCS, vol. 4362, pp. 114–129. Springer, Heidelberg (2007), http://se.ethz.ch/~meyer/publications/lncs/testing_sofsem.pdf

[4] ECMA Technical Committee 39 (Programming and Scripting Languages) Technical Group 4 (Eiffel): Eiffel Analysis, Design and Programming Language, ECMA and ISO standard, June 2005 (revised November 2006)

[5] Eiffel Software: EiffelStudio open-source download, http://www.eiffel.com

[6] Gurevich, Y., Meyer, B. (eds.): TAP 2007. LNCS, vol. 4454. Springer, Heidelberg (2007)

[7] Jézéquel, J.-M., Meyer, B.: Design by Contract: The Lessons of Ariane. In: Computer (IEEE), vol. 30(1), pp. 129–130 (1997), http://se.ethz.ch/~meyer/publications/computer/ariane.pdf

[8] Leavens, G.T., Cheon, Y., Clifton, C., Ruby, C., Cok, D.R.: How the Design of JML Accommodates Both Runtime Assertion Checking and Formal Verification. In: Science of Computer Programming, vol. 55(1-2), pp. 185–208 (March 2005), http://dx.doi.org/10.1016/j.scico.2004.05.015

[9] Leavens, G.T., Cheon, Y.: Design by Contract with JML, draft paper. (with other JML documents from JML), www.eecs.ucf.edu/~leavens/JML/

[10] Leitner, A., Oriol, M., Zeller, A., Ciupa, I., Meyer, B.: Efficient Unit Test Case Minimization. In: proceedings of Automated Software Engineering 2007 (ASE 2007) (to appear)

[11] Leitner, A., Ciupa, I., Oriol, M., Meyer, B., Fiva, A.: Contract Driven Development = Test Driven Development – Writing Test Cases. In: proceedings of ESEC/FSE 2007 (to appear)

[12] Meyer, B.: Reusable Software: The Base Object-Oriented Component Libraries. Prentice-Hall, Englewood Cliffs (1994)

[13] Meyer, B.: Object-Oriented Software Construction, 2nd edn. Prentice-Hall, Englewood Cliffs (1997)

[14] Meyer, B.: Attached Types and their Application to Three Open Problems of Object-Oriented Programming. In: Black, A.P. (ed.) ECOOP 2005. LNCS, vol. 3586, pp. 1–32. Springer, Heidelberg (2005), http://se.ethz.ch/~meyer/publications/lncs/attached.pdf

[15] Nienaltowski, P.: Practical framework for contract-based concurrent object-oriented programming, PhD thesis, ETH Zurich (February 2007), http://se.ethz.ch/people/nienaltowski/papers/thesis.pdf

[16] Schoeller, B., Widmer, T., Meyer, B.: Making Specifications Complete Through Models. In: Reussner, R., Stafford, J., Szyperski, C. (eds.) Architecting Systems with Trustworthy Components. LNCS, Springer, Heidelberg (2006), se.ethz.ch/~meyer/publications/lncs/model_library.pdf

A   Discussion on Bertrand Meyer's Presentation

Greg Nelson

Bertrand, I was intrigued by your remark in passing that Eiffel's type system has recently been extended, so that null-dereference errors are no longer possible in a type-safe program, if I understood you correctly, and I was wondering if this meant that your type checker uses automatic theorem proving techniques, or whether it means, that there is a new class of error, where a general expression is assigned to a variable, declared to be of a non-null type?

Bertrand Meyer

The solutions are not very different from those of Spec#, except we think they are better, and a good reason for this is that we took quite a few ideas from them, and it's of course always easier to improve on someone else's design than to start from scratch. In particular I think our approach is simpler.

Type checking is theorem proving already. So it is just a matter of making the theory a bit more powerful. In just two words: First, one of the differences with the Spec# work is that we decided that by default types are non-void—"attached", as we call them. That default seems to match reality, as in practice most business objects have to be there. Second, the key issue is automatic variable initialization. It seems that's all I have the time to say.

Can We Build an Automatic Program Verifier? Invariant Proofs and Other Challenges

Myla Archer

Code 5546, Naval Research Laboratory,
Washington, DC 20375
archer@itd.nrl.navy.mil

Abstract. This paper reviews some common knowledge about establishing correctness of programs and the current status of program specification and verification. While doing so, it identifies several challenges related to the grand challenge of building a verifying compiler. The paper argues that invariants are central to establishing correctness of programs and that thus, a major part of an automatic program verifier must be automated support for verifying invariants, a significant problem in itself. The paper discusses where the invariants come from, what can be involved in establishing that they hold, and the extent to which the process of finding and proving invariants can be automated. The paper also discusses several of the related challenges identified, argues that addressing them would make the significance to global program behavior of feedback from a verifying compiler clearer, and recommends that many of them should be included within the scope of the grand challenge.

1   Introduction

In undertaking to construct and exploit an automatic program verifier, one must first focus in on the problems to be solved. There are several natural questions that arise, e.g.:

- What does it mean to verify a program?
- What does it mean for a program to be correct? (Is "verified" sufficient?)
- Assuming program verification involves proving a set of properties:
  - What types of properties are to be established?
  - Where do the properties come from?
  - Are the properties capable of automatic proof?
- Finally, what support should be provided by the automatic program verifier to allow a user to best exploit it?

This paper will explore these issues, summarizing some common knowledge about program specification, verification, and correctness, and arguing that one major problem on which to focus is the automation of invariant proofs. The paper will then note several additional challenges related to establishing invariants and other correctness properties of programs, and take the position that, given

B. Meyer and J. Woodcock (Eds.): Verified Software, LNCS 4171, pp. 308–317, 2008.
© IFIP International Federation for Information Processing 2008

the numerous challenges, the notion of a verifying compiler as a grand challenge should be given a broad scope.

Sections 2 through 5 discuss the questions listed above. Section 6 discusses related challenges. Finally, Section 7 presents some conclusions and discusses our current and future research that relates to some of the challenges.

2   What Does It Mean to Verify a Program?

Program verification can be approached in more than one way. Two major approaches are *assertion-based verification* and *model-based verification*. As will be expanded on below, to be used for complete program verification, the second (model-based) approach needs to be combined with the first (assertion-based) approach.

Assertion-Based Verification. Since the seminal work in [12] and [7], program verification is often thought of in terms of assertions that can be proved to hold at various points in the program. In particular, for programs designed to run to completion while performing some computation, assertions at the beginning and end of the program can be used to specify the expected result of the computation. The approach is also valid for programs that run indefinitely; in this case, assertions (about input and output streams) before reads and after writes can be used to specify the expected visible behavior of the program.

Model-Based Verification. In model-based program verification, desired program properties are specified by way of a model. Certain programs, particularly ones intended to run indefinitely, are primarily intended to react to events in their environment. Such programs are often better specified not by providing assertions at points in the program but by giving an operational model, usually accompanied by invariant properties of the model. This is the approach used, for example, in SCR (Software Cost Reduction) [14], TIOA (Timed Input/Output Automata) [18,13] and other software development tools. What then needs to be established in verifying the program is that it refines the specification in the sense that there is a refinement mapping or relation from a state machine representation of the program to the state machine of the operational model. When the operational model (specification) is intended to capture all or most of the intended behavior of the program, verification that the program refines the specification can be done by relating preconditions and postconditions in the model to assertions known to hold at appropriate locations in the program. Here, rather than serving as the program specification, the assertions serve as proof obligations about the program. The benefit of establishing a refinement relation from program to model is that any properties proved of the model will translate into properties of the program. The "refinement" approach can be generalized to allow alternative notions of implementation of a specification: e.g., forward simulation. This approach (establishing an implementation) is one version of model-based verification.

To many, the term "verification" principally means another form of model-based verification: model checking. Model checking has been used more often in the context of hardware verification than software verification, but recent advances such as automated abstraction refinement (see, e.g., [8]) have extended the degree of its applicability to software. When used for true verification rather than testing for counterexamples, model checking involves exhaustively examining a set of cases that covers all the reachable states of the model in some manner (individually, or intelligently grouped). For this reason, the size of the state space becomes a limitation, and model checking for program verification usually compares a very spare model of the program to a second model that captures one property (or a small set of properties) at a time.

Models used to capture just one or a small set of properties rather than the full functional behavior of a program can be termed *property models*. In verification using model checking, the specification to be met is given as a set of properties that are represented (directly or by transformation) as property models. Thus model checking for full program verification requires 1) a sufficient set of property models to adequately specify the program; 2) for each property model, an abstract model of the program that can be given as input to the model checker together with the property model to establish a refinement; and 3) some form of proof that each abstract program model used is a correct abstraction of the program—i.e., that the program refines or implements the abstract model. The use of property models is not limited to the model checking context: Property models are also important for capturing properties of full operational models of programs (as, for instance, in TIOA—see, e.g., [22,23]).

Verification, Specification, and Correctness. Both verification methods discussed above show that a program *satisfies a specification*. However, as will be argued in the next section, this is not necessarily the same as showing that the program is "correct".

3   What Does It Mean for a Program to Be Correct?

As noted in Section 2, the term "program verification" in any sense means establishing that the program satisfies a specification. The specification may be defined by assertions associated with various points in the program, by an operational model to which the program must conform, or by other assertions about the program as a whole (such as liveness, or absence of deadlock or livelock), which often are captured as specialized property models. However, *correctness* of a program means that the program's behavior matches a set of (behavioral) *requirements*. Thus, for verification of a program to be equivalent to establishing the program's correctness, it is necessary for the specification against which it is verified to capture these requirements.

For some programs, the requirements are clear. For example, a program that sorts a list needs to take a list as input and produce a sorted version of the list as output. For simple programs of this type, assertion-based verification is an appropriate approach.

For a very complex program, e.g., a graphical editor, the requirements for completely correct behavior are equally complex, and it can even be unclear what correctness ought to mean, precisely. A specification, even an operational model, that captures all the desired behavior can be so complex as to make reasoning about it in full detail an intractable problem. For such programs, one may be most interested in only some particular subset of the required behavior. This subset may cover "good" behavior from the user's and operating system's point of view: Will the program terminate unexpectedly due to a segmentation fault? Are there possible buffer overflows or deadlocks? Many properties of this type can be captured in a straightforward way as program assertions.

Another subset of required behavior that is of interest as a program correctness criterion (short of full functional correctness) is security relevant behavior. For cases in which only the security relevant behavior is considered critically important, correctness can mean conformance to a particular security model, and thus model-based verification is especially appropriate.

Whatever the verification method used, verification will only establish correctness of a program if the specification the program is verified against correctly captures the requirements for the program. But, it is only possible to capture requirements in a well-formed specification if they are consistent. Completeness of the requirements can also be particularly important, e.g., if all exceptional behavior must be described. Thus, analysis of well-formedness properties of requirements specifications has a role in the overall effort of establishing the correctness of programs.

4   Properties: Formulation and Proof

4.1   What Types of Properties Are to Be Established?

All the program correctness properties mentioned above can be formulated as invariants of some state machine. The simplest category from the point of view of proof is that of state invariants: program assertions, absence of deadlock, and many specified properties of models fall in this category. Conformance to a model can also be cast as a state invariant of a composition automaton (representing some composition of the model and the program). Almost as simple are safety properties, which involve at most a bounded sequence of transitions. More difficult to prove are liveness properties, which can involve reasoning about an unbounded sequence of states and may involve some fairness assumptions.

4.2   Where Do the Properties Come From?

In the interest of separation of concerns, one can assume, in tackling the challenge of building an automatic program verifier, that the properties that must be established of the program are given. However, it is clear that an automatic verifier will not be much help in establishing program correctness if properties that imply its correctness have not been formulated by someone. Thus, a related challenge is to persuade developers (or other stakeholders in a piece of software) to specify in some form what the software is to do (i.e., its required behavior). A further related challenge is to create a tool that, given appropriate information, can derive assertions about a program to be used by an automatic program verifier from assertions about an abstract model of the program's behavior.

In the context of asserted programs, there has been some work [11] on dynamically discovering likely program invariants that could produce some of the needed assertions in a program (which would then be subject to proof). There has also been work on generating known invariants, starting from [9] and [10], which consider program assertions. Later work includes [4], which also considers program assertions, and [15], which considers invariant properties of specifications. Although these approaches can help furnish some of the assertions, the connection between the assertions and program correctness would need to be established by someone who understands what the program is supposed to do, or how a model is supposed to behave. Creating automated support for generating program assertions from assertions about a model appears to be an open problem.

4.3 Are the Properties Capable of Automatic Proof?

Some program assertions can be established without induction: e.g., input assertions can be assumptions, other assertions can be established through weakest precondition computations, and further assertions can be established from existing ones by the application of decision procedures. A challenge in this connection is to develop additional decision procedures to be integrated into existing ones that can handle data types (beyond numerical, boolean, and enumerated types) for which many assertions are decidable.

However, for certain classes of assertions, induction is required. For example, induction is generally needed to establish loop invariants. Induction in some form is also generally needed to establish liveness properties. For a finite model, one can sometimes avoid induction: properties of finite models can (if state explosion is manageable) be established by exhaustive search (model checking). However, establishing invariant properties of infinite (and sometimes, very large finite) models requires theorem proving, and, typically, induction.

Thus, even though some program properties can be established by other means, a general truly *automatic* program verifier would need to be able to do induction proofs automatically. A completely general approach to doing this is not possible, because the general problem of establishing whether an assertion is an invariant is undecidable. In principle, provided the induction scheme is known (as is the case, e.g., for state invariants, where induction is over the reachable states), and provided the base and induction cases can be stated in first order logic, *valid* invariants can be established by induction automatically. However, efficiency is an issue; so is the problem that some properties being checked are false—as may be the case for the induction step when one is trying to prove a possibly true invariant by proving that it is inductive. In particular, proofs by induction of invariants also often require strengthening of the invariants, a process that is not always automatable. Strengthening *can* be automated, to a degree, as has been illustrated in SCR. Note that an equivalent approach to strengthening is the introduction of additional invariants as lemmas. In the context of SCR, it has been possible to create an induction proof strategy that uses automatically generated invariants [15] as lemmas and that proves many properties of SCR specifications automatically without user guidance; see, e.g., [20].

Thus, automating induction proofs of program properties is itself a challenge. The goal would be to create a technique that would cover the kinds of assertions that normally arise in practice. Techniques such as proof planning with rippling [6,5] have had some success, but are still not sufficiently universal.

Mechanical proofs—by induction or otherwise—of correctness properties of abstract models are often best constructed interactively. This is because for abstract models, correctness properties can contain quite complex predicates (e.g., the `Authenticated` predicate in the basic TESLA protocol model in [2] involves existential quantifiers and is recursively defined) and are potentially higher-order. As shown by our experience with TAME [3], efficient interactive construction of proofs can be made more feasible if an appropriate special domain tool or prover interface is provided. (TAME is discussed further in Section 5, and in more detail in Section 7.)

5 How to Exploit an Automatic Program Verifier?

As has been noted above, an automatic verifier presupposes some form of specification against which to verify the program. A user better equipped to specify is thus better equipped to verify. But such a user is also better equipped to *test*. To state the obvious: the user should test the assertions before using the program verifier, because verification is expensive; only after one has evidence that a set of properties is likely correct should one undertake to prove the properties. Thus, a program verifier is best used in conjunction with a testing tool.

Equally important to knowing that a program has certain properties is knowing *why* it has those properties. For example, one usually does not want a property to be vacuously true, as might happen (in a program) for the postcondition of an unintentionally nonterminating loop, or (in a model) when all preconditions of transitions are false. Thus, in addition being able to prove properties, it is desirable for the verifier to produce some degree of proof explanation. A variety of theorem proving techniques provide some form of explanation. Several automatic proof techniques provide proof explanation; examples include ACL2 [16,17] and approaches based on proof planning such as [19]. Our tool TAME [3] provides explanations for invariant proofs produced with interactive guidance.

However explanations are produced, the same techniques used in proof explanation can be adapted to provide some explanation of proof failure—i.e., what point and proof goal did the proof reach when the automatic verifier was unable to continue? When the automatic verifier is unable to verify a program, the next action needs to be either modification of the program or modification of the specification. While performing the proper corrective action is an art form, understandable feedback from the automatic verifier is an important prerequisite to making the correction.

Addressing some other challenges related to the automatic program verifier would allow the automatic verifier to be exploited as fully as possible as a tool for establishing program correctness. The next section discusses a number of these challenges and notes how addressing them would help.

6   Related Challenges

As noted above, the challenge of building an automatic invariant prover is a part of the challenge of building an automatic program verifier. The challenge of improving and expanding the scope of decision procedures also falls into this category. But there are other challenges that, if addressed, would increase the usefulness of an automatic verifier. Two have already been mentioned.

First, it would be helpful if software developers could be convinced to provide some form of specification of what the software is supposed to do. With respect to low level specification, this is not an unreasonable hope: for example, the inclusion of assertions with C and Java code is provided for and beginning to come into practice. It is likely unrealistic to hope that *all* software developers will provide requirements specifications that capture the intended behavior of the code. However, when the correctness of the code is essential, such specifications are more likely to be developed.

Next, as noted in Section 2, when an operational specification of the required behavior is available, one approach to establishing that a program refines this specification is to relate assertions in the specification (e.g., pre- and postconditions associated with transitions) to assertions in the code. This leads to a second challenge: automating as far as possible the mapping of assertions in the specification to assertions in the code, based on information provided by the user that relates program states to abstract (specification-level) states and program segments to transitions in the specification. Even if there are no decidability issues here, deriving code assertions from assertions in the specification may not be straightforward in cases where there is not a direct relation between individual variables in the program to variables in the specification, or when the relation of program states to abstract states is not a simple mapping. The design and development of generic tool support for this part of the program verification process can thus be complicated problem.

There is a third, additional challenge related to the second: To develop sound procedures for transforming requirements specifications expressed in forms such as natural language or a set of logical properties into an operational requirements specification. Implicit in this challenge is the ability to analyze requirements specifications for such properties as consistency and completeness.

A further, fourth challenge is to develop methods that can be applied by developers in designing programs for verifiability, and induce the developers to use them. While some such guidance already exists (e.g., avoid certain constructs), this guidance is mostly of a "local" nature. An open question is whether guidance can be provided for structuring programs so that particular properties (e.g., for security, separation of data) are easier to establish.

Addressing these challenges would help ensure first, that the automatic program verifier is proving properties of interest and second, that the automatic verifier's task is made as simple as possible.

7   Conclusions, Recommendations, and Plans for the Future

A verifying compiler that verifies assertions in programs is only part of the answer to the problem of producing verifiably correct programs. The challenge of building an automatic program verifier can be conceived more generally as covering not only a (possibly interactive) mechanical verifier of assertions in programs but a mechanical verifier (almost necessarily interactive!) that a program conforms to a model. For either the program-assertion-based or model-based verification style, the automation of (or, failing full automation, mechanized support for) proofs of invariants, and in particular induction proofs, will play a central role.

This paper has identified several related challenges to be met; some of them are directly implied by the challenge of building an automatic program verifier. Others are associated with additional parts of the process of establishing correctness properties of programs. Because addressing these others will increase the effectiveness of the automatic program verifier, it is worth considering including them as part of the overall challenge. Below is a summary of our current and future work that does (or will) address *some* of the related challenges.

The challenges identified that relate to requirements specifications are addressed in part by the SCR tool set [14]. In particular, the SCR tool set provides for consistency and completeness checking of SCR specifications, which define operational models. Moreover, SCR specifications can include an associated set of properties. While the tool set does not provide a means for transforming properties to an operational model, the associated set of properties can be used to express a property-based version of the specification, and several tools in the tool set can be applied to showing consistency between the properties and the operational specification.

Two of the other challenges identified above are addressed to some degree for model-based verification by the tool TAME (Timed Automata Modeling Environment) [1,3], a specialized interface to PVS [24] for proving properties of timed I/O automata [21,22]. In particular, by providing specification templates, TAME attempts to make specification of models easier.[1] It also partially automates proofs of invariants, including state invariants, transition invariants, and abstraction properties such as refinement and forward simulation [23] by providing a set of high level proof steps that allow a proof sketch to be mechanically checked. For SCR specifications, TAME can prove many invariant properties automatically. TAME provides user feedback for failed proofs both inside the prover at the point of a proof dead end and in saved TAME proofs through

---

[1] The SCR tool set also aims at simplifying the specification of models, but uses a quite different approach based on tables.

structure, proof step names, and automatically generated comments. A prototype proof tool that translates TAME proofs into English has been implemented. Work is continuing on improving TAME in all these areas.

It is also planned to extend the work on TAME by increasing the degree to which proofs of invariants can be automated. This will be done by 1) developing techniques that can prove more invariants automatically by building on previously proved invariants, by finding useful alternative instantiations of the inductive hypothesis, and so on; and 2) exploring the possible use of techniques such as rippling in proving invariants of TAME models.

Other plans for the near future include:

- The use TAME or a similar "special domain" PVS interface to model some medium-sized programs and establish their correctness. The goal is to build on the techniques used in TAME to permit program verification on a level nearer to the level of program assertions.
- Development of prototype automated support for translating assertions at the model level into assertions at the program level.

Some interesting lessons, and perhaps some new associated challenges, are likely to result from these efforts.

Acknowledgements

I thank Elizabeth Leonard and Sandeep Shukla for helpful discussions, and Elizabeth for comments on an earlier version of this paper. I also thank the anonymous reviewer whose thoughtful observations have helped to improve the paper.

References

1. Archer, M.: TAME: Using PVS strategies for special-purpose theorem proving. Annals of Mathematics and Artificial Intelligence 29(1-4), 139–181 (2001)
2. Archer, M.: Proving correctness of the basic TESLA multicast stream authentication protocol with TAME. In: Workshop on Issues in the Theory of Security (WITS 2002), Portland, OR, January 14–15 (2002)
3. Archer, M., Heitmeyer, C., Riccobene, E.: Proving invariants of I/O automata with TAME. Automated Software Engineering 9(3), 201–232 (2002)
4. Bjørner, N., Browne, I.A., Manna, Z.: Automatic generation of invariants and intermediate assertions. Theoretical Computer Science 173(1), 49–87 (1997)
5. Bundy, A., Stevens, A., van Harmelen, F., Ireland, A., Smaill, A.: Rippling: A heuristic for guiding inductive proofs. Artificial Intelligence 62, 185–253 (1993)
6. Bundy, A.: The use of proof plans for normalization. In: Boyer, R.S. (ed.) Automated Reasoning: Essays in Honor of Woody Bledsoe. Automated Reasoning Series, vol. 7, pp. 149–166. Kluwer, Dordrecht (1991)
7. Hoare, C.A.R.: An axiomatic basis for computer programming. Communications of the ACM 12(10), 576–583 (1969)
8. Clarke, E., Grumberg, O., Jha, S., Lu, Y., Veith, H.: Counterexample-guided abstraction refinement. In: Emerson, E.A., Sistla, A.P. (eds.) CAV 2000. LNCS, vol. 1855, pp. 154–169. Springer, Heidelberg (2000)

9. Cousot, P., Cousot, R.: Abstract interpretation: A unified lattice model for static analysis of programs by construction or approximation of fixpoints. In: Proc. 1977 Symp. on Principles of Programming Languages (January, 1977)
10. Cousot, P., Halbwachs, N.: Automatic discovery of linear restraints among variables. In: Proc. 1978 Symp. on Principles of Programming Languages (January, 1978)
11. Ernst, M.: Dynamically Discovering Likely Program Invariants. PhD thesis, Univ. of Washington (2000)
12. Floyd, R.W.: Assigning meanings to programs. In: Proceedings of Symposia in Applied Mathematics. Mathematical Aspects of Computer Science, vol. 19, pp. 19–32. American Mathematical Society, Providence, RI (1967)
13. Garland, S.: TIOA User Guide and Reference Manual. Technical report, MIT CSAIL, Cambridge, MA, URL (2006), http://tioa.csail.mit.edu
14. Heitmeyer, C., Archer, M., Bharadwaj, R., Jeffords, R.: Tools for constructing requirements specifications: The SCR toolset at the age of ten. International Journal on Computer System Science and Engineering 20(1), 19–35 (2005)
15. Jeffords, R., Heitmeyer, C.: Automatic generation of state invariants from requirements specifications. In: Proc. 6th International Symposium on the Foundations of Software Engineering (FSE-6), Orlando, FL (November 1998)
16. Kaufmann, M., Manolios, P., Moore, J.S.: Computer-Aided Reasoning: An Approach. Kluwer Academic Publishers, Dordrecht (2000)
17. Kaufmann, M., Manolios, P., Moore, J.S. (eds.): Computer-Aided Reasoning: Case Studies. Kluwer Academic Publishers, Dordrecht (2000)
18. Kaynar, D., Lynch, N.A., Segala, R., Vaandrager, F.: A mathematical framework for modeling and analyzing real-time systems. In: The 24th IEEE Intern. Real-Time Systems Symposium (RTSS), Cancun, Mexico (December 2003)
19. Kerber, M., Kohlhase, M., Sorge, V.: Integrating computer algebra into proof planning. Journal of Automated Reasoning 21(3), 327–355 (1998)
20. Kirby Jr., J., Archer, M., Heitmeyer, C.: SCR: A practical approach to building a high assurance COMSEC system. In: Proc. 15th Annual Computer Security Applications Conference (ACSAC 1999), IEEE Comp. Soc. Press, Los Alamitos (1999)
21. Lynch, N., Tuttle, M.: An introduction to Input/Output automata. CWI-Quarterly 2(3), 219–246 (1989)
22. Lynch, N., Vaandrager, F.: Forward and backward simulations – Part II: Timing-based systems. Information and Computation 128(1), 1–25 (1996)
23. Mitra, S., Archer, M.: PVS strategies for proving abstraction properties of automata. Electronic Notes in Theor. Comp. Sci. 125(2), 45–65 (2005)
24. Shankar, N., Owre, S., Rushby, J.M., Stringer-Calvert, D.W.J.: PVS Prover Guide, Version 2.4. Technical report, Comp. Sci. Lab. SRI Intl. Menlo Park, CA (November 2001)

Verified Software: The *Real* Grand Challenge

Ramesh Bharadwaj

Center for High Assurance Computer Systems,
Naval Research Laboratory,
Washington DC, 20375, USA
`ramesh@itd.nrl.navy.mil`

Abstract. This position paper addresses, and attempts to propose solutions for, critical issues in software engineering that need to be resolved before the Verified Software grand challenge as proposed by Professor Tony Hoare can be usefully exploited in industry to increase the assurance of software intensive systems.

1 Introduction

The following assumptions about programs and their correctness (which I refer to in the sequel as "assumptions") are implicit in the problem description of the Verifying Compiler Grand Challenge: 1) Associated with each program are types, assertions, and other annotations[1] that are readily available. 2) They are unassailable, inviolable, and invariant. 3) Their correctness is both necessary and sufficient for the correctness of the programs they annotate. In this paper, I argue that for programs that are intended to solve real-world problems, the subject of my research for more than fifteen years, none of these assumptions necessarily holds. I proceed to explain how this problem may be addressed, and conclude with what I think are more realistic expectations on the impact of the grand challenge problem and its solutions on real-world software development projects.

2 Problem Statement

For programs whose behavior is easily specified as mathematical functions, it is conceivable that the assumptions are valid. An example of such a program is one that implements the 4-coloring algorithm for planar graphs. If we assume that program annotations can characterize the function being computed by the program, the proof of its correctness is probably derivable from the proof of correctness of the 4-coloring problem. However, even for such programs, the correctness of its annotations is often predicated upon extraneous factors in the program's execution environment, such as the word length of the processor, the size of the address space, or the amount of available memory. This is because

---

[1] I shall loosely use the term "annotations" to refer to this redundant information.

B. Meyer and J. Woodcock (Eds.): Verified Software, LNCS 4171, pp. 318–324, 2008.

program code is generically written for an abstract machine; the program may execute on a real machine that may not correctly implement some of these abstractions. In such an event, the program will fail in unexpected ways. Also, program annotations may never be able to capture quantitative aspects such as the space and time requirements of the program. Such properties are central to the program's "correctness" since correctness often entails user expectations about the time and space requirements for successful execution on specific data sets. Even if we assume that it is feasible to precisely characterize such machine requirements and non-functional properties, it is not clear to me how their correctness could possibly be established by a verifying compiler.

The situation becomes hopeless for programs the correctness of whose annotations depends upon extraneous factors. This is the case even when the specification of a program is precisely characterized as a mathematical function; the problem is, it is often impossible to ascertain with 100% accuracy what this function is. My favorite example is sales tax computation. In a bygone era, when I used to write programs for a living, I was under the naive impression that the precise nature of mathematical logic makes the problem of program correctness a mere exercise in calculation. Imagine my surprise when, in response to my Management's decision to start charging for certain transactions, I had my first brush with sales tax laws. In the United States, for businesses that conduct transactions with customers in more than one state, correctly figuring out the sales tax for a specific transaction can be a daunting challenge [12]. Sales tax collection falls within the purview of more than 7,500 state and local administrations, each with its own specific set of rules and regulations. A business located in the United States is required to comply with all the regulations in effect at the location of *each* of its customers. Clearly, computing the correct sales tax is crucial to the very survival of the business.

Consider a program that is required to compute the sales tax associated with a sale: the correct tax rate varies with the location of the sale (which may not necessarily be the location of the computer on which the program is run), the sales tax to be levied at that location, and all applicable legislation(s) pertaining to the transaction[2]. For example, California law provides for the exemption of sales tax on food products subject to the following restrictions:

> Sales of food for human consumption are generally exempt from tax unless sold in a heated condition (except hot bakery items or hot beverages, such as coffee, sold for a separate price), served as meals, consumed at or on the seller's facilities, ordinarily sold for consumption on or near the seller's parking facility, or sold for consumption where there is an admission charge.

It is inconceivable that the above conditions and restrictions could be specified precisely in the form of program assertions. For example, how does one formalize notions such as "except hot bakery items" or "near the seller's parking facility?"

---

[2] An interesting discussion on Sales and Use taxes for transactions carried out via the Internet in the United States is found at [12].

How can one ascertain that the formulations are correct? How will a programmer devise algorithms for their computation? How is the correctness of these algorithms established? Automatically?

One could argue that since the tax code is vague, confusing, and open to interpretation, the above example does not invalidate the aims of the grand challenge. Therefore, the argument goes, no methodology, formal or informal, can ever produce a system that is correct with respect to such an imprecise specification. An optimist may therefore suggest that one of the benefits that society will derive from this grand challenge would be to make the notion of precise and ambiguous specification a widely known and accepted concept of humankind. But, I'm too wizened and all too familiar with the fraility of human beings that I remain a skeptic. I put forth three arguments in my defence: (1) The pace of current day systems development, coupled with ever-changing requirements, and the non-technical background of major decision makers, precludes such optimistic thinking. There's never going to be enough time or money to maintain two distinct, yet accurate descriptions of the same system. (2) Even if we assume that we have the time and money to maintain a mathematically precise specification, how (who) is this going to be maintained (by)? Let's face it, we're never going to become a technocratic society. Technology is, and will continue to be understood by a small minority whose job is, and will continue to be, the "dumbing down" of systems to make them usable by the masses. Since specifications are never intended to be "run" (I consider the term "executable specification" to be an oxymoron) the social processes necessary to weed out bugs are never going to be in place. According to reliable sources [11], the "specification" in Z of the IBM CICS system was understood and read by only one member of the project team, i.e., the writer of the specification; subsequent attempts to wean developers away from their informal specification proved futile, which is when, as a last resort, English text was derived manually from the formal specification for developers to comment upon. (3) It is not the case that specifications are always clearer, more concise, or more comprehensible than the corresponding implementations (i.e., code). Case in point: In the '70s, incompleteness in the formal specification of something as trival as the routine "sort" went unnoticed by several great minds, including members of this august body. Therefore, it is my firm belief that the social processes needed to weed out the bugs in specifications are likely to be more expensive (and unnecessary) in comparison to the weeding out of bugs in the code. Specifications may not be always worth the trouble.

3   Requirements Specifications

My exposure to programs that solve real-world problems led me to the world of software engineering, where one addresses the problem of determining customer needs and their precise characterization in the form of a specification. By *specification* I mean a description of the *required behavior* of a system, sub-system, or component. In general, a specification describes *what* is being computed, omitting details of *how* this is achieved. Two important goals are to make the specification of a system understandable to the users of the system (to enable its *validation*) and making it precise, i.e., avoiding overspecification (also known implementation bias) as well as underspecification[3].

This is a tall order, since the two goals are often in conflict: On the one hand, the specification must be understandable to the users; therefore, its vocabulary must only include user-visible (or environmental) quantities and exclude variables and other artefacts used in the implementation. On the other hand, since a specification is also a "build-to" document, i.e., it is the specification of the behavior of the implementation, its vocabulary must be linked to implementation detail. One solution to this conundrum is to specify a mapping between the two behavioral descriptions (the so-called refinement mapping) – the specification and the implementation. However, providing this is infeasible in practice and I advocate instead an approach [5,6,9] where the implementation vocabulary includes the user vocabulary, i.e., environmental quantities associated with the externally visible behavior of the system.

This approach has two limitations: it does not address the problem of legacy systems; it also unnecessarily constrains design choices. A more general solution to this problem (also known as the "traceability problem" in requirements engineering) remains a daunting challenge. By traceability we mean a formal argument that establishes a relationship between two artefacts that describe a system at different levels of abstraction. We do not mean the manual generation and maintenance by developers of ad-hoc links (akin to hyperlinks in html) whose semantics are not interpreted or captured by the analysis tools. The set of problems whose solutions remain elusive are: 1) Reverse Engineering: Given a legacy implementation, how can one automatically extract a user-understandable description? 2) System verification: Given a user-visible specification of system behavior, how does one ensure that an implementation satisfies the specification? 3) Refinement Mapping: How are relations between user-visible and system-specific vocabularies established? 4) Requirements Traceability: Given an instance of user-visible behavior, which components of the implementation are responsible for implementing this behavior? 5) Trojans and Dead Code: Given a requirements specification, which components, sub-systems, or lines of code in the system are irrelevant to the correct operation of the system?

4 Domain Models

I have also explored another area in software engineering where precise notation and mathematical analysis prove to be very useful. This is in *requirements engineering*, i.e., the processes and methods employed by users and system developers to gain an understanding of the problem being solved in building the system. This is complementary to the specification based approach above and can be used in addition to or instead of requirements specifications. In contrast to the

---

[3] In other words, every implementation that satisfies the specification must be acceptable to the customer and the specification must describe every acceptable implementation.

conventional approach, which can be costly and time consuming, requirements engineering advocates the creation and analysis of "domain models" just for the purpose of answering specific questions about the domain [8]. The effort involved in creating such models is minimal and is comparable to the effort required to peruse prose requirements to find answers to the same questions (which often turn out to be incorrect). Using domain models, not only is there the advantage of arriving at the right answer with mathematical certainty, but as an added bonus, they uncover anomalies and raise issues about the domain that informal approaches do not. Research challenges in this area include the automatic transformation of domain models into requirements specifications, their verification, validation, and maintenance. Other challenges are related to the challenges I enumerate above pertaining to Requirements Specifications.

5   Architectural Patterns

Today's systems are built using highly reusable software or hardware components using the so called "system of systems" approach. Systems are typically built by integration of highly disparate components that interact with one another via a middleware infrastructure [14]. Some of these components may be Commercial Off The Shelf (COTS) or standard IP hardware components which may have been developed without taking into account the requirements of the system in which they are deployed. Further, during the design of a component, consideration of non-functional requirements such as reliability may complicate the design. Therefore, satisfying certain requirements of the system, such as fault-tolerance, is better done at later stages of the development cycle during hardware/software integration. Since the sub-components are not easily modified during system integration, the only alternative is to implement these requirements by appropriately configuring the components so as to alter their behavior at run-time. Architectural patterns are a means to rapidly develop such mechanisms by reusing existing solutions to "similar" requirements. Using such patterns, the system integrator can quickly develop architectural models by assembling existing patterns to meet specific dependability requirements of an application. The research challenges include the automatic translation of these models into efficient runnable code, automated deployment of code on a secure, perhaps distributed platform, and initiation of repair actions in the case of hardware, network, or software failures.

We have conducted an initial study in formal verification of architectural patterns in support of dependable distributed applications [10]. This initial study has shown that it is relatively straightforward to associate safety properties with generic modules that implement such architectural patterns. Proofs of these properties were carried out using the standard induction technique [7] using an assumption/guarantee proof system for compositional reasoning similar to [13]. Although we have automated the proofs of safety properties for concrete instances of an architectural pattern, an open problem is to develop automatic proof strategies for the generic case. Also required is a polymorphic type system and generalized proof methodologies in support of *architectural frameworks*, which are the generators of architectural patterns.

6 Dependable Middleware

A goal of the NRL dependable middleware project [1,2,3,4] is to develop infrastructure to support secure deployment, coordination, security, and encapsulation mechanisms for untrusted software COTS components. With such middleware, it should be feasible to compose and deploy untrusted components in mission-critical applications, while guaranteeing the compliance of the application with performance-critical properties. Such middleware is also the enabler in the creation of service-oriented architectures (SOAs), where organizations can delegate to other organizations the responsibility of implementing, deploying, and maintaining certain functions constituting a mission-critical application. For instance, most businesses routinely use third-party vendors for carrying out credit card transactions. Getting back to the problem of sales tax computation, a business may delegate to a third party responsibility (and associated legal liability) for computing this function within an application. The correctness of such an application is obviously predicated upon the correctness of these outsourced functions. Therefore, to ensure compliance, organizations must enter into Service Level Agreements (SLAs) that are legally binding contracts similar to design contracts in object oriented programming. Automatic discovery of services relevant to an application's requirements, protocols for automatically drawing up service level agreements, ensuring the compliance of services provided by vendors with the SLAs, dynamic composition of available services to meet the requirements of a specific mission-critical application, and verifying that the composed application meets its performance-critical properties, are some of the multitude of challenges posed by application development for service-oriented architectures.

7 Conclusion

In this position paper, I have made an attempt to put into perspective the daunting challenges associated with Verified Software. In my opinion, the Verified Software grand challenge is merely a good start for developing methods and tools to solve the more challenging problems of the software development industry. It is hoped that the attendees of the IFIP Working Conference on Verified Software: Theories, Tools, Experiments, will give thought to these additional challenges, and propose a road map for tackling some of these more pressing problems. I think the Computer Science community has abdicated responsibility for improving the state-of-practice of software development many years ago. It is my earnest hope that this forum will serve as a springboard to invigorate the community into making genuine research contributions that have the potential to truly transform the software development process into an engineering activity. In other words, to put the "engineering" back into software engineering.

References

1. Bharadwaj, R.: SINS:a middleware for autonomous agents and secure code mobility. In: Proc. Second International Workshop on Security of Mobile Multi-Agent Systems (SEMAS 2002), Bologna, Italy (July 2002)
2. Bharadwaj, R.: Verifiable middleware for secure agent interoperability. In: Proc. Second Goddard IEEE Workshop on Formal Approaches to Agent-Based Systems, Greenbelt, MD (October 2002)
3. Bharadwaj, R.: A framework for the formal analysis of multi-agent systems. In: Proc. Formal Approaches to Multi-Agent Systems, Warsaw, Poland (April 2003)
4. Bharadwaj, R.: Development of dependable component-based applications. In: Margaria, T., Steffen, B. (eds.) ISoLA 2004. LNCS, vol. 4313, Springer, Heidelberg (2006)
5. Bharadwaj, R., Heitmeyer, C.: Hardware/software co-design and co-validation using the SCR method. In: Proceedings of the IEEE International High Level Design Validation and Test Workshop (HLDVT 1999), San Diego, CA (November 1999)
6. Bharadwaj, R., Heitmeyer, C.: Developing high assurance avionics systems with the SCR requirements methods. In: Proc. 19th IEEE Digital Avionics Systems Conference, Philadelphia, PA (October 2000)
7. Bharadwaj, R., Sims, S.: Salsa: Combining constraint solvers with BDDs for automatic invariant checking. In: Proc. 6th International Conference on Tools and Algorithms for the Construction and Analysis of Systems, pp. 378–394 (March 2000)
8. Bharadwaj, R.: Formal analysis of domain models. In: Proc. International Workshop on Requirements for High Assurance Systems (RHAS 2002), Essen, Germany (September 2002)
9. Heitmeyer, C., Bharadwaj, R.: Applying the SCR requirements method to the Light Control Case Study. JUCS 6(7) (2000)
10. Jeffords, R.L., Bharadwaj, R.: Formal verification of architectural patterns in support of dependable distributed systems. (Submitted 2005)
11. D.L. Parnas. Private Communication.
12. TurboTax. FAQs on Sales and Use Taxes and the Internet, http://www. turbotax. com/articles/FAQonSalesandUseTaxesandtheInternet.html
13. Xie, F., Browne, J.C.: Verified systems by composition from verified components. In: Inverardi, P. (ed.) Proc. Joint 9th Eur. Softw. Eng. Conf (ESEC) and 11th SIGSOFT Symp. on Foundations of Softw. Eng (FSE-11), Helsinki,Finland, pp. 277–286 (September 2003)
14. Yau, S.S., Mukhopadhyay, S., Bharadwaj, R.: Specification, analysis, and implementation of architectural patterns for dependable software systems. In: Proc. 10th IEEE Int'l Workshop on Object-Oriented Real-Time Dependable Systems (WORDS 2005), Sedona, AZ (February 2005)

Linking the Meaning of Programs to What the Compiler Can Verify

Egon Börger

Università di Pisa, Dipartimento di Informatica, I-56125 Pisa, Italy
`boerger@di.unipi.it`

Abstract. We formulate some research and development challenges that relate what a verifying compiler can verify to the definition and analysis of the application-content of programs, where the analysis comprises both experimental validation and mathematical verification. We also point to a practical framework to deal with theses challenges, namely the Abstract State Machines (ASM) method for high-level system design and analysis. We explain how it allows one to bridge the gap between informal requirements and detailed code by combining application-centric *experimentally validatable system modeling* with *mathematically verifiable refinements* of abstract models to compiler-verifiable code.

This paper is a position paper, triggered by the formulation of the program verifier challenge in [46]. By its definition, Hoare's challenge is focussed on the correctness of programs: software representations of computer-based systems, to-be-compiled by a verifying compiler. As a consequence, "the criterion of correctness is specified by types, assertions and other redundant annotations associated with the code of the program", where "the compiler will work in combination with other program development and testing tools, to achieve any desired degree of confidence in the structural soundness of the system and the total correctness of its more critical components." [46] Compilable code however is the result of two program development activities, which have to be checked too:

- turning the requirements into *ground models*, accurate "blueprints" of the to-be-implemented piece of "real world", which define the application-centric meaning of programs in an abstract and precise form, prior to coding,
- linking ground models to compilable code by a series of *refinements*, which introduce step by step the details *resulting from the design decisions* for the implementation.

We propose to broaden the program verifier challenge by relating the verification of the correctness for compilable programs to the experimental validation of the application-domain-based semantical correctness for *ground models* and to the mathematical verification of their *refinements* to compilable code, using Abstract State Machine (ASM) ground models [11] (Sect. 1) and ASM refinements [12] (Sect. 2). This leads us to formulate a broadening of Hoare's challenge, together with a series of milestones towards the overall goal (Sect. 4).

B. Meyer and J. Woodcock (Eds.): Verified Software, LNCS 4171, pp. 325–336, 2008.

1   ASM Ground Models (System Blueprints): A Semantical Foundation for Program Verification

Compilable programs, though often considered as the true definition of the system they represent, in many complex applications do however not "ground the design in reality", since they provide no correspondence between the extra-logical theoretical terms appearing in the code and their empirical interpretation, as requested by a basic principle of Carnap's analysis of scientific theories [24]. By ground models for software systems I mean mathematical application-centric models, which define what Brooks [23] calls "the conceptual construct" or the "essence" of code for a computer-based system and thus "ground the design in reality". Ground models are the result of the notoriously difficult and error prone elicitation of requirements (see [45,47]), largely a *formalization* and clarification task realizing the transition from mostly natural-language problem descriptions to a sufficiently precise, unambiguous, consistent, complete and minimal formulation, which represents the algorithmic content of the software contract.

By its epistemological role of relating some piece of "reality" to a linguistic description, the fundamental concept of ground model has no purely mathematical definition, though it can be given a scientific definition in terms of basic epistemological concepts which have been elaborated for empirical sciences by analytic philosophers, see for example [43,44]. We limit ourselves here to cite from [11] the essential properties which characterize the notion of ground models and can all be satisfied by ASM ground models. Ground models must be:

- *precise* at the appropriate level of detailing yet *flexible*, to satisfy the required accuracy exactly, without adding unnecessary precision;
- *simple and concise* to be understandable and acceptable as contract by both domain experts and system designers. ASM ground models allow one to achieve this property mainly by avoiding any extraneous encoding and by reflecting "directly", through the abstractions, the structure of the real-world problem. This makes ground models manageable for inspection and analysis, helps designers to resolve the "lack of scientific understanding on the part of their customers (and themselves)" [46, p.66] and enables experts to "clearly explain why ... systems indeed work correctly" [3];
- *abstract (minimal) yet complete. Completeness* means that every semantically relevant feature is present, that all contract benefits and obligations are mentioned and that there are no hidden clauses. In particular, a ground model must contain as interface all semantically relevant parameters concerning the interaction with the environment, and where appropriate also the basic architectural system structure. The completeness property "forces" the requirements engineer, as much as this is possible, to produce a model which is "closed" modulo some "holes", which are however explicitly delineated, including a statement of the assumptions made for them at the abstract level and to be realized through the detailed specification left for later refinements. Model closure implies that no gap in the understanding of "what to build" is left, that every relevant portion of implicit domain knowledge has been

made explicit and that there is no missing requirement—avoiding a typical type of software errors that are hard to detect at the level of compilable code [53, Fact 25]. *Minimality* means that the model abstracts from details that are relevant either only for the further design or only for a portion of the application domain which does not influence the system to be built;

- *validatable* (see [45])and thus in principle falsifiable by experiment and rigorous analysis, satisfying the basic Popperian criterion for scientific models [52];
- equipped with a simple yet *precise semantical foundation* as a prerequisite for rigorous analysis and reliable tool support.

2 ASM Refinements: Management of Design Decisions (Documentation and Verification)

The *ASM refinement notion* I have proposed[1] generalizes Wirth's and Dijkstra's classical refinement method [69,27]. Using stepwise ASM refinements offers the practitioner a technique to cope with the "explosion of 'derived requirements' (the requirements for a particular design solution) caused by the complexity of the solution process" and encountered "when moving from requirements to design" [53, Fact 26], a process that precedes the definition of compilable code. The ASM refinement method supports practical system validation and verification techniques that split checking complex detailed properties into a series of simpler checks of more abstract properties and their correct refinement, following the path the designer has chosen to rigorously link through various levels of abstraction the system architect's view (at the abstraction level of a blueprint) to the programmer's view (at the level of detail of compilable code). Successive ASM refinements also provide a systematic code development documentation, including behavioral information by state-based abstractions and leading to "further improvements to quality and functionality of the code ... by good documentation of the internal interfaces" [46, p.66].

In choosing how to refine an ASM M to an ASM M^*, one has the freedom to define the following items, as illustrated by Fig. 1:

- a notion (signature and intended meaning) of *refined state*,
- a notion of *states of interest* and of *correspondence* between M-states S and M^*-states S^* of interest, i.e. the pairs of states in the runs one wants to relate through the refinement, including usually the correspondence of initial and (if there are any) of final states,
- a notion of abstract *computation segments* $\tau_1, \ldots, \tau_m$, where each τ_i represents a single M-step, and of corresponding refined computation segments $\sigma_1, \ldots, \sigma_n$, of single M^*-steps σ_j, which in given runs lead from corresponding states of interest to (usually the next) corresponding states of interest (the resulting diagrams are called (m, n)-diagrams and the refinements (m, n)-refinements),

---

[1] The proposal goes back to [6,7,9] where it was used to define what became the ISO standard of Prolog [15]. For a recent survey see [12].

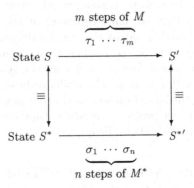

With an equivalence notion ≡ between data in
locations of interest in corresponding states.

Fig. 1. The ASM refinement scheme

- a notion of *locations of interest* and of *corresponding locations*, i.e. pairs of
  (possibly sets of) locations one wants to relate in corresponding states,
- a notion of *equivalence* ≡ of the data in the locations of interest; these local
  data equivalences usually accumulate to a notion of equivalence of corresponding states of interest.

Once the notions of corresponding states and of their equivalence have been
determined, one can define that M^* is a correct refinement of M if and only if
every (infinite) refined run simulates an (infinite) abstract run with equivalent
corresponding states. More precisely: fix any notions ≡ of equivalence of states
and of initial and final states. An ASM M^* is called a *correct refinement* of an
ASM M if and only if for each M^*-run $S_0^*, S_1^*, \ldots$ there are an M-run $S_0, S_1, \ldots$
and sequences $i_0 < i_1 < \ldots, j_0 < j_1 < \ldots$ such that $i_0 = j_0 = 0$ and $S_{i_k} \equiv S_{j_k}^*$
for each k and either

- both runs terminate and their final states are the last pair of equivalent
  states, or
- both runs and both sequences $i_0 < i_1 < \ldots, j_0 < j_1 < \ldots$ are infinite.

The M^*-run $S_0^*, S_1^*, \ldots$ is said to simulate the M-run $S_0, S_1, \ldots$. The states
$S_{i_k}, S_{j_k}^*$ are the corresponding states of interest. They represent the end points of
the corresponding computation segments (those of interest) in Fig. 1, for which
the equivalence is defined in terms of a relation between their corresponding
locations (those of interest). The scheme shows that an ASM refinement allows
one to combine in a natural way a change of the signature (through the definition of states and of their correspondence, of corresponding locations and of the
equivalence of data) with a change of the control (defining the "flow of operations" appearing in the corresponding computation segments), thus integrating
declarative and operational techniques and classical modularization concepts.

The survey in [10] refers to numerous successful practical applications of the above definition, which generalizes other more restricted refinements notions in the literature [55,56] and scales to the controlled and well documented development of large systems. In particular it supports modularizing ASM refinement correctness proofs aimed at mechanizable proof support, see [55,64,16,21].

3 Summary of Work Done Using the ASM Method

The ASM method to high-level system design and analysis, which is explained in the AsmBook [22], is characterized by the three notions of ASM, ASM ground model and ASM refinement.

ASMs are naturally defined as extension of Finite State Machines [13]: just replace the two fixed FSM locations *in* and *out*, used for reading input and writing output symbols, by any set of readable and/or writable, possibly parameterized, locations $(l, (p_1, \ldots, p_n))$ that may assume values of whatever types. Such sets of updatable locations represent arbitrarily complex abstract memory or states, what logicians call Tarski structures. Otherwise stated, ASMs are FSMs with generalized instructions of form *If Condition Then Updates*, where the FSM-input-event $in = a$ is extended to an arbitrary first-order expression *Condition* and the FSM-output-operation $out := b$ to an arbitrary set *Updates* of assignments $l(t_1, \ldots, t_n) := t$. This definition supports the intuitive understanding of ASMs as pseudo-code operating on abstract data structures.

Using ASMs as precise mathematical form of ground models [11] that are linked to compilable programs by ASM refinements [12], allows one to address the two sides of the software correctness problem in one framework, namely whether the ground model (read: the specification) faithfully reflects the intentions of the requirements and whether the code satisfies the ground model. For this purpose, the ASM method has been linked to a multitude of analysis methods, in terms of both experimental *validation* of models and mathematical *verification* of their properties.

The validation (testing) of ASM models is supported by numerous tools to mechanically execute ASMs (*ASM Workbench* [25], *AsmGofer* [59], an Asm2C++ compiler [60], C-based *XASM* [4], .NET-executable *AsmL* engine [32], CoreASM Execution Engine [31,30]). The verification of model properties is possible due to the mathematical character of ASMs, which means precision at the desired level of rigour. As a consequence any justification technique can be used, from proof sketches over traditional or formalized mathematical proofs [63,51] to tool supported proof checking or interactive or automatic theorem proving, e.g. by model checkers [68,26,39], KIV [57] or PVS [28,38]. Also assertion-based techniques can be applied to the state-based run-time ASM models, thus combining so-called declarative (static logical) and operational (run-time state-based) methods and avoiding the straitjacket of purely axiomatic descriptions. Various combinations of such verification and validation methods have been supported and used also for the correctness analysis of compilers [29,49] and hardware [66,65,61,42].

As a consequence, the ASM method supports practical program design and analysis by the following four activities:

- formulate relevant ground model properties ("assertions as specifications in advance of code" [46, p.66]) in traditional mathematical terms, still free from any further burden and restriction that typically derive from additional concerns about a formalization in a specific logic language underlying a proof calculus one may want to use for logical deduction purposes,
- experimentally validate ground model properties by mental or mechanical simulation, performing experiments with the ground model as systematic attempts a) to "falsify" the model in the Popperian sense [52] against the to-be-encoded piece of reality, and b) to "validate" characteristic sets of scenarios, where "testing gives adequate assurance of serviceability" [46, p.69],
- mathematically verify desired ground model properties (e.g. their consistency), using traditional mathematical or (semi-) automated techniques,
- link ground models in a mathematically verifiable way to compilable code via ASM refinements.

4   A Research Challenge and Some Milestones Ahead

The main goal we want to propose, to lift Hoare's challenge from program verification to a discipline of verifiable system development, is a long-term and general methodological goal. It is clearly independent of the ASM system design and analysis method, but from the preceding sections it should have become clear that the ASM framework is appropriate to uniformly support the work on the overall challenge. The challenge is to provide (read: define and implement) an integrated tool support for hierarchies of mechanically verifiable and validatable model refinement patterns, which link in a provably correct and modular way the application-content of systems, as defined by ground models, to to-be-verified compilable programs. This implies extensions and enhancements of the currently available software development and analysis tools, targeted at combining in one project the *definition* of abstract models and their stepwise refinements with their *simulation* and *verifications* of their properties.

This main goal implies various subgoals, some of which we are going to describe as possible milestones of the overall challenge. The first group is related to the refinement method, the second group to the construction of ground models.

A *refinement generator milestone* consists in defining—and where possible mechanically generating—practical and provably correct model refinement schemes, which turn model properties into software interface assertions comprising behavioral component aspects. Such refinement schemes are to be used where run-time features are crucial for a satisfactory semantically founded correctness notion for code.

A *refinement verifier milestone* is to enhance leading mechanical verification systems by means to prove the correctness of model refinement steps. Such a verifier may exploit the modularity character of the underlying refinement schemes.

There are various subgoals of this milestone. An example consists in linking ASMs to Event-B [1,2] along the lines of [14], so that the B verification tool set can be exploited to verify properties of ASMs and in particular the correctness of ASM refinement steps.

Another subgoal example consists in supporting verifications of the stepwise definition of programs written in widely used programming languages and their implementation on virtual machines. Such verifications are needed to close the model verification chain by linking verified abstract models to the generation of executable code. A concrete example in the literature has the form of mappings of Java to the Java Virtual Machine respectively of C# to the .NET Common Language Runtime, which have been provided in [64] respectively in [17,34] with the goal of modeling and analyzing within a uniform framework the source language, the virtual machine and a compilation scheme linking the first to the second. This subgoal comes with a series of near milestones, e.g. to verify by existing mechanical theorem proving systems the following theorems, proved in [64] using layered ASM models for interpreters of Java and the JVM: Type safety of Java (Thm.8.4.1); Correctness of a Java2JVM compilation scheme (Thm.14.1.1); JVM invariants for the soundness of Bytecode Type Assignments (Thm.16.4.1); Completeness of the scheme for certifying Java2JVM compilation (Thm.16.5.1,16.5.2); Soundness of the bytecode verifier (Thm.17.1.1). A way to achieve this may be to extend the computer-based Java-subset verification documented in [5,50].

An interesting practical outcome one can expect of such an endeavor for theorem proving systems is a set of reusable modular proof schemes that reflect hierarchies of layered abstract models, adding to the theorem-prover-oriented analysis provided in [54,55,56] for the ASM refinement notion [12]. Schellhorn's analysis came out of the KIV verification, reported in [57,58], of the mathematical proof for the correctness of a compilation scheme of Prolog programs to Warren Abstract Machine code provided in [21], starting from the ASM model for ISO Prolog developed in [6,7,8,20]. This leads to another near milestone, namely reusing the Java/JVM-related proof schemes to establish the corresponding verifications for C# and the .NET CLR, based upon their ASM models developed and verified in [17,48,34,36,33,37,35].

For language compilation there is also a *compiler verification milestone*, where real-life target processors take the place virtual machines occupy in the preceding milestones. It consists in developing methods supporting the verification of verifying compilers themselves in a general manner, adaptable for different source languages and target processors. A particular effort in this direction has been pursued in the Verifix [41] project, where ASM ground models were used extensively to describe the semantics of the underlying language and machines.

A related milestone consists in building a framework to guarantee forms of off-device pre-verification of compiled code. For example for proving at compile time that the generated bytecode will pass the verifier one could extend the certifying compilation scheme developed for Java in [64, Sect.16.5], where the instructions are annotated with type information that can be and is used in [64, Thm. 16.5.1

pg.266 sqq.] for the proof that the generated code is typable. This milestone is part of a more general challenge, namely to provide a practical theory to support the verification and validation of concepts and tools for *generative programming* techniques. Here the classical compile-link-run model of the semantics of programs has to be extended by a multistage- and meta-programming model for code, which is generated from components or code patterns or fragments, possibly written in low-level languages, according to directives that are expressed through metadata.

A *refinement validation milestone* consists in linking the refinement of ground models to model execution tools to make the generation and systematic comparison of corresponding test runs of abstract and refined machines possible. In particular relating system and unit level test results should be supported.

A *runtime verification milestone* consists in instrumenting current model execution tools to monitor the truth of selected properties at runtime, enabling in particular the exploration of ground models to detect undesired or hidden effects or missing behavior.

A *re-engineering milestone* is to define methods to extract ground models from legacy code as basis for analysis (and re-implementation where possible). The middle-size industrial case study described in [19] illustrates the feasibility of this goal.

A *system certification milestone* is to integrate ground model validation and analysis into industrial system certification processes. This effort can build upon the use that has been made of ASM ground models to formulate industrial standards, e.g. for the forthcoming standard of the Business Process Execution Language for Web Services [67], for the ITU-T standard for SDL-2000 [40], for the de facto standard for Java and the Java Virtual Machine [64], the ECMA standard for C# and the .NET CLR [17,62], the IEEE-VHDL93 standard [18]. This effort is certainly a long-term endeavor, but it appears to us to be both feasible and necessary to formulate the technical content of software reliability for embedded systems.

5   Concluding Remark

One reviewer asks what the advantages of the ASM method are over other approaches, whether it is "just a difference of notation" or whether there are "fundamental advantages". The *conceptual simplicity* of ASMs as FSMs updating arbitrary locations (read: general states), coupled to the use of *standard algorithmic notation*, constitutes a practical advantage: it makes ASMs understandable for application-domain experts and familiar to every software practitioner, thus supporting the mediation role ground models play for linking in an objectively checkable way informal requirements (read: natural-language descriptions of real-world phenomena) to mathematical models preceding compilable code. A further practical advantage of the ASM method is that it allows designers, programmers, verifiers and testers a) to exploit the abstraction/refinement pair, within one coherent mathematical framework, for a *systematic separation of different concerns* and b) to use any fruitful *combination of whatever precise techniques* are available—whether or not formalized within a specific logic or programming language or tool—*to define*, experimentally *validate* and mathematically *verify* a series of accurate system models leading to compilable code.

References

1. Abrial, J.-R.: Event based sequential program development: application to constructing a pointer program. In: Araki, K., Gnesi, S., Mandrioli, D. (eds.) FME 2003. LNCS, vol. 2805, pp. 51–74. Springer, Heidelberg (2003)
2. Abrial, J.-R.: Event driven distributed program construction. Version 6 (August 2004)
3. Abrial, J.-R.: On constructing large computerized systems (a position paper). In: Proc. VSTTE, ETH Zürich (October 2005)
4. Anlauff, M., Kutter, P.: Xasm Open Source (2001), http://www.xasm.org/
5. Betarte, G., Gimenez, E., Loiseaux, C., Chetali, B.: Formavie: Formal modelling and verification of the java card 2.1.1 security architecture. In: Proc. eSmart (2002)
6. Börger, E.: A logical operational semantics for full Prolog. In: Börger, E., Kleine Büning, H., Richter, M.M. (eds.) CSL 1989. LNCS, vol. 440, pp. 36–64. Springer, Heidelberg (1990)
7. Börger, E.: A logical operational semantics of full Prolog. In: Rovan, B. (ed.) MFCS 1990. LNCS, vol. 452, pp. 1–14. Springer, Heidelberg (1990)
8. Börger, E.: A logical operational semantics for full Prolog. In: Moschovakis, Y.N. (ed.) Part III: Built-in predicates for files, terms, arithmetic and input-output, Berkeley Mathematical Sciences Research Institute Publications. Logic From Computer Science, vol. 21, pp. 17–50. Springer, Heidelberg (1992)
9. Börger, E.: Logic programming: The Evolving Algebra approach. In: Pehrson, B., Simon, I. (eds.) IFIP 13th World Computer Congress. Technology/Foundations, vol. I, pp. 391–395. Elsevier, Amsterdam (1994)
10. Börger, E.: The origins and the development of the ASM method for high-level system design and analysis. J. Universal Computer Science 8(1), 2–74 (2002)
11. Börger, E.: The ASM ground model method as a foundation of requirements engineering. In: Dershowitz, N. (ed.) Verification: Theory and Practice. LNCS, vol. 2772, pp. 145–160. Springer, Heidelberg (2004)
12. Börger, E.: The ASM refinement method. Formal Aspects of Computing 15, 237–257 (2003)
13. Börger, E.: The ASM method for system design and analysis. In: Gramlich, B. (ed.) FroCos 2005. LNCS (LNAI), vol. 3717, Springer, Heidelberg (2005)
14. Börger, E.: From Finite State Machines to Virtual Machines (Illustrating design patterns and event-B models). In: Cohors-Fresenborg, E., Schwank, I. (eds.) Präzisionswerkzeug Logik–Gedenkschrift zu Ehren von Dieter Rödding, Forschungsinstitut für Mathematikdidaktik Osnabr(2006) ISBN 3-925386-56-4
15. Börger, E., Dässler, K.: Prolog: DIN papers for discussion. ISO/IEC JTCI SC22 WG17 Prolog Standardization Document 58, National Physical Laboratory, Middlesex, England, (1990)
16. Börger, E., Durdanović, I.: Correctness of compiling Occam to Transputer code. Computer Journal 39(1), 52–92 (1996)
17. Börger, E., Fruja, G., Gervasi, V., Stärk, R.: A high-level modular definition of the semantics of C#. Theoretical Computer Science 336(2–3), 235–284 (2005)

18. Börger, E., Glässer, U., Müller, W.: The semantics of behavioral VHDL 1993 descriptions. In: EURO-DAC 1994. European Design Automation Conference with EURO-VHDL 1994, pp. 500–505. IEEE Computer Society Press, Los Alamitos (1994)

19. Börger, E., Päppinghaus, P., Schmid, J.: Report on a practical application of ASMs in software design. In: Gurevich, Y., Kutter, P.W., Odersky, M., Thiele, L. (eds.) ASM 2000. LNCS, vol. 1912, pp. 361–366. Springer, Heidelberg (2000)

20. Börger, E., Rosenzweig, D.: A mathematical definition of full Prolog. Science of Computer Programming 24, 249–286 (1995)

21. Börger, E., Rosenzweig, D.: The WAM – definition and compiler correctness. In: Beierle, C., Plümer, L. (eds.) Logic Programming: Formal Methods and Practical Applications. Studies in Computer Science and Artificial Intelligence, vol. 11, ch. 2, pp. 20–90. North-Holland, Amsterdam (1995)

22. Börger, E., Stärk, R.F.: Abstract State Machines. In: A Method for High-Level System Design and Analysis, Springer, Heidelberg (2003)

23. Brooks, F.P.J.: No silver bullet. Computer 20(4), 10–19 (1987)

24. Carnap, R.: The methodological character of theoretical concepts. In: Feigl, H., Scriven, M. (eds.) Minnesota Studies in the Philosophy of Science, vol. 2, pp. 33–76. University of Minnesota Press (1956)

25. Del Castillo, G.: The ASM Workbench. A Tool Environment for Computer-Aided Analysis and Validation of Abstract State Machine Models. PhD thesis, Universität Paderborn, Germany (2001)

26. Del Castillo, G., Winter, K.: Model checking support for the ASM high-level language. In: Schwartzbach, M.I., Graf, S. (eds.) ETAPS 2000 and TACAS 2000. LNCS, vol. 1785, pp. 331–346. Springer, Heidelberg (2000)

27. Dijkstra, E.W.: Notes on structured programming. In: Dahl, O.-J., Dijkstra, E.W., Hoare, C.A.R. (eds.) Structured Programming, pp. 1–82. Academic Press, London (1972)

28. Dold, A.: A formal representation of Abstract State Machines using PVS. Verifix Technical Report Ulm/6.2, Universität Ulm, Germany (July 1998)

29. Dold, A., Gaul, T., Vialard, V., Zimmermann, W.: ASM-based mechanized verification of compiler back-ends. In: Glässer, U., Schmitt, P. (eds.) Proc. 5th Int. Workshop on ASMs, Magdeburg University, pp. 50–67 (1998)

30. Farahbod, R., et al.: The CoreASM Project, http://www.coreasm.org

31. Farahbod, R., Gervasi, V., Glässer, U.: CoreASM: An Extensible ASM Execution Engine. Fundamenta Informaticae XXI (2006)

32. Foundations of Software Engineering Group, Microsoft Research. AsmL (2001), http://research.microsoft.com/foundations/AsmL/

33. Fruja, N.G.: The Correctness of the Definite Assignment Analysis in C#. J. Object Technology 3(9), 29–52 (2004)

34. Fruja, N.G.: A Modular Design for the.NET CLR Architecture. In: Beauquier, A.S.D., Börger, E. (eds.) 12th International Workshop on Abstract State Machines, ASM 2005, Paris, France, pp. 175–199 (March 2005)

35. Fruja, N.G.: Type Safety of Generics for the.NET Common Language Runtime. In: Sestoft, P. (ed.) ESOP 2006 and ETAPS 2006. LNCS, vol. 3924, pp. 325–341. Springer, Heidelberg (2006)

36. Fruja, N.G., Börger, E.: Analysis of the.NET CLR Exception Handling. In: Skala, V., Nienaltowski, P. (eds.) 3rd International Conference on .NET Technologies, NET 2005, Pilsen, Czech Republic, pp. 65–75 (May–June 2005)

37. Fruja, N.G., Börger, E.: Modeling the.NET CLR Exception Handling Mechanism for a Mathematical Analysis. Journal of Object Technology 5(3), 5–34 (2006)

38. Gargantini, A., Riccobene, E.: Encoding Abstract State Machines in PVS. In: Gurevich, Y., Kutter, P.W., Odersky, M., Thiele, L. (eds.) ASM 2000. LNCS, vol. 1912, pp. 303–322. Springer, Heidelberg (2000)
39. Gawanmeh, A., Tahar, S., Winter, K.: Interfacing ASMs with the MDG tool. In: Börger, E., Gargantini, A., Riccobene, E. (eds.) ASM 2003. LNCS, vol. 2589, pp. 278–292. Springer, Heidelberg (2003)
40. Glässer, U., Gotzhein, R., Prinz, A.: Formal semantics of sdl-2000: Status and perspectives. Computer Networks 42(3), 343–358 (2003)
41. Goerigk, W., Dold, A., Gaul, T., Goos, G., Heberle, A., von Henke, F.W., Hoffmann, U., Langmaack, H., Pfeifer, H., Ruess, H., Zimmermann, W.: Compiler correctness and implementation verification: The verifix approach. In: Fritzson, P. (ed.) Int. Conf. on Compiler Construction, Proc. Poster Session of CC 1996, Linköping, Sweden (1996); IDA Technical Report LiTH-IDA-R-96-12
42. Habibi, A.: Framework for System Level Verification: The SystemC Case. PhD thesis, Concordia University, Montreal (July 2005)
43. Haeberer, A.M., Maibaum, T.S.E.: Scientific rigour, an answer to a pragmatic question: a linguistic framework for software engineering. In: International Conference on Software Engineering, Toronto, vol. 23 (2001)
44. Haeberer, A.M., Maibaum, T.S.E., Cengarle, M.V.: Knowing what requirements specifications specify (typoscript 2001)
45. Heimdahl, M.P.E.: Let's not forget validation. In: Meyer, B., Woodcock, J.C.P. (eds.) Verified Software: Theories, Tools, and Experiments (VSTTE 2005). LNCS, vol. 4171. Springer, Heidelberg (2008) (this volume)
46. Hoare, C.A.R.: The verifying compiler: A grand challenge for computing research. J. ACM 50(1), 63–69 (2003)
47. Jones, C.B.: What can we do (technically) to get the right specification. In: Meyer, B., Woodcock, J.C.P. (eds.) Verified Software: Theories, Tools, and Experiments (VSTTE 2005). LNCS, vol. 4171, pp. 64–69. Springer, Heidelberg (2008) (this volume)
48. Jula, H.V., Fruja, N.G.: An Executable Specification of C#. In: Beauquier, A.S.D., Börger, E. (eds.) 12th International Workshop on Abstract State Machines, ASM 2005, Paris, France, pp. 275–287 (March 2005); University Paris 12
49. Kalinov, A., Kossatchev, A., Petrenko, A., Posypkin, M., Shishkov, V.: Using ASM specifications for compiler testing. In: Börger, E., Gargantini, A., Riccobene, E. (eds.) ASM 2003. LNCS, vol. 2589, p. 415. Springer, Heidelberg (2003)
50. Klein, G., Nipkow, T.: A machine-checked model for a Java-like language, virtual machine and compiler. ACM Trans. Prog. Lang. Syst. (2006)
51. Nanchen, S., Stärk, R.F.: A security logic for Abstract State Machines. TR 423 CS Dept., ETH Zürich (2003)
52. Popper, K.: Logik der Forschung. Zur Erkenntnishtoeire der modernen Naturwissenschaft. Wien (1935)
53. Glass, R.L.: Facts and Fallacies of Software Engineering. Addison-Wesley, Reading (2003)
54. Schellhorn, G.: Verifikation abstrakter Zustandsmaschinen. PhD thesis, Universität Ulm, Germany (1999)
55. Schellhorn, G.: Verification of ASM refinements using generalized forward simulation. J. Universal Computer Science 7(11), 952–979 (2001)
56. Schellhorn, G.: ASM refinement and generalizations of forward simulation in data refinement: A comparison. Theoretical Computer Science 336(2-3), 403–436 (2005)
57. Schellhorn, G., Ahrendt, W.: Reasoning about Abstract State Machines: The WAM case study. J. Universal Computer Science 3(4), 377–413 (1997)

58. Schellhorn, G., Ahrendt, W.: The WAM case study: Verifying compiler correctness for Prolog with KIV. In: Bibel, W., Schmitt, P. (eds.) Automated Deduction – A Basis for Applications, volume III: Applications, pp. 165–194. Kluwer Academic Publishers, Dordrecht (1998)

59. Schmid, J.: Executing ASM specifications with AsmGofer, http://www.tydo.de/AsmGofer

60. Schmid, J.: Compiling Abstract State Machines to C++. J. Universal Computer Science 7(11), 1069–1088 (2001)

61. Schmid, J.: Refinement and Implementation Techniques for Abstract State Machines. PhD thesis, University of Ulm, Germany (2002)

62. Stärk, R.F., Börger, E.: An ASM specification of C# threads and the.NET memory model. In: Zimmermann, W., Thalheim, B. (eds.) ASM 2004. LNCS, vol. 3052, Springer, Heidelberg (2004)

63. Stärk, R.F., Nanchen, S.: A logic for Abstract State Machines. J. Universal Computer Science 7(11), 981–1006 (2001)

64. Stärk, R.F., Schmid, J., Börger, E.: Java and the Java Virtual Machine: Definition, Verification, Validation. Springer, Heidelberg (2001)

65. Teich, J., Kutter, P., Weper, R.: Description and simulation of microprocessor instruction sets using ASMs. In: Gurevich, Y., Kutter, P.W., Odersky, M., Thiele, L. (eds.) ASM 2000. LNCS, vol. 1912, pp. 266–286. Springer, Heidelberg (2000)

66. Teich, J., Weper, R., Fischer, D., Trinkert, S.: A joint architecture/compiler design environment for ASIPs. In: Proc. Int. Conf. on Compilers, Architectures and Synthesis for Embedded Systems (CASES 2000), November 2000, pp. 26–33. ACM Press, San Jose (2000)

67. Vajihollahi, M.: High level specification and validation of the business process execution language for web services. Master's thesis, School of Computing Science at Simon Fraser University (March 2004)

68. Winter, K.: Model checking for Abstract State Machines. J. Universal Computer Science 3(5), 689–701 (1997)

69. Wirth, N.: Program development by stepwise refinement. Commun. ACM 14(4) (1971)

Scalable Software Model Checking Using Design for Verification*

Tevfik Bultan and Aysu Betin-Can

Department of Computer Science
University of California
Santa Barbara, CA 93106, USA
{bultan,aysu}@cs.ucsb.edu

Abstract. There has been significant progress in automated verification techniques based on model checking. However, scalable software model checking remains a challenging problem. We believe that this problem can be addressed using a design for verification approach based on design patterns that facilitate scalable automated verification. We have been investigating a design for verification approach based on the following principles: 1) use of stateful, behavioral interfaces which isolate the behavior and enable modular verification, 2) an assume-guarantee style verification strategy which separates verification of the behavior from the verification of the conformance to the interface specifications, 3) a general model checking technique for interface verification, and 4) domain specific and specialized verification techniques for behavior verification. So far we have applied this approach to verification of synchronization operations in concurrent programs and to verification of interactions among multiple peers in composite web services. The case studies we conducted indicate that scalable software verification is achievable in these application domains using our design for verification approach.

1 Introduction

Automated software verification techniques based on model checking have improved significantly in recent years. When combined with the increasing computing power, these techniques are capable of analyzing complex software systems as demonstrated by numerous case studies. However, most applications of software model checking succeed either by requiring some manual intervention or by focusing on a specific type of software or a specific type of problem. It is still unclear if there is a general framework for scalable software model checking.

Scalability of software model checking depends on extracting compact models from programs that hide the details that are not relevant to the properties being verified. This typically requires a reverse engineering step in which either user guidance or static analysis techniques (or both) are used to rediscover some information about the software that may be known to its developers at design time. A design for verification approach, which enables software developers to document the design decisions that can be useful

---

* This work is supported by NSF grant CCR-0341365.

B. Meyer and J. Woodcock (Eds.): Verified Software, LNCS 4171, pp. 337–346, 2008.

for verification, may improve the scalability and therefore the applicability of model checking techniques significantly.

We believe that it is possible to develop a general design for verification approach based on stateful, behavioral interfaces which can be used to decouple behavior of a module from its environment. This decoupling enables an assume-guarantee style modular verification strategy which separates verification of the behavior from the verification of the conformance to the interface specifications. Interface verification can be performed using software model checking techniques that work at the code level (e.g., [22]) whereas behavior verification can be performed using domain specific and specialized verification techniques (e.g., [25]). The modularity and the specialization of the verification tasks are crucial for the scalability of our approach.

We proposed a set of design patterns which facilitate modular specification of interfaces and behaviors. These design patterns are supported by a set of helper classes which are used as is. Based on these helper classes we automate the model extraction and environment generation steps required for model checking.

So far we have applied our design for verification approach to verification of synchronization operations in concurrent programs [1,2,5,25] and to verification of interactions among multiple peers in composite web services [3,4]. We believe that this approach can be extended to a general framework in which software developers write behavioral interfaces while they are building different modules, and these interfaces are used by the model checking tools to achieve scalable software verification.

Related Work. Earlier work on design for verification focused on verification of UML models [19] and use of design patterns in improving the efficiency of automated verification techniques [17]. There has been some work on behavioral interfaces in which interfaces of software modules are specified as a set of constraints, and algorithms for interface compatibility checking are developed [8]. Also, there has been work on extending type systems with stateful interfaces [9], suggesting an approach in which interface checking is treated as a part of type checking. Assume guarantee style verification of software components has also been studied [18] in which LTL formulas are used to specify the environment (i.e., the interface) of a component. Automated environment generation for software components has been investigated using techniques such as inserting nondeterminism into the code and eliminating or restricting the input arguments by using side effect and points-to analyses [14,20,21]. Finally, ESC Java [11] uses an approach based on design by contract and automated theorem proving which is similar to what we are proposing here for model checking.

Below, we will first discuss interfaces and modularity and interface-based verification in general terms. Later, we will discuss application of these principles to verification of synchronization operations in concurrent programs and to verification of interactions among multiple peers in composite web services. We will end the paper with a brief discussion of what needs to be done to generalize our approach.

2   Interfaces, Modularity and Interface-Based Verification

Modularization of the verification task is necessary for its scalability. Modularization requires specification (or discovery) of the module interfaces. In order to achieve modularity in verification, the module interfaces have to provide just the right amount of information. If the interfaces provide too much information, then they are not helpful in achieving modularity in verification. On the other hand, if they provide too little information, then they are not helpful for verifying interesting properties. Interface of a module should provide the necessary information about how to interact with that module without giving all the details of its internal structure.

Current programming languages do not provide adequate mechanisms for representing module interfaces because they provide too little information. Think of an object class in an object oriented language. The interface of an object class consists of names and types of its fields, and names, return and argument types of its methods. Such interface specifications do not contain sufficient information for most verification tasks. For example, such an interface does not contain any information about the order the methods of the class should be called. In order to achieve modular verification, module interfaces need to be richer than the ones provided by the existing programming languages.

We believe that finite state machines provide an appropriate tool for specification of module interfaces. Such interface machines can be used to specify the order of method calls or any other information that is necessary to interact with a module. As an example, consider the verification of a concurrent bounded buffer implementation. Access to the buffer operations can be protected with user defined synchronization operations. For example, one requirement could be that the synchronization method *read-enter* should be called before the *read* method for the buffer is called. Such constraints can be specified using an interface machine which defines the required ordering for the method calls. For complex interfaces one could use an extended state machine model and provide information about some of the input and output parameters in a module's interface. Another possible extension is to use hierarchical state machines for interfaces [3].

Behavioral interfaces enable an assume-guarantee style verification strategy which separates behavior and interface verification steps. Interfaces enable isolation of the behavior of interest by separating it from its environment. The behavior of interest could be the behavior of an object encapsulated in an object class or it could be the interaction among multiple components in a distributed system. A behavioral interface for the object class can be used to isolate the object behavior by decoupling it from its environment. Similarly, interfaces of different components can be used to isolate the interaction among multiple components from the component implementations.

Behavior Verification: In our interface-based verification approach, during behavior verification it is assumed that there are no interface violations in the software. Based on this assumption, interfaces are used as environment models. Environment generation is a crucial problem in software model checking [14,21]. We are suggesting the use of a design for verification approach to attack this problem. Software developers are required to write interfaces during the software development process so that these interfaces can then be used as a model of the environment during behavior verification. Using such interfaces we can encapsulate the behavior in question and perform the verification on this encapsulated behavior separately. Note that, interfaces should represent all the constraints about the environment that are relevant to the behavior of interest, i.e., the interfaces should provide all the information about the environment that is necessary to verify the behavior. This is analogous to requiring programmers to declare types to enable type checking.

During behavior verification one could use domain specific verification techniques. Recall the concurrent buffer example above and assume that this buffer is implemented as a linked list. During behavior verification we can assume that the threads that access to this buffer obey its interface and we can verify the correctness of the linked list implementation without worrying about the interface violations. For the verification of the linked list we can use specialized verification techniques such as shape analysis [23] or infinite state model checking [6,24]. Since, interfaces allow isolation of the behavior, application of domain specific verification techniques (which may not be applicable or scalable in general) becomes feasible. These domain specific verification techniques may enable verification of stronger and more complex properties than that can be achieved by more generic techniques.

Interface Verification: During interface verification we need to verify that there are no interface violations. If interfaces of different modules are specified uniformly, for example using finite state machines, then they can be verified using a general interface verification technique. The verification techniques developed for the purpose of applying model checking directly to existing programming languages can be used for interface verification [13,22].

During interface verification, the interfaces can be used to abstract the behavior that is verified during behavior verification. Recall the concurrent buffer example. Interface verification step for this example requires that each thread which has access to the concurrent buffer has to be checked for interface violations. During the verification of a thread, the behavior of the concurrent buffer can be abstracted by replacing the concurrent buffer by its interface machine. Note that, here, we are assuming that the concurrent buffer itself does not make calls to its methods directly or indirectly. If that is not the case, the behavior of the concurrent buffer and any other part of the code which is not relevant to the interface violations can be abstracted away using static analysis techniques such as slicing, since we are only interested in interface violations.

3   Applications

So far we have applied the approach discussed above to verification of synchronization operations in Java programs and to verification of interactions among multiple peers participating to a web service implemented in Java.

3.1   Application to Concurrent Programming

We applied the above principles in developing a design for verification approach for concurrent programming in Java with the goal of eliminating synchronization errors from Java programs using model checking techniques [1,2,25]. We developed a design pattern, called concurrency controller pattern, in which synchronization policies for coordinating the interactions among multiple threads are specified using concurrency controller classes. The behavior of a concurrency controller is specified as a set of actions (forming the methods of the controller class) where each action consists of a set of

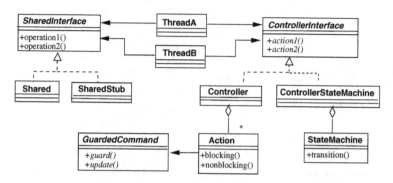

Fig. 1. Concurrency Controller Pattern Class Diagram

guarded commands. The controller interface is specified as a finite state machine which defines the order that the actions of the controller can be executed by each thread.

Figure 1 shows the class diagram for the concurrency controller pattern. The ControllerInterface is a Java interface which defines the names of the controller actions. The Controller class contains the actions specifying the controller behavior. The Action class is the helper class containing a set of guarded commands and implements the semantics of action execution. This class is provided with the concurrency controller pattern, i.e., the developers do not need to modify it. Same holds for the GuardedCommand Java interface. The ControllerStateMachine class is the controller interface. This class has an instance of the StateMachine which is a finite state machine implementation provided with the pattern and can be used as is. The SharedInterface is the Java interface for the shared data. The actual implementation of the shared data is the Shared class. The class SharedStub specifies the constraints on accessing the shared data based on the interface states of the controller.

Recall the concurrent buffer example. We can coordinate the concurrent accesses to this buffer with a controller class which implements a bounded buffer synchronization protected by a reader-writer lock. The synchronization strategy implemented by this controller will allow multiple threads to read the contents of the buffer at the same time but it will only allow a thread to insert or remove an item from the buffer when there is no other thread accessing the buffer. Additionally, this concurrency controller will ensure that a thread that wants to insert an item to the buffer will wait while the buffer is full. Similarly, a thread that wants to remove an item from the buffer will wait while the buffer is empty. We call the concurrency controller which implements this synchronization BB-RW.

The BB-RW controller can be implemented using four variables and five actions. The variables are nR denoting the number of readers in the critical section, busy denoting if there is a writer in the critical section, count denoting the number of items in the buffer, and size denoting the size of the buffer. The actions are r_enter, r_exit, w_enter_produce, w_enter_consume, and w_exit. A part of the BB-RW controller implementation is given in Figure 3. The interface of the BB-RW controller is shown in Figure 2 where the transitions of the interface machine are labeled with the actions of the BB-RW controller.

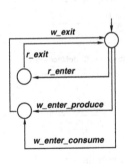

```
class BBRWController implements BBRWInterface{
  int nR; boolean busy; int count; final int size;
  r_enter=new GuardedCommand() {
    public boolean guard() {return (!busy);}
    public void update() {nR = nR+1;}};
  r_exit=new GuardedCommand() {
    public boolean guard() {return true;}
    public void update() {nR = nR-1;}};
  w_enter_produce=new GuardedCommand() {
    public boolean guard() {
      return (nR == 0 && !busy && count<size);}
    public void update() {
      busy = true; count=count+1;}};
  w_exit_consume=new GuardedCommand() {
    public boolean guard() {
      return (nR == 0 && !busy && count>0); }
    public void update() {
      busy = true; count=count-1;}};
  w_exit= new GuardedCommand() {
    public boolean guard() { return true; }
    public void update() { busy = false; } };
  ...
}
```

Fig. 2. Interface of BB-RW   **Fig. 3.** BB-RW Controller Implementation

We developed a modular verification strategy based on the concurrency controller pattern. We first verify automatically generated infinite state models of concurrency controllers using the symbolic and infinite state model checker Action Language Verifier [24], assuming that the threads using the controllers obey their interfaces. Next, we verify this assumption using the explicit and finite state model checker Java PathFinder [22]. In this modular verification strategy the two verification steps are completely decoupled. Moreover, during the verification of the threads for interface violations there is no need to consider interleavings of different threads since we are only interested in the order of calls to the controller methods by each individual thread, and since the only interaction among different threads is through shared objects that are protected using the concurrency controllers, i.e., we can verify each thread in isolation [5].

We conducted two case studies to demonstrate the effectiveness of this approach. The first case study was a concurrent editor which was implemented with 2,800 lines of Java code using a client-server architecture [2]. The concurrent editor allows multiple users to edit a document concurrently as long as they are editing different paragraphs and maintains a consistent view of the shared document among the client nodes and the server. In this case study there were 4 mutex controller instances, one reader-writer controller per paragraph, one bounded buffer (with mutex lock) controller per paragraph, and one barrier controller. The concurrent editor had 4 threads in the client node and 2 threads in the server node. The second case study [5] was conducted on a safety critical air traffic control software called Tactical Separation Assisted Flight Environment (TSAFE) [10]. We reengineered the distributed client-server version of TSAFE which consists of 21,000 lines of Java code. The server node stores flight trajectories in a database, receives current flight data from a radar feed through a network connection to update the database, and monitors the conformance of the flights to their trajectories. The client nodes display the flight status information. The reengineered system used 2 reader-writer controller instances and 3 mutex controller instances. TSAFE had 3 threads in the client node and 4 threads in the server node. In both of these case studies, the behavior verification of the controllers took less than a few seconds and used less than 11 MB memory. In these case studies we isolated the threads for interface verification with automatically synthesized drivers and stubs, i.e., the interface verification was performed thread modularly. Interface verification for some threads took several hundreds seconds and for some of them it took a few dozen seconds. The longest interface verification time we recorded was 1636.62 seconds. The maximum memory consumption recorded during interface verification was less than 140 MB.

3.2 Application to Web Services

We also developed a design for verification approach for verification of web services based on the above principles [3,4]. We focused on composite web services which consist of asynchronously communicating peers. Our goal was to automatically verify properties of interactions among such peers. We modeled such interactions as conversations, the global sequence of messages that are exchanged among the peers [7]. We proposed a design pattern for the development of such web services which enables a modular, assume-guarantee style verification strategy. In the proposed design pattern, called peer controller pattern, each peer is associated with a behavioral interface description which specifies how that peer will interact with other peers. Assuming that the participating peers behave according to their interfaces, we verify safety and liveness properties about the global behavior of the composite web service during behavior verification. During interface verification, we check that each peer implementation conforms to its interface. Using the modularity in the proposed design pattern, we were able to perform the interface verification of each peer and the behavior verification as separate steps. Our experiments showed that, using this modular approach, one can automatically and efficiently verify web service implementations.

The class diagram of the peer controller pattern is shown in Figure 4. The application logic is implemented with the `ApplicationThread`. Each instance of this thread is identified with a session number. The application thread communicates asynchronously with other peers through the `Communicator` which is a Java interface that provides standardized access to the communication implementation. The `CommunicationController` class is a servlet that performs the actual communication. Since it is tedious to write such a class, we provide a servlet implementation (`PeerServlet`)

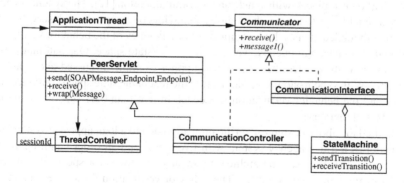

Fig. 4. Peer Controller Pattern Class Diagram

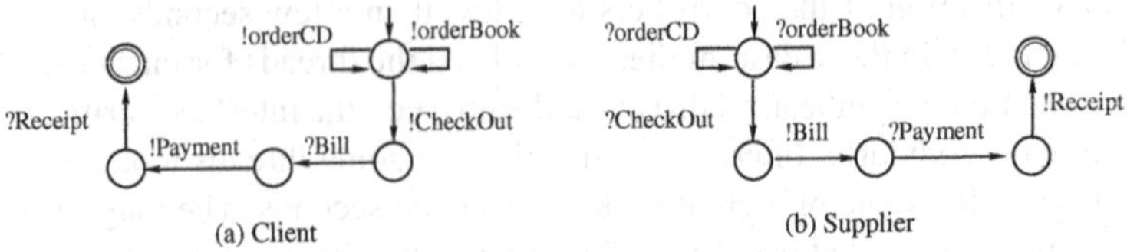

(a) Client   (b) Supplier

Fig. 5. Client-Supplier Example

that uses JAXM [16] in asynchronous mode. The `PeerServlet` is associated with a `ThreadContainer` which contains application thread references indexed by session numbers. When a message with an associated session number is received from the JAXM provider, it is delegated to the thread indexed with that session number. The behavioral interface of each peer is written as an instance of the `Communicator-Interface` class and contains a finite state machine specification written using the provided `StateMachine` helper class.

Consider a composite web service with two peers: one client and one supplier. The client peer places arbitrary number of CD and book orders. After ordering the products, the client issues a *CheckOut* message. The supplier calculates the total price and sends a bill to the client. Client sends the payment and gets a receipt from the supplier. The state machines defining the contracts of these peers are shown in Figure 5. We verified the behavior of this example with different queue sizes using the Spin model checker [15]. Note that, using the behavioral interfaces in the peer controller pattern, we can easily extract the behavior specification characterizing the interactions of a web service composition. For the example shown in 5, the state space of the behavior specification increases exponentially with the size of the queues. In fact, the number of reachable states for this example is infinite if unbounded queues are used. The exponential growth in the state space affects the performance of the Spin model checker significantly. In fact, Spin ran out of memory when the queue size was set to 15.

We adapted the synchronizability analysis [12] into our framework in order to verify properties of composite web services in the presence of asynchronous communication with unbounded queues. A composite web service is called synchronizable if its global interaction behavior (i.e., the set of conversations) does not change when asynchronous communication is replaced with synchronous communication [12]. The synchronizability analysis enables us to reason about global behaviors of composite web services with respect to unbounded queues. It also improves the efficiency of the behavior verification by removing the message queues, which reduces the state space. Our automated synchronizability analyzer identified the client-supplier example discussed above as synchronizable. With synchronous communication the reachable state space contained only 68 states and the behavior verification succeeded in less than 0.01 seconds using less than 1.5 MB of memory.

We applied the above design for verification approach to a loan approval system with three peers [4], a travel agency system with five peers, and an order handling system with five peers [3]. We used hierarchical finite state machines for specifying the peer interfaces of the latter two examples. The behavior verification for all these examples took a few seconds. Using the automated synchronizability analysis, we identified that all of these examples are synchronizable. This result lead to improvements in the behavior verification since synchronous communication results in less number of states. The travel agency system mentioned above had an infinite set of reachable states. Using synchronizability analysis, we were able to verify the global behavior of this example for unbounded message queues. During the verification of the peer implementations, we used the peer interfaces to isolate the peers. This caused a significant reduction in the state space which improved the performance of the interface verification. The interface verification for any of the peers in these examples took a few seconds (at most 9.72 seconds) and did not consume a significant amount of memory (at most 19.69 MB).

4   Conclusions

Our experience in design for verification of concurrent and distributed software systems leads us to believe that software model checking can become a scalable verification technique as long as the software developers write behavioral interfaces which can be exploited for modular verification. In the application domains discussed above, we implemented this approach by providing design patterns that enable specification of behavioral interfaces in existing programming languages. Alternatively, one can extend the programming languages with primitives that allow the specification of behavioral interfaces. Either way, for scalability of model checking, we need to investigate more ways of collecting information about the structure of software during the design phase rather then reverse engineering programs to discover their structure during verification.

There are numerous challenges to be addressed in the behavior and interface verification steps discussed above. We need a large set of domain specific verification techniques to handle different types of behavior verification. The interface-based verification approach discussed above can be used to integrate a diverse set of verification techniques under a single framework. One of the biggest challenges in the presented approach is the development of a uniform interface verification technique. Although this is a challenging problem it is less challenging than the general software model checking problem since it only focuses on interface violations. Automated abstraction techniques may be used more effectively to exploit this focus, and, when combined with a modular verification strategy, this can lead to scalable verification.

References

1. Betin-Can, A., Bultan, T.: Interface-based specification and verification of concurrency controllers. Proc. SoftMC, ENTCS, vol. 89 (2003)
2. Betin-Can, A., Bultan, T.: Verifiable concurrent programming using concurrency controllers. In: Proc. 19th IEEE Int. Conf. on ASE, pp. 248–257 (2004)
3. Betin-Can, A., Bultan, T.: Verifiable web services with hierarchichal interfaces. In: Proc. IEEE Int. Conf. on Web Services, pp. 85–94 (2005)
4. Betin-Can, A., Bultan, T., Fu, X.: Design for verification for asynchronously communicating web services. In: Proc. 14th WWW Conf. pp. 750–759 (2005)
5. Betin-Can, A., Bultan, T., Lindvall, M., Topp, S., Lux, B.: Application of design for verification with concurrency controllers to air traffic control software. In: Proc. 20th IEEE Int. Conf. on ASE (to appear, 2005)

6. Boigelot, B., Godefroid, P., Williams, B., Wolper, P.: The power of QDDs. In: Proc. 4th Static Analysis Symp. pp. 172–186 (1997)
7. Bultan, T., Fu, X., Hull, R., Su, J.: Conversation specification: A new approach to design and analysis of e-service composition. In: Proc. 12th WWW Conf. pp. 403–410 (2003)
8. Chakrabarti, A., de Alfaro, L., Henzinger, T.A., Jurdziński, M., Mang, F.Y.C.: Interface compatibility checking for software modules. In: Brinksma, E., Larsen, K.G. (eds.) CAV 2002. LNCS, vol. 2404, pp. 428–441. Springer, Heidelberg (2002)
9. DeLine, R., Fahndrich, M.: Typestates for objects. In: Odersky, M. (ed.) ECOOP 2004. LNCS, vol. 3086, pp. 465–490. Springer, Heidelberg (2004)
10. Dennis, G.: TSAFE: Building a trusted computing base for air traffic control software, Master's Thesis (2003)
11. Flanagan, C., Leino, K.R.M., Lillibridge, M., Nelson, G., Saxe, J.B., Stata, R.: Extended static checking for java. In: Proc. POPL, pp. 234–245 (2002)
12. Fu, X., Bultan, T., Su, J.: Analysis of interacting BPEL web services. In: Proc. 13th WWW Conf. pp. 621–630 (2004)
13. Godefroid, P.: Model checking for programming languages using VeriSoft. In: Proc. POPL, January 1997, pp. 174–186 (1997)
14. Godefroid, P., Colby, C., Jagadeesan, L.: Automatically closing open reactive programs. In: Proc. PLDI, June 1998, pp. 345–357 (1998)
15. Holzmann, G.J.: The model checker spin. IEEE Transactions on Software Eng. 23(5), 279–295 (1997)
16. Java API for XML messaging (JAXM). http://java.sun.com/xml/jaxm/
17. Mehlitz, P.C., Penix, J.: Design for verification using design patterns to build reliable systems. In: Proc. Work. on Component-Based Soft. Eng. (2003)
18. Pasareanu, C.S., Dwyer, M.B., Huth, M.: Assume guarantee model checking of software: A comparative case study. In: Dams, D.R., Gerth, R., Leue, S., Massink, M. (eds.) SPIN 1999. LNCS, vol. 1680, pp. 168–183. Springer, Heidelberg (1999)
19. Sharygina, N., Browne, J.C., Kurshan, R.P.: A formal object-oriented analysis for software reliability: Design for verification. In: Hussmann, H. (ed.) ETAPS 2001 and FASE 2001. LNCS, vol. 2029, pp. 318–332. Springer, Heidelberg (2001)
20. Tkachuk, O., Dwyer, M.B.: Adapting side-effects analysis for modular program model checking. In: Proc. ASE, pp. 116–129 (2003)
21. Tkachuk, O., Dwyer, M.B., Pasareanu, C.: Automated environment generation for software model checking. In: Proc. ESEC/FSE, pp. 188–197 (2003)
22. Visser, W., Havelund, K., Brat, G., Park, S.: Model checking programs. Automated Software Engineering Journal 10(2), 203–232 (2003)
23. Wilhelm, R., Sagiv, M., Reps, T.: Shape analysis. In: Proc. 9th Int. Conf. on Compiler Construction, pp. 1–17 (2000)
24. Yavuz-Kahveci, T., Bartzis, C., Bultan, T.: Action language verifier, extended. In: Etessami, K., Rajamani, S.K. (eds.) CAV 2005. LNCS, vol. 3576, pp. 413–417. Springer, Heidelberg (2005)
25. Yavuz-Kahveci, T., Bultan, T.: Specification, verification, and synthesis of concurrency control components. In: Proc. ISSTA, pp. 169–179 (2002)

Model-Checking Software Using Precise Abstractions

Marsha Chechik and Arie Gurfinkel

Department of Computer Science, University of Toronto,
Toronto, ON M5S 3G4, Canada
{chechik,arie}@cs.toronto.edu

1   Introduction

Formal verification techniques are not yet widely used in the software industry, perhaps because software tends to be more complex than hardware, and the penalty for bugs is often lower (software can be patched after the release). Instead, a large amount of time and money is being spent on software testing, which misses many subtle errors, especially in concurrent programs. Increased use of concurrency, e.g., due to the popularity of web services, and the surge of complex viruses which exploit security vulnerabilities of software, make the problem of creating a verifying compiler for production-quality code essential and urgent.

Many formal techniques can effectively analyze *models* of software. However, obtaining these models directly from the program text is non-trivial. Not only are there language issues (pointers, dynamic memory allocation, object-orientation, dynamic thread creation) to deal with, but the most important problem is automatically determining the level of abstraction for creating such a model: it should be simple enough to analyze and yet detailed enough to be conclusive on the properties of interest. Thus, we believe that part of the challenge of creating a verifying compiler is creation of fully automated light-weight verification and validation techniques which help detect bugs and yet scale to handle large complex software. Furthermore, the techniques should be supported by a methodology that enables developers to pose questions about correctness of their programs and effectively understand the results of the analysis.

Software model-checking [BPR01, VHB+03] checks the program by either forcing it to "run" all of its behaviours up to a certain number of steps, or by static analysis. Pioneered by Microsoft's SLAM project, software model-checking has been successfully applied to checking Windows device drivers [BCLZ04], demonstrating that effective verification of single-threaded C programs is possible.

We believe that the existing techniques based on the CEGAR framework (see Figure 1) that use a theorem-prover for constructing models and a model-checker for exploration is a reasonable way to go for analyzing realistic programs. However, such methods should be enhanced in a number of directions if our goal is to create a truly effective program verifier. In Section 2, we describe our existing work on creating better abstractions. In Section 3, we discuss two approaches that we believe are essential for scaling automated analysis: reuse (via compositional analysis and regression verification) and combining static and dynamic reasoning. We conclude in Section 4.

B. Meyer and J. Woodcock (Eds.): Verified Software, LNCS 4171, pp. 347–353, 2008.
© IFIP International Federation for Information Processing 2008

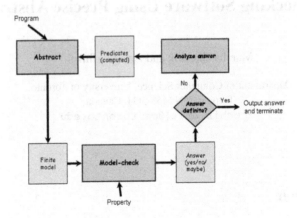

Fig. 1. Abstraction-refinement cycle

```
        int x;
        x = 0;                            ;
        if (x > 0)                        if (*)
(a)     {x++}                    (b)      {;}
        else                              else
           {x--}                             {;}
        P1:                               P1:
```

Fig. 2. (a): a C program where line P1 is not reachable; (b): an abstraction of (a) without predicates

2 Creating Precise Abstractions

Paraphrasing Reps and Sagiv [RSW04], we need abstractions that allow lack of precision and still enable reasoning. Thus, an abstraction is "good" if it can identify whether
the analysis of a property of interest is conclusive (i.e., when the property is true/false
in abstract model, it is true/false in the concrete one). With such an abstraction, we can
trust all of the answers except those that explicitly indicate "no information". Experience in static analysis [RSW04] showed that a logic with values other than just True and
False can be used effectively to create abstractions that preserve both truth and falsity:
when a property is inconclusive in the abstraction, the analysis simply returns a special
value Maybe.

Traditional model-checking approaches already build such abstractions. For example,
suppose we are interested in checking whether P1 is reachable in a program in Figure 2(a).
The initial abstraction for this program is just its control-flow graph, shown in Figure 2(b),
and it is clear that P1 is reachable by every path, i.e., regardless of the evaluation of the
condition of the if statement. However, since the conditions is "unknown", i.e., it is
neither True nor False, it is not possible to convert it into a boolean model, expected by

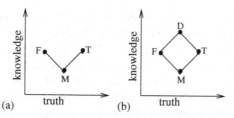

Fig. 3. Truth order vs. knowledge order of (a): Kleene and (b): Belnap logics

classical model-checking algorithms. Here, two choices are available. The standard approach, employed by such model-checkers as SLAM and BLAST, is to treat "unknown" as "non-deterministic", i.e., as *either* True or False, which looses some of the information available in the abstraction, but allows the use of classical model-checking algorithms. An alternative approach is to extend the analysis to partial models that can represent "unknown" explicitly. In fact, several such alternatives, based on Kleene and Belnap logics (see Figure 3, where the additional values stand for "maybe" and "disagreement") have been proposed over the years (e.g. [LT88, BG99, CDEG03, DGG97, GWC06]), but have not found their way into software model-checking practice because it is generally believed that they cannot be implemented efficiently. Thus, the additional power of already available rich abstractions remains untapped. Instead, the classical analysis needs to know exactly which execution of the if statement in the example in Figure 2(b) is feasible, which leads to generating an additional predicate and a refined abstraction. Clearly, this can and should be avoided.

To show that the additional reasoning power can be obtained without sacrificing performance, we have recently built a prototype software model-checker YASM [GC06] which implements the CEGAR framework using Belnap logic. The "disagreement" value is used to improve precision of our models. The remainder of this section comments on how our approach differs from the classical one, phase by phase.

The abstraction phase builds an abstract model, using a theorem-prover (YASM uses CVCLite [BB04]) to approximate the effect of each statement by a propositional formula over the available predicates. Abstracting each line of the program can take up to 2^n calls to the theorem prover, where n is the current number of predicates [GS97, BR01]. This number can be minimized by the application of constraint-satisfaction algorithms [Dec03], and we are currently experimenting with several CSP techniques to improve the performance of our tool. Overall, our abstraction phase is quite standard and is independent of our use of Belnap logic for the analysis.

For the model-checking phase, our current implementation uses a modification of our existing model-checker $\mathcal{X}$Chek [CDG02] which can naturally analyze models expressed in Belnap and Kleene logic. Just as other implementations of the CEGAR framework, we extended $\mathcal{X}$Chek's algorithms to exploit the control-flow graph of the program. We also discovered that it is relatively straightforward to incorporate and extend existing advances in software model-checking technology, such as interpolant-based predicate discovery [HJMM04] and lazy abstraction [HJMS02], into our framework.

Multi-valued witnesses and counterexamples produced by $\mathcal{X}$Chek correspond to partial proofs of correctness [GC03]. Thus, in the refinement phase, it is not necessary to check whether the execution produced by model-checking is feasible. Instead, we simply refine abstractions that produce the Maybe answer, by extracting new predicates for refinement from such partial proofs. Existing SLAM-like techniques can handle safety properties only (e.g., x is always positive, null pointer is never dereferenced, an assertion is always satisfied), partly because the traditional CEGAR framework depends on the linearity and the finiteness of generated counterexamples. Our approach can work regardless of the structure of the property, and thus can be applied to a larger set of properties, such as non-termination (to complement the technique of Cook et. al. [CPR05]) and liveness, as well as to programs with explicitly-defined *fair* computations.

The current version of the tool can check properties of C programs with complex language features such as structures, pointers, and recursion. We have also implemented lazy and eager abstraction and a limited form of non-determinism, which will lead to the analysis of concurrent programs. Our experience showed that the introduction of additional logic values does not reduce the feasibility of the analysis. In fact, the analysis remains as feasible as the classical one while making it possible to effectively reason about a larger class of properties.

3   Other Approaches to Effective Software Model-Checking

A verifying compiler should be able to effectively compile arbitrarily large and complex programs, from device drivers which can be effectively analyzed by state-of-the-art tools, to multi-user multi-threaded distributed systems. Thus, the problem of "scaling up" of software model-checking will remain pressing, and in this section we discuss two directions which we believe are essential for tackling this problem.

3.1   Reuse: Compositional and Regression Verification

Complexity of software is often addressed by decomposing a system into components. Thus, one way to improve scalability of a verification technique is by making it *compositional*. Over the years, various "assume-guarantee" techniques have been proposed to partition the verification effort across system components, and these can be adopted to reasoning about software. For example, to analyze a given thread, we can generate a most general environment that is sufficient to ensure that the desired property holds, and then check that the combination of other threads satisfies this environment. We also propose to apply symmetry reduction to build abstractions of concurrent systems with several similar components [WGC05]. We believe that a similar approach can be taken to facilitate the analysis of component-based and parameterized systems.

A major reason for SLAM's ability to analyze *recursive* programs is its compositional approach to processing functions. Instead of handling function calls by inlining, SLAM treats each function as a component, analyzes it once, and uses the computed *function summary* in the rest of the analysis.

However, the traditional notion of a component (i.e., a function, a module, a library, a thread), is not sufficient to effectively capture the complexity of software. This is especially highlighted by the recent popularity of non-traditional decomposition techniques such as aspect-based programming [EFB01].

An approach complementary to compositional verification is *regression verification*. As software gets changed frequently and needs to be "recompiled" (and thus reverified), the goal of this approach is to determine how much of the modified program needs to be reverified and reusing results of previous analyses whenever possible. In particular, it is necessary to determine when previous abstractions can be reused in checking the modified program. Further, changes in software often affect a large number of components, and we believe that the re-verification effort must be proportional to the amount of change, not to the number of affected components.

The lack of support for regression verification is particularly evident in the current applications of the CEGAR framework. In this framework, the abstraction of the program is constructed incrementally, with each new abstraction being a "small change" of the old. However, with the notable exception of [HJMS02, GC06], this is not taken into account during the verification phase. Early experience with regression verification shows a lot of promise. For example, Henzinger et al. [HJMS04] have demonstrated an almost "on-line" verification of some properties, where the program is verified as it is being written. Our own experience [GC06] shows that program analysis using Belnap logic that precisely identifies which results of a verification can be trusted, is particularly well suited to localizing the effort of regression verification. Moreover, our current work on merging [UC04] allows us to combine function and other component summaries obtained during different analysis passes through the program being modified.

3.2 Combining Static and Dynamic Approaches

The goal of static analysis is to establish a property of all executions of a program. In theory, it promises to completely eliminate dynamic analysis such as testing and runtime monitoring; moreover, this has been possible in practice, for analyzing relatively small components such as device drivers. We believe that static techniques alone may not scale to reasoning about large distributed programs that are routinely being built today, and may need to be supplemented by a careful application of dynamic analysis.

There are numerous ways in which static and dynamic analysis can be combined. For example, program execution can supplement theorem-proving in construction of abstract models [KGC04]: if the program reaches the desired state, then the value of the transition should be True; otherwise. no information is available.

Another approach is to combine results of testing to help navigate static analysis towards a possible error. We are currently exploring a variation of this approach by building an abstract model from regression test suites. Such suites are available with most large-scale software systems and can be thought of as detailed scenarios describing the system. We can combine these into partial behavioural models [UC04, WS00] to use in formal analysis.

4   Position

In this paper, we briefly discussed our position on using software model-checking for creating a verifying compiler. We are firm believers in automated symbolic verification which combines static and dynamic analyses, theorem-proving and model-checking, and think such techniques can be effectively extended to reasoning about complex software systems. We also believe that capturing the distinction between "the abstraction is not precise" and non-determinism is a key to pushing symbolic approaches towards reasoning about concurrency.

Currently, the automated verification research community has several competing approaches to analyzing software. We hope that bringing us together will facilitate tool sharing, so we can evaluate improvement of our tools against the state-of-the-art. We also hope that we can create and share a set of agreed-upon "requirements" for a verifying compiler. These requirements can take a form of a benchmark suite combining programs of varying complexity and size, with different language features and different correctness criteria.

References

[BB04]   Barrett, C., Berezin, S.: CVC Lite: A New Implementation of the Cooperating Validity Checker. In: Alur, R., Peled, D.A. (eds.) CAV 2004. LNCS, vol. 3114, pp. 515–518. Springer, Heidelberg (2004)

[BCLZ04]   Ball, T., Cook, B., Lahiri, S.K., Zhang, L.: "Theorem Proving for Predicate Abstraction Refinement". In: Alur, R., Peled, D.A. (eds.) CAV 2004. LNCS, vol. 3114, Springer, Heidelberg (2004)

[BG99]   Bruns, G., Godefroid, P.: Model Checking Partial State Spaces with 3-Valued Temporal Logics. In: Halbwachs, N., Peled, D.A. (eds.) CAV 1999. LNCS, vol. 1633, pp. 274–287. Springer, Heidelberg (1999)

[BPR01]   Ball, T., Podelski, A., Rajamani, S.: Boolean and Cartesian Abstraction for Model Checking C Programs. In: Margaria, T., Yi, W. (eds.) ETAPS 2001 and TACAS 2001. LNCS, vol. 2031, pp. 268–283. Springer, Heidelberg (2001)

[BR01]   Ball, T., Rajamani, S.: The SLAM Toolkit. In: Berry, G., Comon, H., Finkel, A. (eds.) CAV 2001. LNCS, vol. 2102, pp. 260–264. Springer, Heidelberg (2001)

[CDEG03]   Chechik, M., Devereux, B., Easterbrook, S., Gurfinkel, A.: "Multi-Valued Symbolic Model-Checking". ACM Transactions on Software Engineering and Methodology 12(4), 1–38 (2003)

[CDG02]   Chechik, M., Devereux, B., Gurfinkel, A.: χChek: A Multi-Valued Model-Checker. In: Brinksma, E., Larsen, K.G. (eds.) CAV 2002. LNCS, vol. 2404, pp. 505–509. Springer, Heidelberg (2002)

[CPR05]   Cook, B., Podelski, A., Rybalchenko, A.: Abstraction Refinement for Termination. In: Hankin, C., Siveroni, I. (eds.) SAS 2005. LNCS, vol. 3672, pp. 87–101. Springer, Heidelberg (2005)

[Dec03]   Dechter, R.: Constraint Processing. Morgan Kaufmann, San Francisco (2003)

[DGG97]   Dams, D., Gerth, R., Grumberg, O.: Abstract Interpretation of Reactive Systems. ACM Transactions on Programming Languages and Systems 2(19), 253–291 (1997)

[EFB01]   Elrad, T., Filman, R., Bader, A.: Aspect-Oriented Programming: Introduction. Communications of the ACM, pp. 29–32 (October 2001)

[GC03]   Gurfinkel, A., Chechik, M.: Proof-like Counterexamples. In: Garavel, H., Hatcliff, J. (eds.) ETAPS 2003 and TACAS 2003. LNCS, vol. 2619, pp. 160–175. Springer, Heidelberg (2003)

[GC06]   Gurfinkel, A., Chechik, M.: Why Waste a Perfectly Good Abstraction? In: Hermanns, H., Palsberg, J. (eds.) TACAS 2006 and ETAPS 2006. LNCS, vol. 3920, pp. 212–226. Springer, Heidelberg (2006)

[GS97]   Graf, S., Saïdi, H.: Construction of Abstract State Graphs with PVS. In: Grumberg, O. (ed.) CAV 1997. LNCS, vol. 1254, pp. 72–83. Springer, Heidelberg (1997)

[GWC06]   Gurfinkel, A., Wei, O., Chechik, M.: Systematic Construction of Abstractions for Model-Checking. In: Emerson, E.A., Namjoshi, K.S. (eds.) VMCAI 2006. LNCS, vol. 3855, pp. 381–397. Springer, Heidelberg (2005)

[HJMM04]   Henzinger, T.A., Jhala, R., Majumdar, R., McMillan, K.L.: Abstractions from Proofs. In: Proceedings of 31st ACM SIGPLAN-SIGACT Symposium on Principles of Programming Languages (POPL 2004), Venice, Italy, January 2004, pp. 232–244. ACM Press, New York (2004)

[HJMS02]   Henzinger, T., Jhala, R., Majumdar, R., Sutre, G.: Lazy Abstraction. In: Proceedings of 29th SIGPLAN-SIGACT Symposium on Principles of Programming Languages (POPL 2002), Portland, Oregon, January 2002, pp. 58–70. ACM Press, New York (2002)

[HJMS04]   Henzinger, T.A., Jhala, R., Majumdar, R., Sanvido, M.: Extreme Model Checking. In: Dershowitz, N. (ed.) Verification: Theory and Practice. LNCS, vol. 2772, pp. 332–358. Springer, Heidelberg (2004)

[KGC04]   Kroening, D., Groce, A., Clarke, E.: Counterexample Guided Abstraction Refinement via Program Execution. In: Proceedings of International Conference on Formal Engineering Methods, November 2004, pp. 224–238 (2004)

[LT88]   Larsen, K.G., Thomsen, B.: A Modal Process Logic. In: Proceedings of 3rd Annual Symposium on Logic in Computer Science (LICS 1988), pp. 203–210. IEEE Computer Society Press, Los Alamitos (1988)

[RSW04]   Reps, T.W., Sagiv, M., Wilhelm, R.: Static Program Analysis via 3-Valued Logic. In: Alur, R., Peled, D.A. (eds.) CAV 2004. LNCS, vol. 3114, pp. 15–30. Springer, Heidelberg (2004)

[UC04]   Uchitel, S., Chechik, M.: Merging Partial Behavioural Models. In: Proceedings of 12th ACM SIGSOFT International Symposium on Foundations of Software Engineering, November 2004, pp. 43–52 (2004)

[VHB+03]   Visser, W., Havelund, K., Brat, G., Park, S., Lerda, F.: Model Checking Programs. Journal of Automated Software Engineering 10(2) (April 2003)

[WGC05]   Wei, O., Gurfinkel, A., Chechik, M.: Identification and Counter Abstraction for Full Virtual Symmetry. In: Borrione, D., Paul, W. (eds.) CHARME 2005. LNCS, vol. 3725, pp. 285–300. Springer, Heidelberg (2005)

[WS00]   Whittle, J., Schumann, J.: Generating Statechart Designs from Scenarios. In: Proceedings of 22nd International Conference on Software Engineering (ICSE 2000), May 2000, pp. 314–323. ACM Press, New York (2000)

Toasters, Seat Belts, and Inferring Program Properties

David Evans

University of Virginia, Department of Computer Science
Charlottesville, Virginia
evans@cs.virginia.edu

Abstract. Today's software does not come with meaningful guarantees. This position paper explores why this is the case, suggests societal and technical impediments to more dependable software, and considers what realistic, meaningful guarantees for software would be like and how to achieve them.

> *If you want a guarantee, buy a toaster.*
> Clint Eastwood (*The Rookie*, 1990)

1 Introduction

Software today doesn't come with guarantees. Should it? What kinds of guarantees should they be?

I wouldn't want to argue with "Dirty Harry", but toasters don't really come with guarantees either, certainly not in the sense of a mathematical proof that they will satisfy a set of precisely defined requirements. What a toaster does come with is: (1) a reasonable expectation that a semi-intelligent user will be able to get the toaster to transform a typical slice of bread into toast; (2) a warranty that the manufacturer promises to replace the toaster if it is defective, and (3) in the United States to a large degree, and to varying degrees in other countries, the assurance that if the defectively designed or manufactured toaster causes your house to burn down, you will be able to sue the toaster manufacturer for damages far in excess of the cost of the toaster.

Software is a long way from satisfying any of those properties: (1) purchasers of software do not expect it to work correctly; instead of returning misbehaving software, users are conditioned to blame themselves; (2) software usually comes with an offer to replace defective disks, by no warranty on correct behavior; and (3) software vendors, to date, have managed to be immune from liability lawsuits even in cases where negligent implementations produce serious losses. We do, however, have many of the essential technologies in place to provide meaningful guarantees regarding software systems. Research tools have been developed to check properties of large programs [5, 10, 12, 14, 20, 22], and dozens of companies are now offering analysis tools and services (e.g., Coverity, Fortify, Ounce Labs, PolySpace, Reflective).

The rest of this paper discusses four of the major impediments that remain before routine software comes with effective guarantees: a lack of mechanisms for providing the necessary incentives to encourage software vendors to invest resources and delay products to improve dependability; inadequate ways to identify properties worth checking; insufficient theoretical understanding of how to interpret the outcome of

B. Meyer and J. Woodcock (Eds.): Verified Software, LNCS 4171, pp. 354–361, 2008.
© IFIP International Federation for Information Processing 2008

checking, especially unsound analyses, as meaningful guarantees; and deficiently educated developers unable to effectively use and insist on the use of appropriate program verification tools and techniques.

> *The first principle was security... A consequence of this principle is that every occurrence of every subscript of every subscripted variable was on every occasion checked at run time against both the upper and the lower declared bounds of the array. Many years later we asked our customers whether they wished us to provide an option to switch off these checks in the interests of efficiency on production runs. Unanimously, they urged us not to—they already knew how frequently subscript errors occur on production runs where failure to detect them could be disastrous. I note with fear and horror that even in 1980, language designers and users have not learned this lesson. In any respectable branch of engineering, failure to observe such elementary precautions would have long been against the law.*
> Tony Hoare, describing Elliott Brothers' Algol 60 implementation
> *The Emperor's Old Clothes*, 1980 Turing Award Speech

2 Incentivizing Verification

Twenty-five years after Hoare's speech, computing is still not a "respectable branch of engineering": software developers and language designers continue to release code where memory references are unchecked and no one has yet been sent to jail or even fined for doing it. The technologies for preventing this particular type of error have been available for many decades, yet vendors still ship software without using them. If jail sentences had been established in 1980 for the CEO of any company that sells a product containing a buffer overflow vulnerability, I suspect there would have been no programs with buffer overflow vulnerabilities sold in 1981, and certainly not in 2005. Alas, I know of no jurisdiction that has made programming in C++ or designing a language without bounds checking a criminal offense [8]. This is an incentive problem, not a technology problem.

An automobile company could not sell a car that suffers from a problem like unchecked array references, without losing billions of dollars in lawsuits. As a result, technologies that improve safety are quickly deployed throughout the industry. Some parallels can be drawn between safety belts in cars and bounds checking in software. Safety belts were introduced in the 1950s because of biomechanical research suggesting their effectiveness; they were, however, rarely used by car occupants until mandatory belt wearing laws were passed [16]. As with bounds checking, a very effective technology was available but largely unused for many decades. However, unlike the case with software, legal mechanisms in the form of both regulation and liability, placed pressure on vendors to incorporate the best known technology in their products. In 1986, General Motors became the first US auto manufacturer to decide to install lap/shoulder belts in the rear seats of cars, instead of lap-only belts. GM began installing lap/shoulder belts in selected 1987 model cars. The other auto companies followed within a few years, and it later became a government standard. GM faced a $200M lawsuit (which was settled under seal) claiming that GM was negligent in not making the change sooner since its internal research indicated that lap-only belts were less effective than previous government estimates [16, 17].

Software in embedded systems is subject to potential lawsuits if the containing device fails with disastrous results. As a result, the development and validation practices for such software is quite different from that typically used for software-only systems. With a few notable exceptions, critical software in embedded systems today is remarkably reliable compared to software in software-only systems.

Applying product liability to software is not without risks, however. If companies that do not deploy the best known technology can be liable for negligence, this provides a strong disincentive to developing new technologies and stifles creativity and innovation. Software liability also raises serious issues for open source developers and academic researchers who wish to develop and distribute software without fear of lawsuits or needing approval from lawyers.

An alternative is to use market forces. This has proven difficult so far with software, primarily because of the difficulty in measuring software quality, especially security. A research community is emerging that considers economic approaches to improving security [3, 4] as well as measuring it [23]. Good ideas for software security metrics, however, remain elusive. One promising direction is work on measuring relative attack surfaces [19].

There are no easy answers here, but it seems many of the challenges we face in improving software dependability and security are not so much in developing tools and techniques to analyze programs, but in making using those tools cost effective in a business sense. This involves the technical challenges of decreasing the costs of using them and increasing the value they provide, but also the large contextual challenge of making the costs of improving software quality economically justifiable by increasing the cost disadvantages associated with low qualify software. The trends are in the right direction as evidenced most clearly by Microsoft's trustworthy computing initiative [18] and increasing willingness to sacrifice functionality and delay product releases to enhance security over that past few years [21].

> *It is easier to write an incorrect program than understand a correct one.*
>
> Alan Perlis

3 Identifying Properties

We can group properties into three categories:

1. Generic language semantics properties.
2. Documented application properties.
3. Unknown (but necessary) application properties.

The first category comprises those properties that should always be true of all programs, such as all memory references are in bounds and the program never leaks memory. Since these properties are universal, they should be identified once by the programming language designers and there is no need to identify them for a particular application. Most program analysis tools available today are focused on checking or detecting violations of this type of property. Few viable excuses remain for releasing software today that suffers from these kinds of flaws.

In most cases, documented application-specific properties do not exist. There is no precise description of required application properties, and even the developers don't know what those properties are. Efforts to improve education for software developers (discussed in Section 5) may increase the likelihood of there being documented properties, but progress here will be slow and limited. Except for the most safety-critical (and thus expensive) software, it is unreasonable to expect required application properties to be clearly documented in the near future. Even when developers are willing to spend the effort required to formally document these properties, they often do not know what properties are necessary for correctness or would be useful to document.

Our efforts should focus, then, primarily on the third category – unknown and undocumented, but necessary, application properties. Over the past few years, several research groups have developed tools for inferring those properties. Daikon infers data invariants on programs by analyzing execution traces on a test suite [13]. Other researchers have developed techniques for inferring specifications of programs from their dynamic behavior [2, 9, 31] and static analysis of their program texts [1, 30, 31].

My research group's work in this area is motivated by the observation that many properties in the third group are true during many or all test executions, but when they are violated during real executions they produce serious consequences. We have developed a tool, Perracotta [29], that takes a program and a test suite and produces a set of inferred properties. We have focused primarily on inferring simple temporal properties that constrain the order and occurrence of events in the program such as calls to a particular method (such as all calls to the lock method must be followed by calls to the corresponding unlock method) or combinations of temporal and data properties (such as, object O is never modified between events A and B). The goal is not to produce a specification of the program for human use, but rather to infer properties that are useful for other purposes. We have used inferred properties to identify undesirable behaviors [27]; unexpected differences between similar programs or different versions of a program [28]; and as input to a model checker [29]. When a counterexample to an inferred property is found, it may reveal a bug in the program or a deficiency in the testing approach. By inferring properties this way and using them with automatic checking and comparison tools, we are able to discover essential properties about a program that developers would not think to document.

4 Towards Software Guarantees

Let's return to the rather degenerate toaster example and the toaster guarantee is shown in Figure 1. The guarantee does not claim that the toaster will always behave according to a particular specification. Rather, it states that if the toaster "goes wrong" it will be replaced, provided the user does not misuse, "neglect", modify, or damage the toaster. Despite its limitations, this guarantee has some value to the purchaser, and it would be a major advance if software came with a similar guarantee.

The technical challenge is to determine the equivalent of "goes wrong" for a complex software system. Automatic property inference and checking is a step towards this goal. Instead of attempting to formally specify the exact behavior for software, by using property inference techniques to infer properties that are true of the "normal"

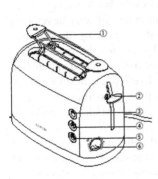

safety

- Burnt food can catch fire, so:
- never leave your toaster on unattended;
- keep your toaster away from anything (eg curtains) that could catch fire;
- set the browning control lower for thin or dry bread;
- set the browning control no higher than ⊗ when using the warming rack; and
- never warm food with a topping or filling (eg pizza): if it drips into the toaster, it could catch fire.
- To avoid electric shocks, never:
- let the toaster, cord or plug get wet; or

guarantee

If your toaster goes wrong within one year from the date you bought it, we will repair or replace it free of charge provided:

- you have not misused, neglected or damaged it;
- it has not been modified (unless by Kenwood);
- it is not second-hand;
- it has not been used commercially;
- you have not fitted a plug incorrectly; and
- you supply your receipt to show when you bought it.

This guarantee does not affect your statutory rights.

Fig. 1. Kenwood TT360/TT390 Toaster Instructions (excerpted)

behavior of the software, and checking (or ensuring at run-time) that they are always true we can establish claims about the scope of executions covered by the testing strategy. If the inferred properties capture enough of the behavior of the software, then we can claim that executions that satisfy those properties are "okay", and executions that do not satisfy them have "gone wrong". In such circumstances, measures can be taken to put the software right again to return to the "normal" behavior. Rinard and his colleagues' work on acceptability-oriented computing [11, 24, 25] and Swift et al.'s work on hiding device driver failures from executing programs [26] illustrate the possibility of executing programs in ways that programming errors are automatically recovered from. When unsound analysis techniques are used, we cannot expect to make full correctness guarantees; instead, we should strive to find ways to formalize guarantees more like the toaster guarantee of nothing "goes wrong", and to develop tools and techniques that allow us to make such guarantees.

> The use of COBOL cripples the mind;
> its teaching should, therefore, be regarded as a criminal offence.
> Edsger W.Dijkstra, *How do we tell the truths that might hurt?* (EWD 498), June 1975

5 Education

The single most important factor in determining the quality of software is the knowledge, experience and attitudes of people who design and implement it. People choose the programming languages, compilers, analysis tools and testing and validation approaches to use. Hence, it is unlikely that software quality will improve dramatically without also changing the ways we educate programmers. Although increasing automation can make analysis tools accessible to less sophisticated developers, it will be up to developers to decide to use those tools and to correctly interpret their results.

Computer science curricula have traditionally followed industry, not led it. With rare exceptions, the choices of programming languages and tools used in most introductory software engineering courses follow a few years behind the current needs of industry rather than envisioning the future and focusing on producing graduates with conceptual understanding and the ability to lead industry forward. To improve the state of software engineering, academia needs to take the lead in teaching students in introductory software engineering courses the theories, tools and techniques that will be important for verified programming. Instead of focusing on the technical details of complex programming languages that are popular in industry, introductory software engineering courses should be teaching students to think about preconditions, postconditions, data invariants, and temporal properties and to understand what program analysis tools and testing techniques can allow them to state about their programs. At the University of Virginia, we are developing a curriculum towards these goals [6, 7] (which draws heavily from the MIT curriculum), and have experimented with introducing static analysis tools in our introductory software engineering course [7]. Although the state of the art in available tools presents some challenges, and it is difficult for students in introductory courses to formally document complex invariants, we are optimistic that incorporating automatic property inference tools into the process can help [15] and that this approach can provide students with the necessary background to develop more secure and dependable software.

6 Summary

The research and industrial communities have made tremendous progress in program analysis and verification tools over the past several years, and these tools have now reached the point where they can be usefully applied to large, complex programs. In order for their use to become prevalent, however, the appropriate incentive structure must be in place. Technical challenges remain in determining useful properties to check that go beyond generic language properties, and in better understanding the claims that can be made as a result of unsound analyses. Promising directions for research towards these goals include automatic property inference and automatic detection of and recovery from errors. Full program verification against a precise specification will remain expensive and rare, but perhaps advances in technology and changes in incentive structure will make meaningfully guaranteed software commonplace.

References

1. Alur, R., Černý, P., Madhusudan, P., Nam, W.: Synthesis of Interface Specifications for Java classes. In: Proceedings of the ACM Symposium on Principles of Programming Languages (2005)
2. Ammons, G., Bodik, R., Larus, J.R.: Mining Specifications. In: Proceedings of the ACM Symposium on Principles of Programming Languages (January 2002)
3. Anderson, R.: Economics and Security Resource Page,
   http://www.cl.cam.ac.uk/users/rja14/econsec.html
4. Camp, L.J., Lewis, S. (eds.): Economics of Information Security, September 2004. Kluwer Academic Publishers, Dordrecht (2004)

5. Chen, H., Dean, D., Wagner, D.: Model Checking One Million Lines of C Code. In: Proceedings of the 11th Annual Network and Distributed System Security Symposium (NDSS) (February 2004)
6. CS150: Computer Science from Ada and Euclid to Quantum Computing and the World Wide Web. University of Virginia Course, http://www.cs.virginia.edu/cs150
7. CS201j: Engineering Software. University of Virginia, http://www.cs.virginia.edu/cs201j
8. CS655: Graduate Programming Languages. University of Virginia Course. (Spring, 2000), http://www.cs.virginia.edu/evans/cs655-S00/mocktrial/
9. Cook, J.E., Du, Z., Liu, C., Wolf, A.L.: Discovering Models of Behavior for Concurrent Workflows. Computers in Industry 53(3), 297–319 (2004)
10. Das, M., Lerner, S., Seigle, M.: ESP: Path-Sensitive Program Verification In Polynomial Time. In: Proceedings of the ACM SIGPLAN Conference on Programming Language Design and Implementation (June 2002)
11. Demsky, B., Rinard, M.: Data Structure Repair Using Goal-Directed Reasoning. In: Proceedings of the 2005 International Conference on Software Engineering (May 2005)
12. Engler, D., Chelf, B., Chou, A., Hallem, S.: Checking System Rules Using System-Specific Programmer-Written Compiler Extensions. In: Symposium on Operating Systems Design and Implementation (October 2000)
13. Ernst, M.D., Cockrell, J., Griswold, W.G., Notkin, D.: Dynamically Discovering Likely Program Invariants to Support Program Evolution. IEEE Transactions on Software Engineering (February 2001)
14. Evans, D.: Static Detection of Dynamic Memory Errors. In: Proceedings of the ACM SIGPLAN Conference on Programming Language Design and Implementation (May 1996)
15. Evans, D., Peck, M.: Simulating Critical Software Development. University of Virginia Computer Science Technical Report, UVA-CS-TR2004-04 (February 2004)
16. Evans, L.: Traffic Safety. Science Serving Society Press (2004), http://scienceservingsociety.com/traffic-safety.htm
17. Evans, L.: Personal communication (April 2005)
18. Gates, B.: Trustworthy Computing Initiative (memo to all Microsoft employees) (January 15, 2002)
19. Howard, M., Pincus, J., Wing, J.M.: Measuring Relative Attack Surfaces. In: Proceedings of Workshop on Advanced Developments in Software and Systems Security, Taipei (December 2003)
20. Larochelle, D., Evans, D.: Statically Detecting Likely Buffer Overflow Vulnerabilities. In: USENIX Security Symposium (August 2001)
21. Microsoft Corporation. Trustworthy Computing, http://www.microsoft.com/twc
22. Musuvathi, M., Park, D., Chou, A., Engler, D.R., Dill, D.L.: CMC: A Pragmatic Approach to Model Checking Real Code. In: Proceedings of the Fifth Symposium on Operating Systems Design and Implementation (December 2002)
23. Ozment, A.: Bug Auctions: Vulnerability Markets Reconsidered. In: Workshop on Economics and Information Security (May 2004)
24. Rinard, M.: Acceptability-Oriented Computing. In: ACM SIGPLAN Conference on Object-Oriented Programming Systems, Languages, and Applications Companion (OOPSLA 2003 Companion) Onwards! Session, California (October 2003)
25. Rinard, M., Cadar, C., Dumitran, D., Roy, D.M., Leu, T., Beebee Jr, W.S.: Enhancing Server Availability and Security Through Failure-Oblivious Computing. In: Proceedings of the 6th Symposium on Operating Systems Design and Implementation (December 2004)

26. Swift, M., Annalamai, M., Bershad, B., Levy, H.: Recovering Device Drivers. In: Proceedings of the 6th Symposium on Operating Systems Design and Implementation (December 2004)
27. Yang, J., Evans, D.: Dynamically Inferring Temporal Properties. In: ACM SIGPLAN-SIGSOFT Workshop on Program Analysis for Software Tools and Engineering (June 2004)
28. Yang, J., Evans, D.: Automatically Inferring Temporal Properties for Program Evolution. In: 15th IEEE International Symposium on Software Reliability Engineering (November 2004)
29. Yang, J., Evans, D., Bhardwaj, D., Bhat, T., Das, M.: Perracotta: Mining Temporal API Rules from Imperfect Traces. In: 28th International Conference in Software Engineering (May 2006)
30. Weimer, W., Necula, G.: Mining Temporal Specifications for Error Detection. In: Halbwachs, N., Zuck, L.D. (eds.) TACAS 2005. LNCS, vol. 3440, pp. 461–476. Springer, Heidelberg (2005)
31. Whaley, J., Martin, M.C., Lam, M.S.: Automatic extraction of object-oriented component interfaces. In: International Symposium on Software Testing and Analysis (July 2002)

On the Formal Development of Safety-Critical Software

Andy Galloway, Frantz Iwu, John McDermid, and Ian Toyn

Department of Computer Science, University of York
Heslington, York, YO10 5DD, UK
{andyg,iwuo,jam,ian}@cs.york.ac.uk

Abstract. We reflect on the formal development models applicable to embedded control systems in light of our experience with safety-critical applications from the aerospace domain. This leads us to propose two complementary enhancements to Parnas' four-variable model, one elaborating the structure outside the control computer, and the other elaborating the structure inside the control computer. We then identify several challenges which illustrate why formal development in this domain is difficult, and report our own progress in meeting these challenges. Finally, we outline the residual issues, which form the agenda for our future work.

1 Introduction

It has often been argued that formal development is necessary in order to achieve the extremely low failure rates demanded for safety-critical software. Accordingly, this principle is embodied in a number of standards [1,2]. However, whilst there are good examples of the application of static program analysis techniques to safety-critical software, e.g. [3], there are very few examples of the use of "classical" formal approaches such as those based on the notion of refinement ([4] is a rare example). Indeed, there are many practical and theoretical difficulties in applying such models.

The purpose of this paper is to outline a sound technical basis for the formal development of safety-critical systems, identify recent progress in developing such a process (along with associated tools), and highlight future research challenges.

The paper starts by considering development models applicable to safety-critical systems, and uses them to reflect on the scope and limitations of classical approaches to formal development. We propose two complementary, but orthogonal, enhancements of Parnas' four variable model. The first enhancement identifies additional structure outside the control computer, whilst the second focuses on the structure inside the computer.

The analysis is then expanded by considering some of the challenges that arise in the practical development of safety-critical systems, reflecting our experience with a range of avionics applications. This is used to propose a model for formal development of safety-critical software, to outline progress being made towards realising such a model, and to identify residual research challenges.

2 Development Models

In developing safety-critical systems we need to model the environment (air, passengers, roads, etc.), the top-level system, e.g. an aero-engine, which we term the "platform", the

B. Meyer and J. Woodcock (Eds.): Verified Software, LNCS 4171, pp. 362–373, 2008.

control, or embedding, system, e.g. a Full Authority Digital Engine Controller (FADEC) and the embedded system (computing system and software). Few software development models relate the software to the embedding system/environment; counterexamples are Dave Parnas' four variable model [5] and Michael Jackson's Problem Frames [6]. Parnas' model distinguishes:

- monitored variables;
- controlled variables;
- input variables;
- output variables.

The first two represent the environment and/or platform; the control system senses the monitored variables and attempts to control the environment by influencing the controlled variables (both the sensing and influencing processes may be indirect i.e. via other real-world variables). For example a FADEC senses cockpit thrust demands, various air temperatures and pressures along with engine shaft speeds (the monitored variables), and modifies fuel flow (amongst other things) in order to influence the level of thrust (the controlled variable) in the required way.

The input and output variables are the values seen or produced by the computer – perhaps the output of an analogue to digital (A/D) converter at the input, and the contents of a register which goes through digital to analogue (D/A) conversion to produce a current to drive a motor or valve.

Abstractly, *requirements* for the control system are stated in terms of relationships over the monitored and controlled variables, whilst *specifications* for the computer system are stated in terms of input and output variables. To give a complete specification also requires a definition of the relationship between the monitored variables and the inputs, as well as between the output variables and controlled variables. (Parnas' approach does not distinguish between the environment and platform; our proposed enhancement makes such distinctions explicit, in a way which we believe adds engineering value.)

Jackson's approach is not constrained to embedded systems, and so does not identify specific classes of variables. It does however introduce the notion of domain models, which encapsulate properties of the wider system; these can be used to represent the nature of the environment, platform and embedding system. Thus, for example, a domain model could be used to explain the relationship between the monitored and input variables in Parnas' approach. Both approaches are relevant to the development of embedded systems; but experience with embedded systems such as FADECs suggests the need for an elaboration of these models.

In Parnas' approach the behaviour of the physical environment (Nature) is described by a relation, NAT. The basic model is illustrated in Fig. 1, which shows the system decomposition on the left and the relationship of elements of the specification set on the right:

The arrows from the platform are the monitored variables; the reverse arrow is the controlled variable. In the case of an engine controller many of the inputs are environmental properties, e.g. air pressures, at defined points in the engine; other are specific properties of the engine, e.g. shaft speeds.

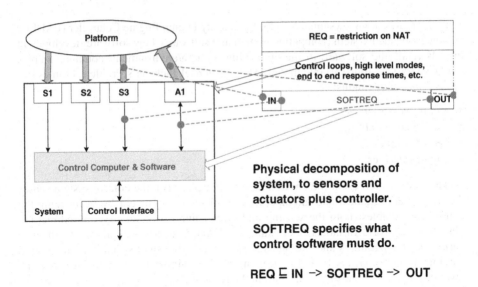

Fig. 1. Representation of Parnas' Four Variable Model

The input and output variables relate to the control computer and software. The sensors (e.g. S1) map the monitored variables to inputs, represented by relation[1] IN, and the actuators (e.g. A1) map the outputs to the controlled variables, represented by relation OUT. (Here we have made the decision to align IN and OUT with elements of the embedding system.) REQ gives the required behaviour in "real world" terms (environment and platform); SOFTREQ is the analogous specification at the level of computing system and software. A control interface is also shown; this would be a cockpit interface if the platform were an engine. The interface can be thought of as a further set of monitored, controlled, input and output variables, albeit with a very different inter-relationships determined by the design of other systems on the aircraft.

In problem frames, the domain models would encompass necessary properties of the environment, platform, the embedding system, the sensors and actuators – NAT (with a wide scope), IN and OUT in Parnas' terms.

3   Development Models – First Proposed Enhancement

An important practical consideration regarding domain modelling and the elucidation of NAT, REQ, IN and OUT is how to manage the considerable complexity that may be inherent. From our experience with aerospace applications we are aware of many subtleties to be addressed. A key concern is to reflect better the role of the embedding system, and to distinguish it from the environment and platform. Our view is that such distinctions provide a useful basis for abstraction, and that they need to be acknowledged and clarified within the development model. By achieving a greater separation

---

[1] Note that by a relation Parnas is referring to a *trajectory* or *time-indexed* relation between variables.

of concerns, we believe it will be easier to develop and validate specifications and to handle change.

A further problem that we need to contend with is the difficulty of sensing key properties of the environment/platform. For example it is not practical to manage engine thrust directly – although it is a key controlled variable – instead it is necessary to use surrogates such as shaft speed or engine pressure ratio.

Our first proposal is, therefore, to enhance the environmental model by adding additional variables. Thus, in addition to monitored/controlled variables and inputs/outputs, we might further distinguish:

- sensed and actuated variables: those real-world variables[2] which are affected directly by the system under development, and which are influenced by/influence the monitored/controlled variables;
- embeddingInput and embeddingOutput variables: those variables which represent the inputs and outputs of the embedding system.

Thus, for instance, whilst REQ might still define the high-level requirements (thrust in terms of demand), we could also distinguish EFFECTREQ over sensed and actuated variables and EMBEDDINGREQ over EmbeddingInput and EmbeddingOutput variables. We would also need to provide the equivalent of the IN/OUT relations to define how the new variables are related. For example, IN_{Emb} could describe the relationship between the real-world "sensed" variables and the inputs to the embedding system. See Fig. 2.

We can illustrate the above principle by revisiting the earlier engine example. The monitored variables are demands, temperatures, pressures and shaft speeds; the controlled variable is thrust. The sensed variables are the same as the monitored variables, whereas the actuated variable is fuel flow. The inputs to the embedding system might be analogue electronic signals from several sensing devices (with multiplex redundancy for some of the sensed variables). The output might be control signals to a stepper motor which changes the "throat" on a control valve. Finally, the inputs to the computer are digital representations of the analogue sensor inputs, and the output is a digital representation of the stepper motor signal. The relation IN_{Emb} in this context would relate the sensed input signals to the real-world variables they are sensing – this might reflect assumptions, for instance, about "noise".

It is now possible to state the relationships between the various abstractions:

$$EMBEDDINGREQ \sqsubseteq IN \rightarrow SOFTREQ \rightarrow OUT$$
$$EFFECTREQ \sqsubseteq IN_{Emb} \rightarrow EMBEDDINGREQ \rightarrow OUT_{Emb}$$

Where $\sqsubseteq$ is the appropriate refinement relation, and $\rightarrow$ represents composition of Parnas' relations.

The above is a generalisation of the usual relationship between REQ and IN, SOFTREQ and OUT. However, once in the "real world" this generalisation, whilst valid, may be impractical to define as the relationships between sensor/actuator variables and monitored/control variables are likely to be too complex to represent as

---

[2] E.g. shaft speed.

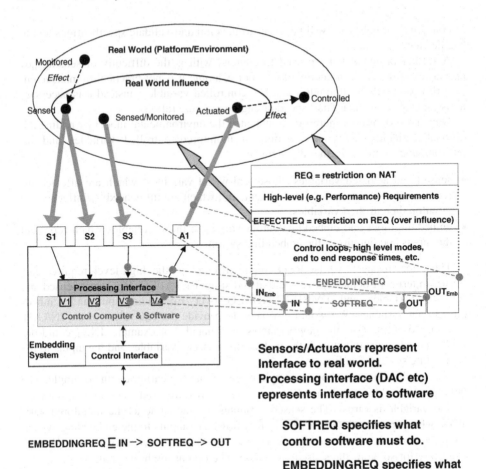

Fig. 2. Elaboration of Environmental Model

IN/OUT style relations between interface[3] variables (c.f. closed-loop control). Instead we would propose the following:

NAT is defined as a relation over all monitored/controlled and sensed/actuated variables, representing a model of the *real world*.

REQ is defined as a relation over monitored and controlled variables, with the condition that:

$$\text{NAT} \sqsubseteq \text{REQ}$$

i.e. that REQ is consistent with (a refinement of) NAT.

---

[3] I.e. between monitored and sensed, and between actuated and controlled.

EFFECTREQ is defined as a relation over sensed and actuated variables, with the condition that:

$$REQ \setminus ((monitored \cup controlled) \setminus (sensed \cup actuated)) \subseteq EFFECTREQ$$

i.e. that EFFECTREQ is consistent with REQ (where all monitored/controlled variables that are not also sensed/actuated variables have been hidden).

Finally, although we have distinguished *an* embedding system, for certain applications there may be a *hierarchy* of embedding systems. Thus, it may be desirable to distinguish more than one set of embedding system variables and requirements etc. We presented the "simple" case as an example of the general case.

4 Development Models – Second Proposed Enhancement

SOFTREQ is expressed rather monolithically. In fact there will be computing hardware, application software and also other software elements, e.g. an operating system, functions for managing faults, etc. Our second proposal is to elaborate the four variable model as shown in Fig 3.

This expanded model shows further decomposition of the software specification, reflecting the hardware structure of the embedding system. The control system software will include device drivers (represented as I/P and O/P) which will map the

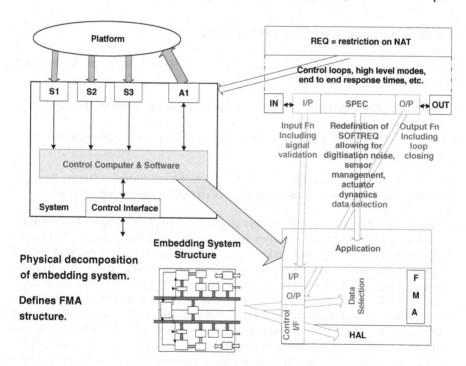

Fig. 3. Representation of Software Structure

output of the sensors to meaningful values in software, e.g. the output of a 6 bit A/D converter to a temperature in degrees C, represented as an Ada variable; similarly O/P represents drivers for actuators (note these may be complex and read back values from actuators, running them "closed loop"). A hardware abstraction layer (HAL), or primitive operating system, provides basic services such as scheduling, timers, etc.

The controller computer hardware is usually multiplex redundant, and there are often multiple sources of sensed data. Thus there is fault management and accommodation (FMA), or data selection, logic deriving "healthy" values from the various inputs to provide validated data to the application. A "disconnect" is shown between IN and I/P, and O/P and OUT to reflect that input/output variables may correspond to different embedding system inputs and outputs depending on which input values are selected. In highly critical applications, e.g. aircraft flight control, the validation and data selection logic (dealing with redundant processing hardware, sensors and actuators) might account for 80% or more of the embedded code.

In problem frame terms, the controller structure is another (part of the) domain model. There is another important factor in such a development, the introduction of a software architecture to structure the code. Jackson has been developing problem frames in this direction [7]; this is important, but for brevity we focus here on more "black box" specifications. Finally the definition of HAL seems to be a "free choice"; in practice the application-programming interface (API) is likely to be defined by a standard, e.g. ARINC653 [8].

5 Challenges for Formal Development

At one level the challenge for formal development is stated simply; provide a formal process which:

- acknowledges the structure of the environment (cf. sensed/actuated, EmbeddingInput/EmbeddingOutput variables);
- respects and supports the relationship of physical design decomposition and specifications outlined in Fig 3.

It is possible to illustrate the challenge by considering formal software development alongside some of the essential features of embedded safety-critical systems.

- refinement – the development process sits uneasily with the usual rules of refinement, e.g. weakening pre-conditions and strengthening post-conditions. For example, requirements will be met under normal conditions and under certain classes of input failure, but will be violated when inadequate input data is available. The important thing to note is that the precondition representing "inadequate input data" can not easily be expressed over the program variables; it is a "real world" property. Thus, without adequate treatment of the problem structure external to the software, one might have no recourse but to weaken the post-condition in this situation. From a development process perspective, one abstract data value (monitored), e.g. air pressure, may have multiple representations at different points in the environment and software – "real-world", "raw" values from sensors, value after fault accommodation for that sensor, value after voting between alternative data sources or derivation from other sensors etc. These "design steps" are not supported by the classical rules of refinement;

- continuous (e.g. closed loop) control – most embedded safety-critical systems use some form of continuous control, at least for part of the system. Thus the software is required to implement discrete approximations to continuous transfer functions, transforming not just the values of interest but also their integrals and differentials. The control engineers are interested in properties such as jitter, stability, etc. The issue for formal development is linking the discrete specification (e.g. SPEC) back to the continuous requirement, i.e. REQ;

- abstraction – it is hard to employ abstraction. The data being manipulated is a simple reflection of real-world properties, e.g. temperatures and pressures, making classical data abstraction of little value. Other approaches, e.g. loose or algebraic specifications, are also of limited relevance – it is necessary to specify precisely what happens under all physically permissible circumstances to ensure safety, and so on. Some state abstraction is possible, but abstraction is a "much weaker tool" for embedded systems than in more classical "IT" systems;

- non-functional properties – the non-functional properties, e.g. timing, numerical accuracy (to ensure stability of control algorithms) etc. are crucial aspects of "correctness". Further, the functional and non-functional properties are not always separable. For instance, the functional requirements for fault detection will depend on timing requirements (e.g. the larger the interval between one reading and the next, the wider the error bands which have to be set on valid inputs).

There are some proposed approaches to these problems, e.g. the work on retrenchment [9] and some direct approaches to deriving control system specifications [10], but none of these address the range of problems outlined above.

6 Models for Safety-Critical Formal Development

Producing a formal development process which fully addressed all of the issues outlined above would be an enormous undertaking – and also, we would argue, unhelpful. To address the above issues within a single formal notation it would be necessary to formalise the relevant aspects of physics, including atmospheric and oceanic models for aircraft and ships, respectively, thermal properties of materials, e.g. fuels, sensor dynamics, and so on. Clearly this is not practical – and, in any event, there are well-established approaches for dealing with such issues in engineering practice. No one (formal) technique can adequately incorporate all of the essential features of the control system. For example, embedding *control theory* into a discrete formal method is impractical (if not impossible), and one cannot rigorously analyse discrete software elements in control theory.

Thus it seems that the strategy that should be adopted is to formalise "where formality adds engineering value", and make the links between formal development of software and the relevant aspects of domain models external to the formalism itself. However, this approach yields a secondary *meta-modelling* problem.

In many cases different dimensions to the problem space can be "separated" and targeted by different forms of analysis, e.g. the concerted use of control theory, formal specification and refinement, numerical analysis, scheduling theory and probabilis-tic/risk-based analysis. However, it is vital that the relationships between the various techniques are properly understood, in order for example to ensure their mutual con-sistency. The *meta-modelling* problem is crucial to the successful application of for-mal methods.

In the approach we have been developing, known as Practical Formal Specification (PFS), the interpretation of "where formality adds engineering value" has been to re-cord assumptions which reflect the key parts of the domain models, and to conduct validation of the specifications in the context of these assumptions. The term assump-tion is used because these are properties which have to be assumed by the software developers, and which cannot be "proven" as part of the (pure) software development process. These assumptions often reflect properties of the embedding system or plat-form, e.g. maximum rate of change of temperature (given thermal mass, and software iteration rate). Thus the assumptions bring relevant parts of relations such as IN_{Emb} into the realm of formal analysis.

7 Progress on Practical Formal Development

Our work on PFS initially started as a general analysis of where formality can add most value; more recent work has centred on Matlab/ Simulink/Stateflow (MSS), the development tool suite widely used by control systems engineers in industry. Our aim has been to add formalism to MSS specifications in a non-obtrusive manner so that the approach can be used by those already familiar with the tool without the need for substantial retraining. There are three core elements to PFS [11]:

- notational restrictions to ensure that sound specifications are produced (MSS is, in effect, a graphical programming language and it is possible to write very poor specifications in MSS);
- representation of assumptions about the domain through annotations on the MSS specifications, e.g. on the states of Stateflow (state machine) diagrams, represent-ing the maximum rate of change of the model variables. These can be proven con-sistent with assumptions on the root state, which are in turn rewritten (in weakest-precondition style) into assumptions on the domain variables (these need to be vali-dated with domain experts, and can not be further analysed formally);
- rules for "healthiness" of specifications, e.g. disjointedness/completeness of transi-tion triggers, self-consistency of specification and assumptions. These rules are checked by an analysis tool known as SSA [12,13] (Simulink/Stateflow Analyser) which extracts a semantic model of the MSS specification, a representation of the assumptions and generates proof obligations for the healthiness conditions. These conditions are discharged formally using a combination of automated proof and model checking.

The PFS approach and SSA tool are influenced by the development models out-lined above, and are intended to be a step towards resolving the identified challenges for formal development. In terms of these challenges, progress (within PFS and SSA) is as follows:

- refinement – the approach allows for the sorts of development steps outlined above, especially stating and relating assumptions at different levels and checking healthiness properties of the specifications. The relationships between the assumptions at different levels are checked, but the rules are probably too strict making engineering practicalities, such as requirements concessions (for example to deal with loss of sensor data), difficult to handle. There is an issue here regarding the right balance between formally justifying model assumptions and relying on validation by other means;
- continuous (e.g. closed loop) control – as stated earlier, a controller represents a *transfer* function, which maps inputs plus their differentials and integrals into outputs plus their differentials and integrals. Crucially, the PFS weakest precondition analysis is based on (discrete representations of) differential pre- and postconditions, which allows us to do meaningful analysis of the transfer function properties of the model. Currently, we can analyse, for example, simple assumptions which can be justified in terms of transfer function behaviour (e.g. a differentiator or integrator). However, the analysis is never going to be a substitute for control theory, and again there is a trade-off to be made between formalisation and other forms of validation;
- abstraction – PFS and SSA support as much relevant abstraction as possible. Loose definition of sub-system behaviour allows for a compositional approach. Loose definitions are especially important for abstracting away from the details of continuous functions – such as those derived empirically from the domain. Such subsystems can at one level be described relationally – as function *envelopes* – carrying enough information to ensure consistency with other parts of the model. In addition *rate of change* assumptions are particularly useful for abstraction in requirements modelled as state-machines. The assumptions effectively *scope* the set of circumstances to which the state-machine must react;
- non-functional properties – these are largely outside the scope of the method and toolset at present. There are good tools for dealing with timing properties, but this does not address the meta-modelling issue of their integration into the overall formal development process.

PFS and SSA focus on validation of specifications; they are complementary to approaches, such as ClawZ [14,15], which focus primarily on the verification of code against Simulink models.

8 Residual Research Challenges

There is much to be done towards an effective model of formal development; the PFS/SSA approach addresses only some of the issues identified. There remain many open problems, both at the modelling and meta-modelling levels, including:

- adequate treatment of control laws, i.e. validation of important control properties such as stability. Note that this requires addressing timing properties within the formal models;

- review of current restrictions on the approach with a view to enabling a wider class of specifications to be addressed (without imposing any unnecessary constraints on control engineers);
- dealing with non-functional properties in specifications;
- providing stronger links with the safety[4] process, including effective treatment of failure management code – for example, by using a concession-like approach such as "otherwise clauses", or by auto-generating fault accommodation code from safety analysis results, e.g. failure modes and effects analyses.

Some of these issues are being addressed by projects of which the authors are aware (many outside York); producing an integrated and usable approach remains a major challenge.

9 Conclusions

Development of safety-critical software is, in many respects, a "natural" domain for application of formal methods. Despite the dictates of standards and some successes, the use of "classical" formal techniques on embedded safety-critical code remains the exception, not the rule. This paper has tried to articulate the technical (as opposed to commercial and cultural) reasons for the limited use of formal methods on safety-critical software, and outlined some of the characteristics which a formal development process would need to have to be useful in such a domain.

We have outlined some of our work which addresses part of this broad challenge – but acknowledge that there is much to be done, and many other "pieces of the jigsaw" which need to be put in place to provide a fully fledged formal development process for safety-critical software. It is hoped that, by articulating the vision for such a process, it will help foster a better understanding of the technical challenges which need to be met in this area, and thus stimulate constructive and collaborative work on the issues.

Acknowledgements

The ideas presented here have been influenced by discussions with colleagues at York and elsewhere. Discussions with Dave Parnas and Michael Jackson over a number of years have been particularly influential.

We acknowledge the support of the UK MoD for the PFS project, and of the EPSRC through MATISSE (GR/R70590/01), for some of the more detailed work which underpins the philosophy set out above.

We are also grateful to our industrial collaborators, especially Airbus, BAE Systems, QinetiQ and Rolls-Royce. Without them we would not have gained the understanding of the practical safety-critical systems development issues outlined here.

---

[4] Including probabilistic and risk-based analyses.

References

1. UK Ministry of Defence, Defence Standard 00-56 Issue 2: Safety Management Requirements for Defence Systems (1996)
2. Australian Department of Defence, Australian Defence Standard Def(Aust) 5679: Procurement of Computer-based Safety Critical Systems (1998)
3. A German, Software Static Code Analysis, Lessons Learned, Crosstalk(November 2003)
4. King, S., Hammond, J., Chapman, R., Pryor, A.: Is Proof more Cost-Effective than Tesing? IEEE Transactions on Software Engineering 26(8) (2000)
5. Parnas, D., Madey, J.: Functional Documents for Computer Programs. Science of Computer Programming 25(1) (1995)
6. Jackson, M.A.: Problem Frames. Addison Wesley, Reading (2001)
7. Rapanotti, L., Hall, J.G., Jackson, M.A., Nuseibeh, B.: Architecture-driven Problem Decomposition. In: Proceedings of RE 2004, IEEE Computer Society Press, Los Alamitos (2004)
8. Airline Electronic Engineering Committee, ARINC, Supplement 1 to ARINC Specification 653: Avionics Application Software Standard Interface, Standard 03-116/SWM-89, Annapolis Maryland (2003)
9. Poppleton, M., Banach, R.: Retrenchment, Refinement and Simulation. In: P. Bowen, J., Dunne, S., Galloway, A., King, S. (eds.) B 2000, ZUM 2000, and ZB 2000. LNCS, vol. 1878, Springer, Heidelberg (2000)
10. Hayes, I., Jackson, M., Jones, C.B.: Determining the Specification of a Control System from that of its Environment. In: Araki, K., Gnesi, S., Mandrioli, D. (eds.) FME 2003. LNCS, vol. 2805, Springer, Heidelberg (2003)
11. Iwu, F., Galloway, A., Toyn, I., McDermid, J.A.: Practical Formal Specification For Embedded Control Systems. In: Proceedings of the 11th IFAC Symposium on Information Control Problems in Manufacturing, INCOM 2004, Salvador, Brazil, April 5-7 (2004)
12. Galloway, A., Toyn, I., Iwu, F., McDermid, J.A.: The Simulink/Stateflow Analyzer. In: FAA and Embry-Riddle Aeronautical University (ERAU) Software Tools Workshop, Florida, USA, May 18 -19 (2004)
13. Toyn, I., Galloway, A.: Proving Properties of Stateflow Models using ISO Standard Z and CADiZ. In: Treharne, H., King, S., C. Henson, M., Schneider, S. (eds.) ZB 2005. LNCS, vol. 3455, Springer, Heidelberg (2005)
14. Arthan, R., Caseley, P., O'Halloran, C., Smith, A.: ClawZ: Control Laws in Z. In: Liu, S., McDermid, J.A., Hinchey, M.G. (eds.) Proceedings of ICFEM 2000, IEEE Computer Society, Los Alamitos (2000)
15. Cavalcanti, A., Clayton, P., O'Halloran, C.: Control Law Diagrams in Circus. In: Fitzgerald, J.S., Hayes, I.J., Tarlecki, A. (eds.) FM 2005. LNCS, vol. 3582, Springer, Heidelberg (2005)

Verify Your Runs

Klaus Havelund and Allen Goldberg

Kestrel Technology, Palo Alto, California, USA
{havelund,goldberg}@kestreltechnology.com
http://www.kestreltechnology.com

1 Introduction

A program verifier determines whether a program satisfies a specification. Ideally verification is achieved by static analysis without executing the code. However, program verification is unsolvable in general. The interactive approach, for example with a human guiding a theorem prover, does not in practice scale to large software systems. Some restricted kinds of specifications can, however, be checked automatically, for example type definitions. Also static analysis of properties such as un-initialized variables, null-pointer de-referencing, and array-bound violations scales to production programs on the order of hundreds of thousands of lines of code. Even concurrency-related problems such as data races and deadlocks can to some extent be checked statically, although often resulting in false positives. However, going beyond these simple properties to arbitrarily complex behavior specification and scaling to ever-growing production program size is undoubtedly a challenge, and in our opinion we cannot expect regular economic use of program verification of arbitrary properties to be fully achieved within the 15 year time horizon of the challenge.

Hence, we will probably have to accept that parts of the verification task will remain as proof obligations. It is reasonable to not throw such proof obligations away, but to monitor them during program testing, or in the operations phase. In the latter case, one can program reactions to property violations to achieve some form of fault protection. We call the scientific discipline that studies the monitoring of properties during program execution *runtime verification* [1]. Much work has been done in this area within recent years.

In this paper we shall outline and classify some current approaches to runtime verification and describe our contributions. We shall describe how we intend to further contribute to this work in the framework of the Grand Verification Challenge. The paper does not address the topic of test *case generation* although runtime verification is a part of this subject. That is, an effectful test case generation framework needs to support the generation of test cases, where a test case consists of inputs to the program together with an oracle that will inspect the output of the program (including inspection of its internal behavior) when executed on that input. Generation of the oracle is the runtime verification part. We believe that runtime verification is a rich subject on its own.

B. Meyer and J. Woodcock (Eds.): Verified Software, LNCS 4171, pp. 374–383, 2008.

2 Specification-Based Runtime Verification

Specification-based runtime verification consists of monitoring a program's execution against a *user-provided specification* of intended program behavior. The many approaches to program specification logics have lead to differing styles of runtime verification. One can consider a spectrum of monitoring approaches, ranging from monitoring of predicate assertions stating properties about a single state at a single program location, to monitoring of temporal assertions stating properties about temporally separated states at multiple program locations identified by automated program instrumentation. We shall discuss the techniques along four dimensions:

- *Location quantification:* whether the logic allows to quantify over locations in the program to be monitored. Monitors evaluate when certain program locations are reached during program execution. If the monitoring code is executing *in-line*, these locations will contain the monitoring code itself. If monitoring is *off-line*, the locations will contain event generators, that will send events to the monitors that run in some more or less loose form of synchronization with the code. Locations can either be specified individually, by identifying each of them explicitly, or they can be *quantified* over, as in Aspect Oriented Programming, covering many locations with one declaration, for example "before every call of any method defined in class C, evaluate monitor M".
- *Temporal quantification:* whether the logic allows quantification over time points. For example, whether one can express properties of the form: "whenever a call of method **close** occurs then in the past there has been a call of the **open** method". Some temporal logics only allow to state ordering relationships, while others go further and allow to state relative or absolute time values.
- *Data quantification:* whether the logic allows binding and referral (forward or backward in time) to values across states. For example, "whenever a call of method **close**(f) occurs, with a file argument f, then in the past there has been a call of **open**(f) of the same file f." Obviously, data quantification presumes temporal quantification.
- *Abstract data specification:* whether abstract states mapping variable names to values can be defined together with an abstraction that relates concrete program states to abstract specification states.

In the following we shall classify a collection of monitoring approaches along these dimensions.

Assertions. Runtime checks are assertions inserted at specific locations in the code. Assertions were introduced in Java 1.4 such that the programmer can write assertions of the form **assert** ψ for a Java predicate ψ, at explicit program locations. Assertions do not directly support location, temporal or data quantification, nor abstract data specification.

Pre-Post Conditions. Pre-post conditions is an extension of the assert statement, where the programmer explicitly indicates where checks should be performed, namely before and after method calls, hence not supporting location quantification. However, a post condition typically relates the value of variables at the start and the end of the method. Thus this is a restricted form of temporal and data quantification. The Eiffel language [25] has long embodied this idea, and recently so has JML [41], the Java Modeling Language. In Eiffel there is no provision for abstract data specification, while in JML there is. The Larch Shared Language approach [44] supports abstract (axiomatic) data specification in combination with pre-post conditions.

Invariants. Invariants, as found in for example Eiffel and JML, express properties about a single state, and are required to hold at *all* locations where data consistency can be expected, specifically at the completion of method calls, and at the limit after every variable update. Hence this is an example of a logic supporting location quantification. Since an invariant asserts a property of just the current state it does not support temporal or data quantification.

State Machine Notations and Process Algebras. In state machines/automata and process algebras, the specification is an *abstract program*, and runtime verification dynamically checks that the executing program is a *refinement* of the abstract program. That is, the instrumented program locations correspond to abstract program states, and monitoring checks the required state sequencing and that each concrete program state satisfies (via an abstraction function) the properties of a corresponding abstract state. This form of specification supports temporal quantification. The Jass system [40] monitors a combination of JML and CSP process algebra. Alternating automata, supporting AND as well as OR states, have shown to be particularly convenient for monitoring logics as demonstrated in [22,28,27]. Also state charts [32] offer this combination of AND and OR states. An example illustrating the use of state machines for monitoring is the TLChart system [24], that monitors a combination of temporal logic and state machines. An extension of simple state machines are timed automata, where time constraints can be put on states (one can only be in a state for a certain time period) and on transitions. One such system for runtime verification of timed automata is T-UPPAAL [56] and another similar system is described in [13]. T-UPPAAL also generates test cases. All the systems mentioned above monitor finite traces against finite trace automata. In [20] is described a technique for monitoring against Omega automata: automata that normally accept infinite traces. This is specifically useful for monitoring automata generated from specifications originally targeted for model checkers such as SPIN [54]. In [30] is described an algorithm for synthesizing finite trace monitoring algorithms from LTL specifications, inspired by similar algorithms used for synthesizing infinite trace Omega automata from LTL specifications.

Temporal Assertions. While automata and process algebras are operational in nature, temporal logics are declarative. *Temporal logics* have operators that relate arbitrary states, and hence support full temporal quantification, and can in many cases allow more succinct specifications. Pre-post conditions support a simple form of temporal quantification by relating two states (the pre-state and the post-state). In the commercial Temporal Rover system [22], one writes past time and future time temporal logic formulas at specific program locations, that get evaluated whenever that program location is reached. This tool hence supports temporal quantification but not location quantification. The MaC system [43] supports temporal past time assertions and location quantification by allowing instrumentation of method calls and variable updates. MaC also allows abstract data specifications referenced as the propositions of the temporal logic. An interesting logic is the future time temporal logic PSL [46] adopted by the hardware industry. In metric temporal logics one can state properties about time. Several such systems have been developed, for example [22,57]. Regular expressions, and extended regular expressions allowing negation, appear to be very useful for writing certain properties that in temporal logic would become more complicated to state. Such a system is described in [51]. A generalization of metric logics are data logics supporting data quantification, where one can reason about data values existing at different time points. Such systems are described in [23,27,21]. Temporal logics are often mapped to automata, although other interpretations are possible, such as for example described in [49,36], where rewriting is used to interpret temporal logic for monitoring.

General Purpose Specification Languages. A monitoring language may be a complete formal specification language, in the style of ASML [7], Maude [17], PVS [47], VDM [60], RAISE [48] or Specware [53]. This is the approach taken at Microsoft where ASML (Abstract State Machine Language) [7] is used for runtime verification as part of a general test case generation framework. Clearly such an approach supports abstract data specification. These full specification languages usually have executable subsets which resemble a programming language, be it functional or state-based. This observation can be exploited by having the specification language be an extension of the programming language, an approach taken in Spec# [9], Microsoft's extension of the work in [7].

3   Predictive Runtime Verification

As with testing, the effectiveness of runtime verification depends on the choice of test suite. For concurrent systems this becomes even more serious because this is compounded by the many possible execution paths of a non-deterministic program. This raises the question of whether there are properties that can be checked on one or a small number of execution traces and still identify bugs with high probability (if such exist). The answer is affirmative due to recent work on what we call *predictive runtime verification*.

In predictive runtime verification a property P to be monitored is replaced with a stronger property Q, i.e. for all inputs x, $Q(x) \rightarrow P(x)$. Furthermore if $\forall x P(x)$ then $Q(x)$ for most x (few false positives) but if $\exists x \neg P(x)$ then $\neg Q(x)$ for most x (good detection). It turns out that for certain problems finding such Q is possible.

One of the earliest successes was the Eraser algorithm [50] for detecting data races, that was implemented in Compaq's Visual Threads tool [33]. This algorithm checks a single execution trace in order to determine whether there are any *potentials* for data races: the situation where two threads access a shared variable simultaneously. This work has later been extended to cover other forms of data races, such as higher level data races [5] and atomicity violations [6,29,63]. Also deadlocks of the dining philosopher format can be checked in this manner [15]. A generalized predictive analysis framework is presented in [52]. In most of the above mentioned systems, the properties are programmed directly as algorithms in a traditional programming language. Attempts have, however, been made to express the properties in logic [10]. These are often data oriented properties that are best expressed in a monitoring logic appropriate for expressing data quantification and location quantification.

Concurrent target systems may be modified by inclusion of wait statements or modifications to schedulers, so that a fuller range of non-deterministic behaviors are exhibited during testing. Such modifications can be combined with predictive analysis. This is discussed in the overview paper [26] and in [14].

4   Instrumentation

Instrumentation is the modification of the target system with additional code that informs the monitor of events and data values relevant to the monitored properties, such as the taking of a lock, the entry into a method, or the update of a variable. This can be achieved through source code instrumentation, for example using Aspect Oriented Programming (AOP) as supported by AspectJ [8]; through byte-code instrumentation, BCEL [12] being an example byte-code instrumentation tool; or through object code instrumentation, with Valgrind [58] being an example. The Java-MOP system described in [16] is a generalized framework for instrumenting Java programs specifically for runtime verification. Instrumentation can, however, also be done through debugging interfaces, modification of the runtime system or virtual machine, or through operating system or middleware services. In our work we have used byte-code instrumentation and aspect oriented programming to instrument code.

It is worth noting that runtime verification techniques are starting to appear within the aspect oriented programming community. In a traditional AOP language such as AspectJ [42], an aspect specifies augmentations/modifications to a program, that may add functionality or specify a correctness property and appropriate actions to be executed when the property is violated. Traditionally actions are weaved into the program at program points, specified by so called pointcuts. A recent trend is to augment the pointcut language to include predicates on the execution trace. Solutions have been offered for augmenting AOP with regular expressions [2], future time linear temporal logic [55,19], state machines [59], and grammars [62].

Naive instrumentation can cause significant degradation of performance and is a significant concern for most systems, especially real time systems. Static analysis can be used as a technique for optimizing runtime monitoring. This is a dual but equivalent view to that presented in the introduction, namely that runtime monitoring is used to verify residual properties that remain unverified by (static) program verification.

5   Our Previous Work

In this section we briefly outline our own and close colleague's work in runtime verification. Some of our early work [34] was done in predictive runtime verification of concurrent Java programs and resulted in a tool for performing predictive deadlock and Eraser-like data race analysis on Java programs, guiding the Java PathFinder (JPF) model checker [61] to confirm the warnings discovered by the much faster predicative analysis. Instrumentation was done by modifying the Java Virtual Machine of JPF. The work on predictive runtime verification was later re-implemented and elaborated in the Java PathExplorer (JPaX) tool [37,35]. Specifically the deadlock analysis algorithm was improved to yield fewer false warnings [15]. In [14] is described an approach where such deadlock warnings are fed into a testing framework, where detected potential deadlock cycles are used to control the execution of the program in an attempt to confirm the deadlocks. Other recent results on predictive runtime verification includes work that goes beyond low-level data races on single variables, and includes detection of high-level data races on collections of variables [5], and detection of out-dated copies of shared variables [6]. JPaX also supports specification-based runtime verification. The Maude rewriting system [17] is used to define new logics [49,36]. This has proved extremely elegant since Maude is well suited for defining the syntax and semantics of a logic. In [38,39] we describe how to synthesize very efficient algorithms based on dynamic programming for monitoring past time logic.

In more recent work we decided to develop a runtime verification framework for Java *in Java*. Eagle [11] is a powerful temporal kernel language supporting temporal quantification and capable of modeling all of the temporal logics and most of the specification paradigms mentioned in this overview. Eagle is an extension of propositional logic with three temporal kernel operators, recursion, and parameterization over formulas in the logic as well as over data values. Formula parameterization allows the user to define new temporal combinators, and hence new temporal logics. The language therefore directly supports the definition of new specification patterns of the kind illustrated in [45]. Data parameterization allows to define properties relating data values from different points in time, hence supporting data quantification. Due to these constructs Eagle can define various forms of past and future time linear temporal logics, real-time logics, interval logics, extended regular expressions and state machines. Eagle furthermore supports abstract data specification in that formulas are interpreted on an abstract state defined as a Java class, and referred to as the Eagle state. In principle there is a stratification of the propositional language and the logic proper so that Java may be replaced by a high-level specification language. The user must define an abstraction mapping from concrete program states to abstract Eagle states. At each instrumentation location in the monitored target system, a method representing the abstraction function is called to update the Eagle state. Noting that Eagle supports the definition of state machines, we see that Eagle hence supports both data refinement and control refinement. A recent extension of Eagle supports automated program instrumentation [19], hence location quantification, using the aspect oriented programming tool AspectJ [8]. In previous work we developed the jSpy tool [31], which instruments Java byte-code. A jSpy instrumentation specification consists of a set of rules, each of which consists of a condition on byte-code and an instrumentation action stating what to report when byte-codes satisfying the condition are executed. The reported events are then picked up by the monitors that in turn check for various user provided properties. Eagle has been used within a test-case framework as described in [3,4].

6   Future Work

As a scientific discipline specification-based runtime verification does not face the same difficult problems as, say, model checking or theorem proving, and is likely closer to become part of practical software development environments. However, the discipline faces unsolved problems concerned with choice of specification notations, monitoring algorithms, code instrumentation, as well as social issues such as the usual resistance amongst software developers to write formal specifications in addition to the code itself. We feel that predictive runtime verification should be part of any development system since it is very effective, fully automated, requires no specifications, and essentially imposes only minor cost to the programmer. The challenge is to identify other problems that lend themselves to this form of analysis. Concerning specification-based runtime verification, choosing the right specification formalism is critical to the success of the approach. The formalism must be simple, yet powerful, and/or, it could be an already accepted notation, such as UML. We will continue experimenting with Eagle, but we will also investigate other formalisms in order to achieve the optimal balance between simplicity, efficiency and effectiveness. Amongst work not mentioned is that on generating specifications from runs [18]. We intend to extend our work in this direction.

References

1. 1st – 5th Workshops on Runtime Verification (RV 2001 - RV 2005). ENTCS, vol. 55(2), 70(4), 89(2), 113. Elsevier Science Direct. Amsterdam (to be published, 2001–2005), http://www.runtime-verification.org
2. Allan, C., Avgustinov, P., Kuzins, S., de Moor, O., Sereni, D., Sittamplan, G., Tibble, J., Christensen, A.S., Hendren, L., Lhoták, O.: Adding Trace Matching with Free Variables to AspectJ. In: OOPSLA 2005 (2005)
3. Artho, C., Barringer, H., Goldberg, A., Havelund, K., Khurshid, S., Lowry, M., Pasareanu, C., Rosu, G., Sen, K., Visser, W., Washington, R.: Combining Test-Case Generation and Runtime Verification. Theoretical Computer Science 336(2–3), 209–234 (2005), Extended version of [4]

4. Artho, C., Drusinsky, D., Goldberg, A., Havelund, K., Lowry, M., Pasareanu, C., Roşu, G., Visser, W.: Experiments with Test Case Generation and Runtime Analysis. In: Börger, E., Gargantini, A., Riccobene, E. (eds.) ASM 2003. LNCS, vol. 2589, pp. 87–107. Springer, Heidelberg (2003)
5. Artho, C., Havelund, K., Biere, A.: High-Level Data Races. Software Testing, Verification and Reliability 13(4) (2004)
6. Artho, C., Havelund, K., Biere, A.: Using Block-Local Atomicity to Detect Stale-Value Concurrency Errors. In: 2nd International Symposium on Automated Technology for Verification and Analysis, Taiwan, October–November (2004)
7. ASML. http://research.microsoft.com/fse/asml
8. AspectJ. http://eclipse.org/aspectj
9. Barnett, M., Leino, K.R.M., Schulte, W.: The Spec# Programming System: An Overview. In: Barthe, G., Burdy, L., Huisman, M., Lanet, J.-L., Muntean, T. (eds.) CASSIS 2004. LNCS, vol. 3362, Springer, Heidelberg (2005)
10. Barringer, H., Goldberg, A., Havelund, K., Sen, K.: Program Monitoring with LTL in Eagle. In: Parallel and Distributed Systems: Testing and Debugging (PADTAD 2004), Santa Fee, New Mexico, USA, April (2004)
11. Barringer, H., Goldberg, A., Havelund, K., Sen, K.: Rule-Based Runtime Verification. In: Steffen, B., Levi, G. (eds.) VMCAI 2004. LNCS, vol. 2937, Springer, Heidelberg (2004)
12. BCEL. http://jakarta.apache.org/bcel
13. Bensalem, S., Bozga, M., Krichen, M., Tripakis, S.: Testing Conformance of Real-Time Applications by Automatic Generation of Observers. In: Proceedings of the 4th International Workshop on Runtime Verification (RV 2004) [1], pp. 19–38 (2004)
14. Bensalem, S., Fernandez, J.-C., Havelund, K., Mounier, L.: Confirmation of Deadlock Potentials Detected by Runtime Analysis. In: Parallel and Distributed Systems: Testing and Debugging (PADTAD 2006), Portland, Maine, USA (July 2006)
15. Bensalem, S., Havelund, K.: Scalable Dynamic Deadlock Analysis of Multi-Threaded Programs. In: Parallel and Distributed Systems: Testing and Debugging (PADTAD - 3), IBM Verification Conference, Haifa, Israel, November 2005. LNCS (2005)
16. Chen, F., D'Amorim, M., Roşu, G.: Checking and Correcting Behaviors of Java Programs at Runtime with Java-MOP. In: Proceedings of the 5th International Workshop on Runtime Verification (RV 2005) [1] (2005)
17. Clavel, M., Durán, F.J., Eker, S., Lincoln, P., Martí-Oliet, N., Meseguer, J., Quesada, J.F.: The Maude System. In: Narendran, P., Rusinowitch, M. (eds.) RTA 1999. LNCS, vol. 1631, pp. 240–243. Springer, Heidelberg (1999)
18. Daikon. http://pag.csail.mit.edu/daikon
19. D'Amorim, M., Havelund, K.: Runtime Verification for Java. In: Workshop on Dynamic Program Analysis (WODA 2005) (March 2005)
20. D'Amorim, M., Rosu, G.: Efficient Monitoring of Omega-Languages. In: Etessami, K., Rajamani, S.K. (eds.) CAV 2005. LNCS, vol. 3576, Springer, Heidelberg (2005)
21. D'Angelo, B., Sankaranarayanan, S., Sanchez, C., Robinson, W., Finkbeiner, B., Sipma, H.B., Mehrotra, S., Manna, Z.: LOLA: Runtime Monitoring of Synchronous Systems. In: 12th International Symposium on Temporal Representation and Reasoning (TIME 2005), pp. 166–174 (2005)
22. Drusinsky, D.: The Temporal Rover and the ATG Rover. In: Havelund, K., Penix, J., Visser, W. (eds.) SPIN 2000. LNCS, vol. 1885, pp. 323–330. Springer, Heidelberg (2000)

23. Drusinsky, D.: Monitoring Temporal Rules Combined with Time Series. In: Hunt Jr., W.A., Somenzi, F. (eds.) CAV 2003. LNCS, vol. 2725, pp. 114–118. Springer, Heidelberg (2003)
24. Drusinsky, D.: Semantics and Runtime Monitoring of TLCharts: Statechart Automata with Temporal Logic Conditioned Transitions. In: Proceedings of the 4th International Workshop on Runtime Verification (RV 2004) [1], pp. 2–18 (2004)
25. Eiffel. http://www.eiffel.com
26. Eytani, Y., Havelund, K., Stoller, S., Ur, S.: Toward a Framework and Benchmark for Testing Tools for Multi-Threaded Programs. In: Concurrency and Computation: Practice and Experience (to appear, 2005)
27. Finkbeiner, B., Sankaranarayanan, S., Sipma, H.: Collecting Statistics over Runtime Executions. In: Proceedings of the 2nd International Workshop on Runtime Verification (RV 2002) [1], pp. 36–55 (2002)
28. Finkbeiner, B., Sipma, H.: Checking Finite Traces using Alternating Automata. In: Proceedings of the 1st International Workshop on Runtime Verification (RV 2001)[1], pp. 44–60 (2001)
29. Flanagan, C., Freund, S.: Atomizer: A Dynamic Atomicity Checker for Multi-threaded Programs. SIGPLAN Not. 39(1), 256–267 (2004)
30. Giannakopoulou, D., Havelund, K.: Automata-Based Verification of Temporal Properties on Running Programs. In: Proceedings, International Conference on Automated Software Engineering (ASE 2001), Coronado Island, California. ENTCS, pp. 412–416 (2001)
31. Goldberg, A., Havelund, K.: Instrumentation of Java Bytecode for Runtime Analysis. In: Fifth ECOOP Workshop on Formal Techniques for Java-like Programs (FTfJP 2003), Darmstadt, Germany (July 2003)
32. Harel, D.: Statecharts: A Visual Formalism For Complex Systems. Science of Computer Programming 8, 231–274 (1987)
33. Harrow, J.: Runtime Checking of Multithreaded Applications with Visual Threads. In: Havelund, K., Penix, J., Visser, W. (eds.) SPIN 2000. LNCS, vol. 1885, pp. 331–342. Springer, Heidelberg (2000)
34. Havelund, K.: Using Runtime Analysis to Guide Model Checking of Java Programs. In: Havelund, K., Penix, J., Visser, W. (eds.) SPIN 2000. LNCS, vol. 1885, pp. 245–264. Springer, Heidelberg (2000)
35. Havelund, K., Roşu, G.: Monitoring Java Programs with Java PathExplorer. In: Proceedings of the 1st International Workshop on Runtime Verification (RV 2001)[1], pp. 97–114 (2001)
36. Havelund, K., Roşu, G.: Monitoring Programs using Rewriting. In: Proceedings, International Conference on Automated Software Engineering (ASE 2001), Coronado Island, California. Institute of Electrical and Electronics Engineers, pp. 135–143 (2001)
37. Havelund, K., Roşu, G.: An Overview of the Runtime Verification Tool Java PathExplorer. Formal Methods in System Design 24(2) (March 2004)
38. Havelund, K., Roşu, G.: Efficient Monitoring of Safety Properties. Software Tools for Technology Transfer 6(2), 158–173 (2004)
39. Havelund, K., Roşu, G.: Synthesizing Monitors for Safety Properties. In: Katoen, J.-P., Stevens, P. (eds.) ETAPS 2002 and TACAS 2002. LNCS, vol. 2280, pp. 342–356. Springer, Heidelberg (2002), Best paper award
40. Jass. http://csd.informatik.uni-oldenburg.de/~jass
41. JML. http://www.cs.iastate.edu/~leavens/JML

42. Kiczales, G., Hilsdale, E., Hugunin, J., Kersten, M., Palm, J., Griswold, W.G.: An Overview of AspectJ. In: Knudsen, J.L. (ed.) ECOOP 2001. LNCS, vol. 2072, pp. 327–353. Springer, Heidelberg (2001)
43. Kim, M., Kannan, S., Lee, I., Sokolsky, O.: Java-MaC: a Run-time Assurance Tool for Java. In: Proceedings of the 1st International Workshop on Runtime Verification (RV 2001)[1] (2001)
44. Larch. http://www.cs.iastate.edu/larch-faq-webboy.html
45. Patterns. http://patterns.projects.cis.ksu.edu
46. PSL/Sugar. http://www.pslsugar.org
47. PVS. http://pvs.csl.sri.com
48. RAISE. http://spd-web.terma.com/Projects/RAISE
49. Roşu, G., Havelund, K.: A Rewriting-based Approach to Trace Analysis. Automated Software Engineering 12(2), 151–197 (2005)
50. Savage, S., Burrows, M., Nelson, G., Sobalvarro, P., Anderson, T.: Eraser: A Dynamic Data Race Detector for Multithreaded Programs. ACM Transactions on Computer Systems 15(4), 391–411 (1997)
51. Sen, K., Roşu, G.: Generating Optimal Monitors for Extended Regular Expressions. In: Proceedings of the 3rd International Workshop on Runtime Verification (RV 2003)[1], pp. 162–181 (2003)
52. Sen, K., Roşu, G., Agha, G.: Detecting Errors in Multithreaded Programs by Generalized Predictive Analysis of Executions. In: Steffen, M., Zavattaro, G. (eds.) FMOODS 2005. LNCS, vol. 3535, Springer, Heidelberg (2005)
53. Specware. http://www.specware.org
54. SPIN. http://spinroot.com
55. Stolz, V., Bodden, E.: Temporal Assertions using AspectJ. In: Fifth Workshop on Runtime Verification (RV 2005). Electronic Notes in Theoretical Computer Science, Elsevier Science Publishers, Amsterdam (2005)
56. T-UPPAAL. http://www.cs.aau.dk/~marius/tuppaal
57. Thati, P., Rosu, G.: Monitoring Algorithms for Metric Temporal Logic Specifications. In: Proceedings of the 4th International Workshop on Runtime Verification (RV 2004)[1], pp. 131–147 (2004)
58. Valgrind. http://valgrind.org
59. Vanderperren, W., Suvé, D., Augustina Cibrán, M., De Fraine, B.: Stateful Aspects in JAsCo. In: Workshop on Software Composition, ETAPS 2005 (2005)
60. VDM. http://www.csr.ncl.ac.uk/vdm
61. Visser, W., Havelund, K., Brat, G., Park, S.: Model Checking Programs. In: Proceedings of ASE 2000: The 15th IEEE International Conference on Automated Software Engineering, September 2000, IEEE CS Press, Los Alamitos (2000)
62. Walker, R.J., Viggers, K.: Implementing Protocols via Declarative Event Patterns. In: Taylor, R.N., Dwyer, M.B. (eds.) 12th International Symposium on the Foundations of Software Engineering, ACM, New York (2004)
63. Wang, L., Stoller, S.: Run-Time Analysis for Atomicity. In: Proceedings of the 3rd International Workshop on Runtime Verification (RV 2003) [1] (2003)

Specified Blocks

Eric C.R. Hehner

Department of Computer Science, University of Toronto
Toronto ON, M5S 2E4, Canada
hehner@cs.utoronto.ca

Abstract. This paper argues that specified blocks have every advantage over the combination of assertions, preconditions, postconditions, invariants, and variants, both for verifying programs, and for program development. They are simpler, more general, easier to write, and they make proofs easier.

1 Introduction

Assertions, invariants, variants, preconditions, and postconditions, are often claimed to be useful annotations for the verification of software. I shall refer to all of these as "assertion", by which I mean something that is intended to be true whenever execution passes the point in the program where it is located. This paper argues that assertions are superseded by the more general, easier to use, idea of specification.

The kind of specification I am advocating is not new; for a full account see [0]; for a shorter account see [2]. I hope that the version and presentation in this paper will make the idea more palatable to those who still cling to assertions.

All I ask of a programming language (for my present purpose) is that there be some way to make a block of code, such as the { } brackets in C and Java, and a way to label a statement or block. I will use ordinary ( ) parentheses to make a block, and an identifier followed by a colon for a label, but I make no case for any particular syntax.

2 First Example

To illustrate the idea, I will start with a standard programming pattern: do something to every item of a list. To make the example specific, given a natural number n , and a variable L of type lists of length n of integers, add one to every item of L . The program fragment is easily written.

$i := 0$; **while** $i \ne n$ **do** $(L[i] := L[i] + 1; \ i := i + 1)$

A specification describes the purpose of a block of code. Any block of code may have a specification. The only code that needs to have a specification is loops and procedures (methods, functions). For this example, I specify the whole, and also the loop within it.

add_1_to_every_item_of_L:
  ($i := 0$;
    add_1_to_remaining_items_of_L: **while** $i \ne n$ **do** $(L[i] := L[i] + 1; \ i := i + 1)$
)

We must also tell the verifier the formal specifications. So we define

B. Meyer and J. Woodcock (Eds.): Verified Software, LNCS 4171, pp.384–391, 2008.

add_1_to_every_item_of_L $=$ ($\forall j$: 0,..n· $L'[j] = L[j] + 1$)
add_1_to_remaining_items_of_L $=$ ($\forall j$: 0,..i· $L'[j] = L[j]$) $\land$ ($\forall j$: i,..n· $L'[j] = L[j] + 1$)

I am using an unprimed variable to stand for a variable's value at the start of the block to which the specification is attached, and a primed variable to stand for a variable's value at the end of the block to which the specification is attached. (The asymmetric notation a,..b starts with a and includes $b-a$ integers.) The programmer is now finished, unless the automated verifier needs help. The verifier has to make one proof per label. It must prove

add_1_to_every_item_of_L $\Leftarrow$ (i:= 0; add_1_to_remaining_items_of_L)
add_1_to_remaining_items_of_L $\Leftarrow$ **while** $i \neq n$ **do** ($L[i]$:= $L[i]$+1; i:= i+1)

For the first of these, notice that the loop is represented only by its specification. In general, any specified block is represented in a proof only by its specification. Starting with the right side,

$\quad$ (i:= 0; add_1_to_remaining_items_of_L) $\qquad\qquad$ replace informal spec with formal spec
$=$ (i:= 0; ($\forall j$: 0,..i· $L'[j] = L[j]$) $\land$ ($\forall j$: i,..n· $L'[j] = L[j] + 1$))
$\qquad\qquad\qquad\qquad\qquad\qquad\qquad\qquad\qquad\qquad$ replace i by 0 in what follows
$=$ ($\forall j$: 0,..0· $L'[j] = L[j]$) $\land$ ($\forall j$: 0,..n· $L'[j] = L[j] + 1$) $\qquad$ first $\forall$ has *null* domain
$=$ ($\forall j$: 0,..n· $L'[j] = L[j] + 1$)
$=$ add_1_to_every_item_of_L

For the second, the verifier uses the refinement semantics of loops [1]. That means proving

$\quad$ add_1_to_remaining_items_of_L
$\Leftarrow$ **if** $i \neq n$ **then** ($L[i]$:= $L[i]$+1; i:= i+1; add_1_to_remaining_items_of_L) **else** ok

For the proof, the verifier needs to know
$\quad$ **if** b **then** P **else** Q $=$ $b \land P \lor \neg b \land Q$
and it needs to know that if the variables are L and i, then
$\quad$ ok $=$ $L'=L \land i'=i$
Proofs, in general, are substitutions and simplifications, with few inventive steps. For brevity, we do not pursue this proof further.

$\quad$ Specifications do not have to be complete. We might be interested only in some property of the computation. Suppose we are interested in its execution time. Then, if you will allow me a freer syntax of labels, we can specify

$t'=t+n$:
$\quad$ (i:= 0;
$\quad\quad$ $t'=t+n-i$: **while** $i \neq n$ **do** ($L[i]$:= $L[i]$+1; i:= i+1; t:= t+1)
$\quad$)

The specification $t'=t+n$ says that the final time t' is the initial time t plus n, measuring time as iteration count. The specification $t'=t+n-i$ says that the time remaining at the start and end of each iteration of the loop is $n-i$.

So why is this better than assertions? First, there is the well-known problem that an assertion (abstraction of a single state) cannot relate the output to the input. And there is the usual work-around: introduce some specification variables (constants?) of uncertain status (they ought to be quantified to make them local to the assertions that use them). In our example, we need two of them: one to capture the initial state of the list, and the other to capture the initial state of the variant. In the usual style, here is the annotated program.

$\{L = M\}$
$i := 0;$
$\{(\forall j: 0,..i \cdot L[j] = M[j] + 1) \land (\forall j: i,..n \cdot L[j] = M[j]) \land 0 \leq n-i\}$
while $i \neq n$ **do**
      $\{(\forall j: 0,..i \cdot L[j] = M[j] + 1) \land (\forall j: i,..n \cdot L[j] = M[j]) \land 0 < n-i = V \land i \neq n\}$
      $(L[i] := L[i]+1;\ i := i+1)$
      $\{(\forall j: 0,..i \cdot L[j] = M[j] + 1) \land (\forall j: i,..n \cdot L[j] = M[j]) \land 0 \leq n-i < V\}$
$\{(\forall j: 0,..i \cdot L[j] = M[j] + 1) \land (\forall j: i,..n \cdot L[j] = M[j]) \land i=n\}$
$\{(\forall j: 0,..n \cdot L[j] = M[j] + 1)\}$

VDM eliminated the need for specification variables in its procedure postconditions, but not in general.

Second, look at the number of assertions (six) needed, versus the number of specifications (two) needed. The loop rule we are using here

> if $\{I \land b \land 0<v=V\}\ P\ \{I \land 0\leq v<V\}$
> then $\{I \land 0\leq v\}$ **while** b **do** P $\{I \land \neg b\}$

is standard, and does indeed require all the assertions we have used.

Third, and more importantly, I think it makes more sense to programmers to say what a block of code is intended to do than to try to say what is true at strategic points in the code. In other words, it's easier to write specifications than preconditions and postconditions and invariants and variants. This point is elaborated in Section 2.

Fourth, and most importantly, specifications are not limited to talking about initial and final values of variables, nor are they limited to talking about terminating computations. They can talk about intermediate values of variables, and about communication sequences. They can talk about space usage. They work for loops with intermediate exits, and loops with deep exits, which are problematic for assertions. They work for general recursion, and for parallel composition, and a great many other things. This point is elaborated in Section 3.

3 Binary Search

Here is an example to illustrate the difference between writing assertions and writing specifications. Given a nonempty sorted list L , assign natural variable h to indicate a position where x occurs, if any. Adding natural variables i and j , here is a solution.

$h := 0;\ j := \#L;$ **while** $j-h>1$ **do** $(i := (h+j)/2;$ **if** $L[i] \leq x$ **then** $h := i$ **else** $j := i)$

We need a specification for the whole thing, and one for the loop. For the moment, I use meaningless labels A and B because the choice of meaning is the point of the example.

```
A:  (  h:= 0;  j:= #L;
       B:  while j–h>1 do
           (  i:= (h+j)/2;
              if L[i]≤x then h:= i else j:= i
           )
    )
```

The proof obligations are

$A \Leftarrow h:= 0; j:= \#L; B$

$B \Leftarrow$ **while** $j–h>1$ **do** $(i:= (h+j)/2;$ **if** $L[i]≤x$ **then** $h:= i$ **else** $j:= i)$

The first proof (after defining A and B) is two substitutions: replace j by $\#L$ and then h by 0 in B . The second proof is

$$B \Leftarrow \quad j–h>1 \wedge (i:= (h+j)/2; \quad L[i]≤x \wedge (h:= i; B)$$
$$\vee \quad L[i]>x \wedge (j:= i; B))$$
$$\vee \quad j–h≤1 \wedge h'=h \wedge i'=i \wedge j'=j$$

Specification A is, informally, to find x in L . Formally, it is

$$(\exists i: 0,..\#L· L[i]=x) = L[h']=x$$

If x occurs in L anywhere from the beginning to the end, then the final value of h will be a position of x ; and if x does not occur anywhere in L , then the final value of h will be a position of some other value. (Obviously our search will be followed immediately by the test $L[h]=x$ to determine whether x was found.) For specification B we have a choice. The sensible choice is

$$h<j \Rightarrow ((\exists i: h,..j· L[i]=x) = L[h']=x)$$

which says: given that the list segment from (incl.) h to (excl.) j is nonempty, search in there. It describes what remains to be done at the start and end of each iteration. There is an alternative choice for B which says: given what's true at the start and end of each iteration, fulfill the original task. Formally,

$$h<j \wedge \neg(\exists i: 0,..h· L[i]=x) \wedge \neg(\exists i: j,..\#L· L[i]=x)$$
$$\Rightarrow ((\exists i: 0,..\#L· L[i]=x) = L[h']=x)$$

The antecedent (first line) is an invariant (as was the antecedent of the "sensible" choice). This example illustrates that we can, if we choose to, encode invariant assertions within specifications. It also illustrates that it is simpler and more direct to say what's left to be done, rather than to formulate an invariant.

4 Exponentiation

This example is an extremely efficient program for raising a number to a natural power. It gains its efficiency, in part, by using goto's in an unstructured way, including a jump into the middle of a loop. Nonetheless, it causes no problem for verification by specification blocks.

Let x and z be real variables, and let y be a natural variable. The following code makes the final value of z be the initial value of x raised to the power of the initial value of y. Formally, $z'=xy$, which is both briefer and clearer.

```
A: (  z:= 1;
        if even(y) then goto C
        else B:(  z:= z×x;  y:= y–1;
                  C:  if y=0 then goto E
                      else D: (  x:= x×x;  y:= y/2;
                                 if even(y) then goto D
                                 else goto B
                              )
               )
   );

E:
```

Straight from the code, what needs to be proven is the following:

$A \;\Leftarrow\;$ $z:= 1;$ **if** $even(y)$ **then** C **else** B
$B \;\Leftarrow\;$ $z:= z×x;$ $y:= y–1;$ C
$C \;\Leftarrow\;$ **if** $y=0$ **then** E **else** D
$D \;\Leftarrow\;$ $x:= x×x;$ $y:= y/2;$ **if** $even(y)$ **then** D **else** B

for appropriate formalizations of labels A, B, C, D, and E, as follows:

$A \;=\;$ $z_i=xy$
$B \;=\;$ $odd(y) \Rightarrow z' = z×xy$
$C \;=\;$ $even(y) \Rightarrow z' = z×xy$
$D \;=\;$ $even(y) \wedge y>0 \Rightarrow z' = z×xy$
$E \;=\;$ ok

A specifies the computation being performed. B, C, and D say: given what we know entering the block, here's what remains to be done. And E says there's nothing more to be done. It is well-known that a tail-recursive call can be compiled as a branch. In fact, any tail call, whether recursive or not, can be compiled as a branch (recursion is irrelevant). And conversely, a branch (which cannot be followed by live, unlabeled code) can be decompiled as a tail call. That, in effect, is what we are doing here. When we specify the purpose of a block that includes goto's, we include the computation that results from following the goto, as if the goto were a call.

Apparently, unstructured goto's pose no more verification problem than structured loops.

5 Product of Power Series

Here is an example to illustrate some of the general applicability of specified blocks. Write a procedure to read from channel a an infinite sequence of coefficients $a_0\ a_1\ a_2\ a_3\ ...$ of a power series $A = a_0 + a_1 \times x + a_2 \times x^2 + a_3 \times x^3 + ...$ and in parallel to read from channel b an infinite sequence of coefficients $b_0\ b_1\ b_2\ b_3\ ...$ of a power series $B = b_0 + b_1 \times x + b_2 \times x^2 + b_3 \times x^3 + ...$ and in parallel to write on channel c the infinite sequence of coefficients $c_0\ c_1\ c_2\ c_3\ ...$ of the power series $C = c_0 + c_1 \times x + c_2 \times x^2 + c_3 \times x^3 + ...$ equal to the product of the two input series.

procedure *PowerSeriesMultply* (**chan** *c*)
(**var** *a0, a1, aa, b0, b1, bb, dd*: *real*;   **chan** *d*: *real*;
   (**read** *a0* **from** *a* ‖ **read** *b0* **from** *b*);   **write** *a0×b0* **to** *c*;
   (*PowerSeriesMultply(d)*
   ‖   ((**read** *a1* **from** *a* ‖ **read** *b1* **from** *b*);   **write** *a0×b1 + a1×b0* **to** *c*;
       write_remaining_coefficients_on_c_reading_from_a_b_and_d:
        while *true* **do**
        ((**read** *aa* **from** *a* ‖ **read** *bb* **from** *b* ‖ **read** *dd* **from** *d*);
          write *a0×bb + dd + aa×b0* **to** *c*
)
)
)
)
)

The procedure has a channel parameter; the channel supplied as argument will get the output. It also has a local channel declaration for use within the procedure. This procedure is nonterminating, reading and writing infinite sequences of coefficients; it has dynamic process generation (because a parallel composition occurs within each recursive call); it has synchronization (otherwise known as sequential composition); it has dynamic storage allocaton (declarations occur within each recursive call). A parallel composition is just a conjunction of its operands. The same input can be read by different processes, each at its own speed.

Just two specifications are needed, the procedure name and the loop name, and they are already present. The verifier requires formal definitions, as follows.

PowerSeriesMultiply(c) $=$ $C = A \times B$
write_remaining_coefficients_on_c_reading_from_a_b_and_d $=$ $C = a0 \times B + D + A \times b0$

where D is the power series $d_0 + d_1 \times x + d_2 \times x^2 + d_3 \times x^3 + ...$ formed from the messages $d_0\ d_1\ d_2\ d_3\ ...$ written to and read from local channel d. It would be nice to allow procedures and loops and other blocks to be named with a formal specification, rather than just an identifier, particularly when, as here, the formal specification is shorter.

The prover needs to be told what it means to multiply power series. We tell it that $C = A \times B$ means $c_n = \Sigma i: 0,..n+1 \cdot a_i \times b_{n-i}$. We also tell the prover what it means to multiply a power series by a scalar, as in $a0 \times B$, and what it means to add power series. After that, the proof is straightforward, well within reach of an automated verifier; it can be found in complete detail in [0].

6 Conclusion

The proposal in this paper is applicable to initial program development, to program modification, and to verification of completed programs. For program development, proof can be made when a specification is formalized, even before its block has been written. For program modification, specifications are the information needed to make the modification. For verification, the specifications need to be invented if they are not already present.

From the fact that my examples are small, some people draw the conclusion that the method is only applicable to small programs. That inference is ridiculous; that conclusion is wrong. There is no upper limit on the size of blocks that can be specified. Scaling up works because a specified block is represented in a proof only by its specification.

A specification says what a block of code is intended to do; an assertion says what is true at a strategic point in the code. The former is often easier to write and briefer than the latter. Furthermore, specifications are not limited to talking about initial and final values of variables, nor are they limited to talking about terminating computations. They can talk about intermediate values of variables, communication sequences, time usage, and space usage. Without inventing new proof rules, they work for loops with intermediate and deep exits, for general recursion, for parallel composition, and a great many other things.

When there are two scientific theories, each having a merit over the other, it makes sense to keep them both. For example, Einstein's theory of motion is more accurate than Newton's, applying to a broader range of motion; but Newton's theory is simpler than Einstein's, so we keep it and use it whenever it is accurate enough for our purpose. But sometimes one theory has all the merits. For example, Galileo's theory of elliptical orbits around a stationary sun is both more accurate and simpler than Ptolemy's theory of cycles within cycles around a stationary earth. So it would be scientifically irresponsible to continue to use the worse theory when a better one is available.

There is an interesting variety of ways of approaching verification. Some of them have at least one merit not shared by the others, and so they deserve continued attention. Assertions (invariants, preconditions, postconditions), however, are completely subsumed by specifications in the form of a single boolean expression; the latter are both simpler and more widely applicable than the former. It would be scientifically irresponsible to continue to use the worse theory.

7 Progress and Further Work

We have a working prover [4], an adaptation of HOL, that knows the necessary theory of programming, and keeps track of frames. It is aimed entirely at program development, and includes a syntax-directed editor that confines the user to a limited selection of programming constructs. Further work is needed to broaden the applicability and usability of the tool.

A recent PhD thesis by I.T.Kassios [3] has made specified blocks applicable to the full range of object oriented programming features, including modularity, encapsulation, inheritance, reuse, polymorphism, and unrestricted pointers.

Acknowledgements

I thank Doug McIlroy for the Power Series example. I thank Albert Lai and Yannis Kassios for discussion concerning specification style.

References

[1] Hehner. E.C.R.: a Practical Theory of Programming, Springer, New York, 1993; current edition available free at www.cs.utoronto.ca/ hehner/aPToP

[2] Hehner, E.C.R., Gravell, A.M.: Refinement Semantics and Loop Rules. In: Woodcock, J.C.P., Davies, J., Wing, J.M. (eds.) FM 1999. LNCS, vol. 1709, pp. 1497–1510. Springer, Heidelberg (1999), `www.cs.utoronto.ca/~hehner/RSLR.pdf`

[3] Hehner, E.C.R.: Specifications, Programs, and Total Correctness. Science of Computer Programming, 34, 191–205. Elsevier, Amsterdam (1999), `www.cs.utoronto.ca/~hehner/SPTC.pdf`

[4] Kassios, I.T.: A Theory of Object Oriented Refinement, Ph.D. thesis, University of Toronto (2006)

[5] Lai, A.Y.C.: A Tool for a Formal Refinement Method, MSc thesis, University of Toronto (2000)

A Case for Specification Validation

Mats P.E. Heimdahl

Department of Computer Science and Engineering, University of Minnesota
University of Minnesota Software Engineering Center (UMSEC)

Abstract. As we are moving from a traditional software development process to a new development paradigm where the process it largely driven by tools and automation, new challenges for verification and validation (V&V) emerge. Productivity improvements will in this new paradigm be achieved through reduced emphasis on testing of implementations, increased reliance on automated analysis tools applied in the specification domain, verifiability correct generation of source-code, and verifiably correct compilation. The V&V effort will now be largely focused on assuring that the *formal specifications* are correct and that the *tools* are trustworthy so we can rely on the results of the analysis and code generation without extensive additional testing of the resulting implementation. Most effort has traditionally been devoted to the verification problem. In this position paper we point out the importance of validation and argue that if we fail to adequately address the validation problem problem the impact of verifying code generation and compilation will be limited.

1 Introduction

In software engineering we make a distinction between the *validation* and the *verification* of a software system under development. Verification is concerned with demonstrating that the software implements the functional and non-functional requirements. Verification answers the question *"is this implementation correct with respect to its requirements?"* Validation, on the other hand, is concerned with determining if the functional and non-functional requirements are the right requirements. Validation answers the question *"will this system, if build correctly, be safe and effective for its intended use?"* There is ample evidence that most safety problems can be traced to erroneous and inadequate requirements. Incomplete, inaccurate, ambiguous, and volatile requirements have plagued the software industry since its inception. In a 1987 article [6], Fred Brooks wrote

> The hardest single part of building a software system is deciding precisely what to build. No other part of the conceptual work is as difficult as establishing the detailed technical requirements... No other part of the work so cripples the resulting system if done wrong. No other part is as difficult to rectify later.

We know that the majority of software errors are made during requirements analysis [5,12,34,29], and that requirements errors are more likely to affect the safety of a system than errors introduced during design or implementation [24,26].

B. Meyer and J. Woodcock (Eds.): Verified Software, LNCS 4171, pp. 392–402, 2008.

Therefore, to improve the safety of software intensive systems it is critical that the requirements are properly *validated*. Unfortunately, current certification standards, for example, DO-178B [31], as well as the research effort outlined in the Verifiable Software Project focus almost exclusively on various *verification* activities. We find this unfortunate since one of the most critical problems with current certification standards and development practices is a lack of robust and reliable ways of assessing whether the requirements are correct; to gain the full advantage of verifying code generators and compilers we have to develop techniques to determine if the requirements have been adequately validated.

There is a significant effort in the avionics and medical technology industry to reduce the high cost of software development. The current trend is to focus on tools and automation, for example, automatically generating certifiably correct production code from a formal requirements specification or generating MC/DC tests for certification could provide dramatic cost savings. This approach is commonly referred to as model-based development. Since this approach relies heavily on the correctness of the model (or specification) for the correctness of the derived system, our current inability to adequately validate our requirements raises a serious concern regarding the adoption of this type of automation. In the remainder of this position paper we will discuss model-based development in more detail and point to some concerns that must be considered as we adopt verifying translators in software development.

2   Model-Based Development

Traditionally, software development has been largely a manual endeavor. Validation that we are building the right system has been achieved through requirements and specification inspections and reviews. Verification that the system is developed to satisfy its specification is archived through inspections of design artifacts and extensive testing of the implementations (Figure 1). In critical embedded control systems, such as the software controlling aeronautics applications and medical devices, the validation and verification phase (V&V) is particularly costly and consume approximately 50%–70% of the software development resources. Thus, if we could devise techniques to help us reduce the cost of V&V, dramatic cost savings could be achieved. The current trend towards *model-based development* (or specification-centered development [3,32]) is one attempt to address this problem.

In model-based development, the development effort is centered around a formal description of the proposed software system. For validation and verification purposes, this *formal specification* can then be subjected to various types of analysis, for example, completeness and consistency analysis [17,19] model checking [15,9,10,20,11], theorem proving [1,2], and test case generation [8,14,13,4,28,21,30]. Through manual inspections, formal verification, and simulation and testing we convince ourselves (and any regulatory agencies) that the software specification possesses desired properties. The implementation is then *automatically and correctly generated* from this specification and little or

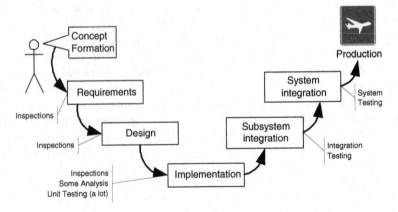

Fig. 1. Traditional Software Development Process

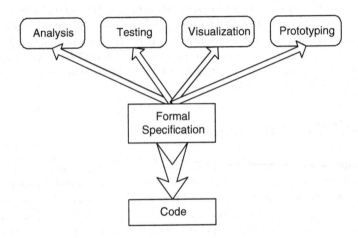

Fig. 2. Specification Centered Development

no additional testing of the implementation is required (Figure 2). There are currently several commercial and research tools that attempt to provide these capabilities—commercial tools are, for example, Esterel and SCADE from Esterel Technologies, Statemate from i-Logix [16], and SpecTRM from Safeware Engineering [25]; and examples of research tool are SCR [18], RSML^{-e} [32], and Ptolemy [23].

The capabilities of model-based development enable us to follow a different process. The development is centered around the formal specification and the V&V has been largely moved from testing and analyzing the code (Figure 1) to analyzing and testing the specification (Figure 3)—the traditional (and, in the critical systems domain, very costly) unit testing of code is replaced with testing and analysis of the specification in a hope to provide higher quality at a lower cost.

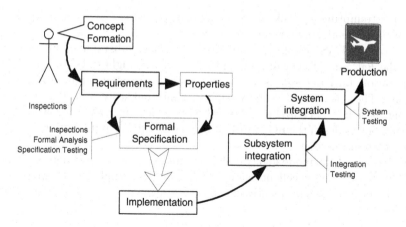

Fig. 3. Specification Centered Development Process

Note here that, in our opinion, the possibility of reducing or fully automating the costly unit-testing efforts are key to success of specification centered development. We have found very little support for this type of development if modeling and analysis are to be performed in *addition* to what is currently done—these new techniques must either make current efforts more efficient or replace some currently required V&V activity. In either case, our increased reliance on tools requires that they can be trusted—a prime opportunity for verifying translators as well as analysis tools that provide proof justifications and proof explanations. On the other hand, we are now demanding that the formal specification serving as the basis for our development is correct with respect to the customers' true needs; a demand that can only be met through extensive model validation.

In an ongoing project with Rockwell Collins Inc. and NASA Langley Research Center we have investigated model-based development and focused mainly on the verification aspects of the problem. Below we provide a short overview of one of our case examples and discuss some issues that have arisen during the course of this project.

2.1 Overview of a Flight Guidance System

A Flight Guidance System (FGS) is a component of the overall Flight Control System (FCS). It compares the measured state of an aircraft (position, speed, and attitude) to the desired state and generates pitch and roll guidance commands to minimize the difference between the measured and desired state. These guidance commands are both displayed to the pilot as guidance cues on the Primary Flight Display (PFD) and sent to the Autopilot (AP) that moves the control surfaces of the aircraft to achieve commanded pitch and roll.

The internal structure of the FGS can be broken down into the mode logic and the flight control laws. The flight control laws accept information about the aircraft's current and desired state and compute the pitch and roll guidance commands. The mode logic determines which lateral and vertical modes are armed (attempting to lock on to a navigation source) and active (providing guidance to the aircraft) at any given time.

The overall FGS system consists of two identical subsystems, one associated with the left side of the aircraft and one with the right side. In most modes of operation, only one side is active and responds to pilot inputs and produces outputs. The inactive side simply copies its internal state from the active side, serving as a hot backup. In a few critical modes such as Approach and Go Around, both sides of the FGS are active and generate outputs that are compared before they are used.

We have used the mode logic of a FGS as an example in several previous studies [7,22,33]. It is an excellent example because it is complex and representative of a class of problems frequently encountered in the design of embedded control systems.

2.2 Modeling Process

In the project, we collected the system requirements as informal "shall" statements. These requirements were relatively mature and well-understood. The next phase, modeling, consisted of constructing by hand an executable model that we believed exhibited the behavior informally stated in the shall statements; in this case we used the RSML^{-e} notation developed at the University of Minnesota. Throughout creation of the model, we continually used the simulation capabilities of the RSML^{-e} execution and analysis environment NIMBUS to execute the model and informally confirm that it behaved as we expected. As we built the model, we discovered and corrected numerous ambiguous, unclear, and inconsistent informal requirements.

In the formal verification phase, we manually translated the shall statements into formal properties stated over the model in CTL and merged these formal properties with the translation of the RSML^{-e} model into NuSMV created using a translator developed by the University of Minnesota. Again, the formalization process helped us improve the informal requirements. The NuSMV model checker was then used to confirm whether the property held over the model or not.

When completed, the model of the FGS mode logic consisted of 41 input variables (Boolean and enumerated), 16 small, tightly synchronized hierarchical finite state machines, 122 macro or function definitions, 29 output variables (Boolean and enumerated), and was roughly 160 pages long in its typeset version. We developed 300+ CTL properties based on the informal requirements. A detailed description of the model and its simulation environment is available in [27].

3   The Specification Will Be Wrong

As mentioned above, the process of creating a model from the English prose requirements caused us to go back and clarify the English statement of the requirements. In the same way, translating the English statements into SMV also prompted us to go back and clarify the English statement. In addition, the verification that the model satisfied the requirements (formalized as CTL properties) led to some insight into the validation problem. For example, consider the well-validated and non-controversial requirement below.

If Heading Select mode is not selected, Heading Select mode shall be selected when the HDG switch is pressed on the Flight Control Panel.

After formalization into CTL, this property did not verify in our model. Using the model-checker we discovered two ways in which this property will not be true. First, if another event arrived at the same time as the HDG switch was pressed, that event could preempt the HDG switch event. Second, if this side of the FGS was not active, the HDG switch event was completely ignored by this side of the FGS. These were two scenarios that were correctly handled in the implementation of the FGS systems, but not captured in any specification. The counterexamples from NuSMV led us to modify the requirement to state

If this side is active and Heading Select mode is not selected, Heading Select mode shall be selected when the HDG switch is pressed on the FCP (providing no higher priority event occurs at the same time).

While longer and more difficult to read than the original statement, it has the advantage of being a more accurate description of the system's behavior. Of course, we also had to clearly define what a "higher priority"' event was.

We found that the process of proving the properties forced us to go back and modify virtually all of our original English requirements; consequently, all formal specification properties also had to be modified.

It also became clear to the engineers formalizing the properties that great care needs to be taken when formulating SMV properties to ensure that their proofs are meaningful. For example, in the modelling of the FGS we frequently used macros to encapsulate commonly used properties, for example, we might encapsulate a complex condition in a macro named "When_Lateral_Mode_Manually_Selected". The macros were frequently used when the properties were stated as SMV properties. In most cases, the macro was used as the antecedent of an implication, for example,

```
AG(m_When_Lateral_Mode_Manually_Selected.result ->
   Onside_FD_On)
```

Naturally, if the macro "When_Lateral_Mode_Manually_Selected" was over-constrained in the model (or even contradictory and thus always false) this proof would succeed but it would be rather meaningless.

To summarize, when developing formal models of any substantial system, the models will most likely be incorrect with respect to the real needs of the system. In our case, the three complementary models—informal English language requirements, requirements formalized as CTL properties, and an executable formal model—served to check each other in a rigorous validation process. Had we only built the executable model and validated it through testing, chances are significant flaws would have remained. Similarly, had we been blessed with a correct-by-construction tool that would have helped us refine our 300+ CTL properties to an implementation, the implementation would certainly have been grossly incorrect with respect to the customers' real needs. It is clear that a *rigorous validation process* must be in place to ensure that any formal artifacts serving as the basis for downstream automation are correct; without this validation any breakthroughs in verifiably correct code generation and compilation will achieve limited success.

4   Loss of "Collateral Validation"

The goal of adopting model-based development is to reduce the high cost of software development. The hope is that by relying on tools and automation, for example, automatically generating certifiably correct production code from a formal requirements specification or generating MC/DC tests for certification, we could provide dramatic cost savings. These cost savings will be achieved by replacing time consuming and costly manual processes, for example, design, coding, and definition of test-cases, with tools. As mentioned above, our current inability to adequately validate our requirements raises a serious concern regarding the adoption of this type of automation. Manual processes, may that be design, coding, testing, or putting a medical device through clinical studies, draw on the collective experience and vigilance of many dedicated software professionals; professionals that provide *"collateral validation"* as they are working on the software. Experienced professionals designing, developing code, or defining test cases provide additional validation of the software system; if there is a problem with the specified functionality of the system, they have a chance of noticing and taking corrective action. As an example, consider the requirements example from the previous section. Although the facts that the FGS had to be active and that no higher-priority events were received at the same time were not explicitly sated in the requirements, the engineers implemented the FGS functionality correctly; these problems were caught in the manual development process. When replacing these manual efforts with automation, proper validation of the formal requirements specifications on which the automation is based becomes absolutely essential; there may be no safeguards in the downstream development activities to catch critical flaws in the formal model—the collateral validation is lost.

Naturally, the tools we use in the validation process may lead to additional problems. For example,

1. If the specification execution environment misrepresents the semantics of the specification language, all testing and validation done in the specification domain is invalid.
2. If the code generation is incorrect, the resulting implementation will naturally be wrong (and it may not be caught since we are now reducing testing in the code domain).

3. If any of our analysis tools applied in the specification domain provide false negatives (they fail to catch a faulty specification), we may mistakenly accept a specification as correct and use it for code generation (again, this problem is unlikely to be caught with the reduced code testing).

Solutions to such problems must be provided before these promising techniques can be effectively used in the development of critical systems. The research agenda laid out in this workshop promises to address some of the concerns related to the tools used in model-based development, for example, verifying translators and trusted proof checkers would address issues 2 and 3 above. Unfortunately, execution environments, code generators, and analysis tools are not simple pieces of software and it is highly unlikely that we will be able to provide the level of confidence necessary to trust a specific tool as a development tool [31] in critical systems development. Also, consider tool evolution and the cost of reverification of evolving tools and the situation looks grim.

5   No Need for Perfection

As we ponder how new analysis techniques and development tools can be effectively deployed in the critical systems domain, we cannot loose track of one important fact—*although perfection and full verification is the goal, perfection is not necessary for deployment and highly effective use.* After all, our aim with increased use of tools is to replace costly, time consuming, and error prone manual tasks such as inspections and testing, and all that is really necessary from our tools is that they are *better* than the manual tasks they replace. Unfortunately, we do not know much about how error prone our manual processes really are, nor do we know how to compare the effectiveness of an automated process to a manual process—much important analytical and empirical research is needed to help answer this question.

6   Summary

The emergence of formal modeling languages acceptable to practicing engineers and the development of powerful analysis tools, for example, model checkers, will enable a new development paradigm relying heavily on the use of automated tools for analysis and code generation—a development paradigm often referred to as model-based development. As a community, we are now in a position to bring the full power of formal software development to fruition. As discussed in this position paper, however, we have to approach this opportunity cautiously. All formal development efforts rely on a correct specification as a basis for development and verification; this puts enormous demands on the validation of the specification—the specification simply must be correct with respect to the customers' needs. Unfortunately, research efforts outlined in the Verifiable Software Project focuse almost exclusively on various *verification* activities. We find this troublesome; to gain the full advantage of verifying code generators and compilers we have to concurrently develop techniques to determine if the specifications have been adequately validated. It would be highly disappointing if the enormous advantages in verification technology we have seen the last decade, and will most likely see in the future, are used to verify that faulty specifications are implemented correctly. A few well publicized failures are enough to make widespread industry adoption and regulatory acceptance very difficult and set our efforts back a decade—let us make sure that this does not happen.

Acknowledgements

The author wishes to acknowledge the contributions of Dr. Steven P. Miller, Dr. Michael W. Whalen, and Dr. Alan Tribble of Rockwell Collins for their modeling and analysis efforts, and valuable discussions; the ongoing support of this work by Ricky Butler, Kelly Hayhurst, and Celeste Bellcastro of the NASA Langley Research Center; and the efforts of his current and former graduate students Anjali Joshi, Ajitha Rajan, Yunja Choi, Sanjai Rayadurgam, George Devaraj, and Dan O'Brien of the University of Minnesota.

References

1. Archer, M., Heitmeyer, C., Sims, S.: TAME: A PVS interface to simplify proofs for automata models. In: User Interfaces for Theorem Provers (1998)
2. Bensalem, S., Caspi, P., Parent-Vigouroux, C., Dumas, C.: A methodology for proving control systems with Lustre and PVS. In: Proceedings of the Seventh Working Conference on Dependable Computing for Critical Applications (DCCA 7), San Jose CA, January 1999, pp. 89–107. IEEE Computer Society Press, Los Alamitos (1999)
3. Valdis, B.L., Yehudai, A.: Using transformations in specification-based prototyping. IEEE Transactions on Software Engineering 19(5), 436–452 (1993)
4. Blackburn, M.R., Busser, R.D., Fontaine, J.S.: Automatic generation of test vectors for SCR-style specifications. In: Proceedings of the 12th Annual Conference on Computer Assurance, COMPASS 1997 (June 1997)
5. Boehm, B.: Software Engineering Economics. Prentice-Hall, Englewood Cliffs (1981)
6. Brooks, F.: No silver bullet: Essence and accidents of software engineering. IEEE Computer, 10–19 (April 1997)
7. Butler, R., Miller, S., Potts, J., Carreno, V.: A formal methods approach to the analysis of mode confusion. In: 17st Digital Avionics Systems Conference (DASC 1998), Belllevue, WA, pp. C41/1 – C41/8 (October 1998)
8. Callahan, J., Schneider, F., Easterbrook, S.: Specification-based testing using model checking. In: Proceedings of the SPIN Workshop (August 1996)
9. Chan, W., Anderson, R.J., Beame, P., Burns, S., Modugno, F., Notkin, D., Reese, J.D.: Model checking large software specifications. IEEE Transactions on Software Engineering 24(7), 498–520 (1998)
10. Choi, Y., Heimdahl, M.: Model checking RSML^{-e} requirements. In: Proceedings of the 7th IEEE/IEICE International Symposium on High Assurance Systems Engineering, Tokyo, Japan, October 2002, pp. 109–118 (2002)

11. Clarke, E.M., Grumberg, O., Peled, D.: Model Checking. MIT Press, Cambridge (1999)
12. Davis, A.: Software Requirements: Object, Function, and States. Prentice-Hall, Englewood Cliffs (1993)
13. Engels, A., Feijs, L.M.G., Mauw, S.: Test generation for intelligent networks using model checking. In: Brinksma, E. (ed.) TACAS 1997. LNCS, vol. 1217, pp. 384–398. Springer, Heidelberg (1997)
14. Gargantini, A., Heitmeyer, C.: Using model checking to generate tests from requirements specifications. Software Engineering Notes 24(6), 146–162 (1999)
15. Grumberg, O., Long, D.E.: Model checking and modular verification. ACM Transactions on Programming Languages and Systems 16(3), 843–871 (1994)
16. Harel, D., Lachover, H., Naamad, A., Pnueli, A., Politi, M., Sherman, R., Shtull-Trauring, A., Trakhtenbrot, M.: Statemate: A working environment for the development of complex reactive systems. IEEE Transactions on Software Engineering 16(4), 403–414 (1990)
17. Heimdahl, M.P.E., Leveson, N.G.: Completeness and consistency in hierarchical state-base requirements. IEEE Transactions on Software Engineering 22(6), 363–377 (1996)
18. Heitmeyer, C., Bull, A., Gasarch, C., Labaw, B.: SCR*: A toolset for specifying and analyzing requirements. In: Haveraaen, M., Dahl, O.-J., Owe, O. (eds.) Abstract Data Types 1995 and COMPASS 1995. LNCS, vol. 1130, Springer, Heidelberg (1996)
19. Heitmeyer, C.L., Jeffords, R.D., Labaw, B.G.: Automated consistency checking of requirements specifications. ACM Transactions on Software Engineering and Methodology 5(3), 231–261 (1996)
20. Heitmeyer, C., Kirby Jr., J., Labaw, B., Archer, M., Bharadwaj, R.: Using abstraction and model checking to detect safety violations in requirements specifications. IEEE Transactions on Software Engineering 24(11), 927–948 (1998)
21. Jasper, R., Brennan, M., Williamson, K., Currier, B., Zimmerman, D.: Test data generation and feasible path analysis. In: Proc. of Int'l Symp. on Software Testing and Analysis, August 1994, pp. 95–107 (1994)
22. Joshi, A., Miller, S.P., Heimdahl, M.P.E.: Mode confusion analysis of a flight guidance system using formal methods. In: 22nd Digital Avionics Systems Conference (DASC 2003), pp. 2.D.1-1 – 2.D.1-11(October 2003)
23. Lee, E.A.: Overview of the ptolemy project. Technical Report Technical Memorandum UCB/ERL M03/25, University of California, Berkeley, CA, 94720, USA (July 2003)
24. Leveson, N.: Safeware: System Safety and Computer. Addison-Wesley, Reading (1995)
25. Leveson, N.G., Heimdahl, M.P.E., Reese, J.D.: Designing Specification Languages for Process Control Systems: Lessons Learned and Steps to the Future. In: Nierstrasz, O., Lemoine, M. (eds.) ESEC 1999 and ESEC-FSE 1999. LNCS, vol. 1687, pp. 127–145. Springer, Heidelberg (1999)
26. Lutz, R.: An overview of REFINE 2.0. In: Proceedings of the First ACM SIGSOFT Symposium on the Foundations of Software Engineering (1993)
27. Miller, S., Tribble, A., Carlson, T., Danielson, E.: Flight guidance system requirements specification. Technical Report CR-, -212426, NASA Langley Research Center (June 2003),
http://techreports.larc.nasa.gov/ltrs/refer/2003/cr/NASA-2003-cr212426.refer

28. Offutt, A.J., Xiong, Y., Liu, S.: Criteria for generating specification-based tests. In: Proceedings of the Fifth IEEE International Conference on Engineering of Complex Computer Systems (ICECCS 1999) (October 1999)

29. Ramamoorthy, C., Prakesh, A., Tsai, W., Usuda, Y.: Software engineering: Problems and perspectives. IEEE Computer, 191–209 (October 1984)

30. Rayadurgam, S., Heimdahl, M.P.E.: Coverage based test-case generation using model checkers. In: Proceedings of the 8th Annual IEEE International Conference and Workshop on the Engineering of Computer Based Systems (ECBS 2001), April 2001, IEEE Computer Society, Los Alamitos (2001)

31. RTCA. Software Consideration. In: Airborne Systems and Equipment Certification. RTCA (1992)

32. Thompson, J.M., Heimdahl, M.P.E., Miller, S.P.: Specification based prototyping for embedded systems. In: Nierstrasz, O., Lemoine, M. (eds.) ESEC 1999 and ESEC-FSE 1999. LNCS, vol. 1687, pp. 163–179. Springer, Heidelberg (1999)

33. Tribble, A., Miller, S.: Safety analysis of a flight guidance system. In: 21st Digital Avionics Systems Conference (DASC 2002), Irvine, CA, October 2002, vol. 2, pp. 13C1–1 – 13C1–10 (2002)

34. van Schouwen, A.: The A-7 requirements model: Re-examination for real-time systems and an application to monitoring systems. Technical Report 90-276, Queens University, Hamilton, Ontario (1990)

Some Verification Issues at
NASA Goddard Space Flight Center

Michael G. Hinchey[1], James L. Rash[2], and Christopher A. Rouff[3]

[1] Loyola College in Maryland
Department of Computer Science
Baltimore, MD 21210, USA
mhinchey@loyola.edu
[2] Advanced Architectures and Automation Branch
NASA Goddard Space Flight Center
Greenbelt, MD 20771, USA
james.l.rash@nasa.gov
[3] Advanced Technology Laboratories
Lockheed Martin Corporation
Arlington, VA 22203, USA
crouff@atl.lmco.com

Abstract. NASA is developing increasingly complex missions to conduct new science and exploration. Missions are increasingly turning to multi-spacecraft to provide multiple simultaneous views of phenomena, and to search more of the solar system in less time. Swarms of intelligent autonomous spacecraft, involving complex behaviors and interactions, are being proposed to accomplish the goals of these new missions. The emergent properties of swarms make these missions powerful, but simultaneously far more difficult to design, and to verify that the proper behaviors will emerge. In verifying the desired behavior of swarms of intelligent interacting agents, the two significant sources of difficulty are the exponential growth of interactions and the emergent behaviors of the swarm. NASA Goddard Space Flight Center (GSFC) is currently involved in two projects that aim to address these sources of difficulty. We describe the work being conducted by NASA GSFC to develop a formal method specifically for swarm technologies. We also describe the use of requirements-based programming in the development of these missions, which, it is believed, will greatly reduce development lead-times and avoid many of the problems associated with such complex systems.

1 Introduction

It is planned that future NASA missions will exploit exciting new paradigms for space exploration [22,23]. To perform new science and exploration, traditional missions, reliant upon the use of a single large spacecraft, are being replaced with missions that will involve several smaller spacecraft. These new missions will behave as a "system of systems," operating in collaboration, analogous to swarms in nature [11].

This offers several advantages: the ability to send spacecraft to explore regions of space where traditional craft simply would be impractical, greater redundancy and, consequently, greater protection of assets, and reduced costs and risk, to name but a few.

B. Meyer and J. Woodcock (Eds.): Verified Software, LNCS 4171, pp. 403–412, 2008.

Planned missions entail the use of several unmanned autonomous vehicles (UAVs) flying approximately one meter above the surface of Mars, which will cover as much of the surface of Mars in approximately three seconds as the now famous Mars rovers did in their entire time on the planet; the use of armies of tetrahedral walkers to explore the Mars and Lunar surface; constellations of satellites flying in formation; and, the use of miniaturized pico-class spacecraft to explore the asteroid belt, where heretofore it was impossible to send exploration craft without high likelihood of loss [18].

However, these new approaches to exploration missions simultaneously pose many challenges. The missions will be unmanned and necessarily highly autonomous. They will also exhibit all of the properties of *autonomic* systems, being self-protecting, self-healing, self-configuring, and self-optimizing [12]. Many of these missions will be sent to parts of the solar system where manned missions are simply not possible, and to where the round-trip delay for communications to spacecraft exceeds 40 minutes, meaning that the decisions on responses to problems and undesirable situations must be made *in situ* rather than from ground control on Earth. The degree of autonomy that such missions will possess would require a prohibitive amount of testing. Furthermore, learning and continual improvements in performance will mean that emergent behavior patterns simply cannot be fully predicted [19].

2 Formal Approaches to Swarm Technologies

These missions are orders of magnitudes more complex than the traditional missions and verifying these new types of missions will be impossible using current techniques. New verification methods will be needed to address the added complexity resulting from the nondeterminate nature of these systems as well as the emergent behavior of swarms. To support the level of assurance that NASA missions require, formal specification techniques and formal verification will play vital roles in the future development of NASA space exploration missions. The role of formal methods will be in the specification and analysis of forthcoming missions, enabling software assurance and proof of correctness of the behavior of the swarm, whether or not this behavior is emergent (as a result of composing a number of interacting entities, producing behavior that was not foreseen). Formal models derived may also be used as the basis for automating the generation of much of the code for the mission to further reduce the probability of adding new errors during coding.

To address the challenge in verifying the above missions a NASA project, *Formal Approaches to Swarm Technology* or *FAST*, is investigating the requirements of appropriate formal methods for use in such missions, and is beginning to apply these techniques to specifying and verifying parts of a future NASA swarm-based mission.

2.1 FAST

As part of the FAST project, the planned ANTS (Autonomous Nano Technology Swarm) mission is being used as an example swarm-based mission. The ANTS submission PAM (Prospecting Asteroid Mission) will involve the launch of 1000 picoclass satellites into the asteroid belt [11,21]. Many of these will be lost on first launch, others through collisions with asteroids and with other ANTS spacecraft. The surviving spacecraft (approximately 30% to 40%) will form subswarms under the control of a leader or *ruler*. *Worker* spacecraft will carry individual instruments (e.g., a magnetometer, x-ray, gamma-ray, visible/IR, neutral mass spectrometer, etc.) which will be used to collect various types of data. Based on these data, the ruler will determine which asteroids are worthy of further investigation. Because of distances, low bandwidth, and roundtrip delays in communication with Earth, the mission will be required to operate more or less autonomously. It must also be able to recover from collisions, loss of instruments, loss of rulers or *messengers* (used to facilitate communication between spacecraft and/or with ground control), in addition to solar storms, whereby charged particles from the Sun can damage spacecraft and/or the solar sails (panels) that they use to obtain power from the sun.

2.2   Properties of an Appropriate Formal Method for Intelligent Swarms

An effective formal method must be able to predict the emergent behavior of 1000 agents operating as a swarm, as well as the behavior of the individual agent. Crucial to the mission will be the ability to modify operations autonomously to reflect the changing nature of the mission. For this, the formal specification will need to be able to track the goals of the mission as they change, and to modify the model of the Universe as new data comes in. The formal specification will also need to allow for specification of the decision making process to aid in the determination of which instruments will be needed, at what location, with what goals, etc.

Most importantly, the formal specification must allow for verification, and for the analysis of various properties and conditions within the evolving system. The ANTS mission details are still being determined and are constantly changing as more research is conducted. The formal specification technique employed must be sufficiently flexible to allow for efficient changes and re-prediction of emergent behavior.

Bearing all of this in mind, the following list summarizes the properties necessary for effective specification and emergent behavior prediction of the ANTS swarm and other swarm-based missions, and looks to existing formal methods to provide some of the desired properties [10].

Process representation: Processes can be specified using the various manifestations of transition functions.

Reasoning: Other forms of possibly non-standard logics may need to be employed to allow for intelligent reasoning with uncertain and possibly conflicting information.

Choosing Action Alternatives: A means of expressing probabilities and frequencies of events (as in WSCCS) is most beneficial in choosing between different enabled actions. A modified version of the WSCCS ability may be used to supply an algebra for choosing between possible actions.

Asynchronous messaging: Asynchronous messaging will need to be supported, as this is the most common type of messaging in swarm applications. This is not a significant problem as most synchronous messaging is implemented via asynchronous "handshakes". There are variants of CSP and other process algebras that support asynchronous messaging, either by having all processes be receptive (as in Receptive Process Theory), or through infinite buffering as in ACSP.

Message buffering: Message buffering may be needed due to the possibly asynchronous nature of messaging between members of the swarm. Several asynchronous variants of CSP achieve this through infinite buffering.

Concurrent agent states for each spacecraft: This requirement is well supported by available process algebras.

Communication protocols between agents: Available process algebras are highly effective in this area.

Adaptability to programming: Any formal specification languages that are developed will need to keep in mind the ease of converting the formal specification to program code and as input to model checkers.

Determining whether goals have been met: The goals of each spacecraft are constantly under review. We will need to be able to specify a method by which the spacecraft will know when the goals have been met. A modification to X-Machines may be able to solve this since the goals could be tracked using X-Machines (effectively finite state machines with memory).

Method for determining new goals: Once goals are met, new goals must be formed. We need to be able to specify a method for forming these goals.

Model checking: Model checking will help to avoid semantic inconsistencies in the specifications. Notations employed will need to be suitable for use as input to a model checker.

Tracking Models: X-Machines have the ability to track the universe model in memory but we need a more robust way to detail what the model is, how it is created, and how it is modified.

Associating agent actions with priorities and frequencies: A suitable formal method requires a means of expressing the probability of certain actions being enabled, and the frequency with which this will occur.

Predicting emergent behavior: Current approaches are not robust enough for the purpose of predicting individual and swarm emergent behavior and will need to be enhanced by greater use of Probability, Markov Chains, and/or Chaos Theory.

3   An Integrated Formal Method

The requirements detailed above point to the need to employ multiple formal methods in order to provide both a sufficiently expressive specification notation (that can deal with concurrency, real-time constraints, data manipulation, goal-oriented operation, etc.) *and* to facilitate verification.

The FAST project has surveyed various formal methods examining them for application to swarm technologies, and more generally "systems of systems" [20]. Various formal specification notations have been applied to parts of the ANTS mission (such as it currently stands, realizing that much of it will change before its launch) to provide feedback on the appropriateness of various approaches.

The project has concluded, unsurprisingly, that no single formal method will be appropriate for dealing with such a complex mission, and has consequently been concentrating on blending together various notations to provide a sufficiently expressive notation [10]. Future work on the project will include developing support tools for the integrated notation, and developing verification techniques for swarm-based missions.

4   Formal Requirements-Based Programming

Requirements-Based Programming (RBP) has been advocated [4,5] as a viable means of developing complex evolving systems. The idea that it embodies is that requirements can be systematically and mechanically transformed to executable code.

This may seem to be an obvious goal in the engineering of computer-based systems, but requirements-based programming does in fact go a step further than current development methods. System development, typically, assumes the existence of a model of reality, called a design (more correctly, a design specification), from which an implementation will be derived [8]. This model must itself be derived from the system requirements, but there is a large 'gap' in going from requirements to design. Requirements-Based Programming seeks to eliminate this 'gap' by ensuring that the ultimate implementation can be traced fully back to the actual requirements. NASA's experience has been that emphasizing sufficient effort at the requirements phase of development can significantly reduce cost overruns later [2]. RBP promises a significant payoff for increasing effort at the requirements phase by reducing the level of effort in subsequent verification.

R2D2C (Requirements-to-Design-to-Code) is a NASA patent pending approach to the engineering of complex computer systems, where the need for correctness of the system, with respect to its requirements, is significantly high [7,9]. In this category, we include NASA mission software, most of which exhibits both autonomous and autonomic properties, and must continue to do so in order to achieve survivability in harsh environments.

4.1   R2D2C

In the R2D2C approach, engineers (or others) may write requirements as scenarios in constrained (domain-specific) natural language, or in a range of other notations (including UML use cases). These will be used to derive a formal model that is guaranteed to be equivalent to the requirements stated at the outset, and which will subsequently be used as a basis for code generation. The formal model can be expressed using a variety of formal notations. Currently we are using CSP, Hoare's language of Communicating Sequential Processes [13,14], which is suitable for various types of analysis and investigation, and as the basis for fully formal implementations as well as automated test case generation, etc.

R2D2C is unique in that it allows for full formal development from the outset, and maintains mathematical soundness through all phases of the development process, from requirements through to automatic code generation. The approach may also be used for reverse engineering, that is, in retrieving models and formal specifications from existing code (Figure 2). The method can also be used to "paraphrase" (in natural language, etc.) formal descriptions of existing systems.

In addition, the approach is not limited to generating executable code. It may also be used to generate business processes and procedures, and we have been experimenting (successfully) with using a rudimentary prototype to generate instructions for robotic devices to be used on the Hubble Robotic Servicing Mission (HRSM) [16]. We are also

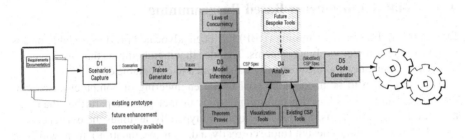

Fig. 1. The R2D2C approach and current status of the prototype

experimenting with using it as a basis for an expert system verification tool, and as a means of capturing expert knowledge for expert systems [17].

4.2   Technical Approach

The R2D2C approach involves a number of phases, which are reflected in the system architecture described in Figure 1. The following describes each of these phases.

D1 Scenarios Capture: Engineers, end users, and others write scenarios describing intended system operation. The input scenarios may be represented in a constrained natural language using a syntax-directed editor, or may be represented in other textual or graphical forms.

D2 Traces Generation: Traces and sequences of atomic events are derived from the scenarios defined in D1.

D3 Model Inference: A formal model, or formal specification, expressed in CSP is inferred by an automatic theorem prover – in this case, ACL2 [15] – using the traces derived in phase 2. A deep[1] embedding of the laws of concurrency [6] in the theorem prover gives it sufficient knowledge of concurrency and of CSP to perform the inference. The embedding will be the topic of a future paper.

D4 Analysis: Based on the formal model, various analyses can be performed, using currently available commercial or public domain tools, and specialized tools that are planned for development. Because of the nature of CSP, the model may be analyzed at different levels of abstraction using a variety of possible implementation environments. This will be the subject of a future paper.

D5 Code Generation: The techniques of automatic code generation from a suitable model are reasonably well understood. The present modeling approach is suitable for the application of existing code generation techniques, whether using a tool specifically developed for the purpose, or existing tools such as FDR [1], or converting to other notations suitable for code generation (e.g., converting CSP to B [3] and then using the code generating capabilities of the B Toolkit).

It should be re-emphasized that the "code" that is generated may be code in a high-level programming language, low-level instructions for (electro-) mechanical devices,

---

[1] "Deep" in the sense that the embedding is semantic rather than merely syntactic.

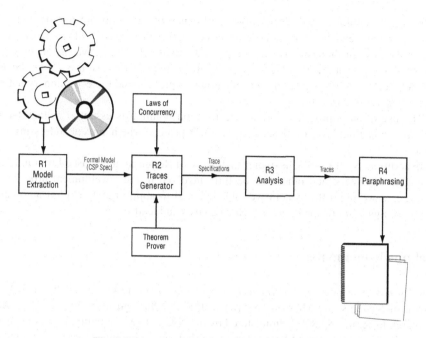

Fig. 2. Reverse engineering a system using R2D2C

natural-language business procedures and instructions, or the like. As Figure 2 illustrates, the above process may also be run in reverse:

R1 *Model Extraction*: Using various reverse engineering techniques [24], a formal model expressed in CSP may be extracted.
R2 *Traces Generation*: The theorem prover may be used to automatically generate traces based on the laws of concurrency and the embedded knowledge of CSP.
R3 *Analysis*: Traces may be analyzed and used to check for various conditions, undesirable situations arising, etc.
R4 *Paraphrasing*: A description of the system (or system components) may be retrieved in the desired format (natural language scenarios, UML use cases, etc.).

Paraphrasing, whereby more understandable descriptions (above and beyond existing documentation) of existing systems or system components are extracted, is likely to have useful application in future system maintenance for systems whose original design documents have been lost or systems that have been modified so much that the original design and requirements document do not reflect the current system.

5   Conclusion

NASA scientists and engineers are setting goals for future NASA exploration missions that will greatly challenge all of us. Future missions will exhibit levels of complexity that have never been seen before. They will be autonomous, pervasive, autonomic, surviving in harsh environments and with strict constraints on their behavior.

Swarm technologies will be widely used in such missions, exploiting the fact that more complex behaviors can emerge from the combination of several (in many cases hundreds, or even thousands) more simple individual behaviors. Swarms augur great potential, but pose a great problem for verification. Such systems simply cannot be adequately tested, both because of their inherent complexity, and the evolutionary nature of the systems due to learning.

The use of an appropriate formal specification notation is essential to facilitating formal verification. We have described the FAST project, which aims at addressing this issue.

In addition, NASA GSFC is exploring the use of Requirements-Based Programming to enable engineers, and others, to be fully involved in the development process, to ensure that we build the system we intended, and to appropriately exploit automatic programming, with the prospect of reducing costs and lead-times.

Acknowledgements

The *Formal Approaches to Swarm Technologies (FAST)* project is funded by the NASA Office of Systems and Mission Assurance (OSMA) through its Software Assurance Research Program (SARP), administered by the NASA IV&V Facility, Fairmont, WV.

The Requirements-Based Programming work described in this paper is supported in part by the Information Systems Division and the Technology Transfer Office at NASA Goddard Space Flight Center.

Research described in this paper was performed while Mike Hinchey was with NASA Software Engineering Laboratory, NASA Goddard Space Flight Center, and Chris Rouff was with SAIC. The work benefited from collaborations with Walt Truszkowski (NASA GSFC), Denis Gračanin (Virginia Tech), John Erickson (University of Texas at Austin), and Roy Sterritt (University of Ulster), amongst others.

References

1. Failures-Divergences Refinement: User Manual and Tutorial. Formal Systems (Europe), Ltd. (1999)
2. Bowen, J.P., Hinchey, M.G.: Ten commandments revisited: A ten year perspective on the industrial application of formal methods. In: Proc. FMICS 2005, 10th International Workshop on Formal Methods for Indutrial Critical Systems, Lisbon, Portugal, September 5 – 6, 2005, ACM Press, New York (2005)
3. Butler, M.J.: csp2B: A Practical Approach To Combining CSP and B. In: Declarative Systems and Software Engineering Group, University of Southampton (February 1999)
4. Harel, D.: From play-in scenarios to code: An achievable dream. IEEE Computer 34(1), 53–60 (2001)
5. Harel, D.: Comments made during presentation at "Formal Approaches to Complex Software Systems" panel session. In: ISoLA 2004 First International Conference on Leveraging Applications of Formal Methods, Paphos, Cyprus, October 31 (2004)
6. Hinchey, M.G., Jarvis, S.A.: Concurrent Systems: Formal Development in CSP. In: International Series in Software Engineering, McGraw-Hill International, London, UK (1995)

7. Hinchey, M.G., Rash, J.L., Rouff, C.A.: Requirements to design to code: Towards a fully formal approach to automatic code generation. Technical Report TM-2005-212774, NASA Goddard Space Flight Center, Greenbelt, MD, USA (2004)

8. Hinchey, M.G., Rash, J.L., Rouff, C.A.: A formal approach to requirements-based programming. In: Proc. IEEE International Conference and Workshop on the Engineering of Computer Based Systems (ECBS 2005), April 3–8, 2005, IEEE Computer Society Press, Los Alamitos, Calif (2005)

9. Hinchey, M.G., Rash, J.L., Rouff, C.A., Gračanin, D.: Achieving dependability in sensor networks through automated requirements-based programming. Journal of Computer Communications, Special Issue on"Dependable Wireless Sensor Network" 29(2), 246–256 (2006)

10. Hinchey, M.G., Rash, J.L., Rouff, C.A., Truszkowski, W.F.: Requirements of an integrated formal method for intelligent swarms. In: Proc. FMICS 2005, 10th International Workshop on Formal Methods for Industrial Critical Systems, Lisbon, Portugal, September 5–6, 2005, ACM Press, New York (2005)

11. Hinchey, M.G., Rash, J.L., Truszkowski, W.F., Rouff, C.A., Sterrit, R.: Autonomous and autonomic swarms. In: Proc. The 2005 International Conference on Software Engineering Research and Practice (SERP 2005), Las Vegas, Nevada, USA, June 27, pp. 36–42. CSREA Press (2005)

12. Hinchey, M.G., Rash, J.L., Truszkowski, W.F., Rouff, C.A., Sterritt, R.: You can't get there from here! Problems and potential solutions in developing new classes of complex systems. In: Proc. Eighth International Conference on Integrated Design and Process Technology (IDPT), Beijing, China, June 13–17, The Society for Design and Process Science (2005)

13. Hoare, C.A.R.: Communicating sequential processes. Communications of the ACM 21(8), 666–677 (1978)

14. Hoare, C.A.R.: Communicating Sequential Processes. Prentice Hall International Series in Computer Science. Prentice Hall International, Englewood Cliffs, NJ (1985)

15. Kaufmann, M., Manolios, P., Moore, J.S.: Computer-Aided Reasoning: An Approach. Advances in Formal Methods Series. Kluwer Academic Publishers, Boston (2000)

16. Rash, J.L., Hinchey, M.G., Rouff, C.A., Gračanin, D.: Formal requirements-based programming for complex systems. In: Proc. International Conference on Engineering of Complex Computer Systems, Shanghai, China, June 16–20, 2005, IEEE Computer Society Press, Los Alamitos, Calif (2005)

17. Rash, J.L., Hinchey, M.G., Rouff, C.A., Gračanin, D., Erickson, J.D.: Experiences with a requirements-based programming approach to the development of a NASA autonomous ground control system. In: Proc. IEEE Workshop on Engineering of Autonomic Systems (EASe 2005) held at the IEEE International Conference and Workshop on the Engineering of Computer Based Systems (ECBS 2005), April 3–8, 2005, IEEE Computer Society Press, Los Alamitos, Calif (2005)

18. Rouff, C., Vanderbilt, A., Hinchey, M., Truszkowski, W., Rash, J.: Formal methods for swarm and autonomic systems. In: Proc. 1st International Symposium on Leveraging Applications of Formal Methods (ISoLA), Cyprus, October 30–November 2 (2004)

19. Rouff, C., Vanderbilt, A., Hinchey, M., Truszkowski, W., Rash, J.: Properties of a formal method for prediction of emergent behaviors in swarm-based systems. In: Proc. 2nd IEEE International Conference on Software Engineering and Formal Methods, Beijing, China (September 2004)

20. Rouff, C.A., Truszkowski, W.F., Rash, J.L., Hinchey, M.G.: A survey of formal methods for intelligent swarms. Technical Report TM-2005-212779, NASA Goddard Space Flight Center, Greenbelt, Maryland (2005)

21. Sterritt, R., Rouff, C.A., Rash, J.L., Truszkowski, W.F., Hinchey, M.G.: Self-* properties in NASA missions. In: 4th International Workshop on System/Software Architectures (IWSSA 2005) in Proc. 2005 International Conference on Software Engineering Research and Practice (SERP 2005), Las Vegas, Nevada, USA, June 27, pp. 66–72. CSREA Press (2005)
22. Truszkowski, W., Hinchey, M., Rash, J., Rouff, C.: NASA's swarm missions: The challenge of building autonomous software. IEEE IT Professional 6(5), 47–52 (2004)
23. Truszkowski, W.F., Hinchey, M.G., Rash, J.L., Rouff, C.A.: Autonomous and autonomic systems: A paradigm for future space exploration missions. IEEE Transactions on Systems, Man and Cybernetics, Part C: Applications and Reviews 36(3), 279–291 (2006)
24. van Zuylen, H.J.: The REDO Compendium: Reverse Engineering for Software Maintenance. John Wiley and Sons, London, UK (1993)

Performance Validation on Multicore Mobile Devices

Thomas Hubbard, Raimondas Lencevicius, Edu Metz, and Gopal Raghavan

Nokia Research Center, 5 Wayside Road, Burlington, MA 01803, USA
Thomas.Hubbard@nokia.com, Raimondas.Lencevicius@nokia.com
Edu.Metz@nokia.com, Gopal.Raghavan@nokia.com

Abstract. The validation of modern software systems on mobile devices needs to incorporate both functional and non-functional requirements. While some progress has been made in validating performance (including power consumption) on current mobile devices, future mobile devices will incorporate multiple processing units, more complex software and hardware that will raise additional challenges. This paper outlines ideas for future directions in performance validation on multicore devices, based on the current work in model-based validation, application state monitoring and performance assertions.

1 Motivation

Today personal communication devices are more than voice call terminals. Mobile phones serve as platforms for a variety of mobile applications including text and picture messaging as well as personal information management, including data synchronization with remote servers and desktop computers. Many mobile phones today are equipped with imaging devices and are capable of taking still images and video clips. The images may be sent over wireless networks to other phones or may be transferred to a remote server or a desktop computer for storage or forwarding. Mobile phones also have a number of local connectivity interfaces such as USB, Bluetooth, and WLAN that can be used for a variety of applications involving local data transfer, remote execution, and other types of interaction with surrounding computing resources. For example, a phone can serve as a wireless modem for a laptop computer over Bluetooth connecting it to a wide area network over circuit switched data call or GPRS (General Packet Radio Service) packet data connection.

The above description shows that mobile devices host complex software systems subject to numerous non-functional requirements. This paper concentrates on performance requirements. In particular we focus on two areas of performance: software response time and power consumption, although our methods may be also applicable to other performance areas, such as memory consumption.

Software response time and power consumption requirements are somewhat at odds with each other: decreasing response time by using more powerful hardware usually means increased power consumption, while decreasing power consumption may lead to slower response times. However, they are tightly connected, since they both depend on the hardware specifications and on the software execution.

Both of these requirements have been partially ignored in the generic computing environments subject to Moore's law and constantly connected to power outlets. In a

B. Meyer and J. Woodcock (Eds.): Verified Software, LNCS 4171, pp. 413–421, 2008.

mobile environment, both are very important. Mobile device processors lack the speed of their personal computer counterparts for cost and size reasons, while the mobile software is as complicated as the software running on desktop computers. This forces mobile application developers to spend a lot of time optimizing software performance. Mobile device power consumption is primarily important for two critical reasons: battery lifetime and heat dissipation. Extending battery lifetime supports other non-functional requirements such as usability and availability of the device since the device does not have to be connected to the power outlet and charged as often. Heat dissipation is a key requirement because if too much heat is dissipated in too short amount of time, the device may overheat. It then has to be shut down or it risks being destroyed.

While some approaches for performance validation in mobile devices have been proposed [9][11], additional research is needed in the future. An important issue in the near future is the upcoming use of multiple processors on a single mobile device. While some mobile devices already use two general CPUs and two DSPs, devices with even more processors are projected in the future. More and more complex software is developed for mobile devices, which requires high performance processors. However, such processors consume a lot of power. A single processor needed to satisfy the application power needs in the next couple years would consume about 800mW, which is a considerable amount of power from battery capacity and heat dissipation point of view. Replacing such a processor with multiple slower and more energy efficient processors becomes a realistic alternative. ARM has already released MPCore [1] multicore solution that supports such approach. Even in the PC industry Intel and AMD are moving towards multiprocessor solutions in their future processor roadmaps [6].

This move towards multicore systems brings new challenges to non-functional requirement validation. The rest of this paper describes these challenges and proposes possible adaptation and extension of current research techniques for multicore systems.

Section 2 outlines an existing method of validating power consumption on mobile devices. Section 3 then describes the challenges of applying current methods to complex devices in the future. Sections 4 and 5 propose two new methods to deal with complexities described: application state monitoring and performance assertions. We finish with related work and conclusions.

2   Energy Consumption Validation with Power Profiles

It may be possible to create performance validation methods for multicore mobile devices by extending current approaches [9][11]. Already now, performance validation has to take into account the multiple hardware devices controlled by the software. These hardware devices have a large influence on the functionality and performance of the system. For example, an audio player is a simple application that uses a number of devices: LCD, backlight, flash storage, RAM memory, CPU, DSP, speakers, keypad, and headset. If the audio is fetched from the network then the wireless modem must be used as well. All of these devices affect response time, throughput and power consumed by the audio player. Validating performance for such a device may be not very different from validation for upcoming multicore devices. The remainder of this section reviews the energy validation approach we have proposed previously [9].

Our energy consumption validation approach consists of three parts: power requirements, a device power model, and system power measurements.

Using this approach, the device's software is modeled as a set of run-time functions that are executed, possibly in parallel. A set of hardware devices is associated with software functions. The efficient energy consumption requirement is that only hardware devices associated with active software functions should be active. In other words, any device not associated with the active software function should be inactive.

The device being validated is modeled as a collection of hierarchical state machines [2] that represent the power consuming devices in the system. Each device, or a component, is described as a state machine containing a set of power functions.

For example, let us consider the model of an audio subsystem. Figure 1 represents the state machine of an abstract audio subsystem component. It shows that the subsystem can be in the "Audio Idle" state or in the "Audio Standby" state. The "Audio Standby" state shows the nesting of parallel sub-states that describe microphone and earpiece activity. Looking at the parallel states, it is clear that the microphone and the earpiece can transition independently between active and idle states when the audio subsystem is in the "Audio Standby" state.

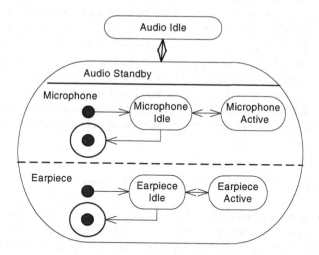

Fig. 1. Audio subsystem state transition model

Every state and transition in the state machine has an associated power level function. In the simplest case, the power level function is a constant for a state and zero for a transition. The power consumption in a state may also depend on parameters. For example, the power consumption in a processor depends on executed instructions, cache misses, memory accesses, etc. The power consumption in a radio antenna depends on the transmission frequency, signal strength, transmission protocol and other parameters. It is possible to use only constant power functions and to model any parameter dependencies by introducing additional states and transitions. However, such approach is cumbersome. For example, while a very detailed state transition diagram could potentially model the processor power consumption, such diagram would have enormous number of states and would be difficult to construct and understand. Non-constant power functions allow us to use higher-level system abstractions in state transition diagrams.

The power function of a composite state combines the power functions of the state's components. For example, the Audio Standby state's power function combines the constant standby power of the audio subsystem $PConstant_{AudioStandby}$ and the power functions of the microphone $P_{microphone}$ and the earpiece $P_{earpiece}$:

$$P_{AudioStandby} = PConstant_{AudioStandby} \circ P_{microphone} \circ P_{earpiece}$$

In simple cases, the composite function is a sum of the component functions.

Transitions between the power states in the model are controlled by global system events. These events are applied to all concurrent parts of the state machine so that when an event occurs, all parts perform the state transition triggered by the event. The overall power consumption of the entire system can then easily be determined by examining the power function of each state in the system.

In order to perform energy requirement validation the following information is needed: the model described above, the observation of the global system event triggers that generate state transitions, and the power measurements at the time of the trigger. The events are observed by using software traces. The power measurements are part of a power measurement test framework. When validation is being performed, the events observed from the trace are applied to the model in time sequence. At each point in time, the calculated power function of the model is compared to the measured power of the system. If there is any discrepancy between the actual and the modeled power levels, it means that the efficient energy consumption requirement is violated. Further analysis can indicate whether the system implementation is faulty or the system model is incorrect.

3   Challenges of Validating Complex Devices

Adjusting the approach described in section 2 for multicore devices is simple in principle. It only requires inclusion of the multicore hardware model into the hierarchical state machines. However, in practice this is not straightforward, because the hardware model and the relationship of the software to the hardware become much more complex in multicore devices. For example, resource conflicts have to be modeled when multiple processors access common bus, memory or peripherals. Timing relationships among multiple processors have to be modeled at very fine grain level, which leads to very fine grain (machine instruction level) modeling of software as well.

These issues are not unique to multicore devices. General complexity of hardware devices is increasing due to advanced features and power savings functionality. For example, new processors allow multiple voltage and frequency settings based on the current processing demands of the device. Modeling of these processors will be more-complex, since the transition times between voltage and frequency levels must be modeled as well as any lag time when moving from high frequency to low frequency states. WLAN adapters have different modes of operation, such as power save mode, constant aware mode, and so on. Each of these modes has different capabilities and power profiles. This means that hardware models become much more complex and building them may become a bottleneck in power validation process.

To illustrate these issues, let us consider an example of validating the power consumption for a web browser downloading five web pages from the network. The browser consists of 2 processes and uses the CPU, RAM, flash storage, LCD, backlight (at various brightness levels), keypad, and wireless modem over the entire test. The test takes 5 minutes to complete. During that 5-minute period on a typical mobile device with no other foreground application running, 42 threads belonging to 33 different processes are scheduled, not counting the browser. Also due to the asynchronous nature of wireless protocols and embedded devices many interrupts are scheduled causing the browser to suspend. On some executions of the tests, some thread not belonging to the browser may have previously activated the wireless modem. In such case, a browser thread does not have to do this again. In other test runs the browser may have to perform this power costly function thereby changing the power consumption. This results in a very complex system whose performance still needs to be validated.

Matching the software with the hardware is a non-trivial issue. It is easy to do for single core and multicore CPUs, since the operating system scheduler generally keeps track of which process or thread is active. For other resources reconciling the software using a resource with the resource requires a few levels of indirection. For example, under Linux it takes one call to enter system space and interact with the driver, and then the return call requires a callback to the kernel followed by a thread reschedule to the caller. In other, microkernel operating systems, for example, Symbian, this involves more levels of indirection and the application-resource mapping is difficult to track due to interactions with intermediate system servers.

Due to these considerations we cannot directly use the approach from section 2 for complex multicore devices. We need to find ways to adjust it so that it becomes applicable in practice. Sections 4 and 5 describe two possible directions.

4 Application State Based Validation

One way to resolve the issues raised in previous section would be to abstract the power consumption validation to the level of application states.

Generally, applications are specified as a set of features and requirements on those features. A logical state of an application can be viewed as a set of paths that combine to accomplish a goal and has a meaningful characteristic use of power and resources. This can be represented as a simple grammar in Bachus Naur form:

<application> ::= <state> { <state> }
<state> ::= <path> {<path>}
<path> ::= <instruction> {<instruction>}

The application level is too coarse for performance validation, while paths and instructions are too complex and granular to validate effectively. For this reason we propose to validate power and resource use at the application state level. An application can be instrumented to track application states and their transitions together with resources used in every state.

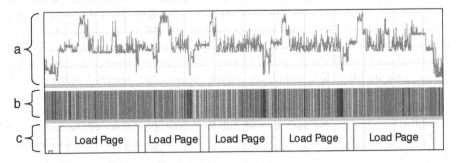

Fig. 2. Application State Technique

Consider Figure 2 that shows the information obtained from an executed application, including the application state information and power measurements. In Figure 2, a) represents the power measurements taken from the browser test described in section 3, b) represents time slices of activity of the system (each color in the actual visualization represents a different thread in the system), and c) represents the different states that the browser enters during the verification process. In this example, the "Load Page" application state uses the CPU, RAM disk (for caching), Backlight (level 2), LCD, and wireless modem. Information about all the application states in the system along with software traces indicating which application is using which resource makes finding violations of power requirements more straightforward. The power consumed by the devices that an application is using in each state can be compared to the power consumption model abstracted to the application state level.

A possible drawback of this approach is that application states are more abstract than paths or instructions. Therefore the modeled power consumption may be approximate. The comparison of the model to the measurements would need to use some analytic approximate comparison techniques.

5 Assertion Based Validation

An alternative approach to the application-state based validation is to use performance assertions. Assertions have long been used to validate the functionality of software systems [4][12]. Because assertions became well-known and easy to use tool, researchers and practitioners tried to extend them for validation of non-functional requirements, such as performance [10][15]. Such assertions track the software events corresponding to the ones specified in requirements and check the performance constraints. For example, a constraint *"Deleting a number of scheduled meetings in a calendar application should take less than 1 second plus 10 ms for each deleted meeting"*, can be checked by a performance assertion:

```
int Calendar::calendarStartDeleteFunction (...)
{
    ...
    pa_start(CALENDAR_DELETE);
    ...
}

int Calendar::calendarFinishedDeletingFunction (...)
{
    ...
    pa_end(CALENDAR_DELETE,
    assertion_interval(CALENDAR_DELETE)
    < 1000 + numberdeleted * 10);
    ...
}
```

Here the pa_start event starts the assertion interval and pa_end event finishes it and checks the assertion. We have proposed a performance assertion framework for mobile devices that handles assertions in a multitasking environment (for example, Symbian OS [14] that uses client-server model inside the device) and resolves a number of other issues with previous performance assertion proposals [8].

Performance assertions allow programmers to specify performance constraints corresponding to the requirements directly in program code. For example, the following constraints may be specified and checked:

1. *During GPRS session lower layer packets arrive every 10 ms.*
2. *Screen redraw should take no more than 10% of the time needed to insert an appointment into a calendar application*
3. *Opening a scheduled meeting in a calendar application should take less than 1 second*
4. *Reading of a file should take at most 10ms multiplied by the number of blocks read and multiplied by the ratio of total and consecutive blocks in the file*

Assertions incorporate all the parts needed for validation: requirements are expressed as the assertion constraint and the device model is implicit in the constraint. The response time is communicated to the assertion checker by the assertion mechanism. Performance assertions avoid the complexity of profile-based validation by specifying and checking very specific requirements in a single spot. The complexity of building the model of the whole system is split into the more manageable complexity of using implicit partial models inside the assertion formulas. It remains to be seen whether such shift is justifiable in terms of overall complexity when numerous assertions are present.

Performance assertions can be adjusted to specify power constraints. Consider the example constraint we discussed above *"Deleting a number of scheduled meetings in a calendar application should take less than 1 second plus 10 ms for each deleted meeting*". It could be rewritten in terms of energy model: "*Deleting a number of scheduled meetings in a calendar application should take less than 100mW plus 100μW for each deleted meeting*". The assertion start and end events in the code would remain almost the same as before:

```
int Calendar::calendarStartDeleteFunction (...)
{
    ...
    pa_start(CALENDAR_DELETE);
    ...
}

int Calendar::calendarFinishedDeletingFunction (...)
{
    ...
    pa_end(CALENDAR_DELETE,
    assertion_interval_power(CALENDAR_DELETE)
    < 100 + numberdeleted * 0.1);
    ...
}
```

Instead of time measurements, power measurements would need to be provided to the assertion checker. Obtaining such measurements inside a device may be complicated. Additionally care should be taken to exclude energy spent in tasks unrelated to the one mentioned in a constraint. This is similar to tracking "process specific" time intervals, where time spent in other processes is excluded from the total time.

6 Related Work

Researchers from Duke University have proposed an energy consumption model for a Palm™ device [3], which they used for the Palm™ device simulation, but not for the validation. We formalized and extended their model using state machine diagrams and extended message sequence charts [9].

A research group at MIT has implemented JouleTrack [13] - a web based system for software energy profiling. JouleTrack simulates only the energy used by a processor in application execution. Such a system could provide a detailed model and power function for a processor.

Real-time system modeling is a large research field. Our power consumption model has some similarities with timed transition systems [5] and modecharts [7]. Neither timed transition systems nor modecharts were previously used to model the energy consumption of the real-time systems.

7 Conclusions

In this paper we presented the position that non-functional requirement validation is very important for future complex multicore mobile devices. We discussed the expected validation issues and our ideas for solving these issues based on the current work in model-based validation, application state monitoring, and performance assertions. We believe that these approaches outline a feasible path towards solving the non-functional requirement validation issues in the future.

References

[1] ARM MPCore (2005),
     http://www.arm.com/products/CPUs/ARM11MPCoreMultiprocessor.html
[2] Booch, G., Rumbaugh, J., Jacobson, I.: The Unified Modeling Language User Guide. Addison-Wesley, Reading (1999)
[3] Cignetti, T., Komarov, K., Ellis, C.: Energy Estimation Tools for the Palm™. In: Proceedings of ACM MSWiM 2000: Modeling, Analysis and Simulation of Wireless and Mobile Systems (August 2000)
[4] Floyd, R.W.: Assigning Meanings to Programs, Proceedings of the Symposium in Applied Mathematics, Vol XIX, pp. 19–32. American Mathematical Society, Providence, RI (1967)
[5] Henzinger, T.A., Manna, Z., Pnueli, A.: Temporal proof methodologies for timed transition systems. Information and Computation 112, 273–337 (1994)
[6] Intel Platform 2015, http:// www.intel.com/ technology/computing/ archinnov/ platform2015/?iid=search& (2005)
[7] Jahanian, F., Mok, A.: Modechart: A Specification Language for Real-Time Systems. In: IEEE Transactions on Software Engineering, vol. 20(12) (December 1994)
[8] Lencevicius, R., Metz, E.: Proposal of Performance Assertions for Mobile Devices, Technical Report (2005)
[9] Lencevicius, R., Metz, E., Ran, A.: Software Validation using Power Profiles. In: 20th IASTED International Conference on Applied Informatics (AI 2002) (February 2002)
[10] Perl, S.E.: Performance Assertion Checking, Ph.D. Thesis, MIT (1992)
[11] Raghavan, G., Salomaki, A., Lencevicius, R.: Model Based Estimation and Verification of Mobile Device Performance. In: Proceedings of the International Conference on Embedded Software (EMSOFT 2004) (September 2004)
[12] Rosenblum, D.S.: Towards a method of programming with assertions, Proceedings of the 14th international conference on Software Engineering, Melbourne, Australia, pp. 92–104 (1992)
[13] Sinha, A., Chandrakasan, A.: JouleTrack - A Web Based Tool for Software Energy Profiling. In: Proceedings of the 38th Design Automation Conference, Las Vegas (June 2001)
[14] Symbian OS (2005), http://www.symbian.com
[15] Vetter, J., Worley, P.H.: Asserting Performance Expectations. In: Proceedings of the SC 2002 (2002)

Tool Integration for Reasoned Programming*

Andrew Ireland

School of Mathematical and Computer Sciences
Heriot-Watt University
Edinburgh, Scotland, UK
a.ireland@hw.ac.uk

Abstract. We argue for the importance of tool integration in achieving the Program Verifier Grand Challenge. In particular, we argue for what we call *strong integration, i.e.* a co-operative style of interaction between tools. We propose the use of an existing planning technique, called *proof planning*, as a possible basis for achieving strong integration.

1 Introduction

The renewed interest in the mechanical verification of software, we believe, can be attributed in part to the following three factors:

- A focus on property based verification, rather than full functional verification.
- Progress in terms of mechanizing abstractions.
- Greater integration of tools.

Below we highlight some software verification projects in which these factors played a key role:

- SLAM [1] provides an integrated toolkit for checking safety properties of software interfaces written in C. SLAM has been applied very successfully to the validation of device driver software. Predicate abstraction and model checking are used to identify potential defects. Using a theorem prover, the potential defects are then refined to identify true defects.
- ESC/Java [12] is a tool for identifying defects in Java programs. Using a theorem prover, ESC/Java can verify that a program is free of run-time exceptions. In general, annotations are required in order to support the theorem proving. In order to address this annotation burden, ESC/Java has been integrated with the Houdini [11] *annotation assistant*. Houdini is based upon predicate abstraction, and uses refutations to refine candidate annotations.

---

* The work discussed was supported in part by EPSRC grants GR/R24081 and GR/S01771. We are grateful for feedback on this position paper from Alan Bundy. Thanks also goes to Praxis High Integrity Systems Ltd, in particular Peter Amey and Rod Chapman for their support.

B. Meyer and J. Woodcock (Eds.): Verified Software, LNCS 4171, pp. 422–427, 2008.

- Caveat [3] is a static analysis tool for software written in C, and was used during the development of the flight-control software for the Airbus A380. Caveat includes a theorem prover that supports the verification of annotated C programs. A tool called Cristal supports the automatic generation of annotations (preconditions) for run-time exception freedom proofs. Currently, abstract interpretation [26] is being explored as a basis for generating loop invariants [25].
- NuSPADE[1] [9,10,20] builds upon the SPARK approach to high integrity software development [2]. The SPARK approach has been used extensively on safety [22] and security [15] critical applications. The NuSPADE project developed an integrated approach to program reasoning, based upon the use of proof-failure analysis to constrain the generation of program annotations. NuSPADE focused in particular on automation for run-time exception freedom proofs.

The above list is by no means complete. The aim is simply to highlight the role of property-based verification, mechanized abstract and tool integration within current software verification projects. The remainder of this position paper focuses on the importance of tool integration for software verification.

2 Tool Integration

The importance of tool integration for software verification is not a new observation. For instance, the potential benefits of having a close relationship between heuristic guidance, *i.e.* annotation generation, and theorem proving were anticipated by Wegbreit in his early work on program verification [31]. Achieving a "close relationship", what we will refer to as *strong integration*, requires a co-operative style of interaction between tools. Note that strong integration is closely related to the notion of *tightly coupled integration* presented in [8]. The use of counterexamples in guiding the search for program annotations is an example of strong integration. As an aside, the importance of counterexamples within the context of software verification is discussed in more detail in [30]. This is in contrast to a black box style of integration, or *weak integration*, where interaction between tools is minimal, *e.g.* success and failure.

In terms of automated reasoning, the benefits of strong integration are illustrated in [4] where Boyer and Moore report on the experimental integration of their theorem prover with a decision procedure for linear arithmetic. They found that the decision procedure was directly applicable to very few subgoals generated by the theorem prover – so weak integration gave poor performance. In contrast, strong integration, *i.e.* allowing the theorem prover and decision procedure to interact co-operatively, gave significant performance improvements. However, the customization associated with such strong integration is costly. Boyer and Moore reported that implementing strong integration was time-consuming, involving extensive and complex changes to both the theorem prover and decision

---

[1] More details can be found at http://www.macs.hw.ac.uk/nuspade

procedure. An in-depth discussion of the trade-offs that need to be considered when addressing the challenge of tool integration can be found in [8].

If one accepts strong integration as an important factor in addressing the task of software verification, then alleviating the costs associated with strong integration is an important milestone on the road to meeting the Program Verifier Challenge. We believe that approaches that support the kind of "customization" outlined above will play a vital role in alleviating such costs. We propose planning, and in particular *proof planning* [5], as a possible approach to achieving the level of customization that is required in order reduce the cost of strong integration.

Proof planning is a computer-based technique for automating the search for proofs. At the core of the technique are high-level proof outlines, known as *proof plans*. Proof planning builds upon tactic-based reasoning [14]. Starting with a set of general purpose tactics, plan formation techniques are used to construct a customized tactic for a given conjecture. A key feature of proof planning is that it separates proof search from proof checking. This gives greater flexibility in the strategies that can be used in guiding proof search as compared to conventional proof development environments. An example of this greater flexibility is the *proof critics* mechanism [16,18] that supports the automatic analysis and patching of proof planning failures. Proof critics have been very successful in automating the generation of auxiliary lemmas, conjecture generalizations and loop invariants [17,18,19,29,21].

Inspired by [4], the value of proof planning as a basis for strong integration was first observed in [6], where part of a decision procedure was rationally reconstructed as a proof plan. The modularity imposed by the proof plan enabled flexibility in the application of the decision procedure, *e.g.* auxiliary information such as lemmas, could be easily incorporated. In terms of tool integration, the value of proof planning as a basis for a co-operative style reasoning has been demonstrated through the Clam-HOL [28] and NuSPADE projects, the details of which are outlined below.

In the case of Clam-HOL, the Clam proof planner [7] was integrated with the Cambridge HOL interactive theorem prover [13]. The Boyer and Moore integration example, highlighted above, was re-implemented within the Clam-HOL framework with positives results [27].

Within the NuSPADE project, proof plans were used to increase the level of proof automation available via the SPARK toolset. Part of this effort involved the development of new proof plans, as well as the reuse of existing proof plans, *i.e.* proof plans developed for mathematical induction. The NuSPADE project also broadened the role of proof plans, *i.e.* proof patching was extended to incorporate light-weight program analysis. That is, common patterns of proof-failure were identified with constraints on missing properties. These constraints were used by our program analyzer to guide the introduction of auxiliary program annotations, *e.g.* loop invariants. It should be noted that the program analyzer also initiated interactions with the proof planner, *i.e.* the program analyzer called upon the proof planner to discharge simple equational reasoning goals. In terms of automation for run-time exception freedom proofs, NuSPADE was evaluated on a number of industrial applications, including SHOLIS [22], the first system developed to meet the UK Ministry of Defence Interim Defence Standards 00-55 [24] and 00-56 [23]. Our techniques are aimed at verification conditions that arise in loop-based code. While industrial strength critical software systems are engineered to minimize the number and complexity of loops, we found 80% of the loops that we encountered were provable using our techniques. That is, our program analysis, guided by proof-failure analysis, automatically generated auxiliary program annotations that enabled subsequent proof planning and proof checking attempts to succeed.

3   Conclusion

Tool integration is prevalent within current software verification projects. We have argued for the value of strong integration, *i.e.* a co-operative style of tool interaction, within the context of software verification. To achieve strong integration, we have proposed the use of proof planning, an approach which has a track-record in the development of reasoning systems which embody a co-operative style of interaction. We believe that strong integration will accelerate the development and sharing of tools and techniques on the road to achieving the Program Verifier Grand Challenge.

References

1. Ball, T., Rajamani, S.K.: The SLAM project: Debugging system software via static analysis. In: Conference Record of POPL2002: The 29th ACM SIGPLAN-SIGACT Symposium on Principles of Programming Languages, Portland, Oregon, pp. 1–3 (2002)
2. Barnes, J.: High Integrity Software: The SPARK Approach to Safety and Security. Addison-Wesley, Reading (2003)
3. Baudin, P., Pacalet, A., Raguideau, J., Schoen, D., Williams, N.: Caveat: A tool for software validation. In: International Conference on Dependable Systems and Networks (DSN 2002), IEEE Computer Society Press, Los Alamitos (2002)
4. Boyer, R.S., Moore, J.S.: Integrating decision procedures into heuristic theorem provers: A case study of linear arithmetic. In: Hayes, J.E., Richards, J., Michie, D. (eds.) Machine Intelligence, vol. 11, pp. 83–124 (1988)
5. Bundy, A.: The use of explicit plans to guide inductive proofs. In: Lusk, R., Overbeek, R. (eds.) 9th International Conference on Automated Deduction, pp. 111–120. Springer, Heidelberg (1988); Longer version available from Edinburgh as DAI Research Paper No. 349
6. Bundy, A.: The use of proof plans for normalization. In: Boyer, R.S. (ed.) Essays in Honor of Woody Bledsoe, pp. 149–166. Kluwer, Dordrecht (1991); Also available from Edinburgh as DAI Research Paper No. 513
7. Bundy, A., van Harmelen, F., Horn, C., Smaill, A.: The Oyster-Clam system. In: Stickel, M.E. (ed.) CADE 1990. LNCS (LNAI), vol. 449, pp. 647–648. Springer, Heidelberg (1990)

8. de Moura, L., Owre, S., Rueb, H., Rushby, J., Shankar, N.: Integrating verification components: The interface is the message (2005), http://www.csl.sri.com/users/shankar/shankar-drafts.html

9. Ellis, B.J., Ireland, A.: Automation for exception freedom proofs. In: Proceedings of the 18th IEEE International Conference on Automated Software Engineering, pp. 343–346. IEEE Computer Society, Los Alamitos (2003); Also available from the School of Mathematical and Computer Sciences, Heriot-Watt University, as Technical Report HW-MACS-TR-0010

10. Ellis, B.J., Ireland, A.: An integration of program analysis and automated theorem proving. In: Boiten, E.A., Derrick, J., Smith, G.P. (eds.) IFM 2004. LNCS, vol. 2999, pp. 67–86. Springer, Heidelberg (2004); Also available from the School of Mathematical and Computer Sciences, Heriot-Watt University, as Technical Report HW-MACS-TR-0014

11. Flanagan, C., Rustan, K., Leino, M.: Houdini, an annotation assistant for ESC/Java. In: Oliveira, J.N., Zave, P. (eds.) FME 2001. LNCS, vol. 2021, Springer, Heidelberg (2001)

12. Flanagan, C., Rustan, K., Leino, M., Lillibridge, M., Nelson, G., Saxe, J., Stata, R.: Extended static checking for Java. In: Proceedings of PLDI (2002)

13. Gordon, M.J.: HOL: A proof generating system for higher-order logic. In: Birtwistle, G., Subrahmanyam, P.A. (eds.) VLSI Specification, Verification and Synthesis, Kluwer, Dordrecht (1988)

14. Gordon, M.J., Milner, A.J., Wadsworth, C.P.: Edinburgh LCF. LNCS, vol. 78. Springer, Heidelberg (1979)

15. Hall, A., Chapman, R.: Correctness by construction: Developing a commercial secure system. IEEE Software 19(2) (2002)

16. Ireland, A.: The Use of Planning Critics in Mechanizing Inductive Proofs. In: Voronkov, A. (ed.) LPAR 1992. LNCS, vol. 624, pp. 178–189. Springer, Heidelberg (1992); Also available from Edinburgh as DAI Research Paper 592

17. Ireland, A., Bundy, A.: Extensions to a Generalization Critic for Inductive Proof. In: McRobbie, M.A., Slaney, J.K. (eds.) CADE 1996. LNCS, vol. 1104, pp. 47–61. Springer, Heidelberg (1996); Also available from Edinburgh as DAI Research Paper 786

18. Ireland, A., Bundy, A.: Productive use of failure in inductive proof. Journal of Automated Reasoning 16(1–2), 79–111 (1996); Also available as DAI Research Paper No 716, Dept. of Artificial Intelligence, Edinburgh

19. Ireland, A., Bundy, A.: Automatic Verification of Functions with Accumulating Parameters. Journal of Functional Programming: Special Issue on Theorem Proving & Functional Programming 9(2), 225–245 (1999); A longer version is available from Dept. of Computing and Electrical Engineering, Heriot-Watt University, Research Memo RM/97/11

20. Ireland, A., Ellis, B.J., Cook, A., Chapman, R., Barnes, J.: An integrated approach to high integrity software verification. Journal of Automated Reasoning: Special Issue on Empirically Successful Automated Reasoning 36(4), 379–410 (2006)

21. Ireland, A., Stark, J.: Proof planning for strategy development. Annals of Mathematics and Artificial Intelligence 29(1-4), 65–97 (2001); An earlier version is available as Research Memo RM/00/3, Dept. of Computing and Electrical Engineering, Heriot-Watt University

22. King, S., Hammond, J., Chapman, R., Pryor, A.: Is proof more cost effective than testing? IEEE Trans. on SE 26(8) (2000)

23. MoD. Hazard analysis and safety classification of the computer and programmable electronic system elements of defence equipment. Interim Defence Standard 00-56, Issue 1, Ministry of Defence, Directorate of Standardization, Kentigern House, 65 Brown Street, Glasgow G2 8EX, UK (April, 1991)

24. MoD. The procurement of safety critical software in defence equipment (part 1: Requirements, part 2: Guidance). Interim Defence Standard 00-55, Issue 1, Ministry of Defence, Directorate of Standardization, Kentigern House, 65 Brown Street, Glasgow G2 8EX, UK (April, 1991)

25. Nguyen, T., Ourghanlian, A.: Dependability assessment of safety-critical system software by static analysis methods. In: International Conference on Dependable Systems and Networks (DSN 2003), IEEE Computer Society Press, Los Alamitos (2003)

26. PolySpace-Technologies, http://www.polyspace.com/

27. Slind, K., Boulton, R.: Iterative dialogues and automated proof. In: Proceedings of the Second International Workshop on Frontiers of Combining Systems (FroCoS 1998), Amsterdam, The Netherlands (October, 1998)

28. Slind, K., Gordon, M., Boulton, R., Bundy, A.: System description: An interface between CLAM and HOL. In: Kirchner, C., Kirchner, H. (eds.) CADE 1998. LNCS (LNAI), vol. 1421, Springer, Heidelberg (1998); Earlier version available from Edinburgh as DAI Research Paper 885

29. Stark, J., Ireland, A.: Invariant discovery via failed proof attempts. In: Flener, P. (ed.) LOPSTR 1998. LNCS, vol. 1559, Springer, Heidelberg (1999); An earlier version is available from the Dept. of Computing and Electrical Engineering, Heriot-Watt University, Research Memo RM/98/2

30. Steel, G.: The importance of non-theorems and counterexamples in program verification. In: Submitted to the IFIP Working Conference on Verified Software: Theories, Tools, Experiments (2005)

31. Wegbreit, B.: The synthesis of loop predicates. Comm. ACM 17(2), 102–122 (1974)

Decision Procedures for the Grand Challenge[*]

Daniel Kroening

Computer Systems Institute
ETH Zürich

Abstract. The *Verifying Compiler* checks the correctness of the program it compiles. The workhorse of such a tool is the reasoning engine, which decides validity of formulae in a suitably chosen logic. This paper discusses possible choices for this logic, and how to solve the resulting decision problems. A framework for reducing decision problems to propositional logic is described, which allows the surprising improvements in the performance of propositional SAT solvers to be exploited. The only assumption the framework makes is that an axiomatization of the desired logic is given.

1 Introduction

The solution to the *Grand Challenge* proposed by Tony Hoare [1] is close to millions of programmers' daydream: a compiler that automatically detects all the bugs in their code.

More realistically, the goal is to prove or refute assertions given together with a program. Writing assertions is common practice. It will certainly remain difficult to write a specification that is strong enough to capture the designer's intent, but leaving this problem aside, just checking what we are able to specify would be tremendously useful already.

The way these assertions are specified is intentionally left open; this may range from simplistic assert() statements inserted into the code to a formula given in a temporal logic like LTL to even another higher-level program, which serves as specification. In general, it is to be expected that the specification or the assertions themselves will not be strong enough to serve as inductive invariants for loop constructs. Part of the challenge, therefore, is to strengthen the property to allow reasoning about the loops.

Manifold methods have been proposed to address this challenge, ranging from interactive theorem proving to automated methods such as Model Checking [2,3]. The workhorse of basically all software verification techniques is an efficient decision procedure, which decides validity of formulae in a suitably chosen assertion logic.

This paper discusses possible choices for this logic, and how to solve the resulting problems. We argue that any choice of assertion logic has to be sufficiently rich to permit expressions over the operators offered most commonly by the major programming languages. It also has to permit reasoning about dynamic data structures. Even for simplistic data structures, this requires support for quantification, either explicitly, in the form of universal and existential quantifiers, or implicitly, in the form of predicates that are defined by means of quantifiers.

---

[*] This research is supported by an award from IBM Research.

B. Meyer and J. Woodcock (Eds.): Verified Software, LNCS 4171, pp. 428–437, 2008.

A decision procedure for program analysis also needs to deal with decision problems that arise from refutation attempts, which are encodings of the feasibility of certain program paths. Given a large program, the paths can become very long, and consequently, the resulting formulae can become very large. The formulae often have a non-trivial propositional structure. Many decision procedures still perform case-splitting on the propositional structure, which limits the capacity of these tools severely.

Outline. In Section 2, we introduce the existing decision procedures that are used by program analysis tools, and discuss their suitability for this task. In Section 3, we propose a framework for encoding decision problems into propositional logic assuming an axiomatization of the assertion logic is given.

2   Decision Procedures for Program Verification

2.1   Existing Approaches

Almost all program verification engines, such as symbolic model checkers and advanced static checking tools, employ automatic theorem provers for symbolic reasoning. For example, the static checkers ESCJAVA [4] and BOOGIE [5] use the Simplify [6] theorem prover to verify user-supplied invariants.

The SLAM [7,8,9,10,11,12] software model-checker uses ZAPATO [13] for symbolic simulation of C programs. The BLAST [14] and MAGIC [15] tools use Simplify for abstraction, simulation and refinement. Other examples include the Invest tool [16], which uses the PVS theorem prover [17]. Further decision procedures used in program verification are CVC-Lite [18], ICS [19], and Verifun [20].

However, the fit between the program analyzer and the theorem prover is not always ideal. The problem is that the theorem provers are typically geared towards efficiency in the mathematical theories, such as linear arithmetic over the integers. In reality, program analyzers rarely need reasoning for unbounded integers. Linearity can also be too limiting in some cases. Moreover, because linear arithmetic over the integers is not a convex theory (a restriction imposed by the Nelson-Oppen and Shostak theory combination frameworks), the real numbers are often used instead. Program analyzers, however, need reasoning for the reals even less than they do for the integers.

Program analyzers must consider a number of program constructs that are not easily mapped into the logics supported by the theorem provers. These constructs include pointers, pointer arithmetic, structures, unions, and the potential relationship between these features.

CBMC [21], a Bounded Model Checker for ANSI-C programs, uses a different approach: the program is unwound into a bit-vector logic formula, which is satisfiable if and only if there exists a trace up to a given length that refutes the property. This decision problem is reduced to propositional logic by means of circuit-encodings of the arithmetic operators. This allows supporting all operators as defined in the ANSI-C standard. The propositional formula is converted into CNF and passed to a propositional SAT solver. If the formula is satisfiable, a counterexample trace can be extracted from the satisfying assignment, which the SAT solver provides.

In [22], we proposed the use of such propositional SAT-solvers as a reasoning engine for automatic program abstraction. The astonishing progress SAT solvers made in the past few years is given in [1] as a reason why the grand challenge is feasible today. Solvers such as ZChaff [23] can now solve many instances with hundreds of thousands of variables and millions of clauses in a reasonable amount of time.

In [24], we report experimental results that quantify the impact of replacing ZAPATO, a decision procedure for integers, with Cogent, a decision procedure built using a SAT solver: The increased precision of Cogent improves the performance of SLAM, while the support for bit-level operators resulted in the discovery of a previously unknown bug in a Windows device driver.

This approach is currently state-of-the-art for deciding validity of formulae in a logic supporting bit-vector operators. It is implemented by Cogent and CVC-Lite, while ICS is still using BDDs to reason about this logic.

2.2   Open Problems

The existing approaches are clearly not satisfying:

1. First of all, the word-level information about the variables is lost when splitting bit-vector operators into bits. A solver exploiting this structure is highly desirable. Word-level SAT-solvers (sometimes called circuit-level SAT solvers) attempt to address this problems, but provide only a very small subset of the required logic. In order to compute predicate images or to perform a fixed-point computation, we need to solve a quantification (or projection) problem, not a decision problem, which is typically considered to be harder than the decision problem.
2. Second, the logic supported by this approach is still not sufficient. A major goal of a *Verifying Compiler* is to show pointer-safety. In the presence of dynamic data structures, this requires support for a logic such as separation logic [25]. The combination of such a non-standard logic with bit-vector logic in a joint efficient decision procedure is a challenging problem.
3. Programs involving complex data structures will certainly require formulae that use quantifiers, e.g., to quantify over array indices. Due to the high complexity of these decision problems, there are currently no practical decision procedures available. The progress that solvers for QBF (quantified boolean formulae) make is encouraging, and promises to enable new applications just as the progress of SAT-solvers did.

A successful decision procedure for program analysis has to support a very rich logic, and be able to scale to large problem instances. In the next section, we discuss a framework for reducing decision problems to propositional logic assuming an axiomatization of the desired assertion logic is given.

3   Encoding Decision Problems

3.1   Propositional Encodings

Definition 1 (Propositional Encoding). *Let ϕ denote a formula that ranges over variables $v_1 \ldots, v_n$ from arbitrary domains $D_1, \ldots, D_n$. Let ϕ_P denote a propositional* *function ranging over the Boolean variables* $b_1, \ldots, b_m$. *The function* ϕ_P *is called a* Propositional Encoding *of* ϕ *iff* ϕ_P *is equi-satisfiable with* ϕ:[1]

$$\exists v_1, \ldots, v_n \in D_1 \times \ldots \times D_n.\phi(v_1, \ldots, v_n)$$
$$\Longleftrightarrow \exists b_1, \ldots, b_m \in \{0,1\}^m.\phi_P(b_1, \ldots, b_m)$$

Once we have computed a propositional encoding of a given formula ϕ, we can decide satisfiability of ϕ by means of a propositional SAT solver. Linear-time algorithms for computing CNF for ϕ_P are well-known [26].

The first efficient proof-based reduction from integer and real valued linear arithmetic to propositional logic was introduced by Ofer Strichman [27]. The proof is generated using Fourier-Motzkin variable elimination for the reals and the Omega test for the integers [28]. We generalize the approach in [27] to permit arbitrary logics as long as a (possibly incomplete) axiomatization is provided.

Definition 2 (Propositional Skeleton)

Let $\mathcal{A}(\phi)$ *denote the set of all atoms in a given formula* ϕ *that are not Boolean variables. The* i-*th distinct atom in* ϕ *is denoted by* $\mathcal{A}_i(\phi)$. *The* Propositional Skeleton ϕ_{sk} *of a formula* ϕ *is obtained by replacing all atoms* $a \in \mathcal{A}(\phi)$ *by new Boolean variables* $e_1, \ldots, e_\nu$, *where* $\nu = |\mathcal{A}(\phi)|$. *We denote the identifier to replace atom* $\mathcal{A}_i$ *by* $e(\mathcal{A}_i)$.

As an example, the propositional skeleton of

$$\phi = (x = y) \wedge ((a \oplus b = c) \vee (x \neq y))$$

is $e_1 \wedge (e_2 \vee \neg e_1)$ and $\mathcal{A}(\phi)$ is $\{x = y, a \oplus b = c\}$.

Let E denote the set of variables $\{e_1, \ldots, e_\nu\}$, and let $\bar{e}$ denote the vector of the variables in E. Furthermore, let $\psi_a(p)$ denote the atom a with polarity $p \in \{\text{true}, \text{false}\}$:

$$\psi_a(p) := \begin{cases} a & : p \\ \neg a & : \text{otherwise} \end{cases} \qquad (1)$$

Thus, $\psi_a(\text{true})$ is the atom a itself, whereas $\psi_a(\text{false})$ is the negation of a.

Lazy vs. Eager Encodings. Many decision procedures compute propositional encodings. All of them use the propositional skeleton as one conjunct of ϕ_P. The algorithms differ in how the non-propositional part is handled.

Let $x : \mathcal{A}(\phi) \longrightarrow \{\text{true}, \text{false}\}$ denote a truth assignment to the atoms in ϕ. Let $\Psi_{\mathcal{A}(\phi)}(x)$ denote the conjunction of the atoms $a_i \in \mathcal{A}(\phi)$ where a_i is in the polarity given by $x(a_i)$:

$$\Psi_{\mathcal{A}(\phi)}(x) := \bigwedge_{a \in \mathcal{A}(\phi)} \psi_a(x(a)) \qquad (2)$$

Intuitively, $\Psi_{\mathcal{A}(\phi)}(x)$ is the constraint that must hold if the atoms have the truth values given by x. An *Eager Encoding* considers all possible truth assignments x before invoking the SAT solver, and computes a propositional encoding $\phi_E(x)$ such that

$$\phi_E(x) \Longleftrightarrow \Psi_{\mathcal{A}(\phi)}(x) \qquad (3)$$

---

[1] Note that we do not require that the reduction is done in polynomial time, and thus, we can handle logics outside of *NP*.

The number of cases considered while building ϕ_E can often be dramatically reduced by exploiting the polarity information of the atoms, i.e., whether an atom a appears in negated form or without negation in the negation normal form (NNF) of ϕ. After computing ϕ_E, ϕ_E is conjoined with ϕ_{sk}, and passed to a SAT solver. A prominent example of a decision procedure implemented using an eager encoding is UCLID [29].

A *Lazy Encoding* means that a series of increasingly stronger encodings $\phi_L^1, \phi_L^2, \ldots$ and so on with $\phi \implies \phi_L^i$ is built. Most tools implementing a lazy encoding start off with $\phi_L^1 = \phi_{sk}$. In each iteration, ϕ_L^i is passed to the SAT solver. If the SAT solver determines ϕ_L^i to be unsatisfiable, so is ϕ. If the SAT solver determines ϕ_L^i to be satisfiable, it also provides a satisfying assignment, and thus, a truth assignment x^i to the atoms $\mathcal{A}(\phi)$.

The algorithm proceeds by checking if this assignment is consistent with the theory, i.e., if $\Psi_{\mathcal{A}\phi}(x^i)$ is satisfiable. If so, ϕ is satisfiable, and the algorithm terminates. If not so, a subset of the atoms $\mathcal{A}' \subseteq \mathcal{A}(\phi)$ that is already unsatisfiable under x^i is determined. The algorithm builds a *blocking clause* c, which prohibits this truth assignment to the atoms $\mathcal{A}'$. The next encoding ϕ_L^{i+1} is $\phi_L^i \wedge c$. Since the formula only becomes stronger, the algorithm can be tightly integrated into one run of a SAT-solver, which preserves the learning done by the solver in prior iterations. Advanced implementations of lazy encodings also preserve learning done within the decision procedure for the non-propositional theory.

Among others, CVC-Lite implements a lazy encoding of integer linear arithmetic. The decision problem for the conjunction $\Psi_{\mathcal{A}\phi}(x^i)$ is solved using the Omega test.

3.2 Propositional Encodings from Proofs

Proofs in any logic follow a pre-defined set of *proof rules*. A proof rule consists of a set of antecedents $A_1, \ldots, A_k$, which are the premises that have to hold for the rule to be applicable, and a consequence C. The rule is written as follows, where α denotes the "name" of the rule:

$$\frac{A_1, \ldots, A_k}{C}\ \alpha$$

A logic can be axiomatized by defining a set of special proof rules called axioms or axiom schemata, which define true statements in that logic. Many useful logics do not permit a complete axiomatization, but the set of axioms is usually sufficient to prove many theorems of practical interest.

Definition 3 (Proof Steps). *A Proof Step s is a triple $(r, p, \mathcal{A})$, where r is a proof rule, p a proposition (the consequence), and $\mathcal{A}$ a (possibly empty) list of antecedents $A_1, \ldots, A_k$.*

The fact that the dependence between the proof steps is directed and acyclic is captured by the following definition.

Definition 4 (Proof Graph). *A Proof Graph is a directed acyclic graph in which the nodes correspond to the steps, and there is an edge (x, y) if and only if x represents an antecedent of step y.*

Definition 5 (Proof-Step Encoder). *Let $\perp$ denote a contradiction, or the empty clause. Given a proof step $s = (r, p, \mathcal{A})$, its* Proof-Step Encoder *is a function $e(s)$ such that:*

$$e(s) = \begin{cases} false & : p = \perp \\ \neg e(p') & : p = \neg p' \\ new\ propositional\ variable & : otherwise \end{cases}$$

For a proof step $s = (r, p, \mathcal{A})$, we denote by $c(s)$ the constraint that the encoders of the antecedent steps imply the encoder of s, or more formally: if $\mathcal{A} = A_1, \ldots, A_k$ are the antecedents of s, then

$$c(s) := \left(\bigwedge_{i=1}^{k} e(A_i) \right) \longrightarrow e(p)$$

Definition 6 (Proof Constraint). *A proof $P = \{s_1, \ldots, s_n\}$ is a set of proof steps in which the antecedence relation is acyclic. The* Proof Constraint *$c(P)$ induced by P is the conjunction of the constraints induced by its steps:*

$$c(P) := \bigwedge_{s \in P} c(s)$$

A proof P is said to prove validity of ϕ if $e(\neg \phi) \wedge c(P)$ is unsatisfiable.

Theorem 1. *For any proof P and formula ϕ, ϕ implies $\phi_{sk} \wedge c(P)$.*

Thus, the idea of [27] is applicable to any proof-generating decision-procedure:

- All atoms $\mathcal{A}(\phi)$ are passed to the prover *completely disregarding the Boolean structure* of ϕ, i.e., as if they were conjoined. A proof P is obtained.
- Build ϕ_P as $\phi_{sk} \wedge c(P)$.
- The prover must be modified to obtain *all* possible proofs, i.e., must not terminate even if the empty clause is resolved.

Example. We illustrate the algorithm above with the following Hoare triple:

$$\{b = 5 \wedge (p \mapsto a \vee p \mapsto b)\} *p := 3 \{b = 5\}$$

Informally, let '$p \mapsto a$' denote the fact that a pointer p points to some variable a. We denote the dereferencing operation of a pointer p by $*p$. Let $c?x : y$ denote x if c holds, and y otherwise. Given a suitable definition of assignment to $*p$, the following verification condition ψ could be generated for the triple above:

$$\begin{aligned} \psi := \quad & (b' = 5 \wedge (p \mapsto a \vee p \mapsto b) \wedge \\ & (p \mapsto a?a = 3 : a = a') \wedge \\ & (p \mapsto b?b = 3 : b = b')) \\ & \longrightarrow b = 5 \end{aligned}$$

As we aim at showing validity of ψ, we form $\phi := \neg\psi$, and check satisfiability of ϕ. A propositional encoding of ϕ can be obtained using the following mapping from atoms to variables:

$$
\begin{aligned}
e(b' = 5) &= v_0 & e(a = a') &= v_4 \\
e(p \mapsto a) &= v_1 & e(b = 3) &= v_5 \\
e(p \mapsto b) &= v_2 & e(b = b') &= v_6 \\
e(a = 3) &= v_3 & e(b = 5) &= v_7
\end{aligned}
$$

Consequently, the propositional skeleton ϕ_{sk} is:

$$
\begin{aligned}
&v_0 \wedge (v_1 \vee v_2)\wedge \\
&(v_1 \longrightarrow v_3) \wedge (\neg v_1 \longrightarrow v_4)\wedge \\
&(v_2 \longrightarrow v_5) \wedge (\neg v_2 \longrightarrow v_6)\wedge \\
&\neg v_7
\end{aligned}
$$

Reasoning for equality logic is sufficient to prove or disprove claims of the form of our example. The only proof rule needed is transitivity of equality[2]:

$$
\frac{a = b, b = c}{a = c}
$$

An instance of this rule is $(b = 3 \wedge b = b') \longrightarrow b = 5$, which yields the constraint

$$
(v_0 \wedge v_6) \longrightarrow v_7
$$

Let this constraint conjoined with ϕ_{sk} be denoted by ϕ_{enc}. The formula ϕ_{enc} can be passed to a SAT solver. One of the satisfying assignments that the SAT solver could produce is $v_0, \neg v_1, v_2, \neg v_3, v_4, v_5, \neg v_6, \neg v_7$, i.e., $p \mapsto b$, and $b = 3$, which refutes the claimed post-condition.

3.3 Proofs for Program Verification

As motivated above, reasoning for integers is a bad fit for lower-level software, and is basically useless to prove properties of system-level software or even hardware. We would therefore like a proof-based method for a bit-vector logic, enriched with reasoning support for pointers. The main challenge is that any axiomatization for a reasonably rich logic permits too many ways of proving the same fact, and the completeness of the procedure as described above relies on enumerating *all* proofs.

Even if great care is taken to obtain a small set of axioms, the number of proofs is still too large. Furthermore, in the case of bit-vector logic, the proofs will include derivations that are based on reasoning about single bits of the vectors involved, resulting in a flattening of the formula, which resembles the circuit-based models used for encodings of bit-vector logic into propositional logic.

We therefore propose to sacrifice precision in order to be able to reason about bit-vectors, and compute an over-approximation of ϕ_P. This does not necessarily imply

---

[2] We also use the fact that equality is symmetric and axioms about integers; however, these facts are usually hard-coded into the procedure that applies the transitivity rule.

that the program analysis tool will become unsound. In fact, most existing program analysis tools, e.g., SLAM and BLAST, use decision procedures that compute over-approximations in order to save computational effort. Such over-approximations can be refined automatically if needed, e.g., based on UNSAT cores as in [30] or based on interpolants as in [31].

One trivial way to obtain an inexpensive over-approximation of ϕ_P is for example, bounding the depth of the proofs. Future research could, for example, focus on better proof-guiding heuristics.

The technique described above is applicable to decision problems, e.g., for checking verification conditions, and to quantification problems, as arising in fixed-point computations. For an explanation how this technique can be applied to quantification problems arising in predicate abstraction, we refer the reader to [32,33].

4   Conclusion

Program verification engines rely on decision procedures. However, despite many years of research in this area, the available decision procedures are not yet geared towards program analysis. Program analysis requires a logic with many features commonly not found in today's decision procedures, such as bit-vector operators, and ways to handle structs, unions, and pointers. A possible logic to model the pointer operations is separation logic.

The current state-of-the-art for deciding bit-vector logic is an ad-hoc approach using propositional SAT-solvers. An efficient decision procedure that supports a logic as needed for program analysis is an open problem that has to be solved to succeed in the grand challenge.

References

1. Hoare, T.: The verifying compiler: A grand challenge for computing research. J. ACM 50, 63–69 (2003)
2. Clarke, E., Grumberg, O., Peled, D.: Model Checking. MIT Press, Cambridge (1999)
3. Clarke, E.M., Emerson, E.A.: Synthesis of synchronization skeletons for branching time temporal logic. In: Kozen, D. (ed.) Logic of Programs 1981. LNCS, vol. 131, pp. 52–71. Springer, Heidelberg (1982)
4. Flanagan, C., Leino, K.R.M., Lillibridge, M., Nelson, G., Saxe, J.B., Stata, R.: Extended static checking for Java. In: PLDI 2002: Programming Language Design and Implementation, pp. 234–245 (2002)
5. Barnett, M., DeLine, R., Fahndrich, M., Leino, K.R.M., Schulte, W.: Verification of object-oriented programs with invariants. Journal of Object Technology 3, 27–56 (2004)
6. Detlefs, D., Nelson, G., Saxe, J.B.: Simplify: A theorem prover for program checking. Technical Report HPL-2003-148, HP Labs (2003)
7. Ball, T., Majumdar, R., Millstein, T., Rajamani, S.K.: Automatic predicate abstraction of C programs. In: PLDI 2001: Programming Language Design and Implementation, pp. 203–213. ACM, New York (2001)
8. Ball, T., Rajamani, S.K.: Generating abstract explanations of spurious counterexamples in C programs. Technical Report MSR-TR-2002-09, Microsoft Research (2002)

9. Ball, T., Cook, B., Das, S., Rajamani, S.K.: Refining approximations in software predicate abstraction. In: Jensen, K., Podelski, A. (eds.) TACAS 2004. LNCS, vol. 2988, pp. 388–403. Springer, Heidelberg (2004)

10. Ball, T., Rajamani, S.K.: Bebop: A symbolic model checker for Boolean programs. In: Havelund, K., Penix, J., Visser, W. (eds.) SPIN 2000. LNCS, vol. 1885, pp. 113–130. Springer, Heidelberg (2000)

11. Ball, T., Rajamani, S.K.: Automatically validating temporal safety properties of interfaces. In: Havelund, K., Penix, J., Visser, W. (eds.) SPIN 2000. LNCS, vol. 1885, pp. 113–130. Springer, Heidelberg (2000)

12. Ball, T., Rajamani, S.K.: Bebop: A path-sensitive interprocedural dataflow engine. In: PASTE 2001: Workshop on Program Analysis for Software Tools and Engineering, pp. 97–103. ACM, New York (2001)

13. Ball, T., Cook, B., Lahiri, S.K., Zhang, L.: Zapato: Automatic theorem proving for predicate abstraction refinement. In: Alur, R., Peled, D.A. (eds.) CAV 2004. LNCS, vol. 3114, pp. 457–461. Springer, Heidelberg (2004)

14. Henzinger, T.A., Jhala, R., Majumdar, R., Qadeer, S.: Thread modular abstraction refinement. In: Hunt Jr., W.A., Somenzi, F. (eds.) CAV 2003. LNCS, vol. 2725, pp. 262–274. Springer, Heidelberg (2003)

15. Chaki, S., Clarke, E., Groce, A., Strichman, O.: Predicate abstraction with minimum predicates. In: Geist, D., Tronci, E. (eds.) CHARME 2003. LNCS, vol. 2860, pp. 19–34. Springer, Heidelberg (2003)

16. Lakhnech, Y., Bensalem, S., Berezin, S., Owre, S.: Incremental verification by abstraction. In: Margaria, T., Yi, W. (eds.) ETAPS 2001 and TACAS 2001. LNCS, vol. 2031, pp. 98–112. Springer, Heidelberg (2001)

17. Owre, S., Shankar, N., Rushby, J.: PVS: A prototype verification system. In: Kapur, D. (ed.) CADE 1992. LNCS, vol. 607, pp. 748–752. Springer, Heidelberg (1992)

18. Barrett, C., Berezin, S.: CVC Lite: A new implementation of the cooperating validity checker. In: Alur, R., Peled, D.A. (eds.) CAV 2004. LNCS, vol. 3114, pp. 515–518. Springer, Heidelberg (2004)

19. Filliatre, J.C., Owre, S., Rue, H., Shankar, N.: ICS: Integrated canonizer and solver. In: Berry, G., Comon, H., Finkel, A. (eds.) CAV 2001. LNCS, vol. 2102, Springer, Heidelberg (2001)

20. Flanagan, C., Joshi, R., Ou, X., Saxe, J.B.: Theorem proving using lazy proof explication. In: Hunt Jr., W.A., Somenzi, F. (eds.) CAV 2003. LNCS, vol. 2725, pp. 355–367. Springer, Heidelberg (2003)

21. Kroening, D., Clarke, E., Yorav, K.: Behavioral consistency of C and Verilog programs using bounded model checking. In: Proceedings of DAC 2003, pp. 368–371. ACM Press, New York (2003)

22. Clarke, E., Kroening, D., Sharygina, N., Yorav, K.: Predicate abstraction of ANSI–C programs using SAT. Formal Methods in System Design 25, 105–127 (2004)

23. Moskewicz, M., Madigan, C., Zhao, Y., Zhang, L., Malik, S.: Chaff: Engineering an efficient SAT solver. In: DAC, pp. 530–535. ACM, New York (2001)

24. Cook, B., Kroening, D., Sharygina, N.: Cogent: Accurate theorem proving for program verification. In: Etessami, K., Rajamani, S.K. (eds.) CAV 2005. LNCS, vol. 3576, pp. 296–300. Springer, Heidelberg (2005)

25. Reynolds, J.: Separation logic: A logic for shared mutable data structures. In: Proceedings of LICS, pp. 55–74. IEEE Computer Society, Los Alamitos (2002)

26. Plaisted, D.A., Greenbaum, S.: A structure-preserving clause form translation. J. Symb. Comput. 2, 293–304 (1986)

27. Strichman, O.: On solving Presburger and linear arithmetic with SAT. In: Aagaard, M.D., O'Leary, J.W. (eds.) FMCAD 2002. LNCS, vol. 2517, pp. 160–170. Springer, Heidelberg (2002)

28. Pugh, W.: The Omega test: a fast and practical integer programming algorithm for dependence analysis. Communications of the ACM, 102–114 (1992)
29. Bryant, R.E., Lahiri, S.K., Seshia, S.A.: Modeling and verifying systems using a logic of counter arithmetic with lambda expressions and uninterpreted functions. In: Brinksma, E., Larsen, K.G. (eds.) CAV 2002. LNCS, vol. 2404, pp. 78–92. Springer, Heidelberg (2002)
30. Jain, H., Kroening, D., Sharygina, N., Clarke, E.: Word level predicate abstraction and refinement for verifying RTL Verilog. In: Proceedings of DAC, vol. 2005, pp. 445–450 (2005)
31. Henzinger, T., Jhala, R., Majumdar, R., McMillan, K.: Abstractions from proofs. In: POPL, pp. 232–244. ACM Press, New York (2004)
32. Lahiri, S.K., Ball, T., Cook, B.: Predicate abstraction via symbolic decision procedures. In: Etessami, K., Rajamani, S.K. (eds.) CAV 2005. LNCS, vol. 3576, pp. 24–38. Springer, Heidelberg (2005)
33. Kroening, D., Sharygina, N.: Approximating predicate images for bit-vector logic. In: Hermanns, H., Palsberg, J. (eds.) TACAS 2006 and ETAPS 2006. LNCS, vol. 3920, pp. 242–256. Springer, Heidelberg (2006)

The Challenge of Hardware-Software Co-verification*

Panagiotis Manolios

College of Computing
Georgia Institute of Technology
Atlanta, GA 30318
manolios@cc.gatech.edu

Abstract. Building verified computing systems such as a verified compiler or operating system will require both software and hardware verification. How can we decompose such verification efforts into mostly separate tasks, one involving hardware and the other software? What theorems should we prove? What specification languages should we use? What tools should we build? To what extent can the process be automated? We address these issues, using as a running example our recent and on-going work on refinement-based pipelined machine verification.

1 Introduction

The ultimate goal of the formal verification community is to mechanically verify computing systems from the subatomic level up to high-level specifications. In principle, we know that this is possible. It is possible to describe the standard model, quantum mechanics, string theory, and, in general, whatever physical or computational theory we desire, using first-order logic.

However, it does not currently seem feasible to do this: the human effort required is daunting. The differences in size and speed between the subatomic level and higher-level subsystems such as disk arrays are astronomical. In addition, the subatomic level is inherently continuous and probabilistic; in fact, current semiconductor devices not only depend on quantum effects, but even take advantage of them. On the other hand, higher-level abstractions tend to be discrete and (non)deterministic.

The main focus of this paper is on hardware-software co-verification, a central part of the verification challenge which exhibits many of the characteristics of the general problem, *e.g.*, it spans multiple abstraction levels. Hardware verification has been an active area of research for the last few decades and software verification is currently receiving renewed attention. Eventually, these now mostly disparate fields will have to be combined, if we are to truly verify computing systems. It is not just that it is desirable to have a verified hardware base for our software; many challenge problems, *e.g.*, building a verified compiler [7] or operating system, inherently involve both software and hardware.

In the remainder of this paper, we briefly expand upon some of the issues that arise in extending current work on hardware verification to enable software verification. Our viewpoints are shaped by our recent and on-going work on automating proofs of correctness for pipelined machines, which we use as a running example.

* This work was funded in part by NSF grants CCF-0429924, IIS-0417413, and CCF-0438871.

B. Meyer and J. Woodcock (Eds.): Verified Software, LNCS 4171, pp. 438–447, 2008.

We start in Section 2 by considering what Dijkstra called the "pleasantness" problem: what theorems should we prove? We outline a theory of refinement, our answer to the pleasantness problem as it pertains to pipelined machine verification, in Section 3. We then look at pragmatics such as: what specification language to use (Section 4) and how to automate (Section 5) and evaluate (Section 6) the results. In Section 7, we discuss some of our recent work on hardware-software co-verification. This work has led us to start developing tools, a topic discussed in Section 8. We conclude in Section 9.

2   The Pleasantness Problem

One of the major challenges in verification is what Dijkstra called the "pleasantness" problem [5]: how do we determine the "right" theorems to prove? For example, what theorems establish that a device driver works correctly? Well, it depends, but it is worth noting that the pleasantness problem can be mitigated by good design. It is also worth noting that many problems are inherently complex. For example, what does it mean for floating-point arithmetic to be correct? It took many years to settle on the IEEE floating-point arithmetic standards 754 and 854, and William Kahan was awarded the Turing award for his contributions to this effort.

Let us consider the pleasantness problem in the context of pipelined machine verification: what set of properties establishes that a pipelined machine behaves correctly? Such a set might include a property that describes the behavior of the branch misprediction logic. This property might specify what should happen during a branch mispredict: what instructions are invalidated, what latches are affected, how the program counter is updated, etc. The problem with this approach is that it is not clear when one has "complete coverage," which leaves open the possibility that erroneous corner cases remain. Another problem involves the maintenance of such properties, as any design changes will necessitate an update of the properties. Designs will undergo numerous changes, making the tracking of such correctness properties problematic.

For the above reasons, we use a correctness criterion based on refinement that tackles the pleasantness problem by taking advantage of the instruction set architecture interface. This leads to a notion of correctness that is not affected by changes to the pipelined machine. The idea is to show that, to an external observer, the implementation behaves in a fashion that is consistent with the specification, the much simpler instruction set architecture. The instruction set architecture is arguably the most important interface in computer science. On the one hand, it has allowed programmers to think in terms of a machine that executes one instruction at a time. On the other, it has allowed hardware designers to build inherently parallel machines, with features such as superscalar execution and deep pipelines, which simultaneously process numerous instructions at various stages of completion.

There is still the question of what kind of refinement theorem to prove and, more generally, the question of what correctness statements constitute a good answer to the pleasantness problem. An important property of such correctness statements is that, once established, they enable us to ignore the internals of the system under consideration in subsequent verification efforts. For example, a suitable notion of correctness for pipelined machines would allow us to reduce the proof that software running on a pipelined machine satisfies its specification, to a proof that the software runs correctly on the instruction set architecture. To actually achieve this decomposition requires a notion of correctness that preserves not only safety properties, but also liveness properties. To see why, suppose that we have a proof of correctness of the pipelined machine which does not preserve liveness properties. Now, consider proving that a simple program, say to sort an array of numbers, is correct. This requires a total correctness proof at the instruction set architecture level. But, it also requires taking the details of the pipelined machine into account in order to establish that no deadlock or livelock occurs for any execution of this particular program. Variants of the well-known Burch and Dill notion of correctness for pipelined machines [4] suffer from this problem [13]. The refinement theorems we prove do not, as they preserve both safety and liveness properties.

It is especially important to prove theorems that encapsulate the behavior of systems when many layers of abstraction are involved, as otherwise, the verification problem becomes unmanageable. An early pioneering body of work on the use of theorem proving to verify systems from the netlist level up to a high-level language is the CLI stack [24].

Finally, we briefly discuss performance and dependability properties, considered by many to be beyond the reach of formal verification. For example, how do we *prove* that a microprocessor performs well? The problem with this question is that it is vague, *not* that it is beyond the reach of formal methods. This is really just an instance of the pleasantness problem. The best known methods of making the performance question precise depend on the use of benchmarks, sets of programs meant to be "representative" of the kinds of applications the microprocessor will be used to run. Microprocessor performance is then measured with respect to the benchmarks. Performance is now very easy to reason about formally: just execute the model of the microprocessor on the benchmarks and keep track of the time. Similarly, if we know what is meant by "dependability," then we can analyze dependability properties formally.

3   Refinement-Based Verification of Pipelined Machines

In this section we informally review the theory of refinement we use to manage the pleasantness problem in the context of our work on pipelined machine verification; for a full account see [14,15]. A theory of refinement defines when a concrete implementation refines (implements) an abstract specification. In applying refinement to pipelined machine verification, the idea is to show that MA, a machine modeled at the microarchitecture level, a low level description that includes the pipeline, refines ISA, a machine modeled at the instruction set architecture level. A refinement proof is relative to a *refinement map*, r, a function from MA states to ISA states. The refinement map, r, shows us how to view an MA state as an ISA state, *e.g.*, the refinement map has to hide the MA components (such as the pipeline) that do not appear in the ISA. That MA refines ISA means that for every pair of states w, s such that w is an MA state and $s = r(w)$, we have that for every infinite path σ starting at s, there is a "matching" infinite path δ starting at w, and conversely. That σ and δ "match" implies that applying r to the states in δ results in a sequence that is equivalent to σ up to finite stuttering (repetition of states). This notion of refinement is based on stuttering bisimulation and implies that related states satisfy the same next-time-free temporal logic formulas (*e.g.*, CTL* \ X) [2].

Stuttering is a common phenomenon when comparing systems at different levels of abstraction, *e.g.*, if the pipeline is empty, MA will require several steps to complete an instruction, whereas ISA completes an instruction during every step. We note that stuttering bisimulation differs from weak bisimulation [23] in that weak bisimulation allows infinite stuttering. Distinguishing between infinite and finite stuttering is important, because (among other things) we want to distinguish deadlock (which usually indicates an error) from stutter.

The above formulation of refinement requires reasoning about infinite paths, something that is difficult to automate [25]. WEB-refinement is an equivalent formulation that can be more readily verified mechanically, as it only requires local reasoning involving MA states, the ISA states they map to under the refinement map, and their successor states [14]. WEB-refinement is a generally applicable notion. However, since it is based on bisimulation, it is often too strong a notion and in this case refinement based on stuttering *simulation* should be used (see [14,15]).

An important feature of our theory of refinement is that it is compositional. This allows us to verify machines in stages: if M refines M', which refines M'', then M refines M'' (with respect to the composition of the refinement maps).

We have been pleasantly surprised by how many opportunities there have been to exploit the generality of our theory of refinement. For example, that the refinement map used is just a parameter of our theory has enabled us to explore alternative refinement maps, some of which led to orders of magnitude improvements in verification times [21]. That our theory is compositional has allowed us to verify complex machines one feature at a time, making it possible to obtain tremendous savings in terms of verification times and in terms of the complexity of counterexamples when errors are discovered [19].

4 Specification Languages

Having addressed what to prove, we next consider what specification language to use. The available specification languages are quite varied, with foundations ranging from higher-order logics, to first-order logics, to constructive type theory, to decidable fragments of various logics, to temporal logics, etc. The main issues are not so much issues of fundamental power, rather they are about expressiveness and convenience. A good analogy is the situation in programming languages, where languages are judged on their ability to effectively describe computational processes, not on their fundamental power, as many simple languages encompass all that can be effectively computed. Similarly, most of mathematics can be embedded in first order logic, say ZFC, and since our focus is on *mechanical* verification, any proof theory where the notion of proof is decidable can be easily handled in a simple first-order setting.

The connection between programming languages and specification languages is deeper than the analogies above indicate. The systems to be verified are written in a particular programming language. To verify such systems, we must be able to embed the programming language in our specification language. In fact, some specification languages are just extensions of a programming language, *e.g.*, ACL2 [9,11] can be thought of in this way, as it allows any ACL2 program to be used as part of a specification. This makes it simpler for a single person to both write code and be involved in the verification process, something that we expect will eventually become routine practice. We also expect that new languages will eventually be developed with verification as a first-class concern: they will have formal semantics, a proof theory, various libraries and APIs providing basic verification functionality, proof checkers, theorem provers, verified modules and libraries, etc. In fact, now seems like a good time to create such a language, something that will require researchers with expertise in programming languages and verification.

In our work, we found it important to have a general-purpose specification language that allows us to clearly state the theorems of interest, that allows us to efficiently execute and test models, that has structuring mechanisms to manage large scale verification efforts, and that has existing libraries of theories. It is also important that the theorem proving engines used are highly efficient. This topic is discussed in more detail in the next section. We did not find a single tool that suited all our needs and decided to integrate UCLID with ACL2, as we discuss in Section 8.

5   Automation

A major verification challenge concerns automation. While it is not possible to build a general system which given a theorem produces a proof, it is possible to build, tune, or extend systems so that they can be used in a highly automated fashion on a sufficiently restricted class of problems.

As an example, we consider our experiences with pipelined machine verification. Applying our refinement theorem requires, among other considerations, the construction of a suitable refinement map and well-founded rank functions. While there is no general recipe for doing this, we have been exploring how to automate these constructions in the context of pipelined machine verification. The main idea is to discover widely applicable schemes that can be easily (even mechanically) specialized for the particular machine in question. The commitment refinement map [13,14] is an example of a refinement map that can be easily specialized for particular machines. This map produces an instruction set architecture state from a pipelined machine state by simply invalidating all the partially executed instructions and projecting out the instruction set architecture components. An inductive invariant is required, but here, too, a general scheme can be given: a state satisfies the invariant if, after invalidating all of its partially executed instructions, we can reach an equivalent state within a fixed number of steps determined by the pipeline length. Finally, a rank function is needed and, again, a general scheme is used that gives the number of steps the pipelined machine must take before it changes state visible at the instruction set architecture level.

The next step is to simplify the statement of the refinement theorem. Here too, we can specialize and simplify matters by strengthening the main refinement proof obligation. The result is a formula expressible in the CLU logic [3], which can be decided by the UCLID tool [12]. The major restriction is that the models we use are at the *term level*: they abstract away the datapath, require the use of numerous abstractions, implement a small subset of the instruction set, and are far from executable.

Using the WEB-refinement framework as described up to this point has allowed us to significantly extend what can be done in a highly automated fashion. For example, a big advantage over previous work is that we can handle liveness; in fact, we show that with our approach the time spent proving liveness accounts for only 5% of the total verification time [17].

We discovered that the refinement maps used for pipelined machine verification can have a drastic impact on verification times. This led to the introduction of a new method of defining the commitment refinement map which gives a 30-fold improvement in verification times over the standard flushing and commitment refinement maps [20]. We also discovered a new class of refinement maps, that partly commit and partly flush, that can provide several orders of magnitude improvements in verification times over pure flushing or pure commitment refinement maps [21].

All of the above work can be automated. In fact, we have a Web-based tool for generating complex pipelined machine models, including the correctness statements [16].

We end this section with a final example showing how to leverage the compositional nature of our theory of refinement. We developed a set of convenient, easily-applicable, and complete compositional proof rules and showed how this allows us to greatly extend the applicability of decision procedures by verifying a complex, deeply pipelined machine that state-of-the-art tools cannot currently handle. Our approach allows us to reduce the previous monolithic approaches to pipelined machine verification into a sequence of much simpler refinement steps. Not only are there benefits in terms of verification times, but even counterexamples are generally much simpler [19].

6   Evaluation

Any verification effort will invariably require many decisions, including which specification language to use, what theorems to prove, what theory to develop, etc. In this section, we make some observations about the evaluation of such efforts and advocate the use of end-to-end evaluations.

We start with a list of basic evaluation questions. First, what was mechanically verified and at what level? For example, there is a big gap between the trivial proof that an abstract floating-point adder is correct and a proof that a netlist description of the floating-point adder in a current microprocessor is correct. The devil *is* in the details. In addition, it often seems that work which depends on special paper and pencil "meta" theorems is valued more than work which develops such theorems inside a formal framework. But, if the point is to mechanically verify as much as possible, the latter approach should be preferred, even if it was not "automatic."

Another basic question is: how much human effort was required? Measuring this can be subtle, but the practice of classifying methods as either being "fully" automatic or not is counterproductive. For example, we have found that aspects of our work that are considered "automatic" by the research community (*e.g.*, defining refinement maps) have taken far longer than aspects that are not considered automatic (*e.g.*, defining invariants). One should account for all user time, including the time to define and formalize the problem and to determine and mechanically verify the theorems constituting correctness.

Claims by authors should be backed up with enough data to replicate the work reported. This is a basic rule of science that is too often ignored. If there is a good reason why the data cannot be released, then every effort to release a sanitized version of the reported work should be made. When we co-edited a book on the applications of ACL2 [8], we required every submission to include ACL2 proof scripts justifying every formal claim made. This material is available on the Web [10]. For example, Russinoff and Flatau used ACL2 to verify several of the floating-point arithmetic operations in the AMD Athlon processor. Obviously, AMD did not want to release these proof scripts, as they contain Athlon floating-point designs. However, the authors were able to release a precise description of their RTL language and the library of theorems used. They also defined, verified, and released a sanitized version of the floating-point multiplier [26]. Others researchers who could neither release their proof scripts nor produce sanitized versions of their work were not able to contribute.

As a general principle, the evaluation of verification efforts should focus on end-to-end arguments. By this we mean that the stated contribution should be related to the larger context in which the verification is taking place. For example, consider a paper that shows how abstraction α leads to faster verification times than abstraction β. However, if abstraction α is harder to mechanically justify than abstraction β, then from an end-to-end perspective, the use of abstraction α is a net loss. As another example, a negative end-to-end evaluation of a method that provides increased automation is possible under various scenarios, *e.g.*, the method may require a complex preprocessing step, or may generate counterexamples that are hard to understand, or may require extensive tool support, etc.

The end-to-end evaluation should also consider how the work can be used in the context of long-term verification. For example, there are often one-time verification costs such as embedding the semantics of some language into a theorem prover or developing a library of theorems applicable to a wide class of related problems. The floating-point work we mentioned previously is a good example, as these one-time costs were leveraged in subsequent verification efforts, leading to drastic reductions in manual effort required to verify subsequent floating-point operations.

7   Hardware Verification That Enables Software Verification

Recently, we have started thinking about how to prove that low-level programs executing on a pipelined machine behave correctly. The idea is to use WEB-refinement to prove that software running on a pipelined machine satisfies its specification by first proving that the pipelined machine refines the instruction set architecture and then showing that the software running on the instruction set architecture satisfies its specification. But, this requires the use of executable pipelined machine models, because the correctness of software depends on the semantics of instructions. However, in order to take advantage of decision procedures, previous work on hardware verification has focused on term level models that abstract away the datapath, require the use of numerous abstractions, implement a small subset of the instruction set, and are far from executable. To bridge the gap between term level models and bit-level, executable models is a major challenge, requiring that all of the abstractions employed in term level modeling are mechanically justified. We now briefly discuss the issues.

First, term-level models abstract away the datapath, hiding much of the real complexity in an executable model. For example, decoding is modeled using a set of uninterpreted functions. However, decoders for bit-level machines are complicated and notoriously difficult to get right in modern designs.

Even the ALU is modeled using uninterpreted functions, but to prove theorems about software, we need a model of the machine in which the ALU is interpreted.

Another form of abstraction concerns the instruction set itself, which is abstracted away by only modeling one instruction per instruction class. But, again, we really need a model with the full instruction set in order to verify software.

The refinement theorem cannot be expressed in UCLID. Instead, we check what we call the "core theorem," whose proof accounts for most of the verification time. The core theorem requires "polluting" both the pipelined machine and the instruction set architecture by adding extra inputs, control logic, and state to control when and how the refinement map is applied, among other things. This is quite complicated and it is easy to introduce errors, as we have often discovered. A proof is required to show that refinement proofs based on polluted models imply refinement proofs for the original models.

As a final example, we consider branch prediction. Branch prediction schemes are sometimes abstracted using an integer to represent the state of the branch predictor and uninterpreted functions which, given the current state of the branch predictor, return the next state and a guess (taken or not) [27]. This seems simple enough, but using this abstraction turns out to be quite cumbersome. Here's why. The branch predictor depends on the program counter, which depends on the program we are executing and if all we have is one integer to represent the state of the branch predictor, we have to use some kind of Gödel encoding scheme to encode the state of the machine with a single integer. The amount of work required to justify the abstraction is more than the savings it provides. Furthermore, if we have an infinite memory, this abstraction is not sound. A much simpler abstraction which is easily justified just makes nondeterministic choices.

We end with two final observations. First, having an efficiently executable pipelined machine can be quite useful in industrial settings, as it makes it possible to have a single "golden" reference model that can be used both for simulation-based testing and for formal verification. For example, Rockwell Collins used ACL2 to develop, test, and validate executable, bit- and cycle-accurate microprocessor models that ran at close to C speeds [6]. Second, as mentioned in Section 2, it is crucial that the notion of refinement used for hardware-software co-verification preserves liveness properties.

8   Tools

Addressing the above issues requires the use of a tool that can describe executable bit-level designs, can reason about total correctness, can manage the proof process, etc. ACL2 or any industrial-strength theorem prover can be used for this purpose. However, specialized decision procedures have the potential to significantly extend what can be handled automatically. For example, in one experiment, a proof that took about 3 seconds with UCLID required $15\frac{1}{2}$ days with ACL2 [18]. We therefore integrated UCLID with ACL2, and were able to use ACL2 to reduce the proof that an executable, bit-level machine refines its instruction set architecture to a proof that a term level abstraction of the bit-level machine refines the instruction set architecture, which is then handled automatically by UCLID. We also used our system to develop, execute, test, and verify a dynamic programming solution to the Knapsack problem. Thus, we can exploit the strengths of the two systems to prove theorems that are not possible to even state using UCLID and that would require heroic efforts using just ACL2 [22].

An interesting observation is that verification tools have matured to the point where they can handle complex enough subproblems to make the kind of coarse-grained integration described above worthwhile. This allows us to avoid the well-known problems with fine-grained integration [1]. We see many opportunities currently for this kind of tool integration, *e.g.*, we are currently looking at combining static analysis techniques with theorem proving.

9   Conclusions

Building truly reliable systems will require hardware-software co-verification. In this paper we have outlined some of the issues, challenges, and opportunities, using as a running example our recent work on automating refinement proofs involving pipelined machines.

References

1. Boyer, R.S., Moore, J.S.: Integrating decision procedures into heuristic theorem provers: a case study of linear arithmetic. In: Machine intelligence, vol. 11, pp. 83–124. Oxford University Press, Inc. Oxford (1988)
2. Browne, M., Clarke, E.M., Grumberg, O.: Characterizing finite Kripke structures in propositional temporal logic. Theoretical Computer Science 59 (1988)
3. Bryant, R.E., Lahiri, S.K., Seshia, S.: Modeling and verifying systems using a logic of counter arithmetic with lambda expressions and uninterpreted functions. In: Brinksma, E., Larsen, K.G. (eds.) CAV 2002. LNCS, vol. 2404, pp. 78–92. Springer, Heidelberg (2002)
4. Burch, J.R., Dill, D.L.: Automatic verification of pipelined microprocessor control. In: Dill, D.L. (ed.) CAV 1994. LNCS, vol. 818, pp. 68–80. Springer, Heidelberg (1994)
5. Dijkstra, E.W.: Science fiction and science reality in computing, EWD 952 (1986), http://www.cs.utexas.edu/sers/EWD
6. Greve, D., Wilding, M., Hardin, D.: High-speed, analyzable simulators. In: Kaufmann et al., (eds.), [8] pp. 113–135.
7. Hoare, T.: The verifying compiler: A grand challenge for computing research. J. ACM 50(1), 63–69 (2003)
8. Kaufmann, M., Manolios, P., Moore, J.S. (eds.): Computer-Aided Reasoning: ACL2 Case Studies. Kluwer Academic Publishers, Dordrecht (2000)
9. Kaufmann, M., Manolios, P., Moore, J.S.: Computer-Aided Reasoning: An Approach. Kluwer Academic Publishers, Dordrecht (2000)
10. Kaufmann, M., Manolios, P., Moore, J.S.: Supporting files for Computer-Aided Reasoning: ACL2 Case Studies (2000), http://www.cs.utexas.edu/users/moore/acl2
11. Kaufmann, M., Moore, J.S.: ACL2, http://www.cs.utexas.edu/users/moore/acl2
12. Lahiri, S., Seshia, S., Bryant, R.: Modeling and verification of out-of-order microprocessors using UCLID. In: Aagaard, M.D., O'Leary, J.W. (eds.) FMCAD 2002. LNCS, vol. 2517, pp. 142–159. Springer, Heidelberg (2002)
13. Manolios, P.: Correctness of pipelined machines. In: Johnson, S.D., Hunt Jr., W.A. (eds.) FMCAD 2000. LNCS, vol. 1954, pp. 161–178. Springer, Heidelberg (2000)

14. Manolios, P.: Mechanical Verification of Reactive Systems. PhD thesis, University of Texas at Austin (August, 2001),
    http://www.cc.gatech.edu/~manolios-publications.html
15. Manolios, P.: A compositional theory of refinement for branching time. In: Geist, D., Tronci, E. (eds.) CHARME 2003. LNCS, vol. 2860, pp. 304–318. Springer, Heidelberg (2003)
16. Manolios, P., Srinivasan, S.: A parameterized benchmark suite of hard pipelined-machine-verification problems
17. Manolios, P., Srinivasan, S.: Automatic verification of safety and liveness for XScale-like processor models using WEB-refinements. In: Design Automation and Test in Europe, DATE 2004, pp. 168–175 (2004)
18. P. Manolios and S. Srinivasan. A suite of hard ACL2 theorems arising in refinement-based processor verification. In M. Kaufmann and J. S. Moore, (eds.), Fifth International Workshop on the ACL2 Theorem Prover and Its Applications (ACL2-2004) (November, 2004)
    http://www.cs.utexas.edu/users/moore/acl2/workshop-2004/
19. Manolios, P., Srinivasan, S.: A complete compositional reasoning framework for the efficient verification of pipelined machines. In: ICCAD-2005, International Conference on Computer-Aided Design (to appear, 2005)
20. Manolios, P., Srinivasan, S.: A computationally efficient method based on commitment refinement maps for verifying pipelined machines models. In: ACM-IEEE International Conference on Formal Methods and Models for Codesign, pp. 189–198 (2005)
21. Manolios, P., Srinivasan, S.: Refinement maps for efficient verification of processor models. In: Design Automation and Test in Europe, DATE 2005, pp. 1304–1309 (2005)
22. Manolios, P., Srinivasan, S.: Verification of executable pipelined machines with bit-level interfaces. In: ICCAD-2005, International Conference on Computer-Aided Design (to appear, 2005)
23. Milner, R.: Communication and Concurrency. Prentice-Hall, Englewood Cliffs (1990)
24. Moore, J.S.: Special issue on system verification. Journal of Automated Reasoning 5(4) (1989)
25. Namjoshi, K.S.: A simple characterization of stuttering bisimulation. In: Ramesh, S., Sivakumar, G. (eds.) FST TCS 1997. LNCS, vol. 1346, pp. 284–296. Springer, Heidelberg (1997)
26. Russinoff, D.M., Flatau, A.: RTL verification: A floating-point multiplier. In: Kaufmann et al (eds.), [8], pp. 201–231
27. Velev, M.N., Bryant, R.E.: Formal verification of superscalar microprocessors with multicycle functional units, exceptions, and branch prediction. In: Proceedings of the 37th conference on Design Automation, pp. 112–117. ACM Press, New York (2000)

From the How to the What

Tiziana Margaria[1] and Bernhard Steffen[2]

[1] Chair Service and Software Engineering, Universität Potsdam, August-Bebel-Str. 89, 14482 Potsdam (Germany)
margaria@cs.uni-potsdam.de
[2] Chair Programming Systems, Universität Dortmund, Otto-Hahn-Str. 14, 44227 Dortmund (Germany)
steffen@cs.uni-dortmund.de

Abstract. In this paper, we consider the Grand Challenge under a very specific perspective: the enabling of application experts without programming knowledge to reliably model their business processes/applications in a fashion that allows for a subsequent automatic realization on a given platform. This goal, which aims at simplifying the tasks of the many at the cost of ambitious and laborious tasks for the few, adds a new dimension to the techniques and concepts aimed at by the Grand Challenge: the application-specific design of platforms tailored for the intended goal. We are convinced that the outlined perspective provides a realistic and economically important milestone for the Grand Challenge.

1 Motivation

Since the very beginning of computer science, the mismatch between design for machines and design for brains has been a constant pain, and a constant driver for innovation: it was always clear that descriptions that are good for machine processing are inadequate for an intuitive human understanding, and that descriptions which are structured for easy comprehension contain a lot of 'syntactic overhead', that typically slows down their automatic processing.

Compilers were designed to overcome, or better to weaken, this mismatch: Rather than trying to construct machines that work as humans think, it seemed more appropriate to translate comprehensible descriptions into machine-adequate representations. Besides classical compilers that translate high-level programming language into machine code there are also other means of automated code generation from more abstract descriptions: to this group belong parser generators, data flow analysis generators, compiler generators, and all the modern OO-tools that translate, e.g., UML descriptions into code fragments. Most drastic are those versions of Model Driven Design (MDD) that aim at totally replacing the need of programming for most application development using model construction. Thus the original desire to lift low-level machine code (prescribing **How** to run the machine) to more abstract programs (describing **What** to achieve) has become reality at increasing levels of abstraction from the hardware, and leading to extreme approaches like requirements-based programming, which aims at automatically making the user's or customer's requirements executable.

B. Meyer and J. Woodcock (Eds.): Verified Software, LNCS 4171, pp. 448–459, 2008.

2   Background

The fact that writing a parser, or even a compiler (which has been a real enter-prise in the '60s and early '70s) has become meanwhile almost a trivial exercise, and, perhaps even more surprisingly, the fact that global heterogeneous software systems comprising several hundreds of millions of lines of code do quite a re-liable service, certainly bases on conceptual advances. In particular techniques like type checking have had a strong impact on theory and practice: they filter out e.g. typos extremely efficiently and user friendly, and at the same time they guarantee an abstract notion of consistency. However, in our opinion, the cur-rent reliability of huge systems that run on heterogeneous platforms and that are increasingly based on third party legacy components, like middleware, container software, security protocols etc., is due to other, less scientific reasons:

1. Extensive use of *exception mechanisms*, especially in the presence of third party legacy components. In particular the code for internet applications often comprises more than 80% of such non-functional code in order to deal with the uncertainties of the net-based context.
2. *Pattern-based* programming styles, which do not focus on conciseness or ef-ficiency of the code but on its comprehensibility.
3. Syntax-based *tool support*. Of course, semantics-based tools have a much higher potential, but, except for some niche success stories like the SLAM-project [2,3], they did not really reach so far the broad industrial practice.
4. *Testing* and post-release *debugging* by a huge user community.

These four mechanisms have a huge combined pragmatic impact, which is probably the reason for the absence of the 'software crisis' forecasted long ago. However, they are in our opinion not a real safeguard: ultimately, they do not scale. They carry a long way, but they are deemed to fail in the long run as complex software is inherently meta-stable. A tested system may run for years, apparently very reliably, until some apparently minor modification leads to some totally uncontrollable effects. We all experienced situations where such minor modifications to systems considered stable suddenly revealed some deeper hidden bugs, which then took an enormous effort to repair. The larger the systems, the more distributed the features, the larger the project teams, the more likely is the long-term meta-stability of the product. The reason for this is that systems evolving over the years escape more and more our comprehension and thus our prevention and control. Late discovered errors may be so fatal that it is almost impossible to repair the system. Thus they are business-critical for organizations that produce and use those systems.

3   Our Proposal: Application-Specific Solutions

We believe that there is no general cure to this problem. Rather, we are convinced that we can only maintain control of complex systems if we develop tailored so-lutions for application-specific scenarios, since only for very restrictive settings

- based on clear patterns with predefined meaning - we will be able to capture enough semantics to regain sufficient control. This is important since with the variety of systems, platforms, technologies, communication and execution paradigms comes the need to bridge all this diversity in a harmonic way.

Our approach, called Aggressive Model Driven Design (AMDD), aims at decomposing the problem of compatibility and consistency of software (mass-) construction and customization into a

- (global) application-level problem, where compatibility and consistency is not a platform issue, but an issue of application/business process modelling, and therefore a matter of a considerably higher level of abstraction, and a
- platform-oriented synthesis/compilation issue, which provides the adequate 'technology mapping' that bridges the gap from the modelling-level over the programming language level to the target code.

The ultimate goal of this approach is to enable application experts without programming knowledge to reliably model their business processes in a fashion that allows for a subsequent automatic realization on a given platform. Thus, in contrast to usual compiler scenarios, which are designed to economically cover a wide range of source languages and target machines, our approach aims at automatically putting application/business-level models into operation. This is valuable and appreciated even at the price of a very expensive source/target mapping for each individual application/platform pair, and comes together with specific restrictions (e.g to respect standards and platform constraints) and supported patterns. This approach of domain/application-specific solutions goes far beyond established approaches based on domain-specific languages, as it essentially sees the role of the IT as a domain/application-specific platform *provider*. In fact, with AMDD the IT people (in contrast with the business/application experts), are active mainly *prior* to the application/process development to:

- support the domain modelling,
- design the most relevant patterns,
- provide the vital analysis, synthesis and compilation methods, and
- define constraints that guide the pattern-based application development in a way that guarantees the applicability of the provided methods and the reliability of the applications when running on their dedicated platform.

4   Grand Challenge: The AMDD-Persective

We are convinced that products that provide such application/platform-pairs for specific business solutions will have an enormous market already in the near future, as many current businesses complain about the delays imposed by the usual 'loop' via the IT section, even when the current business process only needs some minor modification.

On the other hand, this new scenario also provides a very interesting opportunity for the compiler community, as it allows one to set the scene in such a way that powerful analysis and verification methods work. In fact, rather than being confronted with a fixed scenario, typically a programming language and a class of architectures, and with the question, what can be done under these circumstance, the new setting is goal oriented: We must provide a scenario, where the application expert is able to reliably control his business processes by himself.

As indicated in the previous section, this comprises not only the development of powerful synthesis and compilation techniques, but also

- the development of adequate domain modelling and design patterns (design for verification/synthesis/compilation), and
- the definition of (constraint-based) guiding mechanisms for the application expert that guarantee the safe deployment of the developed applications on its dedicated platform. In particular, this comprises a new quality of diagnostic information and feedback: it is the application expert who must be able to correct his processes in case of problems.

The applicability range of this perspective of the Grand Challenge is, of course, quite restrictive, as it requires the development of very specific setups. On the other hand, it goes beyond the vision of a 'Verifying Compiler', as it explicitly includes the definition of adequate setups, and significantly extends the corresponding requirements.

The next section will briefly sketch a framework and some, admittedly still rather restrictive, scenarios where this goal has been achieved: in the definition of Value-Added Telecommunication Services, for Test Management of Computer/Telephony Applications, and for Personalized Online Services.

5   AMDD and the ABC Framework

AMDD aims at the top-down organization of Service interoperation, which moves most of the recurring problems of compatibility and consistency of software (mass) construction and customization from the coding and integration level to the modelling level (see Fig. 1). Rather than using component models - as usual in today's Component Based Development paradigm - just as a means of specification, which

- need to be compiled to become a 'real thing' (e.g., a component of a software library),
- must be updated (but typically are not), whenever the real thing changes
- typically only provide a local view of a portion or an aspect of a system,

we use *application models* (called Service Logic Graphs (SLGs) in the jABC [6]). Application models are the center of the design activity, becoming *the* first class entities of the *global* system design process. In such an approach, as briefly sketched in Sect. 5.1,

- *libraries* are established at the modelling level: building blocks are (elementary) models, rather than software components,

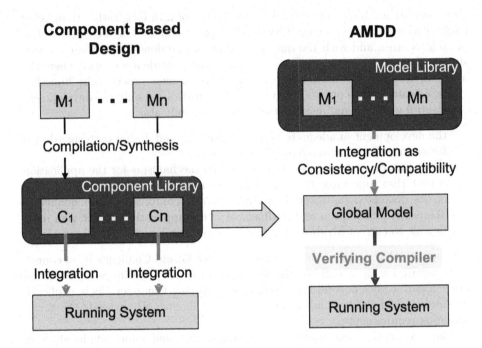

Fig. 1. AMDD: From the How to the What

- *applications* are specified by model combinations (composition, configuration, superposition, conjunction...), viewed as a set of constraints that the implementation needs to satisfy,
- global model combinations are *compiled* (or synthesized, e.g. by solving all the imposed constraints) into a homogeneous solution for a desired platform,
- *application changes* (upgrades, customer-specific adaptations, new versions, etc.) happen primarily (and ideally, only) at the modelling level, with a subsequent global recompilation or re-synthesis.

This *aggressive* style of *model-driven development* [21] strictly separates compatibility and migration issues from model/functionality composition and heavily relies on compilable and synthesisable models. This way it is possible to better control or even in some cases overcome the problem of incompatibility between (global) models, (global) implementations, and their components, because, due to the chosen setups, compatibility can be established and guaranteed at development time, and later-on maintained by (semi-) automatic compilation and synthesis.

In fact, AMDD, when applicable, has the potential to drastically reduce the long-term costs due to version incompatibility, system migration and upgrading. Thus it helps protecting the investment in the software infrastructure. We are therefore convinced that this aggressive style of model-driven development will become the development style at least for mass-customized software in the future.

5.1 An AMDD-Realization

The Java Application Building Center (jABC) [6] promotes the AMDD-style of development in order to move the application development for certain classes of applications towards the application expert. The jABC and its predecessor ABC have been successfully used in the design and customization of Intelligent Network Services [17], test environments [16,20], distributed online decision support systems [12,11], and Web Services [18][23], and it is currently being used in project for Enterprise Resource Planning (ERP) and Supply Chain Management (SCM) [5].

Even though the jABC should only be regarded as a first step of AMDD approach, it comprises the essential points of AMDD, that concern dealing with a heterogeneous landscape of models, supporting a number of formal methods, providing tools that enforce formal-methods based validation and verification, and providing automatic deployment and maintenance support [22] [18]. The rest of the paper will briefly sketch some running application scenarios.

6 Running Scenarios

This section presents three practically relevant applications, ranging from an enhancement of the workflow capabilities of a content management system for non-experts, over our Integrated Test Environment, which enables test experts without deep programming knowledge to create and modify their testing scenarios, to the Online Conference Service, a rather complex distributed, role-based, and personalized online decision support system.

6.1 Enhancing Workflows of a Content Management System

In this project, we used the restrictive workflow management functionalities of a commercial content management system (CMS) as a basis for a component library in the ABC, added global features, like e.g. a version management functionality, and taxonomically classified the resulting library of functionalities. This directly enabled us to graphically design workflows far beyond the capabilities of the original CMS and to embed them in other projects.

Besides increasing the modelling power and the range of applicability, using the ABC also allowed us to check the consistency of the workflows. A simple but important constraint we checked was that 'a new page will never be published before it is approved'. After a simple translation into temporal logic, this constraint can now automatically be model checked for any of the workflows within a small fraction of a second. It turned out that already this constraint did not hold for quite some standard workflows of the CMS.

Thus, using the model checking feature of the ABC, it was straightforward to enhance the CMS environment to avoid such mistakes once and forever, and to combine the CMS features for an editorial workflow with additional features like version control, automated update cycles, and features for fault tolerance, e.g. for taking care of holidays or illness during the distribution of labor.

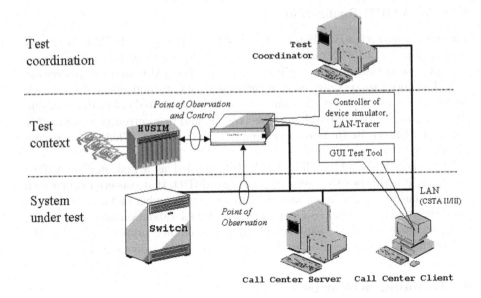

Test coordination

Test context

System under test

Fig. 2. Architecture of the Test Setting for the CTI Application

6.2   ITE: The Integrated Test Environment

A completely different application is the Integrated Testing Environment (ITE) for system level test of complex distributed systems [24,16] developed in a project with Siemens ICN in Witten (Germany). The core of the ITE is the test coordinator, an independent system that drives the generation, execution, evaluation and management of the system-level tests. In general, it has access to all the involved subsystems and can manage the test execution through a coordination of different, heterogeneous test tools. These test tools, which locally monitor and steer the behavior of the software on the different clients/servers, are technically treated just as additional units under test, which led to the system depicted in Fig. 2. The ITE has been successfully applied along real-life examples of IP-based and telecommunication-based solutions: the test of a web-based application (the Online Conference Service described below [25]) and the test of IP-based telephony scenarios (e.g. Siemens' testing of the Deutsche Telekom's Personal Call Manager application [16], which supports among other features the role based, web-based reconfiguration of virtual switches).

In this project we practiced the AMDD approach at two levels:

– the modelling of the test environment itself, and
– the modelling of test cases.

The benefits of the AMDD approach became apparent once a drastic change of the requirements of the test scenario in the telephony application occurred, which meant a new quality of complexity along three dimensions ([16]):

- testing over the internet,
- testing virtual clusters, and
- testing a controlling system in a non-steady state (during reconfiguration).

We could inherit a lot of the conceptual structure of the 'old' ITE for the new version of the test environment. Even more striking was the fact that the test cases hardly needed any adaption, except for some specific changes directly related to the functionality changes. Thus a change that Siemens considered to be 'close to impossible' became a matter of a few weeks [21].

6.3   OCS: The Online Conference Service

The OCS (Online Conference Service) is a server-based Java application that customizes a heavily workflow-oriented application built with the ABC [12,11,15]. It proactively helps authors, Program Committee chairs, Program Committee members, and reviewers to cooperate efficiently during their collaborative handling of the composition of a conference program. The service provides a timely, transparent, and secure handling of the papers and of the related tasks for submission, review, report and decision management. Several security and confidentiality precautions have been taken, in order to ensure proper handling of privacy and of intellectual property sensitive information. In particular,

- the service can be accessed only by registered users,
- users can freely register only for the role Author,
- the roles Reviewer, PC Member, and PC Chair are sensitive and conferred to users by the administrator only,
- users in sensitive roles are granted well-defined access rights to paper information,
- users in sensitive roles agree to treat all data they access within the service as confidential.

The service has been successfully used for over 60 computer science conferences, including the full ETAPS Conferences (with 5 instances of the OCS running in parallel). The Online Conference Service allows fully customizable, role-based business-process definitions, it is tailored for personalized support of each participant in the course of the operations of a virtual Program Committee meeting, and it is customizable and flexibly reconfigurable online at any time for each role, for each conference, and for each user [8].

The AMDD approach drastically simplified the realization and organization of the steady evolution of the OCS, which was guided by the growing demands of the users. It allowed to completely separate the issues of functionality implementation from the process modelling (in term of SLG's), to reuse in particular the constraints for the permission handling. In fact, this property remained even true when developing an Online Journal Service (OJS), which required to change most of the processes, and the addition of new functionality.

7 Further Applications

Since the VSTTE Conference in Zürich we have adopted and successfully applied the AMDD paradigm in a variety of other scenarios including industrial application areas. The most prominent examples are grouped here below.

Our **industrial projects** span a variety of business processes, as well as a project for process-based system migration.

- IKEA: design of an integrated document management system for its worldwide delivery management process [5].
- ThyssenKrupp Systems: modelling a distributed supply chain management process.
- SUN/Ricoh: (CeBIT 2006) Design and execution of mashups overlaying data from geographical information systems with local information and using high-end printers as process-driving engine.
- Samsung/Xythos/SUN: (CeBIT 2007) Exam & Go: heterogeneous distributed process for the examination management at universities, including single-sign-on, document management, and high-end business printers as thin clients.
- DNW (Deutsches Niederländische Windtunnel): reengineering and repurposing of the (business critical) application that steers DNW's 11 wind tunnels [27]

In **bioinformatics for systems biology**, we cooperate in the following four quite different subdomains:

- complex workflow for retrieving orthologous promoters [14],
- the analysis with statistical methods of large data sets from the LC/MS analysis for protein identification and discovery[9],
- the service-oriented redesign of GeneFisher, a popular and successful tool for PCR primer design [10], and
- the derivation of models for cellular processes by means of active learning techniques [13].

Concerning **Autonomous and Embedded Systems**, we have addressed three different scenarios:

- the mission modelling and execution for Lego Mindstorms [7], which contained a challenging compilation to the Lego platform,
- the modelling at the mission and task levels of the ESA Mars Rover mission, and its formal verification with a game beased model checker [1],
- enhancing the model-driven roundtrip engineering of NASA's R2D2C approach with model learning capabilities [4]

In the **Semantic Web** domain, we participate to the Semantic Web Service Challenge [26], where we face a Supply Chain Management case study concerning a purchase order scenario.

- in the Mediation scenario, AMDD is applied to the design, engineering, and automatic synthesis of a mediator process between two parties implemented as web services [23]
- in the Discovery scenario, we apply semantic discovery and ranking of services.

8 Conclusions and Perspectives

We have presented our favorite perspective of the Grand Challenge: the technical realization of Aggressive Model Driven Design (AMDD). This concerns enabling application experts without programming knowledge to reliably model their business processes in a fashion that allows for a subsequent automatic realization on a given platform. In contrast to usual compiler scenarios, which are designed to economically cover a wide range of source languages and target machines, this requires the dedicated treatment of each individual application/platform-pair together with its specific restrictions and supported patterns. This approach of domain/application-specific solutions goes far beyond established approaches based on domain-specific languages, as it essentially sees the role of the IT as a domain/application-specific platform provider, active mainly *prior* to the application/process development.

In order to achieve this goal, which makes application development *difficult for the few* (the providers of domain-specific platforms), but *easy for the many* (the application experts), the domain-specific platform must enforce all the necessary constraints necessary for a safe deployment of the designed processes/applications, and it must give application-level feedback to the process designers. This is only possible on the basis of very strong analysis and verification techniques, specifically adapted and applied to the domain-specific scenarios.

Of course, AMDD will never replace genuine application development, as it assumes techniques to be able to solve problems (like synthesis or technology mapping) which are undecidable in general. On the other hand, more than 90% of the application development costs arise worldwide at a rather primitive development level, during routine application programming or software update, where there are no technological or design challenges. There, the major problem faced is software quantity rather than achievement of very high conceptual complexity, and automation should be largely possible. AMDD is intended to address (a significant part of) this 90% 'niche', which we consider a particularly interesting and realistic scenario also for the Grand Challenge.

References

1. Bakera, M., Margaria, T., Renner, C., Steffen, B.: Game-Based Model Checking for Reliable Autonomy in Space, JACIC. Journ. of Aerospace Computing, Information, and Communication (Publ. by AIAA, American Institute of Aeronautics and Astronautics) (to appear)
2. Ball, T., Rajamani, S.: Automatically Validating Temporal Safety Properties of Interfaces. In: Dwyer, M.B. (ed.) SPIN 2001. LNCS, vol. 2057, pp. 103–122. Springer, Heidelberg (2001)

3. Ball, T., Rajamani, S.: Debugging System Software via Static Analysis. In: POPL 2002, pp. 1–3 (January, 2002)

4. Hinchey, M., Margaria, T., Rash, J., Rouff, C., Steffen, B.: Enhanced Requirements-Based Programming for Embedded Systems Design. In: Proc. MBEES 2006, Dagstuhl Workshop Modellbasierte Entwicklung eingebetteter Systeme II, January 2006, Tech. Rep. TU-Braunschweig 2006-01, pp. 43–52 (2006)

5. Hörmann, M., Margaria, T., Mender, T., Nagel, R., Schuster, M., Steffen, B., Trinh, H.: The jABC Appraoch to Collaborative Development of Embedded Applications. In: Proc. CCE 2006, Int. Workshop on Challenges in Collaborative Engineering – State of the Art and Future Challenges on collaborative Design, Prag (CZ), April 19-20, 2006 (2006) (Industry day)

6. Jörges, S., Kubczak, C., Nagel, R., Margaria, T., Steffen, B.: Model-Driven Development with the jABC. In: Bin, E., Ziv, A., Ur, S. (eds.) HVC 2006. LNCS, vol. 4383, Springer, Heidelberg (2007)

7. Jörges, S., Kubczak, C., Pageau, F., Margaria, T.: Model Driven Design of Reliable Robot Control Programs Using the jABC. In: Proc. EASe 2007, IEEE Conf. on Engineering of Autonomic and Autonomous Systems - Special Session on Autonomous and Autonomic Space Exploration Systems, Loyola College, Baltimore, MD, USA, March 2007, IEEE CS Press, Los Alamitos (2007)

8. Karusseit, M., Margaria, T.: Feature-based Modelling of a Complex, Online-Reconfigurable Decision Support Service. In: WWV 2005, 1st Int'l Workshop on Automated Specification and Verification of Web Sites, Valencia, Spain, March 14-15, 2005 (2005) (final version appears in ENTCS)

9. Kubczak, C., Margaria, T., Fritsch, A., Steffen, B.: Biological LC/MS Preprocessing and Analysis with jABC, jETI and xcms. In: Proc. ISoLA - 2nd IEEE Int. Symp. on Leveraging Applications of Formal Methods, Verification and Validation, Paphos, Cyprus, November 2006, pp. 308–313. IEEE Computer Society Press, Los Alamitos (2006)

10. Lamprecht, A.-L., Margaria, T., Steffen, B.: GeneFisher-P: Variations of Gene-Fisher as Processes in Bio-jETI. In: P. N. (ed.) Proc. NETTAB 2007, A Semantic Web for Bioinformatics: Goals, Tools, Systems, Applications, Pisa (Italy) (June 2007, to appear)

11. Lindner, B., Margaria, T., Steffen, B.: Ein personalisierter Internetdienst für wissenschaftliche Begutachtungs- prozesse. In: Proc. GI-VOI-BITKOM- OCG-TeleTrusT Konferenz on Elektronische Geschäftsprozesse (eBusi- ness Processes), Universität Klagenfurt (September, 2001), http://syssec.uni-klu.ac.at/EBP2001/

12. Margaria, T.: Components, Features, and Agents in the ABC. In: Ehrich, H.-D., Meyer, J.-J., Ryan, M. (eds.) Components, Features, and Agents, PostWorkshop Proceedings of the Dagstuhl Seminar on Objects, Agents and Features. LNCS, Springer, Heidelberg (2003)

13. Margaria, T., Hinchey, M., Raffelt, H., Rash, J.L., Rouff, C.A., Steffen, B.: Completing and Adapting Models of Biological Processes. In: Proc. of IFIP Conf. on Biologically Inspired Cooperative Computing (BiCC 2006), Santiago, (Chile) (2006)

14. Margaria, T., Kubczak, C., Njoku, M., Steffen, B.: Model-based Design of Distributed Collaborative Bioinformatics Processes in the jABC. In: Proc. ICECCS 2006 - 11th IEEE Int. Conf. on Engineering of Complex Computer Systems, Stanford University, CA (USA), August 2006, pp. 169–176. IEEE Computer Society Press, Los Alamitos (2006)

15. Margaria, T., Karusseit, M.: Community Usage of the Online Conference Service: an Experience Report from three CS Conferences. In: 2nd IFIP Conference on e-commerce, e-business, e-government (I3E 2002), Lisboa (P), Towards the Knowledge Society - eCommerce, eBusiness and eGovernment, Dordrecht (October 7-9, 2002), pp. 497–511. Kluwer Academic Publishers, Dordrecht (2002)
16. Margaria, T., Niese, O., Steffen, B., Erochok, A.: System Level Testing of Virtual Switch (Re-)Configuration over IP. In: Proc. IEEE European Test Workshop, Corfu (GR), May 2002, IEEE Society Press, Los Alamitos (2002)
17. Margaria, T., Steffen, B.: METAFrame in Practice: Design of Intelligent Network Services. In: Olderog, E.-R., Steffen, B. (eds.) Correct System Design. LNCS, vol. 1710, pp. 390–415. Springer, Heidelberg (1999)
18. Margaria, T., Steffen, B.: Second-Order Semantic Web. In: Proc. SEW-29, 29th Annual IEEE/NASA Software Engineering Workshop, Greenbelt, (USA), April 2005, IEEE Computer Soc., Los Alamitos (2005)
19. Margaria, T., Steffen, B.: Backtracking-free Design Planning by Automatic Synthesis in METAFrame. In: Astesiano, E. (ed.) ETAPS 1998 and FASE 1998. LNCS, vol. 1382, pp. 188–204. Springer, Heidelberg (1998)
20. Margaria, T., Steffen, B.: Lightweight Coarse-grained Coordination: A Scalable System-Level Approach. STTT, Int. Journal on Software Tools for Technology Transfer (to appear, 2003)
21. Margaria, T., Steffen, B.: Aggressive Model Driven Development of Broadband Applications. invited contribution for the book: Delivering Broadband Applications: A Comprehensive Report, IEC, Int. Engineering Consortium, Chicago (USA) (2004)
22. Margaria, T., Steffen, B.: Service Engineering: Linking Business and IT. IEEE Computer, issue for the 60th anniversary of the Computer Society, 53–63 (2006) (issue for the 60th anniversary of the Computer Society)
23. Margaria, T., Winkler, C., Kubczak, C., Steffen, B., Brambilla, M., Ceri, S., Cerizza, D., Della Valle, E., Facca, F., Tziviskou, C.: The SWS Mediator with WebML/Webratio and jABC/jETI: A Comparison. In: Proc. ICEIS 2007, 9th Int. Conf. on Enterprise Information Sys-tems, Funchal (P) (June 2007)
24. Niese, O., Margaria, T., Hagerer, A., Nagelmann, M., Steffen, B., Brune, G., Ide, H.: An automated testing environment for CTI systems using concepts for specification and verification of workflows. Annual Review of Communication. In: Int. Engineering Consortium Chicago (USA), vol. 54, pp. 927–936, IEC (2001)
25. Niese, O., Margaria, T., Steffen, B.: Demonstration of an Automated Integrated Test Environment for Web-based Applications. In: Bošnački, D., Leue, S. (eds.) SPIN 2002. LNCS, vol. 2318, pp. 250–253. Springer, Heidelberg (2002)
26. Semantic Web Service Challenge Website (2007), http://sws-challenge.org
27. Wagner, C., Margaria, T., Pagendarm, H.-G.: Comparative Analysis of Tools for automated Software Re-Engineering purposes. In: Proceedings of IEEE-ISoLA 2006 and WWV 2006, Paphos, Cyprus, pp. 446–452 (November, 2006)

An Overview of Separation Logic

John C. Reynolds[*]

Computer Science Department
Carnegie Mellon University
john.reynolds@cs.cmu.edu

Abstract. After some general remarks about program verification, we introduce *separation logic*, a novel extension of Hoare logic that can strengthen the applicability and scalability of program verification for imperative programs that use shared mutable data structures or shared-memory concurrency.

1   Introduction

Proving programs is not like proving mathematical theorems. A mathematical conjecture often gives no hint as to why it might be true, but a program is written by a programmer who inevitably has at least an informal understanding of why the program might behave as it should. The goal of program verification is not to search some huge proof space, but to formalize the programmer's own reasoning to the point where any flaws become evident.

Thus, I believe that programs should be proved as they are written, and that the programmer must be intimately involved in the proof process.

At Syracuse University, from 1972 to 1986, I taught a course on structured programmming and Hoare-style program proving to at least a thousand students, mostly master's candidates in computer science. This experience convinced me that good programmers can annotate and prove their programs rigorously, and in doing so achieve vast improvements in the quality of these programs.

No mechanical aids were used — not even a compiler. Indeed, much of the effectiveness of the course came from forcing the students to produce logically correct programs without debugging.

To scale from classroom examples to modern software, however, effective mechanical assistance will be vital. Since proofs are as prone to errors as programs are, they must be checked by machine. Moreover, to avoid drowning in a sea of minutiae, the programmer must be freed from trivial arguments that are amenable to efficient decision procedures.

On the other hand, interaction with the programmer is vital. The ultimate goal of creating error-free software will not be met by filtering the results of

---

[*] Portions of the author's own research described in this position paper were supported by National Science Foundation Grants CCR-9804014 and CCR-0204242, by the Basic Research in Computer Science (http://www.brics.dk/) Centre of the Danish National Research Foundation, and by EPSRC Visiting Fellowships at Queen Mary, University of London, and Edinburgh University.

B. Meyer and J. Woodcock (Eds.): Verified Software, LNCS 4171, pp. 460–469, 2008.

conventional programming through any form of post-hoc verification. Instead specification and verification must be tightly interwoven with program construction — and thus require a logic that is concise and readable.

2 Separation Logic

Around the turn of the millenium, Peter O'Hearn and I devised an extension of Hoare logic called "separation logic" [1,2,3,4]. Our original goal was to facilitate reasoning about low-level imperative programs that use shared mutable data structure. Extensions of the logic, however, have proven applicable to a wider conceptual range, where access to memory is replaced by permission to exercise capabilities, or by knowledge of structure. In a few years, the logic has become a significant research area, with a growing literature produced by a variety of researchers.

For conventional logics, the problem with sharing is that it is the default in the logic, while nonsharing is the default in programming, so that declaring all of the instances where sharing does not occur — or at least those instances necessary for correctness — can be extremely tedious.

For example, consider the following program, which performs an in-place reversal of a list:

$$LREV \stackrel{\text{def}}{=} j := \mathbf{nil}\,;\mathbf{while}\ i \neq \mathbf{nil}\ \mathbf{do}\ (k := [i+1]\,;[i+1] := j\,;j := i\,;i := k)\,.$$

(Here the notation $[e]$ denotes the contents of the storage at address e.)

The invariant of this program must state that i and j are lists representing two sequences α and β such that the reflection of the initial value α_0 can be obtained by concatenating the reflection of α onto β:

$$\exists \alpha, \beta.\ \mathsf{list}\ \alpha\ i \wedge \mathsf{list}\ \beta\ j \wedge \alpha_0^\dagger = \alpha^\dagger{\cdot}\beta\,.$$

(Here the predicate $\mathsf{list}\ \alpha\ i$ can be read "i is a list representing the sequence α.")

However, this is not enough, since the program will malfunction if there is any sharing between the lists i and j. To prohibit this in Hoare logic, we must extend the invariant to assert that only **nil** is reachable from both i and j:

$$(\exists \alpha, \beta.\ \mathsf{list}\ \alpha\ i \wedge \mathsf{list}\ \beta\ j \wedge \alpha_0^\dagger = \alpha^\dagger{\cdot}\beta)$$
$$\wedge\ (\forall k.\ \mathbf{reachable}(i, k) \wedge \mathbf{reachable}(j, k) \Rightarrow k = \mathbf{nil})\,.$$

In separation logic, however, this kind of difficulty can be avoided by using a novel logical operation $P * Q$, called the *separating conjunction*, that asserts that P and Q hold for *disjoint* portions of the addressable storage. Since the prohibition of sharing is built into this operation, our invariant can be written succinctly as

$$(\exists \alpha, \beta.\ \mathsf{list}\ \alpha\ i\ *\ \mathsf{list}\ \beta\ j) \wedge \alpha_0^\dagger = \alpha^\dagger{\cdot}\beta\,.$$

A second, more general, advantage of separation logic is the support it gives to *local reasoning*, which underlies the scalability of the logic. For example, using the invariant given above, one can prove the following specification of the list-reversal program:

$$\{\text{list } \alpha \text{ i}\} \; LREV \; \{\text{list } \alpha^\dagger \text{ j}\} \; .$$

The semantics of this specification implies that the addressable storage described by the precondition $\{\text{list } \alpha \text{ i}\}$, which is the storage containing the list i representing α, is the *only* addressable storage touched by the execution of $LREV$ (often called the *footprint* of $LREV$). If $LREV$ is a part of a larger program that also manipulates some separate storage, say containing a list k representing a sequence γ, then one can use an inference rule due to O'Hearn, called the *frame rule* [3]:

$$\frac{\{p\} \; c \; \{q\}}{\{p * r\} \; c \; \{q * r\}}$$

(where c does not assign to the free variables of r), to infer directly that the additional storage is unaffected by $LREV$:

$$\{\text{list } \alpha \text{ i} * \text{list } \gamma \text{ k}\} \; LREV \; \{\text{list } \alpha^\dagger \text{ j} * \text{list } \gamma \text{ k}\} \; .$$

In a realistic situation, of course, $LREV$ might be a substantial subprogram, and the description of the separate storage might also be voluminous. Nevertheless, one can still reason *locally* about LREV, i.e., while ignoring the separate storage, and then scale up to the combined storage by using the frame rule.

There is little need for local reasoning in proving toy examples. But it has been critical in proving more complex programs, such as the Schorr-Waite marking algorithm [5,6] or the Cheney copying garbage collector [7].

It should also be mentioned that the assertion list α i is only true for an addressible storage containing the relevant list and nothing else. Thus either of the above specifications of $LREV$ indicates that $LREV$ does not cause a memory leak.

3   Semantics of the Logic

Separation logic describes programs in an extension of the simple imperative language with commands for allocating, accessing, mutating, and deallocating data structures, but without garbage collection. A critical feature of this language is that any attempt to dereference a dangling pointer causes program execution to abort.

In Hoare logic, the state of a computation is a mapping from variables to integers, which we will henceforth call a *store*. Thus:

$$\text{Stores}_V = V \rightarrow \text{Integers} \; ,$$

where V is a set of variables. In separation logic, however, there is a second component of the state, called a *heap*, which formalizes the addressable storage where mutable structures reside. Specifically, the heap maps some finite set of *active* addresses into integers, where *addresses* are a proper subset of the integers:

$$\text{Addresses} \subset \text{Integers}$$

$$\text{Heaps} = \bigcup_{A \subseteq_{\text{fin}} \text{Addresses}} (A \rightarrow \text{Integers})$$

$$\text{States}_V = \text{Stores}_V \times \text{Heaps}.$$

The nature of the novel commands in our programming language can be illustrated by a sequence of state transitions:

		Store : x: 3, y: 4
		Heap : empty
Allocation	$x := \mathbf{cons}(1, 2)$;	$\downarrow$
		Store : x: 37, y: 4
		Heap : 37: 1, 38: 2
Lookup	$y := [x]$;	$\downarrow$
		Store : x: 37, y: 1
		Heap : 37: 1, 38: 2
Mutation	$[x + 1] := 3$;	$\downarrow$
		Store : x: 37, y: 1
		Heap : 37: 1, 38: 3
Deallocation	$\mathbf{dispose}(x + 1)$	$\downarrow$
		Store : x: 37, y: 1
		Heap : 37: 1

The indeterminacy of allocation must be emphasized; for example, $x := \mathbf{cons}(1, 2)$ could augment the domain of the heap with any two consecutive addresses that are not already in that domain.

It should also be noted that **cons** and the square brackets are part of the syntax of command forms, rather than parts of expressions. As a consequence, expressions do not depend on the heap and do not have side-effects.

A second example shows the effect of an attempt to mutate a dangling pointer:

		Store : x: 3, y: 4
		Heap : empty
Allocation	$x := \mathbf{cons}(1, 2)$;	$\downarrow$
		Store : x: 37, y: 4
		Heap : 37: 1, 38: 2
Lookup	$y := [x]$;	$\downarrow$
		Store : x: 37, y: 1
		Heap : 37: 1, 38: 2
Mutation	$[x + 2] := 3$;	$\downarrow$
		abort

Similar faults are also caused by out-of-range lookup or deallocation.

The assertions of separation logic go beyond the predicate calculus used in Hoare logic by providing four new forms for describing heaps:

- **emp**

  The heap is empty.
- $e \mapsto e'$

  The heap contains a single cell, at address e with contents e'.
- $p_1 * p_2$

  The heap can be split into two disjoint parts such that p_1 holds for one part and p_2 holds for the other.
- $p_1 \twoheadrightarrow p_2$

  If the current heap is extended with a disjoint part in which p_1 holds, then p_2 holds for the extended heap.

The separating conjunction $*$ is associative and commutative, with **emp** as its neutral element. The operation $\twoheadrightarrow$, called the *separating implication*, is adjoint to $*$. Neither the law of contraction nor the law of weakening hold for $*$.

It is useful to introduce several more complex forms as abbreviations:

$$e \mapsto - \stackrel{\text{def}}{=} \exists x'. \, e \mapsto x' \quad \text{where } x' \text{ not free in } e$$

$$e \hookrightarrow e' \stackrel{\text{def}}{=} e \mapsto e' * \mathbf{true}$$

$$e \mapsto e_1, \ldots, e_n \stackrel{\text{def}}{=} e \mapsto e_1 * \cdots * e + n - 1 \mapsto e_n$$

$$e \hookrightarrow e_1, \ldots, e_n \stackrel{\text{def}}{=} e \hookrightarrow e_1 * \cdots * e + n - 1 \hookrightarrow e_n$$

$$\text{iff } e \mapsto e_1, \ldots, e_n * \mathbf{true} \, .$$

By using $\mapsto$, $\hookrightarrow$, and the two forms of conjunction, it is easy to describe simple sharing patterns concisely:

1. $x \mapsto 3, y$ asserts that x points to an adjacent pair of cells containing 3 and y (i.e., the store maps x and y into some values α and β, α is an address, and the heap maps α into 3 and $\alpha + 1$ into β).

2. $y \mapsto 3, x$ asserts that y points to an adjacent pair of cells containing 3 and x.

3. $x \mapsto 3, y * y \mapsto 3, x$ asserts that situations (1) and (2) hold for separate parts of the heap.

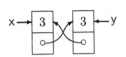

4. $x \mapsto 3, y \wedge y \mapsto 3, x$ asserts that situations (1) and (2) hold for the same heap, which can only happen if the values of x and y are the same.

5. $x \hookrightarrow 3, y \wedge y \hookrightarrow 3, x$ asserts that either (3) or (4) may hold, and that the heap may contain additional cells.

It is also possible (and, except in trivial cases, necessary) to define predicates by structural induction over abstract data types. For example, the predicate list α i:

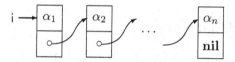

can be defined by structural induction on the sequence α:

$$\text{list } \epsilon \, i \stackrel{\text{def}}{=} \mathbf{emp} \wedge i = \mathbf{nil}$$

$$\text{list } (a{\cdot}\alpha) \, i \stackrel{\text{def}}{=} \exists j. \, i \mapsto a, j \, * \, \text{list } \alpha \, j \, .$$

A more elaborate representation of sequences is provided by *doubly-linked* list segments. Here, we write dlist α (i, i', j, j') when α is represented by a doubly-linked list segment with a forward linkage (via second fields) from i to j, and a backward linkage (via third fields) from j' to i':

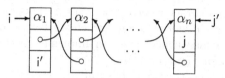

The inductive definition (again on sequences) is:

$$\text{dlist } \epsilon \, (i, i', j, j') \stackrel{\text{def}}{=} \mathbf{emp} \wedge i = j \wedge i' = j'$$

$$\text{dlist } a{\cdot}\alpha \, (i, i', k, k') \stackrel{\text{def}}{=} \exists j. \, i \mapsto a, j, i' \, * \, \text{dlist } \alpha \, (j, i, k, k') \, .$$

It is straightforward to use inductive definitions over any initial algebra without laws. An obvious example is the set S-exps of S-expressions in the sense of LISP, which is the least set satisfying

$$\tau \in \text{S-exps iff } \tau \in \text{Atoms or } \tau = (\tau_1 \cdot \tau_2) \text{ where } \tau_1, \tau_2 \in \text{S-exps}$$

(where atoms are integers that are not addresses).

Suppose we call the obvious representation of S-expressions without sharing a *tree*, and the analogous representation with possible sharing (but without cycles) a *dag*. Then we can define

$$\text{tree } a \, (i) \stackrel{\text{def}}{=} \mathbf{emp} \wedge i = a$$

$$\text{tree } (\tau_1 \cdot \tau_2) \, (i) \stackrel{\text{def}}{=} \exists i_1, i_2. \, i \mapsto i_1, i_2 \, * \, \text{tree } \tau_1 \, (i_1) \, * \, \text{tree } \tau_2 \, (i_2)$$

and

$$\text{dag } a \, (i) \stackrel{\text{def}}{=} i = a$$

$$\text{dag } (\tau_1 \cdot \tau_2) \, (i) \stackrel{\text{def}}{=} \exists i_1, i_2. \, i \mapsto i_1, i_2 \, * \, (\text{dag } \tau_1 \, (i_1) \wedge \text{dag } \tau_2 \, (i_2)) \, .$$

(Notice that tree $\tau\,(i)$ describes a heap containing a tree-representation of τ and nothing else, while dag $\tau\,(i)$ describes a heap that may properly contain a dag-representation of τ.)

4 Extending Hoare Logic

The meaning of the triples used to specify commands is roughly similar to that of Hoare logic. More precisely, however, the partial-correctness triple $\{p\}\ c\ \{q\}$ holds iff, starting in any state in which p holds:

- No execution of c aborts.
- If any execution of c terminates in a final state, then q holds in the final state.

Notice that the universal quantification in this definition extends over both store and heap components of states, and also over the multiple possible executions that arise from the indeterminacy of allocation.

Also notice that, even for partial correctness, specifications preclude abortion. This is a fundamental characteristic of the logic — that (to paraphrase Milner) well-specified programs do not go wrong (when started in states satisfying their precondition). As a consequence, one can implement well-specified programs without runtime memory-fault checking.

An obviously analogous treatment of total correctness is straightforward.

Except for the so-called rule of constancy, which is replaced by the frame rule, all the inference rules of Hoare logic remain sound in separation logic. In addition, there are rules for the new heap-manipulating commands. For instance, for mutation there is a *local* rule:

$$\{e \mapsto -\}\ [e] := e'\ \{e \mapsto e'\}\,,$$

from which one can use the frame rule to infer a *global* rule:

$$\{(e \mapsto -) * r\}\ [e] := e'\ \{(e \mapsto e') * r\}\,.$$

There is also a *backward reasoning* form of the rule that uses separating implication:

$$\{(e \mapsto -) * ((e \mapsto e') -\!\!* p)\}\ [e] := e'\ \{p\}\,.$$

These three rules are interderivable, and the last describes weakest preconditions.

A similar situation holds for allocation, lookup, and deallocation, although the first two cases are complicated by the need to use quantifiers to describe variable overwriting.

5 Present Accomplishments

At present, separation logic has been used to verify manually a variety of small programs, as well as a few that are large enough to demonstrate the potential of local reasoning for scalability [5,6,7]. In addition:

1. It has been shown that deciding the validity of an assertion in separation logic is not recursively enumerable, even when address arithmetic and the characteristic operation **emp**, $\mapsto$, $*$, and $-\!\!*$, but not $\hookrightarrow$ are prohibited [8,6]. On the other hand, it has also been shown that, if the characteristic operations are permitted but quantifiers are prohibited, then the validity of assertions is algorithmically decidable within the complexity class PSPACE [8].
2. A decision procedure has been devised for a restricted form of the logic that is capable of shape analysis of lists [9].
3. An iterated form of separating conjunction has been introduced to reason about arrays [4].
4. The logic has been extended to procedures with global variables, where a "hypothetical frame rule" permits reasoning with information hiding [10]. Recently, a further extension to higher-order procedures (in the sense of Algol-like languages) has been developed [11].
5. Separation logic itself has been extended to a higher-order logic [12].
6. The logic has been integrated with data refinement [13,14].
7. The logic has been extended to shared-variable concurrency with conditional critical regions, where one can reason about the transfer of ownership of storage from one process to another [15,16].
8. Fractional permissions (in the sense of Boyland) and counting permissions have been introduced so that one can permit several concurrent processes to have read-only access to an area of the heap [17].
9. In the context of proof-carrying code, separation logic has inspired work on proving run-time library code for dynamic allocation [18].

6   The Future

As with Hoare logic, it is difficult in separation logic to assert relations between states at different points in a program; one must use ghost variables, but now their values may need to be finite functions or relations. Moreover, the usual notation for such functions or relations is distractingly different from assertions about the current local heap. (These complications are evident in the proof of the Cheney algorithm [7].)

It is likely that the extension to higher-order logic mentioned above will alleviate this problem; for example, it should be possible to use ghost variables to denote the past values of heaps.

Recent advances in generalizing the logic have outstripped our experience in proving actual programs. We particularly need further experience proving programs where the sharing patterns of data structures convey semantic information — for example, when a cyclic graph is used to represent a network. And we have just begun to explore concurrent programs.

If separation logic is going to have an impact on verification, we must be able to automate proof-checking, at a high enough level to avoid trivial details. Judging by recent preliminary research, the likely route here is to express separation logic in a system such as Coq (as in [18]) or Isabelle, so that the inference rules of separation logic become theorems in the underlying logic.

Moreover, the logic must be adapted to real-world languages. This is likely to be relatively straightforward for languages such as C or assembly languages, but a number of issues arise for higher-level languages. These include the treatment of complex type systems (including typed values in the heap), garbage collection [19] (perhaps coexisting with explicitly allocated storage or some form of regions), and the presence of code pointers or closures in the heap [4,20].

A final goal is an integration of logic and type systems. One would like to have a type system for shared mutable data structures, with at least the expressiveness of Walker and Morrisett's alias types [21], that is a checkable sublanguage of separation logic.

References

1. Reynolds, J.C.: Intuitionistic reasoning about shared mutable data structure. In: Davies, J., Roscoe, B., Woodcock, J. (eds.) Millennial Perspectives in Computer Science, Houndsmill, Hampshire, Palgrave, pp. 303–321 (2000)

2. Ishtiaq, S., O'Hearn, P.W.: BI as an assertion language for mutable data structures. In: Conference Record of POPL 2001: The 28th ACM SIGPLAN-SIGACT Symposium on Principles of Programming Languages, pp. 14–26. ACM, New York (2001)

3. O'Hearn, P.W., Reynolds, J.C., Yang, H.: Local reasoning about programs that alter data structures. In: Fribourg, L. (ed.) CSL 2001 and EACSL 2001. LNCS, vol. 2142, Springer, Heidelberg (2001)

4. Reynolds, J.C.: Separation logic: A logic for shared mutable data structures. In: Proceedings Seventeenth Annual IEEE Symposium on Logic in Computer Science, Los Alamitos, California, pp. 55–74. IEEE Computer Society, Los Alamitos (2002)

5. Yang, H.: An example of local reasoning in BI pointer logic: The Schorr-Waite graph marking algorithm. In: Henglein, F., Hughes, J., Makholm, H., Niss, H. (eds.) SPACE 2001: Informal Proceedings of Workshop on Semantics, Program Analysis and Computing Environments for Memory Management, IT University of Copenhagen, pp. 41–68 (2001)

6. Yang, H.: Local Reasoning for Stateful Programs. Ph. D. dissertation, University of Illinois, Urbana-Champaign, Illinois (2001)

7. Birkedal, L., Torp-Smith, N., Reynolds, J.C.: Local reasoning about a copying garbage collector. In: Conference Record of POPL 2004: The 31st ACM SIGPLAN-SIGACT Symposium on Principles of Programming Languages, pp. 220–231. ACM Press, New York (2004)

8. Calcagno, C., Yang, H., O'Hearn, P.W.: Computability and complexity results for a spatial assertion language for data structures. In: Hariharan, R., Mukund, M., Vinay, V. (eds.) FSTTCS 2001. LNCS, vol. 2245, pp. 108–119. Springer, Heidelberg (2001)

9. Berdine, J., Calcagno, C., O'Hearn, P.W.: A decidable fragment of separation logic. In: Lodaya, K., Mahajan, M. (eds.) FSTTCS 2004. LNCS, vol. 3328, pp. 97–109. Springer, Heidelberg (2004)

10. O'Hearn, P.W., Yang, H., Reynolds, J.C.: Separation and information hiding. In: Conference Record of POPL 2004: The 31st ACM SIGPLAN-SIGACT Symposium on Principles of Programming Languages, pp. 268–280. ACM Press, New York (2004)

11. Birkedal, L., Torp-Smith, N., Yang, H.: Semantics of separation-logic typing and higher-order frame rules. In: Proceedings Twentieth Annual IEEE Symposium on Logic in Computer Science, Los Alamitos, California, IEEE Computer Society, Los Alamitos (2005)

12. Biering, B., Birkedal, L., Torp-Smith, N.: Bi-hyperdoctrines and higher order separation logic. In: Sagiv, M. (ed.) ESOP 2005. LNCS, vol. 3444, pp. 233–247. Springer, Heidelberg (2005)

13. Mijajlović, I., Torp-Smith, N.: Refinement in a separation context. In: SPACE 2004: Informal Proceedings of Second Workshop on Semantics, Program Analysis and Computing Environments for Memory Management (2004)

14. Mijajlović, I., Torp-Smith, N., O'Hearn, P.W.: Refinement and separation contexts. In: Lodaya, K., Mahajan, M. (eds.) FSTTCS 2004. LNCS, vol. 3328, pp. 421–433. Springer, Heidelberg (2004)

15. O'Hearn, P.W.: Resources, concurrency and local reasoning. In: Gardner, P., Yoshida, N. (eds.) CONCUR 2004. LNCS, vol. 3170, pp. 49–67. Springer, Heidelberg (2004)

16. Brookes, S.D.: A semantics for concurrent separation logic. In: Gardner, P., Yoshida, N. (eds.) CONCUR 2004. LNCS, vol. 3170, pp. 16–34. Springer, Heidelberg (2004)

17. Bornat, R., Calcagno, C., O'Hearn, P.W., Parkinson, M.: Permission accounting in separation logic. In: Conference Record of POPL 2005: The 32nd ACM SIGPLAN-SIGACT Symposium on Principles of Programming Languages, pp. 259–270. ACM Press, New York (2005)

18. Yu, D., Hamid, N.A., Shao, Z.: Building certified libraries for PCC: Dynamic storage allocation. Science of Computer Programming 50, 101–127 (2004)

19. Calcagno, C., O'Hearn, P.W., Bornat, R.: Program logic and equivalence in the presence of garbage collection. Theoretical Computer Science 298, 557–581 (2003)

20. Ni, Z., Shao, Z.: Certified assembly programming with embedded code pointers. In: Research Report YALEU/CS/TR-1294, Yale University, New Haven, Connecticut (2005), http://flint.cs.yale.edu/flint/publications/xcap.html

21. Walker, D., Morrisett, G.: Alias types for recursive data structures. In: Harper, R. (ed.) TIC 2000. LNCS, vol. 2071, pp. 177–206. Springer, Heidelberg (2001)

A Perspective on Program Verification

Willem-Paul de Roever

Christian-Albrechts University of Kiel
wpr@informatik.uni-kiel.de

Abstract. A perspective on program verification is presented from the point of view of a university professor who has been active over a period of 35 years in the development of formal methods and their supporting tools. He has educated until now approx. 25 Ph.D. researchers in those fields and has written two handbooks in the field of program verification, one unifying known techniques for proving data refinement, and the other on compositional verification of concurrent and distributed programs, and communication-closed layers. This essay closes with formulating a grand challenge worthy of modern Europe.

1 Background

Conjecture: It has become a real possibility that Germany's most powerful industrialist, Jürgen Schrempp, heading the largest industry of Germany, DaimlerChrysler, will be fired next year because his company has not spent sufficient attention to improve the reliability of the software of its prime product, Mercedes Benz cars. For, as a consequence of the poor quality of the top range of Mercedes Benz limousines, BMW has now replaced Mercedes Benz as the leading top-range car manufacturer in Germany. And this fact is unpalatable for the main shareholders of DaimlerChrysler (Deutsche Bank, e.g.).[1]

The underlying reason for this fact is that 60% of the current production of Mercedes Benz cars has to be frequently called back because of software failures, the highest percentage of any car manufacturer in the world. And this percentage cannot be changed in, say, a year, the period of time Schrempp has to defend again his industrial strategy to his shareholders (this year his defense took place on April 6, 2005).

This conjecture is at least the second of its kind: The Pentium Bug convinced the top level chip manufacturers that chips should be reliable and bug-free to the extent that any bug occurring after the production phase should be removable, at least to the extent that patches should be applicable circumventing those bugs.

A third fact, not a conjecture, would be that two crashes of a fully loaded Airbus 380 due to software failure in a row would lead to the demise of the European aircraft industry. And one such crash of the Airbus 380 would have

---

[1] Last minute news: Schrempp leaves DaimlerChrysler end of 2005 (Kieler Nachrichten 29.07.05).

B. Meyer and J. Woodcock (Eds.): Verified Software, LNCS 4171, pp. 470–477, 2008.

far more serious human and economic consequences than any Pentium-scale bug could ever have caused.

These three examples suffice to establish that reliable software is now a vital component for the survival of at least three modern key industries: Those of cars, high performance chips, and passenger aircraft. When in ten years from now ecological disaster is inevitable, nuclear reactors will be added to this list.

Conclusion: *The production of reliable software is here to stay.*

2   Producing Reliable Commercial Software: A Distant Grand Challenge

Is currently produced software reliable? The answer is an unequivocal NO.

Can reliable software meeting current demands in volume be produced at his very moment? *No!*

Is reliable software needed in most applications? *Neither.*

For, if the product in which this software is embedded allows for rebooting and if software crashes in this product can be remedied without leading to catastrophe, one can live with sof(t)ware which is only on the average reliable ("sof" means failure in dutch). We do so in our daily lives. So much for the production of "Sof"ware.

Is it possible to produce reliable software? The answer is: Only with the greatest of efforts.

Yet the need for reliable commercial software is not only unarguably there, but also the only forever distant *Grand Challenge* which I can think of within our field of computer science.

3   Why This Challenge Is Real: Impediments to Overcome

In this section I shall argue that the use of synchronous languages for stating specifications, and the use of any modelchecking or theorem-proving tool or any combination thereof, and of any disciplined use of mathematics, has led to tremendous successes in verifying specialized carefully-tuned domain-specific applications, but does not have the potential required for mass production of reliable software in general in the near future.

3.1   Formulating Correct Specifications

As scientists in the area of formal methods our future task is, therefore, as clear as is the fact that formal methods are not the only tool needed to meet the demands for producing reliable software.

For as difficult it may be to verify large programs, it is at least as difficult to formulate their specifications.

For instance, even when these specifications are written in executable languages, such as the synchronous languages Esterel, Lustre, and Signal, or the

Statemate family of languages, the resulting specifications are programs which should be proved correct, too, relative to new specifications, which should be correct in their turn.

Consequently, there will always be a moment when these specifications should be tested, be it by trail and error, by inspection, or by deducing their logical consequences and testing whether these are acceptable. Famous errors made in the recent past point in this direction. For instance, the fact that one part of the positioning system of a recent marslander was written in the metric system, whereas another part was formulated w.r.t. the English systems of weight and measurement, might have been detected by simply testing it in a realistic simulation, as done, e.g., in trials in the Statemate system.

In one case I know of, the efforts involved in producing correct software have been successful once a correct specification has been found: Once a correct specification in a synchronous language has been produced. For compilers translating this kind of specification languages can be proved correct, as has been done for Signal by a team led by Amir Pnueli [5].

However, as soon as asynchronous properties have to be integrated within a synchronous framework, the race is open, as the field of GALS (for Globally Asynchronous Locally Synchronous) specifications shows, initiated by Albert Benveniste.

3.2   Verifying That a Specification Is Satisfied Using Modelchecking

Then, given the availability of correct specifications, is it possible to verify their satisfaction?

In case of finite state spaces, and in case of infinite state spaces of a very special nature, this can be done using modelchecking techniques. Their advocates will claim that their development is one straight success story, whose end is not in sight. Be this as may, in the (recent) theses produced at my chair in Kiel and under the guidance of the late Rob Gerth at the Technical University of Eindhoven one aspect struck me as essential:

> The enormous effort required to mold very carefully chosen examples in a shape fit for being checked by an implementation of a newly proposed modelchecking strategy.

This effort was caused because any slight deviation from the example at hand:

1. would be uncheckable using the newly developed technique in general, and/or
2. run up against the limitations of the resources employed in the particular implementation.

This observation is made not to belittle the efforts of the researchers concerned. Far from it, I have the deepest respect and highest admiration for the researchers involved in this challenging and highly successful field!

My observation only serves to formulate the obvious:

> The efforts involved in, and the very serious impediments imposed by, overcoming the limitations of any implementation of any modelchecking

technique, applied to any serious example I know of during the existence
of this now 25 years old field, are enormous.

Usually, modelchecking is associated with checking the correctness of (synchronous) hardware circuits. Gerard Holzmann has developed the Spin modelchecker for checking (asynchronous) software for Bell-Labs.

He states that one of the reasons for his success is Moore's law, in this case,
the fact that hardware speed and size of memory double every 18 months. This
enabled him, a.o., to verify a concurrent telephone network server for Bell-Labs,
i.e., industrial software.

In a similar vein, Siemens (now Infineon's) modelchecker (which is commercially available), has been reported a few years ago to be able to check the
software of one industrial robot in a production line, e.g., for a steel production
mill. Verifying the correctness of an entire line required at that moment an approximately 6-months effort due to the need to finetune the assumptions of one
robot in order to be logically implied by the accumulated commitments of its
predecessors in the line, which had to be done by a team of engineers.

Finally, nowadays the importance of modelchecking is predominantly that of
a systematic debugging technique, because of its capability to generate traces
leading to the errors found.

3.3 Verifying That a Specification Is Satisfied Using Theorem Proving

The impediments met during modelchecking can be reformulated, mutatis mu-
tandis, for Theorem Proving.

One proud advocate of a draft of a very interesting paper on inclusive end-to-
end verification, which I read a few days ago, observed that his team of verification engineers could now verify one page of code using Hoare style verification
checked by the theorem prover Isabelle in one week.

Which proves my point: Similar limitations as exist for model checkers hold
for verification based on theorem provers. Enormous advances are being made by
the teams of Tobias Nipkow, Wolfgang Paul, John Rushby, Natarajan Shankar,
and others. However, any production of software verified by a theorem prover is
still a major research effort and has been so ever since theorem proving entered
the field of program verification 40 years ago.

Verifying that a specification is satisfied using a combination of modelchecking
and theorem-proving techniques has entered the field by the development of the
tool Invest of Bensalem, Bouajjani, and Lakhnech, integrated into PVS by Sam
Owre, and extended at Saarbrücken by Podelski and his team in the context of
AVACS (see below). Although one may expect that the same objections hold as for
modelchecking and theorem proving, it is clear that verification engineers having
such a powerful tool at their disposal may be able to make considerable progress.

Indicative of the promise of this mixed approach is AVACS [2], a German
consortium of universities, research laboratories, and industries, led by Werner
Damm, aiming at the automated verification of the embedded software of a high
speed train by 2016!

However, clearly in their limit at best semi-automatic tools can result from the combination of modelchecking and theorem-proving techniques, requiring specialist support. This defeats the goal of any large scale production of un-specialized verified software, but makes it possible to verify related families of domain-specific software.

3.4   Verifying a Program by a Disciplined Use of Mathematics

One of the most impressive verification efforts I know of has been undertaken by a team led by Leslie Lamport and resulted in the complete verification of two commercial cache-coherence protocols for Pentium-class processors, produced by AMD.

Clearly a team consisting of top engineers, verification specialists, guided by a person of the stature of Leslie Lamport is able to obtain results which only much later can be emulated using any of the aforementioned techniques. Therefore, cloning Leslie might possibly result in producing correct software for specialized industrial needs. Of course, more than cloning alone would be needed, because two clones of Leslie would be very hard to manage...

I'll come back to this possibility because it symbolizes the partisan endeavor of the extremely gifted individual,[2] who, however gratifying he may be for me as a researcher, contradicts clearly any form of mass production of software, whatsoever.

Yet for extremely complicated algorithms, which are to be implemented in hardware, I see no other realistic solution than the cooperation of very gifted individuals. And this will always be the case, since any time has its own frontier of research.

4   Intermediate Conclusion

The only conclusion that can be formulated thus far is the conjecture that when programs of unrestricted complexity are to be verified, it is in the nature of human beings to find ways of proving these correct, given enough time, an un-bounded number of resources, and an unbounded number of gifted people.

The problem is, e.g., that:

1. current chip manufacturers, have now hit the boundary of the number of available specialists and resources, and do not know how to proceed now that more of everyone and everything is not anymore available, and that, e.g.,
2. modelchecking has to beat exponential bounds, which can be done at best in a limited number of restricted cases at the cost of tremendous intellectual achievement.

However, as the French "approche synchrone" in combination with Harel's StateCharts have shown, once some of the greatest minds of our time start

---

[2] A reviewer of this paper remarked that also Bob Kurshan belongs to this list.

working at the top of their capacity in the restricted area of specifying real-time embedded systems not only as an academic exercise but at a scale required for specifying the full complexity of software required for operating nuclear reactors or gigantic aircraft such as the A 380, the complementarity of the formal academic approach with respect to the one based on industrial trial and error is established.

For it has led to an improvement in quality of the produced code by a factor of at least hundred.[3]

5   Considerations Involving Programming Languages

Originally, I started out by stating that our real Grand Challenge is the production of reliable software at an industrial scale.

In which languages is such software usually written?

C. Operating system software is often written in C, C++, or another dialect of C. Even lightweight verification tools, such as abstract analysis tools have problems with checking software written in C. Some years ago the crash of one of NASA's Marslanders due to software failure could only be tracked after translating its flight software into Java, and then finding the errors using lightweight verification tools for Java, such as those based on abstract interpretations.

An often-heard obstacle against generating correctness proofs for programs written in C is C's reliance on pointer arithmetic. I do not understand this obstacle. Once correctness is crucial, the implementation of integers on a particular family of processors is known and can be easily incorporated in proof systems. Also, the mathematical analysis of pointers is known since its discovery by America and de Boer approximately 20 years ago [9]. However. I do not know of any practical tools based on these particular observations, which work in most practical cases. Important advances have been made by restricting to specific classes of pointer structures, e.g., using monadic second-order logic as specification language for while programs with pointers and by checking the reformulation of the corresponding verification problem using the MONA tool [7].

Very promising and indicative of the state of the art is the effort of proving correctness of a multiprocessor operating system with paged memory techniques written in a seriously curtailed subset of C, undertaken by a team led by Wolfgang Paul [4].

Java. Web software is often written in Java. Although it is in principle possible to prove concurrent multi-threaded Java programs correct, by all practical means and purposes such correctness proofs are unattainable, as remarked in recent work by Erika Abraham c.s. in case of deadlock freedom. (Her thesis [1] contains a sound and relatively complete Hoare-style proof system for a multi-threaded subset of Java.)

---

[3] See, e.g., http://www.esterel-technologies.com/technology/success-stories/
overview.html, especially the table regarding the Airbus aircraft.

Yet enormous advances have been made in building tools for verifying restricted classes of properties for certain subsets of Java. Often these operate on abstract versions of these programs; e.g., the Bandera tool [8].

I have heard from Matt Dwyer that the company-internal Java tools of Microsoft are ahead of the published state of the art. Similarly, it has been remarked by the late Rob Gerth that the company-internal modelcheckers of Intel are ahead of the state of the art.

From the point of view of the production of reliable industrial software these are approximately the most positive remarks one can expect: If the reliability of their programs is of such importance to these companies that their internally produced verification tools are kept secret, this is certainly a sign of maturity of our field.

An altogether different approach is producing High Integrity software is obtained by seriously restricting the use of semantically complicated features in a programming language to such an extent that verification becomes commercially feasible. This is the goal of the SPARK approach, documented by John Barnes [6], focusing on software which is correct by construction.

6   Summarizing the State of the Art

1. The enormous effort required to mold very carefully chosen examples in a shape fit for being checked by a(n implementation of a newly proposed) model checking strategy, theorem prover, or a combination thereof, is still staggering. However, also helped by the effects of Moore's law, ever more programs of industrial importance are being verified using these tools.
2. Once a correct specification in a synchronous language such as Esterel, Lustre, or Signal has been produced, its automatic translation in C is correct when produced by a verifying compiler for that synchronous language. E.g., for the synchronous language Signal, such a verified compiler is available [5]. The associated strategy of producing graphical specifications, e.g., by using the Scade tool, Esterel Studio, or Statemate, and translating them automatically, has led to an improvement in quality of the code produced for real-time embedded systems by a factor of at least hundred.
3. By seriously restricting the use of semantically complicated features in a programming language, it has become feasible to prove the correctness of large programs such as operating systems. The first time this possibility was seriously pursued was in the SPARK-ADA project [6].
4. For extremely complicated algorithms, which are to be implemented in hardware, I see no other realistic solution for their verification than the cooperation of gifted individuals, led by a person of exceptional stature.

7   Grand Challenge

As grand challenge worthy of modern Europe I propose:

Proving the correctness of the safety-critical parts of the software for the Airbus A380.

Acknowledgments. Dennis Dams suggested many improvements, Martin Steffen and Marcel Kyas helped me with getting the paper ready.

References

1. An Assertional Proof System for Multithreaded Java – Theory and Tool Support, Erika Abraham, Thesis, University of Leiden (2005), www.informatik.uni-freiburg.de/~eab
2. AVACS, Automatic Verification and Analysis of Complex Systems (2004), www.avacs.org/
3. Süddeutsche Zeitung (Thursday, 7.04.2005)
4. VERISOFT (2003), http://www.verisoft.de/
5. Pnueli, A., Gordin, I.L., Leviathan, R.: Validating the Translation of an Industrial Optimizing Compiler. In: Wang, F. (ed.) ATVA 2004. LNCS, vol. 3299, pp. 230–247. Springer, Heidelberg (2004)
6. Barnes, J.: High Integrity Software: The SPARK Approach to Safety and Security. Addison-Wesley, Reading (2003)
7. Jensen, J.L., Jørgensen, M.E., Schwartzbach, M.I., Klarlund, N.: Automatic Verification of Pointer Programs using Monadic Second-Order Logic. In: Proceedings of the ACM SIGPLAN Conference on Programming Language Design and Implementation (PLDI-97), pp. 226–234 (1997)
8. Hatcliff, J., Dwyer, M.B., Păsăveanu, C.S., Robby,: Foundations of the Bandera abstraction tool. In: The Essence of Computation, pp. 172–203. Springer, Heidelberg (2002)
9. America, P., de Boer, F.: Reasoning about dynamically evolving process structures. Formal Aspects of Computing 6(3), 269–316 (1994)

Meta-Logical Frameworks
and
Formal Digital Libraries*

Carsten Schürmann

Department of Computer Science
Yale University
carsten@cs.yale.edu

Although the Annals will publish Dr. Hales's paper, Peter Sarnak, an editor of the Annals, whose own work does not involve the use of computers, says that the paper will be accompanied by an unusual disclaimer, stating that the computer programs accompanying the paper have not undergone peer review. There is a simple reason for that, Dr. Sarnak says it is impossible to find peers who are willing to review the computer code. [Economist, March 31, 2005]

1   Introduction

Software verification research has become once again a very exciting research area and simultaneously a melting pot for many different subareas within computer science. In this position paper, I emphasize two of the areas that I am particularly interested in and consider to be of significant importance to this endeavor; meta-logical frameworks and formal digital libraries.

The central concepts in software verification are program code and formal proofs. Proofs vouch for the fact that software adheres to its specification. Specifications may be chosen arbitrarily, while within the confines designated by the specification logic. A first approximation to software correctness is software soundness. Type soundness or resource soundness guarantee that a piece of software doesn't consume too many resources (including time and space) and doesn't crash leaving the computer system in an undefined state that could be exploited by malicious intruders. Memory soundness restricts access to private and protected data. However, the task of software verification goes much beyond soundness in that it requires that any computation always adheres to its specification.

The days when software was written in only one language are long gone. In fact, a program is rarely ever a monolithic construction but almost always draws on a large variety of different functions, written in different programming languages with different semantics. These functions are organized in the form of libraries and usually invoked by name through (possibly even foreign) function

---

* This research has been funded by NSF grants CCR-0325808 and CCR-0133502.

B. Meyer and J. Woodcock (Eds.): Verified Software, LNCS 4171, pp. 478–485, 2008.

interfaces. For example, the infamous *malloc* implemented in C may be called upon by a compiler written in SML.

Correctness proofs, on the other hand, still tend to be monolithic constructs. This is because, logically speaking, it is really not clear in general how specification logics interact. For example, what does it mean to appeal to a lemma proven in constructive type theory from within a classical argument about the correctness of a piece of code. It is not surprising that there is little sharing of libraries of proofs between systems like PVS, Isabelle, Nuprl, Coq, Lego, or Twelf. I argue that for software verification, we need not only worry about the interaction of different programming languages, but also the interaction of different specification logics.

Hence we must carefully distinguish between *libraries of code* and *libraries of proofs*.

There are numerous specification logics, including logics with special connectives for reasoning about time (temporal logics) and mutable state (separation logic). I prefer to think about the meaning of logical propositions prooftheoretically (as opposed to set theoretical or model theoretical), because it often yields a well-understood syntactic way of handling semantics. Those syntactic denotations are also called *proof objects* that can be independently verified and capture the evidence why a proposition holds. Syntactic proof objects have become very popular in the last decade, witnessed by the design of numerous proof carrying code architectures where explicit proof objects are shipped from code producers to code consumers as evidence that the obtained byte code adheres to an a priori defined safety policy. In such an architecture it is the compiler that needs to construct the proof object, possibly drawing on libraries of proofs.

One way of giving the machine access to abstract concepts such as meaning or derivability is by capturing the defining judgments as types in a logical framework. For example, in the logical framework LF [HHP93], the judgment that "an expression e evaluates to a value v" is encoded as a type (eval $\ulcorner e \urcorner \ulcorner v \urcorner$), where $\ulcorner e \urcorner$ corresponds to the encoding of expression e and $\ulcorner v \urcorner$ as an encoding of value v. Similarly, the judgment that F is derivable in HOL may be captured by a type (hol $\ulcorner F \urcorner$) where $\ulcorner F \urcorner$ is an encoding of formula F.

In the judgments as types paradigm, derivations are subsequently encoded as objects of the corresponding type. For example, HOL proof objects are encoded as objects of type (hol $\ulcorner F \urcorner$). The encoding is said to be *adequate* if type-checking automatically entails the validity of a derivation. Over the years, many different and more expressive logical frameworks have been developed with one goal in mind: to sharpen the conciseness of encodings. Please consult [Pfe99] for a survey article.

Thus, software verification goes far beyond one programming language and one specification logic. The effort must be seen holistically, which involves integration of different semantic programming models and the validity of mathematical knowledge beyond the borders of a particular specification logic. I believe it is here where we will find many challenging and interesting research problems in the future.

2   Challenges

2.1   Semantic Modeling

Logical framework technology has provided a reliable representation methodology for a substantial class of programming languages, including the semantic characterization of machine code [Cra03] and a complete encoding of the full semantics for SML (an ongoing project led by Robert Harper and Karl Crary)[1]. There is a large pool of practical programming languages, whose semantical foundations may mathematically not be as clean and as well understood as those of Haskell, yet need to be urgently looked at as well. Scripting languages and query languages form the basis of modern web based computing and must play a central role in any serious verification effort.

And similarly, logical framework technology has proven useful for studying properties of specification logics, including soundness and completeness properties, yet there are other specification logics that have not been looked at, which may influence the design of future logical frameworks. The current state of the art logical framework technology can capture many derivations from higher-order logic to sub-structural non-commutative logics, yet little research has been conducted on how to model modal and temporal logics. Those logics are of particular interest, especially for specifying concurrent programs.

An important challenge arises when proof theoretic means are not enough to capture meaning. In contrast to searching for proof objects, decision procedures that are used increasingly within software verification tools guarantee adherence to a specification by executing a program. Model checkers, for example, traverse large state spaces in the search of *bad* states. Combining the dynamic aspects of decision procedures with the static aspects of deductive reasoning, I believe, is an exciting and important research challenge that is still in its infancy.

2.2   Morphisms

The act of verifying software requires not only a solid understanding of the meaning and behavior of programs written in a single programming language but also the intricate details of the interaction with programs written in other languages. Analogously, proofs need to be understood not only in the context of a single specification logic, but interpreted instead in some desired target logic, be it constructive type theory or separation logic.

I think about a software verification infrastructure as the integrated whole of several programming languages and specification logics together with a set of morphisms between them as indicated by the edges in Figure 1. It is useful to distinguish between *vertical morphisms*, i.e. morphisms that express semantic embeddings among programming languages or logics, and *horizontal morphisms*, i.e. morphisms that encode programming languages and their semantics inside a specification logic. Vertical morphisms are denoted by undirected edges among

---

[1] Personal communication.

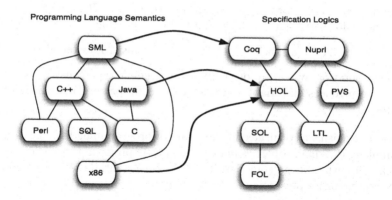

Fig. 1. Vertical and Horizontal Morphisms

programming languages and logics and horizontal morphisms by directed edges between programming languages and logics.

Vertical Morphisms. Consider for example the embedding of HOL into Nuprl pioneered by Howe [How96, How98]. Every theorem and every proof in HOL can be translated into a Nuprl proof. The meta-theoretical argument is constructive and therefore defines a total function for proof translation [SS05]. This function is a *vertical morphism* as it expresses a relation between two specification logics. The judgment that an HOL formula A can be translated into Nuprl formula B is captured by the type (trans $\ulcorner A \urcorner \ulcorner B \urcorner$) where $\ulcorner A \urcorner$ and $\ulcorner B \urcorner$ are encodings of the respective formulas in LF. Not every morphism needs to be total. To keep proof translation practical, morphisms may need to remain partial in oder to translate more expressive specification logics into less expressive ones.

Programming morphisms involves programming with meanings and proof objects. In my group, we are pursuing the development of logical framework specific programming languages for programming (partial) morphisms. The programming language whose term algebra is that of the logical framework LF is called Delphin.

Example 1 (Logic embeddings). Without going into the details over how to write Delphin programs, we give the sample Delphin type of a function f that converts HOL proofs into Nuprl proofs of the translated HOL statement. Let A be the HOL sentence, and H the proof of A in HOL. We can show that there exists a Nuprl sentence B, evidence E that B is in fact the translation of A, and of course the Nuprl proof N of B. In Delphin, we carefully separate between data expressed in the logical framework LF and programs. If $\ulcorner A \urcorner$ is the LF representation of HOL formula A, $\langle \ulcorner A \urcorner \rangle$ stands for the corresponding embedded value in Delphin. Similarly, $\langle \mathsf{hol} \ulcorner A \urcorner \rangle$ is an (atomic) Delphin type that merely states that A is provable in HOL.

$$f \langle \ulcorner A \urcorner \rangle \langle \ulcorner N \urcorner \rangle = (\langle \ulcorner B \urcorner \rangle, (\langle \ulcorner E \urcorner \rangle, \langle \ulcorner N \urcorner \rangle))$$

In Delphin we write $\supset$ for non-dependent function types, Π for dependent ones, and $\star$ and Σ for Cartesian products. Thus, we derive that

$$f \in \Pi \langle A \rangle \in \langle o \rangle . \langle \text{hol } A \rangle \supset \Sigma \langle B \rangle \in \langle o \rangle . \langle \text{trans } A \, B \rangle \star \langle \text{nuprl } B \rangle.$$

The most noteworthy feature of Delphin's dependent type constructors is that binding occurrences of variables are determined by pattern matching, such as $\langle A \rangle$ and $\langle B \rangle$.   □

Vertical morphisms also surface in the realm of programming languages in form of compilers. Proving properties about a high-level program is of little use when compiling it with a buggy compiler. It is therefore essential that the compilation process is semantics preserving.

Example 2 (Compilers). Let S be a valid program written in SML with meaning V and let us assume that this relation can be formally encoded in LF as (sml $\ulcorner S \urcorner \ulcorner V \urcorner$). Similarly, let us assume we can capture the meaning of an intermediate language program M as W, where we encode the relation between M and W in LF as a type (il $\ulcorner M \urcorner \ulcorner W \urcorner$). Furthermore, let us specify a compiler as a relation between SML programs and intermediate code, which is encoded in LF as type (compile $\ulcorner S \urcorner \ulcorner M \urcorner$). Finally we encode an interpretation function of machine language values into SML as LF type (interpret $\ulcorner W \urcorner \ulcorner V \urcorner$). A compiler is semantics preserving, if we can write a program c in Delphin such that

$$c \, \langle \ulcorner S \urcorner \rangle \, \langle \ulcorner V \urcorner \rangle \, \langle \ulcorner D \urcorner \rangle = (\langle \ulcorner M \urcorner \rangle, (\langle \ulcorner W \urcorner \rangle, (\langle \ulcorner C \urcorner \rangle, (\langle \ulcorner E \urcorner \rangle, \langle \ulcorner I \urcorner \rangle)))),$$

and show that c is total. D is evidence that V is the meaning of S, C is evidence that S compiles into M, E is evidence that the meaning of M is indeed W, and I establishes the relation between W and V. In Delphin, c has type

$$\Pi \langle S \rangle \in \langle exp \rangle . \Pi \langle V \rangle \in \langle value \rangle . \langle \text{sml } S \, V \rangle$$
$$\supset \Sigma \langle M \rangle \in \langle mcode \rangle . \Sigma \langle W \rangle \in \langle answer \rangle .$$
$$\langle \text{compile } S \, M \rangle \star \langle \text{il } M \, W \rangle \star \langle \text{interpret } W \, V \rangle.$$

□

Horizontal Morphisms. In specification logic, programs and their meaning are the central subjects of reasoning. Since we propose to formalize both programming languages and specification logics in the same logical framework, it is important to examine how to embed programming languages into the term algebra of the logic. This embedding is made explicit by horizontal morphisms that translate programs and their meanings into the logical domain and make them available for radical scrutiny.

Example 3 (Greatest Common Divisor). The following SML program

$$\begin{aligned} &\textbf{fun } \text{gcd } a \, b = \textbf{if } a \textbf{ mod } b = 0 \textbf{ then } b \\ &\qquad\qquad\qquad \textbf{else } \text{gcd } b \, (a \textbf{ mod } b) \end{aligned}$$

can be represented as an object of type (exp) in LF. Recall that in LF, we write (eval $\ulcorner e \urcorner$ $\ulcorner v \urcorner$) for the encoding of the operational meaning of programs. The property we would like to prove in the specification logic is that if $gcd(a, b)$ returns c, that c is indeed the greatest common divisor of a and b, which means that c divides a and b, and every other divisor of a and b is also a divisor of c.

The proof proceeds by induction on the structure of the derivation that $gcd(a, b)$ returns c. Therefore, for the formal argument to be carried out in Coq, we need to turn the definition of "being an expression" and the "operational meaning" into inductively defined types and make them available to the specification logic by means of reflection.

For example, the fact that a is a valid expression is expressed by an inductive type exp providing a new infix constructor @ for application, and that v is the semantic value of e is encoded as an inductive type as well, eval $\ulcorner e \urcorner$ $\ulcorner v \urcorner$.

$$\forall(a : \mathsf{exp}).\forall(b : \mathsf{exp}).\forall(c : \mathsf{exp}).\mathsf{eval}(\ulcorner gcd \urcorner @ a @ b)\ c$$
$$\supset (c \mid a) \wedge (c \mid b) \wedge (\forall(d : \mathsf{exp}).(d \mid a) \wedge (d \mid b) \supset (d \mid c)).$$

$\square$

A *meta-logical framework* extends a logical framework with tools for programming and reasoning with deductive systems, including programming languages and specification logics together with a collection of vertical and horizontal morphisms. Reflection is only one of the challenges that arises when designing a meta-logical framework as the foundation of a software verification infrastructure. A reflective meta-logical framework that supports standard induction principles was described by Basin and Meseguer [BCM04]. However, it remains yet to be investigated on how to extend their result to accommodate non-standard induction principles, which are prevalent implicitly in (almost all) LF encodings. Therefore, I consider research on meta-logical frameworks, in general, an important part of the grand challenge for software verification.

2.3   Organization of Mathematical Knowledge

Many verification tasks rely on domain-specific knowledge. For example, numerical applications may have to appeal to properties of floating point arithmetic or even stability results for solutions of sets of differential equations. But what shall one do, if the specification logic is Isabelle/HOL yet all desired theorems were already proven in PVS? It seems to be a waste of effort to redo all those parts from scratch. Thus, I have become very interested on how to share mathematical knowledge and proofs across logic specific boundaries.

In a *formal digital library* we store a collection of mathematical facts together with their respective meanings in form mathematical proofs. Vertical morphisms help cast mathematical knowledge from one formalism into another. A formal digital library should be extensible, meaning that new logical systems and vertical morphisms can be easily added. Furthermore, it should provide adequate functionality to retrieve and maintain mathematical knowledge in a database.

I speculate that such a formal digital library is not only applicable for libraries of proofs, but that it also helps organize libraries of code. Moreover, if invariants and their proofs are stored in conjunction with code, the query engine could use this information and retrieve library functions, not by name, but by a semantic description.

Example 4 (Relative primality). Assume that a programmer tries to write a function to compute if two numbers a and b are relatively prime. He or she might formulate the following (speculative) query: Is there a program S in SML, that has the following invariant provable in Coq?

$$\forall a : \mathsf{exp}.\forall b : \mathsf{exp}.\forall c : \mathsf{exp}.(c \mid a) \wedge (c \mid b) \supset c = 1$$

The answer should be: Yes, choose

$$S = (\gcd (a,b) = 1 \text{ } \mathbf{andalso} \text{ } \gcd (b,a) = 1).$$

$\square$

At least two different formal digital library projects are currently underway. The FDL project led by Cornell University, the California Institute of Technology, and the University of Wyoming focuses on the organization of mathematical knowledge. The Logosphere project conducted at Carnegie Mellon University, SRI International and Yale University concentrates on the organization of libraries of mathematical proof and the specification of vertical morphisms.

3 Conclusion

The enormously difficult task of verifying software involves a colorful variety of programming languages and specification logics and is intimately connected to mathematical truth. Sometimes this truth can be retrieved, other times it must be constructed. It is common knowledge that the performance of verification technologies depends on the kind of verification problems it is applied to, and each technology has its weaknesses and its strengths. The more we can draw on all areas of automated deduction and formal methods, the faster we can reach the goal of software verification. Thus, a common meta-logical framework infrastructure that facilitates the construction of libraries of code and libraries of proofs will help us make strides towards a solution of the grand challenge.

Returning to the original opening quote to this position paper, a formal digital library may help Dr. Hales to completely formalize the proof of Kepler's conjecture in HOLlight, his chosen target logic. The vertical morphisms will help to convert pieces of the proof formulated in different logical formalisms and the horizontal morphisms allow him to reason about the correctness of the programs he used to obtain the proof, leading up to one huge monolithic proof object in HOLlight, that can be subsequently checked by a small and well-understood proof checker. Trusting the checker means trusting the proof, which simplifies the job of the referee who does not even have to look at the proof at all any more.

References

[BCM04]   Basin, D., Clavel, M., Meseguer, J.: Reflective metalogical frameworks. ACM
          Transaction on Computational Logic 5(3), 528–576 (2004)
[Cra03]   Crary, K.: Toward a foundational typed assembly language. In: Proceedings
          of the 30th Symposium on Principles of Programming Languages (POPL),
          New Orleans, Louisiana, USA, pp. 198–212 (2003)
[HHP93]   Harper, R., Honsell, F., Plotkin, G.: A framework for defining logics. Journal
          of the Association for Computing Machinery 40(1), 143–184 (1993)
[How96]   Howe, D.J.: Importing mathematics from HOL into Nuprl. In: von Wright,
          J., Harrison, J., Grundy, J. (eds.) TPHOLs 1996. LNCS, vol. 1125, pp. 267–
          282. Springer, Heidelberg (1996)
[How98]   Howe, D.J.: Toward sharing libraries of mathematics between theorem
          provers. In: Proceedings of Frontiers of Combining Systems, FroCoS 1998,
          ILLC, University of Amsterdam, October 2–4, 1998, Kluwer Academic Pub-
          lishers, Dordrecht (1998)
[Pfe99]   Pfenning, F.: Logical frameworks. In: Robinson, A., Voronkov, A. (eds.)
          Handbook of Automated Reasoning, Elsevier Science Publishers, Amster-
          dam (1999) (in preparation)
[SS05]   Schürmann, C., Stehr, M.-O.: An executable formalization of the
          HOL/Nuprl connection in the meta-logical framework Twelf. In: Sutcliffe,
          G., Voronkov, A. (eds.) Proceedings of Logic for Programming, Artificial
          Intelligence, and Reasoning (LPAR), Montego Bay, Jamaica, Springer, Hei-
          delberg (2005) (to appear)

Languages, Ambiguity, and Verification

The SPARK Team

Praxis High Integrity Systems
20 Manvers Street,
Bath BA1 1PX
UK
sparkinfo@praxis-his.com

Abstract. This position paper is based on presentations given at the Grand Challenge workshops held at Gresham College in March 2004 and in Newcastle in July 2005. It reports some of our experience from building the SPARK language and its verification tools. We argue that the provision of an unambiguous semantics for a programming language is crucial if the verification framework is to be sound, deep and efficient. Secondly, we offer some reflections on the (mostly non-technical) barriers that we encounter in trying to deploy SPARK within organizations. Finally, we try to set some goals for future work.

1 Design Goals for a Program Verification System

A programming language and verification system that aim to meet this Grand Challenge might have the following design goals:

- Soundness – the system must not give a false-negative result.
- Completeness – the system should issue as few false-positive results (aka "false alarms") as possible.
- Depth – the verification system should be able to verify useful and non-trivial properties of our programs.
- Efficiency – the system must be fast enough to enable constructive and interactive use. If it takes all night to verify anything useful, then no-one will use it! Ideally, the system should be so fast as to wean programmers away from the lure of compilation and test.
- Composition – "separate verification" (somewhat akin to "separate compilation") must be possible. Addition of new program units must not invalidate the verification of existing units.
- Expressive Power – the language must be large enough for use on industrial-scale projects. (It's easy to meet the first five goals for a toy language that no-one else uses...)

2 Languages and Ambiguity

In program verification, we are asking questions of the form "What does this program mean?" or "Does this program have property X?" It seems a reasonable expectation

B. Meyer and J. Woodcock (Eds.): Verified Software, LNCS 4171, pp. 486–490, 2008.

that questions of the first form should only have *one* answer, while the second form should be ideally answered "Yes" or "No".

A central goal then is the provision of an *unambiguous* semantics for our programming language, since any ambiguity can lead to incomplete "Don't know" answers or (worse) unsoundness. Consider the case of a simple evaluation-order dependence—a language feature that is *implementation-dependent* in C, C++ or Ada. If a verification tool encounters a compound expression, should it assume left-to-right, right-to-left, or both evaluation orders? The first two options possibly lead to unsoundness if a compiler disagrees with the choice made by the verification tool. The latter choice leads to an unacceptable explosion in analysis complexity.

Another approach is to define a language (or a subset of some suitable parent language) so that either evaluation order is allowed, but the choice can never make any difference to the program's meaning. This is a rather more subtle trick, but has significant benefit: the system is sound, efficient, and the language can be a true subset of its parent so that standard industrial compilers can be used.

This is the approach taken by SPARK[1], which aims for an unambiguous semantics through:

- Careful sub-setting of Ada95 to remove troublesome language features such as unrestricted use of tasking and generics, and
- Provision of design-by-contract "annotations" in the language to strengthen the specification of units with just the right information required for analysis, and
- Static analyses, such as information flow analysis and aliasing analysis, which are mandatory.

The latter are important: the SPARK Verification-Condition Generator (VCG) is built on the assumptions that programs are free from aliasing of names, function side-effects, and the use of uninitialized variables. These analyses ensure the required properties hold before the VCG can be enabled, and the language is designed so that these analyses are sound, complete and efficient.

3 SPARK in the Real World

We now have a small, but non-trivial set of customers using the SPARK system to prove real properties of real programs. These programs range from about 10000 lines of code to several million lines. Most customers attempt proof of the absence of "run-time errors" (e.g. buffer overflow, division by zero etc.) first, since the side-conditions for these are "built in" to the VCG (no additional annotations are required) so it provides an approachable first rung on the ladder. Our theorem prover is typically about 97% complete for the resulting VCs. Machines resources are now available that proof of such properties can be attempted on whole programs with an hour or so, and on a particular subsystem or package within minutes.

We have observed one other effect through the use of the SPARK proof system: it mandates a clarity and precision of expression that offer benefits far beyond the simple verification of program fragments. In trying to complete a proof for a routine, engineers find (with alarming frequency) that their requirements or specifications are incomplete, ambiguous, or contradictory. Finding these mistakes sooner rather than later has an obvious beneficial impact on a project's risk, time-scale and overall defect rate.

3.1 Barriers to SPARK Adoption

In SPARK's natural application domain (hard real-time, embedded and critical systems), the technical argument in favour of strong static verification is easily won. The commercial advantage of a low-defect rate is also well established[4]. In spite of these, we often struggle to convince organizations to adopt the technology. The reasons are rarely technical, but seem to fall into the following general categories:

Process-ism
The rise of software process capability models such as CMM has led to a rather unfortunate relegation of technical considerations. We often hear arguments along the lines of "Our process is CMM level X, therefore it doesn't matter what programming language we use..." We also see much "process improvement" effort focused on detection of defects (i.e. "speed up code/test/debug") rather than their prevention earlier in the life-cycle.

Some software process standards, such as DO-178B, give little or no credit for formal approaches, so projects prefer to follow the letter of the standard regardless of the utility of alternative approaches. Ironically, the UK's Def-Stan 00-55 does call for formally-based approaches, yet this seems to have made little difference.

Resistance to change
The SPARK approach implies changing many aspects of software development practice and process—design style, code review, subsequent testing and so are all modified as a result of using static verification. These changes are often perceived as a risk by project managers, who see changing nothing as less risk-prone than adopting something seen as disruptive or new. Large organizations (e.g. defence prime contractors) exhibit a near-glacial inertia that prevents change—this mindset does not prevent the purchase of additional tools as long as they don't require any true change of process or life-style; unfortunately, it is usually the process that is most in need of change.

Snake-oil, wizards, gurus...
The software development industry is rife with approaches, -isms, tools, magics, and wizards—most of which fail to deliver all that they promise. Differentiating SPARK from this crowd remains a constant battle.

Secondly, some engineers are indeed very capable at working with imperfect technologies and processes, and produce excellent results. These "gurus" become the "heroes" of a project, and management come to depend on their skills and advice for this and future efforts. SPARK undermines these witch-doctors, and so we (ironically) find that the most talented engineers in an organization often find SPARK or similar approaches to be a threat.

Procurement practice
In some industries, there seems to be very little pressure for developers to improve or change their ways. Procurers let contracts that allow for the delivery of a defective

product, which is, unsurprisingly enough, what they often get. Procurers rarely ask for any sort of meaningful warranty.

SPARK is mostly associated with highly critical safety-related systems, so we often hear the mantra "our system's not safety-critical, so we don't need SPARK", conveniently ignoring the issue of whether the system actually has to work! This is reinforced by customers' low expectations of success. Since failure is both expected and tolerated, expending extra effort in the hope of success may seem rather pointless, especially when similar attempts using the latest fashion have failed to deliver.

The "A word" and recruitment

The "A word" is, of course, "Ada" on which SPARK is based. Ada still incites a knee-jerk reaction with some potential customers. Customers shy away from the idea of having to adopt a new or different language—they perceive the cost and effort of changing, but ignore the potential pay-off. Recruitment in the industry also seems very focused on languages and tools rather than skills and domain knowledge. This is a real challenge to the Grand Challenge (!)—the world is wedded to fashionable languages, yet these very languages are incompatible with the aims of the Grand Challenge.

3.2 Lessons

Technology transfer remains difficult, but several lessons have been learnt that might be useful for the future of the Grand Challenge:

- Technical strength is required as a basis, but is not enough to get beyond the early adopters. Packaging, training, support, the "user experience" and so on are all crucial for the technology to reach a wider audience. We need to "make the maths disappear."
- Success is not the same as dominance within a market. SPARK exists as a successful product within a small niche, but can hardly be described as dominant. Should the Grand Challenge (given the time-scales available) be aiming for success within a particular niche (e.g. high reliability systems), or a wider goal of program verification becoming dominant in more general software engineering?

4 Future Work

This section offers an admittedly incomplete set of ideas for future work, based on our experience and feedback from our customers. Some of these are within reach given time and money. Others seem more challenging. In no particular order:

- Floating point proof. The system does not yet support the proof of floating point numerical algorithms, largely owing to the ambiguity in the popular IEEE specification for such things, and the lack of a notation for expressing relative error in pre- and post-conditions. We need the VCG algorithms, an "equality within relative error" operator, proof rules, and decision procedures for all of this. Recent work in abstract interpretation suggests this ought to be within reach[2].
- Make the language bigger. Some people consider SPARK to be a hopelessly small subset language for general purpose use. It is certainly a *very* small subset of Ada

(a good thing!), but there's lots of room for careful enlargement. Tasking was recently re-introduced in a form that's suitable for hard real-time systems, and a subset of generics seems within reach. Beyond that the list is endless: pointers (plus garbage collection), more OO support (particularly polymorphism), call-backs, interfaces, etc. At the far end of this spectrum, we would simply start again and design a new language from scratch or design a subset of a different suitable language.

- Distributed proof. The theorem prover remains a bottleneck in the system, but can be distributed almost arbitrarily. A truly efficient and interactive verification environment could rely on a network of many hundred CPUs working as a "proof engine."
- User interface. SPARK was originally designed as a largely "batch oriented" system. We sorely need an interactive user-interface, both for the basic static analyses and for the proof system.
- Proof management and replay. The current system is rather fragile in the face of change – a small code change can easily "break" a proof script. Automated support for impact analysis, proof management and proof re-discovery would be useful.
- Counter-example finding. Telling a user not to bother looking for a proof of a non-theorem and offering a counter-example would be a direct benefit and could usefully be applied to the small percentage of VCs that the theorem prover does not discharge. We concur the Steel's position paper on this topic[3].
- Concurrency. Support for proving properties of concurrent programs is very limited in SPARK at present.

References

1. Barnes, J.: High Integrity Software: The SPARK Approach to Safety and Security. Addison Wesley, Reading (2003)
2. Miné, A.: Relational abstract domains for the detection of floating-point run-time errors. In: Schmidt, D. (ed.) ESOP 2004. LNCS, vol. 2986, pp. 3–17. Springer, Heidelberg (2004)
3. Steel, G.: The importance of Non-theorems and Counterexamples in Program Verification. University of Edinburgh. Position paper for this workshop
4. Humphrey, W.: Winning with Software: An Executive Strategy. Addison-Wesley, Reading (2001)

The Importance of Non-theorems and Counterexamples in Program Verification

Graham Steel

School of Informatics,
University of Edinburgh,
Edinburgh, EH8 9LE, Scotland
graham.steel@ed.ac.uk
http://homepages.inf.ed.ac.uk/gsteel

Abstract. We argue that the detection and refutation of non-theorems, and the discovery of appropriate counterexamples, is of vital importance to the Grand Challenge of a Program Verifier.

1 Introduction

In this essay, we make a case for the inclusion of non-theorem (i.e. incorrect conjecture) detection and counterexample generation as a core theme in the research program of the Grand Challenge of a Program Verifier. We will argue that:

- Research in program verification technology will be hindered if counterexample generation research does not catch up and keep pace. We will give the reasons for this in §2.
- Detecting false conjectures and generating counterexamples to them is a fascinating scientific challenge in itself. We will argue this in §3.
- Deduction based approaches for verification, which offer perhaps the best chance of achieving the goals of the grand challenge, must improve in their handling of non-theorems if they are to compete with model checking approaches, which are already able to give counterexamples to false verification conditions.

Our arguments will be followed in §4 by a look at previous and current research on the topic, including our own efforts in the Mathematical Reasoning Group at the University of Edinburgh.

Since the areas of application are the same, and since the problems of program verification and counterexample generation are in a sense 'dual', it seems logical that they should be thought of as part of the same Grand Challenge. Note that we fully support the view that the final goal of the project must be a program verifier, not a system that just finds more and more bugs. However, we will argue in this paper that to achieve this goal, the dual problem of non-theorem detection and counterexample generation must be given due attention.

B. Meyer and J. Woodcock (Eds.): Verified Software, LNCS 4171, pp. 491–495, 2008.

2   The Importance of Counterexample Generation

Even the most diligent and expert programmer will very rarely write a bug-free
first version of a program. The majority of calls to a program verifier will therefore involve an incorrect program. If we want program verification tools to become
widely used, they must deal with buggy programs in a competent manner. Simply
presenting failed verification conditions or open subgoals is not sufficient, since it
leaves the user with no idea whether a bug has been found, or whether the verification system is simply unable to dispose of that particular proof obligation. What
is required is a system which can not only detect an incorrect conjecture, but also
supply a counterexample to allow the user to locate the flaw.

Non-theorem detection is also important to the internal processes of a verification tool. Automated proof attempts, particularly when induction is involved,
will frequently require the conjecturing of lemmas and generalisations. Often
these conjectures will be false, and it is vital that we detect these cases and
prune our search space appropriately.

There is a further, pragmatic argument for the inclusion of counterexample generation within the Grand Challenge. Great scientific problems, from landing a man
on the moon to producing a computer to beat a grand master at chess, have been
solved by making iterative improvements to a prototype and learning from failures. To apply this methodology to our Grand Challenge, we must encourage participation from industry, in order to ensure a supply of case study material, to get
feedback on the tools we produce, and where appropriate, to try to influence software engineering practice. For this, we need to ensure that we are able to make a
financial argument for the use of our tools even when they are at a prototype stage,
and unable to deliver a fully verified end product. Being able to detect and present
counterexamples that allow bugs to be identified is a way of ensuring some pay-
back to our industrial partners. The current industrial preference for model checking over theorem proving can partly be explained by the ability of model checkers
to present counterexample traces. Indeed, the recent interest in formal methods
shown by the world's largest software company, Microsoft, can be traced back to
the PREfix tool, presented to Microsoft by Intrinsa, a small Palo Alto start-up.
This was a Lint-like tool for spotting possible bugs in source code. Microsoft were
sufficiently impressed with the bugs detected to purchase the company, and their
formal methods research has proceeded from there. It seems clear that the way to
get our research into industrial use, and so to develop it to its full potential, is to
develop tools which detect and handle counterexamples intelligently.

3   The Challenge of Counterexample Generation

The non-theorems that arise in program verification can sometimes be easy
to find. They often occur close to the base case of a recursive data type, and
evaluating the conjecture at some small values can be sufficient to detect the
bug. However, there are a large number of cases where the counterexample is
a far more subtle object, and it is here that the scientific challenge lies. An

example of a success story in this area is the application of formal methods to discovering attacks on security protocols. Here, the attacks are counterexamples to conjectures about the security of a system. The counterexamples may be quite large, for example up to 14 messages in [19], and may require an intruder to exploit quite subtle flaws in the protocol. Further challenges remain: for example, taking into account the mathematical properties of the cryptofunctions in use.

Other problems are well outside the scope of current techniques. For example, the book 'Numerical recipes in C' contains Knuth's code for a (pseudo-)random number generator, [15, p. 283]. The code is designed to return a floating point number between 0 and 1. However, if certain very large seed values are used, the code can return a number outside of this range. With seed value 752 005 709[1], 13 out of the first 10,000 calls return a value very significantly outside the required range. The large seed value may seem ridiculous, but if you were seeding your generator on the number of seconds since 1 Jan 1970, this value would have occurred as a seed during 1993. The generation of these counterexamples remains well beyond the capabilities of current tools, and presents a substantial scientific challenge.

4   Survey of Counterexample Generation

Given how important the detection and presentation of counterexamples is to applications of formal methods, it is surprising how comparatively little attention it has received. A community of researchers interested in the subject is now beginning to emerge, with the third 'Workshop on Disproving' due to be held at IJCAR 2006[2].

Much past research has focused on fast generation of counterexamples to conjectures which are in some sense 'obviously' false. Model generators like MACE, [10], and FINDER, [18], can be used to enumerate finite domains to search for counterexamples. The Isabelle/HOL theorem prover, [12], now includes a tactic to search for small counterexamples, called quick-check, [5]. The Alloy modelling system generates counterexamples using a SAT-solver, [9]. For infinite data structures with recursive definitions, methods have been proposed by Protzen, [16], and Reif, [17]. Both can deal with small problems quite effectively, but are not suitable for large counterexamples, or for domains that cannot be easily enumerated. Model generation has also been proposed as a method for refuting non-theorems, [1,21].

Model checking can be a very effective method for finding counterexamples to false verification conditions, particularly in finite domains. As we have already remarked, the fact that model checking can produce counterexamples as well as provide guarantees is one reason for its increasing popularity in industry. Many researchers are now working on extending model checkers to non-finite domains, using 'lazy' and 'on-the-fly' techniques to construct the infinite models as they

---

[1] Knuth stated in the specification that the seed value can be any (large) number under 1 000 000 000. This is a known bug - the Numerical Recipes in C website contains a patch to fix the code.

[2] http://www.cs.chalmers.se/~ahrendt/FLoC06-ws-disproving/

are checked (e.g. [4]), with good results. Another large branch of current model checking research is in counterexample guided abstraction refinement, [6,3]. Here, the processing of counterexamples is used to guide management of the level of detail that is taken into account when attempting verification of a program, balancing tractability of the model checking problem against over-abstraction. Theorem provers can be used to check the feasibility of counterexample traces, [2]. A further current direction involves passing unproven conjectures from a theorem prover to a model checker to search for counterexamples, [14].

Our work in Edinburgh has lead to the development of the CORAL system[3], which refutes incorrect inductive conjectures using a first-order theorem prover adapted to follow the 'proof by consistency strategy' of Comon and Nieuwenhuis, [7]. Its major successes have been in the field of protocol analysis, where it has been used to discover 6 previously unknown attacks on 3 group protocols, [19,20]. The protocols are modelled inductively following Paulson, [13], and the attacks found as counterexamples to security conjectures. CORAL proved to be particularly suitable for group protocols because they can be formalised very naturally in an inductive model. This is something that rival approaches, such as model checking, struggle with. In future, we plan to experiment with CORAL in other areas of formal verification.

Many of the big problems remain unsolved. For example, how to deal adequately with arithmetic, or how to explore very large or non-trivially enumerable spaces for counterexamples. Some current directions include trying to use more information from failed proof attempts to guide the counterexample search, [8], and to suggest patches for incorrect conjectures, [11].

5   Summary

We have argued that disproof and counterexample generation are vital areas for research in the development of practical program verification systems. There remain many exciting open problems, and milestones to pass, such as the automatic generation of counterexamples for Knuth's random number bug, described above. Non-theorem detection therefore deserves to be included as a core theme in the Grand Challenge of a Program Verifier.

References

1. Ahrendt, W.: Deductive search for errors in free data type specifications using model generation. In: Voronkov, A. (ed.) CADE 2002. LNCS (LNAI), vol. 2392, Springer, Heidelberg (2002)
2. Ball, T., Cook, B., Lahiri, S., Zhang, L.: Zapato: Automatic theorem proving for predicate abstraction refinement. In: Alur, R., Peled, D.A. (eds.) CAV 2004. LNCS, vol. 3114, pp. 457–461. Springer, Heidelberg (2004)
3. Ball, T., Rajamani, S.: The SLAM toolkit. In: Berry, G., Comon, H., Finkel, A. (eds.) CAV 2001. LNCS, vol. 2102, Springer, Heidelberg (2001)

---

[3] http://homepages.inf.ed.ac.uk/gsteel/coral

4. Basin, D., Mödersheim, S., Viganò, L.: An on-the-fly model-checker for security protocol analysis. In: Proceedings of the, European Symposium on Research in Computer Security, pp. 253–270, 2003. Extended version available as Technical Report 404, ETH Zurich (2003)

5. Berghofer, S., Nipkow, T.: Random testing in Isabelle/HOL. In: 2nd International Conference on Software Engineering and Formal Methods (SEFM 2004), pp. 230–239 (2004)

6. Clarke, E., Grumberg, O., Jha, S., Lu, Y., Veith, H.: Counterexample-guided abstraction refinement for symbolic model checking. Journal of the Association for Computing Machinery 50(5), 752–794 (2003)

7. Comon, H., Nieuwenhuis, R.: Induction = I-Axiomatization + First-Order Consistency. Information and Computation 159(1-2), 151–186 (2000)

8. Dennis, L.A.: The use of proof planning critics to diagnose errors in the base cases of recursive programs. In: Basin, D., Rusinowitch, M. (eds.) IJCAR 2004. LNCS (LNAI), vol. 3097, pp. 47–58. Springer, Heidelberg (2004)

9. Jackson, D.: Alloy: a lightweight object modelling notation. ACM Transactions on Software Engineering and Methodology (TOSEM) 11(2), 256–290 (2002)

10. McCune, W.: A Davis Putnam program and its application to finite first order model search. Technical report, Argonne National Laboratory (1994)

11. Monroy, R.: Predicate synthesis for correcting faulty conjectures: The proof planning paradigm. In: Automated Software Engineering, pp. 247–269 (2003)

12. Nipkow, T., Paulson, L.C., Wenzel, M.: Isabelle/HOL. LNCS, vol. 2283. Springer, Heidelberg (2002)

13. Paulson, L.: The Inductive Approach to Verifying Cryptographic Protocols. Journal of Computer Security 6, 85–128 (1998)

14. Pike, L., Miner, P., Torres, W.: Model checking failed conjectures in theorem proving: a case study. Technical Report NASA/TM–2004–213278, NASA Langley Research Center (November 2004),
http://www.cs.indiana.edu/~lepike/pub_pages/unproven.html

15. Press, W., Teukolsky, S., Vetterling, W., Flannery, B.: Numerical Recipes in C: The Art of Scientific Computing. Cambridge University Press, Cambridge (1992)

16. Protzen, M.: Disproving conjectures. In: Kapur, D. (ed.) 11th Conference on Automated Deduction, Saratoga Springs, NY, USA, June 1992. Springer Lecture Notes in Artificial Intelligence, vol. (607), pp. 340–354. Springer, Heidelberg (1992)

17. Reif, W., Schellhorn, G., Thums, A.: Flaw detection in formal specifications. In: Goré, R.P., Leitsch, A., Nipkow, T. (eds.) IJCAR 2001. LNCS (LNAI), vol. 2083, Springer, Heidelberg (2001)

18. Slaney, J.: FINDER: Finite Domain Enumerator. In: Australian National University (1995), ftp://arp.anu.edu.au/pub/papers/slaney/finder/finder.ps.gz

19. Steel, G., Bundy, A.: Attacking group multicast key management protocols using CORAL. Electronic Notes in Theoretical Computer Science (ENTCS) 125(1), 125–144 (2004) (Also available as Informatics Research Report EDI-INF-RR-0241. Presented at the ARSPA workshop 2004)

20. Steel, G., Bundy, A., Maidl, M.: Attacking a protocol for group key agreement by refuting incorrect inductive conjectures. In: Basin, D., Rusinowitch, M. (eds.) IJCAR 2004. LNCS (LNAI), vol. 3097, pp. 137–151. Springer, Heidelberg (2004)

21. Weber, T.: Bounded model generation for Isabelle/HOL. In: Basin, D., Rusinowitch, M. (eds.) IJCAR 2004. LNCS (LNAI), vol. 3097, pp. 27–36. Springer, Heidelberg (2004)

Regression Verification - A Practical Way to Verify Programs

Ofer Strichman and Benny Godlin

Technion, Haifa, Israel
ofers@ie.technion.ac.il, bgodlin@cs.technion.ac.il

1 Introduction

When considering the program verification challenge [8] one should not forget a lesson learned in the testing community: when it comes to industrial size programs, it is not realistic to expect programmers to formally specify their program beyond simple assertions. It is well known that large parts of real code cannot be described naturally with high level invariants or temporal properties, and further that it is often the case that the process of describing what a code segment should do is as difficult and at least as complicated as the coding itself. Indeed, high-level temporal property-based testing, although by now supported by commercial tools such as TEMPORAL-ROVER[4], is in very limited use. The industry typically attempts to circumvent this problem with *Regression Testing*, which is probably the most popular testing method for general computer programs. It is based on the idea of reasoning by induction: check an initial version of the software when it is still very simple, and then check that a newer version of the software produces the same output as the earlier one, given the same inputs. If this process results with a counterexample, the user is asked to check whether it is an error or a legitimate change. In the latter case the testing database is updated with the new 'correct' output value. Regression Testing does not require a formal specification of the investigated system nor a deep understanding of the code, which makes it highly suitable for accompanying the development process, especially if it involves more than one programmer. We propose to learn from this experience and develop techniques for *Regression Verification*. The underlying proof engine is still a certifying compiler as envisioned by the grand challenge, so this proposal should be thought of as another application of this technology that makes the verification picture more complete.

While formally proving equivalence between two programs is generally undecidable, if one is willing to sacrifice completeness this becomes not only a decidable problem, but also one that can be built on top of existing tools. Without completeness, the equivalence problem can be reduced to one of proving an assertion on a merged program (see next section), for which functional verification techniques can be used. Thus, Regression verification should be thought of as an additional layer, or dimension, to be dealt with as part of the verification challenge.

B. Meyer and J. Woodcock (Eds.): Verified Software, LNCS 4171, pp. 496–501, 2008.
© IFIP International Federation for Information Processing 2008

When can Regression-verification be useful? A natural question to ask is whether proving equivalence is relevant in the context of a real software development process, as in such a process the program is expected to produce a different output after every revision. While this is in general true, consider the following scenarios, all of which are targeted by our approach:

- Checking side-effects of new code. Suppose, for example, that from version 1.0 to version 1.1 a new flag was added, that changes the result of the computation. It is desirable to prove that as long as this flag is turned off, the previous functionality is maintained. The RV tool we propose will allow the user to express a condition (the inactivation of the flag in this case) under which the two programs are expected to produce equal outputs.
- Checking performance optimizations. After adding an optimization of the code for performance purposes, it is desirable to verify that the two versions of the code still produce the same output.
- Manual *Re-factoring* (a popular set of techniques for rewriting existing code for various purposes). To quote Martin Fowler [6,5], the founder of this field, '*Refactoring is a disciplined technique for restructuring an existing body of code, altering its internal structure without changing its external behavior. Its heart is a series of small behavior preserving transformations. Each transformation (called a 'refactoring') does little, but a sequence of transformations can produce a significant restructuring. Since each refactoring is small, it's less likely to go wrong. The system is also kept fully working after each small refactoring, reducing the chances that a system can get seriously broken during the restructuring.*' Equivalence proof, before and after refactoring, seems valuable in this case.

This list demonstrates, but does not exhaust, the scenarios in which such a tool can be used.

□

At the Technion we are currently developing a method for formally verifying the equivalence of two closely related C programs, under certain restrictions inherited from the functional verification tool we use. One of the main challenges is to find ways to benefit from the similarity of the two programs, in order to scale-up the verification system beyond what is currently possible for verifying a single program. In particular, we are trying to make the complexity depend only on the *differences* between the two programs (including the propagation of these changes to other parts of the program), rather than on their original sizes. We dedicate the next section for giving a brief description of this project, after which we will summarize what we believe are the main challenges in making verification by regression widely used.

2   Proving Equivalence of Two C Programs

In the rest of this note we concentrate on C programs. Automated (incomplete) verification tools that work directly on widely used programming languages such as C were first made available only a few years ago. We are aware of three categories of such tools: 1) Predicate-abstraction-based tools such as BLAST [7], SLAM [2] and MAGIC [3], 2) Symbolic search of a bounded model of the program, as in SATURN [14] and CBMC [10], and 3) Explicit state tools such as SPIN (in combination with FEAVER [9]) and CMC [11]. Each of the tools in these three categories is a candidate for serving as an infrastructure for Regression Verification, although adapting each one of them for this task presents a research challenge by its own right.

Our prototype implementation uses CBMC as the underlying decision procedure, since it is one of the two tools (together with CMC) that supports full C and C++. In the rest of this note we exclusively focus on this category.

2.1 The CBMC Tool

CBMC [10], developed by D. Kroening, is a Bounded Model Checking tool for full ANSI-C and C++ programs. For each loop i in the given program, the user is required to specify a bound k_i on the number of iterations. This enables CBMC to symbolically characterize the full set of possible executions restricted by these bounds, with a propositional formula f. The existence of a solution to $f \wedge \neg a$, where a is a user defined assertion, implies that there is a path in the program that violates a. Otherwise, it is still possible that the given bounds are not sufficiently high. CBMC allows the user to check whether the bounds are high 'enough' by generating special *unwinding assertions* for each loop. An unwinding assertion for a loop i, given k_i, is satisfied iff the condition of this loop cannot be true after iterating k_i times. Thus, CBMC can be thought of as a complete tool as long as all the loops are terminating.

2.2 A Regression Verification Tool for C Programs

We started building a Regression Verification tool that generates a combined C program that is unrolled and checked by CBMC. Our program performs several simplifications and abstractions using Uninterpreted Functions as we explain in Section 2.3. The user is involved in two phases:

– The user needs to supply a list of pairs

$$\langle label\#1, expression\#1 \rangle, \langle label\#2, expression\#2 \rangle \ldots$$

representing his/her specification that *expression*#1 in the location specified by *label*#1 in the first program, should always be equal to *expression*#2 in location *label*#2 in the second program. In other words, the sequence of values of these two expressions in these locations should be equal regardless of the inputs. A special case of this option is specifying that the outputs of the program are equal.
– When a counterexample is found, the user needs to confirm whether it represents an error or a legitimate change resulting from further development of

the investigated program. The problem is that there can be an exponential number of examples due to a single change, so approving them one by one is not a desirable option. We plan to give the user the option of describing symbolically the allowed changes between the two programs, and also of determining dynamically the subset of outputs to concentrate on.

2.3 Optimizations with Uninterpreted Functions

Verification can be made simpler by using automated abstraction and decomposition. In the context of proving equivalence, Uninterpreted Functions has proven to be a highly effective tool (see, for example, the case of Translation Validation [13,12]).

In the following description we use unprimed and primed variables to distinguish between variables that belong to the old (unprimed) and new (primed) versions of the code. Consider, for example, a function $\text{int} f(x_1 \ldots x_n)$ that is syntactically equivalent to its counterpart $\text{int} f'(x_1' \ldots x_n')$ in the new code, and assume that they do not call other functions. We would like in this case to hide the content of f and f' while assuring that if the input to both functions is the same, then so is their output and side effects. Assume that f is reading the values of the global variables in a set G_r and writes to a set of global variables G_w (G_r and G_w are not necessarily disjoint)[1]. We observe that if f and f' are called with the same arguments, and all variables in G_r have the same values as their counterparts in G_r' when f and f' are called, then the return value of f and f' is the same, as well as the values in G_w and G_w'. Based on this observation, we represent the functions f and f' with two new variables of type int, say f_v and f_v', and add the following constraint:

$$(\bigwedge_{i=1}^{n} x_i = x_i' \wedge \forall g_r \in G_r . g_r = g_r') \rightarrow (f_v = f_v' \wedge \forall g_w \in G_w . g_w = g_w') \qquad (1)$$

This type of (conservative) abstraction can be seen as a simple extension of a method suggested by Ackermann [1], who considered the case in which there are no side effects. There are various complications when using this kind of simplification, some of which are:

- Recursive and mutually recursive functions require proofs by induction.
- A change in a function renders all its ancestors in the call-graph unsuitable for replacement with Uninterpreted Functions. We attempt to minimize this effect in two ways. First, we attempt to prove that although the two functions are syntactically different, they are still semantically the same. Second, we consider *Uninterpreted Scopes*, which are more fine-grained than Uninterpreted Functions, and hence less sensitive to the propagation of changes.

---

[1] We consider here local variables declared as `static` as a special case of global variables.

– Function arguments and global variables can be pointers, which makes Equation (1) unusable (obviously the two pointers represent different memory addresses). We are currently investigating various syntactic analysis methods in order to be able to check, at least in some cases, whether two pointers point to two isomorphic objects.

2.4 Summary

Compared with existing C verification tools, all of which are property based, Regression Verification has two things to offer. First, code that cannot be easily checked against a formal specification can still be checked throughout the development process by examining its evolving effect on the output (or, in fact, on internal variables as well, which helps pin-pointing the cause for the difference). Second, comparing two similar systems is in most cases computationally easier than property-based verification[2]. The reason for this is that there are various optimizations and decomposition opportunities that are only relevant when comparing two closely related systems. We described one such optimization based on Uninterpreted Functions in section 2.3.

3 The Road Ahead

Verification by regression poses numerous technical challenges, some of which are:

– Adapting other existing techniques for formally verifying a single program to proving equivalence, most notably predicate abstraction. Our current choice of the C language and the tool CBMC as a starting point is largely due to the maturity of the tool rather than some deep theoretical reason.
– Achieving scalability and automation beyond what is possible in functional verification. Abstracting portions of the program with uninterpreted functions, as explained above, is one possible technique that is challenging by itself in the presence of dynamic data structures, aliasing, arrays and so forth. Various Static Analysis techniques (like Pointer Analysis and Shape Analysis) seem relevant to this question.
– Identifying (either manually or automatically) what variables (outputs or others) and in which locations should be equal in order to increase the confidence in the correctness of the changes.
– Identifying the connection between functional properties and equivalence properties: assuming that a certain early version of the program satisfies some invariants or other high level property, which variables should be followed through the evolvement of the program to guarantee that this property still holds ? under which conditions this is decidable?

---

[2] The same observation is well known in the hardware domain, where equivalence checking of circuits is considered computationally easier in practice than model-checking.

– Finding the ideal gap between two versions of the same program, for making Regression Verification most effective. There is an apparent tradeoff between larger gaps, which reduce the overhead of proving equivalence, and the effectiveness of comparing the two versions of the code.

References

1. Ackermann, W.: Solvable cases of the Decision Problem. In: Studies in Logic and the Foundations of Mathematics, North-Holland, Amsterdam (1954)
2. Ball, T., Rajamani, S.: Automatically validating temporal safety properties of interfaces. In: Dwyer, M.B. (ed.) SPIN 2001. LNCS, vol. 2057, Springer, Heidelberg (2001)
3. Chaki, S., Clarke, E., Groce, A., Jha, S., Veith, H.: verification of software components in C. In: International Conference on Software Engineering (ICSE) (2003) (to appear)
4. Drusinsky, D.: The Temporal Rover and the ATG Rover. In: Havelund, K., Penix, J., Visser, W. (eds.) SPIN 2000. LNCS, vol. 1885, Springer, Heidelberg (2000)
5. Fowler, M.: http://www.refactoring.com
6. Fowler, M.: Refactoring: Improving the Design of Existing Code. Addison-Wesley, Reading (1999)
7. Henzinger, T.A., Jhala, R., Majumdar, R., Sutre, G.: Lazy abstraction. In: Symposium on Principles of Programming Languages, pp. 58–70 (2002) (BLAST)
8. Hoare, T.: The verifying compiler: A grand challenge for computing research. J. ACM 50(1), 63–69 (2003)
9. Holzmann, G., Smith, M.: An automated verification method for distributed systems software based on model extraction. IEEE Trans. on Software Engineering 28(4), 364–377 (2002)
10. Kroening, D., Clarke, E., Yorav, K.: Behavioral consistency of C and Verilog programs using bounded model checking. In: Proceedings of DAC 2003, pp. 368–371. ACM Press, New York (2003)
11. Musuvathi, M., Park, D.Y., Chou, A., Engler, D.R., Dill, D.L.: Cmc: A pragmatic approach to model checking real code. OSDI 2002 (2002)
12. Pnueli, A., Rodeh, Y., Strichman, O., Siegel, M.: The small model property: How small can it be? Information and computation 178(1), 279–293 (2002)
13. Pnueli, A., Siegel, M., Singerman, E.: Translation validation. In: Steffen, B. (ed.) ETAPS 1998 and TACAS 1998. LNCS, vol. 1384, Springer, Heidelberg (1998)
14. Xie, Y., Aiken, A.: Scalable error detection using boolean satisfability. In: POPL 2005: Proceedings of the 32nd ACM SIGPLAN-SIGACT sysposium on Principles of programming languages, ACM Press, New York (2005)

Programming with Proofs: Language-Based Approaches to Totally Correct Software

Aaron Stump

Computer Science and Engineering
Washington University in St. Louis
St. Louis, Missouri, USA

1 Introduction

Tremendous progress has been made in automated and semi-automated verification since the seminal works on program verification. Automated deductive techniques like model checking have been highly successful for many verification tasks (e.g., [17, 18, 13]). Impressive advances continue to be made in static analysis, type systems, and static bug finding (e.g., [21, 12]). These approaches aim to verify code or find bugs in existing systems as automatically as possible, with as little developer help as possible. This has been the aim of the research community for many years, possibly due in part to the bad reputation that continues to plague full program verification. Theorem proving approaches to program verification have continued to make advances, but indeed, they still are generally applied only to the most critical applications (e.g., [7, 5, 16, 11]).

Despite the continuing advances in fully automated verification, it seems unlikely that essentially automatic techniques will ever be able to scale to full program verification. Given steadily increasing societal reliance on software systems, totally correct code remains a vitally important goal. In this position paper, I advocate an approach to full program verification in which programmers write imperative programs and their computational proofs together as single artifacts (Section 3). Despite the reliance on manual creation of proofs, the approach I advocate is quite different from existing theorem-proving approaches, which I argue are unlikely ever to be feasible for mainstream use (Section 2). In Section 4, I show how the approach I advocate solves critical problems with theorem proving, and I compare the approach to other verification approaches.

2 Problems with Theorem Proving

Program verification based on theorem proving deserves its unfavorable reputation as unreasonably burdensome. Consider a typical contemporary example, the Krakatoa tool for certifying Java and JavaCard programs [8]. The approach implemented in this tool is state-of-the-art, and integrates many sophisticated ideas and tools to provide a complete solution for an important real-world verification problem. Nevertheless, despite its impressive strengths, Krakatoa demonstrates the burdensome nature of current theorem-proving approaches. Krakatoa works

B. Meyer and J. Woodcock (Eds.): Verified Software, LNCS 4171, pp. 502–509, 2008.

as follows. Verification problems consisting of Java programs annotated with JML specifications are translated into verification problems in an intermediate language called WHY. Another tool then generates verification conditions (VCs) for the WHY problem, in the language of the Coq proof assistant. Those VCs must now be proved in Coq. While Coq provides a number of powerful tactics for automated reasoning, this task is of necessity largely a manual one. The proof is conducted with respect to a model in Coq of parts of Java carried through by the WHY tool. The number of highly complex artifacts that the person doing the verification must understand here is simply too great. She must be fluent in:

- the specification language, in this case JML. JML's syntax resembles Java's, but as a logical language it nevertheless relies on mathematical, as opposed to computational, intuitions.
- the proof language, in this case the language of Coq. As a higher-order logic, this is far removed from something most developers are familiar with. Effective verification in a tool like Coq also requires knowledge of a sophisticated tactics library.
- the background theory; in this case, the partial model of Java in Coq.
- in the case of Krakatoa, the WHY intermediate language, and the encoding of Java into WHY. This must be understood since the VCs are generated via WHY. The encoding of Java into WHY is nontrivial, involving, for example, an explicit model of the heap.

It is not reasonable to require a programmer to understand all these unfamiliar artifacts to solve even basic verification problems.

3 Language-Based Verification

Program verification based on proving extracted verification conditions (I will call this "the VC approach") seems destined to remain infeasible for mainstream use. But there is another approach, known for a long time to the type theory community, which does not suffer from these difficulties. This is what Thorsten Altenkirch calls *internal verification* [2]. With internal verification, proofs are data in the programming language, just like booleans or strings. The type of a proof is the theorem it proves. Internally verified functions require, as additional input arguments, proofs of their pre-conditions. They produce, as additional outputs, proofs of their post-conditions. Proofs are connected to the non-proof parts of programs by the type checker. My group[1] has been developing two different languages based on this idea, which I will now describe. The first is nearing a certain degree of maturity, while the second is still in very early stages.

3.1 RSP1

RSP1 is a novel functional programming language that supports type-safe imperative programming with proofs [20]. It builds on ideas from Martin-Löf type

---

[1] See http://cl.cse.wustl.edu

theory, particularly as developed in the logical frameworks community, while adding imperative features. The basic idea of logical frameworks is that proof systems can be encoded as term-indexed datatypes. For example, we can declare a datatype `form` of formulas in a standard way. Then a datatype `pf` of proofs may be declared as a term-indexed datatype, where the index is a formula. If p is an encoded formula, then (`pf` p) is a type. Term constructors are then declared in such a way that mathematical proofs of formulas ϕ are in one-one correspondence with values of type (`pf phi`), where phi is the object of type `form` corresponding to ϕ. For example, we might have a constructor `ModusPonens` which takes in formulas p and q, together with objects of type (`pf` (`implies` p q)) and (`pf` p), and constructs a new term of type (`pf` q). As this example shows, the types of constructors are *dependent* in RSP; the return type of a use of `ModusPonens` depends on (i.e., mentions by name) some of its input values. The static and dynamics semantics of RSP1 have been formalized, and the language has been proved type safe. The major difference between RSP1 and Martin-Löf type theory is that the latter relies on evaluating arbitrary terms at compile-time to doing type checking. This means that imperative features cannot be added to Martin-Löf type theory in any straightforward way, and programs must all be (strongly) normalizing. RSP1 separates representation and computation in such a way that imperative features and general recursion can be handled, while retaining decidable type checking. The essential technical idea is syntactically to keep impure constructs like effectful operations out of types. To refer in a type to something like the result of a possibly non-terminating computation or a read of mutable state, one uses a *hiding let* construct to get a name for the result of the computation. This name can then be used in types. An RSP1 type checker, interpreter, and compiler to Ocaml have been implemented, in around 7000 lines of Ocaml.

We have implemented a number of nontrivial examples in RSP1. One is a proof-producing validity checker called RVC ("Rogue Validity Checker"), which is currently around 8000 lines of RSP1 (see [6] for a description of RVC in its early stages). RVC decides validity of quantifier-free formulas modulo combined background theories of linear integer arithmetic, uninterpreted functions, and arrays. Due to type safety of RSP1, any proof produced by a successful execution is guaranteed to check. Indeed, we have implemented a form of partial evaluation which can slice out proofs from RVC's code after type checking. Other examples include statically validated mesh-manipulating algorithms from Computer Graphics, where internal verification ensures that the data being manipulated always satisfy the property of being a mesh (with a particular Euler characteristic) [3].

3.2   Local Heap Invariants in RSP1

RSP1 can be used to write programs with proofs showing that local invariants of the heap are maintained. This can be done even though RSP1's type system does not allow explict mention of the results of reads and writes to mutable state in types (which serve as specifications). In RSP1, pointers can be set to point from one object to another. To express a local invariant, the programmer can require that a proof of that invariant must be given when the pointer is set. Such a proof is then available when the pointer is dereferenced. Technically, this is done by making the pointer point from the first object to a *dependent record* (as in [15]) containing the second object and the proof of the invariant.

Local heap invariants, while less expressive than global invariants involving, for example, the transitive closure operator, are still quite powerful for specifying mutable data structures. Several examples are explored in a recent paper from my group, the most complex of which is verified insertion into a binary search tree, where we statically verify the binary search tree property [20]. This is done by associating, with each node in the tree, a lower and upper bound for all the data at nodes reachable from the current node. This association is done using an indexed type: nodes have type "node l d u", where l is the lower bound, u is the upper bound, and d is the data stored at the node itself. Setting the pointer to the left subtree of a node requires a proof that the upper bound of the left subtree is less than or equal to the data stored at the current node (and similarly for the right subtree). Insertion then manipulates proofs showing that these local invariants hold. Verification using local heap invariants has also been studied recently by McPeak and Necula [10].

3.3   Reflected Evaluation Proofs

RSP1 is excellent for programming with proofs of properties of data. It can even verify certain properties of mutable data structures, despite the fact that types are forbidden to mention references. But RSP1 is not well suited to verifying total correctness of algorithms, since it provides no way to reason about executions of code. For example, it has no mechanisms to prove that code will not encounter run-time errors like arithmetic exceptions or array-bounds errors. Furthermore, specifications are implemented as datatypes, and proofs must be defined by the programmer.

A more fundamental approach to programming with proofs may possibly be realized along the following lines. First, we adopt assertions as our (computational) specifications. That is, pre- and post-conditions of functions are expressed by saying how certain pieces of code are expected to evaluate before and after the function is called. For example, consider the obvious function which merges two sorted lists to obtain a new sorted list with exactly the same elements. Part of its computational specification is that calling the check_sorted routine on each input list before the function is called should return true. This way of specifying code is likely to be very appealing to programmers, who are already used to writing assertions. But the question then arises, if we are going to program with proofs for these kinds of specifications, what are those proofs? The answer is that they are reflected versions of the evaluation proofs inductively defined by the operational semantics of the language. For each proof rule in the operational semantics of the language, there is a built-in term constructor. Reflected evaluation proofs showing that pieces of code execute in certain ways can then be built by the programmer in the programming language. The type of the proof is the evaluation statement it proves. For example, in the big-step semantics for a language with an if-then-else (ITE) construct, there is a rule that says: if the if-part of the ITE evaluates to true, and the then-part evaluates to X, then the whole ITE evaluates to X. This proof rule is reflected as a term constructor `iftrue` in the programming language. This constructor takes in two reflected proofs corresponding to the two premises of the rule, and constructs a term whose type is (`if I then T else E ==> X`).

The foundational nature of reflected evaluation proofs is appealing, but it is not clear yet how the technical development of the idea should proceed. One approach begins by defining static and dynamic semantics for such a language, and proving the usual meta-theoretic results, in particular type preservation. One technical novelty is that whenever a term is evaluated, the operational semantics states that the corresponding reflected evaluation proof is actually constructed, and placed on a stack. Subproofs are removed from this stack to construct the new proof. These proofs are then accessible to programs via an explicit reflection construct.

A second approach begins by developing a logical theory of executions of a programming language (without embedded proofs). Executions are represented by terms in some logic, most likely higher-order logic, for handling binding constructs in the programming language. Axioms are given defining a relation on executions and pairs of terms, which holds when the first term evaluates to the second according to the execution. An induction principle is formulated for executions. Properties of programs may then be proved in the external verification style using higher-order logic and the axioms about executions. To support internal verification, the programming language is then extended to allow executions as program data. The meaning of a program is partly determined by an elaboration function which maps a program (with its embedded proofs in the internal verification style) into a higher-order logic proof about the computational part of the program (i.e., without its embedded proofs). The goal is then to define a type system which is sound for successful elaboration: well-typed programs elaborate to higher-order logic proofs that are guaranteed to check. The advantage of this approach over the first one is that it naturally supports classical reasoning principles. The first approach seems most naturally to require constructive reasoning.

Whichever approach to the technical development of reflected evaluation proofs succeeds, techniques for proof irrelevance will likely be required to slice away proofs from the computational parts of programs [14].

4   Comparison to Existing Approaches

I will now argue that the two languages described in the preceding Section compare favorably with existing verification approaches, using these metrics:

Automatic: How automatic is the approach? Must the programmer write proofs, specifications, or other annotations, or can raw code be handled?

Strength: Can arbitrary properties be specified and checked of arbitrary systems, or are the specifications or systems that can be handled restricted in some way?

Mainline languages: Does the approach apply to systems developed in mainstream programming languages, or must special languages be used?

Incremental update: How much work is required to re-establish specifications after an incremental change?

Unified language: Is there a single language and single set of tools for specification, implementation, and proof?

Computational approach: Are the languages involved computational or mathematical/logical in character?

Support for imperative features: Can the approach handle imperative features? If so, how directly are they handled?

Figure 1 compares the following approaches with the languages proposed above: fully or mostly <u>automated</u> approaches like model-checking and static analysis, theorem-proving based on manually proving extracted <u>VCs</u>, program development by <u>refinement</u>, and type theoretic approaches like Martin-Löf type theory (<u>MLTT</u> in the Figure). The latter are, of course, the most closely related to <u>RSP1</u> and the reflected evaluation proofs (<u>REP</u> in the Figure). The <u>KeY</u> system supports verification of JavaCard programs using Dynamic Logic [1, 4]. Let me provide some further explanation for the entries in the Figure.

approach	auto	strong	mainline	update	unified	comp.	effects
automated	yes	no	yes	yes	partial	partial	yes
VCs	no	yes	yes	partial	no	no	yes
refinement	no	yes	yes	no	no	no	yes
MLTT	no	yes	no	yes	yes	yes	no
RSP1	no	partial	maybe	yes	yes	yes	partial
REP	no	yes	maybe	yes	yes	yes	yes(?)
KeY	partial	yes	yes	yes	good	partial	yes

Fig. 1. Comparison of verification approaches

Automated approaches cannot handle arbitrary properties of arbitrary systems. Specifications (e.g., temporal logic in model checking) are often more logical than computational. The techniques do apply to mainstream programming languages, and can handle effects. The VC approach has already been discussed. Note that while it is in principle possible to apply the VC approach to any programming language one likes, doing so for a new language typically requires a lot of modeling work in the theorem prover. Refinement requires manual application of refinement steps, which are outside the programming language. The main drawback of the approach of Martin-Löf type theory is that it cannot in any obvious way be extended to mainstream programming languages with general recursion or effects. RSP1 goes some of the way towards dealing with effects in a unified, computational way. The ideas there could probably be incorporated into a mainstream functional programming language like Ocaml. It does require manual creation of proofs, like the VC approach. I do not consider it fully strong because of its limited ability to specify properties of the heap. The reflected evaluation proofs approach has the same strengths as RSP1, with the added potential (not yet realized) to specify properties of the heap. Furthermore, reflected evaluation proofs support an even more computational approach than RSP1, since specifications are just assertions, whereas in RSP1, they are term-indexed datatypes.

The KeY system, while based on a traditional verification paradigm (namely Dynamic Logic), supports a much more viable approach to dispatching verification conditions than is typical of the VC approach. In particular, program fragments are retained in the modal operators of Dynamic Logic, and discharging verification condition requires a mix of symbolic simulation, state simplification, and logical deduction. In this respect, it resembles work on Dynamic Verification [19]. KeY also has some support for incrementally recovering parts of proofs which are still applicable when code is modified. Proofs are separate artifacts from programs, but the KeY tool is able to maintain a close connection between proofs and programs. It remains to be seen how the tightly integrated language-based approach I have advocated here compares in detail with an approach like KeY's.

5   Conclusion

I have argued that traditional approaches based on proving extracted verification conditions are unlikely ever to be widely adopted for verification, due to the heavy burdens they place on developers. I propose that instead, language-based approaches to program verification be developed, where correctness proofs are intertwined with code, in a way that gives them the appearance of being program data just like strings or booleans. Work in this direction is being pursued by my group, based on the RSP1 language, and the still developing idea of reflected evaluation proofs. The intention is that by making specificational and verificational artifacts more computational and less (in the technical sense) logical, program verification will become more usable for regular development. Other projects working toward this vision include the Epigram project and the ATS project [22, 9]. Language-based approaches are also highlighted at the FLoC 2006 workshop entitled "Programming Languages meets Program Verification" (PLPV), organized by Hongwei Xi and the author.

References

[1] Ahrendt, W., Baar, T., Beckert, B., Bubel, R., Giese, M., Hähnle, R., Menzel, W., Mostowski, W., Roth, A., Schlager, S., Schmitt, P.: The KeY tool. Software and System Modeling 4, 32–54 (2005)

[2] Altenkirch, T.: Integrated verification in Type Theory. Lecture notes for a course at ESSLLI 96, Prague (1996) (Available from the author's website)

[3] Brandt, J.: What a Mesh: Dependent Data Types for Correct Mesh Manipulation Algorithms. Master's thesis, Washington University in Saint Louis, April (2005), http://cl.cse.wustl.edu

[4] Harel, D., Kozen, D., Tiuryn, J.: Dynamic Logic. MIT Press, Cambridge (2000)

[5] Harrison, J.: Formal Verification of IA-64 Division Algorithms. In: 13th International Conference on Theorem Proving in Higher Order Logics (2000)

[6] Klapper, R., Stump, A.: Validated Proof-Producing Decision Procedures. In: Tinelli, C., Ranise, S. (eds.) 2nd International Workshop on Pragmatics of Decision Procedures in Automated Reasoning (2004)

[7] Klein, G., Nipkow, T.: Verified Bytecode Verifiers. Theoretical Computer Science 298(3), 583–626 (2003)

[8] Marché, C., Paulin-Mohring, C., Urbain, X.: The Krakatoa Tool for Certification of JAVA/JAVACARD Programs Annotated in JML. Journal of Logic and Algebraic Programming 58(1-2), 89–106 (2004)

[9] McBride, C., McKinna, J.: The View from the Left. Journal of Functional Programming 14(1) (2004)

[10] McPeak, S., Necula, G.: Data Structure Specifications via Local Equality Axioms. In: Etessami, K., Rajamani, S. (eds.) 17th International Conference on Computer-Aided Verification, pp. 476–490. Springer, Heidelberg (2005)

[11] Moore, J., Lynch, T., Kaufmann, M.: A Mechanically Checked Proof of the Correctness of the Kernel of the AMD5k86 Floating-Point Division Program. IEEE Transactions on Computers 47(9) (1998)

[12] Musuvathi, M., Park, D., Chou, A., Engler, D., Dill, D.: CMC: A Pragmatic Approach to Model Checking Real Code. In: 5th Symposium on Operating Systems Design and Implementation (December 2002)

[13] Norman, G., Shmatikov, V.: Analysis of Probabilistic Contract Signing. In: BCS-FACS Formal Aspects of Security (FASec 2002) (2002)

[14] Pfenning, F.: Intensionality, Extensionality, and Proof Irrelevance in Modal Type Theory. In: 16th IEEE Symposium on Logic in Computer Science, IEEE Computer Society Press, Los Alamitos (2001)

[15] Pollack, R.: Dependently Typed Records in Type Theory. Formal Aspects of Computing 13, 386–402 (2002)

[16] Ruess, H., Shankar, N., Srivas, M.: Modular Verification of SRT Division. Formal Methods in System Design 14(1) (1999)

[17] Shlyakhter, I., Seater, R., Jackson, D., Sridharan, M., Taghdiri, M.: Debugging Overconstrained Declarative Models Using Unsatisfiable Cores. In: 18th IEEE International Conference on Automated Software Engineering (2003) (received best paper award)

[18] Velev, M., Bryant, R.: Effective Use of Boolean Satisfiability Procedures in the Formal Verification of Superscalar and VLIW Microprocessors. Journal of Symbolic Computation 35(2), 73–106 (2003)

[19] Wang, C., Musser, D.: Dynamic Verification of C++ Generic Algorithms. IEEE Transactions on Software Engineering 23(5), 314–323 (1997)

[20] Westbrook, E., Stump, A.: A Language-based Approach to Functionally Correct Imperative Programming. In: 10th ACM SIGPLAN International Conference on Functional Programming (2005)

[21] Xie, Y., Aiken, A.: Scalable Error Detection using Boolean Satisfiability. In: Abadi, M. (ed.) Proceedings of the 32nd ACM Symposium on Principles of Programming Languages (2005)

[22] Zhu, D., Xi, H.: Safe Programming with Pointers through Stateful Views. In: Proceedings of the 7th International Symposium on Practical Aspects of Declarative Languages, pp. 83–97. Springer, Heidelberg (2005)

The Role of Model-Based Testing

Mark Utting

The University of Waikato, New Zealand
marku@cs.waikato.ac.nz

Abstract. This position paper gives an overview of model-based testing and discusses how it might fit into the proposed grand challenge for a program verifier.

1 Introduction

Model-based testing [EFW02, BBN04, LPU04, UL06] is a break-through innovation in software testing because it can completely automate the validation testing process. Model-based testing tools automatically generate test cases from a model of the software product. The generated tests are executable and include an oracle component which assigns a pass/fail verdict to each test.

Model-based testing helps to ensure a repeatable and scientific basis for product testing, gives good coverage of all the behaviors of the product and allows tests to be linked directly to requirements. Intensive research on model-based testing in the last 5-10 years has demonstrated the feasibility of this approach, shown that it can be cost-effective, and has developed a variety of test generation strategies and model coverage criteria. Some commercial tools have started to emerge, from the USA (T-Vec, Reactive Systems, I-logix), and also from Europe (Conformiq, Leirios Technologies, Telelogic), as well as a wide variety of academic and research tools [BFS05].

The discussion in this paper is limited to functional testing, rather than the more specialist areas of testing real-time software or concurrent software, because model-based testing is less mature in these areas.

The paper gives an overview of the variety of methods and practices of model-based testing, then speculates on how model-based testing might promote or complement the program verifier grand challenge.

2 Overview of Model-Based Testing

Model-based testing is the automation of black-box test design. It usually involves four stages:

1. **Building an abstract model of the system under test.** This is similar to the process of formally specifying the system, but the kind of specification/model needed for test generation may be a little different to that needed for other purposes, such as proving correctness, or clarifying requirements.

B. Meyer and J. Woodcock (Eds.): Verified Software, LNCS 4171, pp. 510–517, 2008.

2. **Validating the model (via typechecking, static analysis and animation).** This is done to increase the quality of the model, by removing some obvious errors. This validation process is usually incomplete, but this is less crucial in this context, than in the usual refinement-to-code context. With model-based testing, if some errors remain in the model, they are very likely to be detected when the generated tests are run against the system under test (see below).

3. **Generating abstract tests from the model.** This step is usually automatic, but the test engineer can control various parameters to determine which parts of the system are tested, how many tests are generated, which model coverage criteria are used etc.

4. **Refining those abstract tests into concrete executable tests.** This is a classic refinement step, which adds concrete details missing from the abstract model. It is usually performed automatically, after the test engineer specifies a refinement function from the abstract values to some concrete values, and a concrete code template for each abstract operation.

After this, the concrete tests can be executed on the system under test, in order to detect *failures* (where the outputs of the system under test are different to those predicted by the tests).

It is the independence between the test model and the implementation that is important. Experience shows that failures that occur when the tests are run are roughly equally likely to be due to errors in the model or errors in the implementation.

So the process of model-based testing provides useful feedback and error detection for the requirements and the model, as well as the system under test.

The remainder of this section gives a brief overview of the variety of model-based testing practices, under five headings.

Nature of the Model: The model used for test generation can be a functional model of just the system under test, or of the environment of the system (capturing the ways in which the system will be used), or (more usually) a model of both the system and its environment. Models of the system are useful for predicting the outputs of the system, which allows test oracles to be generated, while models of the expected environment are useful for focussing the test generation on an expected usage of the system.

Model Notation: Almost all formal specification notations can and have been used as the basis for model-based testing. Pre/post notations such as Z, B, VDM, JML and Spec# are widely used for model-based testing, but so are transition-based notations such as Statecharts and UML state machines.

Control of Test Generation: It is necessary to be able to control the generation of tests, to determine how many tests are generated and which areas or behaviours of the system they test.

One approach for controlling the generation is to specify (in addition to the model) some patterns or test specifications, and then generate only tests that satisfy these patterns or specifications.

Another approach is to specify a *model coverage criteria* which determines which tests are interesting. Most of the usual code-based coverage criteria (such as statement coverage, decision/condition coverage, MC/DC, full predicate coverage, def-use coverage) have been adapted to work as model coverage criteria.

On-line or Off-line Test Generation: On-line model-based testing generates tests from the model in parallel with executing them. This makes it easy to handle non-determinism in the system under test, since the test generator can see the outputs from the system under test (after its non-deterministic choice) and change the subsequent test generation accordingly.

On the other hand, off-line test generation generates tests independently of executing those tests. This has numerous practical advantages, such as being able to execute the generated tests repeatedly (for regression testing), in different environments etc.

Requirements Traceability: It is highly desirable for model-based testing tools to produce a requirements traceability matrix, which relates each informal requirement to the corresponding tests. This kind of traceability helps with validation of the informal requirements, and can also be used as a coverage criteria (*every requirement is tested*).

Requirements traceability can be obtained by annotating the model with requirements identifiers, then preserving those annotations throughout the test generation process, in order to produce a relation between requirements and test cases.

3   Similarities and Differences

This section discusses several similarities and several differences between using model-based testing to find errors in a program versus using a program verifier.

3.1   Similiarities

Independent Specification. To verify the behavioural correctness of a program, we must have a specification of the expected behaviour of the program. Similarly, model-based testing requires a specification (model) of the expected behaviour. In both cases, we have two descriptions of the program behaviour: one is the specification and the other is the executable code.

It is important that these two descriptions should be as independent as possible, since the goal of model-based testing, and of program verification, is to find discrepancies between the two descriptions (or prove that there are no discrepancies). That is, there must be a large degree of *independence* between the specification/model and the implementation code. For example, it is usually pointless to derive a specification from the code, then use that specification as the basis for verifying or testing the code—one would expect to find no errors, because there is no independence between the two descriptions of behaviour—they are consistent by construction. (The only reason for performing such an exercise would be to try and find errors in the testing/proof tools themselves).

This shows that both model-based testing and program verification have a common overhead of writing the specification. The requirement for independence implies that the specification and the code must both be the result of some human creativity, since if one was derived automatically from the other there would be no independence.

Abstract Specification. We have seen that model-based testing and program verification both require a specification of the expected behaviour of the system. Another similarity between the two approaches is that this specification needs to be *abstract*. That is, we want the specification to be shorter and simpler than the program itself, typically by omitting many of the details of the program. Otherwise, programmers would not be willing to write such lengthy specifications, the cost of writing them and validating them would be prohibitive, and it would be difficult to have confidence in the correctness of the specification. So abstraction is the key to developing practical specifications, and is a key goal of both model-based testing and program verification.

Reasoning Technology. The goal of most model-based testing tools is to fully automate the test generation process. This requires sophisticated reasoning about specifications and sequences of operations. The reasoning technologies that have been used in model-based testing include: model-checking, symbolic execution, constraint-based simulation, automated theorem proving, and even interactive theorem proving.

These are the same kinds of reasoning technologies that are needed and used within program verifiers. Indeed, the needs of the two approaches are almost identical. One difference is that, because model-based testing does not try to test all behaviours, it is often acceptable to restrict data types to be small and finite, to make reasoning decidable and fast. However, if the focus of a program verifier is on finding errors (like ESC/Java2 [1]), and completeness is not an essential goal, then the same technique can be used.

3.2   Differences

Colour. Model-based testing is a black-box approach, which can be applied to binary programs without source code, to embedded software, or even to hardware devices. In contrast, program verification is a white-box approach, which requires the source code of the program to be verified, and also requires a formal semantics of that source code. This means that program verification is more restricted in the kinds of systems that it can verify, than model-based testing.

Partiality. Model-based testing is quite often used to test just one aspect of a complex system. This means that the specification can specify just that aspect, rather than having to specify the complete system behaviour. For example, in a GPS navigation system for a car, we might use model-based testing to test the tracking of the vehicle's position, and ignore all route planning, route display

---

[1] See http://secure.ucd.ie/products/opensource/ESCJava2

and user interaction features. A separate model-based testing project might test the route planning algorithms, while ignoring the other features such as position tracking. Such an approach tests each aspect independently, but does not explore any interactions between the aspects (for example, between route planning and position tracking).

The ability to perform model-based testing from a partial specification means that each partial specification can be more smaller and more abstract than one comprehensive specification would be, which makes it easier to get the specification right and simplifies the test generation task. Furthermore, it seems likely that fewer specifications will be needed for model-based testing than for verification of a program, since a verifier usually requires specifications of all modules within the system, whereas model-based testing requires just a specification of the observable behaviour of the top-level system. One can argue that it is good engineering discipline to require specifications of all modules! However, the point here is simply that the *minimum level* of specification needed for model-based specification is likely to be less than that required for verification, which may help to make model-based testing less costly than verification.

A partial specification may be specifying a subsystem of the system under test, with multiple specifications specifying different subsystems, or it may be specifying a very abstract view of the behaviour, with multiple specifications specifying alternative abstractions of the same system. The former case (verifying subsystems independently) is often used for program verification too, but the latter case (verifying a system with respect to multiple specifications) seems to be rarely used for program verification and may deserve further investigation. It is related to program slicing, which has recently been suggested as an abstraction technique for model-checking programs [VTA04].

Confidence. It is common wisdom that testing can never give a 100% guarantee that a program is bug-free, whereas proof can. This is a fundamental and intrinsic difference between testing and proof.

However, to play devil's advocate, I shall misquote Dijkstra: "Program testing can be used to show the presence of bugs, but [almost] never to show their absence!" [Dij70]. I've added the 'almost' to comment that there are some circumstances, like the following, where testing can 'prove' the absence of bugs.

- Some of the algorithms for generating tests from finite state machines [LY96] can guarantee that if all tests pass, then the system under test has identical behaviour to the specification (the FSM), under the (rather strong!) assumption that the implementation has a maximum number of distinct states that is no greater than the number of states in the specification.
- HOL-Test [BW05] is an interactive model-based testing tool that generates tests from a model, but also generates 'uniformity assumptions' which formalise the assumptions being made about the cases that are not tested and their similarity to the tests. If one could prove these uniformity assumptions, then passing all the tests would imply that the implementation is a refinement of the specification.

– Some algorithms for testing concurrent processes can exhaustively test all interleavings of the processes, which can guarantee that there are no bugs due to concurrency interactions between the processes.
– Cleanroom [Mil93] uses rigorous development techniques (informal proof) to obtain high quality software, and does not use testing as a bug-detection technique. Instead, it uses testing to determine the statistical reliability of the software, by performing random testing based on a profile of the expected usage of the software. This does not guarantee that the software is bug free, but does tell us its mean time between failures.

Of course, we expect that the proposed program verifier will guarantee absolutely no bugs! Well, except for out-of-memory errors, integer overflow errors etc., which are usually considered outside the scope of verification.

The point is that formal verification is relative to a semantics of the programming language that is usually a simplification of the real semantics. Typically, we ignore some difficult issues such as resource limits. In contrast, testing is the only verification technique that executes the program in its real environment, under conditions that are as close as possible to its intended use. So, as Fig. 1 suggests, verification is good at finding *all* errors down to a certain level of abstraction (usually the simplified language semantics, but the long term goal is to push this abstraction level down as far as possible), whereas testing is good at finding *some* errors at all levels of abstraction (down to and including the hardware).

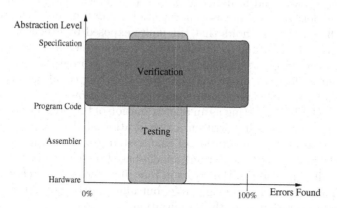

Fig. 1. Strengths of Verification and Testing

For these reasons, it is likely that testing and proof will always be somewhat complementary technologies, and the goal will be to find a suitable balance between them.

4   Relationship to the Program Verifier Grand Challenge

Once the grand challenge of a fully automatic program verifier has been achieved, one might argue that there will no longer be any need for model-based testing, or any kind of functional testing, because it will be easy and cheap to *prove* programs correct, rather than test them. And proof is obviously preferably to testing, since it gives guarantees about *all* behaviours being correct, rather than just detecting some (unknown) proportion of the obvious errors.

However, in the interim, model-based testing obviously has a role to play. Even when the grand challenge has been achieved, model-based testing may still be useful. Its roles could include:

1. Using model-based testing as an introduction to the ideas of formal models and verification. That is, model-based testing is a cost-effective approach to finding errors in non-verified programs.

   The adoption of model-based testing by industry will build experience in formal modelling skills and the use of automated testing/verification tools. These are necessary prerequisites for the use of a full program verifier. Thus, model-based testing can be viewed as an evolutionary step (the missing link!) from the status quo, towards fully automatic program verification by proof. Model-based testing changes the current software lifecycle in a small way (it introduces formal modelling, and modifies the test development processes, but leaves the rest of the lifecycle unchanged), whereas full verification seems likely to require more significant methodological changes.

2. Validating the specification notations which will be used by the program verifier. Similar notations are needed for model-based testing and for full verification. So model-based testing may be a useful way to validate the expressive power and usability of proposed specification notations.

3. Using model-based testing as a specification-validation tool. Experience with model-based testing shows that the faults exposed by executing the generated tests are often due to specification or requirements errors, rather than implementation errors [BBN04]. So if we have a program and a proposed specification for that program, model-based testing could be used to detect errors in the specification, before starting verification.

4. Using model-based testing as an approximation of the program verifier. That is, after an engineer has written a specification of the desired system, and also written an implementation of that system (or done a large refinement step towards an implementation), model-based testing could be used to automatically find some of the errors in that implementation/refinement. This is similar usage as the previous role, but aimed at finding errors in the implementation rather than the specification.
   Model-based testing may give faster and more comprehensible detection of errors than a proof approach. After all errors detected via model-based testing have been corrected, then a proof approach could be started. This is based on the oft-quoted observation that 90% of proofs fail because the conjecture that is being proved is false.

5. Using model-based testing as an alternative to full verification. If we assume that the program verifier requires a significant amount of input to achieve good results (for example, very precise specifications of the system and each module within the system), then full verification may not be cost-effective for some non-critical systems.

Model-based testing is likely to require fewer specifications than full verification (eg. only a top-level system model, rather than a model of each module within the implementation, and a partial model is often sufficient to generate useful test suites). So model-based testing may remain a cost-effective alternative to verification, for applications where we are willing to accept reduced guarantees about program correctness.

References

[BBN04]   Blackburn, M., Busser, R., Nauman, A.: Why model-based test automation is different and what you should know to get started. In: International Conference on Practical Software Quality and Testing (2004),
http://www.psqtconference.com/2004east/program.php

[BFS05]   Belinfante, A., Frantzen, L., Schallhart, C.: Tools for Test Case Generation. In: Broy, M., Jonsson, B., Katoen, J.-P., Leucker, M., Pretschner, A. (eds.) Model-Based Testing of Reactive Systems. LNCS, vol. 3472, pp. 391–438. Springer, Heidelberg (2005)

[BJK⁺05]   Broy, M., Jonsson, B., Katoen, J.-P., Leucker, M., Pretschner, A.: Model-Based Testing of Reactive Systems. LNCS, vol. 3472. Springer, Heidelberg (2005)

[BW05]   Brucker, A., Wolff, B.: Symbolic test case generation for primitive recursive functions. In: Grabowski, J., Nielsen, B. (eds.) FATES 2004. LNCS, vol. 3395, pp. 16–32. Springer, Heidelberg (2005)

[Dij70]   Dijkstra, E.W.: On the reliability of mechanisms. In: Notes On Structured Programming, EWD249 (1970),
http://www.cs.utexas.edu/users/EWD/ewd02xx/EWD249.PDF

[EFW02]   El-Far, I.K., Whittaker, J.A.: Model-based software testing. In: John, J. (ed.) Encyclopedia of Software Engineering, vol. 1, pp. 825–837. Wiley-InterScience, Chichester (2002)

[LPU04]   Legeard, B., Peureux, F., Utting, M.: Controlling Test Case Explosion in Test Generation from B Formal Models. The Journal of Software Testing, Verification and Reliability 14(2), 81–103 (2004)

[LY96]   Lee, D., Yannakakis, M.: Principles and methods of testing finite state machines — A survey. Proceedings of the IEEE 84(2), 1090–1126 (1996)

[Mil93]   Mills, H.D.: Zero defect software: Cleanroom engineering. Advances in Computers 36, 1–41 (1993)

[UL06]   Utting, M., Legeard, B.: Practical Model-Based Testing: A Tools Approach. Morgan Kauffman, San Francisco (2006)

[VTA04]   Vedula, V.M., Townsend, W.J., Abraham, J.A.: Program slicing for ATPG-based property checking. In: 17th International Conference on VLSI Design, Mumbai, India, 2004, January 5-9, 2004, pp. 591–596. IEEE Computer Society Press, Los Alamitos (2004)

Abstraction of Graph Transformation Systems by Temporal Logic and Its Verification

Mitsuharu Yamamoto[1], Yoshinori Tanabe[2,3],
Koichi Takahashi[2], and Masami Hagiya[3,4]

[1] Faculty of Science, Chiba University
[2] Research Center for Verification and Semantics,
National Institute of Advanced Industrial Science and Technology (AIST)
[3] Graduate School of Information Science and Technology, University of Tokyo
[4] NTT Communication Science Laboratories

1 Introduction

Abstract model checking has been studied as a promising technique for applying various model checking methods to infinite state systems. Graph transformation systems [11], which can model many distributed and concurrent algorithms, are examples of such infinite systems.

We have been studying abstraction of several kinds of link structures, which are instances of graph transformation systems. First, we introduced abstraction of heap structures using regular expressions mainly for verifying concurrent garbage collection algorithms [14,15]. In this setting, each cell has a color and a link to another cell. Since cells can be allocated dynamically during execution, it is impossible to enumerate all the execution states of the heap. Thus we need to use abstraction for applying finite verification methods.

The basic strategy is to abstract each cell in a heap structure in terms of regular expressions taken from a fixed finite set. Each regular expression represents a property of a cell concerning its connectivity with other cells. For example, the regular expression w^*g holds at a cell that can reach a gray cell via white cells, where w is the label of a white cell and g is that of a gray cell.

Similarly, one can use branching-time temporal logic formulas in place of regular expressions [16], where temporal operators are used for describing spatial relationship. For example, the temporal formula $E(w \text{ until } g)$ in CTL (computation tree logic) also represents a cell that can reach a gray cell via white cells. In [16], we defined abstraction of elementary graph transformation rules.

Some applications require to mention the inverse direction of links as well as the forward direction. Such situations can be naturally expressed by using inverse modalities in temporal logics. So we proposed the use of two-way CTL (2CTL) for abstraction and applied it to analysis of synchronous and asynchronous cellular automata [8]. In contrast to general graph transformation system, they do not allow to change the connectivity of cells, but the label associated to each cell can be changed according to a given rewrite rules. Representation of a rewrite rule also refers to 2CTL formulas.

B. Meyer and J. Woodcock (Eds.): Verified Software, LNCS 4171, pp. 518–527, 2008.
© IFIP International Federation for Information Processing 2008

To enable analysis be done fully automatically, satisfiability checking of 2CTL formulas plays a central role. For example, adjacency of abstract cells can be derived by checking satisfiability of a 2CTL formula, and if it is shown that they cannot be adjacent, the abstract link between them is deleted.

Another kind of well-known infinite system is that of timed or hybrid systems, whose state contains dense time values. Abstraction methods using a finite set of partitions of time values called regions or zones, are widely known. We proposed timed multiset rewriting systems as a framework that subsumes both timed automata [1] and timed Petri nets [4]. Multiset rewriting can be naturally extended to graph transformation by introducing links between elements of a multiset.

Our current challenge is to extend the abstraction method using temporal logic so that we can provide a uniform framework that works on more general graph transformation systems. We are also planning its timed extension by attaching clock values to each node of a graph.

The rest of the paper is organized as follows. Section 2 compares our framework with related work. Section 3 describes why we use temporal logic for abstraction of graph transformation systems. Section 4 shows possible case studies that we are planning. Implementation status of related tools are described in Sect. 5. Section 6 mentions some aspects of formal verification of the algorithms used in the framework, and Sect. 7 summarizes the paper.

2   Related Work

Separation logic [10] is an extension of Hoare logic, and deals with spatial properties of shared mutable data structures using assertions about disjoint parts of the heap. Though it can reason about data structures that have particular shapes such as lists, basic properties of these structures have to be prepared.

"Shape analysis" methods [5,12] in abstract interpretation also concern representation of spatial properties of pointer structures. Among them, Sagiv et al.'s work [12] on the TVLA system (Three-Valued-Logic Analyzer) is closely related to ours. One of the differences is that they use logical structures for 2-valued first-order logic for representing the concrete space, whereas ours use Kripke structures. What is more crucial is that ours uses decidable temporal logic. Thus we can use satisfiability checking as a tool to promote automation in analysis. We also make some extensions to temporal logic so that it can suit abstraction of graph transformation systems, as detailed in the next section.

3   Why Temporal Logic?

The use of temporal logic for abstraction is the most important feature of our framework. In this section, we explain why we use temporal logic, and what kinds of extensions to temporal logic we have made or we are going to make in order to apply it to abstraction of graph transformation systems.

A concrete graph can be regarded as a Kripke structure $\mathcal{M} = (M, \{R_a\}, \lambda)$ where M is a set of concrete nodes, $\{R_a\}$ is a collection of labeled relations on

M such that $sR_a t$ if and only if there is a link labeled a from s to t, and λ is a function that maps a label to the set of the associated nodes. As already mentioned, the key idea is to use temporal modalities for the purpose of describing spatial properties of nodes. For example, if a node s points to another node t by a link labeled a and property p holds at the node t (i.e., $sR_a t$ and $t \in \lambda(p)$), then $\mathsf{EX}_a p$ holds at the node s (i.e., $\mathcal{M}, s \models \mathsf{EX}_a p$).

An *abstracted node* is characterized by truth values of some temporal formulas. It represents possibly multiple concrete nodes where each formula has the corresponding truth value. In order for abstract nodes to have only a finite number of variations, we first fix a finite set F of temporal formulas in advance. Then each abstract node is determined by $C \subseteq F$ so that $\bigwedge \{\phi \mid \phi \in C\} \wedge \bigwedge \{\neg\phi \mid \phi \in F \setminus C\}$ (denoted by ϕ_C) is satisfied in the corresponding concrete nodes. That is, a concrete node s in a concrete graph $\mathcal{M}$ is represented by an abstract node $C \subseteq F$ if and only if $\mathcal{M}, s \models \phi_C$ holds. Since F is a finite set, the number of abstract nodes is bounded by $2^{|F|}$.

The use of decidable temporal logic enables us to use satisfiability checking as a tool for automated analysis. In general more expressive logics require higher computational complexity. So we may use a subclass of decidable temporal logic such that its satisfiability checking is feasible, or we may do approximate checking that does not violate conservativeness of abstraction.

CTL is a kind of branching-time temporal logic that has been well studied and widely used especially for model checking. However, in order to use it for analysis using abstraction, we sometimes need more expressibility than that of the bare CTL. In the rest of this section, we describe what kinds of extensions we have made as well as our plan of future extensions.

Two-Way Modality and Satisfiability. When we describe spatial properties, we often need to mention not only the modality of the forward direction but also that of the inverse direction. In the example of 1-dimensional cellular automata [8], an abstract cell has to have information on the colors of its left and right neighbors. In that case, it is natural to use inverse modality as well as forward one.

For modality a, the inverse modality of a is denoted as $\bar{a}$ and thus $\bar{\bar{a}} = a$. In this two-way setting, we define *abstract links* between abstract nodes as follows: for abstract nodes C, D and modality a, there is an abstract link labeled a from C to D if and only if both $\phi_C \wedge \mathsf{EX}_a \phi_D$ and $\phi_D \wedge \mathsf{EX}_{\bar{a}} \phi_C$ are satisfiable.

Abstraction of the concrete graph structure is represented as an *abstract graph*, which consists of abstract nodes and abstract links between them. In this paper, to simplify the explanation, we focus on the framework in which an abstract graph is fully induced from a set of abstract nodes, so we denote such a graph by the corresponding set $\mathcal{G} \subseteq 2^F$ of abstract nodes. Satisfiability checking plays a central role in automated generation of the abstract graph as above.

An abstract graph $\mathcal{G}$ is said to be *sound* with respect to a concrete graph $\mathcal{M} = (M, \{R_a\}, \lambda)$ if $\forall s \in M. \exists C \in \mathcal{G}. \mathcal{M}, s \models \phi_C$ holds. Because $C \subseteq F$ satisfying this condition is uniquely determined from s if it exists, we may write such C as $\alpha(s)$ for $s \in M$. If $\mathcal{G}$ is sound with respect to $\mathcal{M}$, then there is an abstract link labeled a from $\alpha(s)$ to $\alpha(t)$ whenever sR_at holds.

As we mentioned, an abstract node is determined by truth values of user-selected two-way temporal formulas that represent characteristic properties of concrete nodes. This method can be regarded as predicate abstraction by two-way temporal formulas. Sagiv et al. [12] proposed parametric framework for shape analysis using predicate abstraction by user-defined predicates on 3-valued logic. Such predicates include not only "pointed to by the variable x" but also "reachable from the variable x". The latter type of predicate is called an "instrumentation predicate", which does not directly appear in the target program but plays an important role in static analysis. How these predicates change according to a program execution step is specified by "predicate update formulas", and automatic generation of those for instrumentation predicates is a difficult problem especially when transitive closure of a predicate is included [9]. Our approach is to use temporal formulas for representing such instrumentation predicates, and to calculate of the weakest precondition of a program execution step. The details are described in Section 5.

Nominal. We also use hybrid temporal logic, which differs from the ordinary temporal logic in that it has two kinds of atomic formulas. One is that of ordinary propositional constants, and atomic formulas of the other kind are called nominals. A nominal has the same role as a propositional constant syntactically, but they are different semantically: in a Kripke structure $\mathcal{M} = (M, R, \lambda)$ for hybrid temporal logic, the domain of λ is the union of the set of propositional constants and the set of nominals, and $\lambda(x)$ is required to be a singleton for a nominal x. That is, a nominal x specifies a unique node in a Kripke structure.

Introduction of nominals increases the power of describing properties of a graph. For example consider the property "node n is in a loop". It can be paraphrased as "n is reachable from n by following the arrows (more than once)," and is therefore expressible as "$x \to \mathsf{EXEF}x$" if x is a nominal that specifies n. If x were just a propositional constant, the formula would not express the property.

In [12], abstract heap structures contain two kinds of nodes: summary nodes and non-summary nodes. A summary node represents "more than one concrete node", and a non-summary one represents "exactly one concrete node." The distinction of these kinds of abstract nodes plays an important role in expressivity and accuracy of abstraction. In our framework, the former kind of abstract node corresponds to a set of usual formulas, while the latter kind corresponds to a set of formulas containing a nominal. Since we cannot express the latter kind of abstract node without nominals, they are essential for doing analysis as in [12].

Shape Analysis is Tableau. We use a tableau method for checking satisfiability of a given two-way temporal formula. We construct a tableau by repeatedly removing inconsistent tableau nodes starting from all of the possible ones. The tableau constructed in this way effectively encodes all models that make the given formula satisfiable.

Tableau construction and shape analysis using abstract graphs are closely related as follows. For an abstract graph $\mathcal{G}$, consider a formula $\psi_{\mathcal{G}} = \mathsf{A} \bigvee \{\phi_C \mid C \in \mathcal{G}\}$, where A denotes a global modality [2] and $\mathsf{A}\phi$ means that ϕ is true at all points in a model. Then a Kripke structure $\mathcal{M} = (M, \{R_a\}, \lambda)$ is a model of $\psi_{\mathcal{G}}$ if and only if $\forall s \in M.\ \mathcal{M}, s \models \bigvee \{\phi_C \mid C \in \mathcal{G}\}$. Suppose that $\mathcal{M}$ is a model. Since $\forall s \in M.\ \exists C \subseteq F.\ \mathcal{M}, s \models \phi_C$ always holds, we have $\forall s \in M.\ \exists C \in \mathcal{G}.\ \mathcal{M}, s \models \phi_C$. This means $\mathcal{G}$ is sound with respect to $\mathcal{M}$.

Therefore, all the concrete graphs for an abstract graph used in the shape analysis is covered by the tableau corresponding to a particular formula constructed by the abstract graph. The use of decidable temporal logic and its satisfiability checking tightly connects tableau method with shape analysis in this sense.

Spatio-Temporal Logic. Although we have used modalities in temporal logic for the purpose of describing spatial properties, they are originally introduced for describing temporal properties, of course. In the example of cellular automata, connectivity of cells are not changed through temporal evolution of cells, because a cell is not generated or destroyed. Therefore one can think of temporal change of spatial properties of a cell such as "for a cell satisfying S, T holds until U via temporal evolution," where S, T, and U are spatial properties.

In general, properties of graphs to be verified involve not only spatial relations but also temporal ones as above. So we are now trying to establish such "spatio-temporal" logic that can describe interaction of both kinds of modalities.

In our software model checking tool TLAT described in Sect. 5, we are trying to grasp both spatial and temporal properties of a cell in the heap. Refer to Section 5 for the detail.

4   Case Studies

In this section, we give some case studies we are planning with our framework.

Asynchronous transformation of link structures such as that in a concurrent garbage collection algorithm is a typical example of graph transformation. In the concurrent GC environment, there are two kinds of processes, a mutator and a collector, running concurrently. The mutator process accesses the heap to change the link structure according to the given program. The collector process also accesses the heap to collect unused cells without stopping the mutator process.

The key features in our framework are characterization of heap properties using temporal logic formulas and the use of their satisfiability checking for automation. We are planning to apply them to the shape analysis through predicate abstraction and model checking [5]. It enables us to do shape analysis on heaps by a generic abstraction algorithm using the calculation of the weakest preconditions instead of specialized abstract interpretation algorithms. We also mention the current status along this direction in Section 5.

Distributed algorithms over networks can also be regarded as graph transformation systems. Examples include mutual exclusion, routing protocols, propagation of DNS information, and leader election algorithms on mobile ad hoc network. Timed extension is crucial for analyzing network protocols that have the notion of timeouts.

Cellular automata are also special cases of graph transformation. The shape of the graph does not change, but the label associated each node (cell) does. Transition on cellular automata can be synchronous and asynchronous. The synchronous transition changes the labels of all the nodes simultaneously. The asynchronous one changes the label of one node at a time. The dining philosopher problem taken in [8] is an example of asynchronous cellular automata. How abstraction by temporal logic can be used in the deadlock analysis of this problem is shown.

5   Tools

Some tools related to our framework have been implemented or under construction.

Satisfiability Checker. As we mentioned, satisfiability checking plays an important role in abstraction under our framework. Although a decidable algorithm is already proposed for two-way modal μ-calculus [20], and for hybrid two-way modal μ-calculus [13], their straightforward implementations cost high computational complexity because of the emptiness problem on infinite tree automata. Moreover, the actual implementation is not reported to the best of our knowledge.

We showed that satisfiability of some subclasses of two-way modal μ-calculus can be effectively checked using a tableau method that is implemented by iterative computation over BDDs [3]. We first implemented a satisfiability checker for two-way CTL [17] with this method. Then it is also applied to alternation-free two-way modal μ-calculus [19] by adding some extra information to the tableau. Overview of this method is explained below.

A simple decision procedure for satisfiability checking in (one-way) CTL, which is a subsystem of the two-way modal μ-calculus, is well-known [6]. By expanding modal formulas (for example, formula $\mathsf{EF}\varphi$ is expanded to $\varphi \vee \mathsf{EXEF}\varphi$), any formula can be regarded as a boolean combination of propositional constants and formulas in the form of $\mathsf{EX}\varphi$ or $\mathsf{AX}\varphi$. We consider a tableau consisting of nodes each of which is a subset of the set of propositional constants and formulas in the form of $\mathsf{EX}\varphi$ and $\mathsf{AX}\varphi$. We regard each formula that belongs to a node is "true" at the node. Starting with the full tableau consisting of all nodes, we repeatedly dispose of "inconsistent" nodes. Among the types of inconsistency, the most important one is the type concerning "eventuality." An example situation is that the formula $\mathsf{EF}\varphi$ is "true" at a node but no node where φ is "true" can be reached from there. In the case of (one-way) CTL, this type of inconsistency can be judged relatively easily. However, in the case of two-way logic, the situation is not so simple because of additional inconsistency induced by the inverse modality. As for two-way CTL, an additional check between adjacent tableau nodes suffices. As for alternation-free two-way μ-calculus, we introduced some relation between formulas in tableau nodes. The details are in [19].

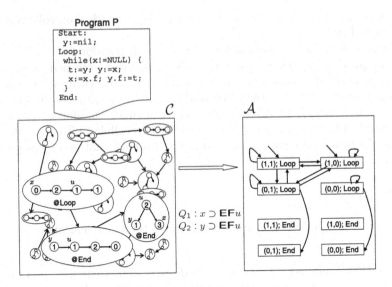

Fig. 1. Abstraction in TLAT

We are also developing a hybrid version (i.e., with nominals mentioned in Sect. 3) of a satisfiability checker using the same method.

TLAT. We are developing a tool that enables software model checking based on the abstraction method described in the paper, which we call Temporal Logic Abstraction Tool (TLAT). TLAT handles heap structures, called pointer structures, consisting of a finite set of nodes and a finite set of variables. A node stores a value (an element of some fixed finite set) and has pointers with names where each pointer points to a node. A variable also points to a node. And we have introduced a small language called PML (Pointer Manipulation Language), which has a minimum set of assignment statements and control statements to describe operations on pointer structures. Figure 1 shows an example of a program P in PML, which reverses a given "list" headed by a node pointed to by variable x at label Start and the resulting list is headed by a node pointed to by variable y at label End. A PML program such as P induces a transition system $\mathcal{C} = (C, \rightarrow)$, where an element of C is a pair of a pointer structure and a value of the program counter.

We consider hybrid two-way CTL with values (stored in nodes) as propositional constants and variables as nominals. We also consider a pair (v, φ) of a program variable and a formula of the hybrid two-way CTL and call it a *p-formula*. A p-formula (v, φ) is also denoted by $v \supset \varphi$, and can be considered as a predicate on pointer structures: it holds on pointer structure S if the node pointed to by v in S satisfies φ. For example, p-formula $x \supset EF_f u$ expresses that the node pointed to by variable x reaches the node pointed to by u by following pointers labeled f. We also introduce notation "@l" meaning that the current execution point is at label l. In TLAT a specification of a program is expressed by an LTL formula with p-formulas and "@l" notations as atomic formulas. For example the specification "Any node in the list headed by the node pointed to by variable x at label Start is contained in the list headed by the node pointed to by variable y at label End" can be expressed by the LTL formula $\Box(\texttt{@Start} \wedge x \supset \mathsf{EF}u \rightarrow \Box(\texttt{@End} \rightarrow y \supset \mathsf{EF}u))$.

It is not possible to verify such a specification by model-checking the transition system $\mathcal{C}$ since it is obviously infinite. TLAT constructs a finite transition system $\mathcal{A} = (A, \rightarrow)$ which is a sound abstraction with respect to LTL formulas in the sense that if an LTL formula holds in $\mathcal{A}$ it is guaranteed that it also holds in $\mathcal{C}$. Let $Q_1, \ldots, Q_n$ be p-formulas appearing in the specification plus p-formulas given by the user as hints for abstraction. An element of A is a pair of a sequence of 0 and 1 of length n and a value pc of the program counter. For $a = (a_1, \ldots, a_n)$ where $(a, pc) \in A$, we denote by $Q(a)$ the conjunction of Q_j (if $a_j = 1$) or $\neg Q_j$ (if $a_j = 0$). Following the spirit of "shape analysis is tableau" in Sect. 3, a heap structure at the program counter pc is abstracted to $(a, pc) \in A$ if and only if it is encoded in the tableau for the formula $\bigwedge\{AQ_i \mid a_i = 1\} \wedge \bigwedge\{A\neg Q_i \mid a_i = 0\}$.

If an assignment statement s is in the location of pc, whether $(a, pc) \rightarrow (a', pc + 1)$ holds or not can be decided by judging whether $Q(a) \wedge \mathrm{wp}(s, Q(a'))$ is satisfiable or not, where $\mathrm{wp}(s, T)$ is the weakest precondition of T with respect to s and can be calculated as in [18]. TLAT performs model checking with the specification against $\mathcal{A}$. If the result is positive, the verification succeeds. Otherwise the user investigates if the counterexample obtained as the result of the model-check corresponds to a real counterexample in $\mathcal{C}$. If not, a new set of p-formulas is to be added to $Q_1, \ldots, Q_n$ to get a more precise abstract system.

Region Analysis Tool. As we already mentioned, we are planning to add clock values to nodes. Traditionally, abstraction of clock values is done by dividing the infinite value space into finite partitions. Because our framework abstracts several concrete nodes into an abstract node, we need to consider an *abstract clock* that represents several concrete clocks whose values are in a certain interval.

We are also planning to develop a checker that does region analysis on abstract clocks. A rough algorithm has been made and we are now trying to implement and evaluate the checker.

6 Formal Verification

Verification algorithms themselves can also be a target of verification. It increases the reliability and confidence of their implementation. In particular, graph algorithms are extensively used in verification, and actually both the satisfiability checking algorithm for two-way temporal logics and the abstract model checking of graph transformation systems are instances of graph algorithms. Our group has some experiences of formal verification on graphs [21,22] using a theorem proving environment, so we are also planning formal verification of graph algorithms used in our framework. In particular, the tableau method used in the satisfiability checker is already fairly complicated and it deserves formal verification.

Besides ensuring correctness, a merit of formal verification is that it leads to better understanding of the target algorithm. Thus we expect that we can grasp the essence of the algorithm and understand both the possibility of extension and its limitation.

7 Summary and Conclusion

We described some results and ongoing projects on abstraction and verification of graph transformation systems by temporal logic. Crucial aspects in the use of temporal logic are decidability, automation by satisfiability checkers, and several kinds of extensions. A brief sketch of the framework, possible case studies, related tools, and some aspects of formal verification are presented. We are now experimenting the effectiveness of the framework through concrete applications.

Acknowledgments. The authors are grateful to anonymous reviewers for their constructive comments.

This research was supported by Core Research for Evolutional Science and Technology (CREST) Program "New High-performance Information Processing Technology Supporting Information-oriented Society" of Japan Science and Technology Agency (JST). This research was also partially supported by the Ministry of Education, Science, Sports and Culture, Grant-in-Aid for Scientific Research on Priority Areas, 16016211, 2004.

References

1. Alur, R., Dill, D.L.: A Theory of Timed Automata. Theoretical Computer Science 126, 183–236 (1994)
2. Blackburn, P., de Rijke, M., Venema, Y.: Modal Logic. Cambridge University Press, Cambridge (2001)
3. Bryant, R.E.: Symbolic Boolean Manipulation with Ordered Binary-Decision Diagrams. ACM Computing Surveys 24(3), 293–318 (1992)
4. Cerone, A., Maggiolo-Schettini, A.: Time-Based Expressivity of Time Petri Nets for System Specification. Theoretical Computer Science 216, 1–53 (1999)
5. Dams, D., Namjoshi, K.S.: Shape analysis through predicate abstraction and model checking. In: Zuck, L.D., Attie, P.C., Cortesi, A., Mukhopadhyay, S. (eds.) VMCAI 2003. LNCS, vol. 2575, pp. 310–323. Springer, Heidelberg (2002)
6. Emerson, E.A.: Temporal and Modal Logic. In: Handbook of Theoretical Computer Science. Formal Models and Semantics, vol. B, pp. 995–1072. Elsevier, Amsterdam (1990)
7. Grädel, E., Thomas, W., Wilke, T. (eds.): Automata, Logics, and Infinite Games. LNCS, vol. 2500. Springer, Heidelberg (2002)
8. Hagiya, M., Takahashi, K., Yamamoto, M., Sato, T.: Analysis of Synchronous and Asynchronous Cellular Automata using Abstraction by Temporal Logic. In: Kameyama, Y., Stuckey, P.J. (eds.) FLOPS 2004. LNCS, vol. 2998, pp. 7–21. Springer, Heidelberg (2004)
9. Reps, T., Sagiv, M., Loginov, A.: Finite Differencing of Logical Formulas for Static Analysis. In: European Symposium on Programming, pp. 380–398 (2003)

10. Reynolds, J.C.: Separation Logic: A Logic for Shared Mutable Data Structures. In: Proceedings of the Seventeenth Annual IEEE Symposium on Logic in Computer Science, pp. 55–74 (2002)
11. Rozenberg, G. (ed.): Handbook of Graph Grammars and Computing by Graph Transformation. Foundations, vol. 1. World Scientific, Singapore (1997)
12. Sagiv, M., Reps, T., Wilhelm, R.: Parametric shape analysis via 3-valued logic. ACM Transactions on Programming Languages and Systems 24(3), 217–298 (2002)
13. Sattler, U., Vardi, M.Y.: The Hybrid μ-Calculus. In: Goré, R.P., Leitsch, A., Nipkow, T. (eds.) IJCAR 2001. LNCS (LNAI), vol. 2083, pp. 76–91. Springer, Heidelberg (2001)
14. Takahashi, K., Hagiya, M.: Abstraction of Link Structures by Regular Expressions and Abstract Model Checking of Concurrent Garbage Collection. In: First Asian Workshop on Programming Languages and Systems, pp. 1–8 (2000)
15. Takahashi, K., Hagiya, M.: Formal Proof of Abstract Model Checking of Concurrent Garbage Collection. In: Workshop on Thirty Five years of Automath, Informal Proceedings, Heriot-Watt University, Edinburgh, April, 2002, pp. 115–126 (2002)
16. Takahashi, K., Hagiya, M.: Abstraction of Graph Transformation using Temporal Formulas. In: Supplemental Volume of the 2003 International Conference on Dependable Systems and Networks (DSN-2003), pp. W-65 – W-66 (2003)
17. Tanabe, Y., Takahashi, K., Yamamoto, M., Sato, T., Hagiya, M.: An Implementation of a Decision Procedure for Satisfiability of Two-Way CTL Formulas Using BDD (in Japanese). Computer Software, Japan Society for Software Science and Technology 22(3), 154–166 (2005)
18. Tanabe, Y., Takai, T., Sekizawa, T., Takahashi, K.: Preconditions of Properties Described in CTL for Statements Manipulating Pointers. In: Supplemental Volume of the 2005 International Conference on Dependable Systems and Networks, June 28 – July 1, 2005, pp. 228–234 (2005)
19. Tanabe, Y., Takahashi, K., Yamamoto, M., Tozawa, A., Hagiya, M.: A Decision Procedure for the Alternation-Free Two-Way Modal μ-Calculus. In: Beckert, B. (ed.) TABLEAUX 2005. LNCS (LNAI), vol. 3702, pp. 277–291. Springer, Heidelberg (2005)
20. Vardi, M.Y.: Reasoning about the Past with Two-Way Automata. In: Larsen, K.G., Skyum, S., Winskel, G. (eds.) ICALP 1998. LNCS, vol. 1443, pp. 628–641. Springer, Heidelberg (1998)
21. Yamamoto, M., Nishizaki, S., Hagiya, M., Toda, Y.: Formalization of Planar Graphs. In: Schubert, E.T., Alves-Foss, J., Windley, P. (eds.) HUG 1995. LNCS, vol. 971, pp. 369–384. Springer, Heidelberg (1995)
22. Yamamoto, M., Takahashi, K., Hagiya, M., Nishizaki, S., Tamai, T.: Formalization of Graph Search Algorithms and Its Applications. In: Grundy, J., Newey, M. (eds.) TPHOLs 1998. LNCS, vol. 1479, pp. 479–496. Springer, Heidelberg (1998)
23. Yamamoto, M., Cottin, J.-M., Hagiya, M.: Decidability of Safety Properties of Timed Multiset Rewriting. In: Damm, W., Olderog, E.-R. (eds.) FTRTFT 2002. LNCS, vol. 2469, pp. 165–183. Springer, Heidelberg (2002)

Program Verification by Using DISCOVERER*

Lu Yang[1], Naijun Zhan[2], Bican Xia[3], and Chaochen Zhou[2]

[1] Software Engineering Institute, East China Normal University
[2] Laboratory of Computer Science, Institute of Software, Academia Sinica
[3] LMAM & School of Mathematical Sciences, Peking University

Abstract. Recent advances in program verification indicate that various verification problems can be reduced to semi-algebraic system (SAS for short) solving. An SAS consists of polynomial equations and polynomial inequalities. Algorithms for quantifier elimination of real closed fields are the general method for those problems. But the general method usually has low efficiency for specific problems. To overcome the bottleneck of program verification with a symbolic approach, one has to combine special techniques with the general method. Based on the work of complete discrimination systems of polynomials [33,31], we invented new theories and algorithms [32,30,35] for SAS solving and partly implemented them as a real symbolic computation tool in Maple named DISCOVERER. In this paper, we first summarize the results that we have done so far both on SAS-solving and program verification with DISCOVERER, and then discuss the future work in this direction, including SAS-solving itself, termination analysis and invariant generation of programs, and reachability computation of hybrid systems etc.

Keywords: semi-algebraic systems, DISCOVERER, program verification, termination, invariant generation, reachability computation.

1 Introduction

In the last decades, since the first modern computer was invented, the performances of computer hardware have been multiplied by 10^{13} or even more. This is a technical revolution. The immediate consequence is that the size of programs executed on these computers has grown in similar proportions. On the other hand, neither the intellectual capacities of programmers nor the sizes of design and maintenance teams can grow in similar proportions. This results in most software products containing many bugs. For example, we are often told that Microsoft Company releases bug repairing programs for its merchandized products on the website of the company. Some of these errors may cause catastrophic consequences which are very costly and sometimes inadmissible (e.g., nuclear control systems). The difficulty to prevent and find errors grows faster than the

* This work is supported in part by NKBRPC-2002cb312200, NKBRPC-2004CB318003, NSFC-60273022, NSFC-60493200, NSFC-60421001, NSFC-60573007, and NKBRPC-2005CB321902.

B. Meyer and J. Woodcock (Eds.): Verified Software, LNCS 4171, pp. 528–538, 2008.
© IFIP International Federation for Information Processing 2008

size of programs which can now be really huge. Classical software verification methods like code reviews, simulations, tests and so on do not scale up. The production of reliable software, their maintenance and their evolution over long periods of time has become a fundamental concern to computer scientists.

Exploiting mathematical methods to strictly prove that a computer program does exactly what is stated in the program specification has been recognized as an effective and efficient approach to produce reliable softwares and in fact has been made lots of achievements, for example applying model-checking techniques [4,5,6,24] to the design of hardware. Since the total program verification problem is undecidable, it is doomed to be impossible to find an universal approach to mechanically verify the correctness of programs without any simplification or restriction. This implies that the possible solution to program verification problem is either by abstract interpretation to simplify the given proof obligation, or by interactive manner to acquire some oracles during verification, or by developing specific methods for specific verification problems which are decidable. Following the above three lines, there are various techniques to program verification that have been well established so far, e.g., the abstraction-based techniques [11] such as static program analysis [12,16] and program typing [13,19], theorem-proving based deductive methods [20,21], model-checking [4,5,6,24], etc. The main disadvantage of the abstraction-based techniques is that complicated properties cannot be dealt with well because complicated properties closely interwind with the actual executions of a program, but normally in abstract executions of the program lots of useful information will be lost. The shortcomings of theorem-proving based deductive methods lie in the following three aspects. First, it is semi-automatic and we cannot get anything if theorem provers fail for the given problem. Second, it is not easy to master theorem provers because they are driven by unformalized heuristics, and these heuristics and their interaction are changed often for improving proof strategies. Third, compatibility with other formal methods is somewhat difficult. By contrast, designing a specific full automatic computer-aided method for some specific problems will be more effective and efficient.

Recent advances in program verification indicate that various verification problems of programs, for instance, termination analysis of programs [28,3], reachability computation of linear hybrid systems [18], and invariant generation [9,25,26], can be reduced to SAS solving. Lots of well-known real symbolic computation tools such as REDLOG [15] and QEPCAD [8] have therefore been applied to program verification [18,9].

Most of the well-known real symbolic computation tools for solving SASs are fundamentally based on the techniques concerning quantifier elimination of real closed fields using the cylindrical algebraic decomposition (CAD) method due to Collins [7], and thus the complexity of the algorithms adopted in these tools is at least double exponential in the number of variables [14]. In order to improve the efficiency of such tools, special methods may be combined with the CAD for specific targets.

Based on the work in [36,33,31], two kinds of specific problems of SASs are studied in [32,30,35]. Reference [30] presented an algorithm to isolate the real solutions of constant SASs, while references [32,35] proposed practical algorithms for real solution classification of parametric SASs. We have partly implemented the theory and algorithms as a Maple package named DISCOVERER which has been successfully used to address many problems studied by other researchers [32,30,35,29]. Specifically, when DISCOVERER is applied to program verification, we found that many verification problems can be more effectively solved. In what follows, we will report some of the results, including termination condition generation of linear loop programs and reachability computation of linear hybrid systems.

2   DISCOVERER

In this section, we will give a brief description on DISCOVERER and refer the reader to [32,35] for details.

All the polynomials discussed in this section are in $\mathbb{Q}[u_1, ..., u_d, x_1, ..., x_s]$, the ring of polynomials in indeterminates $u_1, ..., u_d, x_1, ..., x_s$ with rational coefficients, where $s > 0, d \geq 0$, $u = (u_1, ..., u_d)$ are parameters and $x = (x_1, ..., x_s)$ variables. The following system

$$
\begin{cases}
p_1(u, x) = 0, ..., p_s(u, x) = 0, \\
g_1(u, x) \geq 0, ..., g_r(u, x) \geq 0, \\
g_{r+1}(u, x) > 0, ..., g_t(u, x) > 0, \\
h_1(u, x) \neq 0, ..., h_m(u, x) \neq 0,
\end{cases}
$$

is called a *semi-algebraic system* and is denoted shortly by

$$[[P], [G_1], [G_2], [H]] \tag{1}$$

where P, G_1, G_2 and H represent the sets of polynomials $\{p_1(u, x), ..., p_s(u, x)\}$ $(= 0)$, $\{g_1(u, x), ..., g_r(u, x)\}$ (≥ 0), $\{g_{r+1}(u, x), ..., g_t(u, x)\}$ (> 0) and $\{h_1(u, x), ..., h_m(u, x)\}$ $(\neq 0)$, respectively. An SAS is called *parametric* if $d > 0$ and *constant* otherwise.

Based on the theory of *complete discrimination systems for polynomials* [33,31], which is a set of explicit expressions in terms of the coefficients of a given polynomial that are sufficient for determining the numbers and multiplicities of the real and imaginary roots of the polynomial, and the *RSD* algorithm [36], which enables us to transform equations into triangular form with good properties, we proposed new algorithms for solving SASs which have been implemented partly in DISCOVERER. Our algorithms and DISCOVERER have been applied to many problems such as automated theorem discovering and proving involving inequalities, computer vision, stability analysis etc., e.g., see [32,35,29].

For a constant SAS, T, of the form (1), DISCOVERER can determine the number of distinct real solutions of T, say n, and compute n disjoint cubes with rational vertices. Each of the cubes contains one and only one solution to T and the width of the cubes can be less than any given positive real. The two functions are realized through calling

$$\texttt{nearsolve}([P], [G_1], [G_2], [H], [x_1, ..., x_s])$$

and

$$\texttt{realzeros}([P], [G_1], [G_2], [H], [x_1, ..., x_s], w),$$

respectively, where w is optional and used to indicate the maximum length of the edges of the output cubes.

For a parametric SAS, T, of the form (1) and any integer $N \geq 0$, DISCOVERER can determine the conditions on u such that T has exactly N distinct real solutions for x. The conditions can be obtained by combining two functions of DISCOVERER: tofind and Tofind. First, by calling

$$\texttt{tofind}([P], [G_1], [G_2], [H], [x_1, ..., x_s], [u_1, ..., u_d], N),$$

one obtains the *border polynomial* BP in u of the system T and the necessary and sufficient conditions for T to have N distinct real solutions provided BP$\neq 0$. Second, to determine the situation when parameters are on the "boundary", i.e., BP$= 0$, one need to call Tofind. Suppose R is a factor of BP, one can call

$$\texttt{Tofind}([P, R], [G_1], [G_2], [H], [x_1, ..., x_s], [u_1, ..., u_d], N)$$

to obtain conditions when the parameters are on $R = 0$.

The last argument of tofind and Tofind is one of the following three forms:

- a non-negative integer b, to indicate that T has exactly b distinct real solutions;
- a range $b..c$, where b, c are non-negative integers and $b < c$, to indicate that T has b to c distinct real solutions;
- a range $b..w$, where b is a non-negative integer and w a name, to indicate T has more than or equal to b distinct real solutions.

3   Termination Analysis and Reachability Computation with DISCOVERER

In this section, we summarize the work that we have achieved so far on termination condition generation of linear programs and reachability computation of linear hybrid systems with DISCOVERER.

3.1   Termination Criterion Generation of Linear Programs

The well-known method for establishing termination of programs is the use of well-founded domains together with so-called ranking functions that map the state space of a program to a well-founded domain. Clearly, the existence of such a ranking function implies termination. Some heuristics on generating linear ranking functions for linear programs have been proposed, e.g. [10,23].

Generally speaking, the cost for synthesizing linear ranking functions is very high, for example, the complexity of the algorithm in [10] is exponential and that of the algorithm in [23] could be double exponential. Besides, it is not easy to characterize programs to which such an algorithm can be applied. If the algorithm fails for a given program, we can conclude nothing about the termination of the program. The ideal solution to termination problem is to establish a criterion for each class of programs whose termination problem is decidable so that for a given program contained in the class, it can be decided if the program terminates trivially by computing the criterion, although the cost for generating such a criterion is also expensive.

Reference [28] made an attempt towards the direction by showing the decidability of a class of programs of the form, called linear loop programs,

$$P_1: \texttt{while } (Bx > b) \ \{x := Ax + c\},$$

by relating the termination of P_1 to the positive eigenvalues of A, where A and B are $N \times N$ and $N \times M$ matrices respectively, $Bx > b$ represents a conjunction of linear inequalities in the program variables and $x := Ax + c$ represents the linear assignments to each of the variables. In order to establish criteria for termination of P_1 based on Tiwari's work, theories and tools concerning root classification of parametric SASs on an interval are demanded.

Based on Tiwari's work, we used DISCOVERER and established termination conditions for programs of the following form:

$$P_{11}: \texttt{while } \left(\sum_{i=1}^{n} c_i x_i > 0 \right) \ \{x := Ax\}.$$

For example, suppose the dimension of x is specified, say, three, setting $A = (a_{ij})_{3 \times 3}$, we have:

Theorem 1. *Provided the polynomial system* $\{(a_{11}-\lambda)x_1+a_{12}x_2+a_{13}x_3,\ a_{21}x_1+ (a_{22}-\lambda)x_2+a_{23}x_3,\ a_{31}x_1+a_{32}x_2+(a_{33}-\lambda)x_3,\ c_1x_1+c_2x_2+c_3x_3\}$ *has no nontrivial solutions, the program* P_{11} *terminates if and only if the following formula is satisfied:*

$$(p \geq 0 \wedge q \geq 0 \wedge r \geq 0) \vee (D_3 < 0 \wedge r \geq 0), \tag{2}$$

where

$$
\begin{aligned}
p &= -a_{11} - a_{22} - a_{33}, \\
q &= -a_{21}a_{12} + a_{11}a_{33} - a_{31}a_{13} + a_{22}a_{33} + a_{11}a_{22} - a_{23}a_{32}, \\
r &= -a_{11}a_{22}a_{33} + a_{31}a_{13}a_{22} + a_{21}a_{12}a_{33} + a_{11}a_{23}a_{32} \\
&\quad -a_{31}a_{12}a_{23} - a_{21}a_{13}a_{32}, \\
D_3 &= -4\,q^3 + 18\,p\,q\,r + p^2q^2 - 4\,p^3r - 27\,r^2.
\end{aligned}
$$

One can use various algebraic tools, such as multivariate resultant methods, to check whether a certain polynomial system has a non-trivial solution or not.

4   Reachability Computation of Linear Hybrid Systems

Reachability and safety are now being recognized as central problems in designing hybrid and dynamical systems. Contrast with issues of stability and controllability of hybrid systems which are well-studied in control theory, there are not many results on reachability of those systems in computer science. Known classes of hybrid systems for which the reachability problem is decidable are timed automata [2], multirate automata [1], rectangular hybrid automata [22,17], etc. Recently a most general decidability result of three families of linear hybrid systems whose differential equations of the form $\dot{\xi} = A\xi + Bu$ was obtained in [18], where $\xi(t) \in \mathbb{R}^n$ is the state of the system at time t, $A \in \mathbb{R}^{n \times n}, B \in \mathbb{R}^{n \times m}$ are the system matrices, and $u : \mathbb{R} \to \mathbb{R}^m$ is a piecewise continuous function which is called the control input.

Roughly speaking, computing a reach set in [18] is via the following two steps: firstly, purely mathematically transform a problem of reachability computation to an SAS and therefore the decidability is obtained according to the famous Tarski's results [27]; then use the well-known computer algebra programs REDLOG and QEPCAD to solve the resulting SAS.

Using DISCOVERER instead of REDLOG and QEPCAD in the second step, we found that the results reported in [18] can be much improved. This can be justified by revisiting the examples in [18] that are not dealt well with REDLOG and QEPCAD. We list two of them below.

Example 1 (Example 3.5 of [18]). Consider the linear control vector field given by the diagonal matrix $A \in \mathbb{Q}^{2 \times 2}$ and $\mathcal{U} = \{u\}$ defined as follows:

$$A = \begin{bmatrix} 2 & 0 \\ 0 & -1 \end{bmatrix}, \quad u(t) = \begin{bmatrix} u_1(t) \\ u_2(t) \end{bmatrix} = \begin{bmatrix} -ae^{\frac{1}{2}t} \\ ae^t \end{bmatrix}, \quad \text{with } a \geq 0.$$

Let the initial set be $X = \{(0,0)\}$. Then, after mathematical transformation, we get the reach set from X forwards as:

$$\text{Post}(X) = \{(y_1, y_2) \in \mathbb{R}^2 \mid \exists a \exists z : 0 \leq a \wedge z \geq 1 \wedge h_1 = 0 \wedge h_2 = 0\} \quad (3)$$

where

$$h_1 = y_1 - \frac{2}{3}a(-z^4 + z), \quad h_2 = y_2 z^2 - \frac{1}{2}a(z^4 - 1).$$

Since the quantifiers in (3) cannot be eliminated using REDLOG or QEPCAD alone, reference [18] applied REDLOG to eliminate a first and then using QEPCAD to eliminate z, and thus obtained $\text{Post}(X)$ is

$$\{(y_1, y_2) \in \mathbb{R}^2 \mid (y_2 > 0 \wedge y_1 + y_2 \leq 0) \vee (y_2 < 0 \wedge y_1 + y_2 \geq 0)$$
$$\vee 4y_2 + 3y_1 = 0\} \quad (4)$$

With DISCOVERER, (3) can be solved by calling first

`tofind([`h_1, h_2`], [`$a, z - 1$`], [ ], [ ], [`z, a`], [`y_2, y_1`], 1..`n`);`

and we get that the system has real solutions if and only if

$$y_2 > 0 \wedge y_1 + y_2 < 0$$

provided that

$$y_1 \neq 0, y_2 \neq 0, y_1 + y_2 \neq 0 \text{ and } R \neq 0$$

where

$$R = 192y_2^3 y_1^2 - 63y_1^3 y_2^2 + 112y_1 y_2^4 - 6y_1^4 y_2 + 3y_1^5 + 16y_2^5.$$

Further considering (y_1, y_2) on the "boundaries" with DISCOVERER (by calling Tofind), we get that the system has real solutions if and only if

$$(y_2 > 0 \wedge y_1 + y_2 < 0) \vee (y_1 = y_2 = 0) \vee$$
$$(y_1 < 0 \wedge (y_2 \text{ is the smallest root of } R = 0 \text{ when } y_1 \text{ is specified})). \qquad (5)$$

The whole computation costs no more than 30 seconds on a PC (Pentium III/800 GHz CPU, 256M main memory, Windows XP) with Maple 9.

Note that (5) is inconsistent with (4). We give the following counter-examples by DISCOVERER to show that (4) is not correct. Suppose $y_2 = -1, y_1 = 2$, thus $y_2 < 0 \wedge y_1 + y_2 \geq 0$. It is easy to see that the system has no real solutions under $a \geq 0$ and $z \geq 1$. Another two counter-examples are $y_2 = 1, y_1 = -1$ and $y_1 = 4, y_2 = -3$.

Example 2 (Example 3.7. of [18]). Consider the control linear vector field given by the matrix $A \in \mathbb{Q}^{2 \times 2}$ and $\mathcal{U}$ defined as follows:

$$A = \begin{bmatrix} 0 & -1 \\ 1 & 0 \end{bmatrix}, \quad u(t) = \begin{bmatrix} u_1(t) \\ u_2(t) \end{bmatrix} = \begin{bmatrix} a\cos(2t) \\ -a^{-1}\sin(2t) \end{bmatrix}, \text{ with } a > 0.$$

Let the initial set be $X = \{(0,0)\}$ and the final set be $Y = \{(-1,1)\}$. Then, after some mathematical transformation, Y is reachable from X if and only if the following formula holds:

$$\exists w \exists z \exists a : a > 0 \wedge g_1 = 0 \wedge g_2 = 0 \wedge g_3 = 0, \qquad (6)$$

where $g_1 = w^2 + z^2 - 1$, $g_2 = w((4a^2 - 2)z + 2 - a^2) + 3a$ and $g_3 = (a^2 - 2)(w^2 - z^2 + z) - 3a$.

The solution to (6) in [18] with REDLOG and QEPCAD is as follows: Eliminate w with REDLOG first and then obtain

$$\exists z \exists a : a > 0$$
$$\wedge 16a^6 z^4 - 24a^6 z^3 + 9a^6 z^2 - a^6 z + 48a^5 z^2 - 24a^5 z + 3a^5 - 48a^4 z^4$$
$$+ 84a^4 z^3 - 42a^4 z^2 + 6a^4 z - 9a^4 - 48a^3 z^2 + 60a^3 z - 12a^3 + 36a^2 z^4$$
$$- 84a^2 z^3 + 60a^2 z^2 - 12a^2 z + 18a^2 + 12az^2 - 24az + 12a - 8z^4$$
$$+ 24z^3 - 24z^2 + 8z = 0 \wedge$$
$$16a^4 z^4 - 8a^4 z^3 - 15a^4 z^2 + 8a^4 z - a^4 - 16a^2 z^4 + 20a^2 z^3 + 12a^2 z^2$$
$$- 20a^2 z + 13a^2 + 4z^4 - 8z^3 + 8z - 4 = 0 \qquad (7)$$

with the assumption that $4a^2z - a^2 - 2z + 2 \neq 0$. The resulting formula is so complex that the quantifiers cannot be automatically eliminated using either REDLOG or QEPCAD. Thus $z = 0$ is assumed and it results that (6) holds provided that

$$\exists a : a > 0 \wedge (a^2 \neq 2) \wedge$$
$$3a^4 - 9a^3 - 12a^2 + 18a + 12 = 0 \wedge -a^4 + 13a^2 - 4 = 0 \qquad (8)$$

which is found to be true using QEPCAD. Alternatively, reference [18] also used REDUCE to derive the roots of the polynomials in a of (8) and found the common root $r = \frac{1}{2}(\sqrt{17} + 3) \approx 3.56156$ satisfying $r > 0$ and $r^2 \neq 2$. Hence, $y = (-1, 1)$ is reachable from $x = (0, 0)$ by taking $a = r$.

In contrast, we solve (6) using DISCOVERER simply by executing the following command

`realzeros([`g_1, g_2, g_3`], [ ], [`a`], [ ], [`w, z, a`], 1/1000000)`

and get the following three solutions within 0.3 seconds on the same machine

$$\begin{array}{lll} \left[\left[\frac{-3786927439}{4294967296}, \frac{-30295419511}{34359738368}\right], & \left[\frac{16599516199973}{35184372088832}, \frac{33199032472081}{70368744177664}\right], & \left[\frac{938055701}{268435456}, \frac{938055737}{268435456}\right]\right], \\ \left[\frac{-2797709061}{4294967296}, \frac{-699427265}{1073741824}\right], & \left[\frac{-6517535813}{8589934592}, \frac{-6517535651}{8589934592}\right], & \left[\frac{70273639}{134217728}, \frac{281094637}{536870912}\right]\right], \\ \left[\qquad [1,1], & [0,0], & \left[\frac{14938235}{4194304}, \frac{29876471}{8388608}\right]\right], \end{array}$$

which approximates to

$$\begin{array}{lll} \left[\left[-.8817127531, -.8817127531\right], & \left[.4717866261, .4717866271\right], & \left[3.494529802, 3.494529936\right]\right], \\ \left[\left[-.6513924014, -.6513924012\right], & \left[-.7587410292, -.7587410103\right], & \left[.5235794112, .5235795621\right]\right], \\ \left[\qquad [1., 1.], & [0., 0.], & \left[3.561552763, 3.561552882\right]\right]. \end{array}$$

It is easy to see that the solution given in [18] with REDLOG,QEPCAD and REDUCE is just one of the three solutions we got above using DISCOVERER.

5   Future Work

In this paper, it has been shown that the theory for isolating real solutions of a constant SAS and classifying real solutions of a parametric SAS and the tool DISCOVERER invented in [32,30,35] can indeed improve program verification, e.g., termination condition generation of linear programs and reachability computation of linear hybrid systems. But all what we have done up to now is just a first step, as there are still many challenging problems left in this field from the theory on SASs itself to program verification.

As for future work on program verification, we think that it is worth investigating the following issues: Firstly, as termination condition generation for the simple linear loop programs with DISCOVERER, it deserves to apply this method to more general linear programs or even non-linear programs. In addition, it is also a challenging problem to study reachability for more complicated hybrid systems with DISCOVERER. Finally, we believe that it is possible to produce interesting results by applying the theory and DISCOVERER to invariant generation of programs. The dominant method on finding invariants of a program is by abstract interpretation [11], but this method suffers from the problem of overshooting invariants. With comparison to the abstract interpretation based techniques, references [9,25,26] proposed a new technique for invariant generation by reducing this problem to SAS solving so that the new approach can avoid weak invariant generation. However, the high complexity of the well-known techniques and tools for non-linear constraint solving limits the applicability of this approach, for example, in order to avoid producing non-linear constraints [25,26] had to sacrifice the completeness of the method. Additionally, using the approach of [25,26] all the resulting invariants can only consist of polynomial equations but reject polynomial inequalities, this may thus restrict the expressiveness of resulting invariants.

Regarding future work on DISCOVERER itself, all theories and algorithms implemented in DISCOVERER only concern SASs with 0-dimensional solutions (the number of solutions is finite) until now. But, in fact, many problems in program verification may be reduced to SASs with positive dimensional solutions (the number of solutions is infinite). This demands us to extend the established theories and tool in order that SASs with positive dimensional solutions can be also well addressed. Furthermore, we shall develop special tools based on DISCOVERER for program verification.

Finally, we have to point out that up to now we have no idea on how to generalize our approach to non-numerical problems like determining termination for term-rewriting systems. It seems difficult (impossible) because the set of symbols of a term-rewriting system that play as coefficient in SASs does not satisfy required algebraic properties such as the axioms for field.

Acknowledgement

The authors sincerely thank the anonymous referees for their useful comments which are helpful for improving the presentation of this paper.

References

1. Alur, R., Courcoubetis, C., Halbwachs, N., Henzinger, T.A., Ho, P.-H., Nicollin, X., Olivero, A., Sifakis, J., Yovine, S.: The algorithmic analysis of hybrid systems. Theoretical Computer Science 138(3), 3–34 (1995)
2. Alur, R., Dill, D.: A theory of timed automata. Theoretical Computer Science 126, 183–235 (1994)
3. Bradley, A.R., Manna, Z., Sipma, H.B.: Termination of Polynomial Programs. In: Cousot, R. (ed.) VMCAI 2005. LNCS, vol. 3385, Springer, Heidelberg (2005)
4. Clark, E.M., Emerson, A., Sistla, A.P.: Automatic verification of finite-state concurrent programs using temporal logic. ACM Transaction on Programming Languages and Systems 8(2), 244–263 (1986)
5. Clarke, E.M., Emerson, E.A.: Synthesis of synchronization skeletons for branching time temporal logic. In: Kozen, D. (ed.) Logic of Programs 1981. LNCS, vol. 131, Springer, Heidelberg (1981)

6. Clarke, E.M., Grumberg, O., Peled, D.A.: Model Checking. MIT Press, Cambridge (1999)
7. Collins, G.E.: Quantifier elimination for real closed fields by cylindrical algebraic decomposition. In: Brakhage, H. (ed.) GI-Fachtagung 1975. LNCS, vol. 33, pp. 134–183. Springer, Heidelberg (1975)
8. Collins, G.E., Hong, H.: Partial cylindrical algebraic decomposition for quantifier elimination. J. of Symbolic Computation 12, 299–328 (1991)
9. colón, M., Sankaranarayanan, S., Sipma, H.B.: Linear invariant generation using non-linear constraint solving. In: Hunt Jr., W.A., Somenzi, F. (eds.) CAV 2003. LNCS, vol. 2725, pp. 420–432. Springer, Heidelberg (2003)
10. colón, M., Sipma, H.B.: Synthesis of linear ranking functions. In: Margaria, T., Yi, W. (eds.) ETAPS 2001 and TACAS 2001. LNCS, vol. 2031, pp. 67–81. Springer, Heidelberg (2001)
11. Cousot, P., Cousot, R.: Abstraction interpretation: a unified lattice model for static analysis of programs by construction or approximation of fixpoints. In: ACM POPL 1977, pp. 238–252 (1977)
12. Cousot, P., Cousot, R.: Systematic design of program analysis frameworks. In: ACM POPL 1979, pp. 269–282 (1979)
13. Damas, L., Milner, R.: Principal type-schemes for functional programs. In: ACM POPL 1982, pp. 207–212 (1982)
14. Davenport, J.H., Heintz, J.: Real Elimination is Doubly Exponential. J. of Symbolic Computation 5, 29–37 (1988)
15. Dolzman, A., Sturm, T.: REDLOG: Computer algebra meets computer logic. ACM SIGSAM Bulletin 31(2), 2–9
16. Giacobazzi, R., Ranzato, F., Scozzari, F.: Making abstract interpretation complete. J. ACM 4792, 361–416 (2000)
17. Henzinger, T.A., Kopke, P.W., Puri, A., Varaiya, P.: What's decidable about hybrid automata? J. of Computer Science and System Sciences 57, 94–124 (1998)
18. Lafferrierre, G., Pappas, G.J., Yovine, S.: Symbolic reachability computaion for families of linear vector fields. J. of Symbolic Computation 11, 1–23 (2001)
19. Milner, R.: A theory of polymorphism in programming. J. Computer System Science 17(3), 348–375 (1978)
20. Owre, S., Rushby, J.M., Shankar, N.: PVS: A protype verification system. In: Kapur, D. (ed.) CADE 1992. LNCS, vol. 607, pp. 748–752. Springer, Heidelberg (1992)
21. Paulin-Mohring, C., Werner, B.: Synthesis of ML programs in the system Coq. J. Symbolic Logic 15(5/6), 607–640 (1993)
22. Puri, A., Varaiya, P.: Decidability of hybrid systems with rectangular differential inclusions. In: Dill, D.L. (ed.) CAV 1994. LNCS, vol. 818, pp. 95–104. Springer, Heidelberg (1994)
23. Podelski, A., Rybalchenko, A.: A complete method for the synthesis of linear ranking functions. In: Steffen, B., Levi, G. (eds.) VMCAI 2004. LNCS, vol. 2937, pp. 239–251. Springer, Heidelberg (2004)
24. Queille, J.-P., Sifakis, J.: Verification of concurrent systems in CESAR. In: Dezani-Ciancaglini, M., Montanari, U. (eds.) Programming 1982. LNCS, vol. 137, pp. 337–351. Springer, Heidelberg (1982)
25. Sankaranarayanan, S., Sipma, H.B., Manna, Z.: Non-linear loop invariant generation using Gröbner bases. In: ACM POPL 2004, pp. 318–329 (2004)
26. Sankaranarayanan, S., Sipma, H.B., Manna, Z.: Constructing invariants for hybrid systems. In: Alur, R., Pappas, G.J. (eds.) HSCC 2004. LNCS, vol. 2993, pp. 539–554. Springer, Heidelberg (2004)

27. Tarski, A.: A Decision for Elementary Algebra and Geometry, May 1951. University of California Press, Berkeley (1951)
28. Tiwari, A.: Termination of linear programs. In: Alur, R., Peled, D.A. (eds.) CAV 2004. LNCS, vol. 3114, pp. 70–82. Springer, Heidelberg (2004)
29. Wang, D., Xia, B.: Stability analysis of biological systems with real solution classification. In: Kauers, M. (ed.) Proceedings of the 2005 International Symposium on Symbolic and Algebraic Computation (ISSAC 2005), pp. 354–361. ACM Press, New York (2005)
30. Xia, B., Yang, L.: An algorithm for isolating the real solutions of semi-algebraic systems. J. Symbolic Computation 34, 461–477 (2002)
31. Yang, L.: Recent advances on determining the number of real roots of parametric polynomials. J. Symbolic Computation 28, 225–242 (1999)
32. Yang, L., Hou, X., Xia, B.: A complete algorithm for automated discovering of a class of inequality-type theorems. Sci. in China (Ser. F) 44, 33–49 (2001)
33. Yang, L., Hou, X., Zeng, Z.: A complete discrimination system for polynomials. Science in China (Ser. E) 39, 628–646 (1996)
34. Yang, L., Xia, B.C.: An explicit criterion to determine the number of roots of a polynomial on an interval. Progress in Natural Science 10(12), 897–910 (2000)
35. Yang, L., Xia, B.: Real solution classifications of a class of parametric semi-algebraic systems. In: Proc. of Int'l Conf. on Algorithmic Algebra and Logic, pp. 281–289 (2005)
36. Yang, L., Zhang, J., Hou, X.: A criterion of dependency between algebraic equations and its applications. In: Wen-tsun, W., de Cheng, M.- (eds.) Proceedings of International Workshop on Mathematics Mechanization 1992, pp. 110–134. International Academic Publishers, Beijing (1992)

Constraint Solving and Symbolic Execution[*]

Jian Zhang

State Key Laboratory of Computer Science
Institute of Software, Chinese Academy of Sciences
P.O. Box 8718, Beijing 100080, China

1 Introduction

For many decades, the correctness of programs has been a concern for computer scientists and software engineers. At present, it is still not easy to ensure the correctness of nontrivial programs, although many researchers have made various attempts in this direction.

Recently, the Verifying Compiler is proposed as a grand challenge in computing research [7]. But its goal can be achieved incrementally. The following is quoted from Hoare (page 68 of [7]):

> The progress of the project can be assessed by the number of lines of code that have been verified, and the level of annotation and verification that has been achieved. The relevant levels of annotations are: structural integrity, partial functional specification, total specification. The relevant levels of verification are: by testing, by human proof, by machine assistance, and fully automatic.

For program verification to become mainstream technology in software engineering, we need to convince programmers that the benefit will outweigh the "investment". Obviously, highly efficient and easy-to-use tools are necessary. There are many automatic and efficient tools for testing and program analysis. But they still have some weaknesses.

In the software engineering literature, most testing techniques are *syntactic*, in that they tend to neglect the exact meaning of statements and conditional expressions in the program. For example, one may consider the `def-use` relationship (i.e., where a variable is defined/modified, and where it is used), but not consider how the variable is modified. In the programming language literature, many program analysis techniques focus on certain aspects of the programs. For example, pointer analysis algorithms typically neglect the values of non-pointer variables. This kind of abstraction is necessary for scalability. And most researchers would like to demonstrate that their techniques and tools can be used on large-scale programs. But the price to pay is the loss of accuracy and expressiveness. In fact, it is often very difficult to generate a good test suite for white-box testing, in which every test case is executable/usable. Similarly, it is hard to avoid false alarms in static analysis.

---

[*] Supported in part by the National Natural Science Foundation of China (NSFC).

B. Meyer and J. Woodcock (Eds.): Verified Software, LNCS 4171, pp. 539–544, 2008.

We believe that it is worthwhile and feasible to analyze programs and specifications *accurately* and *automatically*. In this paper, we briefly describe and evaluate a path-oriented approach to (partial) program verification and testing, which is based on Constraint Satisfaction and Symbolic Execution (CoSEx). We think that the approach is quite appealing and can serve as the basis of powerful tools. Although the basic ideas have been known for a long time [1,8,2], serious efforts are needed to demonstrate the full power of the approach.

2   Path-Oriented Analysis Based on Symbolic Execution

As we know, a program can usually be represented by some kind of directed graph, e.g., control flow graph, extended finite-state machine (EFSM). From such a graph, one can generate many paths, each of which starts with the entry of the program (or module).

Path-oriented testing is a common testing strategy. With this kind of strategy, one tries to examine the program's paths one by one. But in general, a non-trivial program has too many (or an infinite number of) paths, and it is impossible to examine all of them within a reasonable amount of time. Thus the concept of "basis paths" was proposed. Such paths are expected to be representatives of the set of all paths. Another way to get around the problem is to restrict the number of times each loop is executed. For example, we may consider just two cases: the loop body is not executed; the loop body is executed once.

Anyway, we assume that only a finite number of paths in the program are examined. But even under this assumption, automated verification and test data generation are still difficult. In software testing, a severe problem is that many program paths generated from the control flow graph are *non-executable* or *infeasible*. A path is *executable* (or *feasible*) if there are input data such that the program is executed along that path. Thus it is interesting to analyze each path accurately. To do this, we have to consider the full semantic information in the statements and conditional expressions.

Path-oriented analysis can also be used for some kind of partial verification. We may verify a program in the following steps:

(1) Annotate the program with assertions (preconditions and/or postconditions).
(2) Generate a set of paths from the program's graphical representation.
(3) For each path, decide whether it is executable/feasible.

In the first step, we attach the negation of a correctness property at the end of the program. If some path is executable, the program is found to be buggy.

The third step is crucial. To decide the feasibility of a path, we can first obtain a set of constraints (called the *path condition*), such that it is satisfiable if and only if the path is feasible.

Symbolic Execution

For a program path, the path condition can be obtained through symbolic execution [1,8], which is a well-known technique for testing and verification. During the execution, each variable's value is a symbolic expression, in terms of the initial values of the input variables. For example, suppose we have the input variable a and b, whose initial values are denoted by a_0 and b_0, respectively. Then, after the assignment $x = a + 2b$, the value of the variable x will be $(a_0 + 2 * b_0)$.

After executing a path symbolically, we get the path condition, which is a relational expression describing the constraints on the initial values of the input variables, e.g., $a_0 + 2 * b_0 > 4$. Given any vector of values satisfying the path condition, the program will be executed along the path. Thus the path condition represents a set of input data. It is a subset of the input space, yet it is usually infinite. Typically, one symbolic execution corresponds to many real executions.

The satisfiability of the path condition can be decided using various techniques, such as decision procedures, theorem proving, constraint solving, etc.

Constraint Solving

Constraint satisfaction problems [9] have been studied extensively in the artificial intelligence community. Informally speaking, such a problem consists of a set of variables, each of which may take a value from some domain. In addition, there are some constraints defined on the variables. Solving the problem means finding a value for each variable, such that all the constraints hold.

Obviously, the class of constraint satisfaction problems is quite general. Many problems fit into this framework, such as graph coloring and SAT (i.e., checking an arbitrary set of propositional clauses for satisfiability). For constraints having special forms, usually there are special methods for solving them. For instance, DPLL is a famous algorithm for solving SAT, and the simplex algorithm is very effective for solving linear arithmetic constraints.

We should note that there is some trade-off between the expressiveness of the constraint language and the difficulty of deciding the satisfiability. In the following, we list several forms of the constraints and the hardness of the associated decision problem:

- Boolean formulas: decidable, NP-hard
- linear constraints over rationals: decidable, linear-time
- linear constraints over rationals and integers: decidable, NP-hard
- non-linear constraints over integers: undecidable

Similarly, the more expressive a programming language is, the more difficult the analysis will be.

In [11,10,12], a prototype toolkit is described, which uses symbolic execution and constraint solving techniques. We call the toolkit SPAR. It analyzes a subset of C programs statically. Non-linear arithmetic is not allowed, but logical operators can be used in the program. Ordinary assertions (in C programs) are accepted, but not quantified formulas. This restriction reduces the complexity of the decision algorithm. Moreover, assertions are actively used by many programmers for various purposes [6]. The constraint solving algorithm [11] is essentially a combination of linear programming and SAT solving. In contrast, earlier works like [1] typically uses linear programming only.

3   Comparison with Related Approaches

We think that there are several factors to consider when comparing different approaches. These factors include:

- generality or applicability (e.g., the restriction to finite-state programs)
- accuracy or preciseness (e.g., full verification, partial verification, finding certain bugs, generating few/many false alarms)
- degree of automation and efficiency (e.g., exponential or double exponential complexity)
- the user's investment (e.g., writing a lot of lemmas, or just writing the precondition and the postcondition, or giving no annotation)

The CoSEx approach performs path-wise analysis, and it analyzes each path accurately (under reasonable assumptions of the syntax of the path). It can be used to verify the correctness of certain programs, e.g., bubble sorting program when the size of the input array is a fixed constant. Such a program has a finite number of (symbolic) execution paths. However, most programs have an infinite number of paths, and the approach can only be used to find bugs (if any).

Compared with traditional testing and static analysis techniques, the CoSEx approach can provide the user with accurate analysis results. False alarms are eliminated in most cases. However, we do not think it will scale up to large programs (such as programs with a million lines of code) in the near future.

Compared with model checking, the CoSEx approach does not require the program to have a finite number of states. Although there have been some extensions to model checking so that it can be used to verify infinite-state systems, their effectiveness has yet to be seen.

Compared with theorem proving, the CoSEx approach is more automatic, but the properties it can prove are not so general. It is more effective to use the approach on buggy programs.

An abstract interpretation-based static program analyzer like ASTRÉE [3] considers a superset of the possible program executions, while the approach outlined in this paper considers a subset of all the executions, because only a finite number of paths are analyzed. But it can avoid many false alarms.

ESC/Java [5] and its successors are impressive static checking tools which can perform similar analysis on Java programs. But the underlying theorem prover, Simplify [4], accepts more expressive formulas which may contain quantifiers.

An Example

In [13], 5 modern static analysis tools (including Splint and PolySpace) are evaluated using a number of nontrivial model programs which contain buffer overflows. It is found that, in some cases, some tools are silent, while other tools can detect the vulnerabilities and signal many false alarms.

Two false alarm examples ("aia2" and "inp") are given in Fig. 5 and Fig. 6 of [13]. We have tried our toolkit on the first example, since the second one has complicated expressions which are beyond the scope of the tools.

In the example "aia2", there are two arrays (x and y), and there is an assignment "y[x[i]] = i" (line 8). Although one element of the array x has the value (-1), that value is never used to index into y. Thus there is actually no underflow. Using our tool ePAT (which is an extension of PAT [11]), we can check that this is indeed the case. Since the array y is of size 2, we run ePAT twice, each time attaching one of the following two assertions to the statements before line 8:   @(x[i] < 0);   @(x[i] >= 2);   Here @ denotes an assertion. So we get two extended paths, one of which is the following:

```
int i;   int x[3], y[2];
{
  x[0] = 1;      i = 0;
 @(i < 3);
  x[i] = i-1;   i = i+1;
 @(i < 3);
  x[i] = i-1;   i = i+1;
 @(i < 3);
  x[i] = i-1;   i = i+1;
 @!(i < 3);
  i = 1;
 @(i < 3);
 @(x[i] < 0);
}
```

It is found that neither of the paths is executable. Thus the index expression x[i] is within the bound, and we have shown that the alarm is false.

4   Concluding Remarks

Up to now, only a few programmers have used program verification technology in developing nontrivial software. Wider use of the technology calls for powerful and efficient supporting tools, although education is also quite important.

An approach is outlined and evaluated in this paper. It is based on the analysis of program paths. The analysis involves detailed semantic information, and uses symbolic execution and constraint solving techniques which are automatic and accurate. Hopefully this approach will lead to rewarding tools for average programmers. With such tools, we should be able to

- verify – or find bugs in – certain programs (like bubble_sort, where the size of the input array is a fixed positive integer)
- check the error messages produced by other static analyzers, to eliminate some false alarms
- automate an important part of unit testing, i.e., generating test cases (input data) for the program
- generate test cases for black-box testing or model-based testing, if a proper specification (like EFSM) is provided.

We can also perform other kinds of analysis which are not so related to the correctness of programs.

In summary, we think that it is very important to analyze programs and specifications accurately and automatically. Such an analysis may use symbolic execution and constraint solving techniques. It can be complementary to other verification/analysis approaches. In the near future, we expect that the approach is applicable to small or medium-sized programs or key modules in software systems. While many other techniques try to scale up to large programs, we are more interested in scalability in the expressiveness of the input language. This may be indicated by the data types and expressions allowed in the program (e.g., Booleans, integers, arrays, pointers; linear arithmetic expressions, mixed logical and arithmetic expressions). We hope that powerful tools will be developed which can accurately analyze programs in more and more expressive languages.

References

1. Boyer, R.S., Elspas, B., Levitt, K.N.: SELECT – A formal system for testing and debugging programs by symbolic execution. In: Proc. of the Int. conf. on Reliable Software, pp. 234–245 (1975)
2. Bush, W.R., Pincus, J.D., Sielaff, D.J.: A static analyzer for finding dynamic programming errors. Software – Practice And Experience 30, 775–802 (2000)
3. Cousot, P., et al.: The ASTRÉE analyzer. In: Sagiv, M. (ed.) ESOP 2005. LNCS, vol. 3444, pp. 21–30. Springer, Heidelberg (2005)
4. Detlefs, D., Nelson, G., Saxe, J.B.: Simplify: A theorem prover for program checking. J. ACM 52(3), 365–473 (2005)
5. Flanagan, C., Leino, K.R.M., Lillibridge, M., Nelson, G., Saxe, J.B., Stata, R.: Extended static checking for Java. In: Proc. of the ACM SIGPLAN Conf. on Programming Language Design and Implementation (PLDI), pp. 234–245 (2002)
6. Hoare, C.A.R.: Assertions in modern software engineering practice, Keynote address. In: 26th Int'l Computer Software and Applications Conf (COMPSAC), Oxford, England (August 2002)
7. Hoare, T.: The verifying compiler: A grand challenge for computing research. J. of the ACM 50(1), 63–69 (2003)
8. King, J.C.: Symbolic execution and testing. Comm. of the ACM 19(7), 385–394 (1976)
9. Mackworth, A.K.: Constraint satisfaction. In: Shapiro, S.C. (ed.) Encyclopedia of Artificial Intelligence, vol. 1, pp. 205–211. John Wiley, New York (1990)
10. Zhang, J.: Symbolic execution of program paths involving pointer and structure variables. In: Proc. of the 4th Int'l Conf. on Quality Software (QSIC), pp. 87–92 (2004)
11. Zhang, J., Wang, X.: A constraint solver and its application to path feasibility analysis. of Software Engineering and Knowledge Engineering 11(2), 139–156 (2001)
12. Zhang, J., Xu, C., Wang, X.: Path-oriented test data generation using symbolic execution and constraint solving techniques. In: Proc. 2nd Int'l Conf. on Software Engineering and Formal Methods (SEFM), pp. 242–250 (2004)
13. Zitser, M., Lippmann, R., Leek, T.: Testing static analysis tools using exploitable buffer overflows from open source code. In: Proc. of the 12th ACM SIGSOFT Int'l Symp. on Foundations of Software Engineering, pp. 97–106 (2004)

Author Index

Lecture Notes in Computer Science

Sublibrary 2: Programming and Software Engineering

For information about Vols. 1– 4498
please contact your bookseller or Springer